INTERNATIONAL MONETARY THEORY AND POLICY

ECONOMICS HANDBOOK SERIES

INTERNATIONAL MONETARY THEORY AND POLICY

Miltiades Chacholiades, Ph.D.

Research Professor of Economics
Georgia State University

McGraw-Hill Book Company

New York   St. Louis   San Francisco   Auckland   Bogotá
Düsseldorf   Johannesburg   London   Madrid   Mexico
Montreal   New Delhi   Panama   Paris   São Paulo
Singapore   Sydney   Tokyo   Toronto

INTERNATIONAL MONETARY THEORY AND POLICY

1 2 3 4 5 6 7 8 9 0 D O D O 7 8 3 2 1 0 9 8 7

This book was set in Times Roman. The editor was J. S. Dietrich and
the production supervisor was David Damstra.
R. R. Donnelley & Sons Company was printer and binder.

Library of Congress Cataloging in Publication Data

Chacholiades, Miltiades.
    International monetary theory and policy.

    (Economics handbook series)
    Includes bibliographies and indexes.
    1. International finance. I. Title.
HG3881.C453   332.4'5   77-4078
ISBN 0-07-010340-2

TO THE MEMORY
OF
MY FATHER

CONTENTS

II. PRICE AND INCOME EFFECTS AND POLICIES FOR INTERNAL AND EXTERNAL BALANCE

9   A Basic Model   190

10   The Income Adjustment Mechanism   203

14   Direct Controls   296

III. MONEY AND CAPITAL MOVEMENTS

FOREWORD

As a textbook writer in international economics, I should perhaps take a jaundiced view of new entries in the field, and as a rule I do. But when it is a former student of ours at M.I.T. who enters the arena, like other students before him, I welcome it. This is what teaching is about—for each generation to extend the frontiers of knowledge and to find new ways of propagating not the faith but an understanding of how economies function. A certain amount of redundancy is inevitable, but redundancy, as an old aphorism of mine goes, is the soul of teaching. Successive generations of instructors stand on the shoulders of their instructors, and through this process we reach higher and higher.

This is not Miltiades Chacholiades' first textbook in international economics. That was *The Pure Theory of International Trade*, published in 1973,† which, as its title makes clear, dealt with the microeconomic aspects of international trade and commercial policy. The present work is the macroeconomic accompaniment to the 1973 volume, equally pure in its classical simplicity. Professor Chacholiades is familiar with empirical testing in international economics, with institutions, economic history in the field, and with policy choices. His comparative advantage, however, lies in the pure theory, set out with the aid of geometry and some algebra in the text, and with further rigorous elaboration in the appendices which grace the majority of the chapters. It relies heavily on the two-country model much maligned in the literature and uses taxonomy. If this is heresy, make the most of it. The classical framework of the subject is set out elegantly and at sufficient length so as to make it crystal clear. Better to set out the underpinnings of the subject, the book eschews pursuit of the new topics which are beginning to intrude from all sides: two-gap models, political aspects of international monetary reform, Euro-currency markets, and crawling pegs. Solid contributions are made in such fields as three-point arbitrage

† At Chicago, by the Aldine Publishing Company.

and forward markets, but "personal piffle," as Paul Samuelson calls it, so often found in textbooks, is totally absent. The book is a faithful and dependable guide for the student interested in absorbing cool, clear draughts of pure reason.

If I am not mistaken, Miltiades Chacholiades broke into print in the field of macroeconomics in 1968 when I asked him to write the mathematical appendices for the Marshall-Lerner condition and the foreign-trade multipliers of the fourth edition of my textbook. They too were elegantly done, I was assured, although already his technical virtuosity was beginning to leave me behind. It gives me great pleasure almost a decade later to observe the fruit of this beginning and to see Professor Chacholiades take his place among the solid contributors to and expositors of the income, monetary and financial aspects of international economic relations.

CHARLES P. KINDLEBERGER

Massachusetts Institute of Technology

PREFACE

This book is addressed primarily to the advanced undergraduate and first-year graduate student. It will also prove invaluable to the professional economist, both the teacher and the policy maker. The main objective of the book is to provide a thorough exposition of the general principles of international finance in a systematic, straightforward, and careful manner, and to do so without using advanced mathematical techniques—except in appendices which can be omitted. The emphasis is on principles as opposed to institutions although some indispensable discussion of institutions is provided where necessary. The present book simplifies and clarifies many difficult aspects of the international adjustment process and synthesizes the various approaches found in the literature into a general theory of the balance of payments and the foreign exchange market.

To maximize the usefulness of the book as a teaching and learning device, the material is deliberately organized in a very logical manner. Thus, the discussion proceeds from partial equilibrium to general equilibrium analysis, and from exchange-rate systems to adjustment mechanisms and then to economic policies. Such an approach should prove very helpful both to the student who seeks a clear understanding of the international adjustment mechanism, and to the policy maker who deals with the formulation of economic policy and perhaps the establishment of institutions and rules for their operation.

Further, great care is taken to develop and synthesize this rather complicated field of economics with tools which are already familiar to the reader from his micro- and macroeconomics courses. Accordingly, while the exposition is honest, accurate, and provides a comprehensive survey of the relevant literature, it relies heavily on geometry. Mathematical appendices are provided at the end of several chapters. These appendices, however, can be safely omitted without interrupting the continuity of the book. The reader who nevertheless wants to pursue the analysis given in these appendices will find extremely useful a special mathematical appendix at the end of the book which provides a self-contained treatment of first-order, linear, ordinary differential equations.

The book is divided into three parts. Part I (chapters 1 to 8) deals with the foreign exchange market and the balance of payments in the short run. In particular, the introductory chapters 1, 2, and 3 discuss, respectively, the fundamental concepts of the foreign exchange market, the balance of payments, and the relationship between the supply of domestic currency and the demand for foreign exchange. Chapter 4 develops the Bickerdike-Robinson-Machlup partial equilibrium model, which is used later to study the workings of the flexible-exchange-rate system (chapters 5 and 6), the gold standard (chapter 7), and the adjustable peg (chapter 8). An important feature of this part is the careful development of the simultaneous equilibrium in the spot and forward markets.

Part II (chapters 9 to 14) deals mainly with the current account of the balance of payments. The Bickerdike-Robinson-Machlup, partial equilibrium model for commodity trade is now generalized to include the income effects. After a brief introduction (chapter 9), this part discusses the income-adjustment mechanism (chapter 10), the flexible-exchange-rate system and the theory of employment (chapter 11), the transfer problem (chapter 12), the conflicts between internal and external balance and Meade's reconciliation (chapter 13), and finally the use of direct controls as an expenditure-switching policy (chapter 14).

Part III (chapters 15 to 19) extends the analysis of Part II to include explicitly the money and capital (securities) markets. In particular, chapter 15 deals with David Hume's price-specie-flow mechanism under the classical assumption of full employment. Chapter 16 discusses the gold standard in the context of a Keynesian-type, fixed-price model. Chapter 17 deals primarily with the Mundellian problem of how fiscal and monetary policies can be applied simultaneously to achieve internal and external balance. Drawing on the analysis of chapter 16, chapter 18 extends the analysis of chapter 17 to a two-country, general-equilibrium model. Finally, chapter 19 provides some new insights into the nature of balance-of-payments disequilibrium and the fundamental role of international financial intermediation. The discussion leads naturally to a concrete proposal for reforming the international monetary system.

Selected bibliographies are provided at the end of each chapter. No attempt has been made to provide exhaustive bibliographies. For the convenience of the reader, a glossary of symbols is also provided.

The appendix to chapter 1 was adapted from the author's *Southern Economic Journal* paper "The Sufficiency of Three-Point Arbitrage to Insure Consistent Cross Rates of Exchange." Similarly, chapter 15 and appendix were adapted from the author's *Econometrica* paper "The Classical Theory of International Adjustment: A Restatement." I wish to thank the editors of both the *Southern Economic Journal* and *Econometrica* for their permission to reproduce the above papers.

I would like to thank Professor Charles P. Kindleberger for reading and commenting on the manuscript and the encouragement he has given me. Special thanks are due to Robert W. Boatler, Alan V. Deardorff, and Heidemarie Sherman who read the entire manuscript and offered numerous suggestions for improvement. In addition to his comments on the text, Deardorff was brave enough to read all the mathematical appendices and identify several errors which existed in an earlier draft. I also wish to thank my colleague John Klein, who offered some editorial comments on the first part of the book, and Professor Fred Massey of the Department of Mathematics who read and commented on the mathematical appendix. Any remaining deficiencies are all mine. In addition, I wish to thank the Economics Editor of the McGraw-Hill Book Company, Mr. Stephen Dietrich, for his assistance in preparing the manuscript and for expediting the publication process. Further, I want to thank Marilyn King for her prompt and efficient typing of a rather technical manuscript, and Leila Kinney, Wanda Cooley, and Lynn Lawrence for assisting her. Thanks are also due to Carlos Nunes and Frank Jennings who assisted me in compiling the indexes. Above all I wish to thank my wife and my children for their understanding during the two years I spent writing the book.

MILTIADES CHACHOLIADES

LIST OF SYMBOLS

ENGLISH SYMBOLS

Upper Case

B_a $\equiv$ country A's balance of payments

B_b $\equiv$ basic balance

B_l $\equiv$ liquidity balance

B_0 $\equiv$ official settlements balance

C $\equiv$ consumption

D $\equiv Z + T \equiv$ aggregate spending on the economy's output by domestic and foreign consumers, producers, and government

$D_\$, D_£$ $\equiv$ amounts of dollars and pounds demanded, respectively

E $\equiv$ errors and omissions

E_{ib} $\equiv$ ith country's excess demand for bonds

F $\equiv C + I$

F_i $\equiv C_i + I_i$

G $\equiv$ government spending

H_i $\equiv$ money supply of the ith country

I $\equiv$ investment

K $\equiv$ capital flow

L_i $\equiv$ ith country's demand for money

LTC $\equiv$ long-term capital flow

M $\equiv$ value of all goods imported

M_c $\equiv$ value of imported finished goods

M_p $\equiv$ value of raw materials

M_a, M_b $\equiv$ physical quantities of imports demanded by countries A and B, respectively

P_A, P_B $\equiv$ A's and B's price index numbers, respectively

P_a $\equiv$ covered-interest arbitrage profit

P_f $\equiv$ expected profit of forward speculation

P_s $\equiv$ expected profit of spot speculation

Q $\equiv$ value of all goods made available to the economy by both domestic and foreign producers

$\tilde{Q}$ $\equiv$ value of total output produced by an economy by employing domestic and foreign resources

Q_d $\equiv$ value of output produced by domestic resources (i.e., value of domestic output)

R $\equiv$ rate of exchange (dollars per pound)

R^* $\equiv 1/R$ (pounds sterling per dollar)

R_f $\equiv$ forward rate (dollars per pound sterling)

R_s $\equiv$ spot rate (dollars per pound sterling)

S $\equiv S_p + S_g =$ total domestic saving done by both the private and public sectors

$S_\$, S_\pounds$ $\equiv$ amounts of dollars and pounds sterling, respectively, supplied

S_g $\equiv T_x - G \equiv$ government (or public) saving

S_p $\equiv$ private saving

STC $\equiv$ short-term capital flow

T $\equiv$ balance of trade expressed in domestic currency

T^* $\equiv$ balance of trade expressed in foreign currency

T_d $\equiv$ B's balance of trade expressed in B's currency

T_f $\equiv$ B's balance of trade expressed in A's currency

T_r $\equiv$ tariff revenue

T_x $\equiv$ net taxes paid to the domestic government

U $\equiv$ unilateral transfer

V_i $\equiv$ ith country's income velocity of circulation of money

X $\equiv$ value of exports

X_a, X_b $\equiv$ physical quantities of exports supplied by A and B, respectively

X_d $\equiv$ part of exports produced by strictly domestic resources

X_f $\equiv$ part of exports produced by strictly foreign resources

Y_i $\equiv$ ith country's national income

Z_i $\equiv C_i + I_i + G_i \equiv$ ith country's domestic absorption

Z_d $\equiv$ part of domestic absorption which uses up strictly domestic resources

Z_f $\equiv$ part of domestic absorption which uses up strictly foreign resources

Lower Case

e_a $\equiv$ elasticity of demand for arbitrage funds

e_f $\equiv$ elasticity of demand for foreign exchange in the forward market

e_s $\equiv$ elasticity of demand for foreign exchange in the spot market

$e_d^\$, e_d^\pounds$ $\equiv$ demand elasticities for dollars and pounds sterling, respectively

$e_s^\$, e_s^\pounds$ $\equiv$ supply elasticities of dollars and pounds sterling, respectively

e_{ma}, e_{mb} $\equiv$ demand elasticities of imports of countries A and B, respectively

e_{xa}, e_{xb} $\equiv$ supply elasticities of exports of A and B, respectively

$\bar{g}$ $\equiv$ total supply of gold in the world economy

g_i $\equiv$ ith country's gold reserve

Δg $\equiv$ net change in gold, gold tranche at the IMF, and holdings of convertible currencies

k_i $\equiv$ ith country's money multiplier

k_{ij} $\equiv$ multiplier relating the total change in the national income of the ith country to the autonomous change in the demand for the products of the jth country

m $\equiv$ foreign-trade multiplier when foreign repercussion is ignored

p $\equiv p_a/p_b \equiv$ A's terms of trade

p^* $\equiv p_a^*/p_b^* \equiv$ A's terms of trade

p_a, p_b $\equiv$ prices of A-exportables and B-exportables, respectively, expressed in dollars (or existing in country A)

p_a^*, p_b^* $\equiv$ prices of A-exportables and B-exportables, respectively, expressed in pounds sterling (or existing in country B)

p_i^j $\equiv$ price of ith commodity in jth country expressed in jth currency

r_a, r_b $\equiv$ A's and B's interest rate, respectively

s $\equiv$ *ad valorem* subsidy

t $\equiv$ *ad valorem* tariff rate

w_a $\equiv$ A's money-wage rate expressed in terms of A's currency

w_b $\equiv$ B's money-wage rate expressed in terms of B's currency

GREEK SYMBOLS

ζ_i $\equiv$ change in ith country's demand for goods and services (domestic and foreign) due to the financing and disposal of a unilateral transfer

ζ_{if} $\equiv$ change in ith country's demand for imports due to the financing and disposal of a unilateral transfer

θ_i $\equiv$ amount of exportables which must be exported by the ith country in order for the importing country to receive one unit

μ $\equiv$ closed-economy national-income multiplier

ξ_a^* $\equiv$ proportion in which A-exportables and B-exportables are made available to country B by country A

ξ_i $\equiv \dfrac{\text{amount of A-exportables consumed by the } i\text{th country}}{\text{amount of B-exportables consumed by the } i\text{th country}}$

PART
ONE

THE FOREIGN EXCHANGE MARKET AND THE BALANCE OF PAYMENTS

THE FOREIGN EXCHANGE MARKET

1.1 THE NEED FOR A FOREIGN EXCHANGE MARKET

Because different countries use different currencies, every economic transaction between a resident of one country and a resident of another (i.e., every *international transaction*) necessarily requires the conversion of one currency into another (i.e., a foreign-exchange transaction). The *foreign exchange market* is nothing else but a market in which foreign-exchange transactions take place. That is, in the foreign exchange market national currencies are bought and sold against one another.

A Closed Economy in Static Equilibrium

To gain further insight into this fundamental function of the foreign exchange market, we consider a simple example. Imagine a closed economy in static equilibrium. All commodity and factor markets are in equilibrium and have been in equilibrium for some time. All producers and consumers are also in equilibrium. Each producer buys the same quantities of factor services and produces the same amount of output which he sells to consumers period after period. Similarly, each consumer offers to the producers the same amounts of factor services and buys from them the same amounts of consumption goods period after period. All transactions take place at the equilibrium prices, profits are normal, and there is no incentive on the part of anybody to change his behavior.

Dividing the Closed Economy into Two Open Economies

Suppose now that a political frontier is drawn, dividing the closed economy into two new countries, A and B. (For simplicity ignore the administrative problem created by this change.) Each of the two countries adopts its own national currency. In particular, A (America) uses dollars and B (Britain) pounds sterling. How do these changes, and, in particular, the existence of two different national currencies, affect the initial static equilibrium?

On reflection, it becomes clear that the introduction of a political frontier *per se* need not affect the static equilibrium. It is true, of course, that once the political frontier is drawn the new governments might interfere with the free flow of trade between A and B by means of tariffs, quotas, etc., and this would most certainly affect the initial static equilibrium. However, such interference is an additional change which we are not interested in studying at the moment.

The Need to Convert One Currency into Another

The emergence of two national currencies gives rise to a complication in relation to economic transactions between residents of A and residents of B. Such international transactions require the conversion of dollars into pounds sterling or vice versa, as the case may be. For instance, when a resident of A sells (exports) commodities to a resident of B, he needs to be paid in dollars while the resident of B has pounds sterling only. Somehow the pounds sterling of B's importer must be converted into dollars; otherwise this transaction cannot take place. Note that it is immaterial as to who (A's exporter or B's importer) undertakes the responsibility of converting pounds sterling into dollars. If A's exporter accepts pounds sterling in the first place, it is he who must make the conversion. But if A's exporter insists on being paid directly in dollars, this responsibility is assigned to B's importer. Nevertheless, the important conclusion to be derived from this analysis is that both A's exporter and B's importer have a *common interest* in converting pounds sterling into dollars. How is this conversion made?

Consider another illustration. A resident of A buys (imports) commodities from a resident of B. In this example, dollars have to be converted into pounds sterling. Again note that it is immaterial who actually makes the conversion and that both A's importer and B's exporter have a common interest in converting dollars into pounds sterling. The important question again is this: how is this conversion of dollars into pounds sterling made?

Obviously international economic transactions cannot take place unless a way is found to effect the conversion of one currency into another. This conclusion is not, of course, true when international barter is practiced; i.e., when a resident of A and a resident of B exchange commodities of equal value. Such barter transactions are not very common and are presently ignored.

Solving the Conversion Problem

Consider again the example where A's importer buys commodities from B's exporter. One rather cumbersome way of solving the problem of converting dollars into pounds sterling is to eliminate the problem altogether as follows. Let A's importer use his dollars to buy commodities from other residents of A and sell them for pounds sterling to residents of B. This procedure, although admittedly cumbersome, would provide A's importer with the necessary pounds sterling to pay for the commodities he buys from B's exporter. Unfortunately, this procedure is awkward and inefficient as it requires every importer to be in the retail business abroad. Certainly, if this solution were actually adopted, the combined production of final consumption goods in A and B would fall short of the production of the same goods in the initial closed economy (i.e., before the introduction of the political frontier); thus the initial static equilibrium would be disturbed. Nevertheless, this procedure is important to us because it gives us the first clue as to how the problem of converting one currency into another may be solved. Thus, we learn that the problem is solved when A's residents export to B's residents commodities which have the same value (expressed in either currency) as the commodities which A's residents import from B's residents. In our illustration, the same individual imported and exported commodities, but this is immaterial.

The above procedure can be easily extended to cover all traders of both countries. Divide the residents of each country into two groups: exporters (i.e., those selling goods to foreign residents) and importers (i.e., those buying goods from foreign residents). It is not inconceivable for an individual to belong to both groups or none at all. However, for expositional purposes, it is convenient to think of these two groups as consisting of completely *different* individuals. Further, those who do not belong to either group can be ignored because their transactions do not present any additional difficulties over those which existed in the initial closed economy (before the introduction of the political frontier). The solution to the problem of conversion is given schematically in fig. 1.1.

On the one hand, we have A's exporters and B's importers who have the *common* interest of converting pounds into dollars. On the other hand, we have A's importers and B's exporters who have the *common* interest of converting dollars into pounds sterling. Neither of these groups can perform alone the necessary conversion (or the transfer of purchasing power from one currency to another, as it is usually called). However, the two groups together can eliminate the problem. This can be done in any of the following four different ways.

1. A's exporters receive payment in terms of pounds sterling which they sell to A's importers. A's importers then use the pounds sterling they receive from A's exporters to pay B's exporters for the commodities they buy from them. This is illustrated in panel (*a*) of fig. 1.1.
2. B's exporters receive payment in dollars which they sell to B's importers. B's importers use the dollars to pay for the commodities they buy from A's exporters. This is illustrated in panel (*b*) of fig. 1.1.

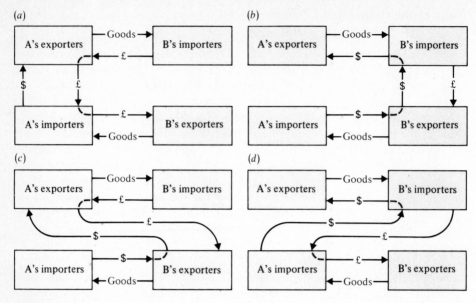

Figure 1.1 The solution to the conversion problem. (*a*) B's importers pay A's exporters in pounds sterling. A's exporters sell the pounds sterling to A's importers and the latter pay B's exporters in pounds. (*b*) A's importers pay B's exporters in dollars. B's exporters sell the dollars to B's importers who in turn pay A's exporters in dollars. (*c*) A's importers pay B's exporters in dollars. B's importers pay A's exporters in pounds sterling. Finally, A's exporters sell pounds sterling to B's exporters. (*d*) A's importers buy pounds sterling from B's importers. Then the importers pay the foreign exporters in the latter's respective currencies.

3. A's exporters accept payment in pounds sterling from B's importers and B's exporters accept payment in dollars from A's importers. Then, A's exporters exchange their pounds sterling for the dollars of B's exporters. This is illustrated in panel (*c*) of fig. 1.1.
4. A's importers exchange their dollars for the pounds sterling of B's importers. The importers can now pay the foreign exporters in terms of the respective currencies of the latter. This is illustrated in panel (*d*) of fig. 1.1.

Note that, since each group of exporters and importers usually includes more than one individual, these four alternatives can be used simultaneously during any time period.

The Possibility of Disequilibrium

⋯g discussion, an important assumption was made: the value of ⋯ntry is equal to the value of its imports. If this condition is not met, ⋯onversion of one currency into another cannot possibly be effected. ⋯rium situation creates difficulties which are the subject matter of the present book. These difficulties are indeed analyzed later on and there is no need for us to be overly concerned with them at the present time.

Note that the possibility of disequilibrium is actually disregarded in our illustration, where the initial closed economy was in static equilibrium to begin with. This can be seen as follows. Suppose that each unit of the old currency is replaced by $R in A and by £1 in B, that £1 exchanges for $R, and that all prices at the initial equilibrium are also replaced by their equivalents in terms of the new currencies. These changes do not affect the static equilibrium of the system at all. Hence, at this equivalent price structure, the receipts of each individual continue to be equal to his payments. The same, of course, must be true of any group of individuals, and, in particular, the residents of each country. Consider now the equality "payments = receipts" of A's residents as a group. Cancelling out the receipts of A's residents from A's residents with the payments of A's residents to A's residents (i.e., all purely domestic transactions), we are left with the equality between the receipts of A's residents from B's residents and the payments of A's residents to B's residents. The same equality can be obtained by starting with the equality "payments = receipts" for B's residents as a group, and then cancelling out all of B's domestic transactions.

International Trade Is Barter Trade

The preceding analysis points to a fundamental principle: the problem of converting one national currency into another is eliminated because at the bottom international trade is indeed barter trade. Go back to fig. 1.1 and observe that in each case the dollars spent by A's importers end up in the pockets of A's exporters. Similarly, the pounds sterling spent by B's importers end up in the pockets of B's exporters. This shows that in effect the importers of a country pay the exporters of that same country. Put differently, a country pays for its imports by means of its exports. That is, a country exchanges its exports for its imports—it practices barter.

1.2 INTRODUCTION OF A FOREIGN EXCHANGE MARKET

We have seen how the problem of converting one currency into another is fundamentally eliminated by means of any one of the four alternative combinations enumerated in the preceding section. But none of these methods is much better than the extreme case where each individual exporter is also an importer with the value of his exports being equal to the value of his imports. It is true that under our new procedure no individual trader need be both exporting and importing commodities to and from the rest of the world as long as he can find somebody else from whom he could buy the required foreign currency or to whom he could sell his foreign-exchange receipts, as the case may be. But obviously such a procedure is still clumsy and inefficient for at least three reasons. First, it requires perfect synchronization of all international transactions in the aggregate; i.e., it requires that the value of exports be equal to the value of imports at every moment, which is something to be desired. Second, even if such perfect synchronization were possible, it would still be difficult for, say, an individual importer to get in touch with another trader from whom he could buy the necessary foreign exchange he needed without the existence of some fairly well-established lines of communication. Third, even if two traders could get together, they would have to synchronize their business, which is almost impossible. Evidently, there is a clearing-house function to be performed. Surely exporters and importers of both countries are willing to pay something for the convenience of making currency exchanges on a smoothly working, impersonal market.

A Clearing House

A clearing house could start with small working balances in both currencies (dollars and pounds sterling) and announce itself willing to exchange *either* currency for the other at a certain rate (say $1.70 per pound sterling) and hope that the inflow of each currency substantially matches the outflow. Thus the initial cash balances in dollars and pounds sterling of the clearing house become a revolving fund. All this is shown schematically in fig. 1.2. Panel (*a*) shows the flow of dollars from the group "A's importers plus B's exporters" to the clearing house and from the clearing house to the group "B's importers plus A's exporters." Note that, as far as the activity in the foreign exchange market is concerned, what really matters is the direction of payment and nothing else. That is, it is immaterial who (the exporter or importer) actually carries out the transaction with the clearing house. For this reason, A's importers have been lumped together with B's exporters—they all have a common interest in converting dollars into pounds sterling. Similarly, B's importers have been lumped together with A's exporters

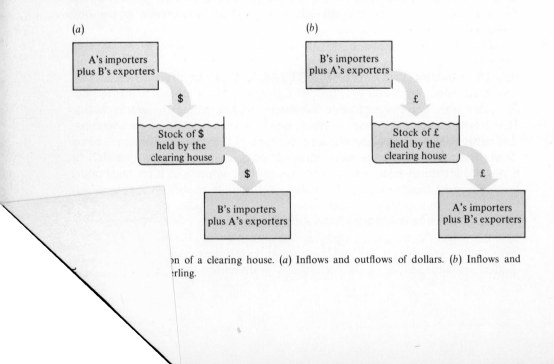

(*a*) Inflows and outflows of dollars. (*b*) Inflows and ...erling.

because they all have a common interest in converting pounds sterling into dollars. Panel (*b*) shows the flow of pounds sterling from the group "B's importers plus A's exporters" to the clearing house and from the clearing house to the group "A's importers plus B's exporters." Note that the position of the two groups of traders is reversed in the two panels. This should be obvious, of course, because when the clearing house buys dollars (see the inflow of dollars in panel (*a*)) it simultaneously sells pounds sterling (see the outflow of pounds sterling in panel (*b*)). The same correspondence exists between the outflow of dollars (panel (*a*)) and the inflow of pounds sterling (panel (*b*)).

Disequilibria: Temporary and Fundamental

When the inflow of a currency into the clearing house does not completely match its outflow, the difference between the two flows is reflected in the level of the stock of that currency held by the clearing house. Thus, when the inflow is larger than the outflow, the stock held by the clearing house tends to rise; when it is smaller, the stock tends to fall. The sole function of the initial stock of dollars and pounds sterling of the clearing house is to bridge any *temporary* gap between the inflow and the outflow of either currency.

It may be thought that the clearing house runs into trouble only when one of its currencies is being depleted, but not when it is augmented. The truth is that when the stock of one of the currencies is augmented, the stock of the other is necessarily depleted. This should be obvious from our previous observation that the inflow of dollars corresponds to the outflow of pounds sterling and the inflow of pounds sterling corresponds to the outflow of dollars. Therefore, if the inflow of dollars is larger than the outflow of dollars, it must also be true that the inflow of pounds sterling is smaller than the outflow of pounds sterling. Accordingly, the stock of neither currency held by the clearing house can increase for ever unless the stock of the other currency (which is depleted continuously) is replenished continuously from outside sources.

The initial stocks of currencies held by the clearing house are good to bridge temporary gaps only between inflows and outflows, but there is no reason to suppose that more permanent and persistent gaps never arise. When such a persistent gap does arise, the situation is usually described as one of *fundamental* disequilibrium. This is a most difficult problem in international monetary theory. It is interesting to note that it raises its ugly head right from the start of our discussion. Its causes and cures are indeed one of the primary objectives of this book. Essentially what needs to be done is to perform some adjustment and effect a better synchronization between the inflows and the outflows of the clearing house.

Fixed Versus Fluctuating Exchange Rates

So far we have been talking about purchases and sales of currencies without specifying the process by which their relative prices are established. This was intentional. We shall return to this particular topic in chaps. 5 to 8. For the moment, it suffices to say that the price of one currency in terms of another (or what is usually called the *rate of foreign exchange*) may be held constant by agreement (as, for instance, in the case of countries on the gold standard); or it may be left free to fluctuate from day to day depending on supply and demand conditions. These are the two major polar cases. Other possibilities exist, of course, but they can always be recognized as some combination of these two polar cases. It should be noted that, in the face of fundamental disequilibrium as described in the preceding paragraph, the precise adjustment process to be followed depends on whether the rate of foreign exchange is supposed to be kept fixed or allowed to fluctuate. As we shall see, any variation in the rate of foreign exchange has a direct impact on the inflows and the outflows of the clearing house. More on this later.

The Clearing-House Function Is Performed by Banks

The term *clearing house* has been used so far to characterize a function rather than any particular institution. In reality, this function is usually performed by banks, partly because for the most part foreign-exchange transactions of any size take the form of an exchange of bank deposits and partly because in case the importer needs credit to finance his imports it is convenient to combine the foreign-exchange transaction with the credit transaction.

Means of Payment

We need not concern ourselves with the various means of payment in international transactions (e.g., bills of exchange, checks, telegraphic transfers, and cash). The distinction between them is legal—not economic. It is sufficient for our purposes to note that because of the competition which exists between these different means of payment, we can speak of the supply and demand for foreign money without paying much attention to the particular document used.†

1.3 THE INTERNATIONAL CHARACTER OF THE FOREIGN EXCHANGE MARKET

The foreign exchange market is not limited to a particular locality. It embraces all financial centers of the world. It is rather an *international* market where national currencies are traded. The force which keeps the various financial centers around the world united into a single market is known as *arbitrage*.

---

† On the various *legal* means of payment and other related matters, the interested reader is referred to Rosenthal (1950).

Definition of Arbitrage

Arbitrage can be defined as simultaneous buying and selling of foreign currencies for the sake of realizing profits from discrepancies between exchange rates prevailing at the same time in different centers. Thus, if 1 pound sterling exchanges for 3 dollars in the financial center of country A while at the same time 1 pound sterling exchanges for only 2 dollars in the financial center of country B, a profit can be realized by buying sterling in B (= selling dollars in B) where it is cheap and selling it in A (= buying dollars in A) where it is expensive. This, of course, can be done by either residents of A or residents of B. Thus, an individual with an initial stock of pounds sterling can first buy dollars in A and then sell them in B, while an individual with an initial stock of dollars can first buy pounds sterling in B and then sell them in A. This kind of arbitrage tends to draw the two prices together by forcing up the price of the dollar in A and depressing it in B, which is equivalent to forcing up the price of pounds sterling in B and depressing it in A.

The preceding example illustrates what is usually called *two*-point arbitrage, because only *two* currencies are involved. This is the simplest kind of arbitrage and it is the only kind that could possibly be practiced in a two-country, two-currency world, like the one we have been studying so far. However, in a multi-country, multicurrency world, other, more complicated forms of arbitrage can take place, namely, *three*-point arbitrage, *four*-point arbitrage, and in general *n*-point arbitrage, corresponding to the simultaneous purchase and sale of three, four, and in general *n* currencies, respectively. The general case of *n*-point arbitrage is rather complicated and is examined further in the appendix to this chapter. For our purposes an illustration of a three-point arbitrage is sufficient.

Three-Point Arbitrage

Consider three countries, A, B, and C, with national currencies the dollar, the pound sterling, and the yen, respectively. The three currencies are traded in three geographically distinct financial centers: New York, London, and Tokyo. Therefore, the price of each currency in terms of another is registered in all three centers. Considering two currencies at a time, two-point arbitrage necessarily establishes the same prices (or rates of foreign exchange) in all three centers. Let us suppose that these rates (prevailing in all financial centers) are as follows: 1 pound sterling sells for either 3 dollars or 1000 yen, and 1 dollar sells for 300 yen. Obviously, two-point arbitrage is no longer profitable, because the price of each currency in terms of any other is the same in all centers. Does this mean that no form of arbitrage is profitable? Absolutely not. Because of the existing inconsistency among the above rates, three-point arbitrage is still profitable. This should be obvious because while 1 pound sterling sells *directly* for 1000 yen, it sells indirectly for 900 yen (i.e., by buying first 3 dollars and then exchanging them for 900 yen). Because of the existing divergence between the *direct rate* of 1000 yen and *indirect* (or cross) *rate* of 900 yen per pound sterling a profit can be follows. Use 900 yen to buy 3 dollars; sell the 3 dollars for 1 pound ste then sell the pound sterling for 1000 yen. A profit of 100 yen is mad

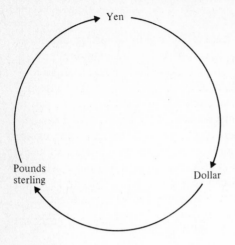

Figure 1.3 Three-point arbitrage. Find a profitable sequence and then arrange the three currencies in a circle using arrows to show the correct sequence. Then you can start with any currency, follow the sequence indicated by the arrows, and make a profit.

Is it necessary for an arbitrager in the above example to start with yen and end up with yen in order to make a profit? No, because when one indirect rate is out of line all of them are. Thus, 1 pound sterling sells for 3 dollars *directly* but for $\frac{1000}{300} = 3\frac{1}{3}$ dollars *indirectly* (i.e., by purchasing first yen and then selling them for dollars). Similarly, 1 dollar sells for 300 yen *directly* while it sells for $\frac{1000}{3} = 333.33$ yen *indirectly* (i.e., by purchasing first sterling and then selling it for yen). Accordingly, an arbitrager can start with any currency and make a profit. The following rule is useful. First determine any profitable sequence.† Then arrange the three currencies in a circle as shown schematically in fig. 1.3. The arrows show the correct sequence. Now it is true that an arbitrager can start with any currency, follow the sequence indicated by the arrows, and make a profit. The reader is encouraged to use the example given above to verify the rule.

Three-point arbitrage, if not prevented, say, by means of exchange control, can eliminate the divergence between the direct and indirect rates very quickly. Thus, in our earlier example, arbitragers of any nationality always sell yen for dollars, dollars for sterling, and sterling for yen. Accordingly, a rudimentary application of the law of supply and demand shows that: (*a*) the price of the dollar in terms of the yen tends to rise, say, to 310; (*b*) the price of sterling in terms of the dollar tends to rise, say, to 3.10; and (*c*) the price of sterling in terms of the yen tends to fall, say, to 961. At these new rates, all indirect rates are equal to the corresponding direct rates and the profitability of all forms of arbitrage is eliminated completely.

---

† To determine a profitable sequence simply start with some *arbitrary* sequence. If it is profitable, you have already found the needed (profitable) sequence. If it is not profitable, then the *opposite* sequence must be profitable. Thus, if moving clockwise in fig. 1.3 generates a loss, moving counterclockwise necessarily generates a profit, and vice versa.

m-Point Arbitrage

In an *n*-country, *n*-currency world the possibility arises for *m*-point arbitrage
($3 < m \leq n$). While the three-point (or triangular) arbitrage is relatively simple, as
the number of currencies traded increases the problem becomes progressively
more difficult. Actually, in practice arbitrage involving more than three currencies
is extremely rare. Is it not possible, then, that arbitragers may miss some profitable
opportunities? And if this is so, does it not follow that the observed rates of
foreign exchange need not be consistent? Fortunately not. In the appendix to this
chapter, the following remarkable theorem is proved: *when three-point arbitrage is
not profitable, then four-point arbitrage, five-point arbitrage, and in general n-point
arbitrage is not profitable either.* Thus, the consistency among a number of foreign-
exchange rates can be established by the relatively simple three-point arbitrage
alone. It is no wonder that in the real world these complicated forms of arbitrage
very rarely, if at all, take place.

Banks and Arbitrage

Most arbitrage in our modern economic system is carried out by banks. Their
foreign-exchange dealers keep in constant touch (by cable, teletype, and tele-
phone) with each other and keep constantly alert to the latest quotations in the
various geographic spots of the market. Even small discrepancies give rise to
voluminous arbitrage which practically wipes out the discrepancies literally
within minutes.

1.4 FORWARD EXCHANGE

The class of foreign-exchange transactions considered so far implied immediate
delivery, or exchange of currencies on the spot. (In practice, the settlement takes
place within two days in most markets.) These transactions are usually called *spot
transactions*, the rate of exchange used in these transactions is the *spot rate*, and
the market itself is the *spot market*. But in addition to spot transactions, another
important class of transactions takes place in the foreign exchange market: the
forward transactions. A forward transaction is an agreement (called the *forward-
exchange contract*) between two parties which calls for delivery at some prescribed
time *in the future* of a specified amount of foreign currency by one of the parties
against payment in domestic currency by the other party, at a price (called the
forward-exchange rate) agreed upon now when the contract is signed. (Thus,
forward exchange is recognized as futures in foreign exchange.)† Consequently,
the forward exchange market deals in current commitments to buy and sell currencies at some specified future time.

---

† On the institutional distinction between *forward* and *futures* markets, the reader is referred to
Snape (1970).

It is often argued that the forward market is separate from the spot market because it has its own prices, and its own methods of determining them, which are different from the spot exchange market. Thus, the current forward rate is in general different from the current spot rate, or even the spot rate prevailing at the time the contract falls due. Nevertheless, as we shall presently see, the forward market is directly and closely connected with the spot market, and this makes it virtually impossible to consider the forward market as separate from the spot market. The forward market is a significant part of the total exchange market and handles the bulk of international trade.

Types of Forward Contract

Ordinarily, forward rates are quoted for one, three, or six months delivery. Nevertheless, each individual contract has to be tailored to suit the needs of the parties involved, as each forward contract calls for delivery at a prescribed date which need not coincide with any one of these even maturities. As a result, a separate forward rate is usually negotiated for each forward contract depending on its maturity. Note also that contracts of up to seven years are known to have been arranged in practice. However, the market for these long maturities is necessarily very thin. Finally, in addition to the forward contract which calls for delivery at a specified future date, another more flexible type of forward contract is available, namely, the *forward-option contract*, which ordinarily calls for delivery at the beginning of the month (i.e., from the 1st to the 10th), the middle of the month (i.e., from the 11th to the 20th), or the end of the month (i.e., from the 21st to the 31st). More refined contracts can also be arranged. Option contracts are necessarily more expensive because the banks work on the assumption that the customer will ask for or make the delivery on the day which is the least favorable from the bank's point of view.

Forward Premium and Forward Discount

The forward rate for a currency, say the pound sterling, is said to be at a premium with respect to the spot rate when 1 pound sterling buys more units of another currency, say the dollar, in the forward than in the spot market. The premium is usually expressed as a percentage deviation from the spot rate on a per annum basis. For instance, if the spot rate for pounds sterling is quoted at $1.680 and the one-month forward rate at $1.687, then sterling is at a 5 percent forward premium (that is, $[(1.687 - 1.680)/1.680] \times 12$ (months) $\times 100 = 5$). Conversely, the forward rate for pounds sterling is said to be at a discount with respect to the spot rate when 1 pound sterling buys fewer dollars in the forward than in the spot market, and the discount is expressed in the same way as the premium. For instance, if the spot rate for pounds sterling is quoted at $1.680 and the one-month forward rate at $1.673, then sterling is at a 5 percent forward discount (that is, $[(1.673 - 1.680)/1.680] \times 12 \times 100 = -5$).

Forward Arbitrage

Profitable arbitrage opportunities arise also in the forward market and give rise to what is called *forward arbitrage* (among different exchange rates of a *given* maturity). No new considerations are introduced by forward arbitrage. Thus, in general we may have two-point, three-point, up to *n*-point forward arbitrage, where *n* indicates the number of currencies traded in the forward market. Note that the forward-arbitrage profits are necessarily realized at the maturity of the forward contracts. As with the case of spot rates, three-point forward arbitrage is sufficient to establish consistent forward rates. Further results on forward arbitrage are noted in the appendix to this chapter.

Exchange Risk

Why should a forward market exist at all? What is it that makes the spot market insufficient to handle all normal foreign-exchange transactions? The usefulness of the forward market becomes obvious when it is realized that ordinarily export and import transactions involve periods of waiting and the future spot rate of exchange is not completely certain. As a result, the slightest unfavorable change in the spot-exchange rate may involve traders (importers and exporters) in losses completely unrelated to their normal business. This *exchange risk* is the only reason for the existence of the forward market.

Note that the exchange risk is not eliminated if the exporters and importers of one country insist on dealing in terms of their own domestic currency. In this case, the exchange risk is simply shifted to the foreigners. Since this procedure might discourage the foreigners, it is almost certain that some advantageous transactions would be ruled out. Thanks to forward exchange, however, this great loss to the international economy can be averted. A few examples are necessary to illustrate the mechanics of forward exchange.

The Exporter's Case

Consider first the case of an American exporter who expects payment in pounds sterling three months from today. If he wants to avoid the exchange risk, he can enter into a contract with his bank and agree to deliver to the bank the pounds sterling he expects to receive three months from today against payment in dollars, at a rate agreed on now. Thus, he avoids the risk of a possible fall in the price of pounds sterling in terms of the dollar. Later, it is shown how the bank avoids the exchange risk.

It is also possible for the American exporter to cover himself against the exchange risk in the following indirect way, without making use of the forward market. He can first borrow sterling for three months in London, sell it today for dollars in the spot market, and in three months, when he receives his export revenue in sterling, pay off his debt. This procedure also eliminates the exchange risk. But it requires the American exporter to have credit facilities in London. Of course, if both methods are available to the exporter, he will definitely choose the one which is most profitable to him. Nevertheless, as shown below, competition causes both methods to produce essentially similar results. As in the case of spot transactions where spot arbitrage keeps the spot rate identical in all geographic centers and commercial traders need not worry about geographic differences in exchange rates, so it is with forward exchange as well. For this reason, the forward market is usually preferred because it is simpler.

The Importer's Case

Next consider the case of an American importer who must make a payment in pounds sterling three months from today. To cover himself against the exchange risk of a possible rise in the dollar price of pounds sterling, he can buy sterling today in the spot market, deposit it with a British bank, and use it (along with the interest accrued) in three months to pay off his debt. But this requires the importer to have either idle cash or credit facilities. A forward contract is simpler. Thus, the importer can sign up a forward contract with his bank, agreeing to buy pounds sterling from the bank three months from today at a (forward) rate agreed on now. (Banks usually sign forward contracts with trusted clients as a matter of routine.) Again, if both options of covering the risk are open to the importer, he will definitely choose the one which is cheaper to him. But as noted in the case of the exporter, competition actually makes the two methods equivalent in normal times, and as a result the forward market is always preferred.

The importer's problem is actually more complicated. In addition to the exchange risk, an importer also runs what might be called a *price risk*, for the dollar price of the goods imported by the American importer is definitely a function of the price of pounds sterling in terms of the dollar. When sterling becomes cheaper, the dollar price of goods imported from England tends to fall because the per-unit-dollar cost of imports falls. As this happens, the American importer who has already covered his exchange risk in the forward market suffers a loss. Accordingly, forward exchange cannot simultaneously protect the importer from both the exchange risk and the price risk. In particular, if the importer actually covers and sterling becomes more expensive, he gains both ways (i.e., he gains by buying pounds sterling at a low price and he also gains by selling his imported goods at a higher price). On the other hand, if he covers but sterling becomes cheaper, he loses both ways. However, if the importer fails to cover the exchange risk through the forward market, the two risks tend to at least partially offset each other. If sterling depreciates, there emerge an adverse price effect and a favorable exchange-rate effect. On the other hand, if sterling appreciates, there emerge an adverse exchange-rate effect and a favorable price effect. Unfortunately, these two effects do not exactly offset each other and the importer might suffer a residual loss after all. This is illustrated by the case where the pound sterling is at a forward discount. If an American importer does not cover his exchange risk (because if he does he will be running a price risk) and the spot rate remains constant, he will be in a disadvantageous position in relation to his competitors who might have bought their sterling at the low forward rate.

There is another complication regarding the American importer. The price risk tends to offset the exchange risk (when the importer does not cover his position) only to the extent that the value of imports not yet sold by the importer equals his debt in pounds sterling. If, for instance, the American importer has a large unsold stock of imported goods after he actually pays for them and sterling becomes cheaper, he suffers an adverse price effect with no offsetting favorable exchange-rate effect. Under these circumstances, the American importer can hedge against this adverse price effect by selling sterling forward (when he pays for his imports) to the extent of the value of his unsold stock. As he sells his stock, at the same time he should buy sterling forward so that his net sterling liabilities match the value of his unsold stock of imported goods. In the future, we shall avoid these complications by assuming that the time required for shipping goods between countries is negligible and that the importers have the goods delivered to them a short time before they sell them.

Tenders and Long Maturities

Industrial firms or contractors tendering for contracts involving expenditure or receipt of foreign currency present an interesting problem: *they simply cannot cover the exchange risk during the time their tenders are being considered.* This is one of the instances in which the forward market does not provide an adequate safeguard against exchange risks. The contractor cannot sign a forward contract because of the uncertainty involved in his foreign-exchange position.

As mentioned earlier, forward contracts of up to seven years are known to have been arranged. These long maturities are of great importance to shipbuilders, aircraft manufacturers, firms undertaking construction of plants abroad, etc. However, because the market for these long maturities is necessarily very thin, such firms might find it necessary to cover their exchange risk by borrowing in terms of the foreign currency in which they are to receive sales revenue and then selling the proceeds of the loan in the spot market for domestic currency. When the sales revenue is received, it can be used to repay the loan.

Banks and Exchange Risk

How do banks cover the risks they assume as they sign forward contracts? They do this in three ways. First, forward purchases and sales of a particular currency by a particular bank ordinarily match to a considerable extent. Hence, a large portion of the risk involved is automatically offset. Second, banks deal among themselves to iron out their net individual positions. But unless the commercial excess demand for forward exchange happens to be zero, there is a residual amount of either forward sales or forward purchases to be covered. Third, banks cover the commercial excess demand (or supply) in the same indirect way an individual importer or exporter who does not wish to use the facilities of the forward market would follow to cover his position. Thus, if, for instance, the commercial excess demand for forward sterling is negative, the banks borrow sterling at short term in London and sell it in the spot market for dollars which they invest at short term in New York. At the maturity of their forward contracts, they buy sterling from their customers (at the forward rate) which they use to repay their short-term loan in London. On the other hand, when the excess demand is positive, the banks buy sterling in the spot market which they invest in London until their forward contracts become due.

In the same way, banks can also cover their working balances of foreign exchange. Essentially, the procedure boils down to a swap of demand deposits between, say, the New York banks and the London banks with a forward contract to reverse the exchange of deposits in, say, three months. It is understood, of course, that these transactions have to be repeated every three months, or whatever the maturity of the forward contract is. A direct application of this principle is the case of the so-called "swaps," by which the monetary authorities of two countries acquire claims on each other by "swapping" demand deposits. As a rule, they simultaneously sign a forward contract reversing the transaction at a specified future date. Such swaps provide the monetary authorities of each country with foreign funds. Thus, they are in a better position to meet a temporary disequilibrium in their international payments.

Some Simplifying Assumptions

As noted earlier, the spot and forward markets are closely linked. In fact, the spot and forward rates are simultaneously determined. We are not ready yet to discuss the joint determination of these two rates. This job is undertaken in chaps. 6 to 8 below. Nevertheless, as an introduction to that analysis, we must examine more rigorously the link between the spot rate and the forward rate. For this purpose, we assume from now on that there is only one period of maturity, say three months, and only one forward rate, even though in reality there are various periods of maturity for forward contracts and therefore many forward rates. In addition, it is useful to view the various transactors in terms of the activities they carry on in the foreign exchange market. These activities include interest arbitrage, speculation, and commercial trade, and they are taken up in this order in the final three sections of this chapter.

1.5 COVERED-INTEREST ARBITRAGE

In addition to the spot and forward arbitrage discussed earlier, there exists a relatively more involved type of arbitrage, called *interest arbitrage*, which provides the link between the spot rate and the forward rate. The theory of interest arbitrage was first expounded clearly by Keynes (1923, pp. 115–139). It rests on the simple proposition that funds available for short-term investments, say, three months, are placed in that center (at home or abroad) which yields the highest return. This is actually part of the normal process of maximizing earnings from investment. In the case of a closed economy (using a single national currency), the problem is trivial indeed: funds move from the region where the interest rate is low to the region where it is high, until the same interest rate prevails everywhere. In the world economy, the problem becomes more complicated because of the existence of exchange risk. Only in the absence of exchange risk is the comparison between interest rates a sufficient guide for the allocation of funds between financial centers. Thus, if the interest rate in New York is 5 percent per annum while it is 10 percent in London, an American investor will find it profitable to invest his funds in London *if* the price of the pound sterling in terms of dollars remains constant (or does not depreciate substantially). The American investor who wishes to invest his funds in London has to buy now (in the spot market) the requisite pounds sterling; then, when he wishes to repatriate his funds at the maturity of his investment, he has to sell the sterling. If the dollar price of the pound sterling remains constant in the meantime, the American investor reaps a return of 10 percent per annum both on the sterling he invested in London and his initial dollar funds. However, if the pound sterling actually depreciates, his return on the sterling he invests in London continues to be 10 percent per annum but his return on his initial dollar funds is lower by the percentage by which sterling depreciates. It is not inconceivable that the sterling depreciation may wipe out completely the 10 percent return on sterling. Of course, if sterling appreciates in the meantime, the return to the American investor (on his initial dollar funds) becomes higher than the London interest rate by the percentage of sterling appreciation.

The Analogy with Fisher's Money and Real Rates of Interest

It is interesting to note the analogy between the present case and Irving Fisher's distinction between the money rate and the real rate of interest. As Fisher (1930, p. 36) notes, a man who lends $100 this year in order to obtain $110 next year is really sacrificing 100 dollars' worth of goods in the hope that he will obtain 110 dollars' worth of other goods next year. While the money rate of interest here is 10 percent, the real rate of interest in terms of real goods may be lower. This happens when (because of inflation) the purchasing power of the dollar falls in the meantime. Thus, one year from now the $110 will not buy 10 percent more goods than the amount which the $100 can buy today—they will buy less. The same goes for the American investor who invests his funds in London. Despite the fact that he receives 10 percent on the sterling he invests in London, the (real) return on his initial dollar funds is less if the pounds sterling he receives in the future have a lower purchasing power (in terms of dollars) than the initial pounds sterling he sacrifices. Conversely, his (real) return is more than 10 percent if the pounds sterling he receives in the future have a higher purchasing power (in terms of dollars) than the initial pounds sterling he sacrifices.

The Keynesian Theory of Covered-Interest Arbitrage

Investing funds in a foreign financial center involves an exchange risk. To rid himself of the exchange risk, the American investor (usually a bank) has to make use of the facilities of the forward market. In particular, he must cover his position by selling forward the sterling he expects to receive in the future. If the forward rate is equal to the spot rate, then it is certainly profitable to transfer funds to London (i.e., the center with the highest interest rate). Further, if the pound sterling is at a forward premium, it is even more profitable to do so because, in addition to the gain due to the favorable interest-rate differential, he makes an additional gain by buying sterling in the spot market where it is cheap and selling it in the forward market where it is expensive. However, if the pound sterling is at a forward discount, the gain from the favorable interest-rate differential must be weighed against the loss he suffers from buying sterling in the spot market where it is expensive and selling it in the forward market where it is cheap. Whether his return is higher than the New York interest rate or not depends on which of these two elements (i.e., the gain from the interest-rate differential or loss on the purchase and sale of sterling) is stronger. Approximately, if the interest-rate differential is higher than the forward discount, it is profitable to transfer funds to London. If the interest-rate differential is smaller than the forward discount, it is not. On the contrary, in the latter case *it is profitable to transfer funds from London to New York*. Covered-interest arbitrage becomes unprofitable when the interest-rate differential is exactly balanced by the loss (or gain, as the case may be) of buying sterling in the spot market and selling it in the forward market, i.e., the forward discount (or the forward premium). Note that the term *covered*-interest arbitrage is used to indicate the fact that the exchange risk is covered.

If it is profitable for an American investor to transfer funds to London, it is necessarily profitable for an Englishman to do so as well. The only difference between the two is that the American starts with dollars and ends with dollars, while the Englishman starts with pounds sterling and ends with pounds sterling. Thus, the Englishman has to borrow dollars first in the New York money market, use the dollars to buy sterling in the spot market, and invest it in London. In addition, he has to sell forward a sufficient amount of sterling to be able to repay his loan (principal plus interest) when it becomes due. Of course, his profit is in sterling. In particular, his profit in sterling is the difference between the amount of sterling he receives from the loan he makes to the London money market (principal plus interest) and the amount of sterling he sells forward to repay the loan (principal plus interest) he receives from the New York money market. The significance of this observation is that it is unnecessary for us, in our future investigations, to distinguish between arbitragers according to their nationality.

Under normal circumstances, covered-interest arbitrage proceeds until the forward difference (premium or discount, as the case may be) equals the interest-rate differential. This may be called the *neutrality condition*. When it holds, any further movement of arbitrage funds ceases as it becomes unprofitable. Precisely how the neutrality condition is established is analyzed later in chaps. 6 to 8.

The fact that the movement of fully covered funds from one financial center to another depends not only on the interest-rate differential but also on the forward difference is of great significance to economic policy. Mainly because of the important role the interest rate plays in maintaining full employment and a healthy rate of economic growth, it is important to know that the movement of covered-arbitrage funds can be influenced through the forward market. For this reason, as we shall see, the forward rate becomes an important instrument of economic policy, because it frees the interest rate to attend to other domestic goals.

Mathematical Formulation

With little effort, the preceding analysis can be made rigorous. Let

r_a = three-months interest rate in A (America)
r_b = three-months interest rate in B (Britain)
R_s = number of dollars required to purchase 1 pound sterling in the *spot* market (i.e., the spot rate)
R_f = three-months forward rate for sterling (i.e., so many dollars per pound sterling)

and define the forward difference (d) as follows:

$$d \equiv \frac{R_f - R_s}{R_s} \qquad (1.1)$$

Thus, if $d > 0$, the pound sterling is at a forward premium, and if $d < 0$, it is at a forward discount.

Consider now an *American arbitrager* endowed with $\$R_s$. If he invests his funds in New York for three months, his rate of return is obviously r_a. On the other hand, he can buy £1 in the spot market and invest it in London for three months. At the end of the three-month period he receives $£(1 + r_b)$. To rid himself of the exchange risk, he sells this amount of sterling forward. He finally receives $\$(1 + r_b)R_f$. Since his initial capital was $\$R_s$, his rate of return is given by

$$r_b^* \equiv \frac{(1 + r_b)R_f - R_s}{R_s} = (1 + r_b)\frac{R_f}{R_s} - 1 = (1 + r_b)(1 + d) - 1 = r_b + (1 + r_b)d$$

where use has been made of eq. (1.1). Note that, in terms of Irving Fisher's (1930) terminology, r_b may be said to be the nominal rate and r_b^* the real rate of interest in B, as viewed by the American investor. The difference between these two rates equals $d + r_b d$, which for all practical purposes can be approximated by the forward difference since the term $r_b d$ is negligible as long as r_b and d are both small fractions.

Where should the American investor place his funds? Obviously in the center where his return is highest. Thus, if

$$r_a < r_b^* = r_b + (1 + r_b)d \qquad (1.2a)$$

or $\qquad r_a - r_b < (1 + r_b)d \cong d \qquad (1.2b)$

it is profitable for the American investor to invest his funds in London. On the other hand, if

$$r_a > r_b^* = r_b + (1 + r_b)d$$

or $\qquad r_a - r_b > (1 + r_b)d \cong d$

he is better off investing his funds in New York. Finally, if the neutrality condition

$$r_a = r_b^* = r_b + (1 + r_b)\, d \qquad (1.4a)$$

or
$$r_a - r_b = (1 + r_b)\, d \cong d \qquad (1.4b)$$

holds, he is indifferent between the two centers because they both offer the same profitability.

Consider now the case of a *British arbitrager*. If inequality (1.2a) holds, he can profit as follows. First, he borrows dollars in New York. For each $\$R_s$ he borrows, he buys £1 in the spot market which he invests in London and receives in three months £$(1 + r_b)$. To cover his position, he sells forward sterling. How much? A sufficient amount to be able to repay his loan (principal plus interest) in three months. In particular, he sells £$(1 + r_a)R_s/R_f$. Finally, his net profit equals £$[(1 + r_b) - (1 + r_a)R_s/R_f] = (r_b^* - r_a)/(1 + d)$ per $\$R_s$ he initially borrows. This amount is necessarily positive because of inequality (1.2a), as can be easily checked.

If, instead of inequality (1.2a), inequality (1.3a) were satisfied, the above expression for the profit of the British arbitrager would be negative (a loss). In this case, it would be profitable for him to invest funds in New York and make a profit as follows. Assuming he is endowed with £1 to begin with, his rate of return by investing in London is obviously r_b. But his rate of return by investing in New York is necessarily higher. Thus, with his £1 he can buy $\$R_s$ in the spot market and invest it in New York. This amount accumulates in three months to $\$(1 + r_a)R_s$. To cover his position, he sells this amount forward. Thus, the initial £1 accumulates to £$(1 + r_a)R_s/R_f$ in three months. Hence, his three-month rate of return is

$$(1 + r_a)\frac{R_s}{R_f} - 1 = \left(\frac{1 + r_a}{1 + d}\right) - 1 = \frac{r_a - d}{1 + d}$$

Accordingly, his return is higher in New York because $(r_a - d)/(1 + d) > r_b$, or $r_a > r_b^*$ which is guaranteed by inequality (1.3a).

Note that when inequality (1.3a) holds, not only the British arbitrager but also the American has an incentive to transfer funds from London to New York. This the American arbitrager can do by first borrowing in London. Suppose he borrows £1 in London and buys $\$R_s$ in the spot market, which he invests in New York. His investment increases to $\$(1 + r_a)R_s$ and his debt increases to £$(1 + r_b)$ in three months. To rid himself of the exchange risk, he sells forward enough dollars to be able to repay his debt (principal plus interest). In particular, he sells forward $\$(1 + r_b)R_f$. His net profit then is given by the difference

$$\$[(1 + r_a)R_s - (1 + r_b)R_f] = \$R_s[(1 + r_a) - (1 + r_b)(1 + d)]$$
$$= \$R_s(r_a - r_b^*) > 0$$

Finally, note that when the neutrality condition holds the profitability of the two centers is identical both from the point of view of the American as well as the British arbitrager.

To summarize: if $r_a > r_b^*$, funds move from B (Britain) to A (America); if $r_a < r_b^*$, funds move from A to B; and, finally, if $r_a = r_b^*$, there is no incentive for funds to move in either direction because the profitability is everywhere the same.

Observe that inequalities (1.2b) and (1.3b) offer a direct comparison between the interest-rate differential and the forward difference which corresponds to our earlier verbal statement. For instance, if the interest rate is higher in New York, that is, $r_a - r_b > 0$, funds can still move to London if the interest loss can be more than offset by a gain in buying sterling spot and selling it forward. This implies, of course, that the pound sterling must be selling at a forward premium ($d > 0$) which is higher than the interest-rate differential.

Interest Parity

When the neutrality condition (1.4a) holds, the forward rate is said to be at *interest parity*. In this case, the following observations follow easily from eq. (1.4a). If the interest rates of the two centers are equal, then the forward rate is equal to the spot rate. On the other hand, if $r_a > r_b$, the pound sterling must be selling at a forward premium and, if $r_a < r_b$, the pound sterling must be selling at a forward discount. Note that when the pound sterling is selling at a forward premium, the dollar is necessarily selling at a forward discount; and when the pound sterling is selling at a forward discount, the dollar is selling at a forward premium. Consequently, in general, *the currency of the country with the lower interest rate must be selling at a forward premium* and *the currency of the country with the higher interest rate must be selling at a forward discount, when the neutrality condition holds.*

The Tendency Toward Interest Parity

Under normal circumstances, the neutrality condition is brought about automatically. For instance, suppose that $r_a < r_b^*$. Funds tend to move from New York to London. This movement of funds, in general, affects both the interest rates (r_a and r_b) and the spot and forward rates; in turn, these changes tend to eliminate the divergence between the forward difference and the interest-rate differential (or the divergence between r_a and r_b^*), and thus eliminate the incentive for transferring funds. In particular, as funds move from New York to London, r_a tends to rise and r_b tends to fall. In addition, R_s tends to rise and R_f tends to fall, which implies that the forward difference (d) tends to fall (algebraically). Accordingly, $r_b^* = r_b + (1 + r_b) d$ tends to fall and r_a tends to rise; if sufficient funds move from New York to London, the neutrality condition, $r_a = r_b^*$, is soon satisfied. The reverse process takes place, of course, when we start initially with the inequality $r_a > r_b^*$. This topic is discussed more extensively in chaps. 6 to 8 below.

The Effect of Spot and Forward Transactions on Reserves

A movement of foreign funds into a country tends to increase that country's reserves of foreign currency and places the receiving country in a better position to meet a temporary disequilibrium in its international payments. We shall return to this point in later chapters. For the moment, it suffices to note that it is only the dealings in the spot market, and not the dealings in the forward market, that affect the reserves. To put it differently, funds actually move from one center to another through the spot market only. Forward transactions are mere agreements for future delivery and they do not affect current reserves directly. Again, this does not mean that the dealings in the forward market do not affect reserves at all. They do, but only indirectly through the spot market. This becomes clear in later chapters when we study the implications of official intervention in forward exchange markets.

Some Implications of the Exchange Risk

It is also important to remember that the main function of the forward market, its *raison d'être*, is to enable businessmen to cover their exchange risks. If the exchange risk did not exist, there would be no need for the forward market. Accordingly, in the absence of exchange risk, uncovered-interest arbitrage tends to equalize the interest rates of all financial centers, as indeed is the case with the various financial centers of a single economy such as the United States. Thus, the interest rate in Chicago, for instance, is usually the same as the interest rate in New York. On the other hand, if there exists perfect confidence that the spot rate will under no circumstances move outside certain limits, as in the case of the gold standard (see chap. 7), then these limits provide an additional constraint on the equilibrium values of the forward difference as well as the interest-rate differential.

Reasons Why Interest Parity May Be Violated

Is the neutrality condition always satisfied in the real world? The answer is " No." First, note that the correct neutrality condition is given by eq. (1.4a) and not by the equality $r_a - r_b = d$. As noted earlier, the difference between these two conditions is the factor $r_b d$, which even though negligible gives rise to a divergence between the interest-rate differential and the forward difference. Nevertheless, there are several other reasons why at times the neutrality condition is violated in the real world. These reasons are summarized as follows:

1. In our discussion, transaction costs were ignored for simplicity. As shown by Kemp (1964, pp. 250–251), when these costs are taken into consideration, covered-interest arbitrage becomes unprofitable when the following inequality is satisfied:

$$\left(\frac{1 + r_a}{1 + r_b}\right)(1 - c)^2 < 1 + d < \left(\frac{1 + r_a}{1 + r_b}\right)\left(\frac{1}{1 - c}\right)^2$$

where c indicates the cost per dollar transacted in the foreign exchange market. (Kemp's inequality reduces to (1.4a) when $c = 0$.) Now, for any given interest rates, r_a and r_b, there exists a wide range of values for the forward difference, implying zero profitability for covered-interest arbitrage. Accordingly, small deviations from our neutrality condition (1.4a) are easily explainable by the existence of transaction costs.

2. Another factor which is believed to have a similar effect to transaction costs is that the arbitragers do not find it worth while to move funds from one center to another unless they can make a certain minimum profit. This minimum profit, which may be called appropriately *arbitrage incentive*, is believed to have fluctuated from one-half of 1 percent per annum prior to World War II to one thirty-second of 1 percent in the postwar period (Stern, 1973, p. 50).

   The idea of a minimum percentage profit is not very convincing, however. In fact, any observed minimum may actually be due to some market imperfection. What is important is absolute (not percentage) profit. By borrowing large amounts, an arbitrager can make huge absolute profits even when the percentage profit is very, very small. Thus, the idea of a minimum percentage profit becomes relevant only when limits are placed on credit. But then it is the imperfection of the credit market which really explains nonneutrality.

   Alternatively, when no limits are placed on credit, the individual transactions may become large enough to affect the relevant market rates. Here an arbitrager will behave like a monopolist-monopsonist. Again a nonnegligible percentage profit may be observed, but such profit, and the resultant breakdown of the neutrality condition, is due to the existing market imperfection.

3. Another complication arises from the fact that the short-term interest rates used in the preceding analysis (that is, r_a and r_b) cannot be unambiguously determined in practice. Usually, a whole structure of interest rates prevails in any financial center. Different rates exist for different maturities. In addition, different rates are charged to different borrowers because of different credit risks among borrowers. Indeed, the observed interest rate might be decomposed into a pure interest element (which is the same for all borrowers) plus a risk premium (which varies depending upon the credit-worthiness of the borrower). This makes the use of our neutrality condition rather hazy.

4. Finally, and perhaps most importantly, the interest parity is violated in the real world because the supply of arbitrage funds is not infinitely elastic. Various reasons are cited in the literature for the low-supply elasticity of arbitrage funds. In the first place, as Tsiang (1959) points out, the use of liquid funds for arbitrage purposes involves increasing opportunity costs in terms of inconvenience and loss of liquidity. Second, in times of political upheaval or financial distress arbitragers avoid the transfer of funds either because governments officially prohibit such movements or because of the possibility that such measures may be adopted before they have the chance to repatriate their funds. Accordingly, the process by which the neutrality condition is established is suspended, and the result is a wide divergence between the interest-rate differential and the forward difference. Third, according to the portfolio-balance theory, diversification of portfolios leads to a reduction in the aggregate risk of the portfolio (even when foreign assets are riskier than domestic assets), but only if carried up to a certain point. Beyond that point diminishing returns set in and arbitrage funds become scarce. Fourth, foreign assets may not be perfect

substitutes for corresponding domestic assets due to the possible need for repatriating funds prior to maturity, in which case a loss may be suffered.

Significance of the Theory of Interest Arbitrage

For all these reasons, the concept of interest parity seems to be losing most of its significance. Certainly, it is no longer inconceivable for our neutrality condition to be flagrantly violated while at the same time no tendency for its restoration exists (due to the lack of a sufficient flow of arbitrage funds). But does the theory of interest arbitrage lose all of its usefulness? No. Despite all the difficulties, it still remains true that specified changes in the interest rates or the forward difference will produce the same qualitative effects on the flow of funds as those predicted by the simple theory presented in this chapter. This fact is of paramount importance to economic policy.

1.6 SPECULATION

Speculation ought to be sharply distinguished from arbitrage. While arbitrage is riskless (except perhaps for a few seconds), speculation is the deliberate assumption of exchange risk in the expectation of a profit. In particular, the speculator has definite expectations about future rates of exchange and is interested in making a profit by buying foreign exchange when it is cheap and selling it when it is expensive. Since there is a deliberate and substantial time interval between his purchase and sale of foreign exchange, the activities of the speculator are necessarily subject to exchange risk. Indeed, the element of exchange risk is "the" characteristic feature of speculation. If the speculator is right in his expectations, he makes a profit. But if he is wrong, he suffers a loss. The possibility of a loss often restrains speculators in their activities. A speculator with pessimistic expectations about the future price of a currency is called a *bear;* one with optimistic expectations, a *bull.* Pure speculation can take place either in the spot or the forward market. The forward market is usually more attractive to speculators because it requires neither immediate command of liquid funds nor access to credit facilities. For example, a bull of sterling buys sterling forward, and if his expectations come true, he accepts the sterling at the maturity of the forward contract and sells it directly in the spot market at the then relatively higher price, thus making a profit. The banks, however, usually discourage forward speculation because a speculator might not be able to carry out the terms of the forward contract. Discussion of the related issue of leads and lags is postponed until chap. 8.

Spot and Forward Speculation

Consider an American speculator who expects the pound sterling to appreciate in terms of the dollar. In particular, assume that sterling is currently selling at $\$R_s^o$ in the spot market and at $\$R_f^o$ in the forward market. The speculator expects that in three months the spot price of sterling will be $\$R_s^e$. How can he make a profit? By buying sterling now, i.e., by assuming a *long position* in sterling. (An individual assumes a long position in a currency, or simply " goes long," when the difference between his total claims minus his total liabilities in that currency is positive. If it is negative, he is said to assume a *short position*, or simply " goes short.") He has two choices: (a) he can buy sterling in the spot market and invest it in London for three months; or (b) he can buy sterling forward.

Obviously, if he chooses to buy sterling forward, his cost for each pound sterling he has available at the end of the three-month period is $\$R_f^o$. On the other hand, if he chooses to buy sterling in the spot market, his cost (per pound sterling available to him in three months) is $\$R_s^o (1 + r_a)/(1 + r_b)$. This follows from the fact that in order to have £1 available in three months he must buy only £$1/(1 + r_b)$ now and let it accumulate to £1 in three months. Hence, his current cost is $\$R_s^o/(1 + r_b)$, which necessarily accumulates to $\$R_s^o (1 + r_a)/(1 + r_b)$ in three months. Nevertheless, his expected revenue for each pound sterling available in three months is $\$R_s^e$ in both cases. Accordingly, his expected profit per pound sterling available to him in three months is

$$(a) \quad P_s \equiv R_s^e - \frac{1 + r_a}{1 + r_b} R_s^o \qquad \text{(if he speculates in the spot market)}$$

or $\quad (b) \quad P_f \equiv R_s^e - R_f^o \qquad$ (if he speculates in the forward market)

Spot Speculation as the Equivalent of Forward Speculation Plus Covered-Interest Arbitrage

The expected profit if he speculates in the spot market (that is, P_s) can be decomposed into two parts as follows:

$$P_s = (R_s^e - R_f^o) + \left(R_f^o - \frac{1 + r_a}{1 + r_b} R_s^o \right) \equiv P_f + P_a$$

The first component $(R_s^o - R_f^o)$ is immediately recognized to be the profit which the speculator expects to make if he speculates in the forward market (that is, P_f). What is the meaning of the second component (P_a)? This is simply covered-interest-arbitrage profit for transferring $\$R_s^o/(1 + r_b)$ from New York to London for three months. Obviously, when covered-interest arbitrage works smoothly and the neutrality condition prevails, this second component becomes zero, and thus the expected profit of our speculator is exactly the same whether he speculates in the spot market or the forward market. But if the neutrality condition does not prevail, this second element may be positive or negative depending on circumstances. If it is negative (i.e., if there is an incentive to transfer funds from London to New York), then the expected speculative profits are higher when the speculator speculates in the forward market than in the spot market. In this case, speculation through the forward market has an additional advantage over and above the fact that no command over liquid funds or access to credit facilities are needed for forward speculation. On the other hand, when there is an incentive to transfer funds from New York to London, the second component (P_a) is positive, and the expected profit of spot speculation (P_s) is higher than the expected profit of forward speculation (P_f).

Even in cases when spot speculation has the advantage and actually takes place, analytically it is useful to decompose it into a transaction of forward speculation plus a transaction of covered-interest arbitrage, and lump the latter transaction with the other covered-interest-arbitrage transactions proper. Accordingly, not much violation is made when from now on we assume that all purely speculative activity takes place in the forward market only.

Spot Speculation as Uncovered-Interest Arbitrage

From another angle, spot speculation may be viewed as *un*covered-interest arbitrage. Thus, to continue our earlier example, our American speculator buys pounds sterling in the spot market and invests them in London. Ordinarily he would have to cover his position by selling his expected proceeds forward at the current forward rate R_f^o. However, in the present case, he does not cover because he expects sterling to be selling in the spot market three months from today at $R_s^e > R_f^o$. Accordingly, he expects to make additional profits by not covering. In essence, our American individual plays two roles: the role of an arbitrager and the role of a speculator. In his role as arbitrager he sells to himself his expected proceeds of sterling at the current forward rate, while in his role as speculator he buys sterling forward from himself. Thus, in his capacity as arbitrager he makes a profit given by $P_a \equiv R_f^o - [(1 + r_a)/(1 + r_b)]R_s^o$ and in his capacity as a pure speculator he expects to make an additional profit given by $P_f \equiv R_s^e - R_f^o$.

1.7 COMMERCIAL TRADE

As noted earlier, traders (exporters and importers) who expect to receive or make payment in a foreign currency in the future are running an exchange risk. These traders have two decisions to make: (*a*) whether or not they wish to cover their exchange risk and (*b*) if they decide to cover, whether they wish to use forward covering (i.e., use the facilities of the forward market) or spot covering (i.e., go through the spot market).

A decision by a trader not to cover his exchange risk is similar to the decision to speculate by a pure speculator. For this reason, this activity of commercial traders is usually called *trader speculation*. Now trader speculation is influenced by the same factors which influence pure speculation. For instance, an American importer, who has to make a future payment in pounds sterling and believes strongly that sterling will be devalued shortly, will avoid covering his exchange risk in the belief that he will be able to buy the necessary sterling when he needs it in the spot market at a much lower price. Since pure speculation was analyzed in the preceding section, no further discussion of trader speculation is needed at the present time. We return to the topic of "leads and lags" in chap. 8.

Spot Covering Versus Forward Covering

Consider now an American importer who has to make a payment to a British exporter in three months and has decided to cover his exchange risk. He has two options: (a) he can buy forward the necessary sterling (forward covering) or (b) he can buy sterling now in the spot market and invest it in London until his debt to the British exporter becomes due (spot covering). Which method should he choose? What are the implications of these two methods on the flow of funds from America to Britain? Or to put it differently, what are the implications of spot covering versus forward covering on the question of which country actually finances the American imports?

Consider the second question first. If the American importer chooses forward covering, obviously no funds move from America to Britain now. The British exporter is paid in three months, at which time the American importer's forward contract matures. Accordingly, in this case of forward covering, it is the British exporter (or, in general, the exporter's country) that provides the financing to the American importer. If the American importer chooses spot covering, though, the financing is provided by America. The American importer borrows dollars and buys sterling in the spot market which he uses either to pay off his debt immediately or make a deposit with a British bank and use the deposit (plus the accumulated interest) in three months to pay off his debt to the British exporter. In either case, funds move now from America to Britain. Accordingly, the financing is provided by America. In general, then, forward covering by an importer implies foreign (from the importer's viewpoint) financing and spot covering implies domestic financing.

The question of which country provides the financing actually has important implications for the distribution of reserves between the two countries. This is dramatized particularly when there is a massive switch from financing commercial transactions in one financial center (or country) to financing them in another. This important question is taken up in chap. 8.

Return now to the first question. Which method should the American importer choose: spot covering ($\equiv$ domestic financing) or forward covering ($\equiv$ foreign financing)? The obvious answer is to choose that method which minimizes his costs. Note that because of the close interconnection between the covering of the exchange risk and the financing of imports, we may speak of either the cost of covering or the cost of financing. We choose the latter approach (cost of financing) presently because it clarifies better the relationship between the present problem and that of covered-interest arbitrage. Which factors then determine which method gives the lowest cost of financing?

Consider an American importer who imports goods from a British exporter worth £1 today. He needs three-month financing, which he can obtain either in London (in which case the exporter himself or a British bank may advance the credit) or in New York. If he obtains credit in London, his debt in three months accumulates to $£(1 + r_b)$. To cover his exchange risk, the American importer buys this amount of sterling forward at the current forward rate (R_f^o). Therefore, his debt in three months becomes $\$(1 + r_b)R_f^o$.

It is important to note here that the effective interest rate which the American importer pays when he obtains British financing (forward covering) is identical with the rate of return which an arbitrager would obtain by investing his funds in London, which we saw earlier to be equal to $r_b^* = r_b + d + r_b d$. Thus, the present value, $\$R_s^o$, of the American importer's debt accumulates to $\$(1 + r_b)R_f^o$ in three months. Accordingly, the implicit three-month interest rate, say x, is the root of the equation: $\$R_s^o(1 + x) = \$(1 + r_b)R_f^o$. Solving this equation for x, we obtain $x = r_b + d + r_b d \equiv r_b^*$.

The American importer may alternatively borrow $\$R_s^o$ in New York, buy £1 in the spot market, and either pay the British exporter immediately or deposit the £1 with a British bank and in three months use the deposit (principal plus interest) to pay off his debt with the British exporter. His debt accumulates now to $\$(1 + r_a)R_s^o$ in three months. Obviously, the interest rate he pays now is r_a.

Which method is cheaper? We could, of course, compare the two expressions giving his accumulated debt in three months in dollars and determine directly which method is cheaper. But there is a simpler way of accomplishing this—a way which actually shows the direct link between the present problem and that of covered-interest arbitrage. We only have to compare the implicit interest rates of the two methods of financing. Accordingly, when $r_a = r_b^*$ (i.e., when the neutrality condition for the movement of arbitrage funds holds), both methods are equally costly to the American importer. When $r_a < r_b^*$ (i.e., when there is a profit to be made by moving funds from New York to London), the American importer finds it cheaper to finance his imports in New York. Finally, when $r_a > r_b^*$ (i.e., when there is a profit to be made by moving funds from London to New York), he finds it cheaper to finance his imports in London.

The identity between the present result and the theory of covered-interest arbitrage is no accident. Borrowing abroad with the exchange risk covered is dual to covered-interest arbitrage. What is actually involved here is the simple rule that one borrows in the cheapest financial center but lends in the dearest.

What was said about the American importer is generally valid. Thus, when it is cheaper for an American importer to finance his imports in London, it is also cheaper for a British importer to do so as well. But note that when $r_a > r_b^*$ and an American importer obtains *foreign* credit (because London is a foreign financial center from the point of view of the American importer), the British importer obtains *domestic* credit (because London is a domestic financial center from the British importer's point of view). Accordingly, the American importer works through the forward market while the British importer works through the spot market. Similarly, when $r_a < r_b^*$, both importers obtain credit in New York. But whereas the credit which the American importer obtains is domestic, the credit which the British importer obtains is foreign. Thus, the American importer works now through the spot market while the British importer works through the forward market. In general, then, when American imports are financed through the spot market, the British imports (or American exports) are financed through the forward market, and vice versa.

Similarly, an exporter who expects to receive foreign exchange in the future and wishes to cover his exchange risk has two choices to do so, as explained earlier: he can seek (a) forward covering or (b) spot covering. If he chooses forward covering, then the exporter (or, in general, the exporter's country) provides the financing. On the other hand, if he chooses spot covering, it is the importer's country which provides the financing. As in the case of the importer, it can be shown that the financing is provided by the center from which covered-interest-arbitrage funds are flowing out. For instance, if $r_a < r_b^*$, the financing will be provided by America and an American exporter would seek forward covering; and if $r_a > r_b^*$, an American exporter would seek spot covering and the financing will be provided by Britain. The arithmetic of the present problem is very similar to that provided earlier for the importer, and there seems no need to repeat it.

Forward Covering as Spot Covering Plus Covered-Interest Arbitrage

Return now to the importer who wishes to cover his exchange risk. As we saw, in this case spot covering implies domestic financing and forward covering implies foreign financing, from the importer's viewpoint. Further, we learned earlier that covered-interest arbitrage implies a transfer of funds from one financial center to another. Is it possible to decompose the two methods of covering (spot and forward) to only a single method plus a covered-interest-arbitrage transaction? It certainly is possible. In particular, all forward covering can be decomposed into spot covering plus a covered-interest-arbitrage transaction moving funds from the foreign financial center (from the importer's viewpoint) to the domestic.

Consider our earlier example of the American importer who finds it profitable to finance his imports (worth £1) in London because $r_a > r_b^*$. He may be considered as doing the following. First, acting in his capacity as importer, he borrows $\$R_s$ in New York, buys £1 in the spot market, and pays off his debt to the British exporter. (This is equivalent to spot covering or financing through the spot market.) Second, acting in his capacity as arbitrager, he borrows £1 in London, sells it in the spot market for $\$R_s^o$ which he invests in New York, in the meantime buying forward $£(1 + r_b)$. (This is merely covered-interest arbitrage.) What is the final outcome of these two transactions? Well, he borrows $\$R_s^o$ in New York but he also invests $\$R_s^o$; therefore, his net position is unchanged here. Next he pays off his debt to the British exporter, but he still owes the £1 he borrowed in London. Thus, in the end he only owes £1 and this obligation is covered by the forward purchase of $£(1 + r_b)$. But this is identical to his position when he simply chooses forward covering right from the start.

Accordingly, we have proved that forward covering by importers can be decomposed into (a) spot covering plus (b) covered-interest arbitrage, transferring funds from the foreign country into the importer's country. This conclusion is important because, if and when we so choose, we can assume that all financing takes place in the importer's country. This, of course, ignores the covered-interest-arbitrage component of those transactions for which foreign financing is secured. But this is no problem. There is no essential difference between this type of interest arbitrage and what may be called interest arbitrage proper. Hence, the two can be lumped together.

A similar decomposition can be made for the exporter as well. Remember that in this case, as well as in the case of the importer, spot covering implies that the financing is provided by the importer's country and forward covering implies that the financing is provided by the exporter's country. Thus, forward covering can be decomposed into (a) spot covering plus (b) covered-interest arbitrage, moving funds from the exporter's country to the importer's. For instance, an American exporter who expects to receive $£(1 + r_b)$ in three months and chooses forward covering can be thought of doing the following. First, he borrows £1 in London which he sells in the spot market for $\$R_s^o$ (spot covering). Second, he spends his $\$R_s^o$ to buy £1 which he invests in London for three months and sells his expected proceeds, $£(1 + r_b)$, forward (covered-interest arbitrage). The final position is identical with his position when he chooses forward covering from the start.

Summary

The preceding discussion can be summarized in the following simple propositions:

1. When spot covering is preferred by American importers, it is also preferred by British exporters as well, and vice versa. The same goes for forward covering.
2. When spot covering (forward covering) is preferred by American importers and British exporters, forward covering (spot covering) is preferred by American exporters and British importers, and vice versa.
3. When spot covering is sought by a trader, the financing is provided by the importer's country, and when forward covering is sought, the financing is provided by the exporter's country.
4. The financing of commercial trade is provided by the country which has the lowest *effective* interest rate. (The word "effective" implies in this context that due allowance is given to the forward difference.)
5. If the effective interest rate is lower in London, American exports (or British imports) are paid cash while American imports (or British exports) are purchased on credit. The opposite is true when the effective interest rate is lower in New York. Then American exports are sold on credit while American imports are paid cash.
6. Forward covering can always be decomposed into (a) spot covering plus (b) covered-interest arbitrage, transferring funds from the exporter's to the importer's country. Hence, in our future discussion, we shall assume that all financing is provided by the importer's country (spot covering), lumping the interest-arbitrage transaction together with the rest of covered-interest-arbitrage transactions proper.

APPENDIX TO CHAPTER ONE. THE SUFFICIENCY OF THREE-POINT ARBITRAGE TO INSURE CONSISTENT CROSS RATES OF EXCHANGE†

This brief note deals with the determination of the necessary and sufficient conditions for the establishment of consistent (spot and forward) exchange rates.

Assume an n-country, n-currency world and let the symbol R_{ij} show the number of units of the ith currency which exchange for one unit of the jth currency in the financial center of the ith country,‡ where $i, j = 1, 2, \ldots, n$. By definition, we must necessarily have:

$$R_{ii} = 1 \qquad (i = 1, 2, \ldots, n) \qquad (A1.1)$$

Table A1.1 summarizes in a convenient way the exchange rates that exist in all financial centers. Since table A1.1 seems self-evident no interpretation appears to be necessary. The elements of table A1.1 form the raw material of the ensuing analysis.

As is well known, the foreign exchange market is *international* in character. The force which keeps the various financial centers around the world united into a single market is known as arbitrage, which involves the simultaneous buying and selling of foreign currencies for the sake of realizing profits from discrepancies that might exist between exchange rates prevailing at the same time in different financial centers.

Table A1.1

Financial centers	Currencies					
	1	2	3	...	$n-1$	n
1	1	R_{12}	R_{13}	...	$R_{1,n-1}$	R_{1n}
2	R_{21}	1	R_{23}	...	$R_{2,n-1}$	R_{2n}
3	R_{31}	R_{32}	1	...	$R_{3,n-1}$	R_{3n}
.	.	.	.	...	.	.
.	.	.	.	...	.	.
.	.	.	.	...	.	.
$n-1$	$R_{n-1,1}$	$R_{n-1,2}$	$R_{n-1,3}$	...	1	$R_{n-1,n}$
n	R_{n1}	R_{n2}	R_{n3}	...	$R_{n,n-1}$	1

Various forms of arbitrage can be distinguished on the basis of the number of currencies which are simultaneously bought and sold. The simplest f⸺

---

† Adapted from Chacholiades (1971).

‡ When a distinction is made between spot and forward rates, the symbols will be used.

two-point arbitrage which involves the simultaneous purchase and sale of *two* currencies. For example, dollars may be used to buy pounds sterling in New York, which are in turn sold for dollars in London, provided this simultaneous buying and selling is profitable. In general, *m*-point arbitrage involves the simultaneous buying and selling of *m* currencies where $2 \leq m \leq n$.

It is obvious that two-point arbitrage will establish the following equalities:

$$R_{ij} R_{ji} = 1 \qquad (\text{for } i, j = 1, 2, \ldots, n) \qquad (A1.2)$$

Therefore, when all profitable opportunities for two-point arbitrage are eliminated, all entries in the northeast triangle (above and to the right of the main diagonal) can be deduced from the entries in the southwest triangle (below and to the left of the main diagonal) of table A1.1, and vice versa. For the rest of the discussion in this note, it is assumed that eqs. (A1.2) are always satisfied. This will enable us to use the symbol R_{ij} as the exchange ratio between currencies i and j (as defined previously) but without regard to the financial center where the rate is actually recorded.

Similarly, three-point arbitrage will establish the following equalities:

$$R_{s, m} R_{m, t} R_{t, s} = 1 \qquad (\text{for } s, m, t = 1, \ldots, n) \qquad (A1.3)$$

The interpretation of eqs. (A1.3) is simple. Starting with one unit of currency s, we can buy $R_{t, s}$ units of currency t; since each unit of currency t sells for $R_{m, t}$ units of currency m, we can buy $R_{m, t} R_{t, s}$ units of currency m.† Finally, selling $R_{m, t} R_{t, s}$ units of currency m for currency s, we can buy $R_{s, m} R_{m, t} R_{t, s}$ units of currency s. Since we originally started with one unit of currency s, the *neutrality condition* (under which there is no incentive for three-point arbitrage) is that we end up with one unit of currency s (hence, eqs. A1.3).

In general, *k*-point arbitrage $(2 \leq k \leq n)$ will establish the following equalities:

$$\underbrace{R_{s, m} R_{m, t} R_{t, r} \cdots R_{v, z} R_{z, s}}_{K} = 1 \text{ (with } s, m, t, r, \ldots, v, z = 1, \ldots, n) \quad (A1.4)$$

The interpretation of eqs. (A1.4), being similar to the interpretation of eqs. (A1.3), is omitted.

It should be obvious that *k*-point arbitrage (where *k* is large) is rather complicated and it could be argued *on the basis of this inherent complexity* that it is a rare phenomenon, if it indeed takes place at all. However, computational difficulty should not be a deterrent to arbitragers for capturing easy and large profits in an age where the use of computers is so widely spread. Therefore, there must exist a

---

† The rate $R_{m, t} R_{t, s}$ is usually called *indirect* (or *cross rate*) because it shows how many units of currency m can be bought indirectly (i.e., through the purchase and sale of currency t) with one unit of currency s. The rate $R_{m, s}$ is called *direct*. It is then obvious that three-point arbitrage will equalize the direct rate $R_{m, s}$ to the indirect rate $R_{m, t} R_{t, s}$. But since $R_{m, s} = 1/R_{s, m}$ (because of two-point arbitrage), eqs. (A1.3) follow immediately.

more fundamental reason why k-point arbitrage $(k > 3)$ does not take place in the real world. The purpose of this appendix is simply to provide the apparently missing justification.

Theorem A1.1 If three-point arbitrage is not profitable, then k-point arbitrage $(k > 3)$ is not profitable either.

In other words, if eqs. (A1.3) are satisfied, then eqs. (A1.4) are necessarily satisfied. Therefore, three-point arbitrage is all that is necessary to eliminate all arbitrage profits; this seems to be the real reason for the absence of k-point arbitrage $(k > 3)$ as opposed to the computational difficulty.

PROOF Theorem A1.1 can be easily proved by mathematical induction. The only thing we have to show is this: assuming that $(k - 1)$-point arbitrage is not profitable, then k-point arbitrage is also nonprofitable.

For nonprofitable k-point arbitrage, it is required that eqs. (A1.4) are satisfied. Since $(k - 1)$-point arbitrage is nonprofitable by assumption, eqs. (A1.5) must necessarily be satisfied:†

$$\underbrace{R_{s,t}R_{t,r} \cdots R_{v,z}R_{z,s}}_{(k-1)} = 1 \quad \text{(with } s, t, r, \ldots, v, z = 1, \ldots, n) \quad \text{(A1.5)}$$

Dividing eqs. (A1.4) by eqs. (A1.5), we get

$$\frac{R_{s,m}R_{m,t}}{R_{s,t}} = 1 \quad \text{(A1.6)}$$

Equations (A1.6) are the same as eqs. (A1.3) because $1/R_{s,t} = R_{t,s}$. Thus, assuming that eqs. (A1.3) and (A1.5) are satisfied, eqs. (A1.4) must necessarily be satisfied as well. This proves the theorem.

Theorem A1.1 is a general theorem that can be applied both to spot and forward rates. However, theorem A1.2 shows that three-point spot arbitrage in conjunction with two-point interest arbitrage‡ renders three-point forward arbitrage nonprofitable.

Theorem A1.2 If three-point spot arbitrage and two-point interest arbitrage are not profitable, then three-point forward arbitrage is not profitable either.

PROOF Three-point spot arbitrage will insure the following equalities:

$$R^S_{s,m}R^S_{m,t}R^S_{t,s} = 1 \quad \text{(for } s, m, t = 1, 2, \ldots, n.) \quad \text{(A1.7)}$$

---

† Equations (A1.5) have been derived from eqs. (A1.4) through elimination of currency m.
‡ On interest arbitrage in general, see the discussion in chap. 1 and the Selected Bibliography.

On the other hand, two-point interest arbitrage will insure the equations:

$$R^F_{s,m}/R^S_{s,m} = (1 + r_s)/(1 + r_m)$$
$$R^F_{m,t}/R^S_{m,t} = (1 + r_m)/(1 + r_t) \qquad (A1.8)$$
$$R^F_{s,t}/R^S_{s,t} = (1 + r_s)/(1 + r_t)$$

where r_i = interest rate in the ith financial center. Solving eqs. (A1.8) for $R^S_{s,m}$, $R^S_{m,t}$, $R^S_{s,t}$, respectively, and substituting into eqs. (A1.7), we get, after some algebraic manipulation,

$$R^F_{s,m} R^F_{m,t} R^F_{t,s} = 1 \qquad (A1.9)$$

This proves the theorem.

In the same way, it can be easily shown that the following theorem is also true.

Theorem A1.3 If three-point forward arbitrage and two-point interest arbitrage are not profitable, then three-point spot arbitrage is not profitable either.

The general conclusion of our discussion must be clear by now. Three-point arbitrage is sufficient to establish consistent exchange rates. Further, considering the spot and forward markets and assuming that two-point interest arbitrage is always working efficiently and eliminates all profitable opportunities (i.e., eqs. (A1.8) are always satisfied), three-point arbitrage is necessary only in one of the two markets. However, if effective three-point arbitrage is missing, k-point arbitrage will be profitable. Hence, the "complexity" arguments do not lose all of their validity. Somewhere, someone is missing the boat, and the trick is to find the rates that are out of line and act quickly.

SELECTED BIBLIOGRAPHY

Auten, J. H. (1963). "Forward Exchange and Interest Differentials." *Journal of Finance* (March), pp. 11–28.

Branson, W. H. (1969). "The Minimum Covered Interest Differential Needed for International Arbitrage Activity." *Journal of Political Economy* (November–December), pp. 1028–1035.

Chacholiades, M. (1971) "The Sufficiency of Three-Point Arbitrage to Insure Consistent Cross Rates of Exchange." *The Southern Economic Journal*, vol. XXXVIII, no. 1 (July), pp. 86–88.

Chalmers, E. B. (Ed.) (1971). *Forward Exchange Intervention.* Hutchinson Educational Ltd., London.

Einzig, P. A. (1961). *A Dynamic Theory of Forward Exchange.* St. Martin's Press, New York.

——— (1966). *A Textbook on Foreign Exchange.* St. Martin's Press, New York.

Fisher, I. (1930). *The Theory of Interest.* Reprints of Economic Classics, Augustus M. Kelley, Bookseller, New York, 1965.

Frenkel, J. A., and R. M. Levich (1975). "Covered Interest Arbitrage: Unexploited Profits?" *Journal of Political Economy* (April), pp. 325–338.

Holmes, A. R., and F. H. Schott (1965). *The New York Foreign Exchange Market.* Federal Reserve Bank of New York, New York.

Kemp, M. C. (1964). *The Pure Theory of International Trade.* Prentice-Hall, Inc., Englewood Cliffs, N.J., chaps. 16 and 17.

Keynes, J. M. (1923). *A Tract on Monetary Reform.* Macmillan and Company, London, pp. 113–139.

Kindleberger, C. P. (1973). *International Economics,* 5th ed. R. D. Irwin, Inc., Homewood, Ill., chap. 17 and app. F.

Klopstock, F. H. (1965). "The International Money Market: Structure, Scope and Instruments." *Journal of Finance* (May), pp. 182–207.

Machlup, F. (1970). "The Forward-Exchange Market: Misunderstandings Between Practitioners and Economists." In G. N. Halm (Ed.), *Approaches to Greater Flexibility of Exchange Rates.* Princeton University Press, Princeton, N.J.

Meade, J. E. (1951). *The Theory of International Economic Policy,* vol. I, *The Balance of Payments.* Oxford University Press, London, chap. XVII.

Officer, L. H., and T. D. Willett (1970). "The Covered-Arbitrage Schedule: A Critical Survey of Recent Developments." *Journal of Money, Credit, and Banking,* vol. II (May), pp. 247–257.

Rosenthal, M. T. (1950). *Techniques of International Trade.* McGraw-Hill Book Company, New York.

Snape, R. H. (1970). "Forward Exchange and Futures Markets." In I. A. McDougall and R. H. Snape (Eds.), *Studies in International Economics.* North-Holland Publishing Company, Amsterdam.

Spraos, J. (1953). "The Theory of Forward Exchange and Recent Practice." *Manchester School of Economics and Social Studies,* vol. 21 (May).

Stein J. L. (1965). "The Forward Rate and the Interest Parity." *Review of Economic Studies* (April), pp. 113–126.

Stern, R. M. (1973). *The Balance of Payments.* Aldine Publishing Company, Chicago, Ill.

Tsiang, S. C. (1959). "The Theory of Forward Exchange and Effects of Government Intervention on the Forward Exchange Market." *International Monetary Fund Staff Papers* (April), pp. 75–106.

Yeager, L. B. (1966). *International Monetary Relations.* Harper and Row, New York, chap. 2.

TWO

THE BALANCE OF PAYMENTS

This chapter is divided into three parts. Part A explains the principles of balance-of-payments accounting. Part B explains the concept of balance-of-payments equilibrium and shows how the actual deficit (or surplus) is officially measured by the U.S. Department of Commerce. Finally, part C discusses briefly the balance of international indebtedness. A short appendix at the end of the chapter summarizes the difficulties which arise in practice in the process of constructing the balance of payments, and illustrates these difficulties by means of examples taken from the actual construction of the U.S. balance of payments.

PART A. BALANCE-OF-PAYMENTS ACCOUNTING

2.1 DEFINITION OF THE BALANCE OF PAYMENTS

A country's balance of payments is usually defined as the systematic record of all economic *transactions* between the *residents* of the reporting country and the residents of the rest of the world *over a specified period of time*. This definition raises several questions. What is an economic transaction? Who is a resident? What is the relevant period of time?

Economic Transactions

Economic transactions comprise transfers of ownership of goods, rendering of services, and transfers of money and other assets (including all financial claims, whether equity or creditor, and immovable property). They are divided into two categories: (*a*) two-way transactions, i.e., exchange of goods, services, or money and other assets against one another (in other words, transactions involving a *quid pro quo*), and (*b*) one-way transactions, i.e., transfer of goods, services, or money and other assets from residents of one country to residents of another *as a gift* (in other words, transactions involving no *quid pro quo*). Thus, the concept of economic transactions is defined as broadly as possible to include (with some notable exceptions) all transactions, both in kind and in cash, regardless of whether or not they involve a *quid pro quo*.

Accordingly, the balance of payments is not restricted to those transactions which take place in the foreign exchange market. For instance, barter practiced between a U.S. resident and a foreigner does not appear in the foreign exchange market but is nevertheless recorded in the balance of payments. On the other hand, as we shall see later in this chapter, there are foreign-exchange transactions (in particular, gross capital transactions) which do not appear in the balance of payments.

Residency

Like all other forms of social accounting, the balance of payments records the transactions not of a single person or institution. It rather records the transactions of a *group* of persons and institutions, namely, those who are identified with the reporting country. For this identification a criterion is needed. This is precisely the purpose of the concept of *residency*. Nationality is not a satisfactory criterion for this purpose, as can be verified by the fact that many immigrants who have disconnected all ties with their motherland retain their original nationality.

Obvious examples of resident individuals are: citizens of the country living there permanently, diplomats and military personnel stationed abroad, and citizens studying or undergoing medical treatment abroad. But complications arise in the case of citizens living abroad. Should they be treated as residents (i.e., should they be considered as *travelers*) or foreigners (i.e., should they be considered as *emigrants*)? For this purpose, the International Monetary Fund (IMF) has adopted the principle "center of interest." According to this principle, citizens living abroad are treated as residents or foreigners depending upon a number of factors, such as the permanence of their stay abroad and the extent to which they concentrate abroad their earning activities and their investments. Surely, these decisions are arbitrary.

Resident institutions of the reporting country include the central and all local governments, and all business enterprises and nonprofit organizations located in the country, as well as agencies stationed abroad. However, foreign branches and subsidiaries are treated as residents of the country of their location, because, according to the IMF, they are considered an integral part of that country's economy. The distinction between "branch" and "agency," as it is drawn in the *IMF Manual*, is made to rest on *whether the local office acts as a principal for its own account or whether it acts for the account of principals abroad.* But as Badger (1951) observed, this does not seem in harmony with the principle that branches and subsidiaries are treated as residents of the country of their location because they are considered an *integral part of that country's economy.*

International institutions (i.e., political, administrative, or financial organizations in which members are governments or official institutions) are not considered residents of the country of their location. They are rather treated as international areas outside national boundaries. Therefore, their transactions with residents of the country of their location are considered international, and thus recorded in its balance of payments. As examples one could cite the International Monetary Fund and the International Bank for Reconstruction and Development.

The application of the concept of resident to concrete situations may involve subtle distinctions, and it is often extremely difficult to determine residence even when all the facts are known. A number of borderline cases and exceptions to the resident-foreigner criterion do exist in practice. These cases (e.g., undistributed profits of subsidiaries, migrants transfers, freight and insurance on exports, gold transactions, short-term capital movements, intergovernment military transfers, and government grants to foreigners) are considered more systematically in the appendix.

Accounting Time Period

Finally, it should be noted that the balance of payments records the *flow* of international transactions of the reporting country *over a specified period of time.* The significance of the length of the balance-of-payments time period cannot be overemphasized at this stage. Suffice it to say that the statistical measurement of the balance-of-payments deficit or surplus is inherently related to the length of the time period over which the balance of payments is drawn up. This point is taken up again later in part B of this chapter when the concept of balance-of-payments equilibrium is discussed.

2.2 PRINCIPLES OF BALANCE-OF-PAYMENTS ACCOUNTING

In principle, the balance of payments is constructed on the basis of double-entry bookkeeping similar to that used by business firms. Two-way transactions (i.e., transactions involving a *quid pro quo*) give rise to two entries: a debit and a credit of equal amounts. On the other hand, one-way transactions (i.e., transactions not involving a *quid pro quo*, such as gifts, donations, etc.) give rise to only one entry: a debit or a credit, as the case may be. However, these transactions are treated as exceptions, and by accounting convention a second entry is made (as shown below) to keep the books in balance.

Debit and Credit Entries

In ordinary business accounting, the following convention is adopted: *a debit entry is used to show an increase in assets or a decrease in liabilities, while a credit entry is used to show an increase in liabilities or a decrease in assets.* These elementary principles can be applied to the recording of transactions in the balance of payments. For example, when a U.S. resident exports goods to a foreigner on credit, a debit entry is made to show the increase in the stock of claims for payment held by U.S. residents and a credit entry is made to show the decrease in the stock of goods held by U.S. residents. In principle, a debit entry is made in the U.S. balance of payments when an international transaction gives rise to a debit entry in the books of a U.S. resident. Similarly, a credit entry is made in the U.S. balance of payments when an international transaction gives rise to a credit entry in the books of a U.S. resident.

Each Side of a Transaction Considered as a Separate Transaction

All this seems straightforward enough. In practice, a minor complication arises because data are usually collected by different authorities and therefore only the debit or credit entry, as the case may be, is made in the balance of payments at any one time. Thus, when a U.S. resident exports goods to a foreigner in exchange for a demand deposit, the customs records show the value of goods exported only, giving no information whatsoever as to how the U.S. exporter's claim is settled. Therefore, based on the customs records, only a single-credit entry ("merchandise exports") can be made in the balance of payments. Information on the other side of the transaction (i.e., the settlement of the exporter's claim) will probably be given by the banking system. The debit entry can be made only after the banking system gives the necessary information.

As a result of this peculiarity, it may be useful to consider *each side* of an economic transaction as a *separate transaction.* Thus, when we refer to a "transaction" in our present discussion, it must be understood—unless stated otherwise—that we refer to only "one side" of the transaction involved. To which side, of course, we refer will be clear from the text. For example, when we refer to "exports" it must be understood that we refer to the transfer of goods and not the settlement of the exporter's claim. Much confusion can be avoided if the reader keeps this convention in mind. All this may sound complicated but actually is very simple. All one has to remember is the accounting convention that a debit entry is made to show an increase in assets or a decrease in liabilities, and a credit entry the opposite.

Construction of a Hypothetical Balance of Payments

We proceed now to illustrate the above principles by means of several examples which lead to the construction of a hypothetical balance-of-payments statement for the United States. A hypothetical list of debit entries is given in table 2.1. The

Table 2.1 Hypothetical list of U.S. debit entries

1. Merchandise imports (or visible imports)

2. Imports of services (or invisible imports)
   (a) Foreign travel abroad
   (b) Shipping and freight services rendered by foreign vessels, airlines, etc.
   (c) Insurance, banking, and brokerage services rendered by foreign concerns
   (d) Expenditure abroad by government agencies to carry on diplomatic, consular, and other functions
   (e) Interest and dividend payments to foreign holders of domestic bonds, stocks, and other assets which yield interest or income
   (f) Miscellaneous services (e.g., motion picture rentals, etc.)

3. Purchases of money and other assets from foreigners
   (a) Purchase of bonds and stocks
   (b) Purchases of titles to property
   (c) New loans and mortgages given to foreigners
   (d) Repayments and redemptions of loans and mortgages received from foreigners in the past
   (e) Purchases of bills of exchange from foreigners
   (f) Purchases of currency and bank deposits from foreigners
   (g) Open-book credit given to foreigners and repayment of open-book credit received from foreigners in the past

4. Unilateral transfers to foreigners (one-way transactions)
   (a) Gifts and grants
   (b) Personal remittances
   (c) Contributions
   (d) Indemnities and reparations
   (e) Other one-way transactions

5. Official purchases of gold and foreign currencies

reasons for classifying all entries in this table as debit entries are summarized in the next few paragraphs.

A debit entry is made for merchandise imports (or visible imports, as they are usually called) because U.S. residents acquire goods. This acquisition of goods by U.S. residents necessarily involves an increase in U.S. assets. Similarly, a debit entry is made for imports of services (or invisible imports). These services are broken down in table 2.1 into several categories. In each case, a debit entry is made for the value of the services rendered to U.S. residents. Thus, foreign travel abroad indicates the value of foreign services rendered to U.S. residents traveling abroad. A similar interpretation holds for all other services listed in table 2.1. In particular, the debit entry "interest and dividend payments to foreign holders of domestic bonds, stocks, and other assets" is made for the use of foreign capital which was made available to U.S. residents when foreigners bought U.S. bonds, stocks, etc.

Before going any further a clarification is necessary for the entry "foreign travel abroad." Usually, in addition to services, travelers abroad purchase commodities, a portion of which is consumed on the spot while the rest is brought home. Strictly speaking, these purchases are merchandise imports and ought to be included in the first category. Nevertheless, they are lumped together with all other purchases of services by these travelers. The reason for this convention is twofold. On the one hand, there is the practical reason that to treat these purchases as merchandise imports would involve major reporting difficulties. On the other hand, these purchases are more closely associated with *travel psychology* rather than with the business considerations which ordinarily govern merchandise imports.

The third category of debit entries concerns purchases of money and other claims from foreigners by U.S. residents. The reader is urged to verify that each and every entry in this category involves either the acquisition by U.S. residents of some asset (or claim) or the reduction of a U.S. liability. Therefore, these entries follow easily from the definition of the debit entry.

The fourth category of debit entries concerns unilateral transfers made by U.S. residents to foreigners. Unilateral transfers are one-way transactions, i.e., transactions which do not involve a *quid pro quo*. Therefore, only one entry can be made according to the definitions of debit and credit entries. For instance, suppose that U.S. residents make a gift of money to their relatives abroad by transferring to them U.S. demand deposits of $1 million held with foreign banks. A credit entry must be made in the balance of payments showing the decrease in U.S. liquid claims on foreigners. But since the U.S. residents receive nothing in return, no debit entry can be made. Yet to fulfill the principle of double-entry bookkeeping, which states that for every credit there must be a corresponding debit entry, and vice versa, a debit entry is made in the balance of payments by convention. This is the rationale for all entries in this category.

Finally, the official purchases of gold and foreign currencies are recorded as debit entries for the same reasons that similar purchases by private U.S. residents are recorded as debit entries: they all involve an increase in U.S. assets. These official purchases are recorded separately because of their importance as international monetary reserves. The imports of nonmonetary gold (e.g., for industrial purposes) are recorded along with other merchandise imports. Also, private purchases of foreign currencies are recorded under "purchases of money and other assets from foreigners."

Looking at the list of debit entries given in table 2.1 from the point of view of the rest of the world, we can construct a corresponding list of credit entries,

Table 2.2 Balance of payments

Debit entries (−)	Credit entries (+)
1. Merchandise imports	6. Merchandise exports
2. Imports of services	7. Exports of services
3. Purchases of money and other assets from foreigners	8. Sales of money and other assets to foreigners
4. Unilateral transfers to foreigners	9. Unilateral transfers from foreigners
5. Official purchases of gold and foreign currencies	10. Official sales of gold and foreign currencies

because by necessity a debit entry in the balance of payments of one country implies a credit entry in the balance of payments of some other country. But there seems to be no need for another table giving us in detail the list of credit entries.

The major categories of debit and credit entries are brought together in table 2.2. This table is the hypothetical balance-of-payments statement promised to the reader earlier.

Errors and Omissions

The fact that the balance of payments is theoretically constructed on the basis of double-entry bookkeeping implies that the sum of total debits must necessarily be equal to the sum of total credits. This is usually expressed by saying that the balance of payments always balances. In practice, however, the collection of statistical data for the construction of the balance of payments is inherently imperfect for reasons to be given later. Therefore, it is not improbable—in fact this is the rule—to get in practice a sum of debits which is unequal to the sum of credits. In this case, an additional entry is made in the balance of payments to restore the equality between the two sides—to fulfill, so to speak, the accounting principle that total credits equals total debits. In the United States this entry used to be called "errors and omissions." Recently, the U.S. Department of Commerce changed its name to "statistical discrepancy" in order to identify it clearly as a residual. The British call it "balancing item." It is usually thought that the entry "errors and omissions" is due to unrecorded short-term capital movements. However, this is not necessarily so, as the appendix on reporting difficulties makes abundantly clear.

The Various Accounts of the Balance of Payments

The balance of payments is usually divided into the following four accounts: (*a*) the current account (consisting of entries 1, 2, 6 and 7); (*b*) the capital account (consisting of entries 3 and 8); (*c*) the unilateral transfers account (consisting of entries 4 and 9); and (*d*) the official reserves account (consisting of entries 5 and 10). In addition to these four accounts, we have the balancing entry "errors and omissions."

A Rough Correspondence Between the Balance of Payments and the Foreign Exchange Market

Before concluding this section it is useful to note that the credit entries give us the *sources* while the debit entries give us the *uses* of foreign exchange of the reporting country. Put differently, the credit entries give us the *actual* sales of foreign exchange while the debit entries give us the *actual* purchases of foreign exchange by the residents and monetary authorities of the reporting country. This correspondence between debit and credit entries in the balance of payments, on the one hand, and purchases and sales of foreign exchange, on the other, is not perfect. As already noted, some transactions are made in the balance of payments even though there are no corresponding foreign-exchange transactions; conversely, some foreign-exchange transactions are not represented by any entries in the balance of payments. Nevertheless, this rough correspondence between the balance of payments and the foreign exchange market is useful and ought to be kept in mind.

2.3 CAPITAL FLOWS

Define the *net-claims position* of the United States as the *stock* of all claims held by U.S. residents against foreigners *minus* the *stock* of all claims held by foreigners against U.S. residents at an instant of time. A careful examination of the entries in the capital account in the U.S. balance of payments reveals the following truth: all debit entries tend to enhance the net-claims position of the United States either by increasing the stock of all claims held by U.S. residents against foreigners or by decreasing the stock of claims held by foreigners against U.S. residents. Similarly, all credit entries tend to deteriorate the net-claims position of the United States either by decreasing the stock of U.S. claims against foreigners or by increasing the stock of foreign claims against U.S. residents (i.e., the stock of U.S. liabilities to foreigners). For example, when a U.S. resident buys a bond from a foreigner, the U.S. stock of net claims against the rest of the world increases by the amount of the bond. This is true whether the bond was originally issued by a foreign government or corporation (in which case the stock of U.S. claims against foreigners increases) or by the U.S. government or a U.S. corporation (in which case the stock of U.S. liabilities to foreigners decreases).

It is of paramount importance to emphasize that we are talking here about *the claim for payment incorporated in the bond only*. It is true that the purchase of the bond may be settled through the transfer of another claim, such as a bank deposit or currency. This is immaterial. As noted in the preceding section, the transfer of the deposit (or currency) should again be considered as a separate transaction. Accordingly, it is wrong to assert that the purchase of the bond involves no change in the net-claims position of the United States because a mere exchange of claims takes place, for to do so means that both sides of the transaction are considered simultaneously, and this is ruled out.

Similar interpretations hold for all other debit entries in the capital account. Consider, for instance, the case of loans. When a U.S. resident makes a loan to a foreigner, the stock of total U.S. claims against foreigners increases. Therefore, the U.S. net-claims position increases also. Again, no confusion should be made between the loan contract, which the foreigner signs and which forms the basis for the increase in the total stock of U.S. claims against the foreigners (i.e., the debit entry), and the cash that the U.S. resident surrenders today to the foreigner (i.e., the credit entry) in exchange for the foreigner's promise to repay him (with interest) at some time in the future. The two sides of the transaction ought to be considered separately.

Similar considerations hold for the case of repayment of a loan which a U.S. resident may have obtained from a foreigner in the past. When the repayment takes place, the stock of U.S. liabilities to foreigners decreases because the U.S. resident receives back the loan contract he initially signed. Again, the cash which the American borrower surrenders to the foreigner in exchange for the loan contract is a separate (credit) entry.

Similarly, when U.S. residents sell bonds to, or receive loans from, foreigners or when foreigners repay U.S. residents for loans which the latter had made to the foreigners in the past, the U.S. net-claims position deteriorates. As we have seen, all these transactions give rise to credit entries in the balance of payments.

Capital Outflow and Capital Inflow

Following the preceding discussion, we define *capital outflow* as all transactions which tend to enhance the net-claims position of the reporting country and *capital inflow* as all transactions which tend to deteriorate it. Accordingly, capital outflow (or capital exports) refers to transactions giving rise to debit entries in the capital account of the balance of payments and capital inflow (or capital imports) refers to transactions giving rise to credit entries.

It should be noted that the term "capital" in this context does not refer to real capital goods such as machinery, buildings, etc. It merely refers to the stock of U.S. claims against foreigners and the stock of foreign claims against the U.S. (i.e., the reporting country). Accordingly, *capital flows* (inflows and outflows) refer to *changes* in these stocks of claims. Much confusion can be avoided if this distinction is kept in mind.

A Hypothetical Illustration

It is often convenient to think in terms of the concepts of capital outflow and capital inflow, although the words "inflow" and "outflow" may sound very confusing to the beginner. Consider the following hypothetical case which is admittedly extreme but seems to illustrate the point well. An American robs the Bank of England and brings *into* the United States £1 million which, say, he sells to an American Bank. The fact that the money is moving into the United States may give the impression that a capital *inflow* is involved. But this is wrong. It is a capital *outflow* because the stock of U.S. *claims* against foreigners *increases* by the amount of foreign currency brought into the United States. Therefore, it is a debit entry. What is the credit entry? Well, it is the act of stealing which is not recorded in the U.S. balance of payments, presumably because of lack of information! Thus, it ends up in the account "errors and omissions."

It may be instructive to compare this hypothetical transaction with a *bona fide* loan transaction. Suppose that the U.S. resident does not rob the Bank of England, but the Bank of England grants a long-term loan to him. In this case, the *loan agreement* between the Bank of England and the U.S. resident is entered as a credit entry in the U.S. balance of payments because the contract signed by the

U.S. resident increases the *stock* of British claims against the United States. Therefore, it is a capital *inflow* into the United States and, thus, a credit entry in the U.S. balance of payments. However, *the actual transfer of the proceeds of the loan into the United States is indeed a capital outflow* (not inflow), because it increases the stock of U.S. claims against the foreigners. In the earlier hypothetical example of robbery, the act of robbery itself takes the place of the loan agreement between the Bank of England and the U.S. resident. Thus, the actual transfer of pounds sterling from England to the United States, which was giving the wrong impression that a capital inflow was involved, is actually a capital outflow. This example shows that extreme care must be exercised in the use of the terms "capital outflow" and "capital inflow."

Gross Versus Net Flows

The capital account records the capital flows (or capital movements) into and out of the reporting country. But it does not record the *gross* flows or movements. It rather records the *net* changes in the reporting country's foreign claims and liabilities. (Foreign equity investments in the country are counted as liabilities.) An important reason for this practice is that stocks and bonds (as well as other claims and liabilities) may be sold and bought several times during a year, and the *turnover* is of less interest than the net change. Another reason is the difficulty of getting data on the gross amounts traded. As a result, most international transactions dealing with claims are not recorded in the balance of payments. They are netted out. Here is, therefore, a notable example of international transactions which go through the foreign exchange market but are not recorded in the balance of payments.

Valuation Changes

The foreign claims and liabilities of a country do not only change when international transactions in them take place. They also change because of valuation changes, such as changes in the market values of securities and revaluations of claims and liabilities because of exchange-rate adjustments. Are these valuation changes recorded in the balance of payments also? No, because they are not international transactions. As a result, the changes recorded in the capital account do not necessarily reflect the total change in the net-claims position of the reporting country during the period covered by the balance of payments.

Short-Term Versus Long-Term Capital Flows

The capital account is usually broken down into short-term and long-term accounts, depending upon the nature of the credit instrument involved. Short-term capital movements are those embodied in credit instruments with an original maturity of one year or less. All others are classified as long-term capital movements. Thus, short-term capital consists of deposits, commercial and financial paper and acceptances, loans and commercial book credits, and items in the process of collection. On the other hand, long-term capital consists of (*a*) ownership instruments (i.e., equity holdings of shares, real estate, etc.) and (*b*) credit instruments with an original maturity greater than one year.

Note that any maturity criterion is necessarily arbitrary. Investments in long-term securities may be made for short periods of time and they may be even more volatile than some short-term loans and commercial credits—which may be, in effect, long term in view of more or less automatic renewal. A very instructive example of the difficulty involved with the maturity criterion is the following. The United States may sell surplus wheat to India for rupees. The accumulation of rupees is, of course, a short-term claim. Nevertheless, if the intention is to use these rupees primarily for grants (or long-term loans) to India, then aid is actually given on a long-term basis at the start. Finally, note that a distinction based on *remaining* (rather than original) maturity may be preferable. However, this criterion would create enormous reporting difficulties because of the ageing of existing assets and the continuous shift from long-term to short-term spectrum.

Direct Investment Versus Portfolio Investment

Long-term capital is usually divided into the following two categories: (*a*) direct investment and (*b*) portfolio investment. (This distinction is made largely because separate investor groups are usually involved whose behavior is quite different and has different economic effects.) *Direct investment* is defined as investment in enterprises located in one country but effectively controlled by residents of another country. Direct investment as a rule takes the form of investment in branches and subsidiaries by parent companies located in another country. Thus, the U.S. direct investments abroad are the U.S. owned portions of foreign business enterprises in which U.S. residents are deemed to have an important voice in management. Similarly, foreign direct investments in the United States are those that involve an important foreign managerial interest. Any other long-term investment is classified as *portfolio investment*. Accordingly, portfolio investment includes long-term securities, commercial credits and bank loans, mortgages, equities in trusts and estates, and miscellaneous other long-term claims.

Several statistical criteria are used to determine which foreign enterprises involve sufficient U.S. managerial interest to be classified as foreign subsidiaries or affiliates, in which U.S. investment is considered to be direct investment. Thus, a foreign corporation qualifies as a U.S. direct investment if 25 percent or more of its voting stock is owned by a U.S. resident or an affiliated group of residents. Analogous U.S. equity interests in an unincorporated foreign enterprise also represent direct investment. In addition, U.S. investment in a foreign corporation is considered direct investment if all U.S. stockholders together hold 50 percent or more of its voting stock, even when no affiliated group holds as much as 25 percent. Similar criteria are used to define foreign direct investment in the United States. In practice, investment in foreign enterprises in which a U.S. resident (or group) has equity ownership of 10 to 25 percent have been included with direct investment in the U.S. balance of payments. Finally, it may be interesting to know that, as far as direct investment is concerned, no distinction is usually made between long-term and short-term capital movements. They are all recorded as long term.

PART B. BALANCE-OF-PAYMENTS EQUILIBRIUM

2.4 INTRODUCTION

As we saw in part A of this chapter, the balance of payments is constructed on the basis of double-entry bookkeeping. As a result, the balance of payments always balances in an accounting sense, i.e., total debits = total credits. (For the moment, ignore any statistical deficiencies giving rise to "errors and omissions.") Does this accounting balance mean that the balance of payments is also in equilibrium? In other words, does the identity "total debits ≡ total credits" mean that the reporting country never experiences any balance-of-payments difficulties? Unfortunately, this is not the case, as any casual observer of international affairs would know.

The question of balance-of-payments equilibrium is a fundamental one and must be handled with great care. For this purpose, we need to distinguish among the various ways in which a balance of payments may be conceived. Machlup (1950) taught us that what is indiscriminately called "the balance of payments" may be (*a*) an *accounting balance*, i.e., a balance of debits and credits; or (*b*) a *market balance*, i.e., a balance of supply and demand; or (*c*) a *programme balance*, i.e., a balance of needs and desires. The meaning of equilibrium within each of these three concepts is by no means clear. In addition, the meaning of a deficit (i.e., excess of payments over receipts) or a surplus (i.e., excess of receipts over payments) is different for each of the three concepts. To avoid confusion and inappropriate balance-of-payments policies, extreme caution needs to be exercised. In the following pages, each of the three basic concepts is studied in some depth.

2.5 THE ACCOUNTING BALANCE OF PAYMENTS

What Machlup calls "the accounting balance of payments" (or, for short, the accounting balance) is what we actually studied in the first part of this chapter. In other words, the accounting balance is a systematic record of all economic transactions between the residents of the reporting country and foreign residents during a certain *past* period of time. Thus, the accounting balance is an *ex post* concept. It describes what actually happened over a past period. It gives absolutely no information about the future except in the limited sense that, based on the information given by the accounting balance over a number of past periods, an econometrician may make projections about the future course of events. But these projections, in addition to the historical information provided by the accounting balance, depend on several assumptions, hypotheses, judgements, and all that is necessary for the successful completion of the required economic and statistical analysis. The accounting balance as such tells us nothing about the future.

The accounting balance of payments always balances because it records *actual* (not *intended*) sales and purchases. But the identity " actual sales ≡ actual purchases " is true by definition and has nothing to do with the concept of equilibrium. When is the accounting balance in equilibrium?

Autonomous Versus Accommodating Transactions

Meade (1951, chap. 1) observed that, in principle, the transactions recorded in the accounting balance can be divided into two major categories: autonomous and accommodating. *Autonomous* transactions are those which are undertaken for their own sake, usually in response to business considerations and incentives but sometimes in response to political considerations as well. Their main distinguishing feature is that they take place independently of the balance-of-payments position of the reporting country. All other transactions are called accommodating. Thus, *accommodating* transactions do not take place for their own sake. Rather, they take place because other (autonomous) transactions are such as to leave a *gap to be filled*. Accommodating transactions may be *automatic* (i.e., unplanned and unforeseen) or *discretionary* (i.e., planned and foreseen). In addition, accommodating transactions may be made by private persons or public authorities.

Examples of autonomous transactions are: virtually all exports of goods and services undertaken for profit, unilateral transfers, most long-term capital movements, as well as many short-term capital movements motivated by a desire either to earn a higher return, to make a speculative profit, or to find a safe refuge. On the other hand, examples of accommodating transactions are: the sale of gold or foreign currencies by the central bank in order to fill the gap between the receipts and payments of foreign exchange by the private residents of the country in question, a gift or loan received by the authorities of a country from foreign governments for the express purpose of filling a gap in the autonomous receipts and payments, and so on.

Accounting Deficits and Surpluses

Imagine a horizontal line drawn through a balance-of-payments statement. Above this imaginary line, place all autonomous transactions (or entries), and below the line, place all accommodating transactions (or entries). When the balance on autonomous transactions in zero (i.e., when "autonomous payments = autonomous receipts "), we shall say that the accounting balance is in equilibrium. When the sum of autonomous receipts is greater than the sum of autonomous payments, we shall say that there is an *accounting surplus*, and when the sum of autonomous receipts falls short of the sum of autonomous payments, we shall say that there is an *accounting deficit*. In each case, the accounting measure of disequilibrium (surplus or deficit) is given by the difference between the sum of autonomous receipts and the sum of autonomous payments.

Because the accounting balance of payments is an identity, we always have

Sum of autonomous transactions + sum of accommodating transactions = 0

or

Sum of autonomous transactions = − sum of accommodating transactions

Accordingly, the accounting measure of balance-of-payments disequilibrium can be determined also as the *negative* of the difference between accommodating receipts and payments. Thus, instead of looking at the gap between autonomous receipts and payments, we can look at the amount of accommodating *financing* which was necessary to fill that gap.

Difficulties with the Distinction Between Autonomous and Accommodating Transactions

All this sounds easy and straightforward, but actually the analytical distinction between autonomous and accommodating transactions, although sound in principle, faces insurmountable difficulties in practical applications. In the first place, there is the possibility of international inconsistency. A transaction may be regarded autonomous for one country but accommodating for another, as when the monetary authorities of the latter, in the face of balance-of-payments difficulties, borrow in the private financial market of the former. Thus, a deficit in one country need not be offset by a surplus in the other, and it is not impossible for all countries to be in deficit at the same time, a situation which may lead to conflicting balance-of-payments policies.

A second and much more fundamental difficulty arises from the fact that the distinction between autonomous and accommodating transactions is an *ex ante* concept depending ultimately on *motives* which cannot be observed in an *ex post* statistical statement like the accounting balance. The problem would not be as difficult if it were possible to infer the motive either from the type of the transaction or the type of transactor. But this is not the case. As a result, in any practical application a subjective judgement is often necessary regarding the ultimate motive behind each transaction. The subjective element necessarily gives rise to differences of opinion among equally competent and honest people.

A very subtle difficulty arises in relation to public policy and, in particular, monetary policy. For instance, suppose that the U.S. monetary authorities are successful in attracting substantial amounts of short-term capital from foreign financial centers by simply raising their interest rate. What is the nature of this short-term capital inflow: autonomous or accommodating? Certainly from the point of view of private arbitragers these transactions are motivated by profit considerations and ought to be classified as autonomous. But their profitability is actually influenced by the action of the monetary authorities who presumably were concerned about the state of the balance of payments. Thus, from the viewpoint of the monetary authorities these transactions are accommodating—they are prompted by monetary policy to fill a gap left by other transactions.

It is indeed tempting to conclude that all transactions influenced by public policy are accommodating. This actually has been proposed by Lary (1963, pp. 137–162). But this view is too simplistic. The economic system is an interacting one. When something happens in one sector or market, it is transmitted sooner or later to the whole economy. In fact, as pointed out by Cooper (1966, p. 385), the sensitivity of various transactions to monetary policy varies along a continuum, so any dichotomy into " policy sensitive " and " not policy sensitive " is necessarily artificial.

The preceding discussion points to a very important conclusion. The *ex post* grouping of transactions into autonomous and accommodating is not unambiguous. The horizontal line through the balance-of-payments entries may be drawn in a number of arbitrary ways, none of which can be considered to be the correct one. Accordingly, we must reach the negative conclusion that there is no unique accounting measure of balance-of-payments disequilibrium. To be sure, several measures can be developed, each one serving a particular purpose. (In sec. 2.8 below, three measures used by the U.S. Department of Commerce are discussed in some detail.) But the feeling must be resisted that a single number can be relied upon to show the precise degree of balance-of-payments disequilibrium.

Accounting Versus Economic Time Period

So far we have been concerned with the distinction between autonomous and accommodating transactions on the assumption that the total population of transactions is known. This was implicitly assumed when it was mentioned that the accounting balance is drawn over a *specified time period*. But the time period itself (determining the total population of transactions) is very crucial. Thus, given any arbitrary criterion to identify autonomous (or accommodating) transactions, the accounting measure of disequilibrium (deficit or surplus) depends crucially on the time period chosen. In principle, a chart could be drawn showing through time the continuous flows of autonomous receipts and payments, and their difference (instantaneous deficit or surplus). Surely, then, the accounting deficit or surplus over *any* specified period of time is the algebraic sum of the instantaneous deficits and surpluses registered within the chosen period. Accordingly, as the accounting period is lengthened or shortened, the accounting deficit or surplus is necessarily altered.

Note that, in addition to the arbitrary character of the accounting measure due to the arbitrary choice of the time period, the accounting deficit or surplus fails to show the *pressures* that mount in the foreign exchange market *during* the accounting period.

The length of the time period is crucial. The actual deficit or surplus in the accounting balance depends on it. In effect, the accounting deficit or surplus can be made almost anything we want by arbitrarily changing the accounting time period. Does it then follow that all balance-of-payments difficulties can be made to evaporate into thin air by manipulating the accounting period? Certainly not. But it behoves us to distinguish between the accounting time period and what may be called the *economic time period*. The latter is that period over which the balance of payments must be in equilibrium on economic grounds. The economic time period need not be equal to the accounting time period (i.e., the period over which the balance of payments is actually drawn) and should not be confused with it.

What is the appropriate length of the economic time period? Is it a day, a week, a month, a year, a decade? The answer to this question is of paramount importance because on it depends not only the correct diagnosis of the balance-of-payments problem but also the formulation of economic policy. Usually economists point out that the economic time period should be long enough to even out the effects of self-correcting short-term disturbances of a daily, weekly, monthly, or seasonal nature. As a result, the year is considered to be the minimum acceptable economic time period. On the other hand, the economic time period should not be too long. Nurske (1949, p. 6) suggested a period which is long enough to cover a whole business cycle. He placed this period between five and ten years. Obviously, the precise length would depend on the cycle, and the cycle is different today than it used to be in the 1940s. The important conclusion, however, to be drawn from this discussion is that there is no unique way to specify the economic time period. A subjective judgement is again involved, and differences of opinion (especially in the formulation of economic policy) may again arise between equally competent and honest people.

Accounting Deficits and Surpluses under Flexible-Exchange Rates

So far, our discussion assumed implicitly a fixed-exchange-rate system. However, since 1973, most major currencies have been allowed to "float," but not entirely freely. Governments have intervened frequently to maintain orderly markets and often to support the external value of their currencies—the so-called "dirty" or managed floating. How should a balance-of-payments deficit be interpreted under this new regime?

Under a completely freely fluctuating exchange-rate system (to be considered later) the rate of exchange is left free to equate supply and demand for foreign exchange. Accommodating transactions do not take place and the balance of payments can register neither a deficit nor a surplus. Any disturbances which under a fixed-exchange-rate system might have given rise to a balance-of-payments disequilibrium are now reflected in exchange-rate fluctuations.

Under a regime of "dirty" or managed floating, the situation is slightly different—a mixture, so to speak, of the fixed and freely fluctuating exchange-rate systems. Here the authorities do intervene to iron out wide fluctuations in the exchange rate. Such intervention, though, is discretionary—not mandatory. Any deficits or surpluses now reflect a mixture of such discretionary intervention plus positive investment decisions. Thus, any change in the reserve position of a country is not the passive consequence of all other international economic transactions.

2.6 THE MARKET BALANCE OF PAYMENTS

The accounting balance of payments is an *ex post* concept. It is an historical statement describing the transactions which actually took place during a specified period in the past. Indeed, this is the reason why we were forced to conclude that it is impossible to determine a correct *accounting measure* of balance-of-payments disequilibrium. What is really needed is an *ex ante* measure.

The market balance of payments is a model of the foreign exchange market. It deals directly with desires, intentions, or plans revealed by supply and demand schedules showing the alternative amounts of foreign exchange which exporters, importers, investors, individuals making or receiving gifts, etc., would like to buy or sell at alternative rates of exchange including the current rate. This is clearly an *ex ante* concept. Our earlier distinction between autonomous and accommodating transactions was really an attempt to capture *ex post* the imbalance in these *ex ante* plans for autonomous transactions at the current rate of exchange. Too much was therefore asked of the accounting balance of payments.

Before proceeding any further there is a methodological point that needs to be cleared up. Earlier in this chapter we saw that the coverage of the balance of payments is different from the coverage of the foreign exchange market. That is, some transactions which are recorded in the balance of payments may not pass through the foreign exchange market; and, conversely, some foreign-exchange transactions are not recorded in the balance of payments. If this is so, can we really use the supply and demand schedules for foreign exchange to determine the degree of disequilibrium in the balance of payments, as we are presently suggesting? Yes, we can. The slight divergence in coverage is of no consequence whatsoever. What is important is not the absolute amount of foreign exchange demanded or supplied but the *excess* demand. When equal amounts are added to intended sales and purchases, the difference between them remains unchanged, and this makes it possible for us to cast our discussion in terms of the excess demand for foreign exchange. We return now to the main theme.

The Concept of Equilibrium

A market is said to be in equilibrium when the price is such that the quantity which the buyers are *willing* to buy equals the quantity which the sellers are *willing* to sell. When this condition prevails, *there is no tendency for change*, unless the economic data which lie behind the supply and demand curves (such as tastes, technology, income, other prices) change. Of course, in any period "actual sales ≡ actual purchases." This is true by definition. But the bare data on the actual amounts traded tell us nothing about the disappointments of those market participants who were unable to fulfill their plans. It is these disappointments, which do not appear on any *ex post* statistical statement, which give the system a tendency to change in the future. No wonder, then, that the accounting balance of payments, which is an *ex post* statistical statement, offered us little help in our search for balance-of-payments equilibrium.

This concept of equilibrium, a balance of desires and plans, can be applied to the foreign exchange market and the balance of payments. But unfortunately the foreign exchange market is not an ordinary market. It is indeed a very complicated market, because it links together the economies of the world. It is therefore impossible to isolate the foreign exchange market from the economy of the rest of the world and study it by itself. This means that the task of defining equilibrium in the foreign exchange market cannot be even attempted unless one is willing to consider simultaneously all other markets in the world economy. The concept of balance-of-payments equilibrium (or equilibrium in the foreign exchange market) is by necessity a concept akin to *general equilibrium* rather than to partial equilibrium. The sooner this is realized the better.

General equilibrium systems are inherently difficult, and the concept of balance-of-payments equilibrium is no exception. In the following chapters, balance-of-payments equilibrium is studied in terms of simplified models which bring out all of the important elements. For the moment, some general comments on the concept of balance-of-payments equilibrium may be useful.

Conditions for Balance-of-Payments Equilibrium

As noted above, when a system is in equilibrium there exists no tendency for change (endogenously). This idea implies that equilibrium in the foreign exchange market (and the balance of payments) requires that the following two conditions are met: (*a*) all markets related directly or indirectly to the foreign exchange market are in equilibrium; and (*b*) all stocks are optimally allocated. The first condition follows from the fact that any tendencies for change in markets linked with the foreign exchange market will necessarily affect the excess-demand schedule for foreign exchange. The second condition requires further explanation and justification.

Economists distinguish between two types of economies: the *stationary state* and the *dynamic state*. The former is an economy in which the fundamental economic data, such as factor supplies, technology, tastes, and factor ownership, remain constant through time. On the other hand, a dynamic state is one in which these fundamental data change either continuously through time or only occasionally. The concept of a stationary state is no more than a theoretical device which permits us to see more clearly some of the aspects of realistic situations. Let us, therefore, restrict our comments to such a model.

Note that the concepts of intended supply and demand refer to *flows* per unit of time. In fact, *all* entries in the balance of payments represent *flows*. Now there are some flows, such as exports and imports of goods and services, which presumably can continue indefinitely, and their existence does not give rise to tendencies for change. But this is not true of all flows that go through the foreign exchange market and are registered in the balance of payments. Take, for instance, long-term capital flows. In a stationary world, it cannot continue forever, for in a stationary world the total stock of capital is by definition fixed and the economic problem is how this given stock is to be allocated. Long-term capital movements may be thought of as the channel through which the optimal allocation of the given stock of capital takes place. Before long-run equilibrium (optimal allocation) is reached, there is a flow of long-term capital from the capital-rich to the capital-poor country. But after the optimal allocation is completed, the flow of long-term capital necessarily comes to a halt. By necessity, the balance of payments and the foreign exchange market undergo changes until the stock of capital is allocated optimally; but later, the flow of long-term capital, and with it the changes in the balance of payments and the foreign exchange market, cease completely. This is, of course, a hypothetical example which is used to illustrate a point. Nevertheless, similar comments hold for all flows whose purpose is merely to allocate optimally a stock. Their very existence gives rise to forces which tend to eliminate them.

Long-Run Versus Short-Run Equilibrium

The condition that all stocks are optimally allocated is, of course, a condition for *long-run* equilibrium. Accordingly, if this condition is not met, there will exist *long-run balance-of-payments disequilibrium*. But if the process of optimally allocating stocks is a lengthy one, with the stock-adjusting flows expected to continue for a long time, it may be more appropriate to say that there exists *short-run balance-of-payments equilibrium*, assuming, of course, that intended sales equal intended purchases of foreign exchange at the current rate of exchange.

Note that the distinction between short-run and long-run equilibrium is again related to the time period. But while in our earlier discussion we were concerned with the equality between autonomous receipts and payments during the economic period, here a new condition is added. Thus, in addition to an equality between intended sales and purchases of foreign exchange at the current rate of exchange, short-run equilibrium requires that this condition is not temporary but lasts for some time. Long-run balance-of-payments equilibrium, on the other hand, requires that the equality between intended sales and purchases lasts forever, if shifts in the fundamental data do not occur. Both types of equilibrium are important.

The concept of short-run equilibrium is not very precise. It implies that certain slow adjustments in the system have not been completed. Depending on which adjustments are considered to be of a short-run nature and which of a long-run nature, one could possibly define an infinite number of short runs ranging from the marshallian momentary equilibrium to the full long-run equilibrium. Alternatively, a short-run time period may be determined according to some arbitrary criterion. The associated short-run supply and demand curves for foreign exchange can be thought of as shifting continuously through time until full long-run equilibrium is reached.† But even this conception is oversimplified because, as pointed out later, there does not exist a unique set of short-run supply and demand curves for foreign exchange but a whole family of them.

The General-Equilibrium Character of the Foreign Exchange Market

What does the preceding analysis suggest? Several things, but the most important for us for the moment is this: the supply and demand schedules for foreign exchange depend on the conditions prevailing in other markets and the extent to which all stocks are optimally allocated. Any adjustment anywhere else in the system is necessarily reflected in a shift of the demand or supply curves for foreign exchange. In the same way, any adjustment in the foreign exchange market may affect other markets, and changes in those markets will, in turn, affect the foreign exchange market. For instance, assume that country A (home country), in an effort to eliminate a current deficit in its balance of payments, imposes restrictions on imports from country B (foreign country). This may bring A's balance of payments in equilibrium momentarily by shifting the demand curve for foreign exchange (B's currency) to the left. However, the reduction in B's exports ($\equiv$ A's imports) causes B's national income and demand for A's products to fall. Thus, the supply curve for foreign exchange also shifts to the left, and so on. These problems are analyzed in detail later on. Here we merely note that it is impossible to draw a unique set of supply and demand curves for foreign exchange and analyze the workings of the foreign exchange market in terms of this unique set of curves. To be sure, in the following chapters of this book we work with a unique set of supply and demand curves. This is necessary in order to clarify some aspects of the foreign exchange market, and the discussion is completed later on in the rest of the book. Changes in other markets may take place not only during the process to equilibrium. Changes can also occur as a result of shifts in the fundamental data which lie behind supply and demand curves, such as shifts in tastes, technical progress, population growth, changes in the level of economic activity, changes in the money supply, etc. When shifts of this kind occur, the long-run equilibrium is disturbed and forces are created pushing the system toward the new equilibrium.

Economic Policy

There are two basic problems with the concept of long-run equilibrium. In the first place, the automatic forces which are at work in the short run and push the economy toward long-run equilibrium may be too slow. In the second place, the automatic long-run equilibrium itself (which might be attained automatically if

---

† To be sure, long-run equilibrium is never reached. The main reason for this is because changes in the fundamental data occur continuously and, therefore, long-run equilibrium shifts continuously through time. The economic system lives always in the short run and never catches up with the shifting long-run target. Yet the latter is very important. It is a target, albeit a moving target, toward which the economic system aims at every point in time.

the system were left alone for a sufficient amount of time) need not be desirable. In either of these cases, appropriate economic policy measures are usually taken to either speed up the adjustment process toward the automatic long-run equilibrium (if that is considered to be a desirable target) or force the system to move toward a different equilibrium which according to the policy-makers' judgement is more desirable. A successful economic policy requires, in addition to the knowledge of a long-run target (or targets), knowledge of how the economic system reacts to alternative policy measures. For this purpose, knowledge of how the economic system works is needed. This is, in fact, the approach followed in the rest of this book. First, knowledge is sought of how the economic system actually works. Second, based on that knowledge, policy alternatives are sought to achieve certain goals, such as full employment and balance-of-payments equilibrium.

Once the problem is cast in these terms, it is immediately realized how deceptive any accounting measure of disequilibrium may be. Even if God gave us enough rope and we came up with an accounting measure which reflects precisely the degree of current disequilibrium in the balance of payments, we would still not be able to formulate the correct economic policy. For this, we must have some knowledge of how the system actually works, how it is expected to behave in the future, and how the moving long-run equilibrium target is expected to shift also. The problem is similar to that of taking a snapshot of a man who seems to have lost his balance on a boat in a turbulent sea. It is impossible to tell from the snapshot whether the man is actually falling or returning to an equilibrium position. For this a movie—not a snapshot—is needed to show all the forces at work.

The present discussion may sound very complicated to the reader, and it is. Nevertheless, it is only in this context that the concept of balance-of-payments equilibrium can be understood. As a brief introduction to what the subject is all about, this discussion has been cast by necessity in very abstract terms. But the following chapters will hopefully elucidate all those points which may appear too obscure or difficult at this time.

The Nurkse-Meade Conditions for Balance-of-Payments Equilibrium

It may be noted in passing that two prominent writers in the field, Nurkse (1945) and Meade (1951), defined balance-of-payments equilibrium subject to two conditions: (a) full employment and (b) absence of trade or payments restrictions for the purpose of keeping the balance of payments in equilibrium. As pointed out by Johnson (1951) and Machlup (1950, 1958), these conditions introduce value judgements into the concept of equilibrium. In addition, by adopting such a definition we implicitly reject the idea that trade and/or payments restrictions, as well as changes in aggregate spending, are legitimate methods for correcting a balance-of-payments equilibrium. Presently, the Nurske-Meade conditions are ignored. Full employment is considered to be an additional target (goal), and chap. 14 analyzes the circumstances in which use of restrictions may be justified on balance-of-payments grounds.

2.7 THE PROGRAMME BALANCE OF PAYMENTS

The programme balance of payments is a record of planned sources and uses of foreign exchange over a future period of time. It is an *ex ante* concept like the market balance of payments. It differs from the latter, though, in that it deals with hopes and desires rather than market supply and demand. In other words, the country sets certain targets for the levels of domestic consumption, capital formation, and exports, and then develops a programme of meeting an excess of requirements over resources by recourse to foreign finance. A deficit in the programme balance of payments is defined to be the excess of foreign exchange required to meet the specified targets over the foreign exchange expected to become available from regular sources, such as exports of goods and services, foreign investments, unilateral transfers from abroad, etc.

The targets set for domestic consumption, capital formation, and exports are matters of political judgement. These targets must conform to some standards widely accepted as reasonable, because the programme is usually submitted in justification of government measures or requests. A deficit on the programme balance of payments is not the same thing as a deficit on the accounting or market balance of payments. It is rather a deficit which is programmed only when there is a chance to finance it. If foreign financing is not forthcoming, then the targets are revised downward until the deficit is removed. For this reason, it is inappropriate to speak of policies of dealing with the programme deficit.

2.8 ACCOUNTING MEASURES OF DISEQUILIBRIUM IN THE U.S. BALANCE OF PAYMENTS

In this section, we describe three accounting measures of the U.S. balance-of-payments deficit: (*a*) the basic balance, (*b*) the liquidity balance, and (*c*) the official-settlements balance. These measures and the ensuing discussion highlight some of the difficulties raised by the accounting balance. Each measure provides the analyst with some useful information. Nevertheless, none of these (or any other) measures can adequately describe the international position of the United States during any given period. For this basic reason, all three measures have now been abandoned by the U.S. Department of Commerce.

To simplify our discussion we adopt the following notation:

$X \equiv$ exports of goods and services
$M \equiv$ imports of goods and services
$U \equiv$ unilateral transfers received from foreigners *minus* unilateral transfers made to foreigners
$LTC \equiv$ long-term capital flow (net)
$STC \equiv$ short-term capital flow (net)
$\Delta g \equiv$ net change in gold, gold tranche at the IMF, and hol convertible currencies

$E \equiv$ errors and omissions
$B_b \equiv$ basic balance
$B_l \equiv$ liquidity balance
$B_o \equiv$ official-settlements balance

The short-term capital flow (STC) needs to be subdivided into two parts: movements of U.S. capital (STC_{US}) and changes in foreign liquid capital (STC_f), the latter consisting of changes of all U.S. short-term liabilities to foreigners and all foreign holdings of U.S. securities, whatever their maturity. In addition, foreign short-term capital is subdivided into *private*, i.e., owned by foreign private individuals, banks, and corporations (STC_{fp}), and *official*, i.e., owned by foreign central banks (STC_{fo}). Accordingly, we have the following identities:

$$STC \equiv STC_{US} + STC_f \tag{2.1}$$

$$STC_f \equiv STC_{fp} + STC_{fo} \tag{2.2}$$

All credit entries in the accounting balance of payments are usually assigned a positive sign; all debit entries, a negative sign. Accordingly, we have $X > 0$, $M < 0$. Further, the inequality $U < 0$ means that the United States makes more unilateral transfers to foreigners than those received from them and the inequality $U > 0$ means the opposite; $LTC < 0$ and $STC < 0$ mean, respectively, net long-term and short-term capital outflow and $LTC > 0$ and $STC > 0$ mean, respectively, net long-term and short-term capital inflow; $\Delta g < 0$ means that U.S. reserves increase and $\Delta g > 0$ means that they decrease; and finally, $E > 0$ means that there is a credit balance and $E < 0$ that there is a debit balance in the account "errors and omissions."

As we saw earlier, the (accounting) balance of payments always balances. This can be expressed by the following identity:

$$(X - M) + U + LTC + STC + \Delta g + E \equiv 0 \tag{2.3}$$

Each of the three measures (basic balance, liquidity balance, and official-settlements balance) divides in some arbitrary fashion the entries in the U.S. balance of payments into autonomous and accommodating, as explained earlier. Given identity (2.3), each of these measures can be given either in terms of the autonomous transactions or in terms of the accommodating transactions. Below the three measures are given in terms of both groups of transactions.

(a) The Basic Balance (B_b)

The basic balance was used in the U.S. official statistics in the late 1940s and was reintroduced in 1961. It is also used in Britain today. It is defined as follows:

$$B_b \equiv (X - M) + U + LTC \equiv -(STC + \Delta g + E) \tag{2.4}$$

Thus, the basic balance places exports and imports of goods and services, unilateral transfers, and long- term capital movements, above the line as autonomous transactions. The rest, i.e., short-term capital movements, changes in official reserves, and errors and omissions, are considered accommodating and are placed below the line.

By definition, equilibrium prevails when $B_b = 0$. When $B_b < 0$, there is a basic-balance *deficit*, and when $B_b > 0$, there is a basic-balance *surplus*.

Kindleberger (1969, pp. 876–877) explains that the basic balance grew out of the preoccupation of economists with the transfer problem. (The transfer problem is taken up in chap. 12 below.) Briefly, the question is whether a country making a unilateral transfer (or a long-term loan) to another would develop an export surplus such as to enable her to make the transfer in *real* terms. That is, the transfer can be said to be effected when $B_b = 0$.

Cooper (1966, p. 384) provides us with another rationale for the basic balance. He notes that the basic balance "represents an attempt to measure the underlying trends, abstracting from such 'volatile' transactions as short-term capital movements and errors and omissions (changes in which are assumed to be largely unrecorded short-term capital movements)." But this thesis has not remained unchallenged. For instance, Fieleke (1971, p. 11) observed that the assumption that the transactions placed above the line (X, M, U, LTC) depict the workings of the "basic," underlying, longer-run forces "is often at variance with the facts; for example, there have been sharp short-run fluctuations in international transactions involving goods and services (transactions placed above the line . . .) and there have been important long-run trends in international transactions in short-term financial obligations (transactions placed below the line . . .)." Essentially, the same position is taken by the Bernstein report (Review Committee for Balance of Payments Statistics, 1965, p. 106).

The statistical separation of short-term from long-term capital is imperfect and of limited analytical significance. Large flows of short-term capital lurk within direct investments and transactions in long-term securities, while credits that are nominally short-term may be repeatedly renewed. Moreover, movements of certain types of short-term capital are often closely related to merchandise trade and to other "basic" transactions which they finance, so that it cannot be said that the two generally respond to different sets of forces. Finally, difficulties arise with the errors and omissions which supposedly represent unrecorded short-term capital movements. As explained earlier, this assumption is not necessarily correct. Accordingly, placing errors and omissions below the line renders the basic balance unreliable, especially when the item is large or when it is changing rapidly. The situation does not improve if the errors-and-omissions item is placed above the line.

Finally, a third rationale for the basic balance has been provided by Lary (1963). He merely asserts that the items placed below the line as accommodating are extremely sensitive to changes in government policy and, in particular, monetary policy. But as was pointed out earlier in this chapter, such division of international transactions into "policy sensitive" and "not policy sensitive" is necessarily artificial. For further comments on this point, see Cooper (1966, pp. 384–385), Johnson (1964, pp. 15–18), and Kindleberger (1969, pp. 880–881).

(b) The Liquidity Balance or Overall Balance (B_l)

About 1955, concerned over the gradually mounting volume of U.S. liabilities to foreigners, the Department of Commerce under the direction of Walter Lederer, Chief of the Balance of Payments Division, adopted a new accounting measure which has been named the *overall* or *liquidity balance*. The objective was to show changes in the liquidity position of the United States. The liquidity balance is defined as follows:

$$B_l \equiv (X - M) + U + \text{LTC} + E + \text{STC}_\text{US} = -(\text{STC}_f + \Delta g) \qquad (2.5)$$

Thus, the liquidity balance places exports of goods and services, unilateral transfers, long-term capital movements, errors and omissions, and changes in U.S. claims against foreigners above the line. It places changes in U.S. liquid liabilities to all foreigners (both private and official) and changes in U.S. monetary reserves below the line.

The differences between the liquidity balance and the basic balance become obvious from the following identity:

$$B_l \equiv B_b + E + \text{STC}_\text{US} \qquad (2.6)$$

To get eq. (2.6), simply substitute B_b as given by eq. (2.4) into eq. (2.5). Equation (2.6) shows that the liquidity balance differs from the basic balance in that the former considers the following to be autonomous (and places them above the line) while the latter considers them to be accommodating (and places them below the line): (a) errors and omissions and (b) changes in U.S. liquid claims against foreigners.

Lederer (1963) argues that the balance of payments should reflect the ability of the U.S. monetary authorities to defend the exchange value of the dollar. Liquid liabilities to foreigners should not mount to a point where the U.S. monetary authorities would be unable to meet them if they were suddenly presented for payment. According to this view, the ability of the U.S. monetary authorities to defend the dollar depends on two things: (a) their monetary reserves and (b) the foreign liquid claims which the foreigners might liquidate. But while all foreign liquid claims ($\equiv$ U.S. liquid liabilities) pose a potential danger for the U.S. official reserves (and for this reason changes in them are placed below the line), the U.S. monetary authorities cannot be certain of being able to liquidate the U.S. (private) liquid claims on foreigners and use them to offset, so to speak, the U.S. liquid liabilities. For this reason, changes in the U.S. liquid claims on foreigners are placed above the line.

The liquidity balance has been severely criticized. (See, for instance, Cooper, 1966, pp. 385–386; Fieleke, 1971, pp. 9–11; Kindleberger, 1969, pp. 879–880; and Review Committee for Balance of Payments Statistics, 1965, pp. 106–109.) For the benefit of the reader, an attempt is made presently to summarize these criticisms.

1. The basic rationale for the liquidity balance is concerned with the relationship between two *stocks:* the U.S. official reserves and U.S. liquid liabilities. The balance of payments records only *changes* in these stocks. Accordingly, a deficit

on the liquidity definition, implying a fall in the net-reserves position of the country (i.e., reserves minus liquid liabilities), need not be a bad thing unless the initial net-reserves position was already below the optimum. Conversely, a surplus on the liquidity definition (assuming that the basic rationale is accepted) need not necessarily imply the absence of balance-of-payments problems, especially when the initial net-reserves position was well below what may be considered normal, optimal, or acceptable. Accordingly, the liquidity position of the United States cannot be considered in terms of *changes* in the net-reserves position. The actual and optimal values of the net-reserve position itself must also be taken into account.

2. Many of the U.S. liquid liabilities to foreigners are really locked in, representing minimum working balances, compensating balances that must be held against U.S. loans to foreigners, balances required to maintain future lines of credit, and so on. Thus, as Kindleberger (1969, p. 879) points out, "it makes no sense to count the minimum balance held against a New York bank loan to a Japanese borrower as subject to withdrawal, when its maintenance is a condition of the loan."

3. The liquidity definition is clearly concerned with the possibility of a crisis in the confidence in the dollar. But in the event of a crisis, dollar balances held by U.S. residents might well pose a bigger threat. If foreign residents can convert their dollar balances into foreign currencies, U.S. residents can do so too. If this concept is taken too seriously, this potential danger could not be assumed away.

4. As a result of the asymmetrical treatment of the domestic (STC_{US}) and foreign (STC_f) short-term capital flows (the former placed above the line and the latter below), all countries could conceivably be in deficit. This observation is dramatized by the following example. Suppose that the Bank of England and the Federal Reserve Bank of New York swap deposits. Even though they may sign a forward contract to reverse the transaction in three months, the U.S. and U.K. balances of payments will be in deficit (assuming they were in equilibrium before this transaction) according to the liquidity definition. If balance-of-payments policies are based on the liquidity balance, the two countries would follow inconsistent and conflicting policies.

5. Kindleberger (1965), following the lead of Lary (1963), emphasized that the United States acts as a financial intermediary for the world. Accordingly, the United States borrows short and lends long. A free and efficient world capital market will necessarily produce U.S. deficits on the liquidity definition. Should these U.S. deficits be removed? To do so would run the risk of destroying this important role of intermediation—the provision of liquidity to the world by the United States—which is mutually advantageous. As Kindleberger observes, the United States is both a firm and a bank, but its liquidity is more akin to that of a bank than of a firm. Therefore, as a world banker it is natural to have a ratio of, say, 1 to 6 or 8 between its reserves and demand liabilities. United States deficits on the liquidity definition are not necessarily bad. On the contrary, they may be quite useful.

(c) The Official-Settlements Balance (B_o)

General concern about the large and continuing deficit (on the liquidity definition) in the U.S. balance of payments since 1958, and persistent and justifiable criticism of the liquidity definition itself, prompted the U.S. government in 1963 to appoint a committee chaired by Edward M. Bernstein to review balance-of-payments statistics and to comment on their adequacy "as a measure of the problem and a framework within which to consider policy alternatives" (Review Committee for Balance of Payments Statistics, 1965, p. iii). The committee correctly stressed that: "No single number can adequately describe the international position of the United States during any given period. . . . We explicitly reject . . . the notion that as a practical matter people must view the balance of payments position in terms of a single summary concept, the surplus or deficit" (Review Committee for Balance of Payments Statistics, 1965, p. 101). Nevertheless, despite this strong opposition to a single number, surplus, or deficit, the committee contributed a new accounting measure known as the official-settlements balance which is defined as follows:

$$B_o \equiv (X - M) + U + \text{LTC} + \text{STC}_{\text{US}} + \text{STC}_{\text{fp}} + E \equiv -(\text{STC}_{\text{fo}} + \Delta g) \quad (2.7)$$

To compare the new definition with the liquidity definition, we substitute B_l as given by eq. (2.5) into eq. (2.7) and obtain

$$B_o = B_l + \text{STC}_{\text{fp}} \quad (2.8)$$

What the review committee actually proposed was the split of foreign short-term capital (STC_f) into private (STC_{fp}) and official (STC_{fo}), with the former placed above and the latter below the line.

The committee (Review Committee for Balance of Payments Statistics, 1965, p. 109) asserts that the purpose of the official-settlements balance is "to measure the gap between the normal supply of and demand for foreign exchange—a gap which the monetary authorities, here and abroad, must fill by adding to, or drawing down, their reserve assets if exchange rates are to be held stable. . . ." But as Cooper (1966, p. 388) observed, the notion of gaps to be filled is *ex ante* in character and cannot be observed.

The official-settlements balance is based on two assumptions: (*a*) that foreign *private* banks, companies, and individuals are willing holders of dollars, whereas foreign *officials* are not; and (*b*) that private ownership of dollar balances in New York can be effectively distinguished from official ownership. Neither of these assumptions is warranted (Cooper, 1966, pp. 387–389; Kindleberger, 1969, pp. 881–882). The first assumption draws too sharp a distinction between private and official bodies, and ignores completely the important role of financial intermediation played by the United States as the world banker. The second assumption is also unwarranted. For instance, foreign private dollar balances in New York may be beneficially owned by foreign central banks when the latter have undertaken spot sales against forward purchases of dollars as a device for taking funds out of the domestic money market. Alternatively, foreign official dollar balances may have been sold forward, so that in effect they are held for private account.

Some Recent Developments in U.S. Official Reporting

In line with the preceding criticisms of the basic balance, the liquidity balance, and the official-settlements balance, and because of major changes in the world economy and in the international monetary system in the past few years—most notably the widespread substitution of "dirty" floating for the regime of par values—the U.S. Department of Commerce has decided recently to abandon the official reporting of overall balances. It retains, though, the goods and services and current account balances, largely because of their relationship to other macroeconomic accounting systems.

PART C. THE BALANCE OF INTERNATIONAL INDEBTEDNESS

In concluding this chapter, it appears desirable to discuss briefly the *balance of international indebtedness* (also known as the international investment position). The balance of international indebtedness is a statement of the *stock* of total claims of the residents of the reporting country against the residents of the rest of the world and the *stock* of total claims of foreign residents against the residents of the reporting country at a certain point in time.

The relation between the balance of international indebtedness and the balance of payments may be seen as follows. As we saw earlier, the capital account of the balance of payments records *changes* in the stocks of foreign claims and liabilities of the reporting country which take place between two points in time. Therefore, *under ideal conditions,* the balance of international indebtedness could be derived as a summation of *all* past debits and credits in the capital account of the balance of payments (i.e., from the time the first international transaction took place until the moment the balance of international indebtedness is being constructed). In practice, however, ideal conditions are never realized, so that the balance of international indebtedness summarizes, in addition to the combined cumulative effects of international capital flows, the effects of a number of other factors over the years, such as changes in foreign-exchange rates, changes in prices of domestic and foreign securities, changes in the legal status of assets,† and

---

† For example, $490 million of U.S. government claims on Japan in settlement of postwar aid were included in the U.S. international investment position for the first time in 1962, the year in which a settlement agreement was signed; they could not be included earlier because of the uncertainty involved. On the other hand, World War I debts which are moribund but not legally cancelled are omitted.

changes in assets resulting from normal write-offs, liquidation losses, and revaluation of fixed assets. (It should be remembered that valuation changes in claims and liabilities are not included in the balance of payments because they are not international transactions.)

The usefulness of the balance of international indebtedness derives from the fact that, on the one hand, it provides a basis for projecting future flows of investment income and, on the other, it gives some indication of the potential that exists for short-term capital withdrawal, i.e., the potential danger for loss of reserves, or, to put it differently, it gives some clues about the adequacy of existing reserves.

However, the usefulness of the balance of international indebtedness should not be overemphasized in view of the enormous difficulties involved in its construction. In the first place, as a result of the enormous gaps in tracing all capital flows for balance-of-payments purposes, the coverage of the stocks of claims and liabilities for purposes of constructing the balance of international indebtedness is necessarily rather poor. Further, the difficulties of valuation are insurmountable. Finally, no automatic check on accuracy exists. Even the imperfect test provided by the *net* errors and omissions for the balance-of-payments accuracy is not available for the accuracy of the balance of international indebtedness.

It will be recalled that because the balance of payments is constructed on the basis of double-entry bookkeeping the balance on errors and omissions should ideally be zero. It is usually assumed that the larger the balance on errors and omissions the more important the *gross* errors made in the collection of data, etc. However, even a small *balance* on errors and omissions does not exclude the possibility of significant errors in both debit and credit entries in the way that they cancel out to leave only a minor *net* errors-and-omissions entry. Nevertheless, even this imperfect test is not available to check the accuracy of the balance of international indebtedness, because the stock of foreign claims need not be equal to the stock of foreign liabilities of the reporting country.

Three different valuation methods are used in estimating the various components of the U.S. balance of international indebtedness. Direct investments are estimated at *book values* (which are probably substantially lower than current market values), portfolio-securities holdings are estimated at *current market values*, and, finally, short-term claims and nonmarketable long-term claims (other than direct investments) are valued at their *face value*. In the case of portfolio-securities holdings a source of possible error (in addition to imperfect coverage) lies in the adjustments made for changes in market prices and in foreign-exchange rates. This error springs from the fact that, in the case of U.S. holdings of foreign securities, the present reporting system shows the nationality of the foreigner involved in a transaction but not the nationality of the security itself that is traded. The usual assumption made is that the two coincide (or some other *arbitrary* assumption).

An interesting question arises in relation to monetary gold holdings by the U.S. government. Since monetary gold is not a claim on any country in particular, the question arises as to whether the U.S. gold stock should be included in the balance of international indebtedness. There are those who believe that it should be so included because it is a special kind of international asset. If this were done, the stock of total world claims would be greater than the stock of total world liabilities.

APPENDIX TO CHAPTER TWO. BALANCE-OF-PAYMENTS REPORTING DIFFICULTIES

Putting together a balance of payments raises questions of *residency* (i.e., how to *identify* international transactions), *coverage* (i.e., how to collect accurately data on *all* international transactions), *valuation* (i.e., how to *value* international transactions, especially those that do not go through the market-place), and, finally, *timing* (i.e., *when* to make the necessary entry in the balance of payments). This appendix illustrates these problems. The present discussion is definitely not an exhaustive examination of all the difficulties involved.

A2.1 RESIDENCY

Theoretically, the balance of payments is defined as a systematic record of all transactions between the residents of the reporting country and foreigners. In practice, there are several exceptions and borderline cases to this principle. These cases are as follows.

(a) Undistributed Profits of Subsidiaries

While the unremitted profits of branches are usually included in the U.S. balance of payments, both as earnings on foreign investments and as capital flows, the undistributed profits of foreign subsidiaries are not included at all. This practice understates both investment earnings and capital flows.

The reasons usually cited for this artificial distinction are as follows. The profits of a branch are credited to the parent concern continuously, thus automatically creating a claim on the branch in favor of the parent concern in another country. In the case of a subsidiary, however, the income is normally distributed in the form of dividends and interest, which constitute economic transactions at the time they are paid. Therefore, it is argued, the earnings of subsidiaries are not effectively at the disposal of the parents and, in addition, they may be subject to foreign tax liabilities that cannot be determined until they are distributed as dividends. These are legal distinctions. The truth is that the decision to reinvest (rather than distribute) earnings is usually similar in its nature and economic effects to the decision to invest new capital. Accordingly, it appears desirable to treat the earnings of subsidiaries in the same way as the earnings of branches. The main reason for omitting undistributed profits of subsidiaries at present in the U.S. balance of payments is simply the unavailability of satisfactory data.

(b) Migrants' Transfers

When people migrate from one country to another, title to their possessions passes from the country of emigration to the country of immigration. This transfer of property is usually entered in the balance of payments. Thus, it is imagined that a person in his capacity as resident transfers (or donates) property to himself in his capacity as foreigner, or vice versa, as the case may be. (Note that one entry is made in the unilateral-transfers account and another in the current account or the capital account, depending on the particular circumstances.)

(c) Transportation Charges for Merchandise

For reasons of international consistency, the IMF recommended that merchandise exports and imports be valued f.o.b. (free on board) the exporting country. Thus, merchandise exports and imports are valued exclusive of transportation charges, which are recorded separately. In overseas trade either party (the exporter or the importer) may pay for the transportation service. But to assure consistency in interpretation and comparison of trade statistics, transportation is treated as if all transactions were actually handled in the same way. Thus, irrespective of who *actually* pays for the transportation service, the convention adopted for balance-of-payments statistics is to *assume* that the importer actually does so. Accordingly, when transportation is supplied by a foreigner vis-à-vis the importer, it becomes an international transaction and is entered in the balance of payments. Otherwise, no entry is made in the balance of payments, because according to the adopted convention no international transaction is involved.

United States merchandise exports are generally valued on an fas (free alongside ship) basis at the foreign port, with all transportation services rendered by U.S. companies (but not those rendered by foreign companies) posted in the transportation account under the general heading "exports of services." If the foreign importer actually pays for the transportation costs there is no problem. But if the U.S. exporter actually does so, an international transaction (i.e., the rendering of the transportation service by foreign companies to the U.S. exporter and the payment for the service) is omitted from the U.S. balance of payments. In this case, the U.S. exporter is considered to act merely as an agent for the foreign importer.

On the other hand, U.S. imports are generally valued on an f.o.b. foreign port basis, with all transportation services rendered by foreign companies (but not those rendered by U.S. companies) posted into the transportation account. Thus, if the foreign exporter actually pays for the transportation costs (and he is subsequently reimbursed by the U.S. importer), the value of the transportation services rendered by U.S. companies is not shown in the U.S. balance of payments even though the transaction is actually between a U.S. resident and a foreigner. Here again, the foreign exporter is assumed to act merely as an agent for the U.S. importer.

(d) Gold Transactions

Purchases and sales of gold by the monetary authorities from private residents of the reporting country are usually included in the balance of payments (despite the fact that no international transaction is involved) because such purchases and sales affect the stock of international monetary reserves of the reporting country.

(e) Short-Term Capital Movements

In practice, short-term capital movements are calculated as changes in outstanding assets and liabilities from the beginning to the end of the period covered by the balance of payments (adjusted to exclude valuation changes, as explained earlier). Changes in *private* assets and liabilities are recorded separately from changes in *official* assets and liabilities. Therefore, any transfers of foreign short-term assets or liabilities between the private and official sectors are included in the balance of payments, even though no international transaction is involved—both parties to the transaction are residents of the reporting country. Again the main reason for this practice is the fact that a country's official reserves, and therefore information with regard to their changes, is of vital importance to the country.

(f) Government Grants

All Peace Corps expenditures as well as all of AID's service payments (both its administrative overheads in Washington and abroad and its payments to other agencies for services in connection with AID programs) are treated as grants in the U.S. balance of payments. (Two balance-of-payments entries are made: a debit to "nonmilitary grants" and a credit to "exports of U.S. government.") But the practice of including administrative expenses in Washington in the U.S. balance of payments is debatable to say the least. As Cooper (1966) comments:

> The balance-of-payments statistics in effect treat these civil servants as lobbyists for foreigners paid by the United States taxpayer. It is difficult to see why these expenditures should be regarded as an international transaction in view of the higher foreign-policy value the United States places on the activities of both of these agencies; or, to go to the other extreme, why all or part of the domestic expenditures of the Department of State, the Foreign Agricultural Service, the National Institutes of Health, or, indeed, the Ford and Rockefeller Foundations are not also considered international transactions. . . . Certainly no other countries consider these "exports" as imports (p. 380).

A2.2 COVERAGE

In principle, the balance of payments is supposed to record *all* international economic transactions. In practice, however, many international economic transactions are hard to capture through any systematic procedures of data collection. As a result, they go unreported. The following examples illustrate this difficulty.

(a) Visible Trade

This item is usually based on customs returns. There are many reasons why these returns do not as a rule cover all transactions of merchandise trade. In the first place, some countries use data on the basis of the principles of *special* as opposed to *general* trade. (The United States follow the principles of general trade.) When trade statistics are gathered on the special trade basis, imports into free ports or bonded warehouses as well as re-exports are not included in the statistics. Second, when the formal border procedures are inadequate to cope with the volume of traffic (as is the case of U.S. exports over the Canadian border), several important transactions by necessity are omitted from the statistics. Finally, certain items regarded as merchandise (such as goods sent by parcel post, ships and aircraft, and fish and other marine products caught in the open sea and sold directly in foreign ports) are often omitted from the customs reports.

(b) Invisible Trade

For most service items, there are usually no comprehensive reports of individual transactions as there are for merchandise exports and imports. Therefore, the data on services are usually arrived at by *estimation* rather than *enumeration*, and this is the main reason for the imperfect coverage of invisible trade. This is well illustrated by the U.S. balance of payments. For example, U.S. receipts for ocean-freight services rendered to foreigners are estimated from a sample of only 63 percent of the estimated total. Estimates for tourist expenditures are based in part on the number of travelers and on a sample of voluntary returns showing destination, length of stay, and expenditures. Further, for a wide variety of services there are little or no data. For instance: (a) no data are available on commission received or paid in international trade or on international advertising expenditures; (b) the data on royalties and on foreign earnings of service-type enterprises, such as construction firms and consultants, are seriously incomplete; and (c) finally, while estimates of income from U.S. direct investments are probably fairly reliable (information on U.S. direct investment is based on reports from 900 corporations, out of an estimated 3000 companies having direct investments abroad, but they appear to account for 90 percent of such investments), there may be large errors in estimating other types of investment income.

(c) Unilateral Transfers

Data on private unilateral transfers are usually seriously incomplete. The point is well illustrated by the balance of payments of the United States. Private unilateral transfers are estimated separately for two groups of donors, namely, personal and institutional. The estimate of institutional remittances seems satisfactory for those organizations that do report. However, there are several institutions (such as labor unions, universities, and smaller foundations) which may be making remittances and are not covered by the reporting system. Estimates of *cash* personal remittances are based on bank reports—on a sample basis. The banks report personal remittances such as those from individuals to individuals, but it is not certain that some types of large remittances (such as those representing inheritances) can be so identified. In addition, it is not inconceivable that many bank remittances or postal money orders that are counted as unilateral transfers in fact constitute payments associated with commodity purchases, tourism, etc.

Gifts of goods sent by parcel post are estimated by assuming that all parcel post shipments to certain countries are gifts of U.S. residents to foreign residents. (The total weight of parcels sent to each country is multiplied by an average value per pound, calculated from a sample of the Customs declaration forms affixed to the parcels.) Note that in the case of gift parcels, unilateral transfers are debited and merchandise exports are credited by the same amount. Thus, no net errors and omissions result. However, in the case of cash remittances, a residual amount most certainly appears in the errors and omissions.

United States receipts of gift parcels are assumed to be negligible and are not estimated. Further, U.S. receipts from personal remittances are almost impossible to detect, except for a few categories. The Post Office Department reports money order receipts on a quarterly basis, and these are considered to represent personal remittances only. In addition, certain outpayments taken from the balances of payments of Austria, Canada, Germany, and the United Kingdom have been recently (beginning in 1960) included as unilateral receipts.

(d) Capital Movements

The collection of data on movements of private long-term portfolio capital and short-term capital presents serious problems of coverage. It is usually extremely difficult to obtain reports of all such movements from all individuals and firms engaging in international transactions. As a rule, no estimates of unreported transactions can be made because the universe of transactors and transactions is not known. The size of omissions is not known, even roughly. The following examples illustrate the difficulties involved.

1. A bank may not know that certain accounts are foreign. As a result, the banking data omit changes of liabilities to foreigners. There is no similar problem, of course, related to the coverage of banking claims on foreigners because the banks do know what assets they hold abroad for their own account or for the account of their domestic customers.
2. Nonbank data usually appear to be incomplete and inaccurate. For example, there is evidence that some deposits of U.S. nonbanking concerns in Canadian banks may not be reported because of misunderstandings concerning the status of the agencies of Canadian banks in the United States. These agencies are not allowed to receive deposits for their own account, but they may accept funds in the name of their head offices abroad. Thus, the possibility arises that some U.S. concerns placing deposits in Canadian banks through the latters' U.S.

agencies may fail to report them as claims on foreigners in the belief that they are making deposits with the agencies and not the head office.

3. United States residents living along the Canadian border with easy access to Canadian banks may hold substantial deposits there as well as other short-term investments. No information is available.

4. Changes in foreign holdings of U.S. currency, and to a lesser extent changes in U.S. holdings of foreign currencies, may be substantial but extremely difficult to estimate.

5. United Kingdom Treasury bills held in custody by a London branch of a U.S. bank for a U.S. firm must be reported by the latter and not the U.S. bank. But if they are held in custody by a bank in the United States, the bank must report them. Therefore, as a result of possible confusion, the assets may be reported twice or not at all.

6. Finally, the following items are not covered by the present reporting system of the United States: investments in mortgages and real estate; interests acquired in estates, trusts, and personal holding companies; minority interests in foreign business concerns; and other nonnegotiable long-term investments.

A2.3 VALUATION

Essentially, the balance-of-payments statisticians attempt to measure the value of the resources transferred from one country to another. To the extent that regular market transactions are involved, resource value is best represented by the actual amount paid (or agreed on), with appropriate treatment of transportation and other related expenses. In practice, however, the actual amounts paid are not always easily available. In addition, great difficulties arise when there is no such market transaction, and therefore some imputed value must be used. The following examples illustrate these problems.

1. In the United States, every import shipment must be documented by a so-called "import-entry" form, executed by the importer or his agent and filed with the Customs Bureau on the arrival of the goods from abroad. On the basis of this document, the Customs Bureau determines whether the goods are dutiable and if so the amount due. In addition, this document forms the basis for the balance-of-payments entry. It is obvious that if the value figure is not involved in the calculation of duty, there is little incentive for accuracy on the part of the importer—especially if the correct figure is not conveniently available. Further, occasionally the price used for tariff purposes is different from the actual price paid. For example, the preferred-tariff valuation method calls for a market value determined as of a principal foreign market which may or may not be a port of loading. Further, the law requires certain goods to be valued at the "American selling price" for purposes of duty assessment. Thus, in these cases, the declared price may be different from the actual price paid by the importer.

2. The U.S. exporter (or his agent) prior to shipment is required to file with the Customs Bureau a document called the "shipper's export declaration." The instructions for this document call for "value at U.S. port of export (selling price or cost if not sold, including inland freight, insurance, and other charges to U.S. port of export)." But while "selling price" is consistent with the balance-of-payments approach, "cost if not sold" (even if it is available) is not. The latter would apply in general to nonmarket transactions, discussed below.

3. The problem of freight and related charges is of particular concern. It was noted earlier that, under the IMF recommendation, exports and imports are valued, for balance-of-payments purposes, f.o.b. the exporting country. In practice, however, it is quite conceivable that freight charges might be improperly included in the merchandise account; and because data on freight charges are primarily collected from transportation companies rather than exporters and importers, the error is independent of the entries in the transportation account.

   For rail or truck exports, another difficulty arises. This is illustrated by the U.S. exports over the Canadian or Mexican borders. Here, the fas rule calls for the inclusion of freight to the border but not beyond. Thus, the total freight must be split—something that is not very likely to be carried out satisfactorily in practice.

4. More important difficulties are posed by nonmarket transactions such as shipments between affiliated companies or branches, immigrants' household effects, gifts, barter transactions, shipments under a government aid program involving an element of subsidy (as is the case when the United States buys commodities at prices above world market prices in order to help another country or when the United States makes loans at low interest rates), etc. Such transactions enter the trade figures at nominal or arbitrary values.

A2.4 TIMING

At what point of time should merchandise trade be recorded in the balance of payments? When the importer's liability is incurred (when he places his order or signs the contract)? When the importer actually pays for the goods? Or when the goods actually move from the exporter to the importer? In this case should the entry be made when the goods leave the exporter or when they reach the importer?

   The point of time when payment is made is important to the foreign exchange market and the reserves of the countries in question. Nevertheless, recording merchandise transactions when payment is made means that goods imported on credit are recorded in the balance of payments a long time after they have been received (and possibly consumed). Similarly, when an advance payment is made, the entry is made much earlier than the actual receipt of goods by the importer. Further, what if payment is actually made in several annual installments? It appears that the position would be much better reflected by the balance of payments if imports were debited and capital inflows credited during the time period in which the contract is signed. But even this method gives rise to difficulties in cases where residents of the reporting country enter into a long-term contract with foreigners to purchase from them commodities (to be transferred into the reporting country) in several future time periods. To record this transaction as merchandise imports into the reporting country's balance of payments would imply that the goods had been imported on credit and stored up (i.e., not consumed) in the reporting country, which is certainly untrue. Had the goods been purchased on credit and stored up in the exporting country, the debit entry in the merchandise trade account might not seem so unnatural.

In practice, the entries in the merchandise trade account are based on customs returns which generally record merchandise as it crosses the customs frontier of the reporting country. Most countries assume that, in general, their customs returns provide a reasonably accurate record of changes in ownership. That is, it is assumed that small discrepancies tend to compensate over time, and that obvious and blatant discrepancies may be corrected by special adjustments. Timing adjustments to customs returns are particularly important when the volume of trade is changing rapidly or when there are large changes in domestically owned stocks held abroad or foreign-owned stocks held in the reporting country. Such adjustments have been made by a few countries. For example, the United Kingdom assumes that its exports change ownership when they reach foreign ports, and it makes adjustments to the customs returns for *changes* in exports in transit.

Finally, note that invisible trade should be recorded in the balance of payments when the actual service is rendered; transfers should be recorded when the gift is legally made; and capital flows should be recorded when the ownership of assets is transferred from residents of one country to residents of another.

A2.5 INTERNATIONAL CONSISTENCY

As noted earlier, when an international transaction gives rise to a debit entry in the balance of payments of a country, say A, it must necessarily give rise to a credit entry in the balance of payments of another country, say B. International consistency is achieved if the debit and credit entries in the balances of payments of countries A and B, respectively, fall in the same major account (i.e., visible trade, invisible trade, capital account, unilateral transfers account, and official reserves account), during the same time period and at the same valuation. In principle, it appears that international consistency can, and indeed should, always be established, provided only that all countries attach consistent meanings to the items which make up their balances of payments. In practice, however, problems might arise in relation to residency, coverage, valuation, and timing.

For international consistency, it is necessary that everyone should be a resident of a single country. However, in practice some confusion may arise in some borderline cases. For example, when a resident of A lives temporarily in country B, the question arises as to whether he retains his original residency (i.e., he is considered a tourist) or becomes a resident of country B. The answer, of course, is based on rather arbitrary criteria. However, it is important that both countries apply the same arbitrary criteria. Any inconsistency in the criteria used necessarily produces inconsistencies in the balances of payments of the countries involved.

In general, there are four possibilities. An individual (say Mr. X) may be considered:

(a) by A and B as resident of A
(b) by A and B as resident of B
(c) by A as resident of A, and by B as resident of B
(d) by A as resident of B, and by B as resident of A

The obvious inconsistency in the concept of residents in cases (c) and (d) leads to international balance-of-payments inconsistency. For instance, in case (c), the transactions of Mr. X with residents of A are not reported in A's balance of payments (because they are not considered international transactions by A), but they are reported in B's balance of payments. Further, the transactions of Mr. X with residents of B are reported in A's balance of payments, but not in B's. The opposite is true in case (d).

In general, the same type of inconsistency arises when one country makes a double entry in its balance of payments for a transaction that is not international, such as purchases and sales of gold by the monetary authorities to private residents or transfers of foreign short-term assets (or liabilities) between the private and official sectors.

International consistency is also violated by the varying degree of efficiency in *covering* (i.e., recording in the balance of payments) international transactions by different countries around the world. The same is true for valuation problems as well. Thus, as noted earlier, for reasons of international consistency, the IMF recommended that merchandise exports and imports be valued f.o.b. the exporting country. But if exports are actually valued f.o.b. and imports cif, international inconsistency arises because total world exports fall short of total world imports by the amount of insurance and shipping costs necessary to transfer the goods from the exporting to the importing countries.

Finally, international inconsistency may arise in relation to timing. This point is illustrated by the merchandise trade account. As noted earlier, merchandise trade transactions are recorded in the balance of payments when the goods cross the customs frontier of the reporting country. When the customs frontiers of the countries involved coincide, no difficulty exists. However, when the customs frontiers do not coincide (as, for example, in the case where the two countries involved are separated by an ocean), the possibility of international inconsistency arises because the goods cross the two customs frontiers not at the same time but at two different points in time. Therefore, the entry in the exporting country's balance of payments may be made at an earlier accounting period than that in which the entry is made in the importing country's balance of payments. Therefore, if adjustments are not made for goods in transit, international inconsistency arises. It should be noted, however, that unless the volume of trade changes rapidly, this point is not likely to be of any major significance.

SELECTED BIBLIOGRAPHY

Badger, D. G. (1951). "The Balance of Payments: A Tool of Analysis." *IMF Staff Papers*, vol. II, no. 1 (September).

Cohen, B. J. (1970). *Balance-of-Payments Policy*. Penguin Books, Inc., Baltimore, Ma.

Cooper, R. N. (1966). "The Balance of Payments in Review." *JPE* (August).

Fieleke, N. S. (1971). "Accounting for the Balance of Payments." *New England Economic Review*. Federal Reserve Bank of Boston, May–June, 1971.

Gardner, W. R. (1961). "An Exchange Market Analysis of the U.S. Balance of Payments." *IMF Staff Papers*. (May).

International Monetary Fund (1949). *Balance of Payments Yearbook 1938–1946–1947*. The Fund, Washington, D.C.

—— (1950). *Balance of Payments Manual*. The Fund, Washington, D.C.

Johnson, H. G. (1951). "The Taxonomic Approach to Economic Policy." *Economic Journal*, vol. LXI (December), pp. 812–832.

—— (1968). "The International Competitive Position of the United States and the Balance of Payments for 1968: A Review Article." *Review of Economics and Statistics*, vol. XLVI (February), pp. 14–32.

Kindleberger, C. P. (1965). *Balance-of-Payments Deficits and the International Market for Liquidity*. Princeton Essays in International Finance, no. 46. International Finance Section, Princeton University, Princeton, N.J.

—— (1969). "Measuring Equilibrium in the Balance of Payments." *Journal of Political Economy*, vol. 77 (November–December), pp. 873–891.

—— (1973). *International Economics*. R. D. Irwin, Inc., Homewood, Ill., chap. 18.

Lary, H. B. (1963). *Problems of the United States as World Banker and Trader*. National Bureau of Economic Research, New York.

Lederer, W. (1963). *The Balance of Foreign Transactions: Problems of Definition and Measurement*. Special Paper in International Economics, no. 5. International Finance Section, Princeton University, Princeton, N.J.

Machlup, F. (1950). "Three Concepts of the Balance of Payments and the So-called Dollar Shortage." *Economic Journal*, vol. LX (March), pp. 46–68. Reprinted in F. Machlup, *International Payments, Debts, and Gold*. Charles Scribner's Sons, New York, 1964.

—— (1958). "Equilibrium and Disequilibrium: Misplaced Concreteness and Disguised Politics." *Economic Journal*, vol. LXVII (March), pp. 1–24. Reprinted in F. Machlup, *International Payments, Debts, and Gold*. Charles Scribner's Sons, New York, 1964.

Meade, J. E. (1951). *The Balance of Payments*. Oxford University Press, London, chaps. I–III.

Mundell, R. A. (1968). *International Economics*. The Macmillan Company, New York, chap. 10.

Nurkse, R. (1945). *Conditions of International Monetary Equilibrium*. Princeton Essays in International Finance, no. 4. International Finance Section, Princeton University, Princeton, N.J. Reprinted in H. S. Ellis and L. A. Metzler (Eds.), *Readings in the Theory of International Trade*. The Blackiston Company, Philadelphia, 1949.

Review Committee for Balance of Payments Statistics (1965). *The Balance of Payments Statistics of the United States: A Review and Appraisal*. Government Printing Office, Washington, D.C.

Salant, W. S. (1966). "Capital Markets and the Balance of Payments of a Financial Center." In W. Fellner, F. Machlup, and R. Triffin (Eds.), *Maintaining and Restoring Balance in International Payments*. Princeton University Press, Princeton, N.J.

—— (1969). "International Reserves and Payments Adjustment." Banca Nazionale del Lavoro, *Quarterly Review*, no. 90 (September), pp. 281–308.

U.S. Department of Commerce (1976). *Survey of Current Business*. Government Printing Office, Washington, D.C., June 1976. Especially pp. 18–27.

Vanek. J. (1962). *International Trade: Theory and Economic Policy*. R. D. Irwin, Inc., Homewood, Ill., chaps. 2 and 3.

THREE

SUPPLY AND DEMAND FOR FOREIGN EXCHANGE

The first two chapters have dealt with the basic concepts of foreign exchange and the balance of payments. These concepts are indispensable preparation for dealing with the great issues of international monetary economics. During that discussion there was repeated reference to exchange rates and balance-of-payments equilibrium. But there was no systematic discussion of the economic forces which keep the foreign exchange market and the balance of payments in equilibrium. The time has come to begin such discussion systematically.

What determines the rate of foreign exchange? What happens when the quantities of foreign exchange supplied and demanded are not equal? These are fundamental questions. A provisional answer is given in this and the following five chapters.

The present chapter, along with chap. 4, lay the foundations for the discussion of the flexible-exchange-rate system (chaps. 5 and 6) and the fixed-exchange-rate system (chaps. 7 and 8). In particular, after a brief introductory section on the two basic institutional arrangements in the foreign exchange market, this chapter deals primarily with (a) the relationship between the supply of domestic currency and the demand for foreign exchange, and (b) the relationship between the demand for domestic currency and the supply of foreign exchange. Chapter 4 discusses the Bickerdike-Robinson-Machlup model. In particular, it shows how the demand and supply curves for foreign exchange and domestic currency are derived from the demand for imports and supply of exports of goods and services of two countries. During this discussion (chaps. 3 and 4) the spot and forward exchange markets are combined into a single foreign exchange market.

3.1 THE TWO BASIC SYSTEMS (INTRODUCTORY)

Our primary purpose is to discover how the rate of exchange is determined and how differences between the quantities of foreign exchange supplied and demanded are dealt with. For this purpose, we shall continue to assume that there are two countries only: A (America) and B (Britain), with national currencies the dollar and pound sterling, respectively.

Broadly speaking, the adjustment process in the foreign exchange market may be viewed as taking place within either of the following two institutional arrangements: (*a*) the flexible-exchange-rate system and (*b*) the fixed-exchange-rate system. Essentially, under the former system the rate of exchange is determined by the market forces of supply and demand for foreign exchange, while under the latter system the rate of exchange is kept fixed. But how is supply brought into equality with demand for foreign exchange if the rate of exchange is to be kept fixed? The supply and demand for foreign exchange depend on many other economic variables besides the rate of exchange. Under a fixed-exchange-rate system these other economic variables are relied upon to vary, either automatically or as a result of deliberate governmental policies, in such a way as to bring about appropriate shifts in the supply and demand curves for foreign exchange (drawn as functions of the rate of exchange) and eliminate any possible divergence between the quantities of foreign exchange supplied and demanded at the fixed rate of exchange.

The two basic systems are illustrated in fig. 3.1. Along the horizontal axis are measured pounds sterling and along the vertical, the rate of exchange (R), i.e., the dollar price of £1. The curves DD' and SS' are assumed to give the maximum quantities of pounds sterling demanded and supplied, respectively, at alternative dollar prices (R values). The two curves intersect each other at E. Under a flexible-exchange-rate system, the rate of exchange would settle at $R = R_e$, where intended demand for sterling equals intended supply. Because of the assumed negative and

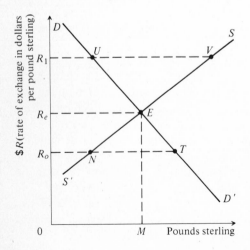

Figure 3.1 The flexible- and fixed-exchange-rate systems. Under a flexible-exchange-rate system, equilibrium occurs at E. Under a fixed-exchange-rate system, the rate of exchange is kept fixed at an agreed-upon level, say $0R_o$ or $0R_1$, which need not be equal to $0R_e$, and, therefore, supply and demand need not be equal.

positive slopes of the demand and supply curves, respectively, any value of $R > R_e$, such as R_1, gives rise to an excess supply of sterling, such as UV, causing the dollar price of sterling (R) to fall. Similarly, any value of $R < R_e$, such as R_0, gives rise to an excess demand for sterling, such as NT, causing the dollar price of sterling (R) to rise. (These comments ignore completely the important factor of speculative activity in the foreign exchange market. The complications of speculation are discussed in later chapters.) Thus, on the surface at least, the flexible-exchange-rate system allows the forces of supply and demand to determine the rate of exchange. In other words, the foreign exchange market organized under the rules of the flexible-exchange-rate system works like any other perfectly competitive market. This system is studied in more detail in chaps. 5 and 6.

The fixed-exchange-rate system, on the other hand, is an institutional arrangement, according to which the rate of exchange is kept fixed at a level agreed upon by governments. More details on such institutional arrangements are given in chaps. 7 and 8. For the moment, note that the agreed-upon rate need not be equal to the equilibrium rate, R_e (fig. 3.1). For instance, the agreed-upon rate of exchange may be given by $R_o < R_e$. At $R = R_o$, there exists an excess demand for pounds sterling, given by the horizontal distance NT. This gap between intended purchases and sales must somehow be filled if the rate of exchange is to be kept at R_o without suspending the free market. Temporarily, the gap may be filled by country A through official sales of reserves of pounds sterling. But then country A will be losing reserves at the rate of NT per unit of time. Since A's reserves are necessarily finite, this process cannot continue for long. An alternative way of filling the gap is for the monetary authorities of B to supply the needed NT pounds sterling either directly to the foreign exchange market or indirectly by making it available in the form of loans to the monetary authorities of country A, which may in turn use it to fill the gap. But none of these alternatives can last for too long either. There is usually a limit for B's intervention. The monetary authorities of B will feel reluctant to either accumulate dollars, which they may not be able to use, or extend unlimited amounts of credit to A. (Essentially both alternatives imply that B extends credit to A. In the first case, B receives, in return, dollar bills while in the second, loan contracts.) We are driven then to the following conclusion. If the rate of exchange R_o is to be maintained either one of the following two things must happen: (a) comprehensive systems of exchange controls may be instituted to allocate in some arbitrary way the limited supply of sterling $(R_o N)$ among those who need it; or (b) by appropriate policy measures a shift may be effected to the supply and demand curves of fig. 3.1 such as to make them intersect each other at $R = R_o$ (if no automatic process with similar effects is at work, or it is too slow, or its side effects are undesirable). The first method suspends the free market; the second does not.

Note that the problem would not have been any easier if R were fixed at a value which is higher than the equilibrium rate R_e, such as R_1. In this case, there would emerge an excess *supply* of pounds sterling which presumably A's monetary authorities could continue buying indefinitely, period after period. But this problem is not different from the problem which B's monetary authorities were facing earlier, when there was an excess demand for pounds sterling per unit of time. Again the conclusion is that A's monetary authorities will refuse to either accumulate pounds sterling or extend continuous credit to B beyond a certain point.

Many economists look at the difficult problems raised by the fixed-exchange-rate system and feel that the flexible-exchange-rate system is better because it is simpler. They point out that any disequilibrium in the foreign exchange market can be quickly and easily removed by a change in the rate of exchange. Why is it so important to maintain exchange rates fixed anyway, if they give rise to imbalances which are not easy to remove? For the moment, we reserve judgement on this important question. We come back to it later.

Both the flexible-exchange-rate system and the fixed-exchange-rate system make use of the supply and demand curves for foreign exchange. The former uses the supply-and-demand apparatus to determine the equilibrium rate of exchange; the latter, to determine at the given rate of exchange the absolute " gap " which must be filled. In addition, the fixed-exchange-rate system requires knowledge of what lies behind the supply and demand curves for foreign exchange for the formulation of appropriate policy measures to bridge the gap. In particular, a curve (supply or demand) is drawn on the assumption that several economic variables (or parameters) remain constant. When any of these parameters change, the curve shifts. The objective of economic policy in the present context is to influence one or more of these parameters and cause appropriate shifts in the supply and demand curves to make them intersect at the fixed rate. The flexible-exchange-rate system also requires knowledge of what lies behind the supply and demand curves for foreign exchange in order to determine the effects of policy changes on the exchange rate and, through it, on the domestic economy.

3.2 RELATIONSHIPS BETWEEN SUPPLY AND DEMAND CURVES FOR FOREIGN EXCHANGE AND DOMESTIC CURRENCY

As we saw in chap. 1, the purchase of one currency involves the sale of another. For instance, if dollars are traded for pounds sterling, the transaction may be thought of as either a purchase of pounds sterling or a sale of dollars. This shows that the demand for pounds sterling is intimately related to the supply of dollars. Similarly, the demand for dollars is intimately related to the supply of pounds sterling. These relationships are clarified in the present section.

Derivation of the Supply-of-Dollars Schedule from the Demand-for-Pounds Schedule

Consider fig. 3.2. All axes are taken to be positive. Along the horizontal axis are measured dollars (absolute quantities) moving from the origin to the right, while moving from the origin to the left are measured dollars per pound sterling, that is, R. Along the vertical axis, moving south from the origin, are measured pounds

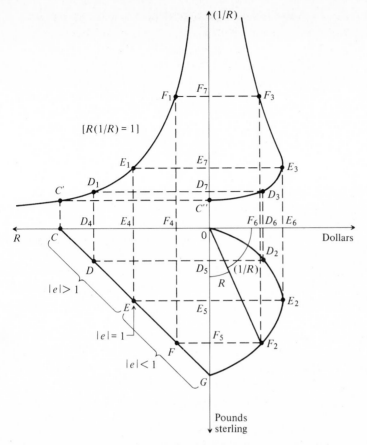

Figure 3.2 The relationship between the demand for pounds sterling and the supply of dollars. Given the demand-for-pounds schedule in the third quadrant, the supply-of-dollars schedule is derived in the first quadrant. In fact, points C, D, E, and F on the demand-for-pounds schedule correspond to points C'', D_3, E_3, and F_3 on the supply-of-dollars schedule.

sterling (absolute amounts), while moving north from the origin are measured pounds sterling per dollar, that is, $1/R$. In the third quadrant a hypothetical demand curve for pounds sterling is drawn ($CDEFG$). The object is to show how the supply curve for dollars, shown in the first quadrant, can actually be derived from the demand curve for pounds sterling given in the third quadrant. (Recall that the price of dollars in terms of pounds sterling is merely the reciprocal of R. The latter is the dollar price of sterling.)

Consider a point on the demand curve for pounds sterling, such as D. At D we are given two things: the total amount of sterling demanded ($0D_5$) and the dollar price of sterling ($0D_4$). Given these data, we can determine (*a*) the corresponding price of dollars in terms of pounds sterling, that is, $1/0D_4$, and (*b*) the amount of dollars supplied, that is, $0D_4 \times 0D_5$, given graphically by the area of the rectangle

$0D_4 DD_5$. These two elements are sufficient to determine a point on the supply curve for dollars, as indeed is shown by point D_3 in the first quadrant.

To facilitate the graphical derivation of the supply curve of dollars, two additional curves have been drawn in the second and fourth quadrants, namely, a *rectangular hyperbola* and an *offer curve*, respectively. The rectangular hyperbola is given by the equation $R(1/R) = 1$. Its purpose is to translate graphically each value of R (i.e., the dollar price of sterling) into $1/R$ (i.e., the price of dollars in terms of sterling). Thus, when $R = 0D_4$, $1/R = D_4 D_1 = 0D_7$. Similarly, the purpose of the offer curve (the term is borrowed from the pure theory of trade†) is to give directly the amount of dollars supplied in exchange for any amount of pounds sterling demanded. For instance, at $R = 0D_4$ the amount of $0D_5$ pounds sterling is demanded and, as we have seen, the corresponding amount of dollars supplied is given by the area of the rectangle $0D_4 DD_5$. The latter is translated into the horizontal distance $D_5 D_2$ ($= 0D_6$) in the fourth quadrant.

What are the properties of the offer curve? It starts at the origin because, when the amount of pounds sterling demanded is zero, the corresponding amount of dollars supplied is also zero. As we travel from C to D to E to F to G along the demand curve for sterling (third quadrant), we correspondingly travel from the origin to D_2 to E_2 to F_2 to G along the offer curve (fourth quadrant). At G both curves meet. From the point of view of the demand curve, the distance $0G$ shows the maximum amount of sterling demanded at $R = 0$. From the point of view of the offer curve, zero dollars are offered in exchange for $0G$ pounds sterling. Note that, as we move from the origin to point G along the offer curve, the latter at first rises until it reaches a maximum at point E_2 and then falls until it reaches G. The behavior of the offer curve depends on the elasticity of demand of the corresponding demand curve. Thus, as R falls from the maximum value $0C$ to zero, the amount of dollars supplied increases, remains the same, or decreases, as the demand elasticity is higher than, equal to, or less than unity. Accordingly, as shown by the curves drawn in fig. 3.2, the elasticity of demand is greater than unity in the region CE; it is exactly equal to unity at point E; and it is less than unity in the region EG.

What we call here "offer curve" is similar to the synonymous curve used in the pure theory of trade. Thus every point on the offer curve in the fourth quadrant of fig. 3.2 shows the amount of dollars offered in exchange for the amount of pounds sterling demanded. For instance, at F_2, $0F_5$ pounds sterling are demanded and $F_5 F_2$ ($= 0F_6$) dollars are offered in exchange. Note also that the dollar price of pounds sterling (R) is given by the ratio of the number of dollars offered to the number of pounds sterling demanded. Graphically, R is given by the slope with respect to the pounds axis of the vector drawn from the origin to the chosen point on the offer curve. Thus, at F_2, the dollar price of sterling is given by the slope of the vector $0F_2$ with respect to the vertical axis. If the slope is taken

---

† On offer curves and related matters see M. Chacholiades (1973), *The Pure Theory of International Trade*, Aldine Publishing Company, Chicago, Ill.

with respect to the horizontal axis, the result is $1/R$, that is, the price of dollars in terms of pounds sterling. The analogy between the present offer curve and the offer curve of the pure theory of trade is exploited further in chap. 5. For the moment, note that the only essential difference between them is that our offer curve deals with *currencies* while the offer curve of the pure theory deals with *commodities*. Technically these curves and their properties are identical, and this is the reason why we presently adopted the same name.

Return now to the derivation of the supply curve for dollars (fig. 3.2). Given a point on the demand curve for pounds sterling (third quadrant), such as D, a corresponding point on the supply curve for dollars (first quadrant) can be determined, such as D_3, by merely completing the rectangle $DD_2D_3D_1$ as shown. The same process can be repeated for all points on the demand curve for pounds sterling, as illustrated by the additional points E and F which give rise to points E_3 and F_3, respectively, on the supply curve for dollars. When a sufficient number of points are so determined in the first quadrant, the supply curve for dollars is traced out by connecting all these points by a continuous line.

Three Important Features of the Supply-of-Dollars Schedule

The supply curve for dollars, as shown in fig. 3.2, has three important features. First, it usually has a strictly positive intercept with the vertical axis (see point C''). This follows from the sensible assumption that the demand curve for pounds sterling has a finite intercept (C) with the R axis. (Should the demand curve for pounds sterling become asymptotic to the R axis, the supply curve for dollars would start at the origin.) Second, the supply curve for dollars is backward bending. This is related to the elasticity of the demand curve for pounds sterling. The region CE, where the demand curve for pounds is elastic, corresponds to the upward-sloping region $C''E_3$ of the supply curve for dollars; and the region EG, where the demand curve is inelastic, corresponds to the backward-bending region of the supply curve. Point E on the demand curve, at which the demand elasticity is unity, corresponds to point E_3 on the supply curve. At E_3, the supply curve is vertical. (Note that the corresponding points E and E_3 give the maximum amount of dollars supplied at any rate of exchange.) Third, the supply curve for dollars approaches the vertical axis asymptotically as $(1/R) \to \infty$. This follows from the fact that $(1/R) \to \infty$ as $R \to 0$. But when R is not exactly zero, the buyers of sterling must pay a positive amount of dollars for the finite amount of pounds they buy. This amount of dollars, however small, is strictly positive, although it tends to zero as $R \to 0$.

None of the above three features of the supply-of-dollars schedule are, of course, necessary properties, even though they follow from reasonable restrictions on the demand-for-pounds schedule. Counterexamples are not hard to find. For instance, should the demand-for-pounds schedule become vertical (as in the case where the demand for pounds arises solely from the need to make a reparations payment specified in pounds), the supply-of-dollars schedule would be given by a rectangular hyperbola with no finite intercept with the R axis. Similarly, the second and third properties are also violated if in the preceding example the reparations payment is specified in dollars. Here the supply-of-dollars schedule becomes vertical (i.e., perfectly inelastic).

Derivation of the Demand-for-Pounds Schedule from the Supply-of-Dollars Schedule

Thus far our discussion has concentrated on the derivation of the supply curve for dollars when the demand curve for pounds sterling is given. Can this procedure be reversed? That is, is it also possible to start with the supply curve for dollars and derive the demand curve for pounds sterling? Such a procedure would present no new difficulties if the rectangular hyperbola in the second quadrant and the offer curve in the fourth quadrant (fig. 3.2) could be determined after the supply curve for dollars is given, for then the demand curve for pounds sterling in the third quadrant could be determined by completing the various rectangles as before. Of course, the rectangular hyperbola (second quadrant) is given by the equation $R(1/R) = 1$, whether the demand curve for pounds or the supply curve for dollars is given initially.

The offer curve (fourth quadrant) is determined as follows. Given any point on the supply curve for dollars, such as D_3, determine the corresponding amount of pounds sterling demanded by forming the product $0D_7 \times 0D_6$, where $0D_7$ is the value of $1/R$ and $0D_6$ is the amount of dollars supplied at point D_3. Thus, the corresponding amount of pounds sterling demanded is given graphically by the rectangle $0D_6 D_3 D_7$ (first quadrant). But knowing the dollars supplied and the sterling demanded, we determine point D_2 on the offer curve. Repeating the same experiment for all points on the supply curve for dollars, we trace out the offer curve in the fourth quadrant.

The preceding discussion has been conducted exclusively in terms of the demand for pounds sterling and the supply of dollars. But surely the same technical relationships exist between the demand for dollars and the supply of pounds sterling. Besides the difference in names, there is no other essential difference. Accordingly, no further discussion is needed.

3.3 MATHEMATICAL ANALYSIS

With a little effort, the discussion of the preceding section can be made rigorous. The advantages of this step are worth the trouble because of new insights to be gained.

Assume that the demand for pounds sterling is given by the equation

$$D_£ = f(R) \tag{3.1}$$

The symbol $D_£$ stands for the amount of pounds demanded and is a function of the dollar price of sterling, that is, R. It is assumed that the derivative $(dD_£)/(dR) \equiv f' < 0$. Determine (a) the functional relationship, say $g(1/R)$, show-
mount of dollars supplied ($S_\$$) as a function of $(1/R)$; and (b) the relation-

ship between the elasticity of demand for pounds sterling and the elasticity of supply of dollars.

The supply-of-dollars function, $g(1/R)$, is easily derived from the demand-for-pounds function given by eq. (3.1). Thus, by definition,

$$S_\$ \equiv g\left(\frac{1}{R}\right) \equiv Rf(R) \tag{3.2}$$

Since we are interested in expressing $S_\$$ as a function of $1/R$, not R, define

$$R^* \equiv \frac{1}{R} \tag{3.3a}$$

Thus

$$R \equiv \frac{1}{R^*} \tag{3.3b}$$

Substitute the value of R, as given by eq. (3.3b), into eq. (3.2), and obtain

$$S_\$ \equiv g(R^*) = \left(\frac{1}{R^*}\right)f\left(\frac{1}{R^*}\right) \tag{3.4}$$

Equation (3.4) gives the amount of dollars supplied ($S_\$$) as a function of the price of dollars in terms of pounds sterling (R^*). It is the supply function we were looking for.

By definition, the elasticity of the demand for pounds sterling ($e_d^\pounds$) is given by

$$e_d^\pounds \equiv f'(R)\frac{R}{f(R)} \quad \left(\frac{p}{6}\right) \tag{3.5}$$

Similarly, the elasticity of the supply of dollars ($e_s^\$$) is given by

$$e_s^\$ \equiv g'(R^*)\frac{R^*}{g(R^*)} \tag{3.6}$$

What is the relationship between these two elasticities?

Differentiating eq. (3.4) with respect to R^*, we obtain

$$g'(R^*) = \left(\frac{-1}{R^{*2}}\right)f\left(\frac{1}{R^*}\right) - \left(\frac{1}{R^{*3}}\right)f'\left(\frac{1}{R^*}\right)$$

$$= -\left(\frac{1}{R^{*2}}\right)\left[f\left(\frac{1}{R^*}\right) + \left(\frac{1}{R^*}\right)f'\left(\frac{1}{R^*}\right)\right]$$

Substituting this result into eq. (3.6), and making use of the definitions given by eqs. (3.2), (3.3a), and (3.5), we obtain

$$e_s^\$ \equiv -Rf(R)\frac{1 + R[f'(R)/f(R)]}{g(R^*)} = -1 - e_d^\pounds$$

or

$$e_s^\$ + e_d^\pounds = -1 \tag{3.7}$$

That is, the sum of the demand elasticity for pounds sterling plus the supply elasticity for dollars is always equal to -1. This is an important relationship.

Based on eq. (3.7) the following propositions can be established:

1. When the demand curve for pounds sterling is elastic ($e_d^£ < -1$), the supply curve for dollars is upward sloping ($e_s^$ > 0$).
2. When the demand curve for pounds sterling is inelastic ($-1 < e_d^£ \leq 0$), the supply curve for dollars is backward bending ($e_s^$ < 0$).
3. When the demand curve for pounds sterling is unit-elastic ($e_d^£ = -1$), the supply curve for dollars is vertical ($e_s^$ = 0$).
4. Assume that $e_d^£ < -1$. Then the higher $e_d^£$ is in *absolute* terms, the higher $e_s^$$ is (i.e., the flatter the supply curve for dollars).
5. Assume $-1 < e_d^£ \leq 0$. The higher $e_d^£$ is in absolute terms, the smaller $e_s^$$ is in absolute terms (i.e., the steeper the backward-bending supply curve for dollars).

The above relationships between the demand for pounds sterling and the corresponding supply of dollars and their respective elasticities are general. In particular, by interchanging the roles of the two currencies in the preceding discussion, we obtain automatically the relationships between the demand for dollars and the corresponding supply of pounds sterling and their respective elasticities.

FOUR

COMMODITY TRADE AND THE FOREIGN EXCHANGE MARKET: THE PARTIAL EQUILIBRIUM MODEL

The preceding chapter dealt with some formal relationships between the demand curve for a currency, say the pound sterling, and the corresponding supply curve of another, say the dollar. During that discussion the assumption was made that these supply and demand curves for currencies were given. The time has now come to see what lies behind these curves.

As we saw in chaps. 1 and 2, there are several categories of transactions which give rise to supply and demand for foreign exchange and domestic currency. For pedagogical reasons, these categories must be considered one by one. This chapter singles out commodity trade for special scrutiny. The present discussion is developed within the context of a partial equilibrium model, the main architects of which are C. F. Bickerdike (1920), Joan Robinson (1937), and Fritz Machlup (1939, 1940), even though others have generously contributed to its development.†
The limitations of this model are noted later. Parts two and three of the book extend the present analysis to a general model which copes with all of the weaknesses of the partial equilibrium approach. The latter may be thought of as a stepping-stone toward that more general analysis.

It is assumed as before that there are two countries, A (home country) and B (foreign country), with national currencies the dollar and the pound sterling, respectively. Further, A's commodity exports are assumed to consist of a single

---

† Samuelson (1971) considers the rigorous foundations of the partial equilibrium model.

homogeneous commodity called for convenience A-exportables. Similarly, B's commodity exports are also assumed to consist of a single homogeneous commodity called B-exportables. A-exportables and B-exportables are by assumption *different* commodities. Both countries are assumed to produce both of these commodities, but only A exports A-exportables, and only B exports B-exportables. It is also assumed that commodity exports are the only source of supply of foreign exchange for either country. Similarly, commodity imports are the only purpose of demand for foreign exchange. Thus, exports and imports of services, capital movements (short-term and long-term, private and official), unilateral transfers, and gold exports and imports are all disregarded. The object is to derive the demand and supply curves for pounds sterling, and also the supply and demand curves for dollars. In the process, several important topics are covered, such as the effects of changes in the rate of exchange on the flows of exports and imports, the domestic and foreign prices of A-exportables and B-exportables, and the terms of trade.

4.1 SUPPLY AND DEMAND FOR COMMODITY EXPORTS AND IMPORTS

The demand for pounds sterling and the supply of dollars depend on the flow of commodities from country B to country A. Similarly, the supply of pounds sterling and the demand for dollars depend on the flow of commodities from A to B. Hence, the derivation of the supply and demand curves for pounds and dollars requires the determination of the commodity flows between the two countries. How are these commodity flows determined?

Elementary economic theory teaches us that these commodity flows are determined by supply and demand. In particular, the commodity flow from B to A depends on A's demand for imports and B's supply of exports of B-exportables; and the commodity flow from A to B depends on A's supply of exports and B's demand for imports of A-exportables. Accordingly, the first step in our analysis is the derivation of the supply and demand curves for exports and imports for both countries.

A's Demand for Imports

A's demand for imports is the excess of A's total demand for consumption over A's domestic supply of B-exportables. Similarly, A's supply of exports is the excess of A's total domestic supply (or production) over A's domestic consumption of A-exportables. B's demand for imports and supply of exports are similarly defined, the only difference being that the roles of A-exportables and B-exportables are reversed.

The derivation of A's demand for imports is illustrated in fig. 4.1. Along the horizontal axes are measured quantities of B-exportables and along the vertical, dollar prices. Panel (*a*) shows A's *total* demand and supply for B-exportables. These supply and demand curves form the raw material, so to speak, for the

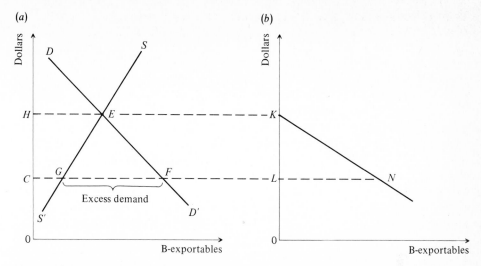

Figure 4.1 The derivation of A's demand for imports. A's demand for imports, as shown in (*b*), is given by the horizontal differences between A's total supply and demand curves for B-exportables below *E*, as shown in (*a*).

partial equilibrium approach followed presently. The demand curve (*DD'*) shows the alternative total amounts of B-exportables demanded for consumption in A at various prices. As usual, it is drawn sloping downwards for the reason that as the price falls the total quantity demanded increases. Note also that this demand curve is drawn on the assumption that tastes, incomes, and prices of other commodities remain constant. When any of these parameters change, the total demand curve shifts either to the right or the left, depending on the particular circumstances which cause the shift. On the other hand, A's supply curve for B-exportables (*SS'*) shows the alternative amounts of B-exportables supplied by A's producers at various prices. In panel (*a*) this supply curve is drawn sloping upwards, implying that higher production of B-exportables in A causes (opportunity) costs to rise. This is no doubt the normal case. It should be noted, however, that a supply curve may behave in a number of ways. It may be horizontal, forward falling, or even backward bending, in addition to being upward sloping. Finally, note that the supply curve is drawn on the assumption that technology and factor prices (or rather rentals) remain constant. When either of these parameters changes, the supply curve shifts.

If country A had no access to foreign trade, equilibrium in the market for B-exportables (in A) would occur at *E*, where A's excess demand is zero, with 0*H* being the equilibrium price (in dollars). But now that international trade is possible, equilibrium need not occur at *E*. Any deficiency in domestic supply to satisfy domestic demand can be made good through imports from abroad. Thus for prices lower than 0*H*, A's total supply falls short of A's total demand. This excess demand is what is called the *demand for imports*. For instance, when the price of B-exportables falls to $0C$, the total quantity demanded by A's consumers is given by CF while the quantity supplied by A's producers is given by CG. The difference between these two quantities, that is, GF, is the quantity of B-exportables which must be imported from B. In short, GF is A's demand for imports when the price is $0C$. This information is registered also in panel (b). Note that $0C = 0L$ and $GF = LN$. All points on A's demand for imports, KN, in panel (b) have been derived in this fashion. In general, then, A's demand for imports, as shown in panel (b), is given by the horizontal differences between the total supply and demand curves for B-exportables, as shown in panel (a), for all prices below the equilibrium price $0H$.

Therefore, the demand curve for imports is part of what is ordinarily called the *excess* demand curve. Because it is derived from the total demand *and* supply curves, it depends on all those parameters which are assumed constant when the latter curves are drawn. Accordingly, like A's total demand curve for B-exportables, A's demand curve for imports depends on tastes, incomes, and other prices. But unlike A's total demand curve for B-exportables, A's demand for imports depends also on technology and factor prices—the parameters which lie behind A's supply curve for B-exportables.

Is the elasticity of A's demand for imports equal to the elasticity of A's total demand for B-exportables? The answer is definitely "No." First note that the elasticity coefficient varies along a demand curve. Hence, when the elasticities of two demand curves are to be compared, the points at which the elasticities are to be evaluated must be specified. In the present case, it is understood that the comparison is to be made for any pair of points which correspond to the same price.

In general, the elasticity of a demand (or supply) curve is given by the ratio $(\Delta Q/Q)/(\Delta P/P)$. The symbols Q and P are, respectively, the quantity demanded and price at the point with reference to which the elasticity is estimated; ΔQ is the change in Q prompted by the change in $P(\Delta P)$. In other words, the elasticity is given by the percentage change in the quantity demanded divided by the percentage change in price. Since P and ΔP are by assumption equal in the present case, any difference between the two elasticities must be attributed to the factor $\Delta Q/Q$, that is, the percentage change in the quantity demanded.

There are two reasons why the elasticity of demand for imports is higher than the elasticity of total demand for B-exportables, assuming only that A's domestic supply curve of B-exportables is upward sloping. First, the quantity imported is in general smaller than the quantity consumed domestically, the difference being the amount of A's domestic production of B-exportables. Thus, the quantity Q in the ratio $\Delta Q/Q$ is smaller for the elasticity of demand for imports than the elasticity for total demand. Second, as the price falls, the quantity imported increases faster than the quantity of total domestic consumption. Thus, the change ΔQ is bigger for the demand for imports than for the total demand curve for any specified change in price. The reason, of course, is that imports are given by the difference between total domestic consumption and total domestic production. Thus, as the price falls, imports increase by the following two amounts: (a) the amount by which total domestic consumption increases, *plus* (b) the amount by which domestic production decreases. The decrease in domestic production is prompted by the fact that, as the price falls, domestic producers find it no longer profitable to maintain their production at the original levels. Clearly, the change ΔQ in the ratio $\Delta Q/Q$ is larger for the elasticity of demand for imports (which takes into account both changes) than for the elasticity of total demand (which takes into account the first factor only). For both of these reasons, the elasticity of demand for imports is higher than the elasticity of total demand. The two coincide when domestic production is nil.

A's Supply of Exports

Turn now to A's supply of exports of A-exportables, which is derived essentially in the same way as A's demand for imports. This is illustrated in fig. 4.2. The quantities of A-exportables are measured horizontally, and dollar prices, vertically. Again panel (a) shows A's total supply (SS') and demand (DD') curves for A-exportables. At point E, A's excess demand for A-exportables is zero. But at higher prices than 0H, the quantity which A's producers are willing to supply is higher than the quantity which A's consumers are willing to buy. For instance, when the price rises to 0C, the quantity supplied *increases* to CG while the quantity demanded *falls* to CF. Thus, an excess supply emerges, given by the horizontal distance FG. The quantity FG is what A is willing to export to B when the price is 0C. This quantity (FG) is also registered in panel (b). Note that FG = LN and 0C = 0L. A similar procedure is followed to determine the alternative amounts of A-exportables which A is willing to export to B for all prices higher than 0C. These

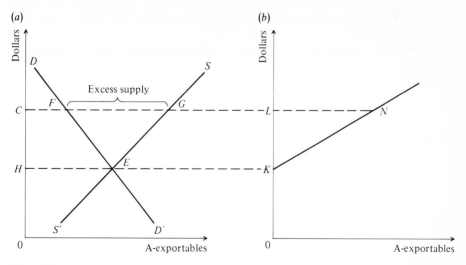

Figure 4.2 The derivation of A's supply of exports. A's supply of exports, as shown in (b), is given by the horizontal differences between A's total supply and demand curves for A-exportables above E, as shown in (a).

amounts are given graphically by the horizontal distances between the total supply and demand curves in panel (*a*) above point *E*. These same horizontal distances are registered also in panel (*b*). The upward-sloping curve (*KN*) in panel (*b*) is A's supply curve for exports.

Note that A's supply of exports depends not only on those factors which lie behind A's total supply curve in panel (*a*) but it also depends on all factors which lie behind A's total demand curve in panel (*a*). Thus, tastes, incomes, and prices of other commodities are all important to A's supply of exports, in addition to technology and factor prices.

The elasticity of A's supply of exports is also higher than the elasticity of A's total supply of A-exportables, for two reasons which are again related to the ratio $\Delta Q/Q$ in the definition of elasticity. First, the quantity Q is higher for the elasticity of total supply than for the elasticity of supply of exports, the difference being the amount of A-exportables consumed domestically by A. Second, as the price of A-exportables increases, the supply of exports increases faster than A's total supply of A-exportables. The reason is that exports, being the difference between domestic production and domestic consumption, increase both by the amount by which domestic production increases *and* the amount by which domestic consumption decreases, as the price of A-exportables increases. For both of these reasons, the percentage increase in exports is always higher than the percentage increase in domestic production. This leads to the conclusion that the elasticity of supply of exports is higher than the elasticity of total domestic supply.

B's Demand for Imports and Supply of Exports

Having derived the demand for imports and supply of exports for country A in a rather exhaustive fashion, it is unnecessary to repeat the same analysis for country B. The above analysis can be used, word for word, for country B as well by merely interchanging the roles of the two countries.

4.2 THE FLOW OF GOODS BETWEEN COUNTRIES

Assume that A's demand for imports and B's supply of exports of B-exportables are given. How can the equilibrium flow of B-exportables from B to A be determined? Similarly, given A's supply of exports and B's demand for imports of A-exportables, how can the equilibrium flow of A-exportables from A to B be determined? These are important questions, and they must be answered before the supply and demand curves for pounds sterling and dollars can be derived.

If A and B were two regions of a single country using the same currency, the volume, price and the value of the commodity flows between them could be determined by superimposing one region's demand curve for imports on the other region's supply of exports. Equilibrium would be determined at the intersection between the two curves as usual. This procedure would give us the equilibrium quantities traded, the equilibrium prices, and, by a mere multiplication of quantities and prices, the values of goods traded. But when A and B are different countries using different national currencies, the problem becomes slightly more difficult, because each country's curves (demand for imports or supply of exports) give quantities (demanded or supplied) as functions of prices expressed in *that* country's currency. Thus, the price axes of A's curves are not commensurate with the corresponding price axes of B's curves, and the approach suggested for two regions is not directly applicable to the present case.

To make each corresponding set of price axes commensurate, it is imperative that all prices be expressed in terms of the same currency; this requires knowledge of the rate of exchange. For instance, if 2 dollars exchange for 1 pound sterling, all dollar prices along A's demand-for-imports and supply-of-exports curves could be converted into prices in pounds sterling by a mere division by 2. This procedure would make the price axes of A's curves (which were initially given in terms of dollar prices) commensurate with the corresponding price axes of B's curves (which are also given in terms of pounds sterling). Alternatively, by multiplying all initial prices in pounds sterling by 2, the initial price axes of B's demand for imports and supply of exports can be converted into axes showing dollar prices. Thus, they can be made commensurate with A's initial price axes.

The above procedure requires knowledge of the rate of exchange. But the rate of exchange is another unknown price which must be determined along with the prices of A-exportables and B-exportables. This is true whether a fixed- or a flexible-exchange-rate system is adopted. As explained later in chaps. 7 and 8, even under a regime of fixed-exchange rates, the rate of exchange is not rigidly fixed. On the contrary, it can vary within certain limits. Does this mean that we have reached an impasse in our development? Fortunately, there is no reason for alarm. As shown later in chaps. 5 to 8, commodity prices and the rate of exchange are determined simultaneously. But before reaching that stage of analysis, there is some preliminary work to be done. Accordingly, it is assumed presently that the rate of exchange is given.

When the rate of exchange happens to be equal to unity, our problem does not differ from the case referred to earlier where A and B are two regions of a single country. The only difference is that presently two currencies (different in appearance but identical in value) circulate. But this presents no analytical difficulty as long as 1 dollar exchanges freely for 1 pound sterling. The solution is illustrated in figs. 4.3 and 4.4. In particular, in fig. 4.3 all prices are given in pounds sterling, while in fig. 4.4 all prices are given in dollars. In both cases, the solid demand-for-imports (DD') and supply-of-exports (SS') curves are drawn precisely as they are given initially in terms of each country's national currency. To emphasize the fact that this is legitimate only when $R = 1$, the latter equation was printed next to the DD' curves of figs. 4.3a and 4.4b and also next to the SS' curves of figs. 4.3b and 4.4a. For simplicity, all curves in all panels are straight lines, and equilibrium always occurs at E_0, with equilibrium prices and quantities denoted by P_0 and Q_0, respectively.

The area $0Q_0 E_0 P_0$ in figs. 4.3a and 4.4a shows the value of B-exportables exported from B to A in terms of pounds sterling and dollars, respectively. In particular, the area $0Q_0 E_0 P_0$ in fig. 4.3a shows the amount of pounds sterling

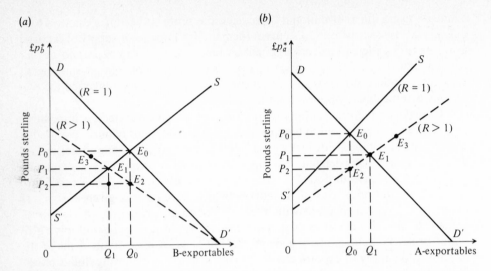

Figure 4.3 The equilibrium flows of goods between countries A and B when all prices are expressed in pounds sterling. (*a*) For each value of the rate of exchange, a different schedule is drawn for A's demand for imports. B's supply of exports is independent of the rate of exchange, i.e., unique. (*b*) For each value of the rate of exchange, a different schedule is drawn for A's supply of exports. B's demand for imports is independent of the rate of exchange, i.e., unique.

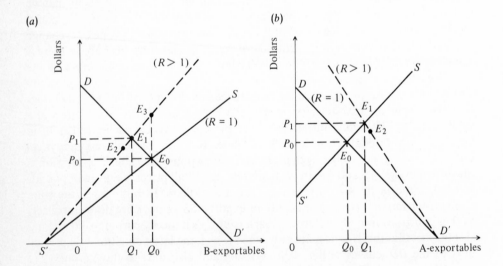

Figure 4.4 The equilibrium flows of goods between countries A and B when all prices are expressed in dollars. (*a*) For each value of the rate of exchange, a different schedule is drawn for B's supply of exports. A's demand for imports is independent of the rate of exchange, i.e., unique. (*b*) For each value of the rate of exchange, a different schedule is drawn for B's demand for imports. A's supply of exports is independent of the rate of exchange, i.e., unique. (*Note:* The solid curves in fig. 4-3*a* are identical to the synonymous curves in fig. 4-4*a*, and similarly for figs. 4-3*b* and 4-4*b*.)

demanded when $R = 1$; the same area in fig. 4.4a shows the amount of dollars supplied when $R = 1$. Similarly, the area $0 Q_0 E_0 P_0$ in figs. 4.3b and 4.4b shows the value of A-exportables exported from A to B in terms of pounds sterling and dollars, respectively. In particular, in fig. 4.3b it shows the amount of pounds sterling supplied at $R = 1$ and in fig. 4.4b, the amount of dollars demanded at $R = 1$.

The reader may feel at this stage that he was cheated in the preceding analysis because of the special assumption that the rate of exchange is unity. But actually this is not so. What was done for $R = 1$ can be done for any other value of R. This becomes clear in the following section, which studies some of the effects of changes in the rate of exchange.

4.3 EFFECTS OF A CHANGE IN THE RATE OF EXCHANGE

What happens when the rate of exchange is different from unity? As emphasized earlier, A's demand for imports and supply of exports are initially given in dollars—not pounds sterling. Similarly, B's demand for imports and supply of exports are initially given in pounds sterling—not in dollars. Accordingly, as the rate of exchange changes to a different value from unity, a shift occurs in A's demand-for-imports and supply-of-exports curves as given by DD' and SS' in fig. 4.3a and b, respectively. In addition, a shift also occurs in B's demand-for-imports and supply-of-exports curves as given by DD' and SS' in fig. 4.4b and a, respectively. Precisely how do all these curves shift? What are the effects of these shifts on the equilibrium prices and quantities traded, and the quantities of dollars and pounds sterling demanded or supplied?

The Effects of Exchange-Rate Adjustments When Prices Are Expressed in Pounds Sterling

Consider first fig. 4.3, where prices are expressed in terms of pounds sterling. B's supply curve for exports (SS' in panel a) and B's demand curve for imports (DD' in panel b) are independent of the rate of exchange. Accordingly, any changes in the latter do not affect them at all. But the same is not true for A's curves (DD' in panel a and SS' in panel b). These curves depend crucially on the rate of exchange, and any change in the latter causes both of these curves to shift. In particular, when the pound sterling becomes more expensive relative to the dollar (i.e., when R increases) both of A's curves in fig. 4.3 shift downward as shown by the broken curves. Why is this so?

Consider A's imports first. According to A's demand curve for imports, given initially in terms of prices expressed in dollars, A's importers are willing to pay alternative prices in dollars for alternative quantities of imports of B-exportables. Because the DD' curve in fig. 4.3a was drawn on the assumption that $R = 1$, the vertical distances between this curve and the horizontal axis show the dollar prices which A's importers are willing to pay for alternative amounts of B-exportables imported from B. In particular, when they import Q_0 units of B-exportables, A's importers are willing to pay $\$P_0$ per unit imported. When $R = 1$, A's importers are in effect willing to pay $£P_0$. But when R increases, the number of pounds sterling to be secured for $\$P_0$ is less than $£P_0$, say $£P_2$, as shown in fig. 4.3a. Thus, as R increases, point E_0 on A's initial demand for imports shifts vertically downward to, say, point E_2. A similar argument holds for all other points on A's initial demand curve for imports. Thus, the whole curve (DD') shifts downwards.

Similarly, A's supply curve for exports (SS') in fig. 4.3b is given initially in terms of prices expressed in dollars. Because the SS' curve in fig. 4.3b was drawn on the assumption that $R = 1$, the vertical distances between this curve and the horizontal axis show the alternative supply prices in *dollars* which A's exporters are willing to accept for alternative amounts of A-exportables exported to B. For instance, A's exporters are willing to export Q_0 units of A-exportables to B at a price $\$P_0$. When $R = 1$, their supply price of $\$P_0$ effectively becomes $£P_0$. But when $R > 1$, their supply price of $\$P_0$ effectively becomes less than $£P_0$, say $£P_2$, as illustrated in fig. 4.3b. This is so because, as the pound sterling becomes more expensive in terms of the dollar, A's exporters are willing to accept fewer pounds sterling because even with the smaller amount of sterling they can still secure the same amount of dollars as before. The latter is indeed their primary consideration. Accordingly, point E_0 on A's initial supply curve for exports (SS') in fig. 4.3b shifts downward to point E_2. The same argument holds for all other points on SS'. Consequently, as R increases, A's supply curve of exports shifts downward.

The downward shifts of A's curves in fig. 4.3 are not parallel shifts. That would have been the case if all dollar prices were reduced by the same *absolute* amount in order to determine the corresponding prices in pounds sterling. But as we have seen, the correct procedure to determine the latter is to *divide* the initial dollar prices by R. Thus, the downward shift of both curves is proportional. In particular, with straight-line demand and supply curves, the downward shift of each curve is nothing but a downward rotation of that curve, with the intercept of the curve with the horizontal axis being the pivotal point.

It is understood that if R falls below unity A's curves in fig. 4.3 rotate upwards.

What is the effect of a devaluation of the dollar, i.e., a rise in R, on A's flows of exports and imports, the prices in sterling of A-exportables and B-exportables, and finally A's expenditure on imports expressed in pounds sterling (i.e., the quantity of pounds sterling demanded) and A's export revenue expressed in pounds sterling (i.e., the quantity of pounds sterling supplied)?

Consider fig. 4.3a first. As R increases, equilibrium shifts from E_0 to E_1. Thus, the price of B-exportables *falls* from $£P_0$ to $£P_1$, and the quantity of B-exportables exported from B to A *falls* from Q_0 to Q_1. For *both* of these reasons, A's expenditure (in pounds sterling) on imports, and therefore the quantity of pounds sterling demanded, necessarily falls. In particular, it falls from the area of the rectangle $0Q_0 E_0 P_0$ to the area $0Q_1 E_1 P_1$. This is actually the reason why the demand curve for pounds sterling is downward sloping.

As shown presently, for any arbitrary rise in R, the quantity of pounds sterling demanded falls. This outcome is embedded, of course, in the assumptions underlying A's demand for imports and B's supply of exports. For instance, if A's demand curve for imports were vertical and passed through point E_0, a change in R would not affect it at all, equilibrium would continue at E_0, and the quantity of pounds sterling demanded would continue to be given by the area $0Q_0 E_0 P_0$. Hence, in this special case, the demand curve for pounds sterling would be vertical also.

Consider also the case where B's supply of exports is backward bending in the neighborhood of the initial equilibrium at E_0, presumably because B's total supply curve for B-exportables is backward bending. Assuming that B's supply curve of exports is steeper than A's demand for imports (for stability), an increase in R would cause the price of B-exportables in terms of pounds sterling to fall. But the quantity exported to A would increase. As a result, the possibility cannot be ruled out that an increase may occur in the quantity of pounds sterling demanded.

These are special cases, of course, and are dismissed in the subsequent discussion. Nevertheless, they make it clear that some exceptions to our general conclusions may exist. In addition, they clear up a misunderstanding which may exist in the mind of the reader, namely, that the demand curve for pounds must slope downwards because A's demand for imports slopes downwards. As we have just seen, this need not always be the case.

Turn now to fig. 4.3b. As R increases, equilibrium moves from E_0 to E_1. Thus, the price of A-exportables *falls* from £P_0 to £P_1, but the quantity of A-exportables exported from A to B *increases* from Q_0 to Q_1. What happens to A's export revenue in pounds sterling (i.e., the quantity of pounds sterling supplied)? It changes from the area $0Q_0 E_0 P_0$ to the area $0Q_1 E_1 P_1$. The latter area is equal to, larger than, or smaller than the former according to whether B's demand for imports is unit-elastic, elastic, or inelastic, respectively. Thus, the outcome depends on B's elasticity of demand for imports. When the latter is unity, the supply curve of pounds sterling is vertical; when it is greater than unity (in absolute terms), it is upward sloping; and when it is less than unity (in absolute terms), it is backward bending. (The special cases referred to in the preceding paragraph are presently ignored.)

The Effects of Exchange-Rate Adjustments When Prices Are Expressed in Dollars

Turn now to fig. 4.4, where all prices are expressed in dollars. Again we wish to study the effects of an increase in R (i.e., devaluation of the dollar) on the equilibrium prices and quantities traded, as well as the quantities of dollars demanded and supplied. Now A's supply of exports (SS' in panel b) and A's demand for imports (DD' in panel a) are independent of R. Therefore, they do not shift when R changes. But B's supply of exports (SS' in panel a) and B's demand for imports (DD' in panel b) do depend on R, and they do shift when R changes. In particular, when R increases, both of B's curves rotate *upwards* through their respective pivotal points, i.e., their respective intercepts with the horizontal axes, with the degree of rotation depending on the *percentage* increase in R. The reason for this upward rotation is simple: the dollar prices which B's traders are willing to accept after the increase in R are higher than the corresponding dollar prices which they were willing to accept before the change, with the precise percentage increase in these prices given by the exact percentage increase in R.

As B's curves in fig. 4.4 rotate upward and equilibrium moves from point E_0 to E_1, the following effects are observed. First, both the dollar price of A-exportables *and* the dollar price of B-exportables rise (from P_0 to P_1 in both panels). This is in sharp contrast with our earlier result regarding the effect of an increase in R on the prices expressed in pounds sterling of both of these commodities. It will be recalled that both prices expressed in terms of pounds sterling *fell* as R rose. Second, the amount of A-exportables exported from A to B increases from Q_0 to Q_1 (fig. 4.4b), while the amount of B-exportables exported from B to A decreases from Q_0 to Q_1 (fig. 4.4a). This is in complete agreement with the conclusion reached earlier in relation to fig. 4.3. In fact, the changes in the quantities of A-exportables and B-exportables are, and indeed must be, identical in the two cases. Third, A's export revenue in dollars increases from the area $0Q_0 E_0 P_0$ to the area $0Q_1 E_1 P_1$ (fig. 4.4b), simply because both the dollar price and the quantity exported from A to B of A-exportables increases as R increases. This is in contrast again with the result reached earlier when A's export revenue was expressed in pounds sterling, where the outcome depended on the elasticity of B's demand for imports. Fourth, A's expenditure on imports changes from the area $0Q_0 E_0 P_0$ to the area $0Q_1 E_1 P_1$, with the latter area being equal to, smaller than, or greater than the former according to whether A's demand for imports is unit-elastic, elastic, or inelastic, respectively. This result is again in contrast with our earlier conclusion that A's expenditure on imports *falls* with an increase in R.

The Terms-of-Trade Effect

What is the effect of the depreciation of the dollar (i.e., the increase in R) on A's *terms of trade?* A's terms of trade (p) are defined as follows: $p \equiv$ (price of A-exportables)/(price of B-exportables). The significance of this concept arises from the fact that p shows the number of units of B-exportables which A receives from B in exchange for 1 unit of A-exportables. Thus, an increase in p is to the advantage of A and is called an improvement in A's terms of trade. On the other hand, a decrease in p is to the advantage of B and is called a deterioration of A's terms of trade or an improvement in B's terms of trade. (B's terms of trade are given by $1/p$.) Does an increase in R (i.e., dollar depreciation relative to the pound sterling) tend to improve or deteriorate A's terms of trade?

Before Robinson (1937) wrote her classic essay, economists took it for granted that depreciation of a country's currency, say the dollar, brought about automatically a deterioration in that country's (A's) terms of trade. Essentially arguing on the basis of the resultant increase in the flow of A-exportables from A to B and the decrease in the flow of B-exportables from B to A (see figs. 4.3 and 4.4), they claimed that A's products became cheaper relative to B's products. That is, they claimed that A's terms of trade necessarily deteriorated. But this view would be correct if A's terms of trade were given by the ratio of the price of A-exportables *in pounds sterling* to the price of B-exportables *in dollars*. In the definition of the terms of trade, however, both prices must be expressed in terms of the *same* currency.

As we saw in the preceding paragraphs, the increase in R causes the prices of *both* A-exportables and B-exportables to rise in A (where they are expressed in dollars) and fall in B (where they are expressed in pounds sterling). Therefore, it is gratuitous to jump to the conclusion that A's terms of trade deteriorate as the dollar depreciates. Our analysis so far does not actually tell us what happens to A's terms of trade. This problem is analyzed in detail in sec. 4.7 below.

The Balance-of-Trade Effect

Another important question relates to the effect of the increase in R on A's balance of trade. The latter is defined as A's export revenue minus A's expenditure on imports, with both magnitudes evaluated in terms of the same currency. Does A's balance of trade improve or deteriorate as the dollar depreciates? Anything is possible. Take, for instance, A's balance of trade expressed in terms of pounds sterling (the foreign currency). As R increases, A's expenditure on imports falls but A's export revenue may go either way depending on B's elasticity of demand for imports (see fig. 4.3). A similar difficulty is observed when A's balance of trade is expressed in terms of dollars (the domestic currency). As R increases, A's export revenue increases but A's expenditure on imports may go either way depending on A's elasticity of demand for imports. In either case, the change in one of the two components is indeterminate and so is the final effect on the balance of trade. Conditions for improvement in A's balance of trade with dollar depreciation are given below in chap. 8.

The Effects on Domestic Production and Consumption

So far, our discussion of the effects of an increase in R has been carried out in terms of figs. 4.3 and 4.4 which work directly in terms of the supply and demand curves for *exports* and *imports* of A and B. Yet an increase in R has dramatic effects on the organization of *production* and *consumption* in *both* countries— effects which are not clearly visible in figs. 4.3 and 4.4. In fact, this is the main reason why the first section of this chapter was devoted to the relationship between the demand for imports and the supply of exports, on the one hand, and the total domestic production and consumption, on the other. The time invested in that analysis begins now to bear fruit. Let us discuss briefly these effects in each country separately.

Consider country A first. As we have just seen, the dollar prices of both A-exportables and B-exportables increase as R increases (i.e., as A's currency depreciates relative to B's). That is, both commodities become *more expensive in A*. What are the implications of these price rises in A? There are several, but we are presently interested in the following two: (*a*) A's *production* of A-exportables *and* B-exportables *expands*; and (*b*) A's *consumption* of A-exportables and B-exportables *contracts*. Similarly, *in country B both commodities become cheaper*, with the following effects on B's consumption and production: (*a*) B's *consumption* of A-exportables and B-exportables *expands*; and (*b*) B's *production* of A-exportables and B-exportables *contracts*.

Our model is not designed to explain how the expansion in A's production is made possible. In addition, it does not tell us precisely how this expansion in production affects A's national income, and, further, how any resultant change in the latter affects A's demand for commodities in general and A's demand for imports in particular. In addition, the partial equilibrium model does not explain what happens to B's national income as B's production of A-exportables and B-exportables contracts, and how any resultant change in B's national income may affect B's demand for commodities in general and its demand for imports in particular. These are serious defects of the partial equilibrium model. As explained earlier, the main justification for using the model at all is that, on the one hand, it clarifies certain (but not all) issues and, on the other, its main weaknesses are removed later in parts two and three of this book.

4.4 THE DEMAND AND SUPPLY CURVES FOR FOREIGN EXCHANGE

With little effort the preceding analysis can be extended to derive the demand and supply curves for pounds sterling.

The Demand-for-Pounds Schedule

Figure 4.5 shows how the demand curve for pounds sterling is derived. The solid supply and demand curves for B-exportables in panel (*a*) are taken directly from fig. 4.3*a*. A's demand curve for imports (DD') is drawn under the assumption that $R = 1$. For this value of R, the amount of pounds sterling demanded is given by the area of the rectangle $0Q_0 E_0 P_0$. This information gives us the coordinates of point M_0 in panel (*b*), where the horizontal distance $0V_0$ corresponds to the area $0Q_0 E_0 P_0$ of panel (*a*).

As noted earlier, when R increases above unity, A's demand curve for imports rotates downward through the pivotal point Q_3. Equilibrium in the market for B-exportables moves downward along B's (unique) supply curve of exports from E_0 toward S'. For instance, for $R = R_1 > 1$, equilibrium occurs at E_1, where the amount of pounds demanded falls to the area of the rectangle $0Q_1 E_1 P_1$; this information is registered in panel (*b*) by point M_1. As R continues to increase, the rectangles giving the amount of pounds sterling demanded continue to shrink—a fact which is reflected by the negative slope of the demand curve for pounds sterling in panel (*b*). When R increases to R_3, A's demand for imports shifts to the position $S'Q_3$ and the quantity of B-exportables demanded by A drops to zero, causing the amount of pounds sterling demanded to drop to zero also. Thus, at

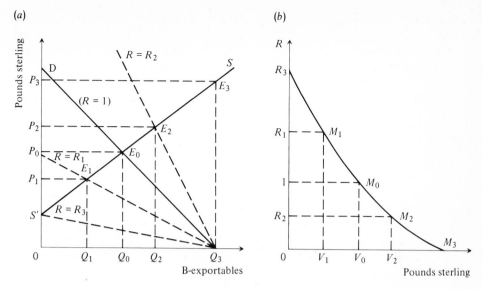

Figure 4.5 Derivation of the demand-for-pounds schedule showing (a) the market for B-exportables and (b) the demand for pounds sterling. For any value of R, say R_1, a schedule is drawn in (a) for A's demand for imports, say $E_1 Q_3$. Given this demand schedule, determine its intersection with B's supply of exports, i.e., point E_1. The area $0Q_1 E_1 P_1$ shows A's expenditure on imports. Knowing R_1 and the area $0Q_1 E_1 P_1$, determine a point on the demand schedule for pounds in (b), as illustrated by M_1. Repeat this experiment for all values of R to obtain the whole demand schedule for pounds.

$R = R_3$, the demand curve for pounds sterling in panel (b) intersects the R axis. Should R rise above the value R_3, A would become an exporter of B-exportables. This possibility is ignored.

When R decreases from unity continuously, A's demand curve for imports rotates upward through Q_3, the price and quantity of B-exportables imported by A increase, and as a result the demand for pounds sterling increases also. Again, this is reflected by the negative slope of the demand curve for pounds sterling in panel (b).

There is an upper limit to the amount of pounds sterling demanded as R tends to zero. This limit is determined by the maximum amount of B-exportables which A is willing to import from B even at zero price *expressed in dollars*. In fig. 4.5a, this maximum is given by the distance $0Q_3$. As $R \to 0$, A's demand curve for imports tends to become vertical through Q_3. Thus, the maximum amount of pounds sterling demanded when $R = 0$ is given by the area $0Q_3 E_3 P_3$ in panel (a) and by the distance $0M_3$ in panel (b).

The Supply-of-Pounds Schedule

Consider now fig. 4.6. It shows how the supply curve of pounds sterling is derived. Panel (a) reproduces the solid supply and demand curves for A-exportables given earlier in fig. 4.3b for $R = 1$. For $R = 1$, the amount of sterling supplied is given by

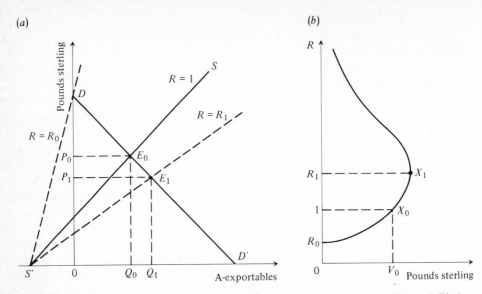

Figure 4.6 The supply-of-pounds schedule showing (*a*) the market for A-exportables and (*b*) the supply of pounds sterling. For any value of R, say R_1, a schedule is drawn in (*a*) for A's supply of exports, say $S'E_1$. Given this supply schedule, determine its intersection with B's demand schedule for imports (DD'), i.e., point E_1. The area $0Q_1 E_1 P_1$ shows A's export revenue ≡ supply of pounds at $R = R_1$. This information is sufficient to determine point X_1 on the supply schedule for pounds (*b*). Repeat the experiment for all values of R and determine the whole supply schedule for pounds.

the area $0Q_0 E_0 P_0$. This information is transferred to panel (*b*), which shows the supply curve for pounds sterling. Thus, the coordinates of point X_0 show that the amount $0V_0$ (= area $0Q_0 E_0 P_0$) is supplied at $R = 1$. As R falls below unity, A's supply curve for A-exportables rotates upward through point S' on the horizontal axis; and as R rises above unity, it rotates downward. Assume that R drops to R_0, causing A's supply curve for A-exportables to shift to $S'D$ as shown in panel (*a*). At $R = R_0$, equilibrium occurs at D (panel *a*) and A exports nothing to B. This is also shown in panel (*b*), where the supply curve for pounds sterling cuts the vertical axis at R_0, implying zero supply of pounds sterling. (If R actually falls below R_0, A would find it profitable to import A-exportables. However, this possibility is ignored.) Now allow R to rise continuously from R_0 and trace out both the various equilibria in the market for A-exportables (panel *a*) and also the supply curve for pounds sterling (panel *b*). As R increases continuously from R_0, A's supply curve for A-exportables rotates downward continuously. The equilibrium point in the market for A-exportables slides downward along B's demand curve for imports from D toward D'. At the beginning, as the equilibrium point moves from D to E_1, B's demand for imports is elastic. Thus, as R increases, the supply of pounds sterling also increases. This is reflected by the positive slope of the supply curve for pounds sterling in the region $R_0 X_1$, which corresponds to the region DE_1 of B's demand curve for imports. B's elasticity of demand for imports is unity at E_1 and less than unity in the region $E_1 D'$. As a result, the supply curve for pounds sterling becomes vertical at point X_1 (which corresponds to point E_1 on B's demand curve for imports) and then it bends backwards, reflecting the fact that as R increases the supply of pounds sterling falls because B's demand for imports is inelastic.

Given that B's demand-for-imports schedule has a finite intercept with the horizontal axis, the supply curve of pounds becomes asymptotic to the vertical axis. This is also seen in fig. 4.6, as follows. As R tends to infinity, A's supply curve of exports rotates downward through S' continuously, tending to coincide with the horizontal axis. But no matter how high R is, A's supply of exports has a positive slope and does not coincide with the horizontal axis. Hence, as $R \to \infty$, the equilibrium point along B's demand curve for imports (panel a) moves closer and closer to point D' (B's demand for imports intercept with the horizontal axis) but never coincides with it. As a result, the amount of pounds sterling supplied tends to zero, but actually never becomes zero. This explains why the supply curve for pounds sterling in panel (b) is asymptotic to the R axis.

The above graphical method used to derive the demand and supply curves for pounds sterling can also be used to derive the supply and demand curves for dollars as well. But this is unnecessary as no new insights can be gained by it. Besides, the technique of chap. 3 could be applied to get directly from the supply curve for pounds sterling, the demand curve for dollars, and from the demand curve for pounds sterling, the supply curve of dollars.

4.5 SOME PROPOSITIONS ABOUT THE ELASTICITY OF DEMAND FOR FOREIGN EXCHANGE

The demand for pounds sterling (foreign exchange) is determined by the equilibrium in the market for B-exportables. Accordingly, the elasticity of demand for pounds sterling is a function of the elasticity of A's demand for imports and B's supply of exports of B-exportables. This statement is made rigorous in sec. 4.7 below. For the moment, the nature of the interdependence among the three elasticities is summarized by the following propositions.

> **Proposition 4.1** When B's elasticity of supply of exports is strictly positive, the demand for pounds sterling is perfectly inelastic, inelastic, unit-elastic, or elastic, according to whether A's demand for imports is perfectly inelastic, inelastic, unit-elastic, or elastic, respectively.

PROOF When A's demand for imports is perfectly inelastic (i.e., vertical), A would import a fixed amount of B-exportables irrespective of R. This is illustrated by the vertical (dotted) curve $Q_0 E_0$ in fig. 4.5a. Given B's unique supply curve for exports, as in fig. 4.5a, this implies that the amount of sterling demanded remains constant, given by the area $0 Q_0 E_0 P_0$. Hence, the demand for pounds sterling is also perfectly inelastic, i.e., vertical. The other parts of the proposition are proved by referring to fig. 4.4a. In this figure, equilibrium occurs always on A's (unique) demand curve for imports. The areas of the rectangles formed at each equilibrium point (such as $0 Q_0 E_0 P_0$) give A's expenditure on imports expressed in dollars. The latter amount is also shown by the area of the rectangle formed at the corresponding point on the demand curve for pounds (see fig. 4.5b). Now, as R falls, equilibrium travels downward on both A's demand curve for imports (fig. 4.4a) and the demand curve for pounds sterling (fig. 4.5b). Given the correspondence between these two curves, it becomes clear that, at any two corresponding points, when one curve is elastic, unit-elastic, or inelastic, the other curve must also be elastic, unit-elastic, or inelastic, respectively.

Proposition 4.2 When B's elasticity of supply of exports is zero, the elasticity of demand for pounds sterling is unity (provided only that A's elasticity of demand for imports is strictly negative).

PROOF Assume that the vertical dotted line $Q_0 E_0$ in fig. 4.4a is B's supply curve for exports. Then equilibrium in the market for B-exportables would always occur at E_0, irrespective of the value of R. (A change in R causes B's supply curve to shift, but because it is vertical the shift leaves the figure essentially unaltered.) This implies that A's expenditure on imports in terms of dollars remains constant (given by the area $0 Q_0 E_0 P_0$), which in turn implies that the demand curve for pounds sterling is a rectangular hyperbola and the elasticity of demand for pounds sterling is unity.

Proposition 4.3 Assuming that the elasticity of B's supply of exports is strictly positive, the higher A's elasticity of demand for imports is, the higher the elasticity of demand for pounds sterling is.

PROOF Consider again fig. 4.4a. As R increases from $R = 1$ to $R = R_1 > 1$, equilibrium slides upward on A's unique demand curve for imports, say from E_0 to E_1. Had equilibrium moved to E_3, with A importing the same amount of B-exportables from B, the quantity of pounds sterling demanded would have remained constant (proposition 4.2). But at E_1, fewer dollars are supplied relative to E_3. This indicates that fewer pounds are demanded, also relative to the initial equilibrium at E_0, i.e., the demand-for-pounds schedule is downward sloping. Had A's elasticity of demand for imports been a little higher at E_0, A's demand curve for imports would have been flatter through E_0, with final equilibrium occurring on B's broker supply curve but at a point below E_1, such as at E_2. At E_2 the amount of dollars supplied is lower than the amount supplied at E_1. Accordingly, the amount of pounds sterling demanded at E_2 is also lower than the amount demanded at E_1, since the corresponding dollar amounts are converted into pounds sterling at the same (higher) rate of exchange. This shows that, as R increases, the amount of pounds sterling demanded falls faster, and thus the demand for pounds sterling is more elastic when A's demand for imports is more elastic.

Proposition 4.4 When A's demand for imports is *elastic*, the *higher* B's elasticity of supply of exports is, the *higher* the elasticity of demand for pounds sterling is. On the other hand, when A's demand for imports is *inelastic*, the *higher* B's elasticity of supply of exports is, the *smaller* the elasticity of demand for pounds sterling is.

PROOF Consider fig. 4.3a. As R increases, equilibrium moves from E_0 to E_1 and the quantity of pounds sterling demanded falls. The object is to show that, as B's supply of exports becomes relatively more elastic at the original equilibrium point E_0, the quantity of sterling demanded falls faster (slower) when A's demand for imports is elastic (inelastic). Observe that when B's supply of exports becomes more elastic, B's supply curve becomes flatter through E_0 and equilibrium occurs along A's broken demand curve for imports above and to the left of point E_1, as illustrated by point E_3. At E_3 the amount of pounds sterling demanded is smaller (larger) than the amount demanded at E_1 (at the higher R), provided that A's demand for imports is elastic (inelastic). This completes the proof.

Similar propositions hold also for the interdependence which exists among the elasticity of demand for dollars, A's elasticity of supply of exports, and B's elasticity of demand for imports.

4.6 SOME PROPOSITIONS ABOUT THE ELASTICITY OF SUPPLY OF FOREIGN EXCHANGE

The supply of pounds sterling is determined by the equilibrium in the market for A-exportables. Accordingly, the elasticity of supply of pounds sterling is a function of the elasticity of A's supply of exports and the elasticity of B's demand for imports of A-exportables. The nature of this interdependence is illustrated by the following propositions.

Proposition 4.5 The elasticity of supply of pounds sterling is positive, zero, or negative according to whether B's demand for imports is elastic, unit-elastic, or inelastic, respectively, assuming that A's elasticity of supply of exports is strictly positive.

PROOF This proposition was proved earlier in sec. 4.4 and no further discussion is necessary.

Proposition 4.6 When B's elasticity of demand for imports is zero, the elasticity of supply of pounds sterling is -1 (i.e., the supply curve for pounds sterling is a rectangular hyperbola).

PROOF By assumption, B imports a fixed amount of A-importables irrespective of price. A is willing to supply this fixed amount to B at a fixed price in terms of dollars (read off A's supply curve of exports). Hence, A's export revenue in dollars remains fixed for all values of R. But A's export revenue in dollars at any R is given graphically by the area of the rectangle formed at the appropriate point on the supply curve for pounds sterling (see fig. 4.6b); if the rectangles formed at all points on the supply curve for pounds remain constant, it follows that the latter is a rectangular hyperbola with elasticity equal to -1.

Proposition 4.7 Assume that B's demand for imports is inelastic, and thus, according to proposition 4.5, the supply of pounds sterling is backward bending. The higher A's elasticity of supply of exports is, the more backward bending the supply curve for pounds sterling becomes (i.e., the higher in *absolute terms* the elasticity of supply of pounds sterling).

PROOF Consider fig. 4.4b. Equilibrium occurs initially at E_0, but as R increases it moves to E_1. By assumption the amount of pounds sterling supplied is smaller at E_1 than at E_0—the supply curve for pounds is backward bending. Proposition 4.7 merely states that the amount of pounds sterling supplied at the higher R, being smaller as it is at E_1 than the original amount supplied at E_0, would have been even smaller had A's supply curve for exports been a little flatter at E_0. In this case, equilibrium would occur on B's broken demand curve for imports at a point below E_1, such as point E_2. Since B's demand curve is inelastic by assumption, it follows that fewer dollars are demanded, and therefore fewer pounds are supplied, at E_2 than E_1.

Proposition 4.8 Assume that B's demand for imports is elastic and A's supply elasticity of exports is strictly positive. Thus, according to proposition 4.5, the supply curve for pounds sterling is upward sloping. Then the higher A's supply elasticity of exports is, the higher the elasticity of supply of pounds sterling is.

PROOF As in the preceding proposition, consider again fig. 4.4b. In the present case, the amount of sterling supplied at E_1 is larger than the amount supplied at E_0, by assumption. The present proposition claims that the amount of sterling supplied at E_2 (had A's supply of exports been a little more elastic at E_0) is also higher than the amount supplied at E_1. But this is necessarily true because in the present case B's demand for imports is elastic, by assumption.

Proposition 4.9 When A's elasticity of supply of exports is zero, the elasticity of supply of pounds sterling is also zero.

PROOF This proposition becomes clear when it is realized that A is willing to export a fixed quantity of A-exportables irrespective of price. B, on the other hand, can be induced to demand that exact quantity if the price of A-exportables in pounds sterling is maintained at a certain fixed level. This implies that A's export revenue in pounds sterling remains fixed irrespective of the rate of exchange. Hence, the supply curve for pounds sterling is perfectly inelastic.

Proposition 4.10 Assume that A's supply elasticity of exports is strictly positive. The higher B's elasticity of demand for imports is, the higher (in algebraic terms) the elasticity of supply of pounds sterling is.

PROOF Consider fig. 4.3b. R increases and equilibrium moves from E_0 to E_1. The essence of the proposition is that the amount of pounds sterling supplied at the higher R would have been larger than the amount indicated by point E_1 had B's elasticity of demand for imports at E_0 been a little higher (i.e., had B's demand curve been a little flatter through E_0). But this should be so because equilibrium would have taken place along A's broken supply curve at a point above point E_1, such as point E_3. Clearly, the rectangle formed with reference to E_3 is larger than $0Q_1 E_1 P_1$.

4.7 MATHEMATICAL FORMULATION OF THE PARTIAL EQUILIBRIUM MODEL

This section develops in mathematical form the partial equilibrium model of the present chapter. The mathematical results derived in this section will be useful in later chapters. For convenience, the following additional notation is adopted (where primes indicate differentiation):

X_a, X_b ≡ physical quantities of exports supplied by A and B, respectively

M_a, M_b ≡ physical quantities of imports demanded by A and B, respectively

p_a, p_b ≡ prices of A-exportables and B-exportables, respectively, expressed in dollars

p_a^*, p_b^* ≡ prices of A-exportables and B-exportables, respectively, expressed in pounds sterling

$$e_{xa} \equiv \frac{X_a' p_a}{X_a} \equiv \text{A's supply elasticity of exports}$$

$$e_{xb} \equiv \frac{X_b' p_b^*}{X_b} \equiv \text{B's supply elasticity of exports}$$

$$e_{ma} \equiv \frac{M_a' p_b}{M_a} \equiv \text{A's demand elasticity of imports}$$

$$e_{mb} \equiv \frac{M_b' p_a^*}{M_b} \equiv \text{B's demand elasticity of imports}$$

$$p \equiv \frac{p_a}{p_b} = \frac{p_a^*}{p_b^*} \equiv \text{A's terms of trade}$$

A bar ($^-$) on any price indicates that it is an equilibrium price. Note also the following identities:

$$p_a = Rp_a^* \tag{4.1}$$

$$p_b = Rp_b^* \tag{4.2}$$

(a) Functional Relationships

Let A's and B's demand functions for imports be given, respectively, by

$$M_a = M_a(p_b) \tag{4.3}$$

$$M_b = M_b(p_a^*) \tag{4.4}$$

Similarly, A's and B's supply functions of exports are given, respectively, by

$$X_a = X_a(p_a) \tag{4.5}$$

$$X_b = X_b(p_b^*) \tag{4.6}$$

By assumption, $M_a' \leq 0$, $M_b' \leq 0$, $X_a' \geq 0$, $X_b' \geq 0$, where primes indicate differentiation.

(b) Market Equilibrium Conditions

Equilibrium in the market for A-exportables requires that the following equation be satisfied:

$$X_a(p_a) = M_b(p_a^*) \tag{4.7}$$

Similarly, equilibrium in the market for B-exportables requires that the following equation be satisfied:

$$X_b(p_b^*) = M_a(p_b) \tag{4.8}$$

Each of these equations has two unknowns. In particular, in eq. (4.7) the unknowns are p_a and p_a^*, and in eq. (4.8), p_b and p_b^*. Accordingly, neither equation can be solved by itself for the equilibrium values of both prices. This reflects the indeterminacy noted earlier in secs. 4.2 and 4.3 regarding the flow of goods between countries. The solution was to determine equilibrium in each of the two markets by assuming that the rate of exchange was given. This amounted to supplying another equation which removed the system's indeterminacy. In terms of our present equations, the approach is to solve eq. (4.7) simultaneously with eq. (4.1), and eq. (4.8) with eq. (4.2). In each case, we have a system of two equations in two unknowns and both systems are determinate. In the following solutions, the rate of exchange is taken as a parameter and all equilibrium prices are expressed as functions of it. This approach coincides with our earlier graphical solution.

First consider the system of eqs. (4.1) and (4.7). Solve equation (4.1) for p_a^* and substitute into eq. (4.7) to obtain

$$X_a(p_a) = M_b\left(\frac{p_a}{R}\right) \tag{4.9}$$

Alternatively, the value of p_a as given by eq. (4.1) could be substituted into eq. (4.7) to obtain

$$X_a(Rp_a^*) = M_b(p_a^*) \tag{4.10}$$

For any value of R, eq. (4.9) could be solved for the equilibrium value of $p_a(\bar{p}_a)$. The latter could then be substituted into eq. (4.5) to obtain the equilibrium amount of X_a. This solution corresponds to the graphical solution given earlier when the price of A-exportables was expressed in dollars. Similarly, for any value of R, eq. (4.10) can be used to determine the equilibrium value of $p_a^*(\bar{p}_a^*)$. Substitution of the latter into eq. (4.4) gives again the equilibrium amount of A-exportables exported from A to B. This solution corresponds to the graphical solution of secs. 4.2 and 4.3, when the price of A-exportables was expressed in pounds sterling.

(c) Comparative-Statics Effects of R Changes on Prices

How do $\bar{p}_a$ and $\bar{p}_a^*$ change as R changes? To answer this question, we differentiate eq. (4.9) totally with respect to R, and then solve for $(d\bar{p}_a/dR)$. We obtain

$$X_a'\left(\frac{d\bar{p}_a}{dR}\right) = M_b' \, \frac{R(d\bar{p}_a/dR) - \bar{p}_a}{R^2}$$

Solving for $(d\bar{p}_a/dR)$ and rearranging using the standard definitions of elasticities, we obtain

$$\frac{d\bar{p}_a}{dR} = \frac{\bar{p}_a^* M_b'}{M_b' - RX_a'} = \frac{\bar{p}_a^* e_{mb}}{e_{mb} - e_{xa}} \geq 0 \tag{4.11}$$

Observe that use has been made of eq. (4.9) in putting the last expression in terms of elasticities.

Equation (4.11) shows that as R increases, $\bar{p}_a$ increases also, except in the limiting case where $e_{mb} = 0$. In the latter case, $\bar{p}_a$ is a constant, independent of R. This verifies the conclusion reached earlier through graphical analysis.

To determine what happens to $\bar{p}_a^*$ as R changes, we could differentiate eq. (4.10) totally with respect to R and proceed as with eq. (4.9). However, there is an indirect and shorter way to get the same result. Differentiate eq. (4.1) totally with respect to R and obtain

$$\frac{d\bar{p}_a}{dR} = \bar{p}_a^* + R\left(\frac{d\bar{p}_a^*}{dR}\right)$$

Solve the latter equation for $(d\bar{p}_a^*/dR)$ to get

$$\frac{d\bar{p}_a^*}{dR} = \frac{(d\bar{p}_a/dR) - \bar{p}_a^*}{R}$$

Finally, substitute eq. (4.11) into the last equation and simplify as follows:

$$\frac{d\bar{p}_a^*}{dR} = \bar{p}_a^* \frac{[e_{mb}/(e_{mb} - e_{xa})] - 1}{R}$$

$$= \left(\frac{\bar{p}_a^*}{R}\right)\left(\frac{e_{xa}}{e_{mb} - e_{xa}}\right) \leq 0 \tag{4.12}$$

Equation (4.12) gives the desired result. It shows that, in general, $\bar{p}_a^*$ falls as R increases. In the limiting case where $e_{xa} = 0$, the equilibrium value of $\bar{p}_a^*$ is a constant, independent of R.

Consider now the system of eqs. (4.2) and (4.8). Solve eq. (4.2) for p_b^* and substitute into eq. (4.8) to obtain

$$X_b\left(\frac{p_b}{R}\right) = M_a(p_b) \tag{4.13}$$

Alternatively, the value of p_b as given by eq. (4.2) could be substituted into eq. (4.8) to obtain

$$X_b(p_b^*) = M_a(Rp_b^*) \tag{4.14}$$

Again, for any value of R, eq. (4.13) could be solved for the equilibrium value of $p_b(\bar{p}_b)$. The latter could then be substituted into eq. (4.3) to obtain the equilibrium M_a. This solution corresponds to the graphical solution given earlier when the price of B-exportables was expressed in dollars. Similarly, for any value of R, eq. (4.14) can be used to determine the equilibrium value of $p_b^*(\bar{p}_b^*)$. Substitution of the latter into eq. (4.6) gives again the equilibrium amount of B-exportables exported from B to A. This solution corresponds to the graphical solution of secs. 4.2 and 4.3, when the price of B-exportables was expressed in terms of pounds sterling.

How do $\bar{p}_b$ and $\bar{p}_b^*$ change as R changes? We could obtain an answer directly by differentiating eqs. (4.13) and (4.14) totally with respect to R, as we did with eqs. (4.9) and (4.10). But this is not necessary. Equations (4.11) and (4.12) contain much more information than what was suggested above. In particular, eq. (4.11) gives general information on how the equilibrium price of any country's exportables, expressed in terms of that country's currency, changes with respect to a change in the price of the foreign currency in terms of the domestic currency. Accordingly, by reversing the roles of the two countries, we obtain immediately, from eq. (4.11),

$$\frac{d\bar{p}_b^*}{dR^*} = \frac{p_b e_{ma}}{e_{ma} - e_{xb}} \geq 0 \tag{4.15}$$

Similarly, from eq. (4.12), we obtain immediately

$$\frac{d\bar{p}_b}{dR^*} = \left(\frac{\bar{p}_b}{R^*}\right)\left(\frac{e_{xb}}{e_{ma} - e_{xb}}\right) \leq 0 \tag{4.16}$$

Of course, what we really want are the derivatives $(d\bar{p}_b^*/dR)$ and $(d\bar{p}_b/dR)$, and not $(d\bar{p}_b^*/dR^*)$ and $(d\bar{p}_b/dR^*)$ as given by eqs. (4.15) and (4.16). But the desired derivatives are only a small step away. (Recall that $R^* \equiv 1/R$.)

Since R^* is a function of R, the needed derivatives can be obtained as follows:

$$\frac{d\bar{p}_b^*}{dR} = \left(\frac{d\bar{p}_b^*}{dR^*}\right)\left(\frac{dR^*}{dR}\right) \tag{4.17}$$

$$\frac{d\bar{p}_b}{dR} = \left(\frac{d\bar{p}_b}{dR^*}\right)\left(\frac{dR^*}{dR}\right) \tag{4.18}$$

Since $R^* = (1/R)$, we also have

$$\frac{dR^*}{dR} = -\frac{1}{R^2} \tag{4.19}$$

Finally, substituting eqs. (4.15) and (4.19) into eq. (4.17) and simplifying, we obtain

$$\frac{d\bar{p}_b^*}{dR} = \left(\frac{\bar{p}_b^*}{R}\right)\left(\frac{e_{ma}}{e_{xb} - e_{ma}}\right) \leq 0 \tag{4.20}$$

with the strict equality holding when $e_{ma} = 0$. Similarly, substituting eqs. (4.16) and (4.19) into eq. (4.18), we obtain

$$\frac{d\bar{p}_b}{dR} = \frac{\bar{p}_b^* e_{xb}}{e_{xb} - e_{ma}} \geq 0 \tag{4.21}$$

with the strict equality holding when $e_{xb} = 0$.

(d) Comparative-Statics Effects of R Changes on the Terms of Trade

How does a change in R affect A's terms of trade, $\bar{p} \equiv (\bar{p}_a/\bar{p}_b)$? As noted earlier, the conclusion that A's terms of trade necessarily deteriorate as the dollar (A's currency) depreciates is not warranted. Presently, we wish to show the conditions under which A's terms of trade may deteriorate or improve.

Differentiating $\bar{p}$ with respect to R, remembering always that both $\bar{p}_a$ and $\bar{p}_b$ are functions of R, we obtain

$$\frac{d\bar{p}}{dR} = \left(\frac{1}{\bar{p}_b^2}\right)\left[\bar{p}_b\left(\frac{d\bar{p}_a}{dR}\right) - \bar{p}_a\left(\frac{d\bar{p}_b}{dR}\right)\right]$$

Substituting from eqs. (4.11) and (4.21) and simplifying, we obtain

$$\frac{d\bar{p}}{dR} = -\left(\frac{\bar{p}_a^*}{\bar{p}_b}\right)\left(\frac{e_{mb}}{e_{xa} - e_{mb}} + \frac{e_{xb}}{e_{xb} - e_{ma}}\right)$$

$$= -\left(\frac{\bar{p}_a^*}{\bar{p}_b}\right)\left[\frac{e_{xb}e_{xa} - e_{ma}e_{mb}}{(e_{xa} - e_{mb})(e_{xb} - e_{ma})}\right] \tag{4.22}$$

From eq. (4.22) it follows that:

1. $(d\bar{p}/dR) > 0$, that is, A's terms of trade improve as the dollar depreciates relative to the pound, if $e_{xa}e_{xb} < e_{ma}e_{mb}$, that is, if the product of the supply elasticities of exports is smaller than the product of the demand elasticities for imports.
2. $(d\bar{p}/dR) < 0$, that is, A's terms of trade deteriorate, if $e_{xa}e_{xb} > e_{ma}e_{mb}$.
3. $(d\bar{p}/dR) = 0$, that is, A's terms of trade remain unaltered, if $e_{xa}e_{xb} = e_{ma}e_{mb}$.

(e) The Demand for Pounds Sterling and the Supply of Dollars

The demand for pounds sterling and the corresponding supply of dollars are given by the following equations, respectively:

$$D_£ = D_£(R) = \bar{p}_b^* X_b(\bar{p}_b^*) \tag{4.23}$$

$$S_\$ = S_\$(R^*) = \bar{p}_b M_a(\bar{p}_b) \tag{4.24}$$

where all prices are equilibrium prices, i.e., they are roots of eqs. (4.13) and (4.14).

What is the precise relationship between the elasticity of demand for pounds sterling and A's demand elasticity of imports and B's supply elasticity of exports? Having come so far, the answer is not too difficult to get.

Differentiating eq. (4.23) with respect to R, remembering that $\bar{p}_b^*$ is a function of R, we obtain

$$\frac{dD_£}{dR} = (X_b + \bar{p}_b^* X_b')\left(\frac{d\bar{p}_b^*}{dR}\right)$$

(The argument of X_b and X_b', that is, $\bar{p}_b^*$, has been omitted for simplicity.) Substituting from eq. (4.20) and making use of the definition of B's elasticity of supply of exports, the preceding expression becomes

$$\frac{dD_£}{dR} = \left(\frac{\bar{p}_b^* X_b}{R}\right)\left[\frac{(1 + e_{xb})e_{ma}}{e_{xb} - e_{ma}}\right] \tag{4.25}$$

By definition, the elasticity of demand for pounds ($e_d^£$) is given by $e_d^£ = (dD_£/dR) \times (R/D_£)$. Accordingly, by multiplying by the factor $(R/D_£)$ both sides of eq. (4.25), we finally obtain

$$e_d^£ = e_{ma}\left(\frac{1 + e_{xb}}{e_{xb} - e_{ma}}\right) \tag{4.26}$$

This is an important formula and the reader is encouraged to use it to verify the propositions which were stated in sec. 4.5 above.

Having derived the formula for $e_d^£$, we can use it along with the equation $e_s^\$ + e_d^£ = -1$, given earlier in chap. 3, to derive an equally important formula for the elasticity of supply of dollars ($e_s^\$$). Thus,

$$e_s^\$ = -1 - e_d^£ = e_{xb}\left(\frac{1 + e_{ma}}{e_{ma} - e_{xb}}\right) \tag{4.27}$$

Note also the following limits:

$$(a) \quad \lim_{e_{xb} \to \infty} e_d^£ = e_{ma}$$

and $\qquad (b) \quad \lim_{e_{xb} \to \infty} e_s^\$ = -(1 + e_{ma})$

(f) The Supply of Pounds Sterling and the Demand for Dollars

The supply of pounds sterling and the corresponding demand for dollars are given by the following equations, respectively:

$$S_£ = S_£(R) = \bar{p}_a^* M_b(\bar{p}_a^*) \tag{4.28}$$

$$D_\$ = D_\$(R^*) = \bar{p}_a X_a(\bar{p}_a) \tag{4.29}$$

where again all prices are equilibrium prices and functions of R.

We could proceed directly to determine the precise relationship between the elasticity of supply of pounds ($e_s^£$) and B's demand elasticity for imports and A's supply elasticity of exports. Nevertheless, this effort is totally unnecessary because the results given in the preceding subsection (e) are valid for the present case as well. The only difference is simply that the roles of the two countries must be reversed. Having this in mind, eq. (4.27) gives directly

$$. e_s^£ = e_{xa} \left(\frac{1 + e_{mb}}{e_{mb} - e_{xa}} \right) \tag{4.30}$$

Similarly, eq. (4.26) gives directly (by interchanging the subscripts a and b)

$$e_d^\$ = e_{mb} \left(\frac{1 + e_{xa}}{e_{xa} - e_{mb}} \right) \tag{4.31}$$

Note also the limits:

$$(a) \quad \lim_{e_{xa} \to \infty} e_s^£ = -(1 + e_{mb})$$

and $\qquad (b) \quad \lim_{e_{xa} \to \infty} e_d^\$ = e_{mb}$

SELECTED BIBLIOGRAPHY

Bickerdike, C. F. (1920). "The Instability of Foreign Exchange." *Economic Journal*, vol. XXX, no. 117 (March).

Dornbusch, R. (1975). "Exchange Rates and Fiscal Policy in a Popular Model of International Trade." *American Economic Review*, vol. LXV, no. 5, pp. 859–871.

Haberler, G. (1949). "The Market for Foreign Exchange and the Stability of the Balance of Payments: A Theoretical Analysis." *Kyklos*, vol. 3, pp. 193–218. Reprinted in R. N. Cooper (Ed.), *International Finance*. Penguin Books, Inc., Baltimore, Md., 1969.

Harberger, A. C. (1957). "Some Evidence on the International Price Mechanism." *Journal of Political Economy* (December).

Hirschman, A. O. (1949). "Devaluation and the Trade Balance." *Review of Economics and Statistics* (February).

Kindleberger, C. P. (1973). *International Economics*, 5th ed. R. D. Irwin, Inc.,. Homewood, Ill., chap. 19.

Machlup, F. (1939 and 1940). "The Theory of Foreign Exchanges." *Economica*, vol. VI (New Series), November, 1939, and February, 1940. Reprinted in American Economic Association, *Readings in the Theory of International Trade*. R. D. Irwin, Inc., Homewood, Ill., 1949.

Meade, J. E. (1951). *The Theory of International Economic Policy*, vol. I, *The Balance of Payments*. Oxford University Press, Inc., New York, pt. IV.

Metzler, L. A. (1948). "The Theory of International Trade." In American Economic Association, *A Survey of Contemporary Economics*. The Blakiston Company, Philadelphia, Pa.

Orcutt, G. H. (1950). "Measurement of Price Elasticities in International Trade." *The Review of Economics and Statistics*, vol. XXXII, no. 2 (May). Reprinted in American Economic Association, *Readings in International Economics*. R. D. Irwin, Inc., Homewood, Ill., 1968.

Robinson, J. (1937). "The Foreign Exchanges." In J. Robinson, *Essays in the Theory of Employment*. Macmillan and Company, London. Reprinted in American Economic Association, *Readings in the Theory of International Trade*. R. D. Irwin, Inc., Homewood, Ill., 1949.

Samuelson, P. A. (1971). "An Exact Hume-Ricardo-Marshall Model of International Trade." *Journal of International Economics*, vol. 1, no. 1, pp. 1–18.

Sohmen, E. (1969). *Flexible Exchange Rates*, revised ed. University of Chicago Press, Chicago, Ill., chap. 1.

Vanek, J. (1962). *International Trade: Theory and Economic Policy*. R. D. Irwin, Inc., Homewood, Ill., chap. 5.

Yeager, L. B. (1966). *International Monetary Relations*. Harper and Row, New York, chap. 9.

THE FLEXIBLE-EXCHANGE-RATE SYSTEM: I. EQUILIBRIUM AND STABILITY IN THE SPOT MARKET

This and the following chapter discuss in some detail the flexible-exchange-rate system. Under this system the rate of foreign exchange is determined daily in the foreign exchange market by the forces of supply and demand. The daily movements of the exchange rate are not restricted in any way by governmental policy, although monetary authorities may intervene in the foreign exchange market to iron out wide fluctuations in these rates. The freedom of the exchange rate to move daily in response to market forces does not necessarily imply that it will actually move significantly and erratically from day to day. It will do so only if the underlying economic forces are themselves erratic, causing erratic shifts in the supply and demand curves for foreign exchange.

The present analysis is carried out in terms of the partial equilibrium model developed in the preceding chapter. In parts two and three this analysis is expanded further to include income effects and to consider the effects of fiscal and monetary policies. This chapter discusses the problem of equilibrium and stability on the assumption that the spot and forward markets are combined into a single foreign exchange market. The next chapter deals with the simultaneous determination of the equilibrium spot and forward rates of exchange.

5.1 EQUILIBRIUM IN THE FOREIGN EXCHANGE MARKET

It will be recalled that we are dealing with two countries: A (home country) and B (foreign country). A's national currency is the dollar and B's the pound. Given the supply and demand curves for foreign exchange (£), the determination of equilibrium is simple: it occurs at the intersection of the two curves. This is shown in fig. 5.1 by point E, whose coordinates show the equilibrium exchange rate (R_e) and amount of pounds traded (P_e), respectively.

The problem of equilibrium could also be cast in terms of the market for dollars. Based on the information given in fig. 5.1, the corresponding supply and demand curves for dollars could be derived as explained in chap. 3; then equilibrium could be determined as in fig. 5.1. But this is not necessary, for when the market for one currency is in equilibrium, the market for the other is also in equilibrium. (The same goes for stability.) Further, any information needed for one market can be recovered from the other. For instance, at the equilibrium point E (fig. 5.1) the amount of dollars traded is given by the area of the rectangle $0P_eER_e$ and the price of the dollar in terms of pounds sterling is given by $(1/R_e)$. Accordingly, only one of the two markets needs to be analyzed explicitly.

Offer Curves

To bring into sharp relief (a) the interrelationship between the market for pounds and the market for dollars, and (b) the formal similarities between the present model which deals with currencies and that of the pure theory of trade which deals directly with commodities, the present problem of equilibrium can be cast in terms of *offer curves*. (The concept of the offer curve was introduced earlier in chap. 3, but the reader may also consult Chacholiades, 1973.)

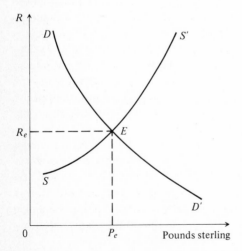

Figure 5.1 The market for pounds sterling. Under the flexible-exchange-rate system, the rate of foreign exchange is determined by the intersection of the supply and demand schedules for foreign exchange (see point E).

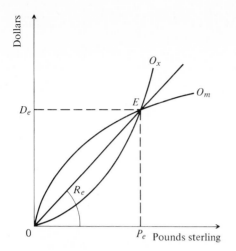

Figure 5.2 Equilibrium in the foreign exchange market in terms of offer curves. Equilibrium in the market for pounds sterling implies equilibrium in the market for dollars. This truth is verified when offer curves are employed, as shown here.

$O_m \equiv$ offer curve of A's importers and B's exporters
$O_x \equiv$ offer curve of A's exporters and B's importers

Consider fig. 5.2. Pounds are measured horizontally and dollars vertically. The offer curve O_m shows the amounts of dollars offered for alternative amounts of pounds sterling demanded by the group A's importers plus B's exporters. Similarly, the offer curve O_x shows the amounts of pounds sterling offered for alternative amounts of dollars demanded by the group A's exporters plus B's importers. Equilibrium occurs at E. The equilibrium amounts of pounds and dollars traded are given, respectively, by the distances $0P_e$ and $0D_e$. The equilibrium rate of exchange (R_e) is given by the slope of the vector $0E$. Note that equilibrium occurs only at an intersection between the offer curves, and at such intersection(s) both the market for dollars and the market for pounds are cleared simultaneously.

Figure 5.2 is important and the reader should study it carefully. To the reader who is already familiar with offer curves, fig. 5.2 gives the opportunity for the direct application of well-known results in the field of the pure theory of trade to the present problem. Formally, there is no difference between fig. 5.2 and the offer curves of the pure theory of trade, except for the insignificant detail that the latter deals with real commodities while the former deals with currencies. This similarity between the pure theory of trade and the foreign exchange market is exploited further in the section on stability. Besides that, no further use is made of offer curves in subsequent analysis.

Multiple Equilibria

Because currency supply curves may be backward bending, equilibrium in the foreign exchange market need not be unique. This is illustrated in fig. 5.3. Panel (*a*) illustrates the case of three equilibria in the market for pounds in terms of the

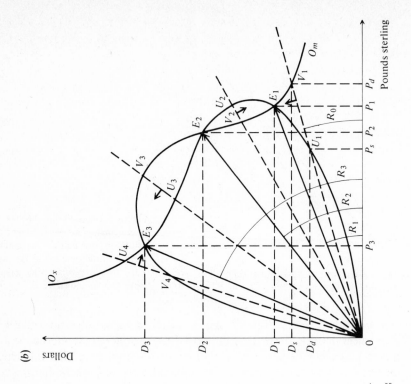

(b)

Dollars

Pounds sterling

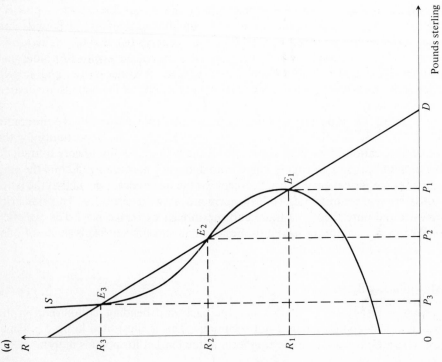

(a)

Pounds sterling

118

ordinary supply and demand curves. Panel (*b*) illustrates the same situation in terms of offer curves. Thus, panel (*b*) portrays directly the market for dollars in addition to the market for pounds. Needless to say, both panels give exactly the same information—no more and no less.

The multiplicity of equilibrium in the foreign exchange market creates difficulties. In the first place, some of the equilibria are *unstable*, as explained in the following section. Second, from the point of view of social desirability each country would probably rank these equilibria differently from the other. This situation will definitely lead to conflicting policies between countries with deleterious effects. Finally, private speculative activity may be such as to cause the system to switch from one equilibrium to the other, giving rise to unnecessary and wasteful reallocation of resources within each country.

5.2 STABILITY OF EQUILIBRIUM

When a market is in equilibrium, each potential buyer can find a seller and each seller can find a buyer. Every market participant does what he desires to do, and no buyer or seller has any incentive to change his behavior. If not disturbed, equilibrium can last forever. But is there any guarantee that a market will be in equilibrium if it is not already there? What happens when a market (or a system of markets) is out of equilibrium? Will the market return to equilibrium? The behavior of a market, or a system of markets, out of equilibrium is the subject matter of stability analysis. The basic question is whether there are economic forces at work which will automatically bring the market (or the system of markets) back to equilibrium. If there are such forces and the market or system does tend to return to equilibrium, then that equilibrium is called *stable;* otherwise, the equilibrium is called *unstable.* Clearly, the concept of stability is an important one because equilibrium cannot be taken seriously unless it is stable.

Static and Dynamic Stability

Two types of stability are usually distinguished: *dynamic* stability and *static* stability. Dynamic stability is concerned with an explicit adjustment process governing the changes of prices and quantities through time, with time entering into the analysis in a crucial manner. Static stability, on the other hand, involves no explicit framework for determining how prices and quantities (demanded or supplied) change through time when the system is out of equilibrium. It merely

---

Figure 5.3 Multiple equilibria in the foreign exchange market. (*a*) The market for pounds. When the supply schedule is backward bending, the possibility of multiple equilibria cannot be excluded. Here there are three equilibria, two of which (E_1 and E_3) are stable and one (E_2) unstable. (*b*) The multiple equilibria of (*a*) are given here in terms of offer curves. Again points E_1 and E_3 are stable while the middle point E_2 is unstable.

establishes the tendencies which exist when the system is out of equilibrium, and whether these tendencies point toward equilibrium or not.

In the neoclassical writings there exist two notions of static stability: the Marshallian and the Walrasian. The Marshallian stability analysis assigns the task of restoring equilibrium to the quantity. It is based on the postulate that, if at the current quantity traded the market price is higher than the supply price (i.e., that price which the producers must receive in order to continue offering the current quantity), the output will tend to expand (presumably because of the existence of abnormal profits); and if the market price is lower than the supply price, output will tend to fall (presumably because of the existence of losses). Thus, an equilibrium is stable according to the Marshallian analysis if, for quantities lower than the equilibrium quantity, the market price is higher than the average cost of production (or the supply price); and if, for quantities higher than the equilibrium quantity, the market price is lower than the supply price.

The Walrasian stability analysis, on the other hand, assigns the task of restoring equilibrium to the price. It rests on the postulate that, when at the current price the quantity supplied is larger than the quantity demanded, the price will tend to fall (presumably because the suppliers who are unable to sell all they want at the current price will lower their bids); and when the quantity supplied is smaller than the quantity demanded, the price will tend to rise (presumably because the buyers who are unable to buy all they want at the current price will raise their bids). Thus, an equilibrium is stable according to the Walrasian analysis if, for prices lower than the equilibrium price, the quantity demanded is larger than the quantity supplied (i.e., the excess demand is positive); and if, for prices higher than the equilibrium price, the quantity demanded is lower than the quantity supplied (i.e., the excess demand is negative).

For the most part, we shall be concerned with the Walrasian analysis for two reasons. First, the Walrasian static-stability analysis is most appropriate for our purposes in comparison with the Marshallian analysis—the rate of foreign exchange is assigned the task of restoring equilibrium. Second, although according to Samuelson the dynamic stability is the true concept of stability, the Walrasian stability analysis is much simpler and, more importantly, implies dynamic stability for most adjustment processes within the framework of our model.

Local and Global Stability

A distinction between *local* and *global* stability ought to be drawn. An equilibrium point is said to be locally stable if, for any *small* displacements around it, the system returns to the original equilibrium. On the other hand, a globally stable equilibrium point requires that there are tendencies for the system to return to equilibrium for *any* displacement, small or large. Thus, a globally stable equilibrium is necessarily a locally stable equilibrium. But the reverse need not be true. That is, a locally stable equilibrium need not be a globally stable equilibrium. In addition, a globally stable equilibrium is necessarily unique, for if a second equilibrium existed, a displacement from the first equilibrium point which puts the economy on the second cannot possibly generate forces that will bring the system back to the original equilibrium; otherwise, the second point would not be an equilibrium point. Our present discussion is concerned with *local* stability only.

Instability Is Possible When the Supply Curve Is Backward Bending

As noted above, the Walrasian stability analysis rests on the postulate that when supply exceeds demand the price tends to fall, and when demand exceeds supply the price tends to rise. When the demand curve is downward sloping and the supply curve upward sloping in the neighborhood of an equilibrium point, as shown, for instance, in fig. 5.1, the equilibrium point is (locally) stable. However, difficulties arise when the supply curve is backward bending—a normal behavior for the supply curve of a currency. As noted in the preceding section and illustrated in fig. 5.3a, a backward-bending supply curve may give rise to multiple equilibria. Some of these equilibria are necessarily unstable. Thus, the reader should verify that in fig. 5.3 points E_1 and E_3 are stable while E_2 is unstable.

When the Market for Pounds Is Stable the Market for Dollars Is Also Stable, and Vice Versa

It was noted in the preceding section that the equilibrium analysis of the foreign exchange market can be cast either in terms of the market for pounds sterling or the market for dollars. The same is true of stability. That is, when the market for pounds sterling is at a stable (unstable) equilibrium point, the corresponding equilibrium in the market for dollars is also stable (unstable). This conclusion follows easily from the following observations: (a) the price of dollars in terms of pounds sterling ($1/R$) is the reciprocal of the price of pounds sterling in terms of dollars (R); and (b) a positive (negative) excess demand for pounds sterling necessarily implies a negative (positive) excess demand for dollars. Thus, when there is a positive (negative) excess demand for pounds sterling, R tends to increase (decrease). But, in addition, there must be a negative (positive) excess demand for dollars causing ($1/R$) to decrease (increase). Since a tendency for R to increase (decrease) is the same thing as a tendency for ($1/R$) to decrease (increase), stability (instability) in the market for pounds sterling necessarily implies stability (instability) in the market for dollars, and vice versa.

The preceding statement is illustrated in fig. 5.3b. Consider a value of R lower than the equilibrium rate R_1, such as the rate R_0 indicated by the slope of the vector $0U_1V_1$. At this low rate of exchange, the amount of pounds sterling demanded is given by the horizontal distance $0P_d$, while the amount of pounds supplied is given by the distance $0P_s$. Since $0P_d > 0P_s$, there is a tendency for the dollar price of the pound sterling, that is, R, to increase, as shown by the arrow. Consider now the quantities of dollars demanded and supplied at $R = R_0$. They are given, respectively, by the vertical distances $0D_d$ and $0D_s$. Since $0D_s > 0D_d$, there is a tendency for the dollar to become cheaper relative to the pound, i.e., there is a tendency for ($1/R$) to fall, which is the same thing as the tendency for R

to rise, calling for a counterclockwise rotation of the vector $0U_1 V_1$. Thus, whether one concentrates on the market for pounds or the market for dollars the outcome is the same—a movement toward the stable equilibrium E_1. The reader is urged to repeat the preceding analysis for other values of R and show that points E_1 and E_3 are stable while E_2 is unstable.

5.3 CONDITIONS FOR STABILITY AND INSTABILITY IN THE FOREIGN EXCHANGE MARKET

What is the *necessary and sufficient* condition for stability in the foreign exchange market? Conversely, what is the *necessary* condition for *instability*? Let us begin with the second question first.

Theorem 5.1 A necessary condition for instability is that both the demand for pounds sterling and the demand for dollars are inelastic at the equilibrium point.

PROOF As observed earlier, instability can occur only if the supply curve of either currency is backward bending at the equilibrium point. But the backward-bending portion of the supply curve for pounds (dollars) corresponds to the inelastic portion of the demand for dollars (pounds). This has been proved in chap. 3. Accordingly, instability can occur only if both the demand for pounds and the demand for dollars are inelastic. If only one of them is inelastic, the equilibrium point is definitely stable. For instance, if the demand for pounds is inelastic but the demand for dollars is elastic, it follows that the supply curve for pounds sterling is upward sloping; hence the market for pounds sterling is stable and by implication the market for dollars is stable also. Finally, note that the present theorem is concerned with a *necessary* condition for instability. That is, it is not true that when both demand curves are inelastic the system is unstable. On the contrary, as shown below, it may very well be stable. However, if either or both demand curves (for dollars and pounds) are elastic, then the system is stable.

Theorem 5.2 A necessary and sufficient condition for stability in the foreign exchange market is that the sum of the elasticity of demand for pounds $(e_d^\pounds)$ plus the elasticity of demand for dollars $(e_d^\$)$ is less than -1. That is, the foreign exchange market is stable when

$$e_d^\pounds + e_d^\$ < -1 \tag{5.1}$$

PROOF Consider the market for pounds sterling. A necessary and sufficient condition for stability is that at the equilibrium point the following inequality be satisfied:

$$\frac{dD_\pounds}{dR} < \frac{dS_\pounds}{dR} \tag{5.2}$$

Multiplying both sides by the ratio $(R/D_£)$ and remembering that at the equilibrium point we necessarily have $D_£ = S_£$, the above inequality is cast in terms of elasticities as follows:

$$e_d^£ < e_s^£ \tag{5.3}$$

Recalling from chap. 3 that $e_d^\$ + e_s^£ = -1$, and substituting into the inequality (5.3) and rearranging, we finally obtain the inequality (5.1).

The preceding discussion and theorems are rather general. They are relevant for any given pair of supply and demand curves for foreign exchange (or domestic currency), irrespective of the fundamental economic model which may lie hidden behind these curves. An example of such a model is the partial equilibrium model studied in the preceding chapter. There it was observed that the supply and demand elasticities for currencies are functions of more fundamental supply and demand elasticities, namely, the supply elasticities for exports and the demand elasticities for imports. Can the stability conditions be cast in terms of these more fundamental elasticities? That this is so is shown by the following important theorem.

Theorem 5.3: Marshall-Lerner condition The foreign exchange market is stable when the sum of the two demand elasticities for imports is less than -1; that is, when the following inequality is satisfied:

$$e_{ma} + e_{mb} < -1 \tag{5.4}$$

Inequality (5.4) is known in the literature as the *Marshall-Lerner condition*.

The Marshall-Lerner condition is in general sufficient but not necessary for stability. It becomes necessary and sufficient in the following two cases: (*a*) when the supply elasticities of exports of *both* countries are infinite; and (*b*) when the demand elasticity for imports of *either* country is zero. In all other cases, the Marshall-Lerner condition is sufficient but' not necessary for stability.

PROOF Our proof is given in several steps. We begin first with the two cases in which the Marshall-Lerner condition is necessary and sufficient for stability.

Infinite Supply Elasticities of Exports

When the supply elasticities of exports are infinite, the price of A-exportables remains fixed in terms of dollars and the price of B-exportables remains fixed in terms of pounds sterling. Without any loss of generality, the units of measurement of A-exportables and B-exportables can be chosen in such a way as to make their respective fixed prices equal to unity. When this is done, A's demand curve for imports of B-exportables coincides with the demand curve for pounds sterling because $p_b = R$ and $D_£ = M_a$. Accordingly, the elasticity of demand for pounds sterling is equal to A's elasticity of demand for imports, that is, $e_d^£ = e_{ma}$. Similarly,

B's demand curve for imports coincides with the demand curve for dollars, and, therefore, the demand elasticity for dollars equals B's elasticity of demand for imports, that is, $e_d^\$ = e_{mb}$. By a mere substitution in inequality (5.1), we obtain the Marshall-Lerner condition, i.e., inequality (5.4).

The experienced reader will note the identity between the present result and the stability analysis for the two-country, two-commodity barter-trade model (see Chacholiades, 1973, especially chap. 6). As noted earlier, technically the offer curves of fig. 5.3 are no different from the offer curves of the barter model. This shows that the inequality (5.1) coincides with the Marshall-Lerner condition of the barter model, with the only difference being that the former deals with currencies while the latter deals with real commodities. Further, when the supply elasticities for exports are infinite, a mere change in the units of measurement (which, as is well known from elementary economics, does not affect the numerical value of the elasticity coefficient) converts the foreign-exchange offer curves into offer curves dealing directly with A-exportables and B-exportables. In this case the identity between the two models is complete. No wonder, then, that the Marshall-Lerner condition becomes necessary and sufficient for stability in both models.

The Demand Elasticity for Imports of Either Country Is Zero

Suppose it is A's elasticity of demand for imports which is zero (that is, $e_{ma} = 0$). As shown in chap. 4, this implies that the elasticity of demand for pounds sterling is also zero. Hence, according to theorem 5.2, stability in the foreign exchange market would prevail if the demand for dollars is elastic, that is, $e_d^\$ < -1$. Again according to the analysis of chap. 4, this is the case when B's demand for imports is elastic (that is, $e_{mb} < -1$). Consequently, the Marshall-Lerner condition must be satisfied for stability. Exactly the same analysis could be provided when B's elasticity of demand for imports is zero.

General Case

Excluding the above exceptional cases, it is clear that the only necessary and sufficient condition for stability in the foreign exchange market is the inequality (5.1). Substituting into (5.1) the values of $e_d^£$ and $e_d^\$$ as given by eqs. (4.26) and (4.31), respectively, we obtain the following general-stability condition:

$$\left[e_{ma}\left(\frac{1 + e_{xb}}{e_{xb} - e_{ma}}\right) \right] + \left[e_{mb}\left(\frac{1 + e_{xa}}{e_{xa} - e_{mb}}\right) \right] < -1$$

Given the reasonable assumption that $e_{xa} - e_{mb} > 0$ and $e_{xb} - e_{ma} > 0$, the above inequality can be simplified to

$$e_{ma}(1 + e_{xb})(e_{xa} - e_{mb}) + e_{mb}(1 + e_{xa})(e_{xb} - e_{ma}) < -(e_{xb} - e_{ma})(e_{xa} - e_{mb})$$

By multiplying out, cancelling equal terms, and rearranging, we finally obtain

$$-e_{xa}e_{xb}(1 + e_{ma} + e_{mb}) + e_{ma}e_{mb}(1 + e_{xa} + e_{xb}) > 0 \qquad (5.5)$$

Inequality (5.5) is the necessary and sufficient condition for stability. Since $e_{ma}e_{mb}(1 + e_{xa} + e_{xb}) \geq 0$, it follows that the Marshall-Lerner condition which guarantees that the first term in inequality (5.5) is also positive is sufficient but not necessary for stability. Note that when an export supply elasticity is zero, say $e_{xa} = 0$, inequality (5.5) is automatically satisfied, assuming only that the corresponding demand elasticity is strictly negative, i.e., $e_{mb} < 0$.

Why does the Marshall-Lerner condition become sufficient for stability in this general case? Recall that it is presently assumed that neither demand elasticity for imports is zero and that neither supply elasticity for exports is infinite. In addition, as shown in sec. 4.5, proposition 4.1, the demand for pounds sterling is perfectly inelastic, inelastic, unit-elastic, or elastic, according to whether A's demand for imports is, respectively, perfectly inelastic, inelastic, unit-elastic, or elastic. The same relationship holds also between the demand elasticity for dollars and B's demand elasticity for imports. Given all this information, it becomes clear that the necessary and sufficient condition for stability, given by inequality (5.1), does not require either demand elasticity for imports to be greater than unity. Consider then the case where both demand elasticities for imports are less than unity (in absolute terms). As it turns out, in this case (see sec. 4.5, proposition 4.4) the demand for pounds sterling is more elastic than A's demand for imports; that is, $-1 < e_d^\pounds < e_{ma} < 0$. Also, the demand for dollars is more elastic than B's demand for imports; that is, $-1 < e_d^\$ < e_{mb} < 0$. If these inequalities are granted, it follows that $e_d^\pounds + e_d^\$ < e_{ma} + e_{mb}$. Hence, inequality (5.1) may be satisfied even though the Marshall-Lerner condition, i.e., inequality (5.4), is not satisfied. In other words, the following situation cannot be ruled out: $e_d^\pounds + e_d^\$ < -1 < e_{ma} + e_{mb}$. Accordingly, the Marshall-Lerner condition is not necessary for stability. However, it is a sufficient condition for stability—when inequality (5.4) is satisfied, inequality (5.1) is also satisfied.

Whether the import-demand elasticities are high enough to guarantee stability is an empirical question. Nevertheless, many economists point to the following three factors as an *a priori* justification for their presumption that these elasticities are high. First, as explained in the preceding chapter, the demand for imports is more elastic than the total domestic demand. A very important factor for this is the supply elasticity of domestic production of import substitutes, as explained earlier. Second, the real world consists of many more than two countries which compete on world markets. As a result, the foreign demand for a country's, say A's, exports is not given by the demand for imports by any single country. It is rather given by the excess demand for imports by the rest of the world (i.e., the difference between the aggregate demand by the rest of the world for imports and aggregate supply of exports of A-exportables). Obviously, the elasticity of the excess demand by the rest of the world for imports of A-exportables can be expected to be high—much higher than the elasticity of demand for imports of A-exportables by any single country. Third, as a country's products become cheaper relative to the products of the rest of the world, the dividing line between exportables and importables (and purely domestic goods) is altered. New commodities fall into the category of exportables while the category of importables tends to shrink. This factor tends to make both the demand for imports and supply of exports more elastic than otherwise, a factor which presumably strengthens the presumption that the stability condition is satisfied in practice. But while a higher import-demand elasticity implies a higher elasticity of demand for foreign exchange, a higher export-supply elasticity implies a higher elasticity of demand for domestic currency only if the foreign demand for imports is elastic. If the foreign demand for imports is inelastic, a higher export-supply elasticity implies a lower elasticity of demand for domestic currency, and thus tends to "reduce the stability of the system." As stated at the beginning of this paragraph, the issue here is an empirical one, and only through econometric studies can it be verified whether the stability condition is indeed satisfied.

5.4 UNILATERAL TRANSFERS AND LONG-TERM CAPITAL MOVEMENTS

So far in our analysis of the foreign exchange market we have focused only on commodity exports and imports. In fact, without much violation, we may assume that the preceding analysis covers more generally exports and imports of goods *and* services, i.e., all current account transactions. Even so, our analysis still ignores completely other major categories of transactions, such as unilateral transfers and long-term capital movements, which are also cleared through the foreign exchange market. The main justification for our approach is that unilateral transfers and long-term capital movements are not very responsive to the rate of exchange. Accordingly, they can be introduced into the analysis separately. This is precisely the purpose of the present section.

Introduction of Unilateral Transfer Payments

Suppose that A's residents have to make a series of large annual payments (on a net basis) to B's residents, so that there emerges an additional demand for pounds sterling (or supply of dollars) over and above the demand for pounds sterling arising from A's imports of B-exportables. The purpose of these additional payments, which for simplicity we shall call *transfer payments*, may be investment in B, or settlement of old debts, or a war reparation, or immigrants' transfer payments, or something of the sort. To get the total demand for foreign exchange, we have to add the demand arising from transfer payments to the demand arising from A's imports of B-exportables. The analysis then can proceed as before in terms of the total demand and supply curves for pounds sterling.

It may be objected that the transfer payments will affect the national incomes in the two countries and consequently the supplies and demands for exports and imports, which in turn will affect the supply and demand for pounds sterling arising from exports and imports. Accordingly, the determination of the total demand and supply of foreign exchange in the presence of transfer payments is not an easy matter, as suggested in the preceding paragraph. This is a strong objection indeed, because such income effects do occur and make the transfer mechanism very complicated and at the same time very interesting. In fact, these income effects are studied in detail in chap. 12, after we have better mastered the necessary analytical framework. At present, we abstract from such income effects and concentrate on what may be called the pure price effects of the transfer. Thus, in what follows we assume that the supplies and demands for exports and imports do not shift as a result of the transfer payments.

In general, the autonomous transfer payments may be fixed in dollars, pounds sterling, or in some other way. However, for simplicity it is assumed that these payments are fixed in pounds sterling. In particular, assume that A's residents make the additional transfer payment of £T to B's residents per unit of time. How does this additional demand for pounds sterling affect the equilibrium-exchange rate, the flow of A-exportables from A to B, the flow of B-exportables from B to A, the prices of A-exportables and B-exportables in A and B, A's terms of trade, and the production and consumption levels of A-exportables and B-exportables in A and B?

Consider fig. 5.4. Along the horizontal axis are measured pounds sterling and along the vertical axis, the exchange rate R (i.e., the dollar price of pounds sterling). The solid curves DD' and SS' show the demand and supply for pounds

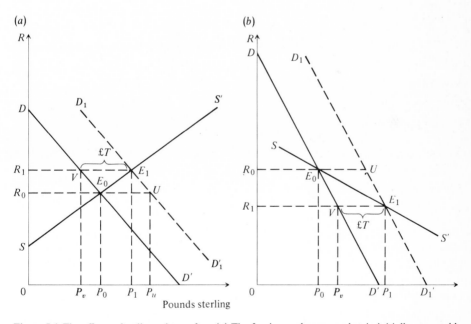

Figure 5.4 The effects of unilateral transfers. (*a*) The foreign exchange market is initially at a stable equilibrium. A unilateral transfer from A to B causes the demand schedule for pounds sterling to shift to the right by the amount of the transfer, as shown by the broken curve through E_1. A's currency depreciates relative to B's (R increases from R_0 to R_1). (*b*) The foreign exchange market is initially at an unstable equilibrium. If the market is at an unstable equilibrium point, such as E_0, before the transfer, the erroneous impression is created that the transferor's currency appreciates relative to the transferee's. Compare points E_0 and E_1. To see that this is wrong, turn to fig. 5.5.

sterling, respectively, arising from exports and imports of goods and services. Thus, when the only economic transactions between A and B are exports and imports of goods and services, equilibrium occurs at E_0 where $0P_0$ pounds sterling are demanded and supplied at $\$R_0$ per pound sterling. Note that panel (a) illustrates the case of a stable equilibrium and panel (b), the case of an unstable equilibrium.

When the transfer payment is introduced, the demand curve for pounds sterling shifts to the broken curve $D_1 D_1'$ and the equilibrium point to E_1. At this new equilibrium, the total amount of pounds sterling supplied by A's exporters and B's importers is given by the distance $0P_1$; the amount of pounds sterling demanded by A's importers and B's exporters, by the distance $0P_v$; and the amount of pounds sterling demanded for net-unilateral transfers, by the distance $P_v P_1$. Thus, $0P_1 = 0P_v + P_v P_1$, that is, A's export revenue = A's expenditure on imports + A's transfers to B. This equation can also be rearranged as follows: $0P_1 - 0P_v = P_v P_1$. That is, A's balance-of-trade surplus is equal to A's transfer payments to B. In other words, the introduction of the transfer payment by A gives rise to a balance-of-trade surplus in A's balance of payments ($\equiv$ deficit in B's balance of payments) equal to A's transfer payment to B. This state of affairs is usually described by saying that the transfer has been totally effected in real terms. That is, while A transfers initially monetary claims to B (monetary transfer), in the end country A makes the transfer in real goods and services (real transfer) by exporting more goods and services to B than B exports to A.

The Effect of Unilateral Transfers on the Rate of Exchange

What is the effect of A's transfer to B on the exchange rate R? A quick glance at fig. 5.4 gives the impression that, if the pre-transfer equilibrium E_0 is stable (panel a), the exchange rate R tends to increase, and if the pre-transfer equilibrium is unstable (panel b), the exchange rate tends to fall. But this conclusion is wrong, for irrespective of whether the pre-transfer equilibrium is stable or unstable, the transfer always gives rise to an excess demand for pounds which always causes the exchange rate to rise. Thus, at the pre-transfer exchange rate R_0, there emerges an excess demand for pounds given by $E_0 U = \pounds T$ in both cases, and the tendency is *always* for the currency of the transferor to depreciate relative to the currency of the transferee. Accordingly, the impression given by the unstable equilibrium of panel (b) is false. But then what actually happens if before the transfer the foreign exchange market happens to be at an unstable equilibrium point?

The mystery is resolved in fig. 5.5. The solid curves are again the pre-transfer supply and demand curves for pounds sterling. Thus, in the pre-transfer situation, there are three equilibria: E_1, E_2, E_3. Two of these equilibria (E_1 and E_3) are stable while the third (E_2) is unstable. When the transfer is introduced the demand curve for pounds sterling shifts to the right, as shown by the broken curve. This gives rise to three new equilibria: E_1', E_2', and E_3'. One may be tempted to say that, if the system is initially at E_i, it will move to E_i' $(i = 1, 2, 3)$. This is true for the stable equilibria (E_1 and E_3) only. The unstable equilibrium E_2 does not follow

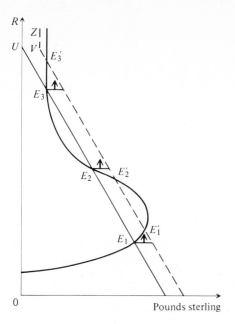

Figure 5.5 The effect of unilateral transfers on the rate of exchange. Whether the initial equilibrium is stable or unstable, the currency of the transferor depreciates relative to the currency of the transferee. Note that all three arrows point upward.

this pattern. If the market is initially at E_2, it will not move to E_2'. It will rather move to E_3'. This should not come as a surprise because E_2' is unstable and the market should not be expected to be driven to it automatically. What actually happens is this. Irrespective of which equilibrium point the foreign exchange market happens to be at before the transfer, the transfer always produces excess demand for pounds and generates a tendency for the exchange rate to rise, as indicated by the arrows in fig. 5.5. Thus, the movement from the unstable equilibrium E_2 is not to the unstable point E_2' but to the next higher stable equilibrium point E_3'.

Other Effects of the Unilateral Transfers

Having established the fact that the transfer causes the currency of the transferor to depreciate relative to the currency of the transferee, the rest of the effects of the transfer are easy to establish. In fact, these effects have already been discussed in chap. 4. For convenience, these effects of the transfer from A to B are briefly summarized below.

1. The prices of A-exportables and B-exportables tend to rise in A (i.e., in dollars) and fall in B (i.e., in pounds sterling).
2. A's production (consumption) of A-exportables and B-exportables expands (contracts). The opposite effects are observed in B.
3. The volume of A-exportables exported from A to B tends to expand, and the volume of B-exportables exported from B to A tends to contract.

4. The effect on A's terms of trade depends on the relationship between the product of the supply elasticities of exports and the product of the demand elasticities for imports of A and B. A's terms of trade improve, deteriorate, or remain the same as the product of the supply elasticities of exports is respectively smaller, larger, or equal to the product of the demand elasticities for imports.

The Upper Limit to the Transfer

Is there an upper limit to the amount of the transfer? Most certainly there is. If the demand curve of fig. 5.5 shifts sufficiently to the right, there might be no possible equilibrium. Surely, this upper limit is nothing else but the maximum excess supply of foreign exchange (excluding the transfer) which may be observed. Making a country pay more than that upper limit would merely result in an endless depreciation of its currency and galloping inflation inside the country.

SELECTED BIBLIOGRAPHY

Chacholiades, M. (1973). *The Pure Theory of International Trade*. Aldine Publishing Company, Chicago, Ill.

(In addition, please see the Selected Bibliography at the end of chap. 6.)

THE FLEXIBLE-EXCHANGE-RATE SYSTEM: II. SIMULTANEOUS EQUILIBRIUM IN THE SPOT AND FORWARD MARKETS

The analysis of the preceding chapter dealt exclusively with the spot market. The present chapter expands that analysis to include the forward market. The object is to study how equilibrium is established simultaneously in the spot and forward markets. For this purpose, it is useful to consider the various transactors in terms of the activities they carry on in the foreign exchange market. Typically these activities are short term in nature and involve commercial trade, speculation, and interest arbitrage. Long-term capital movements (both portfolio and direct investment) as well as unilateral transfers can be incorporated into the analysis later.

The present discussion is based on the following simplifying assumptions: (*a*) all commercial-trade transactions are handled through the spot market; and (*b*) all speculative activity takes place in the forward market. The rationale for this simplification has already been given in chap. 1. Thus, any commercial-trade transaction covered through the forward market can be decomposed into two transactions: spot-covering plus a covered-interest-arbitrage transaction moving funds from the exporter's country to the importer's. Similarly, spot speculation can be decomposed into forward speculation plus a transaction of covered-interest arbitrage. Our simplification then means that the covered-interest-arbitrage component of these compound transactions is lumped with the covered-interest-arbitrage transactions proper.

The reader is urged to review chap. 1 (especially secs. 1.5, 1.6, and 1.7) before proceeding with the present discussion.

6.1 THE SUPPLY SCHEDULE FOR COVERED-INTEREST ARBITRAGE

The link between the spot and forward markets is covered-interest arbitrage. When the equilibrium flow of arbitrage funds is determined the simultaneous equilibrium in the spot and forward markets is also determined. How is the equilibrium flow of arbitrage funds determined? By the law of supply and demand. Accordingly, the first step in our discussion is the development of the supply and demand schedules for covered-interest arbitrage.

We begin with the supply schedule because it is simpler. In fact, it has already been discussed in chap. 1.

The movement of funds from one country to another depends on the rates of return to be realized in the two countries. Because of the exchange risk, these rates of return do not necessarily coincide with the rates of interest of the two countries. As explained in chap. 1, when $r_a > r_b^*$, it is more profitable to invest funds in A; when $r_a < r_b^*$, it is more profitable to invest funds in B; and when $r_a = r_b^*$, the profitability of the two countries is the same. (For the meaning of the symbols the reader is referred back to chap. 1.)

As explained in chap. 1, a positive supply of arbitrage funds from A to B (i.e., a movement of funds from A to B) involves a demand of pounds sterling in the spot market plus a supply of pounds sterling in the forward market. Similarly, a negative supply of arbitrage funds from A to B (i.e., a movement of funds from B to A) involves a supply of pounds sterling in the spot market plus a demand of pounds sterling in the forward market. Also, by the term "supply of arbitrage funds" is meant the *total* supply of funds by both A's and B's residents, including the interest-arbitrage components of transactions by commercial traders and speculators, as explained in chap. 1.

The supply of arbitrage funds between countries A and B may be viewed initially as a function of the difference, $r_b^* - r_a = (1 + r_b)(R_f/R_s) - (1 + r_a)$. But since the interest rates, r_a and r_b, can be taken as parameters which are determined by the monetary authorities, the supply of arbitrage funds may be viewed in the end as a function of the ratio R_f/R_s. This is shown in fig. 6.1. The ratio R_f/R_s is measured along the vertical axis. Along the horizontal axis are measured funds from A to B. (Note that a *negative* amount of funds from A to B actually means a positive amount from B to A.) The curve MUN is an infinitely elastic supply curve of arbitrage funds at $R_f/R_s = 0U$. The vertical distance $0U$ is actually the value of R_f/R_s which satisfies the equation: $r_b^* - r_a = 0$. That is, $0U = R_f/R_s = (1 + r_a)/(1 + r_b)$.

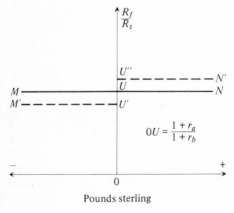

$$0U = \frac{1 + r_a}{1 + r_b}$$

Pounds sterling

Figure 6.1 Supply of arbitrage funds from A to B. The supply of arbitrage funds is, in the first place, a function of the difference $r_b^* - r_a$. However, since the interest rates are treated as parameters, this supply of arbitrage funds is given as a function of the ratio R_f/R_s.

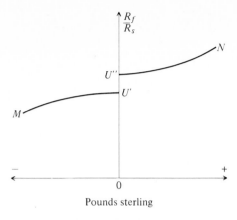

Pounds sterling

Figure 6.2 Supply of arbitrage funds from A to B. As a rule, the supply of arbitrage funds is not unlimited. Therefore, the supply schedule must be drawn upward sloping.

As noted in chap. 1, the supply of funds is not actually perfectly elastic at $R_f/R_s = (1 + r_a)/(1 + r_b)$. When the supply of funds is unlimited but either transaction costs or an arbitrage incentive, or both, are included, the arbitrage supply schedule MUN is distorted to the broken curve $M'U'U''N'$. Thus, unlimited amounts of funds can be supplied from A to B if r_b^* is higher than r_a by a certain margin, say δ. That is, funds move from A to B if $r_b^* = r_a + \delta$, or $R_f/R_s = (1 + r_a + \delta)/(1 + r_b)$. This higher value of R_f/R_s is shown in fig. 6.1 by the vertical distance $0U''$. Similarly, unlimited amounts of funds can be supplied from B to A if r_a is higher than r_b^* by a certain margin. This gives rise to a lower value of R_f/R_s, as shown by the vertical distance $0U'$. Note that the supply of funds is zero for $0U' < R_f/R_s < 0U''$.

So far the amount of funds available for interest-arbitrage purposes has been thought of as unlimited. However, as pointed out in chap. 1, the supply of arbitrage funds is not unlimited and thus the supply schedule of interest-arbitrage funds is not perfectly elastic. Thus, a more realistic supply schedule of arbitrage funds must also take into consideration this aspect of the problem. This is illustrated in fig. 6.2, which is similar to fig. 6.1 except for the shape of the supply function ($MU'U''N$). Note that points U' and U'' have been determined as before for fig. 6.1.

Further note that the supply of arbitrage funds depends crucially on the interest rates of countries A and B. When these interest rates change, the supply curves of figs. 6.1 and 6.2 shift. In particular, when r_a increases (decreases), the supply schedule of arbitrage funds (from A to B) shifts upwards (downwards); and when r_b increases (decreases), the supply schedule shifts downwards (upwards). These propositions can be proved by the reader by studying the effects of interest-rate changes on point U of fig. 6.1.

Finally, the interest rates may be made to depend on the amount of funds moving from one country to another. Such complication would merely affect the shape of the supply curve—it will make it more inelastic. The approach adopted presently is simpler. The supply function is drawn on the assumption that the interest rates assume certain values, and any effect that the flow of funds may have on the interest rates is treated as an independent parametric shift.

The Supply of Arbitrage Funds as a Flow

What is the nature of the supply of arbitrage funds? In particular, is it a supply of a *stock* or a *flow?* This is an important methodological question and deserves a straightforward answer. The relevant literature on the subject treats it as a flow, and this is correct.

It may be objected that the supply of arbitrage funds reflects a desired adjustment in portfolios. That is, given the current spot and forward rates of exchange as well as the rates of interest, portfolio holders determine an optimum composition for their portfolios. The supply of arbitrage funds then reflects the adjustment which is necessary to bring the actual composition in line with the optimum composition of portfolios. Once the divergence between the actual and the optimum composition of portfolios is closed, and for simplicity it may be assumed that this adjustment occurs within one time period, the supply of arbitrage funds drops to zero. Accordingly, it may be argued that the supply of arbitrage funds is a once-and-for-all adjustment to a stock—it is not a flow. But such conclusion is correct as far as it goes. It is true that what is involved is a once-and-for-all portfolio adjustment. But since what is presently involved is a *temporary* transfer of funds from one country to another, to maintain the portfolio adjustment on a *permanent* basis it is necessary to make a new transfer every period. Thus, while the necessary portfolio adjustment must be permanent, the actual adjustment is made for a short time only (say one time period) and has to be renewed at every future time period. For this reason, the supply of arbitrage funds is indeed a supply of a *flow*—not a stock.

6.2 THE DEMAND SCHEDULE FOR COVERED-INTEREST ARBITRAGE

While the concept of supply of arbitrage funds is fairly straightforward, the concept of demand, although implicit in the relevant literature, has not been incorporated explicitly as such in the analysis of the simultaneous equilibrium of the spot and forward markets. The result, of course, of this neglect is the inability to portray graphically the simultaneous equilibrium in the spot and forward markets without making very special and restrictive assumptions. (See, for instance, Sohmen, 1969; Stern, 1973, chap. 2, especially p. 53; and Tsiang, 1959.)

Nature of the Demand for Arbitrage Funds

Where does the demand for arbitrage funds arise from? To answer this question, we must recall that a movement of funds from A to B involves (*a*) a purchase of pounds sterling in the spot market and (*b*) a sale of pounds sterling in the forward market. Accordingly, a demand for arbitrage funds from A to B must reflect an *excess supply* of pounds sterling in the *spot* market (arising from the normal transactions of commercial traders) plus an *excess demand* for pounds sterling in the forward market (arising from the activity of speculators). The arbitrage funds are needed to fill in the gaps, so to speak, created by the activities of nonarbitragers (commercial traders and speculators). Once the excess supply of pounds sterling in the spot market and the excess demand for pounds sterling in the forward market, as determined by the activities of commercial traders and speculators, respectively, are given, a demand schedule for arbitrage funds from A to B can be easily derived. Such a demand schedule will give, at each value of the ratio R_f/R_s, the amount of funds (positive or negative) needed to fill in the gaps between the supply and demand for pounds sterling in both the spot and forward markets.

Derivation of the Demand for Arbitrage Funds

Figure 6.3 illustrates the derivation of the demand curve for arbitrage funds from A to B. Panel (*a*) gives the excess demand curve for pounds sterling in the forward market. This curve reflects all speculative activity. It is derived by summing horizontally the excess demand curves for pounds sterling of all speculators.

It is assumed that each speculator forms some expectations about the future course of the spot rate. When the current forward rate is equal to the expected future spot rate, the speculator's excess demand for pounds is zero. As the current forward rate falls below the expected future spot rate, the speculator demands a positive but finite amount of pounds sterling because he expects to sell it at a higher rate in the future and make a profit. But since the speculator's expectations about the future spot rate are not held with complete confidence, the quantity of pounds sterling demanded by the speculator is not unlimited. In fact, the following reasonable assumption is presently adopted: the lower the current forward rate, the higher the amount of pounds sterling purchased by the speculator. The same analysis, of course, holds for forward rates which are higher than the expected future spot rate. Then the speculator becomes a net supplier of pounds sterling, and the higher the current forward rate, the higher the quantity of pounds sterling supplied by the speculator.

As noted above, the excess demand curve for pounds exhibited in fig. 6.3*a* is the horizontal summation of the excess demand curves for pounds sterling of all speculators. The rate $0H$ is some sort of a weighted average of the expected future spot rates by the various speculators and need not actually coincide with any one of them. Nevertheless, the rate $0H$ may be called the *market* expected future spot rate.

Is the speculators' excess demand a demand for a *flow* or a *stock?* Following the earlier discussion of a similar point in relation to the supply of arbitrage funds, it must be concluded that a flow—not a stock—is involved in the present case as well. The justification for this conclusion is also similar. Given the current and expected rates of foreign exchange, the speculators determine their optimum positions, short or long. The speculators' excess demand then reflects the adjustment which is necessary to bring their current positions in line with their optimum positions. But since the adjustment to their current positions is of a short duration

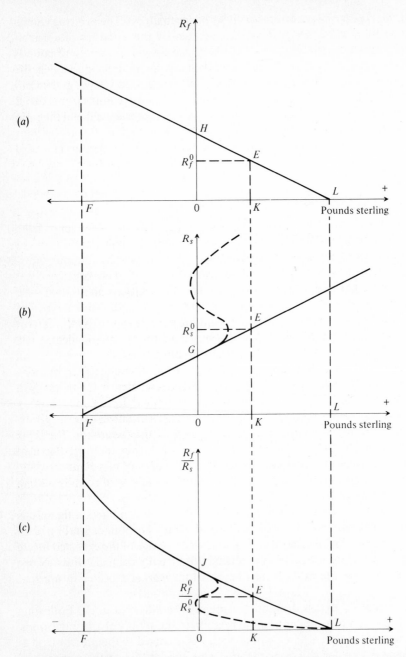

Figure 6.3 The demand curve for arbitrage funds from A to B (c) is derived from the excess demand for pounds sterling for speculative activity in the forward market (a) and the excess supply of pounds sterling for commercial trade in the spot market (b).

(one time period), such adjustment must be repeated at each and every period, unless, of course, expectations change.

Consider now fig. 6.3*b*. It shows the excess supply of pounds sterling in the spot market arising from the activities of commercial traders. This supply curve is drawn sloping upwards throughout its length. This was considered necessary in order to simplify the present discussion. Actually, as we have seen earlier in this book, this excess supply curve will normally bend backwards and intersect the vertical axis more than once, as illustrated by the broken curve in panel (*b*).

Clearly, the excess supply of pounds sterling in the spot market is a *flow*. As we have seen earlier, it is derived from the *flows* of exports and imports of goods and services. Actually, the flow of goods and services between countries is not the only source for the excess supply of pounds sterling in the spot market during the current period. There is an additional source: the amount of pounds sterling (positive or negative) which the speculators had bought forward one period earlier. This is clarified in the next section. For the moment, it is assumed that no earlier forward commitments are falling due.

We are now ready to derive the demand curve for arbitrage funds from A to B. This is done in fig. 6.3*c*. For any arbitrary amount of arbitrage funds moving from A to B, such as $0K$, determine the respective equilibrium rates in the spot and forward markets, such as R_s^0 and R_f^0. (Note that the problem of interest earnings which have to be sold forward as well is presently ignored for simplicity.) This information is sufficient to determine point E on the demand curve for arbitrage funds in panel (*c*). Repeating the same experiment for all other possible values (positive and negative) of arbitrage funds, the whole demand curve may be traced out as shown in panel (*c*).

The demand curve for arbitrage funds reflects the properties of the excess demand for pounds sterling in the spot and forward markets by nonarbitragers. Thus, the demand curve for arbitrage funds (panel *c*) and the excess demand for pounds sterling in the forward market intersect the horizontal axis at the same distance, $0L$. In addition, the demand curve for arbitrage funds becomes vertical when the excess supply for pounds sterling in the spot market intersects the horizontal axis. Further, any twists in the shape of the excess supply curve in the spot market (panel *b*) will be reflected in the shape of the demand curve for arbitrage funds (panel *c*), as illustrated by the broken curves. Finally, note that the demand curve for arbitrage funds is independent of the interest rates in the two countries.

6.3 THE ELASTICITY OF DEMAND FOR ARBITRAGE FUNDS

Theorem 6.1 The elasticity of demand for arbitrage funds is higher, the higher is the elasticity of the excess demand for pounds sterling in the spot or forward markets.

PROOF Let us adopt the following symbols:

$F \equiv$ arbitrage funds moving from A to B

$g(R_s) \equiv$ excess demand for pounds sterling in the spot market

$h(R_f) \equiv$ excess demand for pounds sterling in the forward market

At every point on the demand curve for arbitrage funds (fig. 6.3c) we have:

$$F = -g(R_s) = h(R_f) \tag{6.1}$$

The demand elasticity for pounds sterling spot (e_s) is, by definition,

$$e_s \equiv \frac{g'R_s}{-g} \tag{6.2}$$

Similarly, the demand elasticity for pounds sterling forward (e_f) is given by

$$e_f \equiv \frac{h'R_f}{h} \tag{6.3}$$

(The arguments of the functions $g(R_s)$ and $h(R_f)$ have been ignored for simplicity, and primes have been used to indicate differentiation.)

Finally, the elasticity of demand for arbitrage funds (e_a) is given by

$$
\begin{aligned}
e_a &\equiv \left| \frac{dF}{d(R_f/R_s)} \right| \left(\frac{R_f/R_s}{F} \right) \\
&= \left(\frac{R_s^2 dF}{R_s\, dR_f - R_f\, dR_s} \right) \left(\frac{R_f/R_s}{F} \right) \\
&= \frac{1}{(1/e_f) + (1/e_s)} \tag{6.4}
\end{aligned}
$$

From eq. 6.4, it follows that the higher e_f or e_s is, the higher e_a is.

6.4 SIMULTANEOUS EQUILIBRIUM

Having derived the supply and demand curves for arbitrage funds, we can use them to determine equilibrium in both the spot and forward markets simultaneously. In this effort great care must be exercised, because one period's equilibrium has repercussions on future periods. It is a pity that this aspect of the problem is not brought out explicitly in the literature, although it is often recognized as an afterthought.

Short-Run Equilibria

Consider fig. 6.4. For the moment, ignore the broken curves. This figure is similar to fig. 6.3 except that now the supply schedule of arbitrage funds $(MU'U''N)$ has been added in panel (c). Evidently, equilibrium occurs at E_1 (panel c) where the

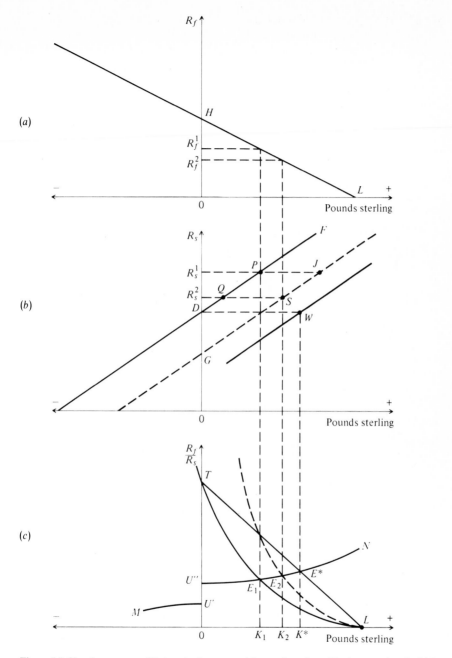

Figure 6.4 Simultaneous equilibrium in the spot and forward markets. The intersection E_1 (c) between the supply and demand curves for arbitrage funds determines a simultaneous, short-run equilibrium in the spot and forward markets. Long-run simultaneous equilibrium occurs at E^* where the auxiliary demand curve TE^*L intersects the supply curve $U''N$.

supply and demand schedules for arbitrage funds intersect. Thus, the amount of $0K_1$ (panel c) pounds sterling are transferred from A to B, as the spot and forward rates assume the equilibrium values R_s^1 and R_f^1, respectively, as shown in panels (a) and (b).

Can the equilibrium at E_1 last for more than one period? Certainly not. The reason is simple. In the following period, the excess supply schedule in the spot market will necessarily shift to the right by the amount of pounds sterling sold forward by the speculators in the current period, that is, $0K_1$. Thus, at the end of the current period (or at the beginning of the next period) the interest arbitragers will essentially exchange their accumulated funds in pounds sterling for the speculators' dollars—this is called for by their current forward contracts. But while the interest arbitragers' portfolios assume at that time the composition they originally had at the beginning of the current period, and, therefore, the interest arbitragers stand ready to go through another cycle, the portfolios of the speculators have more pounds sterling and fewer dollars compared with their composition at the beginning of the current period. Since the intention of the speculators was not to acquire pounds sterling spot, but merely to speculate in the forward market, they will have to sell their new acquisitions of pounds sterling $(0K_1)$ in the spot market. Then they will stand ready again to begin a new cycle of forward speculation.

The preceding analysis is illustrated in fig. 6.4 by the broken curves. Start with the first period's equilibrium at E_1. In the second period, the excess supply schedule for pounds sterling in the spot market (panel b) shifts to the right by the amount $0K_1$, as shown by the broken curve GJ. Accordingly, the demand schedule for arbitrage funds (panel c) shifts upward and to the right, as shown by the broken curve E_2L. Thus, in the second period, equilibrium occurs at E_2 where $0K_2$ pounds sterling are transferred from A to B, and the spot and forward equilibrium rates are, respectively, R_s^2 and R_f^2. (Actually, the balance of payments for the second period will register only the difference $K_1 K_2$ as a short-term capital movement from A to B. The flow of $0K_1$ is registered in the first period.)

In the same way that the first period's equilibrium could not persist at E_1, the second period's equilibrium cannot persist at E_2 either. In the third period, the excess supply of pounds sterling schedule, GJ, will shift further to the right by the additional amount $K_1 K_2$. (Alternatively, we could refer back to the initial excess supply schedule DF and observe that in the third period it shifts to the right by the amount $0K_2$.) Accordingly, in future periods, equilibrium will continue to move northeast along the supply of arbitrage schedule (panel c), and additional funds will continue to flow from A to B. Does this process ever come to an end? Yes, indeed. In fact, the system may be expected to converge to a state of long-run equilibrium rather rapidly, assuming that no further disturbances (such as changes in expectations) occur.

Long-Run Equilibrium

In the present context, long-run equilibrium may be defined as a state which can exist forever unless it is disturbed by some exogenous force, such as a shift in expectations, a shift in a country's supply of exports or demand for imports, or a shift in the supply of arbitrage funds brought about by a change in interest rates. Such a state of affairs exists only when the balance of trade is zero. (Long-term capital movements and unilateral transfers are presently assumed away.) This becomes obvious when one notices that, during any time period, the amount of additional funds transferred from one country to another equals the transferor's balance-of-trade surplus. For instance, referring back to fig. 6.4, it can easily be verified that $0K_1 = R_s^1 P$ and $K_1 K_2 = R_s^2 Q$. Accordingly, the system settles down to a long-run equilibrium when the excess supply schedule in the spot market ceases to shift to the right. This happens when the balance of trade, and thus the flow of additional funds, drops to zero. In terms of fig. 6.4, long-run equilibrium occurs only when the spot rate assumes the value $0D$.

How is long-run equilibrium determined? Go back to fig. 6.4 and imagine that the excess supply schedule in the spot market (panel b) is infinitely elastic (i.e., horizontal) through point D. On the basis of that excess supply schedule draw, in panel (c), a demand schedule for arbitrage funds as before. This is shown by the broken curve TE^*L. Long-run equilibrium is indicated by point E^*, where the auxiliary demand schedule for arbitrage funds intersects the original supply schedule. At E^* the spot rate is necessarily equal to $0D$; A's balance of trade is zero; the speculators buy forward and sell spot $0K^*$ pounds sterling in every period; and the interest arbitragers buy spot and sell forward $0K^*$ pounds sterling in every period.

The technique used to determine the long-run equilibrium point E^* by generating an auxiliary demand schedule for arbitrage funds has general validity. It can be used to determine even a short-run equilibrium point when the excess supply schedule of pounds sterling in the spot market (panel b) is unknown but the equilibrium spot rate is known.

Stability of Long-Run Equilibrium

Is the long-run equilibrium point E^* stable? Will the system be driven to it automatically? The answer is "Yes."

First note that, starting with the initial equilibrium at E_1, the additional flow of funds from A to B is positive but diminishing in every future period. For instance, for the first two periods, it must be true that $0K_1 > K_1 K_2 > 0$. A similar inequality must hold for every other pair of consecutive time periods.

That $K_1 K_2 > 0$ follows from the fact that in the second period the speculators' sale (spot) of the pounds sterling ($0K_1$) which they had bought forward one period earlier causes the demand schedule for arbitrage funds to shift upward and to the right, implying a larger volume of short-term lending from A to B than the first period's volume. Since $0K_2 > 0K_1$, it must be true also that $K_1 K_2 > 0$. A similar reasoning holds for all other future periods.

Consider now the inequality $0K_1 > K_1 K_2$. If $K_1 K_2$ were equal to $0K_1$, the quantity $R_s^1 J$ (panel b) of arbitrage funds would be demanded at least at $R_f / R_s = K_1 E_1$ (panel c). But since the speculators' excess demand schedule for pounds sterling forward is not infinitely elastic, the quantity $R_s^1 J$ is demanded at a lower value of the ratio R_f/R_s than $K_1 E_1$. This result by itself necessarily implies that $0K_2 < R_s^1 J$. Hence, $0K_1 > K_1 K_2$, since $R_s^1 J = 0K_1 + 0K_1$ and $0K_2 = 0K_1 + K_1 K_2$.

So far we have seen that there must exist a positive (and diminishing) additional flow of funds in all future periods. But how do we know that the accumulated lending from A to B will not be higher than $0K^*$ beyond a certain future period? To understand the impossibility of this state of affairs, simply recall that a positive flow of *additional* lending in any period corresponds to a surplus in A's balance of trade and therefore a spot rate of exchange higher than $0D$. But applying the technique we used earlier to determine long-run equilibrium, it becomes evident that for any spot rate higher than $0D$ the total accumulated lending from A to B must be smaller than $0K^*$.

We therefore conclude that the long-run equilibrium point E^* is indeed stable, assuming that all assumptions made earlier remain valid.

An equilibrium point such as E^* can be a true long-run equilibrium point only if an additional condition is satisfied, namely, $R_f = R_s$. Thus, unless $R_f = R_s$, the speculators will sooner or later realize (unless they are extremely naive, which is doubtful) that the future spot rate is equal to the current spot rate and they will revise their expectations accordingly. Thus, the adjustment process has this additional dimension, and depending on the reactions of the speculators a long-run equilibrium may be established quickly or never.

Departure from Interest Parity

Before moving to the next topics, there are several interesting observations that need to be made. First, unless the supply of arbitrage funds is infinitely elastic, interest parity never prevails. In fact, assuming an upward-sloping supply schedule, as in fig. 6.4, the divergence between the forward difference and the interest-rate differential tends to become bigger and bigger as the *accumulated* short-term lending from one country to another increases.

Interaction Among Interest Arbitrage, Commercial Trade, and Speculation

Next consider the question of what activity is primarily responsible for short-term lending between countries. A hasty answer would be: interest arbitrage. Obviously interest arbitragers are the ones who actually effect the transfer of funds between countries, but interest arbitragers cannot act independently of speculators and commercial traders. In the first place, as has been repeatedly mentioned earlier, the flow of additional funds from A to B during any time period corresponds to a surplus in A's balance of trade. That is, commercial trade must make the foreign exchange available to interest arbitragers before the latter can undertake the transfer. But this is not all. Transferring funds from one country to another involves an exchange risk. Somebody must assume that risk; otherwise the transfer of funds cannot be effected. This is where the speculators come in. While the commercial traders make the necessary foreign exchange available to the interest arbitragers, the speculators assume the exchange risk. Accordingly, the activities of commercial traders and speculators accommodate the activities of the interest arbitragers. In the final analysis, it is the three activities of speculation, commercial trade, and interest arbitrage which are simultaneously responsible for short-term lending between countries. The reader can test his understanding of this proposition by referring back to fig. 6.4 and eliminating one activity from the system at a time.

6.5 COMPARATIVE STATICS

The present section considers briefly the comparative statics of three important disturbances to the long-run equilibrium established in fig. 6.4. These cases are: (*a*) a change in speculative expectations; (*b*) a series of annual unilateral transfer payments from A to B; and (*c*) a change in the interest rate of a country. In each of these cases two things will be done. First, the new long-run equilibrium will be determined and compared with the initial equilibrium; and, second, a glimpse into the adjustment process will be offered.

Effects of a Shift in Speculative Expectations

Consider fig. 6.5. It shows a long-run equilibrium at E similar to that of fig. 6.4c. (The other two panels of fig. 6.4 relating to the spot and forward markets are now dropped as unnecessary.) The curves UN and MEL are the initial supply and demand schedules, respectively, for arbitrage funds from A to B. The curve JEL is merely the initial auxiliary demand schedule needed for the purpose of determining the long-run equilibrium point E. At E, country A is lending 0K pounds to B.

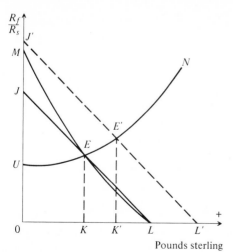

Figure 6.5 The effects of unilateral transfers and shifts in speculative expectations. As the speculators revise upward their expected value of the future spot rate, the auxiliary demand curve for arbitrage funds (*JEL*) shifts upward to *J'E'L* causing (long-run) equilibrium to shift from E to E'. Similarly, a unilateral transfer from A to B causes the auxiliary demand curve for arbitrage funds to shift downward from, say, *J'E'L* to *JEL*. Thus, the transfer prompts a short-term capital inflow into A given by *KK'*.

This lending is renewed period after period and no capital movements are registered in the balance of payments. The balance of trade is also zero.

Assume now that for some reason, rational or irrational, the speculators revise upward their expected value of the future spot rate. How does this change in speculative expectations affect the current long-run equilibrium? The answer is given in fig. 6.5. The upward revision of speculative expectations results in an upward shift of the speculators' excess demand schedule for pounds sterling forward (not shown), which causes the auxiliary demand curve for arbitrage funds (*JEL*) to shift upward also, as illustrated in fig. 6.5 by the broken curve *J'E'L'*. Accordingly, long-run equilibrium shifts from E to E', assuming, of course, that no further shift in speculative expectations takes place. At the new equilibrium, the accumulated volume of lending by A to B has increased from 0K to 0K', but the spot rate is still at the original level and the balance of trade is still zero. The forward rate is necessarily higher at E' than at E simply because the ratio R_f/R_s is higher at E'. Accordingly, the mere expectation for a higher future spot rate causes the forward rate to rise.

Of course, during the adjustment process from E to E' the spot rate rises too. This is necessary in order to generate a temporary surplus in A's balance of trade to finance A's additional lending (*KK'*) to B. But the rise in the spot rate is only temporary. Such a once-and-for-all change in speculative expectations cannot have a permanent effect on the balance of trade. Nevertheless, if such shifts in speculative expectations occur rather frequently, the foreign-trade sectors of the trading countries will be subjected to a continuous and wasteful readjustment.

The exact increase in A's accumulated lending to B (*KK'*) depends on two factors: (*a*) the demand elasticity of the auxiliary demand schedule for arbitrage funds, which necessarily coincides with the demand elasticity of the speculators' demand schedule for pounds sterling forward; and (*b*) the supply elasticity of the supply schedule for arbitrage funds. The higher these elasticities are, the higher the additional amount of lending from A to B is.

Effects of Unilateral Transfers

The long-run (price) effects of unilateral transfers have been analyzed in the preceding chapter. What remains to be done presently is to show that, during the adjustment process until a new long-run equilibrium is attained, short-term capital movements (in the absence of elastic speculative expectations), in the opposite direction to the transfer, reduce the need to effect all of the transfer in real terms.

Figure 6.5 illustrates the present case as well. Assume that the pre-transfer auxiliary demand schedule for arbitrage funds is given by the broken curve *J'E'L'* and that long-run equilibrium occurs initially at E'. A unilateral transfer from A to B causes the excess supply curve in the spot market (fig. 6.4*b*) to shift upward and to the left. Thus, the long-run equilibrium spot rate increases and causes the auxiliary demand schedule for arbitrage funds to shift downward, say to the solid curve *JEL*. A's total lending to B falls from 0K' to 0K. Thus the distance KK' shows the (total) short-term capital inflow into A prompted by the transfer itself. Accordingly, the spot rate does not rise quickly to the higher equilibrium level. On the contrary, during the initial time periods following the transfer, the spot rate starts rising gradually and generates a surplus in A's balance of trade which is only a fraction of the annual transfer. The gap is, of course, filled by the temporary short-term capital flow from B to A, which over time grows smaller and smaller and eventually disappears, making room for a balance-of-trade surplus equal to the annual transfer.

The preceding analysis may have to be amended only slightly if speculators, anticipating the rise in the spot rate, adjust their expectations appropriately.

Effects of Interest-Rate Changes

Consider fig. 6.6, which is similar to fig. 6.5. Long-run equilibrium occurs initially at E. Suppose that country A raises its interest rate. As shown earlier, the increase in A's interest rate causes the supply schedule of arbitrage funds to shift upward from UN to $U'N'$. Long-run equilibrium shifts from E to E', and A gains a total short-term capital inflow equal to $K'K$. This latter amount (KK') is actually spread over several future periods. A's capital inflow is made possible by a temporary deficit in A's balance of trade as the spot rate is temporarily depressed below its long-run equilibrium level. The forward rate, though, is pushed gradually to a higher level which it maintains until something else disturbs the system again. The reason why the forward rate permanently assumes a higher level is, of course, the fact that A's total short-term lending to B is now lower.

Similar effects can be traced out for a *reduction* in B's interest rate also. However, an increase in B's interest rate or a reduction in A's interest rate have diametrically opposite effects to those described for an increase in A's interest rate.

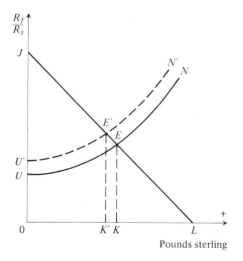

Figure 6.6 The effects of interest-rate changes. When country A (B) raises its interest rate, the supply schedule of arbitrage funds shifts upward (downward).

6.6 STABILIZING AND DESTABILIZING SPECULATION

Does speculation tend to depress or amplify exchange-rate fluctuations through time? This is an extremely important question. On it depends the success or failure of the flexible-exchange-rate system. To simplify the exposition, it is presently assumed that the spot and forward markets are combined into a single foreign exchange market.

Speculation is called *stabilizing* when it depresses exchange-rate variations and *destabilizing* when it amplifies them. This is illustrated in fig. 6.7. By assumption, the curve *CF* describes a sinewave pattern which the exchange rate follows *in the absence of speculation* (and, therefore, in the absence of short-term capital movements). Presumably this cyclical behavior of the exchange rate reflects the influence of cyclical factors on the foreign-trade sectors. The broken curves *CS* and *CD* show how the exchange rate would fluctuate in the presence of stabilizing and destabilizing speculation, respectively.

If speculators had perfect foresight and their transaction costs were zero, speculation would stabilize perfectly the exchange rate as shown by the horizontal line *CE*. The speculators would stand ready to sell foreign exchange whenever the rate rose above 0*C* and they would stand ready to buy foreign exchange whenever the rate fell below 0*C*. Their purchases and sales of foreign exchange would cancel over a whole cycle, and their profits would be zero. These results are guaranteed by perfect competition.

Unfortunately, perfect foresight never exists. Speculators merely form expectations regarding the future course of the rate of exchange, and on the basis of these expectations and the current rate they decide whether to buy or sell and how much. Thus, speculative expectations lie at the heart of speculative activity. When expectations are formed correctly, speculation is stabilizing. Otherwise, speculation is destabilizing.

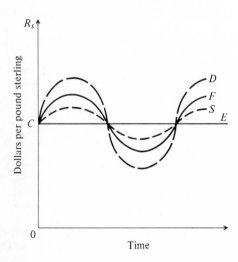

Figure 6.7 Stabilizing and destabilizing speculation, which distort the behavior of the exchange rate from *CF* to *CS* and *CD*, respectively.

Expectations are called *inelastic* when they are formed independently of the current rate or changes in it; they are called *elastic* when changes in the current rate cause the expected future rate to change in the same direction. Inelastic and elastic expectations are *not* synonymous with stabilizing and destabilizing speculation, respectively.

Refer back to fig. 6.7, where 0C is by assumption the long-run equilibrium rate of exchange. Start at time zero. The current rate is 0C and begins to rise. If expectations are formed correctly and speculators expect the rate to return to 0C in the near future, speculation will be stabilizing. Thus, speculators will sell foreign exchange and they will prevent the rate from rising too much (see curve CS). By their activity, the speculators induce a short-term capital inflow which fills the gap (deficit) in A's balance of trade caused by the fact that the rate of exchange was not allowed to rise sufficiently. This short-term capital movement prompted by stabilizing speculation is very desirable, because it minimizes the need for switching resources back and forth. Such switching of resources is obviously wasteful and undesirable.

What happens when expectations are not formed correctly? Suppose again that the rate starts rising from its long-run equilibrium value 0C. Assume that speculators interpret the rise in the current rate as a signal that the rate will go higher. Speculators now *buy* foreign exchange in the hope of selling it in the future at a higher rate. These speculative purchases intensify the rise in the current rate (see curve CD). A's balance of trade now shows a surplus which makes possible a short-term capital flow to B. Accordingly, in the present case, the speculative activity amplifies the initial increase in the current rate and induces a short-term capital flow in the *wrong direction*. The cushioning effect of a desirable short-term capital movement which, as we saw earlier, occurs under stabilizing speculation is totally removed and in fact reversed under destabilizing speculation. The wasteful reallocation of resources which is mitigated under stabilizing speculation is aggravated under destabilizing speculation.

Speculation Under Flexible-Exchange Rates

How does speculation actually behave under flexible-exchange rates? This is an extremely important question. If speculation is actually stabilizing, the case for flexible-exchange rates is strengthened. If speculation is destabilizing, the case for flexible-exchange rates is weakened.

Friedman (1953, p. 175) has a powerful theoretical argument that speculation must be stabilizing. He claims that: "People who argue that speculation is generally destabilizing seldom realize that this is largely equivalent to saying that speculators lose money, since speculation can be destabilizing in general only if speculators on the average sell when the currency is low in price and buy when it is high." Thus, according to Friedman, speculators will continue in the business only so long as it is profitable. This will be the case if they buy cheap and sell dear. But to buy cheap and sell dear is to stabilize.

Friedman's analysis has provoked an interesting controversy as to whether profitable speculation is necessarily stabilizing. Counterexamples against Friedman's thesis have been given by Baumol (1957), Kemp (1963), and Stein (1961). For a review of this controversy the reader is referred to Sohmen (1969, chap. 3), Stern (1973, chap. 3), and Yeager (1966, chap. 11).

The question of whether speculation is stabilizing or destabilizing cannot be settled by recourse to theoretical arguments. Although there may be a presumption that speculation is stabilizing, the question is at bottom an empirical one.

6.7 OFFICIAL INTERVENTION IN THE FOREIGN EXCHANGE MARKET

Stabilizing speculation performs a socially useful function: it irons out temporary fluctuations in the exchange rate and thereby achieves a better allocation of resources over time. Destabilizing speculation, on the other hand, aggravates the fluctuations in the exchange rate and interferes with the optimum allocation of resources over time. How can the ills of destabilizing speculation be cured?

It is often thought that the monetary authorities can control destabilizing speculation by intervening directly in the foreign exchange market. (For the discussion of the present section assume again that the spot and forward markets are combined into a single foreign exchange market.) For this purpose, the monetary authorities may operate an *exchange-equalization fund*, which in principle accommodates all destabilizing speculation. That is, when destabilizing speculation causes the rate of exchange to rise (fall) beyond its long-run equilibrium level, the fund sells (buys) foreign exchange. These purchases and sales of foreign exchange by the fund iron out temporary fluctuations in the rate of exchange caused by destabilizing speculation.

Official intervention may even go a step further. The authorities may attempt not only to offset the undesirable effects of destabilizing speculation but in addition they may pursue an active policy to iron out fluctuations due to other temporary, seasonal, or cyclical factors. Nevertheless, the flexible-exchange-rate system will function smoothly if more permanent and fundamental rate trends are not resisted.

The idea of official intervention in the foreign exchange market is very attractive. In effect, it represents a compromise between fixed and free rates—but a different compromise than the adjustable peg system to be discussed in chap. 8. Unfortunately, in its practical application official intervention faces difficult problems.

The activities of the fund would tend to iron out temporary fluctuations only if the managers of the fund could anticipate correctly the future course of exchange rates. The first problem, therefore, relates to the ability of the managers of the fund relative to the ability of private speculators to predict future movements correctly. Hindsight is not enough. Can the managers of the fund distinguish any better than private speculators between temporary and permanent rate movements? Is there any reason to believe that government officials possess perfect foresight while private speculators do not? There seems to be no compelling reason why this should be so. Besides, if the managers of the fund did actually possess the quality of perfect foresight, they could speculate as private parties and make handsome profits. But in that case, private speculation would be stabilizing and there would be no need for official intervention anyway.

It may be that government officials can predict the future better than private speculators only because the former have access to information that is not available to the latter. In that case intervention would be justified only if the information could not be made public for security or similar reasons. Even in this exceptional case, intervention should be restricted to smoothing out temporary fluctuations.

A second difficulty with official intervention is the danger that the initial policy of ironing out unwarranted fluctuations may gradually drift into a policy of actually pegging the exchange rate, thereby converting a flexible-rate system into the adjustable-peg system.

A third and final difficulty with official intervention is that, under the disguise of ironing out unwarranted fluctuations, the authorities may manipulate the rate of exchange to achieve other objectives, such as full employment, at the expense of other countries. Thus, a country in balance-of-payments equilibrium and wide unemployment may force its currency to depreciate. The depreciation of the domestic currency generates a balance-of-trade surplus which in turn stimulates the domestic economy, as explained later in chap. 11. However, the country's unemployment is reduced at the expense of other countries whose unemployment worsens as their balances of trade deteriorate. In effect, by depreciating its domestic currency that country exports its unemployment to other countries. This is clearly a beggar-thy-neighbor policy. As such, it will most probably provoke retaliation and set the stage for competitive depreciation.

The preceding discussion points to a rather negative conclusion regarding official intervention in the foreign exchange market: official intervention to iron out temporary fluctuations in the exchange rate may do more harm than good. If this is true, the flexible-exchange-rate system can function smoothly if, and only if, destabilizing speculation is not present.

SELECTED BIBLIOGRAPHY

Baumol, W. J. (1957). "Speculation, Profitability, and Stability." *Review of Economics and Statistics*, vol. XXXIX (August), pp. 263–271.

Canterbury, E. R. (1971). "A Theory of Foreign Exchange Speculation Under Alternative Systems." *Journal of Political Economy* (May–June), pp. 407–436.

Caves, R. E. (1963). "Flexible Exchange Rates." *American Economic Review* (May), pp. 120–129.

Chacholiades, M. (1973). *The Pure Theory of International Trade*. Aldine Publishing Company, Chicago, Ill.

Friedman, M. (1953). "The Case for Flexible Exchange Rates." In *Essays in Positive Economics*. University of Chicago Press, Chicago, Ill. Reprinted in AEA, *Readings in International Economics*. Richard D. Irwin, Inc., Chicago, Ill., 1968.

Johnson, H. G. (1970). "The Case for Flexible Exchange Rates, 1969." In G. N. Halm (Ed.), *Approaches to Greater Flexibility of Exchange Rates*. Princeton University Press, Princeton, N.J.

Kemp, M. C. (1963). "Speculation, Profitability, and Price Stability." *Review of Economics and Stastics*, vol. XLV (May), pp. 185–189.

Kindleberger, C. P. (1939). "Speculation and Forward Exchange." *Journal of Political Economy*, vol. XLVII, no. 2 (April), pp. 163–181.

———— (1966). "Flexible Exchange Rates." In *Europe and the Dollar*. The MIT Press, Cambridge, Mass.

Lerner, A. P. (1944). *The Economics of Control*. The Macmillan Company, New York.

Machlup, F. (1970). "The Forward Exchange Market: Misunderstandings Between Practitioners and Economists." In G. N. Halm (Ed.), *Approaches to Greater Flexibility of Exchange Rates*. Princeton University Press, Princeton, N.J.

Marshall, A. (1923). *Money, Credit and Commerce*. Macmillan and Company, London.

Meade, J. E. (1951). *The Theory of International Economic Policy*, vol. I, *The Balance of Payments*. Oxford University Press, Inc., New York, chap. XVII.

———— (1955). "The Case for Variable Exchange Rates." *Three Banks Review* (September), pp. 3–27.

Samuelson, P. A. (1971). "On the Trail of Conventional Beliefs About the Transfer Problem." In J. N. Bhagwati, R. W. Jones, R. A. Mundell, and J. Vanek (Eds.), *Trade, Balance of Payments, and Growth: Papers in International Economics in Honor of Charles P. Kindleberger*. North-Holland Publishing Company, Amsterdam.

Sohmen, E. (1969). *Flexible Exchange Rates*, revised ed. The University of Chicago Press, Chicago, Ill.

Stein, J. L. (1961). "Destabilizing Speculative Activity Can Be Profitable." *Review of Economics and Statistics*, vol. XLIII (August), pp. 301–302.

Stern, R. M. (1973). *The Balance of Payments*. Aldine Publishing Company, Chicago, Ill.

Telser, L. G. (1959). "A Theory of Speculation Relating Profitability and Stability," and "Reply" by W. J. Baumol. *Review of Economics and Statistics*, vol. XLI (August), pp. 295–301.

Tsiang, S. C. (1959). "The Theory of Forward Exchange and Effects of Government Intervention on the Forward Exchange Market." *International Monetary Fund Staff Papers* (April), pp. 75–106.

Williamson, J. (1973). "Another Case of Profitable Destabilizing Speculation." *Journal of International Economics*, vol. 3, no. 1 (February), pp. 77–84.

Yeager, L. B. (1966). *International Monetary Relations*. Harper and Row, New York, chaps. 8 and 11.

THE FIXED-EXCHANGE-RATE SYSTEM:
I. THE GOLD STANDARD

This and the following chapter deal with the fixed-exchange-rate system. In particular, the present chapter deals with the *gold standard* and the following chapter with the *adjustable peg*. The present discussion is restricted to the analysis of how these systems work in the short run. The analysis of long-run adjustment is undertaken later in parts two and three of this book.

7.1 THE RULES OF THE GAME

Under the regime of the gold standard the monetary authorities of all gold-standard countries must obey certain rules of the game. These rules are:

1. The monetary authorities of each country must establish once and for all the gold value of their national currency.
2. There must be free movement of gold among the gold-standard countries.
3. The monetary authorities of each country must tie their domestic money supply to their stock of gold reserves. As the gold reserves increase (decrease) through a persistent inflow (outflow) of gold, the monetary authorities must allow their money supply to increase (decrease).

To implement the first rule, the monetary authorities may adopt any one of the following three mechanisms:

1. *The gold-specie standard.* Under this regime, the actual currency in circulation consists of gold coins of a certain fixed gold content. The coins of the various countries are freely minted at standard rates and freely meltable and exportable.
2. *The gold-bullion standard.* Under this regime, the basis of each local money remains some fixed weight of gold but the actual currency in circulation consists of notes. The monetary authorities of each country stand ready to exchange unlimited amounts of notes for gold and vice versa at fixed prices (gold convertibility).
3. *The gold-exchange standard.* Under this regime, the monetary authorities undertake to buy and sell at fixed prices the money (e.g., notes) of some other country which is operating a gold-specie or gold-bullion standard.

The effect of gold movements on a country's money supply depends on the nature of the banking system. The study of banking systems is a complicated subject. However, for our purposes it is sufficient to note that all systems fall into one of the following three categories:

1. *The 100 percent-money principle.* According to this principle, the money supply is always equal to the gold reserve. Gold movements induce changes in the money supply on a one-to-one basis. It is immaterial whether gold coins of standard specification, or gold certificates with 100 percent gold backing, actually form the circulating medium of exchange.
2. *The fiduciary-issue principle.* According to this principle, the money supply consists of two parts: (*a*) a fixed amount called the *fiduciary* issue which is not backed by gold and (*b*) an amount which is backed by gold 100 percent. Thus, the gold reserve is always less than the total money supply by the fixed-fiduciary issue, but changes in the gold reserve give rise to changes in the money supply on a one-to-one basis, as in the case of the 100 percent-money principle. One danger of the fiduciary-issue principle is that the monetary authorities may run out of gold before the money supply decreases sufficiently to correct a persistent deficit.
3. *The fractional-reserve principle.* According to this principle, the gold reserve is only a fraction of the total money supply and, in addition, any changes in the gold reserve are also less than the consequential changes in the money supply. The simplest case of this principle is when the gold reserve is always a certain fraction (say one-fifth) of the money supply.

7.2 MINT PARITY

The essence of an international gold standard where all countries tie their monies to gold and allow the unrestricted import and export of gold is that the rates of foreign exchange are fixed.

Consider again the model of two countries, A (America) and B (Britain). Suppose that A's and B's monetary authorities declare that they stand ready to buy and sell unlimited amounts of gold at $\$x$ and $\pounds y$, respectively, per ounce of gold of certain specified purity. As a first approximation, assume also that gold can be transported from one country to another in a costless fashion. Then *gold arbitrage* will necessarily establish the following equality: $\$x = \pounds y$, or $\pounds 1 = \$(x/y)$. That is, in the foreign exchange market 1 pound sterling must be selling for $\$(x/y)$. The rate of (x/y) dollars per pound sterling is usually called the *mint rate* or *mint parity*. How is the mint parity established in the foreign exchange market?

Suppose that the current rate of exchange (R_0) is higher than the mint rate (R_m). Then gold arbitragers can make a profit by buying, with dollars, gold from A's monetary authorities and selling it to B's monetary authorities for pounds sterling. Each pound sterling costs them $\$R_m$ and they can sell it in the foreign exchange market at $\$R_0$. Since $R_m < R_0$ by assumption, the gold arbitragers can make a profit. The additional supply of pounds sterling by the gold arbitragers eventually depresses the current rate down to the mint rate.

On the other hand, if the current rate is lower than the mint rate (that is, $R_0 < R_m$), the gold arbitragers can make a profit by buying, with pounds sterling, gold from B's monetary authorities and selling it for dollars to A's monetary authorities. Each dollar they acquire in this fashion costs them $\pounds(1/R_m)$ and they can sell it in the foreign exchange market for $\pounds(1/R_0)$. Since $R_0 < R_m$, it follows that $(1/R_0) > (1/R_m)$. Hence the gold arbitragers can make a profit again. The additional supply of dollars (or demand for pounds sterling) by the arbitragers causes the current rate (R_0) to rise up to the mint rate.

Note that in transferring gold from A to B when $R_m < R_0$, the arbitragers need not start with dollars because their foreign-exchange transaction (i.e., the sale of pounds sterling for dollars) may precede their gold transaction. Similarly, in transferring gold from B to A when $R_m > R_0$, the arbitragers need not start with pounds sterling. For this reason, there is no need to distinguish between American and British arbitragers.

7.3 THE GOLD POINTS

Let us now drop the assumption that the operations of the gold arbitragers are costless. Actually, the remission of gold has a cost, the principal elements in which are the cost of transport, insurance, and interest foregone during the period of transit. In addition, the monetary authorities of either or both countries may adopt a lower price for buying than for selling gold. The monetary authorities may follow this practice either because they want to raise some revenue to cover their operating costs or as a matter of deliberate policy. Finally, the gold arbitragers, like any other businessmen, must make a normal profit (in the form of a commission) to stay in business.

In the presence of these costs, the gold arbitragers are no longer prepared to sell unlimited amounts of pounds sterling at the mint rate. Their supply price must

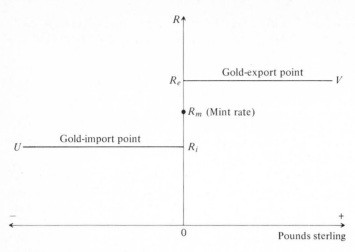

Figure 7.1 Excess supply of pounds sterling by gold arbitragers. The gold arbitragers stand ready to supply unlimited amounts of pounds sterling at A's gold-export point (R_e). They also stand ready to demand unlimited amounts of pounds sterling at A's gold-import point (R_i).

be high enough to cover their costs of buying gold in A and selling it in B including their commission. This is illustrated in fig. 7.1 by the horizontal segment $R_e V$. At the rate R_e, which is higher than the mint rate (R_m) by the cost of remitting one pound's worth of gold from A to B, the supply of pounds sterling by the gold arbitragers becomes infinitely elastic. The rate R_e is called A's *gold-export point* (or B's gold-import point) because at that rate gold is exported from A to B.

But the arbitragers are not prepared to demand unlimited amounts of pounds sterling at the mint rate either. Their demand price must be low enough to cover their costs of buying gold in B and selling it in A including their commission. This is illustrated in fig. 7.1 by the horizontal segment UR_i. At the rate R_i, which is lower than the mint rate by the cost of remitting one pound's worth of gold from B to A, the demand (*negative* supply) for pounds sterling by the gold arbitragers becomes infinitely elastic. The rate R_i is called A's *gold-import point* (or B's gold-export point) because at that rate gold is imported into A from B.

Figure 7.1 illustrates the excess supply of pounds sterling by the gold arbitragers. Because gold arbitrage is carried out at more or less constant costs, this excess supply-of-pounds curve is infinitely elastic at the gold points. As a result, the rate of exchange cannot move outside of the region bounded by the gold points.

The rate of exchange in the foreign exchange market need not coincide with the mint rate. In fact, the only function of the mint rate is the determination of the gold points. Once this is done, the mint rate becomes irrelevant.

The gold points are not rigidly determined and unchanging through time. They are bound to shift with changes in interest rates and transportation costs. Also, with technical progress reducing the cost of transport, the gap between the gold points tends to shrink. Finally, note that the margin between the gold points changes also when the monetary authorities change the margin between their prices for selling and buying gold.

7.4 EQUILIBRIUM IN THE SPOT MARKET

What determines the equilibrium rate of exchange within the gold points? The answer must be obvious from our discussion of the flexible-exchange-rate system: supply and demand for foreign exchange.

Presently, we assume that the spot and forward markets are combined into one and that, initially at least, commercial trade is the only source of international payments besides gold arbitrage. Figure 7.2 reproduces from fig. 7.1 the excess *supply* schedule for pounds sterling by gold arbitragers and, in addition, shows the excess demand schedule for pounds sterling by commercial traders (*DD'*). The latter curve (*DD'*) is drawn sloping downward. However, as explained in the previous chapter, the excess demand schedule *DD'* may twist itself around the vertical axis, giving rise to multiple equilibria. This possibility is presently disregarded for simplicity.

As long as the commercial traders' excess demand schedule for pounds sterling intersects the vertical axis at a rate between the gold points, the present system will behave more or less like the flexible-exchange-rate system. Thus, in fig. 7.2 equilibrium occurs at *E*. The equilibrium rate of exchange 0*E* definitely lies

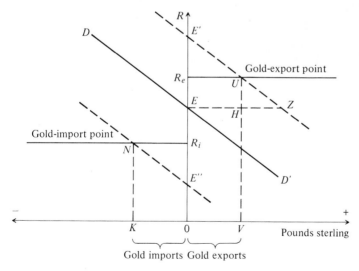

Figure 7.2 Equilibrium in the spot market. Within the gold points, the gold standard behaves more or less like the flexible-exchange-rate system. But when the excess demand schedule (see the broken lines) intersects the vertical axis at points which lie outside the gold points, such as *E'* or *E''*, then the gold arbitragers become active and prevent the rate of exchange from overshooting the gold points (see the equilibrium points *N* and *U*).

between the gold points. The commercial supply of sterling is equal to the commercial demand for sterling, and the gold arbitragers remain idle in the background.

Consider now an autonomous shift upwards and to the right in the commercial excess demand schedule, as illustrated in fig. 7.2 by the broken curve $E'U$. The reasons for this shift are immaterial for our purposes. Under free-market conditions, equilibrium would shift from E to E' and the equilibrium rate of exchange from $0E$ to $0E'$. But the rate $0E'$ is higher than the gold-export point, and, therefore, under our present assumptions, not feasible. What actually happens now is this. The excess demand for pounds sterling ZE at the old rate $(0E)$ causes the rate of exchange to increase. When the rate reaches the gold-export point, the gold arbitragers stand ready to supply unlimited amounts of pounds sterling. Equilibrium occurs now at U. The rate of exchange is equal to the gold-export point, and gold is exported from A to B at the rate of $0V$ (in pounds sterling) per unit of time. The increase in the dollar price of pounds sterling from $0E$ to $0R_e$ has reduced the commercial excess demand by the amount HZ (for reasons which have been analyzed in earlier chapters). The remaining gap $EH = R_e U = 0V$ is filled by gold exports from A to B.

Similarly, should the commercial excess demand schedule for pounds sterling shift downward and to the left, as shown by the broken curve NE'', equilibrium will move to N (not to E''), the rate of exchange will fall to the gold-import point, and gold will be imported into A from B at the rate of $0K$ (in pounds sterling) per unit of time.

The size of the gold flow from A to B $(0V)$ is a measure of the further adjustment required in commercial trade. It depends on three factors: (a) the strength of the initial shift of the commercial excess demand schedule (i.e., the size of EZ); (b) the difference between the initial rate of exchange and the gold-export point (that is, ER_e); and (c) the elasticity of the commercial excess demand schedule which is related to the demand elasticities for imports and supply elasticities of exports, as explained in chap. 4. In general, high import-demand and export-supply elasticities are required for the smooth functioning of the gold standard. Similar comments hold for the size of the gold flow from B to A $(0K)$.

Automatic Stabilizers

Equilibrium points such as U and N (fig. 7.2), implying gold movements between countries, cannot persist for long because sooner or later the gold-losing country will be forced to abandon the gold standard. Accordingly, the gold standard can survive only if powerful economic forces are automatically set into motion to successfully check the gold flow long before the gold reserve of the gold-losing country is completely exhausted. What are these stabilizing forces?

The first economic force to slow down or even cut off completely the gold flow is *speculation*. As the rate of foreign exchange approaches the gold-export point, speculators stand ready to sell large amounts of foreign exchange because their risk is practically nil. The speculators know that the foreign exchange is relatively expensive because the rate cannot rise above the gold-export point. Hence, they sell pounds sterling now in the hope that they will be able to buy them back later at a lower price. On the other hand, as the rate of exchange approaches the gold-import point, the speculators stand ready to buy large amounts of foreign exchange. They know that the pound sterling is relatively cheap—the rate cannot fall below the gold-import point. Hence they buy pounds sterling now in the hope that they will be able to sell them later at a higher price. These speculative purchases and sales of foreign exchange as the rate of exchange approaches the gold-import and gold-export points, respectively, tend to iron out any possible fluctuations in the rate of foreign exchange and, in addition, eliminate (or at least reduce substantially) the need for gold flows between countries.

Implicit in the preceding discussion is an important assumption regarding speculative expectations. It is that the speculators have *absolute confidence* in the ability of the monetary authorities to maintain the gold value of their currencies. Speculation can function successfully in the manner just described as long as there is absolute confidence that the rate of foreign exchange will never move outside the limits set by the gold points. Given this absolute confidence, speculation acts as a powerful stabilizing force in the foreign exchange market. Historically, in the pre-1914 gold-standard days, the gold points were never seriously questioned and speculation did perform this socially useful function.

A second stabilizing force is the movement of covered-interest-arbitrage funds. This is discussed in the following section since it necessarily involves the forward market as well.

A third stabilizing force is David Hume's *price-specie-flow mechanism*. This mechanism is analyzed in detail in chap. 15. Briefly it works like this. Suppose that neither stabilizing speculation nor the movement of interest-arbitrage funds are successful in halting the flow of gold from A to B. According to the third rule of the game, A's money supply contracts while B's money supply expands. The precise changes of the money supplies depend, of course, on the structures of the banking systems of the two countries. For our purposes, however, it is sufficient to know that A's money supply contracts and B's expands. Given the classical world of complete wage and price flexibility (and full employment), A's cost structure and prices tend to fall and B's to rise. In terms of our partial equilibrium model of chap. 4, this means that A's demand curve for imports and supply curve for exports shift downward. Similarly, B's demand curve for imports and supply curve of exports shift upward. Given high elasticities, these shifts imply a reduction in the quantity of pounds sterling demanded and an increase in the quantity of pounds sterling supplied, *at each and every rate of exchange.* Accordingly, the commercial excess demand curve of fig. 7.2 shifts down and to the left. As this happens, the flow of gold from A to B is reduced and eventually eliminated.

Note that, if A's money supply is always equal to or a constant multiple of A's gold reserve, A's monetary authorities will never run out of gold. On the other hand, if A's monetary system is based on the fiduciary-issue principle, the danger that A's monetary authorities may run out of gold before the adjustment process is completed cannot be ruled out.

It is often erroneously stated that there is a presumption in the price-specie-flow mechanism that the gold-losing country will experience a worsening in its (net barter) terms of trade. It is argued that prices in A (the gold-losing country) fall while prices in B rise; hence A's terms of trade deteriorate. This conclusion is wrong. Inflation and deflation as implied by the classical economists are equivalent to exchange-rate changes (in the long run) and, as we have seen in chap. 4, the terms-of-trade effect of a change in the exchange rate is indeterminate. The explanation for this phenomenon is simple. It is true that prices in A fall and prices in B rise. But it is the prices of both A-exportables and B-exportables which fall in A and rise in B, and it is gratuitous to jump to the conclusion that A-exportables become cheaper relative to B-exportables.

Finally, national income changes, which have been excluded from consideration so far, play a major stabilizing role in the adjustment process under a gold-standard regime. This was widely recognized after Keynes published his *General Theory*. This subject is studied in detail in chaps. 10 and 16.

7.5 SIMULTANEOUS EQUILIBRIUM IN THE SPOT AND FORWARD MARKETS

The analysis of the preceding section is presently expanded to include the forward market as well. This will enable us to study the stabilizing effects of covered-interest arbitrage, discount-rate policy, and forward-exchange intervention.

In addition to the three activities (commercial trade, speculation, and covered-interest arbitrage) we considered under the flexible-exchange-rate system of the previous chapter, we now have the activities of the gold arbitragers as well. As with the flexible-exchange-rate system, it is assumed again that all commercial trade is financed through the spot market and all speculation takes place in the forward market. The activities of gold arbitragers are restricted to the spot market.

To determine the simultaneous equilibrium in the spot and forward markets, the supply and demand schedules for arbitrage funds (from A to B) must be determined first. As far as the supply schedule for arbitrage funds is concerned, there is nothing more to add to what has already been discussed in the previous chapter. We therefore concentrate on the demand schedule.

The derivation of the demand schedule for arbitrage funds requires the following two elements: (*a*) the speculator's excess demand schedule for pounds sterling (foreign exchange) in the forward market; and (*b*) the excess supply schedule of pounds sterling in the spot market by commercial traders and gold arbitragers. All this is shown in fig. 7.3.

Figure 7.3 Simultaneous equilibrium under the gold standard. Under the gold standard, the spot rate is maintained within the gold points by the activities of the *gold arbitragers*. The forward rate is also maintained within the gold points by the activities of *speculators*. Accordingly, the gold points restrict the variation of the ratio R_f/R_s within certain limits. Given these new constraints, the simultaneous equilibrium of the spot (*a*) and forward (*b*) markets is determined as with the flexible-exchange-rate system: by the intersection of the supply and demand schedules for arbitrage funds in (*c*).

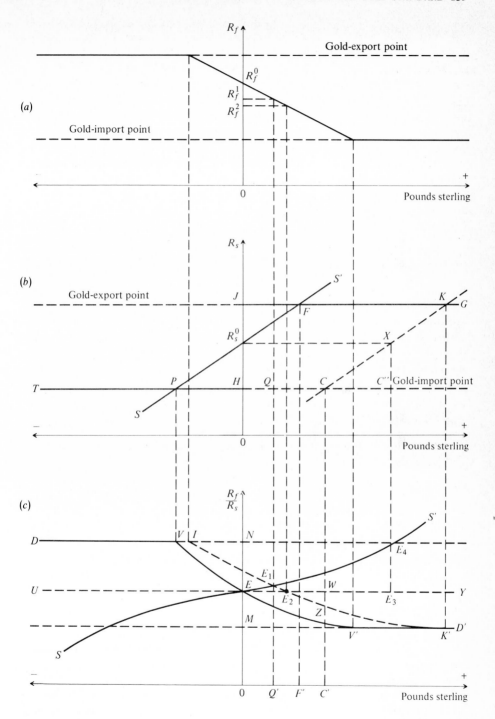

The Speculators' Excess Demand Schedule for Pounds Sterling

Figure 7.3a shows the speculators' excess demand schedule for pounds sterling. Again the rate R_f^0 is the market expected future spot rate. One special and important feature of this demand schedule is that it becomes infinitely elastic at the gold points. This is in line with the argument given in the preceding section regarding the speculators' state of confidence in the gold points. Absolute confidence implies that the speculators are willing to supply (demand) unlimited amounts of pounds sterling at the gold-export point (gold-import point); this is what is reflected by the infinite elasticity of the excess demand schedule in panel (a). Given this excess demand schedule for pounds sterling forward, it must be clear that the forward rate is also bounded by the gold points. But here, it must be remembered, it is the activities of the speculators (not the gold arbitragers) which keep the forward rate within the gold points.

The Excess Supply Schedule of Commercial Traders and Gold Arbitragers

Figure 7.3b illustrates the spot market. The curve SS' shows the commercial traders' excess supply of pounds sterling and the curve $THJG$ shows the gold arbitragers' excess supply of pounds sterling. Both of these curves have been met earlier and further discussion of them is not needed. It is assumed that there are no outstanding forward contracts in the current period. A little reflection shows that the combined excess supply schedule is given by the curve $TPFG$. The gold arbitragers come into play only at the gold points.

The Demand Schedule for Arbitrage Funds

The demand for arbitrage funds (from A to B) is shown in fig. 7.3c by the curve DD'. It is derived in the same way as in the case of the flexible-exchange-rate system (chap. 6), and reference should be made to that discussion for details. Note that the demand schedule for arbitrage funds becomes infinitely elastic at two values of the ratio R_f/R_s, namely, $0M$ and $0N$. These values are determined by the gold points. Thus, the former ($0M$) implies that the forward rate is at the gold-import point *and* the spot rate at the gold-export point, and the latter ($0N$) implies that the forward rate is at the gold-export point *and* the spot rate at the gold-import point.

Simultaneous Equilibrium

Figure 7.3 also illustrates the simultaneous equilibrium in the spot and forward markets. Thus, in panel (c) the supply of arbitrage funds SS' has been introduced. For simplicity, this supply curve has been drawn without any vertical stretch along the vertical axis as was done earlier in chap. 6. Equilibrium occurs at E where the supply schedule intersects the demand schedule. Thus, the equilibrium spot and forward rates are R_s^0 and R_f^0, respectively, and A's balance of trade is zero, as is the flow of funds from A to B. Interest parity also prevails at E.

7.6 THE ADJUSTMENT PROCESS IN THE SHORT RUN

To learn how the gold standard works we must find out how the system reacts to disturbances. This is done in the present section.

Consider again the simultaneous equilibrium at E (fig. 7.3). Assume that the system is disturbed by a shift downward and to the right of the commercial traders' excess supply schedule in panel (b), as shown by the broken curve CK. The reasons for the shift are immaterial for the moment. If speculation and interest arbitrage did not exist, the spot rate would quickly fall to A's gold-import point, and the gold arbitragers would undertake to transfer gold from B to A at the rate HC (in pounds sterling) per unit of time. How do speculation and interest arbitrage modify this result?

During the first time period following the shift in the commercial traders' excess supply schedule, the combined excess supply schedule for pounds sterling spot (panel b) is distorted to $TCKG$. As a result, the demand schedule for arbitrage funds (panel c) is distorted to DIE_1ZK'. Equilibrium for this first time period occurs at E_1. The spot rate falls to A's gold-import point, the forward rate falls to R_f^1, and B's balance-of-trade deficit ($HC = 0C'$) is financed partially by a short-term capital inflow ($0Q' = HQ$) from A. Thanks to this short-term capital movement during this first time period, B's gold outflow is only QC, which is far less than B's balance-of-trade deficit. Will there be additional short-term capital flows from A to B in future time periods to restrict B's gold outflow below B's balance-of-trade deficit? Presently, this is not the case.

In the second time period, as explained in the preceding chapter, the mere execution of the first period's forward contracts will place $0Q'$ pounds sterling in the hands of the speculators. Since the latter never intended to tie up any of their funds in pounds sterling (spot)—they merely intended to buy pounds sterling forward—they will sell this amount of pounds sterling in the spot market. Accordingly, the second period's excess supply schedule of pounds sterling spot (panel b) shifts to the right, causing the demand schedule for arbitrage funds (panel c) to shift to the right also. Under the flexible-exchange-rate system, these shifts are sufficient to guarantee an additional short-term capital flow from A to B in the second period. Not so under the gold standard. For now the horizontal part TC of the first period's excess supply schedule of pounds sterling spot remains unaltered in the second period. Accordingly, equilibrium in the second period continues at E_1. No *additional* short-term capital moves from A to B and B begins to lose gold at the rate of HC per unit of time.

It is not in general true, of course, that, following a disturbance, a desirable short-term capital movement reducing the deficit country's gold outflow occurs during the first time period only. It all depends on (a) the elasticity of the speculative excess demand schedule for pounds sterling forward (panel a) and (b) the elasticity of the supply schedule of arbitrage funds (panel c). The most favorable circumstances prevail when both of these elasticities are infinite. Then short-term capital movements completely eliminate the need for gold movements in *all* time periods. For instance, suppose that the speculators are absolutely convinced that the future spot rate will be R_f^0 and that this expectation makes the speculative excess demand schedule (panel a) infinitely elastic at that rate. Suppose, further, that the supply schedule for arbitrage funds is also infinitely elastic at $R_f/R_s = 0E$ (panel c). Under these conditions, equilibrium in the first period following the shift in the commercial traders' excess supply schedule of pounds sterling spot (panel b) occurs at E_3, because at the ratio $R_f/R_s = 0E$ the quantity $R_s^0 X = EE_3$ of pounds sterling is now demanded for arbitrage. Accordingly, the spot and forward rates remain at their initial levels, R_s^0 and R_f^0, respectively, and B's trade deficit $(R_s^0 X)$ is totally financed by a short-term capital inflow from A. What is more, this state of affairs continues in future periods, for, as is easily verified, the demand for arbitrage funds at $R_f/R_s = 0E$ continues to increase at the rate EE_3 ($=$ B's trade deficit).

When either the speculative excess demand for pounds sterling forward or the supply of arbitrage funds is less than infinitely elastic, short-term capital movements provide temporary relief only to the trade-deficit country. The spot rate gradually moves to the deficit country's gold-export point and from then on the deficit country necessarily finances its trade deficit by means of gold exports. As noted in the preceding section, this gold flow sets into motion the price-specie-flow mechanism which, with some modifications to be discussed in a later chapter, eventually restores equilibrium. Before that happens, is there anything else in the system which can postpone for a little longer the deficit country's loss of gold? Yes there is: monetary policy.

The monetary authorities of B can induce an additional inflow of short-term capital from A by simply raising their interest rate. As we have seen in chap. 6, this increase in B's interest rate causes the supply schedule of arbitrage funds (fig. 7.3c) to shift downward, and the accumulated short-term lending from A to B to increase. Thus, B's loss of gold is put further into the future. Obviously, this policy can produce temporary relief only.

We must, therefore, conclude that the preceding mechanism which relies on the harmonious blend of speculation, covered-interest arbitrage, and monetary policy works effectively to eliminate the need for gold flows and to maintain the rate of exchange within the gold points, only in cases where the basic disturbance is of either a purely *transitory* nature (e.g., a strike or crop failure) or a *reversible* nature (e.g., seasonal or cyclical). On the other hand, if the basic disturbance is of a more permanent nature, either *continuing* or *progressive*, eventually gold will flow from one country to another, the money supplies of both countries will be adjusted according to the third rule of the game, and eventually equilibrium will be restored through price and income adjustments as explained later in chaps. 15 and 16.

7.7 FORWARD-EXCHANGE INTERVENTION

Interest rates influence the flow of funds between countries. But they also influence aggregate spending. Now it may be that the interest-rate change needed for restoring equilibrium in the balance of payments is opposite to the one needed for restoring full employment. For instance, assume that, following a decline in exports, country B suffers from unemployment and at the same time loses gold to the rest of the world. Country B faces the following dilemma: (a) it may raise its interest rate to curb the loss of gold but it will intensify the problem of unemployment by discouraging domestic investment; or (b) it may lower its interest rate to encourage domestic investment and eliminate unemployment but it will intensify the outflow of gold. Obviously there is a conflict here. How can the conflict be resolved?

The conflict can be resolved when the monetary authorities intervene in the forward market. As it may be recalled, the flow of funds from A to B depends directly on the difference $r_b^* - r_a = (1 + r_b)(R_f/R_s) - (1 + r_a)$. Accordingly, the flow of funds from A to B may increase (and thus B's loss of gold may decrease) by either reducing r_a or increasing r_b^*. Since changes in r_a are beyond the power of B's monetary authorities, let us concentrate on increasing r_b^*. This may be accomplished in any one of the following three ways: (a) by increasing r_b; (b) by decreasing R_s; or (c) by increasing R_f. The first alternative (increasing r_b) is ruled out because this is what B's monetary authorities must not do in order to avoid any conflict with the goal of full employment. Similarly, the second alternative (decreasing R_s) is also ruled out because the spot rate (R_s) is already at its lowest point (A's gold-import point) by assumption and cannot be reduced any further. This leaves the last alternative (increasing R_f). This can be accomplished by B's monetary authorities intervening in the forward market and selling dollars forward. This forward-exchange intervention will have the same effect on the flow of funds from A to B as an increase in B's interest rate. Accordingly, B's monetary authorities can attack both problems (balance-of-payments deficit and unemployment) at the same time by reducing their domestic interest rate and simultaneously selling dollars forward.

The preceding analysis illustrates *Tinbergen's principle:* to achieve n targets (or goals), n policy instruments (or tools) must be used (see Tinbergen, 1952). In the preceding example there are two targets (balance-of-payments equilibrium and full employment) and two instruments (the interest rate and the forward rate).

Forward-exchange intervention provides merely short-term *financing* for the country's deficit. The monetary authorities simply substitute a forward commitment to sell gold in the future for the actual loss of gold at the present time. Thus, the monetary authorities merely postpone the loss of gold. Of course, if the basic disturbance is either of a transitory or reversible nature, the balance-of-trade deficit will soon disappear or be converted into a surplus. In that case, temporary financing is all that is needed, and forward-exchange intervention is sufficient to eliminate the need for the gold movement.

However, if the basic disturbance reflects a permanent structural change in the system, the gold movement can be postponed in this fashion for a short period of time only. This is illustrated in fig. 7.3. The most favorable circumstances prevail when the supply schedule of arbitrage funds is infinitely elastic, as shown by the horizontal line UY.

Assume that in the first period following a permanent disturbance in the spot market shifting the excess supply schedule to $TCKG$, equilibrium would move from E to E_2 (panel c) in the absence of any forward intervention. At E_2, country B would start losing gold. However, if the supply of arbitrage funds is infinitely elastic, B's monetary authorities may postpone the loss of gold indefinitely by buying pounds sterling forward. All they have to do is reproduce the most favorable circumstances cited earlier: an infinitely elastic supply of arbitrage funds (which exists by assumption) and an infinitely elastic demand for pounds sterling forward. Accordingly, they may stand ready to buy unlimited amounts of pounds sterling forward† at, say, R_f^2. Actually, in the first period, B's monetary authorities must buy only $E_2 W$ pounds sterling forward. In the second period, they must renew these contracts and buy an additional amount of EW ($\equiv$ B's trade deficit) pounds sterling forward. In the third period, they must renew all previous contracts ($E_2 W$ and EW) and in addition buy the additional amount of EW pounds sterling forward; and so on. The forward commitments of B's monetary authorities will thus tend to grow at the rate EW per unit of time.

This seems to be the sequence of events if the monetary authorities were to pursue blindly their forward-intervention policy under the ideal conditions of a perfectly elastic supply schedule of arbitrage funds. But ordinarily one would expect the monetary authorities, even under these ideal conditions, to realize the nature of their balance-of-payments disequilibrium at an earlier stage and stop their intervention then. And they have a very good reason for doing that. While they buy pounds sterling forward at a relatively high rate (R_f^2), in the presence of a fundamental balance-of-payments disequilibrium they will have to sell them eventually at A's gold-import point, which is definitely lower. Thus, by playing this game B's monetary authorities will lose money. Accordingly, they have a strong inducement to use the forward-exchange policy wisely.

What happens in the more realistic case where the supply of arbitrage funds is not infinitely elastic? In this case, B's monetary authorities cannot induce short-term capital inflows continuously. Given the gold points, the ratio R_f/R_s cannot rise beyond ON (fig. 7.3). Accordingly, the maximum accumulated short-term lending B's monetary authorities can induce from A is NE_4. When this point is reached, there is no way out. B's monetary authorities must start exporting gold.

We therefore conclude that forward intervention may be effective for short-run (temporary or reversible) disturbances. It should not be used to cope with permanent or fundamental disequilibria.

SELECTED BIBLIOGRAPHY

Aghevli, B. B. (1975). "The Balance of Payments and Money Supply Under the Gold Standard Regime: U.S. 1879–1914." *American Economic Review* (March), pp. 40–58.

Beach, W. E. (1935). *British International Gold Movements and Banking Policy, 1881–1913.* Harvard University Press, Cambridge, Mass.

---

† The implicit assumption here is that $r_a < r_b$. (What happens when $r_a > r_b$?)

Bloomfield, A. I. (1959). *Monetary Policy Under the International Gold Standard: 1880–1914*. Federal Reserve Bank of New York, New York.

——— (1963). *Short-Term Capital Movements Under the Pre-1914 Gold Standard*. Princeton Studies in International Finance no. 11, International Finance Section, Princeton University, Princeton, N.J.

Brown, W. A., Jr. (1934). *The Gold Standard Re-interpreted, 1914–1934*. National Bureau of Economic Research, New York.

Hawtrey, R. G. (1947). *The Gold Standard in Theory and Practice*. Longmans, Green and Company, London.

Keynes, J. M. (1930). *A Treatise on Money*, vol. II. Macmillan and Company, Ltd., London, pp. 319–331.

Lerner, A. P. (1944). *The Economics of Control*. The Macmillan Company, New York, chap. 28.

Meade, J. E. (1951). *The Theory of International Economic Policy*, vol. I, *The Balance of Payments*. Oxford University Press, Inc., New York, chaps. XIV and XV.

Stern, R. M. (1973). *The Balance of Payments*. Aldine Publishing Company, Chicago, Ill., chap. 4.

Tinbergen, J. (1952). *On the Theory of Economic Policy*. North-Holland Publishing Company, Amsterdam.

Triffin, R. (1964). *The Evolution of the International Monetary System: Historical Reappraisal and Future Perspectives*. Princeton University Press, Princeton, N.J., especially pp. 2–20.

——— (1968). *Our International Monetary System: Yesterday, Today and Tomorrow*. Random House, New York, chap. 1.

Yeager, L. B. (1966). *International Monetary Relations*. Harper and Row, Publishers, New York, chaps. 4 to 6, 14 to 16, and app. to chap. 6.

(Please see also the Selected Bibliography at the end of chap. 15.)

EIGHT

THE FIXED-EXCHANGE-RATE SYSTEM: II. THE ADJUSTABLE PEG

The present chapter concludes the discussion of how the foreign exchange market works under alternative institutional arrangements which began in chap. 5. Attention is now focused on the adjustable-peg system.

After a quick overview of the adjustable-peg system, the discussion centers on the following important issues: (*a*) how equilibrium is maintained in the spot and forward markets; (*b*) the new dimension which speculation assumes under this system, including the all-important issue of leads and lags; (*c*) the problem of forward intervention; (*d*) exchange-rate adjustments as a means of restoring balance-of-payments equilibrium in the long run; and (*e*) the purchasing power-parity theory.

The present discussion is carried out in terms of the partial equilibrium model but is extended in the rest of the book to more general models.

8.1 AN OVERVIEW

One of the objectives of the International Monetary Fund (IMF), when it was created by the major non-Communist nations of the world at Bretton Woods, New Hampshire, in 1944, was to combine the advantages of both the fixed- and flexible-exchange-rate systems. The system of the *adjustable peg* was adopted for this purpose. As we shall see, the adjustable-peg system provides for exchange-rate stability in the short run (and in this respect it is similar to the gold standard) but it allows for the possibility of exchange-rate adjustment when a country's balance of payments is in *fundamental disequilibrium* (and in this respect it is similar to the flexible-exchange-rate system under which equilibrium is brought about through exchange-rate adjustments). Unfortunately, the adjustable-peg system lacked both the stability, certainty, and automaticity of the gold standard and the flexibility of the flexible-exchange-rate system. As a result of the 1973 crisis, the adjustable-peg system was suspended and replaced temporarily by the present system of *dirty floating*, until something better comes along. Under dirty floating, as opposed to *clean floating*, there is central-bank intervention in the foreign exchange market to iron out wide fluctuations in the exchange rates.

Spot Rates of Exchange

The system of the adjustable peg is similar to the gold standard with respect to the determination and maintenance of the spot-exchange rates in the short run. According to the initial agreement, the dollar was pegged to gold at the fixed parity of $35 per ounce of gold, and dollars held by official monetary institutions were convertible freely into gold as the United States was prepared to buy and sell unlimited amounts of gold at the official rate. Every other country was required to (a) declare the *par value* (or *parity*) of its currency in terms of gold or the U.S. dollar, and (b) stand ready to defend the declared parity in the foreign exchange market by buying or selling dollars, at least in the short run. (For practical reasons, the operative standard for most countries was the dollar as such.) Accordingly, in the short run, the currencies of member countries were kept stable in terms of dollars and thus in terms of each other. Exchange rates were thus fixed, but only in the short run.

Support Points

Exchange rates were not entirely fixed, even in the short run, of course. They were allowed to vary within the so-called *support points* or *intervention points*. These points, which actually replaced the gold points of the gold standard, were initially determined at 1 percent on either side of the parity. Nevertheless, countries could adopt narrower, even asymmetrical spreads, and some countries actually did adopt such spreads. At the upper (lower) support point, the monetary authorities through an exchange stabilization fund stood ready to buy (sell) unlimited amounts of dollars. Thus, the gold arbitragers of the gold standard were replaced by the exchange-stabilization funds, and the gold points by the support points. Nevertheless, the result was the same: exchange-rate variations were maintained within a very narrow band and for all practical purposes exchange rates were said to be fixed.

Forward Rates of Exchange

While the monetary authorities of member countries were required to intervene in the *spot market* and maintain the *spot rates* within the support points, no such requirement was stipulated with respect to the *forward market* and the *forward rates.* Individual countries were free to choose whether to intervene in the forward market or not at their discretion. Accordingly, forward rates would occasionally move outside the limits set for the spot rates. This was mainly the result of heavy speculation, as explained later in this chapter. In fact, a forward rate which lies outside the limits set by the support points can be taken as an indication that a lack of confidence in the maintenance of these support points exists.

The Role of the United States

The United States was not required to intervene, even in the spot market, as it was up to the other countries to maintain fixed dollar parities. As we saw in the appendix to chap. 1, in a system of n currencies there are only $(n - 1)$ independent exchange rates—the nth currency is simply the numeraire. Thus, the $(n - 1)$ countries determined and maintained the $(n - 1)$ independent exchange rates, while the United States assumed the role of the nth country and the dollar the role of the numeraire. The only requirement for the United States was to be prepared to buy and sell gold at $35 an ounce.

The Developments of 1971 and 1973

Incidentally, in August 1971, the United States suspended the link between the dollar and gold and refused to exchange gold for dollars. A few months later, in December 1971, the Smithsonian Agreement was reached. According to this agreement, the major industrial nations agreed on a fundamental realignment of exchange rates. In addition, exchange rates were permitted to fluctuate within a wider band (2.25 percent on either side of the new parities) and the U.S. dollar was devalued by 8 percent (i.e., the price of gold was raised to $38 an ounce from the $35 price which had prevailed since 1934). By February 1973, the United States had announced another 10 percent devaluation of the dollar, raising the official price of gold to $42.22 an ounce. However, the free convertibility of dollars into gold which was suspended in 1971 was never restored.

Exchange-Rate Adjustments in the Presence of Fundamental Disequilibrium

The adjustable-peg system provides for exchange-rate stability in the short run but allows for the possibility of exchange-rate adjustment when a country's balance of payments is in fundamental disequilibrium. The concept of fundamental disequilibrium was never defined in the Fund Agreement. For our purposes, fundamental disequilibrium may be taken to mean a balance-of-payments disequilibrium (deficit or surplus) of a permanent (or persistent) nature. Thus, temporary and reversible deficits and surpluses are excluded. A country with a persistent deficit may choose to lower the dollar parity of its currency, i.e., *devalue* its currency. Similarly, a country with a persistent surplus may choose to raise the dollar parity of its currency, i.e., *revalue* its currency. *Devaluation* and *revaluation* of a currency to correct a fundamental balance-of-payments disequilibrium is a major departure from the gold standard, under which each country was required to determine the gold value of its currency once and for all, and changes in these gold values were unthinkable.

Speculation

Because of the possibility of parity changes, speculation assumes a totally different dimension under the adjustable-peg system than under the gold standard. Under the gold standard, speculation is *stabilizing* because the gold points are totally trusted. Under the adjustable-peg system, however, speculators may come to doubt the support points, and in that case speculation becomes *destabilizing*— short-term capital moves in the wrong direction so to speak. The main reason for this phenomenon is the *one-way option* offered to speculators by the adjustable-peg system. Thus, when a currency is under suspicion there may be some doubt as to whether it will be devalued and to what extent, but there is practically no doubt about the *direction* of change. The only choices are devaluation or no change at all. For instance, speculators observe a country which is running persistently huge deficits and they expect the country to devalue its currency. Accordingly, the speculators sell the currency in the expectation of buying it later at a lower price. If the speculators are right and the country actually devalues, their profits are substantial. On the other hand, if the speculators are wrong, their potential losses are minimal since the narrow band around the par value prevents the currency from appreciating significantly, as might have been the case under a flexible-exchange-rate system.

Note that the assurance that any speculative losses will be minimal applies to spot speculation only. Speculators in the forward market may indeed suffer substantial losses, as they force the forward rate below the lower support point and the currency is not devalued. Nevertheless, even in this case speculators can calculate their maximum possible losses because upward revaluation of the weak currency can be safely ruled out.

Finally, note that such destabilizing speculation can force the deficit country to devalue its currency by bleeding its reserves, even in cases in which the country could have weathered the storm in the absence of destabilizing speculation. The lower the reserves fall, the stronger the incentive for continued bear speculation is, because devaluation becomes more imminent. For this reason, it is often suggested that the adjustable-peg system can operate successfully only if there is some direct control over speculative capital movements. But unfortunately such control is very, very difficult to implement. The controls may be circumvented unless the authorities adopt a comprehensive control system covering nonspeculative current account transactions as well (see sec. 8.4).

Reserves

To maintain fixed-exchange rates in the short run, countries need reserves. Reserves are kept in gold, certain *key currencies* or *reserve currencies* (mainly dollars and to a lesser extent pounds sterling), and *special drawing rights* (SDRs).

Often called "paper gold," SDRs are a new form of international reserve assets whose creation was authorized by amendment to the Articles of Agreement of the IMF. Under this amendment SDRs are allocated annually to member countries in proportion to their IMF quotas. The first allocations were made in 1970.

The creation of SDRs followed a vigorous debate in the 1960s among economists, bankers, and government officials over the weaknesses of the world's system of international reserves. Robert Triffin (1960) was first to notice that reserves were not growing fast enough, and in addition he expressed doubts as to whether the system could indeed generate reserves in sufficient amounts without undermining its very foundations. He argued that, given the slow growth of the stock of monetary gold (less than 1 percent annually), world reserves could increase only if the key-currency countries (mainly the United States) ran huge balance-of-payments deficits to pump into the world monetary system sufficient amounts of reserve-currency deposits. But this, he continued, would undermine confidence in the dollar as the stock of U.S. liabilities to the rest of the world grew larger and larger relative to the U.S. stock of gold. Soon foreign central banks and private holders would become restless and find the dollar weak and redundant. A switch from dollars to gold would cause the system to collapse. Accordingly, Triffin concluded, a way must be found to increase international reserves without breeding instability into the system. Awareness of this problem led eventually to the creation of SDRs which require no disequilibrium in international payments between reserve and nonreserve countries and, unlike gold, use none of the world's scarce resources.

Swaps and the Two-Tier Gold System

Two additional devices were used in the 1960s to cope with the problem of international liquidity: *swap arrangements* (or simply *swaps*), and the *two-tier gold system*. Swaps are a means whereby two central banks acquire claims on each other by merely *swapping* equivalent amounts of their own currencies. Such swaps could be irreversible, i.e., final transactions. Nevertheless, these swaps were almost entirely accompanied by a forward contract reversing the original transaction within three to twelve months.

The two-tier gold system was eatablished in March 1968 by the central banks of the major trading nations of the world. At that time, under pressure of rising demand, gold was draining heavily out of central banks into private hands. The major objective of the two-tier system was to enable central banks to maintain the official price of gold at $35 and at the same time prevent private speculators from raiding their official gold reserves. It was thus agreed to separate the official and private markets. The central banks continued to trade in gold among themselves at the official price but banned the sale of official gold to the private market where the price was higher and fluctuated in response to supply and demand. The two-tier gold system was terminated in November 1973 as a result of the oil crisis.

The Balance of Payments and the Money Supply

Another development which is crucial to our discussion is the removal of the link between the balance of payments and the money supply. Under the rules of the gold standard, the gold-losing (gold-gaining) country is required to allow its money supply to decrease (increase). These money-supply changes supposedly set into motion David Hume's price-specie-flow mechanism which restored balance-of-payments equilibrium. But even under the gold standard it was not uncommon for the monetary authorities to violate the rules of the game by taking offsetting actions and preventing their money supply from changing. Such offsetting actions became widespread in the 1920s, and especially after World War II when full employment was recognized as a primary objective of economic policy. Thus, monetary policy, the main instrument of the balance-of-payments adjustment process under the gold-standard rules of the game, was diverted from its initial function of keeping the balance of payments in equilibrium (external balance) toward the achievement of full employment (internal balance). Thus, the automaticity of the balance-of-payments adjustment process was removed, and this gave rise to the *international disequilibrium system* (Mundell, 1961). This is what made exchange-rate adjustments inevitable.

8.2 THE SPOT MARKET

The functioning of the spot market under the adjustable peg is illustrated in fig. 8.1. It is assumed that A is a reserve country and B a nonreserve country. In particular, A agrees to buy and sell gold at a fixed-dollar price, while B declares a fixed-dollar parity ($0C$) of its currency (pounds sterling) and stands ready to intervene in the spot market and prevent the rate of exchange from moving beyond the support points ($0M$, $0V$). The curve $NMCVU$ represents the excess supply of pounds sterling by B's monetary authorities. This is similar to the gold arbitragers' excess supply of foreign exchange under the gold standard. The curve DD' shows the excess demand for pounds sterling for commercial trade and other purposes, as explained in earlier chapters. Equilibrium occurs at E. By assumption, the equilibrium rate $0E$ lies between the support points and thus B's monetary authorities do not intervene in the foreign exchange market.

Suppose now that the excess demand schedule (DD') shifts downward and to the left, as shown by the broken curve $E_4 E_3$. Under free-market conditions the rate would fall from $0E$ to $0E_3$. However, under the present conditions B's monetary authorities intervene at the lower support point ($0M$) by selling $0ME_4 T$ dollars in exchange for $0T$ pounds sterling per unit of time. Accordingly, equilibrium occurs at E_4.

If the support points are trusted, speculators may consider the rate $0M$ too low. Thus, they may buy pounds sterling in exchange for dollars and thus reduce B's loss of reserves. On the other hand, if speculators anticipate a devaluation of the pound sterling they will sell pounds sterling in exchange for dollars, precipitate B's loss of reserves, and perhaps force B's authorities to devalue.

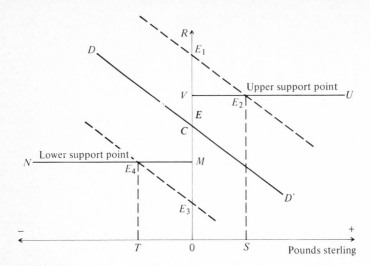

Figure 8.1 The curve *NMCVU* shows the excess supply of pounds sterling by B's monetary authorities. This curve replaces the excess supply by gold arbitragers under the gold standard. Equilibrium occurs at the point where the excess demand for pounds sterling by commercial traders (*DD'*) intersects the excess supply of pounds sterling by B's monetary authorities, as illustrated by points E, E_2, and E_4.

Alternatively, suppose that the excess demand schedule (*DD'*) shifts upwards and to the right, as shown by the broken curve $E_1 E_2$. Under free-market conditions the rate would be bid up from $0E$ to $0E_1$. But under the present system, B's monetary authorities intervene at the upper support point ($0V$) by buying $0VE_2S$ dollars in exchange for $0S$ pounds sterling per unit of time. Again, speculation may decrease or increase B's gain of reserves depending on whether the support points are trusted or an upward revaluation of the pound sterling is expected, respectively.

Equilibria such as those at E_2 and E_4 implying that country B either loses (E_4) or gains (E_2) reserves cannot continue for long. For instance, if the equilibrium at E_4 is the result of a *temporary* disturbance which is expected to be reversed soon, B's monetary authorities will be able to finance the deficit with either owned or borrowed reserves. However, if the excess demand schedule ($E_4 E_3$) is expected to remain at that position permanently, B's monetary authorities will soon run out of reserves and be unable to continue their support of the pound sterling.

It may be recalled that under the gold standard an equilibrium such as E_4 would generate money-supply changes in both countries and set into motion David Hume's price-specie-flow mechanism. Under the present system no such automatic mechanism exists since the money supply is divorced from the balance of payments. Under such circumstances, B's monetary authorities must pursue a deliberate economic policy to restore balance-of-payments equilibrium. Accordingly, B's monetary authorities may either lower the dollar parity of the pound sterling from $0C$ to, say, $0E_3$ (i.e., *devalue* the pound sterling), or pursue other economic policies (to be studied later in the book) to shift the excess demand curve $E_4 E_3$ sufficiently to the right until an equilibrium is established again within the existing support points.

The problem is not much easier at E_2 where B's monetary authorities are gaining reserves. It is true that B's monetary authorities cannot run out of reserves this time, and it is up to them to let the system ride at E_2. But sooner or later, after their foreign-exchange reserves grow well beyond what is considered optimal for financing their international trade, B's monetary authorities will begin to feel unhappy for two reasons. First, A's outstanding short-term liabilities are growing larger and larger relative to A's gold stock, and B's authorities may come to doubt A's ability to maintain the fixed-dollar parity of gold. Second, B's authorities will realize that their economy is actually exchanging real goods and services (through a balance-of-trade surplus) for A's notes or demand deposits, which after all may depreciate relative to gold. Accordingly, B's monetary authorities may either raise the par value of the pound sterling from $0C$ to, say, $0E_1$ (i.e., *revalue* the pound), or pursue economic policies which will shift the excess demand curve $E_1 E_2$ sufficiently to the left until an equilibrium is established again within the current support points.

Country A may also take appropriate measures to correct the imbalance at E_2. Of course, it is not up to country A to let the dollar depreciate relative to the pound sterling. As mentioned earlier, A's only responsibility is the maintenance of the gold value of the dollar. It is country B which declares and maintains a fixed-dollar parity for the pound sterling. Nevertheless, country A may pursue economic policies designed to shift the excess demand curve $E_1 E_2$ to the left. But A may alternatively follow a policy of *benign neglect*, leaving to B the choices of whether to continue to accumulate dollars, to allow its currency to appreciate relative to the dollar, or to pursue other economic policies designed to shift the excess demand curve $E_1 E_2$ to the left. B's authorities, on the other hand, may attempt to force A to carry the burden of adjustment by either converting some of their dollar balances into gold or merely threatening to do so. Accordingly, an agreement may have to be reached between the two countries on who does what.

8.3 SIMULTANEOUS EQUILIBRIUM IN THE SPOT AND FORWARD MARKETS

Let us now expand the preceding analysis to embrace the forward market as well. This is a necessary step in order to study the effects of forward speculation, covered-interest arbitrage, discount-rate policy, and forward intervention.

Consider fig. 8.2, which is similar to fig. 7.3. The only difference between the two figures so far is that the gold points of fig. 7.3 have been replaced in fig. 8.2 by the support points. For the moment it is assumed that the support points are completely trusted by the speculators. Thus the speculators' excess demand schedule (panel *a*) is drawn infinitely elastic at the support points $(0M', 0V')$. As a consequence, the demand schedule for arbitrage funds from A to B (panel *c*) is

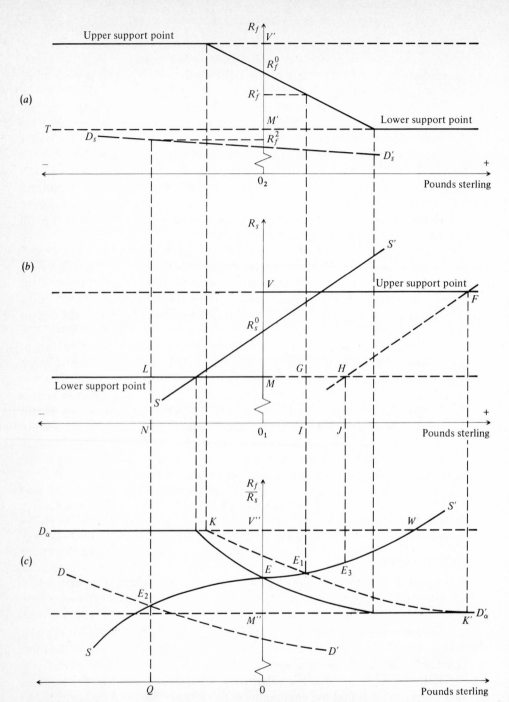

Figure 8.2 Simultaneous equilibrium in the spot (a) and forward (b) markets. When the support points are completely trusted, simultaneous equilibrium is determined as with the gold standard. When the support points are not trusted, then the speculators' excess demand schedule for pounds sterling (a) need not be contained within the support points, as illustrated by the broken curve $D_s D_s'$. The supply and demand curves for arbitrage funds (c) are derived from (a) and (b).

drawn infinitely elastic at the two extreme values: $0M'' = 0_1 M/0_1 V$, and $0V'' = 0_1 V/0_1 M$. Equilibrium occurs at E (panel c), where both the accumulated short-term lending and the current flow of funds from A to B are zero. The equilibrium spot and forward rates are R_s^0 and R_f^0, respectively.

Suppose now that the commercial traders excess supply schedule SS' (panel b) shifts downward and to the right, as shown by the broken curve HF. In the absence of speculation and interest arbitrage, equilibrium in the spot market would shift to H, and country B would start losing reserves at the rate $0_1 JHM$ per unit of time. How do speculation and interest arbitrage modify this result?

When the Support Points Are Completely Trusted

If the support points are completely trusted, the present system will behave like the gold standard. Thus, the speculators' excess demand for pounds sterling forward (panel a) will remain essentially unaltered, the demand schedule for arbitrage funds (panel c) will shift to $D_\alpha KK'D_\alpha'$, and equilibrium will occur at E_1 (panel c). Accordingly, during the first time period following the disturbance, B's loss of reserves is reduced to the area of the rectangle $IJHG$ (panel b) as interest arbitragers transfer $0_1 IGM$ dollars from A to B.

Whether additional funds will move from A to B in future time periods depends on circumstances, as explained in the preceding chapter. Ordinarily one would expect this flow of funds not to last for more than a limited number of time periods. (In fig. 8.2 arbitrage funds move from A to B during the first time period only.) If by that time the original disturbance is not reversed, country B will start losing reserves at the rate $0_1 JHM$.

When the Support Points Are Not Trusted

The situation is much different if the support points are not trusted. Suppose that equilibrium remains at E_1 for a few periods and country B loses reserves at the rate $0_1 JHM$ ($\equiv$ B's trade deficit) per unit of time, as explained in the preceding chapter. Suppose, further, that as this happens speculators come to doubt the ability of B's monetary authorities to preserve the initial dollar parity of the pound sterling. In particular, assume that the speculators anticipate that the pound sterling will be devalued. As a result, the speculators' excess demand schedule for pounds sterling forward (panel a) shifts to the left and downward sharply, as illustrated by the broken curve $D_s D_s'$. This causes the demand schedule for arbitrage funds to shift downward and to the left, as shown by the broken curve $DE_2 D'$ in panel (c). Accordingly, equilibrium shifts to E_2 (panel c), and while the spot rate remains at the lower support point $0_1 M$, the forward rate falls to $R_f^2 < 0_2 M'$. Contrary to what happens under the gold standard, or when the support points are completely trusted, funds now move from B to A—*in the wrong direction*. Instead of B's loss of reserves being mitigated by a short-term capital inflow from A, it is aggravated even further by B's capital outflow ($0_1 MLN$). Thus, B's loss of reserves increases now to $NJHL$.

The short-term capital outflow of B ($0_1 MLN$) is a one-shot affair. It will not be repeated in any future time periods beyond the first unless the speculators' excess demand curve for pounds sterling forward continues to shift to the left and downward. Thus, in the second time period, the mere execution of the first period's forward contracts causes the supply schedule, HF, for pounds sterling spot to shift to the left by LM, but this does not affect the equilibrium at E_2. While country B continues to lose reserves at the rate $0_1 JHM$, the loss of reserves due to the flow of funds from B to A is not repeated. All this must be clear from the analysis of the preceding chapter.

Even though B's loss of reserves due to speculation against the pound sterling is a one-shot affair, it may be quite substantial relative to B's stock of reserves. In that case speculation against the pound sterling may intensify and force a devaluation upon B's authorities, even in cases in which the crisis could have been weathered without devaluing. This kind of self-justifying speculation is obviously destabilizing. The adjustable-peg system can function smoothly if such destabilizing speculation is somehow curbed. What lines of defence are available to B's monetary authorities?

Interest-Rate Policy and Forward Intervention

One line of defence is interest-rate policy. The authorities of B may raise their interest rate and cause the supply schedule of arbitrage funds to shift downward and to the right. If this measure is not accompanied by any adverse effects on speculative expectations, it may be sufficient to restore equilibrium. Nevertheless, this policy measure suffers from at least three drawbacks: (a) it can provide temporary relief only; (b) it may interfere with other domestic goals, such as full employment; and (c) it may be interpreted by speculators as a symptom of basic weakness in B's balance of payments, and in that case speculative selling of pounds sterling forward may increase.

An alternative line of defence is forward intervention. Thus, B's monetary authorities may buy pounds sterling forward in sufficient amounts to cause the demand schedule for arbitrage funds to shift sufficiently to the right and intersect the supply schedule at E_3 (panel c). B's loss of reserves would then shrink to zero. Of course, as explained in the preceding chapter, these forward purchases must be renewed period after period, and in addition they must be augmented by each period's trade deficit. Otherwise, the loss of reserves will be renewed.

Unfortunately, forward intervention suffers from several drawbacks. First, it can provide temporary relief only. As shown in the preceding chapter, the maximum amount of funds which could move from A to B is $V''W$ (panel c). If by the time these funds flow from A to B, B's balance of trade does not improve, B's authorities will begin losing reserves. Second, speculation may intensify if speculators interpret the forward intervention as a sign of weakness. This may happen right at the start, or it may be provoked by large and increasing forward commitments should speculators come to fear that B's monetary authorities will be unable to meet them. Third, if devaluation actually occurs, B's authorities will suffer a loss in fulfilling their forward commitments to speculators.

We therefore conclude that neither interest-rate policy nor forward intervention can be used effectively in the presence of a fundamental weakness in the balance of payments. If the weakness is temporary, forward intervention may provide the necessary relief. Nevertheless, in the presence of a temporary disturbance, if the reserves are large enough to bear the temporary outflow of funds, B's authorities may decide not to intervene at all. Rather they may let the forward rate fall below the spot rate and teach the speculators a lesson by inflicting upon them heavy losses. Needless to say, the success of such a scheme hinges on a correct prognosis of the nature of the balance-of-payments disequilibrium.

During normal times, forward intervention may be used to attract or repel short-term capital flows as a means of increasing or decreasing foreign-exchange reserves. Such forward intervention may even be combined with an interest-rate policy designed to achieve certain domestic objectives (e.g., full employment). The advantages and disadvantages of such a policy mix have been discussed in the preceding chapter.

8.4 LEADS AND LAGS

As noted in sec. 1.7, a decision by a commercial trader *not to cover his exchange risk* is similar to the decision to speculate by a pure speculator. But not covering the exchange risk is not the only form of trader speculation. Another important and in fact more severe form of trader speculation is what is known as *leads and lags*, i.e., the adjustment in the timing of payments, placement of orders, and deliveries for the purpose of avoiding losses or securing profits from an anticipated devaluation or revaluation.

Suppose a devaluation of the pound sterling is suspected. Then B's exporters of goods invoiced in dollars will be anxious to delay (*lag*) receiving payment in the hope of selling their dollar revenue at a more favorable exchange rate. They can do so by merely extending credit to A's importers, perhaps at very attractive terms. For the same reason, B's exporters may delay (lag) their deliveries also.

If B's exports are invoiced in pounds sterling instead of dollars the outcome is still the same except that A's importers assume the initiative now. Thus, it is to the advantage of A's importers to delay (lag) their payments and placement of orders.

B's importers of goods invoiced in dollars will be anxious to accelerate (*lead*) their payments and placement of orders merely to avoid being caught with dollar obligations in the event of a devaluation of the pound sterling. Again, if the goods are invoiced in pounds sterling, A's exporters will take the initiative to accelerate their receipts. In addition, A's exporters may offer better terms to B's importers (presumably because of the anticipated reduction in the dollar price of A-exportables) and induce the latter to accelerate their orders as well.

A delay in the receipt of B's export revenue (= increase in B's claims against A) or an acceleration of B's payments to A (= reduction in B's liabilities to A) amounts to a capital outflow, or an export of *trade capital*, from B to A. Other things remaining equal, such an export of trade capital imposes additional pressure on B's reserves. Similarly, other things remaining equal, a delay in B's export deliveries to A or an acceleration of B's imports implies a deterioration in B's balance of trade and puts additional pressure on B's reserves.

Graphical Illustration of the Adverse Effects of Leads and Lags

The adverse effects of leads and lags are illustrated in fig. 8.3, where for simplicity no distinction between spot and forward markets is drawn and the rate of exchange is assumed to be rigidly fixed by B's monetary authorities. Panel (a) shows B's dollar value of exports (X) and supply of dollars $(S_\$)$ through time. It is assumed that there is a small delay in the receipt of export revenue by B's exporters. The precise amount of delay is shown by the horizontal distance between the curves $X(t)$ and $S_\$(t)$. Panel (b) shows B's dollar value of imports (M) and demand for dollars $(D_\$)$. It is assumed that there is a small delay—given by the horizontal distance between the curves $M(t)$ and $D_\$(t)$—in the payment for imports by B's importers.

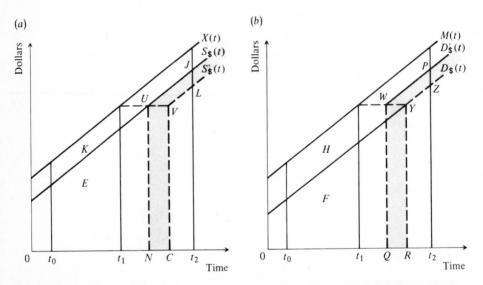

Figure 8.3 (a) B's exports (X) and supply of dollars $(S_\$)$. There is initially a small delay in the receipt of export revenue by B's exporters—the supply-of-dollars schedule $S_\$(t)$ lies to the right of exports schedule $X(t)$. At time t_1, B's exporters delay their receipts for an additional amount of time (UV) because, say, they fear a devaluation of the pound sterling. As a result, B's reserves tend to fall by the amount shown by the shaded area. (b) B's imports (M) and demand for dollars $(D_\$)$. There is initially a delay in the payment of imports, $D_\$(t)$, from the time the goods, $M(t)$, are imported by B's importers. This delay is given by the horizontal distance between the two schedules. At time t_1, B's importers accelerate their payments by reducing their credit period by WY, presumably because they fear a devaluation of the pound sterling. As a result, B's reserves fall by the amount shown by the shaded area.

Consider the time period starting at time t_0 and ending at time t_1. For this time period, the change ($\pm$) in the reserves (Δg) of B's monetary authorities is given by

$$\Delta g = E - F = (E + K) - (F + H) - (K - H)$$

$$= \text{B's trade balance} - \text{B's export of trade capital}$$

The area K shows the increase in the stock of claims of B's exporters against A's importers. This is an export of trade capital from B to A. Similarly, the area H shows the increase in the stock of liabilities of B's importers to A's exporters. It is an import of trade capital into B. Accordingly, the difference $K - H$ shows B's net export of trade capital.

How do leads and lags in commercial payments affect the change in B's reserves? Assume that at time t_1 commercial traders come to expect a devaluation of the pound sterling. B's exporters delay their receipts for an additional amount of time UV. Hence, the supply of dollars continues up to point U along the curve $S_s(t)$—the receipts up to point U reflect commitments prior to the change in the credit period. Beyond point U the supply of dollars jumps to the broken curve $S'_s(t)$. Thus, B's receipts cease completely from U to V, and the stock of claims of B's exporters against A's importers (that is, B's export of trade capital) increases by the shaded area $NCVLJU$. B's reserves will be depleted by this export of trade capital.

Note that if the export revenue is increasing through time, as shown in fig. 8.3, B's loss of reserves will continue into the future. However, if the export revenue remains constant through time, i.e., if the $X(t)$ curve is horizontal, B's loss of reserves following the increase in lags will be contained in the first period only.

Consider now B's imports (panel b). B's importers accelerate their payments by reducing their credit period by WY. Thus, the payments by B's importers follow the $D_s(t)$ curve up to point Y, and then they jump back to W and follow the broken curve $D'_s(t)$. Thus, B's payments during this period increase by the amount shown by the shaded area $QRYZPW$. The latter area shows B's export of trade capital and loss of reserves following the change in the credit terms. Again this loss of reserves will not continue in future time periods if imports are constant through time.

Leads and Lags and the Simultaneous Equilibrium of the Spot and Forward Markets

How do leads and lags fit into the simultaneous equilibrium of the spot and forward markets, as illustrated in fig. 8.2? For this purpose, assume that the $X(t)$ and $M(t)$ curves of fig. 8.3 are horizontal. This is actually required by the static partial equilibrium model. Further assume that the rate of exchange is at the lower support point and country B loses reserves. Commercial traders become convinced that devaluation of the pound sterling is imminent. B's exporters tend to delay their receipts while B's importers accelerate their payments. This phenomenon could be represented graphically by a temporary shift to the right of the excess supply schedule for pounds sterling spot, which lasts for one period only.

But this approach is inconsistent with our earlier decision to let the excess supply schedule for pounds sterling spot show the difference $X(t) - M(t)$ instead of $S_s(t) - D_s(t)$; in addition, it conceals much useful information. Accordingly, the approach suggested by the following theorem is preferred.

Theorem 8.1 A delay in receipts and an acceleration in payments (i.e., an increase in the leads and lags) implies an increased supply of (covered) arbitrage funds from the devaluation-prone country to the rest of the world and a decreased forward demand for the devaluation-prone currency. For instance, an increase in B's leads and lags can be represented graphically in fig. 8.2 by a shift to the left of (a) the supply of arbitrage funds from A to B and (b) the excess demand for pounds sterling forward.

PROOF The proof of the theorem is rather simple. For simplicity, assume that before the increase in leads and lags both exports and imports are paid on delivery, that is, $X(t) = S_s(t)$ and $M(t) = D_s(t)$. A delay in B's export receipts is equivalent to a cash payment on delivery plus an *uncovered* supply of funds from B to A. Similarly, the acceleration in B's payments for imports (payment in advance) is also equivalent to a cash payment on delivery plus an *uncovered* supply of funds from B to A. Further, an *uncovered* supply of funds from B to A is equivalent to a covered supply plus a supply of pounds sterling forward.

Another and perhaps simpler way of looking at this problem is to note that an increase in leads and lags amounts to spot speculation. As we have seen in chap. 1, spot speculation is equivalent to forward speculation plus covered-interest arbitrage. Once the problem of leads and lags is put in the above framework, it becomes evident that speculation through leads and lags is much more severe in its adverse effects on a weak currency than pure forward speculation. This is because leads and lags imply forward speculation *plus* an additional supply of arbitrage funds from the country with the weak currency to the rest of the world.

Similar conclusions can be reached when exports are delayed and imports accelerated as opposed to receipts and payments. This becomes clear when it is observed that delay in exports and acceleration in imports amounts to spot speculation. The only difference is that in the present case speculation is carried out by means of increasing or decreasing the stock of inventories rather than the stock of claims or liabilities. Thus, an increase in B's leads and lags brings about an increase in inventories in B, and a decrease in inventories in A, of both A-exportables and B-exportables. B's loss of reserves due to such leads and lags essentially results from the need to finance the accumulation of inventories by B's exporters and importers.

Finally, note that the reserves lost through leads and lags are eventually recovered when confidence in the devaluation-prone currency is restored either when the anticipated devaluation takes place or when it is realized that the basic balance-of-payments disturbance is only temporary and will be reversed soon. When confidence is eventually restored, exporters and importers return to their normal practices and the disturbing leads and lags are reversed.

8.5 EXCHANGE-RATE ADJUSTMENTS

As explained earlier, long-run balance-of-payments equilibrium exists (in the absence of long-term capital flows and unilateral transfers) only when the balance of trade is zero. Under a flexible-exchange-rate system the market forces are counted on to bring about this state of affairs. But under the adjustable-peg system the authorities at times of fundamental disequilibrium may have to change the par value of their currency. Exchange-rate adjustment is the most potent weapon for correcting a balance-of-payments disequilibrium. What conditions must be satisfied for a successful exchange-rate adjustment—in particular, a deva-luation? In other words, what are the necessary and/or sufficient conditions for a devaluation to improve the devaluing country's balance of trade? This question is answered provisionally in the present section within the context of the partial equilibrium model. We return to this problem later in part two, where the analysis is expanded to include income effects as well.

Let the symbols T_f and T_d stand for country B's balance of trade expressed in terms of foreign currency ($\$$) and domestic currency ($£$), respectively. That is,

$$T_f \equiv S_\$(R^*) - D_\$(R^*) \tag{8.1}$$

$$T_d \equiv D_£(R) - S_£(R) \tag{8.2}$$

$$T_d = R^* T_f \qquad (R^* \equiv 1/R) \tag{8.3}$$

All symbols have been introduced earlier in chap. 3. See also the list of symbols (p. xxiii).

Effects of Devaluation on T_f

To determine the effect of a devaluation of the pound sterling on B's balance of trade expressed in foreign currency, we differentiate eq. (8.1) with respect to R^*:

$$\frac{dT_f}{dR^*} = \left(\frac{dS_\$}{dR^*}\right) - \left(\frac{dD_\$}{dR^*}\right)$$

$$= \left(\frac{1}{R^*}\right)(S_\$ e_s^\$ - D_\$ e_d^\$)$$

$$= RS_\$(e_s^\$ - e_d^\$) + T_f R e_d^\$ \tag{8.4}$$

A successful devaluation requires $(dT_f/dR^*) > 0$.

When either B's balance of trade is zero before devaluation (that is, $T_f = 0$) or when B's demand elasticity for imports is zero (that is, $e_{mb} = 0$, implying $e_d^\$ = 0$), the condition for a successful devaluation reduces to $e_s^\$ - e_d^\$ > 0$. The latter condi-tion is nothing else but the condition for stability in the foreign exchange market. Accordingly, theorem 5.3 (Marshall-Lerner condition) applies to the present case as well. That is, the Marshall-Lerner condition (inequality (5.4)) is in general sufficient (but not necessary) both for stability in the foreign exchange market and successful devaluation; it becomes necessary and sufficient (a) when the supply elasticities of exports of both countries are infinite and (b) when the demand elasticity for imports of *either* country is zero.

In general, when the balance of trade is in deficit ($T_f < 0$) before devaluation and $e_{mb} < 0$, the term $T_f Re_d^\$$ is strictly positive. Hence, the condition $e_s^\$ - e_d^\$ > 0$, and therefore the Marshall-Lerner condition now becomes sufficient (but not necessary) for a successful devaluation.

When B's export supply elasticity is zero (that is, $e_{xb} = 0$), the balance of trade improves with devaluation, assuming only that both demand elasticities for imports are strictly negative ($e_{ma} < 0$, $e_{mb} < 0$). This is so because, in this case, $e_s^\$ = 0$ and $e_d^\$ < 0$. The same is true if $e_{ma} = -1$, $e_{mb} < 0$, and $e_{xb} > 0$.

Finally, devaluation has no effect on T_f in the following two cases: (a) when $e_{xb} = e_{mb} = 0$ (because in this case $e_d^\$ = e_s^\$ = 0$); and (b) when $T_f = e_{xa} = e_{ma} = 0$ (because in this case $e_d^\$ = e_s^\$ = -1$).

Effects of Devaluation on T_d

Are the conditions for improving T_f with devaluation identical with the conditions for improving T_d? Does T_d improve when T_f improves? Is the Marshall-Lerner condition sufficient, in general, for improving T_d with devaluation as is the case with T_f? Unfortunately, the answer to all these questions is a negative one.

To determine the effect of a devaluation of the pound sterling on T_d, differentiate eq. (8.2) with respect to R:

$$\frac{dT_d}{dR} = R^*(D_\pounds e_d^\pounds - S_\pounds e_s^\pounds)$$

$$= R^* S_\pounds (e_d^\pounds - e_s^\pounds) + T_d R^* e_d^\pounds \qquad (8.5)$$

A successful devaluation requires $(dT_d/dR) < 0$.

When B's balance of trade is zero before devaluation, the conditions for improving T_f are indeed identical with the conditions for improving T_d. In all other cases, the conditions for improving T_d are more stringent than those for improving T_f. This can be seen as follows. If $T_d = T_f = 0$, the condition for improving T_f (that is, $e_s^\$ - e_d^\$ > 0$) is identical with the condition for improving T_d (that is, $e_d^\pounds - e_s^\pounds < 0$) because, as we have seen in chap. 3, $e_s^\$ + e_d^\pounds = -1$ and $e_s^\pounds + e_d^\$ = -1$. But if $T_f < 0$ and $T_d < 0$, the inequality $e_s^\$ - e_d^\$ > 0$ is sufficient (but not necessary) for improving T_f with devaluation, while the condition $e_d^\pounds - e_s^\pounds < 0$ is *necessary but not sufficient* for improving T_d since $T_d R^* e_d^\pounds > 0$. Accordingly, it is not inconceivable for T_f to improve and T_d to deteriorate with devaluation. Nevertheless, when T_d improves T_f improves also.

When either $T_d = 0$ or $e_{ma} = 0$ (implying $e_d^\pounds = 0$), devaluation improves T_d if the Marshall-Lerner condition is satisfied (theorem 5.3). However, when $T_d < 0$ and $e_{ma} < 0$, the Marshall-Lerner condition, while necessary, is not sufficient for improving T_d with devaluation. For while the Marshall-Lerner condition guarantees that $e_d^\pounds - e_s^\pounds < 0$, it does not necessarily guarantee that $(dT_d/dR) < 0$ because $T_d R^* e_d^\pounds > 0$ by assumption. Nevertheless, there is one exception to this conclusion: when the devaluing country's demand for imports is elastic (that is,

$e_{mb} < -1$), the Marshall-Lerner condition becomes sufficient for improving T_d. This becomes obvious when one observes that, when $e_{mb} < -1$, $e_s^£ > 0$. (The reader is encouraged to illustrate this result graphically.)

The effect of devaluation on T_d is nil (that is, $(dT_d/dR) = 0$) in the following two cases: (a) when $e_{xa} = e_{ma} = 0$ (because in this case $e_d^£ = e_s^£ = 0$); and (b) when $T_d = e_{xb} = e_{mb} = 0$ (because in this case $e_d^£ = e_s^£ = -1$). Further, T_d always improves with devaluation when $e_{xa} = 0$, assuming only that both demand elasticities for imports are strictly negative. The same is true if $e_{mb} = -1$, $e_{ma} < 0$, and $e_{xa} > 0$.

In comparing the conditions for improving T_d with those for improving T_f, it is interesting to note that $-T_d$ is A's balance of trade expressed in terms of foreign currency (from A's point of view). Hence, the conditions for decreasing B's balance-of-trade *deficit* expressed in domestic currency by means of a devaluation of the pound sterling are identical with the conditions for reducing A's balance-of-trade *surplus* expressed in foreign currency (from A's point of view) by means of a revaluation of the dollar ($\equiv$ devaluation of the pound sterling).

Exchange-Rate Adjustments in Practice

Exchange-rate adjustment has not worked well in practice. Governments dislike it for various reasons. First, devaluation is usually identified with loss of national prestige. Second, the authorities lose to the speculators, as explained earlier. To put it more bluntly, in effect the authorities subsidize speculation. Third, because every exchange-rate adjustment must be kept a secret until it is officially declared in order to thwart massive speculation against the devaluation-prone currency, the authorities are put in the unpleasant position of having to lie to their constituents. Fourth, devaluation is eventually successful only if it restores confidence in the devalued currency. Otherwise speculation would intensify and force a further devaluation. To restore confidence in their currency, convince the public that devaluation was necessary, and regain the lost reserves, the authorities more often than not devalue their currency much more than is otherwise necessary. Accordingly, the deficit is converted into a surplus and creates difficulties for other countries whose earlier surpluses are now converted into deficits. Fifth, as explained earlier in chap. 4, devaluation causes domestic prices to rise; this usually leads labor unions to demand higher money wages. As money wages rise, the competitive advantage gained initially by the devaluation is lost. Finally, exchange-rate adjustment is asymmetrical. It is allowed for the nonreserve countries but disallowed for the reserve country.

8.6 THE PURCHASING-POWER PARITY THEORY: A DIGRESSION

The purchasing-power parity theory is an attempt to explain, and perhaps more importantly measure statistically, the equilibrium rate of exchange and i̶ ̶v̶a̶r̶i̶a̶- tions by means of the price levels and their variations in different countr̶ based on the simple idea that a certain amount of money should purchase the same representative bundle of commodities in different countries. In other words, a certain amount of money should have the same purchasing power in different countries (hence the term *purchasing-power parity*).

The purchasing-power parity theory is usually associated with the Swedish economist Gustav Cassel (1916; 1918; 1922, pp. 137–170; 1928, pp. 1–33; 1932, chap. XX) who also invented the term purchasing-power parity (PPP). Nevertheless, Haberler (1961, p. 45) points out that "essentially the same type of reasoning was employed more than a hundred years ago by members of the classical English school to explain the discount of sterling during the Bank Restriction period, 1797–1821. . . ." The well-known views of David Hume, David Ricardo, and Henry Thornton are all quoted by Haberler (1961, pp. 46–47).

The PPP theory has been severely criticized through the years (Balassa, 1964; Haberler, 1945; Metzler, 1947; Samuelson, 1964; Taussig, 1927, chap. 26). Nevertheless, attempts to prove its validity never ceased (Gailliot, 1970; Hansen, 1948; Houthakker, 1962; Yeager, 1958). Accordingly, we may take it that the issue has not been settled yet.

The Two Versions of the PPP Theory

Two versions of the PPP theory are usually distinguished in the literature: (*a*) the absolute version and (*b*) the relative (or comparative) version. The absolute version declares that at every moment "the rate of exchange between the two countries will be determined by the quotient between the general levels of prices in the two countries" (Cassel, 1916). Cassel (1918) christens this rate "the purchasing power parity." (See also Cassel, 1928, p. 9.) The relative version is a comparative-statics proposition. In particular, it is concerned with the effects of inflation on an initial equilibrium rate of exchange. "When two currencies have undergone inflation, the normal rate of exchange will be equal to the old rate multiplied by the quotient of the degree of inflation in the one country and in the other. . . . This parity I call *purchasing power parity*" (Cassel, 1922, p. 140). Cassel is concerned with fully employed economies only. In the relative version he also abstracts from structural changes in the real sectors, such as technical progress, factor growth, changes in tastes, changes in tariffs, etc.

The PPP Theory as a Trivial Truism

The PPP theory has been criticized by Heckscher and Keynes as a trivial truism (see Samuelson, 1964, p. 147, and 1971, p. 6; Viner, 1937, p. 382). It has been correctly noted that in the absence of transportation costs and trade impediments spatial arbitrage for each commodity ensures that

$$R = \frac{p_i^a}{p_i^b} \tag{8.6}$$

where $p_i^j \equiv$ price of ith commodity in jth country expressed in jth currency (eq. (8.6) is identical to our earlier eqs. (4.1) and (4.2)). Since eq. (8.6) holds for each good, it must also hold trivially for a ratio of any *equally weighted* price index numbers (P_A, P_B). Thus,

$$R = \frac{P_A}{P_B} \tag{8.7}$$

In addition, eqs. (8.6) and (8.7) must hold for all time periods. In particular, for any two time periods indicated by the superscripts 0 and t, eq. (8.7) implies that

$$R^t = \frac{P_A^t/P_A^0}{P_B^t/P_B^0} R^0 \tag{8.8}$$

Equations (8.7) and (8.8) hold trivially for *all* values of the rate of exchange (R). Accordingly, neither can be used to determine *the* equilibrium R. If by the absolute and relative versions of the PPP theory is meant nothing more than the trivial eqs. (8.7) and (8.8), respectively, Cassel's theory is totally useless. Is there anything more to it than this?

The Relative Version as a Comparative-Statics Proposition

First consider the relative version, which incidentally received more attention in the literature than the absolute version. As noted earlier, the relative version is a comparative-statics proposition. In a sense Cassel was invoking the quantity theory of money and was proposing no more than the neutrality of money. This can be illustrated by means of the partial equilibrium model of chap. 4. Let R_0 be an initial equilibrium rate of exchange. Assume that country A increases its money supply by $x\%$. Under conditions of full employment and no structural changes, as explained earlier, A's supply and demand curves shift upward by $x\%$ also. In particular, A's supply-of-exports and demand-for-imports schedules (expressed in B's currency) shift upward in exactly the same way as if the rate of exchange (R) had fallen by $x\%$. Evidently, equilibrium can be reestablished only when R rises by $x\%$ above its initial equilibrium value.

This proposition is no longer a truism and makes the valid point that monetary conditions exert an important influence on the rate of exchange. Nevertheless, the proposition rests on the assumption that changes in technology, tastes, factor supplies, levels of employment, trade impediments, and capital movements do not occur during the transition period. Such changes no doubt take place incessantly in the international economy and do exert a profound influence on the rate of exchange—a fact either completely ignored or heavily discounted by the proponents of the PPP doctrine who believed that monetary factors alone were important. Finally, note that in any statistical verification of the theory, even when all other things do remain equal, extreme care must be exercised in determining the appropriate degrees of inflation in different countries, simply because (a) eq. (8.8) does hold trivially for equilibrium as well as for disequilibrium situations, and (b) the price level of each country depends on the rate of exchange—a fact which follows from the analysis of chap. 4.

The Absolute Version of the PPP Theory

Turn now to the absolute version. Cassel (1922, p. 142) warned that:

> People want to determine by direct means the quotient of the purchasing power of money in the respective countries, and to regard this quotient as the normal level of the exchange rates. *But the problem is not so simple.* It is only if we know the exchange rate which represents a certain equilibrium that we can calculate the rate which represents the same equilibrium at an altered value of the monetary units of the two countries (italics added).

In this statement, and in many others similar to it, Cassel seems to give credence to the relative version while undermining the validity of the absolute version. On another occasion, Cassel (1928, pp. 10–11) explains that:

> Equilibrium in the international balance of trade can evidently only be reached at a rate of exchange which will enable A to sell as much to B as B to A. *This condition may serve as the exact definition of the rate of exchange that represents the Purchasing Power Parity.* Obviously, at this rate of exchange the purchasing power of the one currency is as nearly equal to that of the corresponding amount of the other currency as it is possible to ascertain (italics added).

Some economists (e.g., Haberler, 1936, p. 35; Samuelson, 1971, p. 6, fn. 4) have rejected the absolute version because of the existence of transportation costs. But as we saw earlier and was fully recognized by Samuelson (1964, 1971), even in the absence of transportation costs, eq. (8.7) cannot be used to determine *the* equilibrium R. What is more, Cassel himself tells us in the above-quoted passage that eq. (8.7) cannot be used directly to determine the precise equilibrium R, and he explains that the condition of equilibrium in the balance of trade " may serve as the exact definition of the exchange rate that represents the Purchasing Power Parity." Is Cassel rejecting the absolute version? Is he switching now to the balance-of-trade theory?

Equation (8.7) gives R as the ratio of the price levels of the two countries. But as noted earlier, each price level is a function of R. Which price levels then are to be used? In the absence of transportation costs, eq. (8.7) holds trivially for any R if P_A and P_B are the *current* price levels prevailing *during trade*. This version was rejected earlier as a useless triviality. A very generous interpretation of Cassel (1932, pp. 657–659) reveals that the absolute version of the PPP theory may be equivalent to a well-known proposition of the classical theory of international trade, *if* the price levels used in eq. (8.7) are the *autarkic* price levels of countries A and B.

Consider again countries A and B producing n commodities $(X_1, X_2, \ldots, X_n)$ with labor only. Let a_i and b_i denote the labor requirements for the production of 1 unit of the ith commodity in countries A and B, respectively. Further, assume that $a_1/b_1 < a_2/b_2 < \cdots < a_n/b_n$. In the autarkic equilibrium, the price of the ith commodity is given by $w_a a_i$ and $w_b b_i$ in countries A and B, respectively, where $w_j \equiv$ money wage rate in the jth country expressed in that country's currency $(j = a, b)$. Accordingly, the autarkic price levels of countries A and B are

$$P_A = w_a(\lambda_1 a_1 + \lambda_2 a_2 + \cdots + \lambda_n a_n) \tag{8.9}$$

$$P_B = w_b(\lambda_1 b_1 + \lambda_2 b_2 + \cdots + \lambda_n b_n) \tag{8.10}$$

where the λ_i values are a common set of weights. Taking the ratio of these autarkic price levels and rearranging, we obtain

$$R \equiv \frac{P_A}{P_B} = \left[\frac{(\lambda_1 b_1)(a_1/b_1) + (\lambda_2 b_2)(a_2/b_2) + \cdots + (\lambda_n b_n)(a_n/b_n)}{\lambda_1 b_1 + \lambda_2 b_2 + \cdots + \lambda_n b_n} \right] \frac{w_a}{w_b} \quad (8.11)$$

The expression in the brackets is a weighted average of the ratios a_i/b_i. Hence, R must satisfy the following inequality:

$$(w_a/w_b)(a_1/b_1) < R < (w_a/w_b)(a_n/b_n) \quad (8.12a)$$

or, multiplying through by the ratio w_b/w_a,

$$\frac{a_1}{b_1} < R \frac{w_b}{w_a} < \frac{a_n}{b_n} \quad (8.12b)$$

Inequality $(8.12b)$ is indeed quite familiar to students of the classical theory of international trade (see Chacholiades, 1973, p. 65). Inequality $(8.12a)$ gives only the limits of R; it cannot be used to determine the precise equilibrium value of R. As Cassel pointed out, the precise equilibrium value of R can only be determined by the condition that the value of exports be equal to the value of imports (in the absence of any capital movements).

Conclusion

We therefore conclude that there is a grain of truth in the PPP theory. In particular, the relative version of the PPP theory makes the valid point that monetary factors exert a profound influence on the rate of exchange. But monetary factors are not the only factors influencing the rate of exchange. Structural factors, such as technical progress, factor growth, changes in tastes, tariffs, etc., are also important. On the other hand, the absolute version, even in the light of the preceding generous interpretation, does not add anything to our knowledge—anything, that is, which was not known to Mill, Mangoldt, Marshall, Edgeworth, Taussig, Viner, Graham, Haberler, and Elliot.

SELECTED BIBLIOGRAPHY

Balassa, B. (1964). "The Purchasing-Power Parity Doctrine: A Reappraisal." *Journal of Political Economy*, vol. 72, pp. 584–596. Reprinted in R. N. Cooper (Ed.), *International Finance*. Penguin Books, Inc., Baltimore, Md., 1969.

Bernstein, E. M. (1958). "Strategic Factors in Balance of Payments Adjustment." *Review of Economics and Statistics*, vol. XL (February), pp. 133–137.

Cassel, Gustav (1916). "The Present Situation of the Foreign Exchanges." *Economic Journal* (March).

——— (1918). "Abnormal Deviations in International Exchanges." *Economic Journal* (December), pp. 413–415.

——— (1922). *Money and Foreign Exchange After 1914*. Constable and Company Ltd., London.

——— (1928). *Foreign Investments*. The University of Chicago Press, Chicago, Ill.

——— (1932). *The Theory of Social Economy*, new revised ed. Reprints of Economic Classics, Augustus M. Kelley, Publishers, New York, 1967.

Chacholiades, M. (1973). *The Pure Theory of International Trade.* Aldine Publishing Company, Chicago, Ill.

Einsig, P. (1968). *Leads and Lags: The Main Cause of Devaluation.* St. Martin's Press, New York.

Evans, T. G. (Ed.) (1973). *The Monetary Muddle.* Dow Jones and Company, Inc.

Gailliot, H. J. (1970). "Purchasing Power Parity as an Explanation of Long-Term Changes in Exchange Rates." *Journal of Money, Credit and Banking,* vol. II (August), pp. 348–357.

Haberler, G. (1936). *The Theory of International Trade.* William Hodge and Company, London.

——— (1945). "The Choice of Exchange Rates After the War." *American Economic Review,* pp. 308–318.

——— (1961). *A Survey of International Trade Theory,* revised and enlarged ed. Special Papers in International Economics no. 1, International Finance Section, Princeton University, Princeton, N.J.

Hansen, A. H. (1948). "A Note on Fundamental Disequilibrium." In S. E. Harris (Ed.), *Foreign Economic Policy for the United States.* Harvard University Press, Cambridge, Mass.

——— (1965). *The Dollar and the International Monetary System.* McGraw-Hill Book Company, New York.

Hansen, B. (1961). *Foreign Trade Credits and Exchange Reserves.* North-Holland Publishing Company, Amsterdam.

Hirshman, A. O. (1949). "Devaluation and the Trade Balance." *Review of Economics and Statistics* (February), pp. 50–53.

Houthakker, H. S. (1962). "Exchange Rate Adjustment," In *Factors Affecting the United States Balance of Payments.* U.S. Congress Joint Economic Committee, Washington, D.C., pp. 287–304.

Kenen, P. B. (1965). "Trade, Speculation, and the Forward Exchange Rate." In R. E. Baldwin et al. (Eds.), *Trade, Growth, and the Balance of Payments.* Rand-McNally and Company, Chicago, Ill.

Kindleberger, C. P. (1973). *International Economics.* R. D. Irwin, Inc., Homewood, Ill., chaps. 19, 23 to 25, and app. G.

Meade, J. E. (1951). *The Theory of International Economic Policy,* vol. I, *The Balance of Payments.* Oxford University Press, Inc., New York, chaps. XV to XVII.

Metzler, L. A. (1947). "Exchange Rates and Prices," from "Exchange Rates and the International Monetary Fund," *International Monetary Policies.* Postwar Economic Studies no. 7, Board of Governors of the Federal Reserve System, Washington, D.C. Reprinted in W. R. Allen and C. L. Allen (Eds.), *Foreign Trade and Finance.* The Macmillan Company, New York, pp. 287–295.

Mikesell, R. F. (1954). *Foreign Exchange in the Postwar World.* Twentieth Century Fund, New York.

Mundell, R. A. (1961). "The International Disequilibrium System." *Kyklos,* vol. 14, pp. 154–172.

Officer, L. H. (1972). "International Monetary Reform: A Review Article." *Journal of Economic Issues* (March).

Samuelson, P. A. (1964). "Theoretical Notes on Trade Problems." *The Review of Economics and Statistics,* vol. XLVI (May), pp. 145–154.

——— (1971). "An Exact Hume-Ricardo-Marshall Model of International Trade." *Journal of International Economics,* vol. 1, no. 1, pp. 1–18.

Scammell, W. M. (1961). *International Monetary Policy,* 2d ed. Macmillan and Company, Ltd., London.

Sohmen, E. (1969). *Flexible Exchange Rates,* revised ed. The University of Chicago Press, Chicago, Ill., chap. 3.

Stern, R. M. (1973). *The Balance of Payments.* Aldine Publishing Company, Chicago, Ill., chap. 5.

Taussig, F. W. (1927). *International Trade.* The Macmillan Company, New York.

Tew, B. (1952). *International Monetary Cooperation, 1945–1952,* Hutchinson's University Library, London.

Triffin, R. (1957). *Europe and the Money Muddle.* Yale University Press, New Haven, Conn.

——— (1960). *Gold and the Dollar Crisis.* Yale University Press, New Haven, Conn.

Viner, J. (1937). *Studies in the Theory of International Trade.* Harper and Brothers, New York.

Yeager, L. B. (1958). "A Rehabilitation of Purchasing-Power Parity." *Journal of Political Economy* (December), pp. 516–530.

——— (1966). *International Monetary Relations.* Harper and Row, Publishers, New York, chaps. 10 to 13, 19, and 26 to 28.

TWO

PRICE AND INCOME EFFECTS AND POLICIES FOR INTERNAL AND EXTERNAL BALANCE

NINE

A BASIC MODEL

The analysis of part one has been developed within the context of the Bickerdike-Robinson-Machlup partial equilibrium model for commodity trade. The time has come to replace the partial equilibrium model by a more general model—a model which would include, in addition, the income effects which were completely ignored by the partial equilibrium model. Part two is concerned mainly with this generalization. The present chapter develops a useful framework for the ensuing analysis and serves both as an introduction and an overview of part two.

9.1 THE BASIC ASSUMPTIONS

It is assumed as before that there are two countries, A (home country) and B (foreign country), with national currencies the dollar and the pound sterling, respectively. There are two commodities, called as before A-exportables and B-exportables. However, we shall simplify our analysis from now on by assuming that country A specializes completely in the production of (i.e., produces only) A-exportables, and B specializes completely in B-exportables. This simplification is the price we pay for the introduction of income effects. Fortunately it does not seriously affect any important conclusions. It is further assumed that each country produces its output by means of a single factor of production—labor. Constant returns to scale prevail in each country. In particular, by an appropriate choice of the units of measurement, the labor coefficients of production are reduced to unity. The interest rate in each country is given, perfect competition prevails everywhere, and transportation costs as well as barriers to trade (e.g., tariffs) are zero. Tastes in each country are represented by a nonintersecting social indifference map with regular convexity. Commodity exports are the only source of supply of foreign exchange, and commodity imports are the only purpose of demand for foreign exchange. For the moment, no specific assumption is made regarding the flexibility of the money-wage rate or the relationship between aggregate spending (absorption) and national income in each country. More on this later.

The present model has several limitations. For instance, it excludes the possibility of diversification in production, the existence of nontraded goods, and the multiplicity of factors of production—to mention only a few. Our justification for this model is twofold. First, these simplifications permit us to cut through much detail and go directly to the real issues—any complications may be introduced at a later stage. Indeed, some of the assumptions enumerated presently are modified in later chapters. Second, none of the important conclusions of the model are destroyed when any or all simplifying assumptions are dropped. From the point of view of balance-of-payments theory nothing is gained by unnecessarily introducing more complications into our basic model. Part three of this book expands the present model to include the money and capital markets.

9.2 GENERAL EQUILIBRIUM†

Before commenting on the adjustment process it is natural to consider briefly in the present section the general equilibrium of our basic model. For this purpose, it is tentatively assumed that "aggregate expenditure on commodities = aggregate income" in each country. This is the usual assumption made in the context of the pure theory of trade.

General equilibrium requires that supply equals demand in all markets: the labor markets, the commodity markets, and the foreign exchange market. This is illustrated by the box diagram of fig. 9.1. The distance $0_a 0$ shows A's output of A-exportables when A's supply of labor is fully employed. Similarly, the distance $0_b 0$ shows B's output of B-exportables when B's supply of labor is fully employed. Now imagine that A's social indifference map is drawn with respect to the origin 0_a, as illustrated by the indifference curve $I_a I'_a$. Similarly, imagine that B's social indifference map is drawn with respect to the origin 0_b, as illustrated by the indifference curve $I_b I'_b$. The coordinates of any point in the box with respect to 0_a and 0_b give the amounts of A-exportables and B-exportables allocated to A and B, respectively. Given the assumption of free trade and the absence of transportation costs, the commodity prices and, therefore, the marginal rates of substitution must be the same in the two countries. Accordingly, general equilibrium must occur somewhere along the contract curve $0_a 0_b$, which is nothing but the locus of tangencies between the two sets of indifference curves as illustrated by point E. Which point along the contract curve represents general equilibrium?

† The discussion of this section presupposes some knowledge of the pure theory of international trade. The reader may find useful chaps. 2 and 3 of Chacholiades (1973).

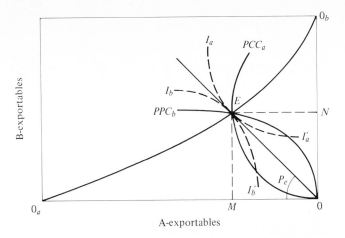

Figure 9.1 General equilibrium. In this box diagram all markets, including the foreign exchange market, are in equilibrium. A's (B's) full-employment output and aggregate spending are given by $0_a 0 (0_b 0)$. Both commodity markets clear at point E, and each country's balance of trade is zero.

By assumption, "aggregate income = aggregate expenditure" in both countries. This means that both A's and B's budget lines must pass through point 0 at all prices. Imagine that a budget line through 0 rotates continuously from the position 00_a to 00_b and determine the two price-consumption curves PCC_a and PCC_b. The curve PCC_a is the locus of tangencies between the rotating budget line and A's indifference curves, while PCC_b is the locus of tangencies between the rotating budget line and B's indifference curves. As is well known, these two price-consumption curves necessarily intersect each other along the contract curve at an odd number of points. For simplicity, fig. 9.1 illustrates the case of a single intersection at E. General equilibrium occurs at E. Note that the coordinates of point E with respect to 0_a ($0_a M$, ME) show A's *absorption* of A-exportables and B-exportables, respectively. (*Absorption* consists of consumption, government spending, and investment, including inventory accumulation. See below, chap. 10.) Similarly, the coordinates of E with respect to 0_b (NE, $0_b N$) show B's absorption of A-exportables and B-exportables, respectively. Finally, the coordinates of E with respect to 0 ($0M$, $0N$) show A's exports of A-exportables and B's exports of B-exportables, respectively.

By definition, A's terms of trade (p) are given by the ratio p_a/p_b, or p_a^*/p_b^* since $p_a = Rp_a^*$, $p_b = Rp_b^*$. For our present purposes, it is more convenient to write A's terms of trade as follows:

$$p \equiv \frac{p_a}{Rp_b^*} \qquad (9.1)$$

This makes it clear that a change in p may come about in any one of the following three ways (or any combination): (*a*) a change in p_a which in our model reflects a change in A's money-wage rate; (*b*) a change in p_b^* which reflects a change in B's money-wage rate; and (*c*) a change in the rate of exchange R.

A's equilibrium terms of trade (p_e) are given by the slope of the vector $0E$ as shown on fig. 9.1. No information on the absolute prices or the exchange rate is given by the diagram. Nevertheless, the information given by fig. 9.1 is sufficient to guarantee equilibrium in the foreign exchange market, for $p_e = ME/0M$, or $p_a/Rp_b^* = ME/0M$, or $p_a \cdot 0M = Rp_b^* \cdot ME$. That is, the dollar value of A's exports of A-exportables equals the dollar value of A's imports of B-exportables.

It is well known to students of the pure theory of trade that given full employment and " aggregate income = aggregate expenditure " the Marshall-Lerner condition is necessary and sufficient for the stability of the long-run equilibrium illustrated in fig. 9.1. Indeed, the equilibrium of fig. 9.1 is stable, as the reader should verify. Further, in the presence of multiple equilibria, each unstable equilibrium is always bounded by two stable equilibria. For a discussion of these propositions, see Chacholiades (1973, chap. 6).

9.3 THE ADJUSTMENT PROCESS: (a) INCOME = DESIRED ABSORPTION

Can the long-run equilibrium of fig. 9.1 be attained automatically? That is, does a disequilibrium state generate automatically forces which tend to restore equilibrium? If such automaticity exists, what is the precise adjustment process? On the other hand, if such automaticity does not exist, what policy measures must be pursued to restore equilibrium? These are important questions. The rest of the book is devoted to them. The rest of the present chapter gives only tentative answers to these questions and prepares the ground for the subsequent discussion.

We are primarily concerned with the problems of equilibrium and adjustment in the foreign exchange market. Nevertheless, as noted in chap. 2, the foreign exchange market is not an ordinary market because it provides the link among the economies of the world. Long-run equilibrium in the foreign exchange market is indeed akin to general equilibrium. Thus, *long-run* equilibrium in the foreign exchange market requires that all other markets are also in equilibrium. In addition, the adjustment process of the foreign exchange market is inherently much more complicated than the adjustment process of any other ordinary market. (These ideas were anticipated in chap. 2.)

Disequilibrium in the foreign exchange market may coincide with (or reflect) a disequilibrium in some other market or markets. But this is not necessary. As shown in sec. 9.4 below, disequilibrium in the foreign exchange market may also exist, even when all other markets are in equilibrium. In fact, the Bickerdike-Robinson-Machlup partial equilibrium model assumes that the markets for all internationally traded goods are *always* in equilibrium, although it remains silent on the state of the labor markets. The rest of the discussion of the present section deals with disequilibrium states in which, in addition to the foreign exchange market, some other market is out of equilibrium. Section 9.4 deals with the important case in which only the foreign exchange market is out of equilibrium.

Throughout the discussion of this section a very important assumption is

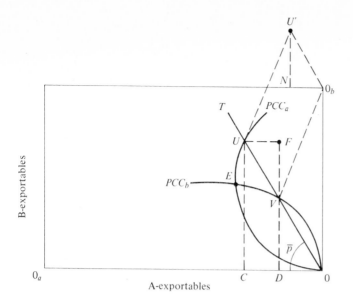

Figure 9.2 International disequilibrium. Points U and V show A's and B's *desired* absorption, respectively. The common *actual* absorption point, however, is F. Hence, A accumulates inventories involuntarily at the rate of UF per unit of time, while B decumulates inventories involuntarily at the rate FV. A pays for the inventory accumulation by means of losses of reserves to B. B's gain of reserves is, of course, the compensation for her involuntary inventory decumulation.

maintained; namely, that "income = desired spending" (or "absorption") in each country. This assumption is removed in sec. 9.4.

Consider fig. 9.2, which is similar to fig. 9.1. The contract curve and the social indifference curves have been omitted for simplicity. Long-run equilibrium occurs at E. However, the current price ratio ($\bar{p}$) given by the slope of the vector $0T$ is by assumption higher than the long-run equilibrium price ratio (p_e). This is clearly a disequilibrium situation.

There are, of course, many types of disturbances (e.g., changes in tastes, technology, factor supplies, etc.) which can cause a system to be out of long-run equilibrium. For our present purposes, the cause of disequilibrium is irrelevant.

What is the nature of the disequilibrium state portrayed in fig. 9.2? That is, what markets are out of equilibrium? Clearly, the labor markets are in equilibrium. Nevertheless, at the current price ratio ($\bar{p}$), country A wants to buy bundle U and country B, bundle V. The aggregate quantities of A-exportables and B-exportables demanded by both countries are given by the vector $0_a U'$ which is the vector sum of the vectors $0_a U$ and $V0_b$. This vector addition is carried out by completing the parallelogram $UV0_b U'$. Thus, the coordinates of point U' with respect to 0_a show the totals of A-exportables and B-exportables demanded by both A and B. On the other hand, the total supplies of A-exportables and B-exportables are given by the coordinates of point 0_b with respect to 0_a (e.g., the sides of the box). Accordingly, there exists an excess demand for B-exportables, given by the vertical distance NU', and an excess supply of A-exportables, given by the horizontal distance $N0_b$. Let us assume for the moment that all buyer plans are realized. That is, A's buyers are allowed to buy bundle U and B's buyers, bundle V. *A's producers are assumed to use the excess supply of A-exportables $(N0_b)$ to increase their inventories, and B's producers are assumed to meet the excess demand for B-exportables (NU') out of inventories.* Thus, the disequilibrium in the commodity markets is, by assumption, reflected in *unplanned inventory changes*.

What is the situation in the foreign exchange market? Observe that A actually exports to B only $D0$ units of A-exportables while B exports to A, CU (or DF) units of B-exportables. Given that the current price ratio $(\bar{p})$ is given by the slope of the vector $0T$, that is, $\bar{p} = DV/D0$, it follows that the value of A's exports falls short of the value of A's imports, that is, A is running an import surplus or a balance-of-payments deficit. This is verified as follows:

$$\bar{p} = \frac{DV}{D0}$$

or
$$\bar{p}D0 = DV$$

or
$$\left(\frac{\bar{p}_a}{R\bar{p}_b^*}\right)D0 = DV$$

or
$$\left(\frac{\bar{p}_a}{R}\right)D0 \equiv \text{supply of pounds sterling}$$

$$= \bar{p}_b^*DV < \bar{p}_b^*DF \equiv \text{demand for pounds sterling}$$

Actually, fig. 9.2 teaches us more. While A's *desired* absorption is indicated by point U, A's *actual* absorption occurs at F. (Recall that A's unplanned inventory accumulation is given by $N0_b$ which equals UF by the similarity of the triangles UFV and $0_b NU'$.) Clearly the value of actual absorption is higher than the value of desired absorption. In particular, A's *deficit* is nothing else but the excess of A's actual absorption over A's national income. Similarly, B's *surplus* is nothing else but the excess of B's national income over B's actual absorption at F. (Recall that B's unplanned inventory decumulation is given by the vertical distance NU' which equals FV.) These are important conclusions. They are summarized by the general identity: "balance of trade = national income − actual absorption." The latter identity, which should be obvious from fig. 9.2, is studied further in chap. 10.

In summary, the disequilibrium portrayed in fig. 9.2 implies disequilibrium in both commodity markets, and disequilibrium in the foreign exchange market. In particular, there exist:

1. An excess supply of A-exportables reflected in an increase in A's inventories per unit of time.
2. An excess demand for B-exportables reflected in a decrease in B's inventories per unit of time.

3. An excess demand for pounds sterling reflected in a decrease (increase) in A's (B's) foreign-exchange reserves. In effect, in this disequilibrium state, A is seen to convert its foreign exchange reserves into unwanted inventories, while B is seen to reluctantly convert its commodity inventories into foreign-exchange reserves.

The disequilibrium of fig. 9.2 can be easily corrected if the price ratio is allowed to fall to p_e, as shown in fig. 9.1. Are there any economic forces at work to bring this result about automatically? A reduction of the price ratio $\bar{p}$ may be accomplished by either (a) a fall in p_a, or (b) an increase in p_b^*, or (c) an increase in R. Based on the disequilibrium states in the markets for A-exportables, B-exportables, and foreign exchange (pounds sterling), a classical economist would hasten to point out that indeed in the current disequilibrium state there is a tendency for p_a to fall (because of the existence of an excess supply of A-exportables), a tendency for p_b^* to rise (because of the existence of an excess demand for B-exportables), and finally a tendency for R to rise (because of the existence of an excess demand for pounds sterling). Thus, in a world of perfect price flexibility one would expect that the price system would adjust quickly to restore equilibrium. Unfortunately, the world economy of today does not justify such optimism. Let us consider each one of these prices separately.

Consider first the rate of foreign exchange R. Although there exists an excess demand for pounds sterling, the question of an exchange-rate adjustment depends largely on the institutional arrangement of the foreign exchange market. Is the foreign exchange market organized on the basis of a fixed- or a variable-exchange rate? If the fixed-exchange-rate system is actually adopted, the rate of exchange will not change even though there exists an excess demand for pounds sterling. As noted in part one, under the gold standard exchange-rate adjustments were unthinkable, while under the adjustable peg there were many reasons why a deficit country would like to avoid devaluation (see sec. 8.5). The classical mechanism of international adjustment under an international gold standard is pursued further in chaps. 15 and 16.

What if a flexible-exchange-rate system is actually adopted, or if A's authorities devalue their currency? Will the system then return to the long-run equilibrium (E) smoothly? As noted in part one, whether a flexible-exchange-rate system functions smoothly depends heavily on whether speculation is stabilizing or destabilizing. In addition, it may be observed that an exchange-rate adjustment affects aggregate spending in a manner studied in detail in later chapters. If this is so, of course, even in the absence of any destabilizing speculation, the system will not move to point E by a mere exchange-rate adjustment simply because aggregate spending will not remain equal to the full-employment income in either country. Finally, another effect of a devaluation (or depreciation) of the dollar is the reduction of A's real income because of the deterioration of A's terms of trade. But such reduction may be resisted by A's workers who may attempt to negotiate higher money wages, causing the cost of production of A-exportables to increase and thus offsetting the adverse effect of devaluation on A's terms of trade. Without a deterioration in A's terms of trade there is no movement toward the long-run equilibrium point E.

We may, therefore, conclude that adjustment through exchange-rate variations is not that simple. The influence of the exchange rate and its variations on the behavior of the world economy is studied below in chaps. 11 and 13.

Turn now to the commodity prices p_a and p_b^*. As we saw earlier, there exists initially a tendency for p_a to fall and a tendency for p_b^* to rise. But a reduction in p_a necessarily implies a reduction in A's money-wage rate. As noted earlier, however, reductions in money wages are resisted. It is a common observation that the money-wage rate is notoriously inflexible in the downward direction. If the money-wage rate cannot be reduced, A's producers will have to cut their production of A-exportables (and employment of labor)—they cannot be expected to accumulate inventories indefinitely. As A's production and income fall, A's spending falls also; this reduction in spending reduces the demand for both A-exportables and B-exportables. As the demand for B-exportables falls, the tendency for p_b^* to rise disappears. Eventually, equilibrium is restored both in the commodity markets and the foreign exchange market. However, a new disequilibrium state is created. because of the massive unemployment which arises in country A.

The preceding process is illustrated in fig. 9.3, which is similar to fig. 9.2. The vector $0T$ and the points U and V of fig. 9.2 are transferred to fig. 9.3. The curve $0_a U$ is A's income-consumption curve for $p = \bar{p}$. Now imagine that A's production falls sufficiently to restore equilibrium in the commodity markets at the current prices. To determine the precise amount by which A's production must fall, simply imagine that, as A's production falls, A's origin (0_a) and income-consumption

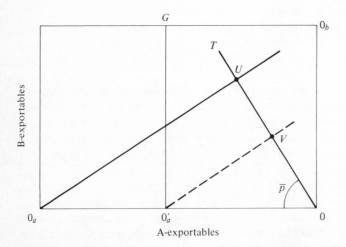

Figure 9.3 Correction of international disequilibrium by means of a reduction in domestic employment causing massive unemployment in A. Points U and V show A's and B's desired absorption, respectively. When A reduces its domestic production by $0_a 0_a'$, the box diagram is reduced to $0_a' 00_b G$, and point V becomes a common desired absorption point.

curve shift continuously to the right until A's income-consumption curve is made to pass through point V, as illustrated in fig. 9.3. Thus, when A's production falls by $0_a 0'_a$, the production box shrinks to $0'_a 00_b G$, and at the current prices ($\bar{p}$) point V becomes an equilibrium point similar to point E of fig. 9.1 or fig. 9.2. Thus, at V, both the commodity markets and the foreign exchange market are in equilibrium. Of course, at V (fig. 9.3) massive unemployment prevails in A. What is even worse, there exists no automatic mechanism to eliminate A's unemployment—A's money-wage rate is inflexible downwards.

9.4 THE ADJUSTMENT PROCESS: (b) INCOME ≠ DESIRED ABSORPTION

So far it has been assumed that in each country national income equals desired absorption (or spending). The time has come to drop this assumption. This opens the way to a new type of balance-of-payments disequilibrium—a disequilibrium in the foreign exchange market which does not coincide with disequilibrium in any other market.

Return to the initial disequilibrium of fig. 9.2. Desired absorption equals full-employment income in each country. But in A actual absorption is higher than desired absorption, leading to an undesired accumulation of inventories. Similarly, in B actual absorption is lower than desired absorption, leading to an undesired decumulation of inventories. These undesired (or unintended) changes in inventories in the two countries tend to reduce production and employment in A and possibly produce inflation in B. (In the preceding section we saw how equilibrium in the foreign exchange market can be reestablished by a cut in A's production and employment.) How would A's and B's authorities react to this situation? According to current macroeconomic thinking, A's authorities, fearing unemployment, would increase aggregate spending by means of expansionary fiscal and monetary policies. Similarly, B's authorities, fearing inflation, would reduce aggregate spending by means of deflationary fiscal and monetary policies. Under certain conditions to be specified below, such policies pursued by A and B simultaneously can restore equilibrium in the commodity markets and eliminate unintended inventory changes. Nevertheless, they give rise to a "fundamental disequilibrium" in the foreign exchange market (and, of course, the balance of payments).

Consider fig. 9.4. The vector $0T$ and points U and V correspond to the synonymous vector and points of figs. 9.2 and 9.3. Thus, at the current terms of trade and levels of spending, A desires bundle U and B, bundle V. Draw A's income-consumption curve through point U, and B's through point V, as shown by the broken curves $0_a UE$ and $0_b EV$. (An income-consumption curve is the locus of points where the marginal rate of substitution—or absolute slope of indifference curves—remains equal to a given price ratio—in our case, $\bar{p}$.) Note that these income-consumption curves have been drawn to intersect at E. Surely point E is recognized as a point on the contract curve (not drawn). If country A increases its

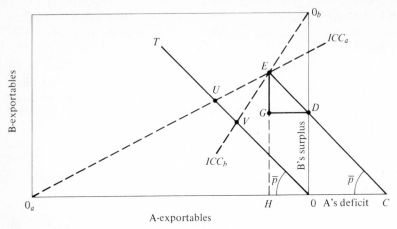

Figure 9.4 Disequilibrium in the foreign exchange market only, all other markets being in equilibrium. A's aggregate spending ($0_a C$) is bigger than A's income ($0_a 0$). B's aggregate spending ($0_b D$) is smaller than B's income ($0_b 0$). Nevertheless, point E is a common desired absorption point.

spending to $0_a C$ (i.e., by $0C$) and B reduces its spending to $0_b D$ (i.e., by $0D$), then both countries' desired absorption would be indicated by point E, and both commodity markets would clear. Accordingly, at point E there exists equilibrium in the commodity markets and the labor markets. Is there equilibrium in the foreign exchange market also? Unfortunately, this is not the case. At E, country A exports GD (or $H0$) units of A-exportables to country B in exchange for HE or $(0D + GE)$ units of B-exportables. Clearly, the value of GD units of A-exportables equals the value of only GE units of B-exportables. Hence, country A (B) suffers from an import (export) surplus of $0D$ units of B-exportables, which is equivalent to $0C$ units of A-exportables since $\bar{p} = (0D/0C) = (GE/GD)$.

It is interesting to note again that A's deficit is identical with the excess of A's absorption over A's income; and B's surplus is identical with the excess of B's income over B's absorption. This is shown clearly on fig. 9.4, which the reader is urged to study carefully, bearing in mind that presently actual absorption equals desired absorption.

Since both the commodity and the labor markets are in equilibrium at point E (fig. 9.4), there is no pressure for change for either commodity prices or money-wage rates. Further, since all unintended inventory changes have disappeared, producers have no incentive to change their production plans. Thus, every consumer and every producer is in equilibrium and yet the foreign exchange market is out of equilibrium: A's authorities lose reserves to B's authorities in every period. Since reserves are limited, this situation cannot continue for too long. Yet a devaluation of A's currency, which is the commonsense medicine for a fundamental balance-of-payments disequilibrium, cannot be relied on to restore equilibrium, even if the Marshall-Lerner condition (or any other more general condition) is satisfied. This conclusion is indeed opposite to the one we reached earlier in part one on the basis of the partial equilibrium model. In this respect, the latter model is indeed misleading.

How can the disequilibrium of fig. 9.4 be corrected? The first thing to be done immediately is to reverse the expenditure changes in A and B and return to the disequilibrium state of fig. 9.2. That is, both countries must pursue *expenditure-adjusting policies* to shift the budget line of fig. 9.4 from the position CE to the original position $0T$. Then, an appropriate exchange-rate adjustment (devaluation or revaluation, as the case may be), or any other *expenditure-switching policy*, can restore general equilibrium. Admittedly, this solution is oversimplified. As noted earlier in the present chapter, an exchange-rate adjustment affects the level of aggregate spending as well, in addition to its *distribution* between A-exportables and B-exportables. These important policy problems are studied in some detail in chaps. 13 and 14. For further thoughts on how to correct the present disequilibrium, see chap. 19.

In the preceding discussion, it was taken for granted that an intersection between the two income-consumption curves (fig. 9.4) always existed above and to the right of vector $0T$, as illustrated by point E. But this is the case only when A's income-consumption curve is flatter than B's, as shown in fig. 9.4. If A's income-consumption curve were steeper than B's, no intersection would exist above and to the right of $0T$, although one might exist below and to the left of $0T$. In general, the two income-consumption curves may intersect each other any number of times or not at all.

Chapter 15 provides an interesting application of the present model in the study of the price-specie-flow mechanism. It is shown that under perfect price and wage flexibility disequilibrium in the foreign exchange market is of the type studied in the present section. Furthermore, if the gold-standard rules of the game are followed and a certain stability condition is satisfied, the system automatically returns to general equilibrium.

9.5 CONCLUDING REMARKS

The object of this chapter was to lay the ground for the analysis in the rest of the book. The outlined model is indeed very simple. But this simplicity should not disturb the reader. On the contrary, in the present case simplicity is a positive advantage. The simple model just outlined can serve remarkably well as the basis for discussing the great issues of international monetary economics. What is actually surprising is the fact that a simple model of this sort can be used to tackle successfully a rather complicated economic problem and deduce far-reaching conclusions.

This chapter's discussion leads to an important conclusion: adjustment may proceed either through *prices* or through *incomes* (i.e., through aggregate spending, production, and employment). The price-adjustment mechanism is already familiar to us from the study of the partial equilibrium model (chap. 4). Nevertheless, the income-adjustment mechanism is a new element and deserves our immediate attention. Accordingly, the next chapter is devoted to a comprehensive study of the income-adjustment mechanism.

SELECTED BIBLIOGRAPHY

Alexander, S. S. (1952). "Effects of a Devaluation on a Trade Balance." *IMF Staff Papers*, vol. II (April), pp. 263–278. Reprinted in AEA *Readings in International Economics*. R. D. Irwin, Inc., Homewood, Ill., 1968.

Chacholiades, M. (1972). "The Classical Theory of International Adjustment: A Restatement." *Econometrica*, vol. 40, no. 3 (May), pp. 463–485.

——— (1973). *The Pure Theory of International Trade*. Aldine Publishing Company, Chicago, Ill.

Johnson, H. G. (1961). *International Trade and Economic Growth: Studies in Pure Theory*. Harvard University Press, Cambridge, Mass., chap. VI. Reprinted in AEA *Readings in International Economics*. R. D. Irwin, Inc., Homewood, Ill., 1968.

Pearce, I. F. (1970). *International Trade*. W. W. Norton and Company, Inc., New York, chaps. 1 to 5.

TEN

THE INCOME-ADJUSTMENT MECHANISM

This chapter is divided into three parts. Part A deals with the historical development of the subject, the basic assumptions, national-income accounting, and finally the circular flow of income. Part B deals with the income-adjustment mechanism in the context of a simple open economy from which all foreign repercussion is assumed away. Finally, part C deals with the income-adjustment mechanism in the presence of foreign repercussion.

PART A.   HISTORICAL DEVELOPMENT, ASSUMPTIONS, AND NATIONAL-INCOME ACCOUNTING

10.1 INTRODUCTION

In the 1920s, at the suggestion of Prof. Frank Taussig, several economists—Williams (1920), Viner (1924), White (1933), and others—studied historical examples of balance-of-payments adjustment under conditions of both fixed- and flexible-exchange rates. The general conclusion was in agreement with classical expectations, namely, that gold flows and relative price changes could be counted on to restore equilibrium in the balance of payments. Nevertheless, Taussig (1928) expressed surprise at the observed smoothness and speed of adjustment in many countries before World War I. Essentially, it was observed that small gold flows and relative price changes seemed to restore equilibrium in the balance of payments quite promptly. This result was too good to believe and led Taussig to suspect that some important economic forces were ignored by the classical theory. The missing link was later found to be the income-adjustment mechanism. This relatively new mechanism is the subject matter of the present chapter.

The income-adjustment mechanism is a direct outgrowth of Keynes' *General Theory* (1936) but Keynes himself had little to do with it. In fact, hints at the income-adjustment mechanism were made by Ohlin (1929) in his debate with Keynes (1929) over the transfer problem (see chap. 12 below). Ironically, in that debate Keynes took the classical position while Ohlin emphasized the income-adjustment mechanism which was later linked with Keynes. After the publication of the *General Theory*, Robinson (1937) and Harrod (1939) were quick to recognize its significance to the problem of international adjustment. Additional contributions were made later by Haberler (1941), Salant (1941), Metzler (1942), Kindleberger (1943), Machlup (1943), and many others.

As we shall presently learn, the income-adjustment mechanism yields two important results: (*a*) international trade is a powerful vehicle for the propagation of business cycles internationally; and (*b*) following a balance-of-payments disturbance which affects the circular flow of income, the resultant national-income changes tend to bring about *partial* (not complete) adjustment in the balance of payments. The first result comes under the *national-income multiplier theory;* the second comes under the *balance-of-trade multiplier theory.*

10.2 THE ASSUMPTIONS

The income-adjustment mechanism rests on several restrictive assumptions which are spelled out explicitly in the present section. The justification for adopting such restrictive assumptions, of course, follows directly from the desire to isolate the effects of national-income changes. The assumptions are:

1. Substantial amounts of unemployment prevail in all countries.
2. Production is carried out under constant returns to scale in both countries.
3. All prices remain constant throughout. That is, all commodity prices, money-wage rates, the rate of exchange, and the rate of interest are assumed fixed.
4. All countries have sufficient stocks of foreign-exchange reserves, e.g., gold.
5. All exports are made out of current production. Thus all expenditure on exports are income generating.

The first assumption (substantial amounts of unemployment) ensures that national income, production, and employment can always change in both directions. If an economy is already at full employment, the income-adjustment mechanism will not work when a disturbance calls for an increase in production. Adjustment will then proceed through price, wage, and interest-rate changes which are presently ruled out by the third assumption. The second assumption (constant returns to scale) and the third (constant prices) are again necessary in order to eliminate all price effects from the adjustment mechanism. The following chapter reconsiders the income-adjustment mechanism in the context of flexible-exchange rates. That analysis, therefore, extends the present theory to include price effects in addition to income effects. The third assumption provides also for constant interest rates. This is necessary in order to eliminate the effect of monetary factors on the circular flow of income. The assumption of constant interest rates is maintained throughout part two but is removed later in part three of this book. The fourth assumption (sufficient reserves) is necessary for the maintenance of fixed-exchange rates. Finally, the fifth assumption (exports are made out of current production) precludes the possibility of exporting goods out of existing inventories without current production to replace them. Such exports out of goods produced in the past do not affect current income—unless inventories are replenished.

The discussion of the income-adjustment mechanism is carried out in terms of comparative statics. Nevertheless, use is made of certain dynamic stability conditions which are derived rigorously in the appendix to this chapter.

It is assumed that the reader is already familiar with the elementary theory of national-income determination and multiplier analysis which is found in any introductory textbook, such as Samuelson (1973, chaps. 11 and 12).

10.3 NATIONAL-INCOME ACCOUNTING

Consider an open economy which over the past time period (e.g., last year) produced an output $\tilde{Q}$ by employing *domestic* resources (labor, capital, land, and entrepreneurship) and *foreign* resources (raw materials). The value of output produced at current market prices is $p\tilde{Q}$, where $p \equiv$ current price of output. Since all prices are assumed constant, by an appropriate choice of the units of measurement we can set $p = 1$. Thus, $\tilde{Q}$ shows both the units and value of output produced.

The factors employed in the production of $\tilde{Q}$, both domestic and foreign, *earn* incomes for their services. The income earned by foreign factors is measured by the value of imported raw materials used up in the production of $\tilde{Q}$. Let the symbol M_p denote the value of these imported raw materials. The domestic factors employed in the production of $\tilde{Q}$ earn wages, interest, rents, and profits. The first three categories of domestic-factor earnings (e.g., wages, interest, and rents) are *contractual*, while the last category (profits) is a *residual* defined by the identity

$$\text{Profits} \equiv \tilde{Q} - (\text{wages} + \text{interest} + \text{rents}) - M_p \qquad (10.1)$$

The sum of all domestic factor earnings, including profits, is called *national income* (Y). That is,

$$Y \equiv \text{wages} + \text{interest} + \text{rents} + \text{profits} \qquad (10.2)$$

Finally, combining the preceding two identities, we obtain the new identity

$$Y \equiv \tilde{Q} - M_p \qquad (10.3)$$

In addition to those raw materials imported for the production of $\tilde{Q}$, our economy imports from the rest of the world *finished* goods mainly for domestic consumption but conceivably domestic investment, government consumption, and even re-exports as well. Let the symbol M_c stand for the imported finished goods, and let us define

$$Q \equiv \tilde{Q} + M_c \tag{10.4}$$

$$M \equiv M_p + M_c \tag{10.5}$$

Thus, Q stands for all goods made available to our economy by both domestic and foreign producers. Similarly, M stands for *all* goods imported from the rest of the world—raw materials *and* finished goods. Combining the last three identities—(10.3) to (10.5)—we finally obtain

$$Y \equiv Q - M \equiv Q_d \tag{10.6}$$

The difference $Q - M$ (or Q_d) is the value of output produced domestically by means of domestic resources. For brevity, we shall refer to Q_d as domestic output or product.

How is Q used up? One portion is used up by domestic consumers for consumption C; a second portion is retained by the business sector for investment I; a third portion is used up by the government sector G; and, finally, a fourth portion is exported to the rest of the world X. That is, we have the following identity:

$$Q \equiv C + I + G + X \tag{10.7}$$

or
$$Y \equiv Q_d \equiv (C + I + G) + (X - M) \tag{10.8}$$

The sum $C + I + G$ is easily recognized as our economy's aggregate *absorption* (or spending). Because of its importance, we adopt the symbol Z for it. That is,

$$\text{let} \qquad Z \equiv C + I + G \tag{10.9}$$

Note that domestic absorption (Z) need not be equal to national income (Y) or domestic output (Q_d). The economy may spend on goods and services (domestic and foreign) more or less than its national income. Although it is statistically impossible, theoretically domestic absorption Z may be split into two parts: (a) the part which uses up strictly domestic resources Z_d and (b) that part which uses up strictly foreign resources Z_f. This gives the additional identity

$$Z \equiv Z_d + Z_f \tag{10.10}$$

The term Z_d (i.e., domestic expenditure on domestic resources) is important for it affects directly the domestic economic activity (employment, domestic output, and national income). The term Z_f (which is part of M) is our economy's spending on foreign resources, and is important to foreign economic activity.

Similarly, total exports X can be split theoretically into two parts: (a) the part which is produced by strictly domestic resources X_d and (b) the part which is produced by strictly foreign resources X_f. Thus, X_f stands for the value of imported raw materials and even finished products which are eventually re-exported (through X). Accordingly, we have also the identity

$$X \equiv X_d + X_f \tag{10.11}$$

From the above discussion, it also follows that imports are made up of Z_f and X_f. That is,

$$M \equiv Z_f + X_f \tag{10.12}$$

Thus, total imports M are either absorbed domestically (Z_f) or re-exported (X_f).

The difference $X - M$ is the economy's balance of trade denoted by T. That is,

$$T \equiv X - M = X_d - Z_f \tag{10.13}$$

Substituting eqs. (10.9), (10.10), and (10.13) into eq. (10.8), we obtain

$$Y \equiv Q_d \equiv Z + T = Z_d + X_d \tag{10.14}$$

The sum $Z + T$ (i.e., the sum of domestic absorption plus the balance of trade) gives aggregate spending by both domestic buyers Z_d and foreigners X_d on the economy's domestic output Q_d. Because of its significance, the sum $Z + T$ is denoted by the symbol D. That is,

$$D \equiv Z + T \tag{10.15}$$

The distinction between Z and D is extremely important and should always be kept in mind. The former (Z) shows the economy's aggregate spending on goods and services in general (domestic *and* foreign). The latter (D) shows aggregate spending on the economy's output by domestic consumers, producers, and government, on the one hand, *and* foreigners, on the other.

Equation (10.14) can be rearranged as follows:

$$T \equiv Y - Z \tag{10.16}$$

Equation (10.16) verifies the important conclusion reached earlier in chap. 9, namely, that a country's balance of trade is given by the difference between national income and aggregate spending.

Finally, the disposition of national income Y is given by the identity

$$Y \equiv C + S_p + T_x + U \tag{10.17}$$

where the meaning of the new symbols is as follows:

$S_p \equiv$ private saving (i.e., saving done by the economy's private sector)
$T_x \equiv$ net taxes to domestic government
$U \equiv$ net unilateral transfers to foreigners

Combining eq. (10.17) with eq. (10.8) and rearranging, we obtain

$$S - I \equiv T - U \tag{10.18}$$

where $S \equiv S_p + S_g$ and $S_g \equiv T_x - G$. Thus, S_g shows government (or public) saving, while S shows total-domestic saving done by both the private and public sectors. Incidentally, the difference $T - U$ is usually referred to as *net-foreign investment*. Equation (10.18) shows, then, that net-foreign investment equals the excess of total-domestic saving over total-domestic investment. Put differently, total saving equals total investment (both domestic *and* foreign).

In what follows, it is assumed that $U = 0$. Accordingly, the net-foreign investment coincides with the balance of trade T.

The accounting identities discussed in the present section apply to all countries. When it is necessary to distinguish between countries A and B, the subscripts a and b will be used.

10.4 THE CIRCULAR FLOW OF INCOME

The relationship between aggregate demand D, domestic output Q_d, and national income Y may be clarified further by means of the circular flow of income in the economy, as illustrated in fig. 10.1. It does not matter where we start, but we must follow the direction of the arrows. For instance, start with domestic output Q_d which generates income Y. In turn, income generates demand D, and demand gives rise to output, and so on ad infinitum.

Before going any further, a comment is necessary on the concepts "income earned" and "income received." As factors of production are used in the production of output they *earn* incomes (wages, interest, rents, and profits) for their services. As explained in the preceding section, "income earned $\equiv$ value of output produced." Nevertheless, the actual receipt of income may either precede or follow the actual earning of income. As a result, income received need not be equal to income earned (or value of output). Empirically, however, the lag between the earning of income and its receipt is rather negligible. For this reason, we always

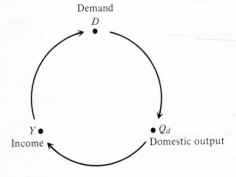

Figure 10.1 The circular flow of income. It does not matter where we start on this circular-flow-of-income diagram as long as we follow the direction of the arrows. For instance, domestic output Q_d generates income Y, income generates demand D, and demand generates output, and so on.

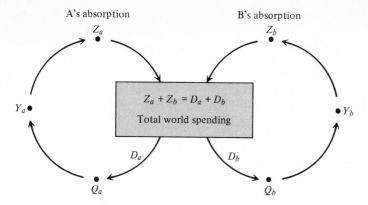

Figure 10.2 The circular flow of income in A and B. As with fig. 10.1, it does not matter where we start as long as we follow the direction of the arrows. But now we have two intertwined circular flows. Start with Z_a and Z_b and allocate D_a to A's domestic output and D_b to B's domestic output. Then D_a generates Q_a, Q_a generates Y_a, and Y_a generates Z_a. Similarly, D_b generates Q_b, Q_b generates Y_b, and Y_b generates Z_b. Now we are back at the starting point and a new cycle is ready to begin.

adopt the assumption that "income earned = income received." Thus, from now on we can talk merely of income (without drawing a distinction between received and earned) and also use the symbol Y for income earned, domestic output, and income received.

Figure 10.1 teaches us something more than the accounting identities of the preceding section—the direction of causation. Thus, output Q_d gives rise to income Y, income Y gives rise to demand D, and demand gives rise to output, and so on. Whereas the accounting identities are *ex post* relationships, the circular flow of income may be viewed as an *ex ante* mechanism which shows how our macroeconomy works. Instead of considering D as the *actual* (*ex post*) expenditure on current output, we may view it as the *desired* (*ex ante*) demand. Viewed in this *ex ante* sense, D need not be equal to current output and income.

The above discussion can be generalized to our two-country model. Consider fig. 10.2, which shows the circular flow of income in a two-country world. As in fig. 10.1, it does not matter where we start as long as we follow the direction of the arrows. The only difference from fig. 10.1 is that we now have two intertwined circular flows. Starting with A's and B's absorption, determine a worldwide demand for goods and services ($Z_a + Z_b$). Then allocate this aggregate demand between A's and B's domestic output. In particular, allocate D_a to A's domestic output and D_b to B's domestic output. The demand component D_a gives rise to A's domestic output Q_a, which in turn gives rise to A's income Y_a, and finally Y_a gives rise to A's absorption Z_a. Similarly, the demand component D_b gives rise to Q_b, which in turn gives rise to B's income Y_b, and finally Y_b gives rise to B's absorption Z_b. We are now back to our starting point and the circular flow is ready to begin on a new cycle.

PART B. THE INCOME-ADJUSTMENT MECHANISM IN THE ABSENCE OF FOREIGN REPERCUSSION

This part studies the national-income multiplier theory as well as the balance-of-trade multiplier theory in the context of a simple open economy. All foreign repercussions from induced changes in the circular flow of income of the rest of the world are presently ignored completely. Foreign repercussion is introduced later in part C of this chapter.

10.5 NATIONAL-INCOME EQUILIBRIUM

The first step in our analysis is to determine national-income equilibrium. As is well known from elementary macroeconomics, national-income equilibrium occurs when desired aggregate demand D equals aggregate supply Q_d. The producers can only be expected to continue production at the current level if and only if there are just enough buyers willing to buy the output produced. When (desired) aggregate demand is higher than current supply, production tends to rise as producers revise upward their production plans. On the other hand, when aggregate demand falls short of current supply, production tends to fall as producers revise downward their production plans.

Determinants of Aggregate Demand for Domestic Output

What determines the desired level of aggregate demand for domestic output D? The determinants of D coincide with the determinants of its components. As we saw in part A, the components of aggregate demand are: consumption C, investment I, government spending G, exports X, and (with a negative sign) imports M. That is, $D = C + I + G + X - M$. Government spending G is exogenous. It assumes the role of a policy parameter in later chapters. Exports X are also exogenous presently because of our simplifying assumption to ignore foreign repercussion. Investment I depends mainly on the interest rate which is presently fixed by assumption. By invoking the *acceleration principle*, investment can also be made a function of either the change or the level of national income. But to make investment a function of the change in income would get us involved unnecessarily in dynamics—a complication which for our purposes can be safely ignored. Nevertheless, the influence of the level of national income Y on investment can be accommodated easily. Further, according to the Keynesian school of thought, consumption depends mainly on income. Finally, imports also depend on income. Ideally one could say that imports consist of two parts: (*a*) the part included in C and I, which necessarily depends on Y; and (*b*) the part included in G and X, which is necessarily exogenous. For our purposes, this fine distinction is not necessary.

The preceding assumptions are summarized as follows:

$$C = C(Y) \text{ (consumption function)} \qquad (10.19)$$

$$I = I(Y) \text{ (investment function)} \qquad (10.20)$$

$$M = M(Y) \text{ (import function)} \qquad (10.21)$$

$$G = \bar{G} \qquad \text{and} \qquad X = \bar{X}$$

Marginal Propensities

The following *marginal propensities* are also introduced here for convenience:

$$\frac{dC}{dY} \equiv C' \equiv \text{marginal propensity to consume}$$

$$\frac{dI}{dY} \equiv I' \equiv \text{marginal propensity to invest}$$

$$\frac{dM}{dY} \equiv M' \equiv \text{marginal propensity to import}$$

$$\frac{dZ}{dY} \equiv Z' \equiv C' + I' \equiv \text{marginal propensity to absorb}$$

The first three marginal propensities are assumed positive and less than unity. The marginal propensity to absorb is positive and usually less than unity, although values greater than unity may be allowed, as explained below.

Average Propensities

To each marginal propensity there corresponds an average propensity. Accordingly, we may define the following *average propensities:*

$$\frac{C}{Y} \equiv \text{average propensity to consume}$$

$$\frac{I}{Y} \equiv \text{average propensity to invest}$$

$$\frac{M}{Y} \equiv \text{average propensity to import}$$

$$\frac{Z}{Y} \equiv \text{average propensity to absorb}$$

Income Elasticities

The ratio between a marginal and a corresponding average propensity is an *income elasticity*. Thus,

$$\frac{dC/dY}{C/Y} \equiv \text{income elasticity of demand for consumption}$$

$$\frac{dI/dY}{I/Y} \equiv \text{income elasticity of demand for investment}$$

$$\frac{dM/dY}{M/Y} \equiv \text{income elasticity of demand for imports}$$

$$\frac{dZ/dY}{Z/Y} \equiv \text{income elasticity of demand for absorption}$$

National-Income Equilibrium

Given the behavioral eqs. (10.19) to (10.21), it becomes obvious that (desired) aggregate demand D is indeed a function of income. Thus,

$$D = C(Y) + I(Y) + \bar{G} + \bar{X} - M(Y) \equiv D(Y) \tag{10.22}$$

and $\dfrac{dD}{DY} \equiv D' = C' + I' - M'$

$$\equiv \text{marginal propensity to spend on domestic output} \tag{10.23}$$

To complete the system, the supply of domestic output is also needed. This is easy. Recall that current domestic output Q_d is equal to current income. Thus,

$$Q_d = Y \tag{10.24}$$

Equilibrium in the commodity market occurs when (desired) aggregate demand equals current aggregate supply. That is, equilibrium occurs when

$$D(Y) = Q_d = Y \tag{10.25}$$

The only unknown in eq. (10.25) is income Y. Accordingly, this equation can be solved for Y; and the value of Y that satisfies eq. (10.25) is the equilibrium level of income, output, and demand.

Graphical Illustration

The above solution is illustrated in fig. 10.3. The 45° line is the graphical representation of eq. (10.24). It shows that the current supply of domestic output always equals current income. The straight line FE is the graphical representation of eq. (10.22). It gives the amount of domestic output that all buyers (domestic and

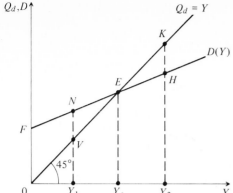

Figure 10.3 Equilibrium in the commodity market occurs at E where the aggregate demand function $D(Y)$ intersects the 45° line.

foreign, private and public, consumers and producers) are willing to buy at alternative levels of current income. Equilibrium occurs at E where the aggregate demand curve FE intersects the 45° line. Thus at E, the current level of income and domestic output (supply) is given by $0Y_e$; desired aggregate demand at $Y = 0Y_e$ is given by $Y_e E$, which is equal to $0Y_e$. At any other level, national income tends to change. For instance, at $Y = 0Y_1$ aggregate demand $(Y_1 N)$ is higher than aggregate supply $(Y_1 V)$, inventories are depleted at the rate of VN units per unit of time, and producers tend to revise upward their production plans. The opposite happens for income levels higher than the equilibrium level, as illustrated by $Y = 0Y_2$. At this level, aggregate supply $(Y_2 K)$ is higher than aggregate demand $(Y_2 H)$, and producers who reluctantly accumulate unsold inventories revise downward their production plans. Accordingly, there is always a tendency for national income to move toward the equilibrium level $0Y_e$. This is expressed by saying that equilibrium is *stable*.

Necessary and Sufficient Condition for Stability

What is the necessary and sufficient condition for stability? A glance at fig. 10.3 reveals that for stability it is required that the slope of the aggregate demand function (at the equilibrium point), or the marginal propensity to spend on domestic output, is smaller than the slope of the 45° line (i.e., smaller than unity). That is, for stability it is required that the following inequality be satisfied:

$$D' \equiv C' + I' - M' < 1 \tag{10.26}$$

Observe that stability does not require the marginal propensity to absorb (Z') to be less than unity. The condition $Z' < 1$ is, of course, necessary for stability in a closed economy, as the reader may know. For this reason, Metzler (1942) calls a system which satisfies the condition $Z' < 1$ "stable in isolation." The conclusion that stability requires only that $D' < 1$ is modified later when foreign repercussion is discussed in part C of this chapter.

National-Income Equilibrium in Terms of Saving, Investment, Imports, and Exports

There is another useful way of defining national-income equilibrium. Substitute eq. (10.17) into eq. (10.25), assuming for simplicity that $U = 0$, and obtain (after some elementary rearrangement of terms)

$$S_p + T_x + M = I + G + X \qquad (10.27a)$$

or
$$S(Y) + M(Y) = I(Y) + \bar{X} \qquad (10.27b)$$

Either eq. (10.27a) or (10.27b) can replace eq. (10.25). Private saving S_p, taxes T_x, and imports M are *leakages* out of the income stream. On the other hand, investment I, government spending G, and exports are *injections* into the income stream. National income is in equilibrium when the leakages are equal to the injections.

Equation (10.27b) can also be rearranged as follows:

$$T \equiv X - M(Y) = S(Y) - I(Y) \qquad (10.28)$$

This last equation shows that the balance of trade is also given by the difference between total-domestic saving and investment.

Equilibrium Income Versus Full-Employment Income

The equilibrium level of income need not coincide with the full-employment level of income. In fact, one of the assumptions of the present analysis is that a substantial amount of unemployment prevails at all times. Furthermore, at the equilibrium level of income there is no necessity for the country's balance of trade to be zero. It may be positive or negative.

10.6 THE OPEN-ECONOMY NATIONAL-INCOME MULTIPLIER

Consider again the national-income equilibrium as illustrated in fig. 10.3 and reproduced for convenience in fig. 10.4. Suppose that the aggregate demand curve shifts upward by ΔD, as illustrated by the broken curve $F'E'$. The reason for this shift is immaterial for the moment. Specific illustrations are given below in sec. 10.8. Obviously, equilibrium shifts from E to E' and national income increases from $0Y_e$ to $0Y'_e$. How is the increase in income (ΔY) related to the upward shift in the aggregate demand function (ΔD)?

From the construction of the diagram, it follows that

$$\Delta Y = EN = NE' = NH + HE' = NH + \Delta D \qquad (10.29)$$

and
$$D' = \frac{NH}{EN} = \frac{NH}{\Delta Y} \qquad (10.30)$$

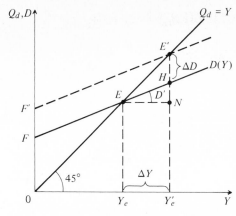

Figure 10.4 The foreign-trade multiplier. As aggregate demand D increases autonomously, the aggregate demand curve shifts upward as shown by the broken curve. National income increases by the increase in aggregate demand (ΔD) times the foreign-trade multiplier. Compare points E and E'.

Solving eq. (10.30) for NH and substituting the result into (10.29), we obtain

$$\Delta Y = D' \, \Delta Y + \Delta D$$

or

$$\Delta Y = \left(\frac{1}{1 - D'}\right) \Delta D \tag{10.31}$$

Accordingly, the change in income (ΔY) is proportional to the change in demand (ΔD), with the factor of proportionality given by the ratio $1/(1 - D')$. The latter ratio is referred to as either the *foreign-trade multiplier* or the *open-economy national-income multiplier*. Because of its significance, we adopt the symbol m for it. That is,

$$m \equiv \frac{\Delta Y}{\Delta D} = \frac{1}{1 - D'} \tag{10.32}$$

As noted earlier, for stability it is required that $0 < D' < 1$. Accordingly, $m > 1$.

The Open-Economy Versus the Closed-Economy Multiplier

The open-economy national-income multiplier m is necessarily smaller than the closed-economy multiplier $\mu \equiv 1/(1 - Z')$. The obvious reason for this result is that for an open economy there is an additional leakage for imports. But there is a deeper reason. From the point of view of the world economy as a whole, imports are *not* a leakage—only saving is a leakage. The world economy is indeed a closed economy! Accordingly, as autonomous spending increases in our economy, a new equilibrium is established only when a corresponding amount of saving is generated in the world economy. But whereas in a closed economy the additional saving is generated only at home, in an open economy the additional saving is generated both at home and abroad—foreign incomes and saving are increasing since our imports from the rest of the world are increasing. Accordingly, following an increase in autonomous spending, a closed economy's national income must increase faster than that of a corresponding open economy simply because more saving needs to be generated in a closed than an open economy.

10.7 BALANCE-OF-TRADE MULTIPLIER THEORY

How does an autonomous shift in aggregate demand affect an open economy's balance of trade? As shown earlier in this chapter, the balance of trade T is given by any one of the following three equations:

$$T = X - M \tag{10.13}$$

$$T = Y - Z \qquad \qquad {}^{\wedge C + I + G} \tag{10.16}$$

$$T = S - I \tag{10.28}$$

Accordingly, any one of these equations may be used to determine the effect on the balance of trade. Very often one of these equations is more convenient to use than the rest, as illustrated in the following section. But no matter which equation (or approach) is used, the following general principle must be kept in mind. The change in T (ΔT) due to an autonomous shift in aggregate demand is made up of two components: (a) an *autonomous part* measuring the effect of the shift in demand *at the initial equilibrium income;* and (b) an *induced part* caused by the resultant change in income from the old to the new equilibrium. Each approach effects the breakdown of the total balance-of-trade change in a different way. The total change is the same for all.

Given the above clarification, the change in T following an autonomous shift in aggregate demand is given by any one of the following three equations:

$$\Delta T = (\Delta X - \Delta M)_{\text{aut}} + (\Delta X - \Delta M)_{\text{ind}} = (\Delta X - \Delta M)_{\text{aut}} \overset{^{\wedge X = Z' = 0}}{-} M' \, \Delta Y \tag{10.33}$$

$$\Delta T = (\Delta Y - \Delta Z)_{\text{aut}} + (\Delta Y - \Delta Z)_{\text{ind}} = -\Delta Z_{\text{aut}} + (1 - Z') \, \Delta Y \tag{10.34}$$

$$\Delta T = (\Delta S - \Delta I)_{\text{aut}} + (\Delta S - \Delta I)_{\text{ind}}$$
$$= (\Delta S - \Delta I)_{\text{aut}} + (S' - I') \, \Delta Y \tag{10.35}$$

The subscripts "aut" and "ind" refer to autonomous and induced changes, respectively. The change in income (ΔY) is the change given by the open-economy national-income multiplier. These formulas are best illustrated by examples. This is done in the following section.

10.8 NUMERICAL ILLUSTRATIONS

In the following examples it is assumed that $D' = 0.9, Z' = 1.1, M' = 0.2, C' = 0.8,$ $S' = 0.2,$ and $I' = 0.3$. These marginal propensities satisfy the following identities:

$$D' = 0.9 = 1.1 - 0.2 = Z' - M'$$

$$Z' = 1.1 = 0.8 + 0.3 = C' + I'$$

$$C' + S' = 0.8 + 0.2 = 1$$

The national-income multiplier equals $1/(1 - 0.9) = 10$.

Example 10.1 Consider a 100-unit autonomous increase of our economy's absorption of domestic output produced solely by domestic resources. That is, $\Delta D_{aut} = (\Delta Z_d)_{aut} = 100$. Determine the effect on national income and the balance of trade.

SOLUTION
(a) *Change in income*

$$\Delta Y = m \, \Delta D_{aut} = 10 \times 100 = 1000$$

(b) *Change in the balance of trade*
Note that in this example $(\Delta X - \Delta M)_{aut} = 0$. Using eq. (10.33), we obtain

$$\Delta T = -M' \, \Delta Y = -0.2 \times 1000 = -200$$

The same result is arrived at when either eq. (10.34) or (10.35) is used. Thus,

$$\Delta T = -\Delta Z_{aut} + (1 - Z') \, \Delta Y$$
$$= -100 + (1 - 1.1)(1000) = -200$$

and $\Delta T = (\Delta S - \Delta I)_{aut} + (S' - I') \, \Delta Y$
$$= -100 + (0.2 - 0.3)(1000) = -200$$

Example 10.2 Consider a 100-unit increase in exports produced solely by domestic resources. That is, $\Delta D_{aut} = (\Delta X_d)_{aut} = 100$. Determine the effect on national income and the balance of trade.

SOLUTION
(a) *Change in income*

$$\Delta Y = m \, \Delta D_{aut} = 10 \times 100 = 1000$$

(b) *Change in the balance of trade*

$$\Delta T = (\Delta X - \Delta M)_{aut} - M' \, \Delta Y = 100 - 0.2 \times 1000 = -100$$

or $\Delta T = -\Delta Z_{aut} + (1 - Z') \, \Delta Y = 0 + (1 - 1.1)(1000) = -100$

or $\Delta T = (\Delta S - \Delta I)_{aut} + (S' - I') \, \Delta Y = 0 + (0.2 - 0.3)(1000) = -100$

The reason why the balance of trade deteriorates in the present example is because $Z' > 1$, which implies also that $S' < I'$. The reader is advised to rework this example by assuming that $Z' < 1$ (and therefore $S' > I'$), and show that in this case ($Z' < 1$) the balance of trade improves.

Example 10.3 Consider an autonomous increase in imports by 100. Determine the effect on national income and the balance of trade.

SOLUTION To determine the precise effect on national income and the balance of trade we need to know to what extent the autonomous increase in imports reflects an autonomous increase in our economy's absorption and to what extent it reflects a shift in the composition of domestic absorption in favor of foreign goods, i.e., a diversion of domestic spending from domestic to foreign products. Presently, we consider two extreme cases:

$$(1) \quad \Delta M_{\text{aut}} = \Delta Z_{\text{aut}} = 100, \text{ and, therefore, } \Delta D = 0$$

$$(2) \quad \Delta M_{\text{aut}} = 100, \Delta Z_{\text{aut}} = 0, \text{ and } \Delta D = -100$$

In the first case the increase in imports reflects an increase in absorption; i.e., our economy's spending on foreign goods only increases autonomously by 100. No change in national income should be expected in this case ($\Delta D = 0$). In the second case a mere shift in demand takes place—domestic expenditures $(C + I + G)$ are reshuffled in favor of foreign goods. That is, Z_f increases and Z_d decreases but their sum Z remains the same at the initial level of income.

Case (1)
(a) *Change in income*

$$\Delta Y = m \, \Delta D = 10 \times 0 = 0$$

(b) *Change in the balance of trade*

$$\Delta T = (\Delta X - \Delta M)_{\text{aut}} - M' \, \Delta Y = -100 - 0 = -100$$

$$\Delta T = -\Delta Z_{\text{aut}} + (1 - Z') \, \Delta Y = -100 + (1 - 1.1)(0) = -100$$

$$\Delta T = (\Delta S - \Delta I)_{\text{aut}} + (S' - I') \, \Delta Y = -100 + (0.2 - 0.3)(0) = -100$$

Case (2)
(a) *Change in income*

$$\Delta Y = m \, \Delta D = 10(-100) = -1000$$

(b) *Change in the balance of trade*

$$\Delta T = (\Delta X - \Delta M)_{\text{aut}} - M' \, \Delta Y = -100 - 0.2(-1000) = +100$$

$$\Delta T = -\Delta Z_{\text{aut}} + (1 - Z') \, \Delta Y = 0 + (1 - 1.1)(-1000) = +100$$

$$\Delta T = (\Delta S - \Delta I)_{\text{aut}} + (S' - I') \, \Delta Y$$

$$= 0 + (0.2 - 0.3)(-1000) = +100$$

Note the paradoxical result of this case. Even though there is a shift in domestic demand in favor of foreign products, giving rise to an autonomous increase in imports, the balance of trade actually improves! This paradox is due to the fact that $Z' > 1$. Figure 10.5 illustrates the case. It gives simultaneously the equilibrium level of national income and the balance of trade. The rationale for this diagram is based on a simple rearrangement of eq. (10.25) into $Y - Z = X - M$. The slope of the $X - M(Y)$ schedule is given by $-M' < 0$. Accordingly,

$$\frac{dX}{dY} - \frac{dM}{dY} = -M'$$

$$= 0$$

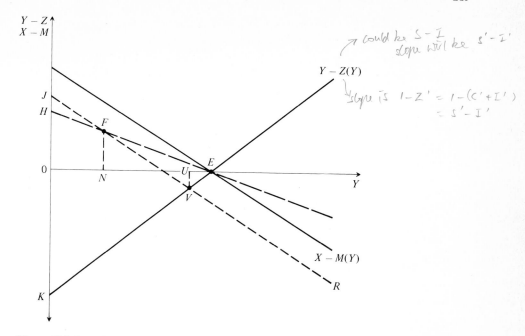

On the figure, handwritten annotations read:

could be $S-I$
slope will be $S'-I'$

slope is $1-Z' = 1-(C'+I')$
$= S'-I'$

Figure 10.5 Some implications of stability in isolation. When $Z' < 1$, the $Y - Z$ schedule slopes upward as shown by the line KVE. In this case, a shift in the composition of domestic demand in favor of foreign products causes the $X - M$ schedule to shift downward (see line JR), bringing about a deterioration in the balance of trade (see the distance VU). On the other hand, when $Z' > 1$, the $Y - Z$ schedule slopes downward, as illustrated by the broken line HFE. Here a change in the composition of domestic demand in favor of foreign products *improves* the balance of trade, as illustrated by the distance NF.

the schedule $X - M$ is always negatively sloped. The slope of the $Y - Z(Y)$ schedule is given by $(1 - Z')$. Thus, when $Z' < 1$, the schedule $Y - Z$ slopes upward as illustrated by the curve KE; but when $Z' > 1$, it slopes downward as illustrated by the broken curve HE. In either case, for stability the schedule $Y - Z$ must intersect the schedule $X - M$ from below. Initially, equilibrium occurs at E. The balance of trade is zero and national income is given by $0E$. When imports increase autonomously while Z remains constant, the schedule $X - M$ shifts downward, as illustrated by the broken curve JR. When $Z' < 1$ (see curve KE), national income falls (from $0E$ to $0U$) and the balance of trade deteriorates (by UV). But when $Z' > 1$ (see curve HE), national income falls faster (from $0E$ to $0N$) and causes imports to fall by a larger amount than the initial autonomous increase. Thus, the balance of trade improves by NF.

The reader is urged to use fig. 10.5 to illustrate the previous example 10.2. (*Hint:* When X_d increases, the $X - M$ schedule shifts upward.)

Example 10.4 Consider an autonomous increase in absorption Z by 200. Determine the effect on national income and the balance of trade.

SOLUTION To proceed with the solution, we must know how the increase in absorption is decomposed into an increase in Z_d and an increase in Z_f. There is no rigid rule for this decomposition. Suppose that $(\Delta Z_d)_{aut} = 100$ and $(\Delta Z_f) = 100$. When the autonomous shift in absorption is decomposed into these two simpler autonomous shifts, it is realized that the effect on national income and the balance of trade is already given in examples 10.1 and 10.3, case (1). The only thing that remains to be done is merely to add up those effects.

(a) *Change in income*

$$\Delta Y = 1000 + 0 = 1000$$

(b) *Change in the balance of trade*

$$\Delta T = -200 - 100 = -300$$

Example 10.5 Consider an increase in exports (X) by 200. Determine the effect on national income and the balance of trade.

SOLUTION As in the preceding example, the increase in X is a composite shift: (a) a shift in X_d and (b) a shift in X_f and, therefore, M. To the extent that the increase in X is due to an increase in X_f, the effect on national income and the balance of trade is zero. Accordingly, the only effects on national income and the balance of trade are those associated with the shift in X_d. These effects have already been analyzed in example 10.2.

PART C. FOREIGN REPERCUSSION

This part extends the preceding analysis to include foreign repercussion. For this purpose two countries, A and B, are explicitly considered. The subscripts *a* and *b* are used to distinguish between countries A and B, respectively.

Section 10.9 discusses the concept of national-income equilibrium in A and B simultaneously. Section 10.10 gives the necessary and sufficient conditions for stability. These conditions are rigorously derived in the appendix to this chapter. Section 10.11 discusses the pure cases of national-income multipliers with foreign repercussion. In addition, it studies some important relationships among the various multipliers. Section 10.12 shows briefly how the effect on the balance of trade of any autonomous change in spending may be calculated. Section 10.13 discusses the effects of some specific cases of autonomous changes in spending. Finally, sec. 10.14 comments briefly on some of the implications of the present analysis for economic policy. The problem of economic policy is properly tackled in later chapters.

10.9 NATIONAL-INCOME EQUILIBRIUM

Based on the preceding analysis of this chapter, the following equilibrium conditions can be formulated at once:

$$Y_a = Z_a(Y_a) + M_b(Y_b) - M_a(Y_a) \equiv D_a(Y_a, Y_b) \qquad (10.36)$$

$$Y_b = Z_b(Y_b) + M_a(Y_a) - M_b(Y_b) \equiv D_b(Y_a, Y_b) \qquad (10.37)$$

Each of these equations corresponds to eq. (10.25) with the only difference that each country's exports are now given as the other country's imports, that is, $X_a = M_b(Y_b)$ and $X_b = M_a(Y_a)$. The system of eqs. (10.36) and (10.37) can be solved for the equilibrium values of Y_a and Y_b, say Y_a^e and Y_b^e. Further, knowing Y_a^e and Y_b^e (which need not coincide with full employment), we can easily determine A's (or B's) balance of trade as follows:

$$T_a = M_b(Y_b^e) - M_a(Y_a^e) = Y_a^e - Z_a(Y_a^e) = -T_b = Z_b(Y_b^e) - Y_b^e \qquad (10.38)$$

The solution of eqs. (10.36) and (10.37) is given graphically in fig. 10.6. Equation (10.36) gives rise to *A's reaction curve FE* and eq. (10.37), to *B's reaction curve HE*. The interpretation of each reaction curve is simple. For instance, A's reaction curve gives the equilibrium value of A's income for each value of B's income (Y_b) and thus for each level of B's imports ($\equiv$ A's exports), as explained in the preceding section. Accordingly, the slope of A's reaction curve is given by $m_a M_b'$ (where

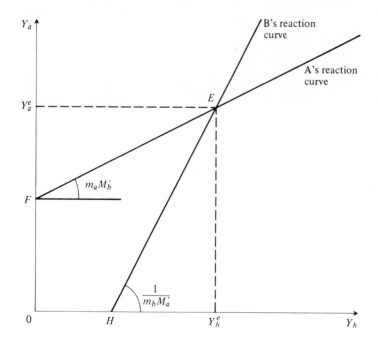

Figure 10.6 National-income equilibrium occurs at the intersection of the two reaction curves, i.e., point E.

$m_a \equiv [1/(1 - Z'_a + M'_a)] \equiv$ A's open-economy national-income multiplier). For each unit increase in Y_b, B's imports and thus A's exports increase by M'_b; hence, A's equilibrium income must increase by $m_a M'_b$. A similar interpretation holds for B's reaction curve. The only difference lies in the fact that the product $m_b M'_a$ gives the slope of B's reaction curve with respect to the Y_a axis, i.e., the *vertical* not the horizontal axis. Nevertheless, in our subsequent discussion we need the slope of B's reaction curve with respect to the *horizontal* axis, which is given by the reciprocal of $m_b M'_a$. These results on the slopes of the two reaction curves can be verified by differentiating totally eqs. (10.36) and (10.37).

Equilibrium in the market for A's output and income occurs along A's reaction curve. Similarly, equilibrium in the market for B's output and income occurs along B's reaction curve. Simultaneous equilibrium in both markets occurs at the intersection of the two reaction curves, as illustrated by point E.

10.10 STABILITY CONDITIONS

The appendix to this chapter shows that the following conditions are necessary and sufficient for local stability:

$$1 - Z'_a + M'_a = \frac{1}{m_a} > 0 \qquad (10.39)$$

$$1 - Z'_b + M'_b = \frac{1}{m_b} > 0 \qquad (10.40)$$

$$(1 - Z'_a + M'_a)(1 - Z'_b + M'_b) - M'_a M'_b > 0 \qquad (10.41a)$$

or
$$\Delta \equiv 1 - m_a m_b M'_a M'_b > 0 \qquad (10.41b)$$

The first two conditions were met in the preceding part (see inequality (10.26)). They merely imply that in the absence of foreign repercussion each country by itself is stable—the open-economy national-income multiplier is positive and finite. The third condition, i.e., inequality (10.41a) or inequality (10.41b), requires that A's reaction curve be flatter than B's, as illustrated in fig. 10.6. This can easily be seen by rearranging inequality (10.41b) as follows:

$$\frac{1}{m_a m_b} > M'_a M'_b \qquad \text{or} \qquad \frac{1}{m_b M'_a} > m_a M'_b$$

When both countries are stable in isolation, i.e., when $Z'_a < 1$, $Z'_b < 1$, all three stability conditions are satisfied. This is obvious, of course, for inequalities (10.39) and (10.40). To verify this proposition for inequality (10.41a) also, rewrite the latter as follows:

$$(1 - Z'_a)(1 - Z'_b) + M'_a(1 - Z'_b) + M'_b(1 - Z'_a) > 0 \qquad (10.41c)$$

When $Z'_a < 1$ and $Z'_b < 1$ all terms on the left-hand side are positive and thus inequality (10.41a) is satisfied.

Stability in isolation in both countries is *sufficient* (but not necessary) for stability. On the other hand, if both $Z'_a > 1$ and $Z'_b > 1$ the system becomes unstable. To see this, merely rearrange inequality (10.41c) as follows:

$$(1 - Z'_a + M'_a)(1 - Z'_b) + M'_b(1 - Z'_a) > 0 \qquad (10.41d)$$

Keeping in mind inequality (10.39), it is obvious that when $Z'_a > 1$ and $Z'_b > 1$, the left-hand side of (10.41d) becomes negative and renders the system unstable. Conversely, a *necessary* condition for stability is that at least one country is stable in isolation. That is, a necessary condition for stability is that either $Z'_a < 1$ or $Z'_b < 1$.

10.11 NATIONAL-INCOME MULTIPLIERS: THE PURE CASES

We proceed now with the national-income multiplier theory. As it turns out, all multiplier formulas which exist in the literature—see, for instance, Kindleberger (1973) and Stern (1973)—are combinations of the following two simple, but important, cases:

1. An autonomous increase (shift) in the demand for A's products with the demand for B's products remaining constant
2. An autonomous increase in the demand for B's products with the demand for A's products remaining constant

The first case implies an upward shift of A's reaction curve while the second case implies a shift to the right of B's reaction curve. To be sure, these two cases are not different since case (2) can be obtained from case (1) by reversing the roles of the two countries, as shown below. Nevertheless, it may be useful to keep these cases apart. We study each in turn.

Case (1): An autonomous increase in D_a with D_b remaining constant Consider fig. 10.7, which reproduces the reaction curves of fig. 10.6. Equilibrium occurs initially at E_0. Suppose now that an autonomous increase in demand for A's products takes place, say ΔD_a. A's reaction curve shifts upward. By how much? Certainly not by ΔD_a. As we saw earlier, for any given value of Y_b and thus A's exports, an autonomous increase in spending on A's products increases A's income by $m_a \Delta D_a$. Consequently, A's reaction curve shifts upward by $m_a \Delta D_a$ (as shown by $F'E_1$). Thus after the autonomous increase in spending, A's equilibrium income is necessarily higher by $m_a \Delta D_a$ at each and every value of Y_b.

Given the shift in A's reaction curve, equilibrium shifts from E_0 to E_1. A's income increases from Y_a^0 to Y_a^1 and B's from Y_b^0 to Y_b^1. How are the income changes $(\Delta Y_a \equiv Y_a^1 - Y_a^0, \Delta Y_b \equiv Y_b^1 - Y_b^0)$ related to the increase in demand for A's products (ΔD_a)? Put differently, what are the national-income multipliers?

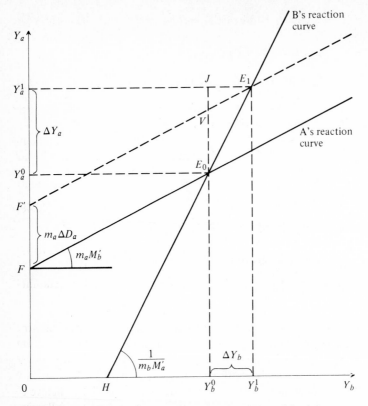

Figure 10.7 The foreign-trade multiplier in the presence of foreign repercussion. An autonomous increase in the demand for A's products (ΔD_a) causes A's reaction curve to shift upward by $m_a \Delta D_a$, as shown by the broken curve $F'E_1$. Equilibrium moves from E_0 to E_1 where both Y_a and Y_b are higher.

Let us adopt the symbol k_{ij} for the multiplier relating the total change in the national income of the ith country to the autonomous change in the demand for the products of the jth country. In particular,

$$k_{aa} \equiv \frac{\Delta Y_a}{\Delta D_a} \tag{10.42}$$

$$k_{ba} \equiv \frac{\Delta Y_b}{\Delta D_a} \tag{10.43}$$

Our object is to determine the multipliers k_{aa} and k_{ba}.

Looking at fig. 10.7 we can easily formulate the following equations:

$$\Delta Y_a = E_0 V + VJ = m_a \Delta D_a + m_a M_b'(JE_1) = m_a \Delta D_a + m_a M_b' \Delta Y_b \tag{10.44}$$

$$\Delta Y_b = JE_1 = m_b M_a'(E_0 J) = m_b M_a' \Delta Y_a \tag{10.45}$$

Substituting the value of ΔY_b as given in eq. (10.45) into eq. (10.44) and then solving (10.44) for ΔY_a, we obtain

$$\Delta Y_a = m_a \, \Delta D_a + m_a M_b' m_b M_a' \, \Delta Y_a$$

or $\qquad\qquad \Delta Y_a = \left(\dfrac{m_a}{1 - m_a m_b M_a' M_b'} \right) \Delta D_a \qquad\qquad\qquad$ (10.46)

Now substitute eq. (10.46) into eq. (10.45) and obtain

$$\Delta Y_b = \left(\frac{m_a m_b M_a'}{1 - m_a m_b M_a' M_b'} \right) \Delta D_a \qquad\qquad\qquad (10.47)$$

Accordingly,

$$k_{aa} = \left(\frac{m_a}{1 - m_a m_b M_a' M_b'} \right) = \frac{m_a}{\Delta} \qquad\qquad\qquad (10.48)$$

and $\qquad\qquad k_{ba} = \left(\dfrac{m_a m_b M_a'}{1 - m_a m_b M_a' M_b'} \right) = \dfrac{m_a m_b M_a'}{\Delta} \qquad\qquad$ (10.49)

Note that both multipliers are strictly positive and finite because of the stability conditions.

Case (2): An autonomous increase in D_b with D_a remaining constant Consider now the second case: an autonomous increase in spending on B's products (ΔD_b). What are the effects on the equilibrium incomes of A and B? This case could be handled in exactly the same way as the first case. Thus, in terms of fig. 10.7, B's reaction curve would shift to the right by $m_b \, \Delta D_b$, and then we could proceed as before to solve for the national-income multipliers (k_{ab}, k_{bb}) defined by the following equations:

$$\Delta Y_a = k_{ab} \, \Delta D_b \qquad\qquad\qquad (10.50)$$

$$\Delta Y_b = k_{bb} \, \Delta D_b \qquad\qquad\qquad (10.51)$$

However, there is an easier approach. As noted earlier, this case is similar to the first case except that the roles of the two countries are reversed. Accordingly, the solutions for k_{bb} and k_{ab} can be obtained directly from eqs. (10.48) and (10.49), respectively, by merely switching the subscripts a and b. Thus,

$$k_{bb} = \frac{m_b}{1 - m_a m_b M_a' M_b'} = \frac{m_b}{\Delta} \qquad\qquad\qquad (10.52)$$

$$k_{ab} = \frac{m_a m_b M_b'}{1 - m_a m_b M_a' M_b'} = \frac{m_a m_b M_b'}{\Delta} \qquad\qquad\qquad (10.53)$$

Properties of National-Income Multipliers

There are some important relationships among the various multipliers we have studied. These relationships are brought out in the next few theorems. First recall that we have three classes of multipliers:

1. The closed-economy multipliers:

$$\mu_i \equiv \frac{1}{1 - Z_i'} \qquad (i = a, b) \qquad (10.54)$$

2. The simple open-economy multipliers (with no foreign repercussion):

$$m_i \equiv \frac{1}{1 - Z_i' + M_i'} \qquad (i = a, b)$$

3. The multipliers k_{ij} $(i, j = a, b)$—given by eqs. (10.48), (10.49), (10.52), and (10.53)—which take into consideration foreign repercussion.

Theorem 10.1 The closed-economy multipliers are larger than the corresponding simple open-economy multipliers. That is,

$$\mu_i > m_i \qquad (i = a, b) \qquad (10.55)$$

PROOF The proof of this theorem was given earlier in part B of this chapter, and the reader is referred to that discussion.

Theorem 10.2 The multiplier k_{ii} is larger than the multiplier m_i. That is,

$$k_{ii} > m_i \qquad (10.56)$$

PROOF From eq. (10.48), we have

$$m_i = k_{ii} \, \Delta = k_{ii}(1 - m_a m_b M_a' M_b')$$
$$= k_{ii} - k_{ii} m_a m_b M_a' M_b' < k_{ii}$$

The last inequality follows from the fact that k_{ii}, m_a, and m_b are all positive because of the assumed stability conditions.

This theorem is illustrated in fig. 10.7 for country A. As the demand for A's products increases autonomously and A's reaction curve shifts upward to $F'E_1$, A's national income increases by $E_0 V$ in the absence of foreign repercussion, and by $E_0 V + VJ$ when foreign repercussion is taken into consideration. What actually happens is this. As A's income increases, A's imports and thus B's exports increase also. When foreign repercussion is allowed, the increase in B's exports causes B's income to increase, which in turn causes B's imports and therefore A's exports to increase further, and so on. It is these induced changes in A's exports which account for the inequality $k_{aa} > m_a$.

Theorem 10.3 Assume that $Z_a' < 1$ and $Z_b' < 1$. Then the closed-economy multiplier μ_i is larger than the foreign-trade multiplier k_{ii}. That is, assuming that $Z_a' < 1$, $Z_b' < 1$, the following inequality is valid:

$$\mu_i > k_{ii} \qquad (10.57)$$

PROOF First observe that

$$\mu_i = \frac{m_i}{1 - m_i M'_i} \tag{10.58}$$

and that

$$\Delta = 1 - m_i m_j M'_i M'_j = (1 - m_i M'_i) + m_i M'_i (1 - m_j M'_j)$$

$$= \left(\frac{m_i}{\mu_i}\right) + m_i M'_i \left(\frac{m_j}{\mu_j}\right) \tag{10.59}$$

where in the last step use is made of eq. (10.58).

Since $k_{ii} = m_i/\Delta$, write

$$\mu_i = k_{ii}\left(\frac{\Delta}{m_i}\right)\mu_i = k_{ii}\left[\left(\frac{1}{\mu_i}\right) + M'_i\left(\frac{m_j}{\mu_j}\right)\right]\mu_i$$

$$= k_{ii} + \left[k_{ii} M'_i m_j \left(\frac{\mu_i}{\mu_j}\right)\right] > k_{ii}$$

where the last inequality follows from the fact that k_{ii}, m_j, μ_i, and μ_j are positive because of the assumption $Z'_a < 1$, $Z'_b < 1$.

The explanation for this result is simple. An autonomous change in demand must be offset by an induced change in saving. In the case of a closed economy the saving must be done at home. Nevertheless, in a two-country world part of the change in saving will occur in the foreign country since foreign income increases and by assumption the foreign marginal propensity to absorp (Z'_j) is less than unity. Hence $\mu_i > k_{ii}$, since the domestic income does not have to increase as much. If $Z'_j > 1$, not saving but *dissaving* occurs in the foreign country and then $\mu_i < k_{ii}$, since the domestic income must increase faster to generate enough saving to match both the autonomous increase in demand and the foreign dissaving.

Theorem 10.4 Assuming that $Z'_i < 1$ ($i = a, b$), the foreign-trade multiplier k_{ii} is larger than k_{ij}. That is,

$$k_{ii} > k_{ij} \tag{10.60}$$

PROOF Consider the relationship between k_{aa} and k_{ab}. From eqs. (10.48) and (10.53), we have

$$k_{aa} = \frac{k_{ab}}{m_b M'_b} = k_{ab}\left(\frac{1 - Z'_b + M'_b}{M'_b}\right)$$

$$= k_{ab} + k_{ab}\left(\frac{1 - Z'_b}{M'_b}\right) > k_{ab}$$

The last inequality follows from the assumption that $Z'_b < 1$. Accordingly, when $Z'_b < 1$, the multiplier k_{aa} is larger than the multiplier k_{ab}—A's income increases faster for an autonomous increase in D_a than for a similar increase in D_b. In a similar way, it can be shown that when $Z'_a < 1$, the multiplier k_{bb} is larger than the multiplier k_{ba}.

In essence theorem 10.4 tells us that an increase in demand for the products of a foreign country causes our country's output to rise by less than it would if the demand for the home products were increased by the same amount as the increase in demand for foreign products, assuming only that the foreign country is stable in isolation. (If the foreign country is unstable in isolation, the impact on domestic income would be higher for an autonomous increase in the demand for foreign than domestic products.) The theorem also tells us that a diversion of either country's spending from A's products to B's products would reduce income and employment in A and increase income and employment in B, assuming both countries are stable in isolation. This last point is discussed further in sec. 10.13.

10.12 BALANCE-OF-TRADE CHANGES

It follows from eq. (10.36) that A's balance of trade is given by

$$T_a \equiv -T_b \equiv M_b(Y^e_b) - M_a(Y^e_a) = Y^e_a - Z_a(Y^e_a) = Z_b(Y^e_b) - Y^e_b \quad (10.61)$$

Accordingly, the total effect on T_a of an autonomous change in either country's demand for the products of either country is given by any one of the following three equations:

$$\Delta T_a = (\Delta M_b - \Delta M_a)_{\text{aut}} + M'_b \, \Delta Y_b - M'_a \, \Delta Y_a \quad (10.62)$$

$$\Delta T_a = -(\Delta Z_a)_{\text{aut}} + (1 - Z'_a) \, \Delta Y_a \quad (10.63)$$

$$\Delta T_a = (\Delta Z_b)_{\text{aut}} - (1 - Z'_b) \, \Delta Y_b \quad (10.64)$$

As in part B, the total change of the balance of trade is divided into two parts: an autonomous part plus an induced part. Various interesting propositions regarding the balance-of-trade multiplier theory are proven in the following section.

10.13 SPECIFIC CASES OF AUTONOMOUS CHANGES IN DEMAND

The principles which have been developed in the preceding two sections are applied to some specific but important cases of autonomous shifts in demand. To keep the present discussion as simple as possible it is presently assumed that each country's exports are totally produced by the exporting country's resources. Accordingly, $M_a = Z_{af}$ and $M_b = Z_{bf}$.

The flow of aggregate spending is given schematically in fig. 10.8. The subscripts d and f have the same meaning as in part B. An autonomous shift in D_a may come about through either an autonomous shift in Z_{ad} or Z_{bf}. Similarly, an

Figure 10.8 The flow of aggregate spending. Assume that each country's exports are produced totally by the exporting country's resources, that is, $M_a = Z_{af}$ and $M_b = Z_{bf}$. Then an autonomous shift in D_a may come about through either an autonomous shift in Z_{ad} or Z_{bf}, as illustrated by arrows (1) and (4). Similarly, an autonomous shift in D_b may come about through either an autonomous shift in Z_{bd} or Z_{af}, as illustrated by arrows (2) and (3).

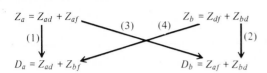

autonomous shift in D_b may come about through either an autonomous shift in Z_{bd} or Z_{af}. The effects on Y_a^e and Y_b^e of these simple shifts in demand have already been studied earlier in sec. 10.11. Nevertheless, some composite shifts may also occur and great care must be exercised in applying the multiplier formulas which we established earlier. We proceed with the study of some specific cases.

Case (1) Consider an autonomous increase in A's demand for its own products produced solely by its own resources. That is, consider an increase in Z_{ad} by ΔZ_{ad}. Determine the effects on the equilibrium levels of Y_a and Y_b (i.e., Y_a^e and Y_b^e), and A's balance of trade T_a.

SOLUTION $\Delta Y_a = k_{aa} \Delta Z_{ad} > 0$; $\Delta Y_b = k_{ba} \Delta Z_{ad} > 0$; and $\Delta T_a = -(1 - Z_b') \times \Delta Y_b < 0$. Observe that A's *balance of trade deteriorates* (assuming that $Z_b' < 1$). Accordingly, as a general proposition we may state that an increase in home demand for home resources (i.e., products produced by home resources) causes incomes everywhere to increase and in addition causes the home country's balance of trade to deteriorate, provided the foreign country's marginal propensity to spend is less than unity.

Case (2) Consider an autonomous increase in B's demand for A's products (Z_{bf}) by ΔZ_{bf}. Determine the effects of Y_a^e, Y_b^e, and T_a.

SOLUTION $\Delta Y_a = k_{aa} \Delta Z_{bf} > 0$; $\Delta Y_b = k_{ba} \Delta Z_{bf} > 0$; and $\Delta T_a = (1 - Z_a') \Delta Y_a$. Whether T_a improves depends crucially on whether A is stable in isolation. If $Z_a' < 1$, then T_a improves; if $Z_a' > 1$, then T_a deteriorates; and if $Z_a' = 1$, then T_a remains the same.

Case (3) Consider an autonomous increase in B's demand for its own output (produced solely by B's resources). That is, assume that Z_{bd} increases by ΔZ_{bd}. Determine the effects on Y_a^e, Y_b^e, and T_a.

SOLUTION $\Delta Y_a = k_{ab} \Delta Z_{bd} > 0$; $\Delta Y_b = k_{bb} \Delta Z_{bd} > 0$; and $\Delta T_a = (1 - Z_a') \Delta Y_a$. As in the previous case, the effect on T_a is indeterminate, depending on whether country A is stable in isolation.

Comparing cases (2) and (3) and making use of theorem 10.4, we can establish the following important proposition: *an increase in B's demand for A's output* (ΔZ_{bf}) *increases* T_a *by more than the same increase in B's demand for B's products* (*that is,* $\Delta Z_{bd} = \Delta Z_{bf}$) *provided that both countries are stable in isolation, that is,* $Z'_a < 1$, $Z'_b < 1$. The proof of this proposition is simple. Assume that $Z'_a < 1$, $Z'_b < 1$ and observe that in both cases $\Delta T_a = (1 - Z'_a)\,\Delta Y_a$. Thus, any difference between the two cases must be attributed to the term ΔY_a. When Z_{bf} increases, $\Delta Y_a = k_{aa}\Delta Z_{bf}$; and when Z_{bd} increases, $\Delta Y_a = k_{ab}\Delta Z_{bd}$. Since $k_{aa} > k_{ab}$, it follows that T_a improves more when Z_{bf} increases. Nevertheless, when $Z'_a < 1$ and $Z'_b > 1$, then $k_{aa} < k_{ab}$ and thus T_a improves more when Z_{bd} increases. Finally, when $Z'_a > 1$ and $Z'_b < 1$, $k_{aa} > k_{ab}$ but T_a actually deteriorates with the deterioration being larger for an increase in Z_{bf}.

Case (4) Consider an autonomous increase in A's demand for B's products (Z_{af}) by ΔZ_{af}. Determine the effects on Y_a^e, Y_b^e, and T_a.

SOLUTION This case is similar to case (2) except that the roles of the two countries are reversed. Thus no further comment is needed.

Comparing cases (1) and (4), the following important proposition can be easily established: *an increase in A's demand for its own products* (*that is,* $Z_{ad}\uparrow$) *causes A's balance of trade to deteriorate by less than would the same increase in A's demand for B's products* (*that is,* $Z_{af}\uparrow$), *assuming that both countries are stable in isolation*. To prove this proposition simply observe that in both cases the change in T_a is given by $\Delta T_a = -(1 - Z'_b)\,\Delta Y_b < 0$. Accordingly, any difference between the two cases must be attributed to the term ΔY_b. When Z_{ad} increases, $\Delta Y_b = k_{ba}\,\Delta Z_{ad}$; and when Z_{af} increases, $\Delta Y_b = k_{bb}\,\Delta Z_{af}$. Since by assumption $\Delta Z_{ad} = \Delta Z_{af}$, it follows (see theorem 10.4) that ΔY_b is higher—and thus T_a deteriorates by more—when Z_{af} increases. Nevertheless, when $Z'_a < 1$ but $Z'_b > 1$, then $\Delta T_a > 0$, and since $k_{bb} > k_{ba}$, the balance-of-trade *improvement* is larger when Z_{af} increases. On the other hand, when $Z'_a > 1$ and $Z'_b < 1$, then $\Delta T_a < 0$, and since $k_{bb} < k_{ba}$, the balance-of-trade deterioration is larger when Z_{ad} increases.

Case (5) Consider a diversion of country B's demand away from its products to the products of country A. That is, assume that Z_{bd} falls by ΔZ and Z_{bf} rises by ΔZ. Determine the effects on Y_a^e, Y_b^e, and T_a.

SOLUTION This is a composite shift. The total change in Y_a^e and Y_b^e is the sum of the changes due to the individual shifts. Accordingly,

$$\Delta Y_a = (k_{aa} - k_{ab})\Delta Z$$

$$\Delta Y_b = (k_{ba} - k_{bb})\Delta Z$$

and
$$\Delta T_a = (1 - Z'_a)\Delta Y_a$$

Assuming that both countries are stable in isolation, it follows that $\Delta Y_a > 0$, $\Delta Y_b < 0$, and $\Delta T_a > 0$. Nevertheless, if $Z_a' > 1$ while $Z_b' < 1$, then $\Delta Y_a > 0$ (since $k_{aa} > k_{ab}$), $\Delta Y_b > 0$ (since $k_{ba} > k_{bb}$), and $\Delta T_a < 0$ (since $(1 - Z_a') < 0$). On the other hand, if $Z_a' < 1$ while $Z_b' > 1$, then $\Delta Y_a < 0$ (since $k_{aa} < k_{ab}$), $\Delta Y_b < 0$ (since $k_{bb} > k_{ba}$), but again $\Delta T_a < 0$ (since $\Delta Y_a < 0$ and $(1 - Z_a') > 0$).

A general autonomous increase in Z_a may be decomposed into two simple shifts we have already studied: (a) an autonomous increase in Z_{ad} plus (b) an autonomous increase in Z_{af}. Similarly, a general autonomous increase in Z_b may be decomposed into: (a) an autonomous increase in Z_{bd} plus (b) an autonomous increase in Z_{bf}.

Another important application of the principles studied in this chapter to a composite shift in demand is studied later in chap. 12 in connection with the transfer problem.

10.14 IMPLICATIONS FOR ECONOMIC POLICY

The preceding discussion shows clearly how the national incomes of countries are linked together. In particular, it shows (a) how income fluctuations in one country (caused by either autonomous changes in spending or by deliberate economic-policy measures) can be transmitted to another country; and (b) how a diversion of demand away from the products of, say, country B to the products of country A normally causes (i.e., when both countries are stable in isolation) B's income and employment to fall and A's to rise. These two cases must be sharply distinguished because of their diametrically opposite effects on foreign incomes. This observation becomes crucial when it comes to economic policy.

A country may influence the level of economic activity at home by influencing aggregate spending on its output. As we saw earlier in this chapter, aggregate demand D for a country's products is given by $D \equiv Z + T$. Accordingly, a change in D may come either through a change in Z or a change in T. For instance, an expansionary fiscal policy or monetary policy affects D through Z. On the other hand, any policy (such as a devaluation of the domestic currency, the imposition of a new tariff or the increase in an old tariff, the reduction of export taxes, etc.) which effects a switch (or diversion) of total world spending from foreign to domestic products affects D through the balance of trade T. *Expenditure-adjusting policies* (i.e., those policies which affect aggregate demand through changes in aggregate absorption) have a favorable effect on foreign incomes. But *expenditure-switching policies* (i.e., those policies which affect aggregate demand through changes in the balance of trade) have an unfavorable effect on foreign incomes.

As already anticipated in chap. 6, the expenditure-switching policies are in the nature of beggar-thy-neighbor policies. They tend to expand domestic income and employment at the expense of foreign incomes and employment. In effect, the country adopting an expenditure-switching policy is exporting unemployment to the rest of the world. Such expenditure-switching policies are bound to provoke retaliation from foreign countries when all countries are suffering from the same ills. Thus, the game of beggar-thy-neighbor is usually played in times of general unemployment. As soon as one country succeeds in increasing its balance of trade, other countries retaliate. Accordingly, the total volume of international trade relative to world activity shrinks continuously. Political, strategic, and sentimental considerations add fuel to the fire, and the flames of economic nationalism blaze ever higher and higher.

We therefore conclude that expansionary fiscal and monetary policies might be preferable to expenditure-switching policies insofar as incomes tend to increase at home and abroad. But there is a drawback: expansionary fiscal and monetary policies have an unfavorable balance-of-trade effect. More on this in chap. 13.

The problem of economic policy is pursued further in much greater detail in later chapters.

APPENDIX TO CHAPTER TEN. STABILITY CONDITIONS OF THE INCOME-ADJUSTMENT MECHANISM

This appendix deals with the stability conditions of the income-adjustment mechanism. Following the analysis of chap. 10, assume that Y_i $(i = a, b)$ tends to increase (decrease) when the aggregate demand for the ith country's output (D_i) is higher (lower) than Y_i. In particular, assume that the rates of change of Y_a and Y_b per unit of time are given by

$$\dot{Y}_a = \lambda_a[Z_a(Y_a) + M_b(Y_b) - M_a(Y_a) - Y_a] \tag{A10.1}$$

$$\dot{Y}_b = \lambda_b[Z_b(Y_b) + M_a(Y_a) - M_b(Y_b) - Y_b] \tag{A10.2}$$

where λ_a, λ_b are positive speeds of adjustment, and $\dot{Y}_a$, $\dot{Y}_b$ are time derivatives.

Expanding eqs. (A10.1) and (A10.2) around the equilibrium point (Y_a^e, Y_b^e) and dropping all nonlinear terms, we get

$$\dot{Y}_a = -\lambda_a[(1 - Z_a' + M_a')(Y_a - Y_a^e) - M_b'(Y_b - Y_b^e)] \tag{A10.3}$$

$$\dot{Y}_b = -\lambda_b[(1 - Z_b' + M_b')(Y_b - Y_b^e) - M_a'(Y_a - Y_a^e)] \tag{A10.4}$$

The solution of eqs. (A10.3) and (A10.4) has the following form:

$$Y_a = Y_a^e + a_{11}e^{\lambda_1 t} + a_{12}e^{\lambda_2 t} \tag{A10.5}$$

$$Y_b = Y_b^e + a_{21}e^{\lambda_1 t} + a_{22}e^{\lambda_2 t} \tag{A10.6}$$

where the constants a_{ij} depend on initial conditions at time $t = 0$ and λ_1 and λ_2 are roots of the following determinantal equation:

$$\begin{vmatrix} -\lambda_a(1 - Z_a' + M_a') - \lambda & +\lambda_a M_b' \\ +\lambda_b M_a' & -\lambda_b(1 - Z_b' + M_b') - \lambda \end{vmatrix} = 0 \tag{A10.7}$$

It is apparent from eqs. (A10.5) and (A10.6) that Y_a and Y_b will not tend to the equilibrium values Y_a^e and Y_b^e, respectively, unless the real parts of λ_1 and λ_2, the roots of (A10.7), are both negative. To determine the conditions under which the real parts of λ_1 and λ_2 are negative, expand the determinant (A10.7) and then express it in the following form:

$$\lambda^2 + C_1\lambda + C_2 = 0 \tag{A10.8}$$

where

$$C_1 \equiv \lambda_a(1 - Z_a' + M_a') + \lambda_b(1 - Z_b' + M_b') \tag{A10.9}$$

$$C_2 \equiv \lambda_a\lambda_b[(1 - Z_a' + M_a')(1 - Z_b' + M_b') - M_a'M_b'] \tag{A10.10}$$

By a well-known theorem,† the real parts of the roots of (A10.8) will be negative if, and only if, $C_1 > 0$ and $C_2 > 0$. Since $\lambda_i > 0$ ($i = a, b$), the second condition reduces immediately to

$$(1 - Z_a' + M_a')(1 - Z_b' + M_b') - M_a'M_b' > 0 \tag{A10.11}$$

Further, since $M_a' > 0$, $M_b' > 0$, it follows that $(1 - Z_a' + M_a')(1 - Z_b' + M_b') > 0$. Accordingly, the two factors, $(1 - Z_a' + M_a')$ and $(1 - Z_b' + M_b')$, must necessarily have the *same* sign. Combining this result with the inequality $C_1 > 0$, we finally obtain

$$1 - Z_a' + M_a' > 0 \tag{A10.12}$$

$$1 - Z_b' + M_b' > 0 \tag{A10.13}$$

In summary, inequalities (A10.11) to (A10.13) are the necessary and sufficient conditions for the stability of the income-adjustment mechanism.

SELECTED BIBLIOGRAPHY

Black, J. (1957). "A Geometrical Analysis of the Foreign Trade Multiplier." *Economic Journal* (June), pp. 240–243.

Haberler, G. (1941). *Prosperity and Depression.* The League of Nations, Geneva, chap. XII.

Harrod, R. F. (1939). *International Economics,* revised ed. Cambridge University Press, Cambridge, chap. V.

Keynes, J. M. (1936). *The General Theory of Employment, Interest and Money.* Macmillan and Company, Ltd., London.

———— (1929). "The German Transfer Problem." *Economic Journal,* vol. XXXIX (March), pp. 1–7. Reprinted in H. S. Ellis and L. A. Metzler (Eds.), AEA *Readings in the Theory of International Trade.* R. D. Irwin, Inc., Homewood, Ill., 1950.

Kindleberger, C. P. (1973). *International Economics,* 5th ed. Richard D. Irwin, Inc., Homewood, Ill., chap. 20 and app. H.

———— (1943). "International Monetary Stabilization." In S. E. Harris (Ed.), *Postwar Economic Problems.* McGraw-Hill Book Company, New York, pp. 375–395.

Machlup, F. (1943). *International Trade and the National Income Multiplier.* The Bakiston Company, Philadelphia.

† See Samuelson (1947, pp. 430–431). See also the Mathematical Appendix at the end of this book.

Meade, J. E. (1951). *The Theory of International Economy Policy*, vol. I. *The Balance of Payments*. Oxford University Press, Inc., New York, pts. II and III.

Metzler, L. A. (1948). "The Theory of International Trade." In H. S. Ellis (Ed.), *A Survey of Contemporary Economics*. The Blackiston Company, Philadelphia.

—— (1942). "Underemployment Equilibrium in International Trade." *Econometrica* (April), pp. 97–112.

Ohlin, B. (1929). "The Reparation Problem: A Discussion." *Economic Journal*, vol. XXXIX (June), pp. 172–178. Reprinted in AEA *Readings in the Theory of International Trade*. R. D. Irwin, Inc., Homewood, Ill., 1950.

Robinson, J. (1937). *Essays in the Theory of Employment*. Basil Blackwell, Oxford, pt. III, chaps. 1 and 2.

Robinson, R. (1952). "A Graphical Analysis of the Foreign Trade Multiplier." *Economic Journal* (September), pp. 546–564.

Salant, W. A. (1941). "Foreign Trade Policy in the Business Cycle." In *Public Policy*, vol. II. Harvard University Press, Cambridge, Mass., pp. 208–231. Reprinted in H. S. Ellis and L. A. Metzler (Eds.), *Readings in the Theory of International Trade*. R. D. Irwin, Inc., Homewood, Ill., 1950.

Samuelson, P. A. (1947). *Foundations of Economic Analysis*. Harvard University Press, Cambridge, Mass.

—— (1973). *Economics*, 9th ed. McGraw-Hill Book Company, New York.

Stern, R. M. (1973). *The Balance of Payments*. Aldine Publishing Company, Chicago, Ill., chap. 6.

Taussig, F. W. (1928). *International Trade*. The Macmillan Company, New York, chaps. XX to XXV.

Viner, J. (1924). *Canada's Balance of International Indebtedness*. Harvard University Press, Cambridge, Mass.

White, H. D. (1933). *The French International Accounts 1880–1913*. Harvard University Press, Cambridge, Mass.

Williams, J. H. (1920). *Argentine International Trade Under Inconvertible Paper Money 1880–1900*. Harvard University Press, Cambridge, Mass.

ELEVEN

THE FLEXIBLE-EXCHANGE RATE AND THE THEORY OF EMPLOYMENT

The preceding chapter considered the income-adjustment mechanism under a regime of fixed prices. The present chapter broadens the scope of our investigation by including relative prices in the manner already suggested in chap. 9. Relative-price (or terms-of-trade) changes are introduced into the model through variations in the rate of foreign exchange, while the price of each country's output in terms of domestic currency continues to remain fixed. The analysis of this chapter is based on the classic works of Harberger (1950) and Laursen and Metzler (1950). Additional contributions to this topic have been made by Stolper (1950), Alexander (1952), White (1954), Spraos (1955, 1957), Pearce (1955), Johnson (1956), and Jones (1960).

The chapter is divided into two parts. Part A deals with the effects on incomes and the balance of trade of a once-and-for-all change in the rate of foreign exchange. Part B considers the theory of employment under the flexible-exchange-rate system. Here the rate of foreign exchange adjusts instantaneously and maintains equilibrium in the balance of trade continuously.

PART A. THE EFFECTS OF EXCHANGE-RATE ADJUSTMENTS

11.1 THE DIRECT EFFECTS OF AN EXCHANGE-RATE ADJUSTMENT

Consider again the two-country model of chap. 10. How does an exchange-rate adjustment affect A's and B's national incomes as well as the balance of trade? Under what conditions would a devaluation of A's currency improve A's balance of trade? More specifically, is the Marshall-Lerner condition sufficient for a successful devaluation? These are important questions and the discussion in this part is devoted to them.

Introduction of the Rate of Foreign Exchange

The first step in our investigation is to incorporate the rate of foreign exchange in the national-income equilibrium equations of chap. 10. It is important now to distinguish between aggregates expressed in dollars and aggregates expressed in pounds sterling. Thus, eqs. (10.36) and (10.37) are now written as follows:

$$Y_a = Z_a(Y_a; R) + RT_a^*(Y_a, Y_b; R) \equiv D_a(Y_a, Y_b; R) \tag{11.1}$$

$$Y_b = Z_b(Y_b; R) - T_a^*(Y_a, Y_b; R) \equiv D_b(Y_a, Y_b; R) \tag{11.2}$$

A's income (Y_a) and absorption (Z_a), as well as the demand for A's products (D_a), are expressed in terms of dollars (A's currency), while A's balance of trade (T_a^*), B's income (Y_b) and absorption (Z_b), and the demand for B's products (D_b) are expressed in terms of pounds sterling (B's currency). The rate of foreign exchange R ($\equiv$ the dollar price of pounds sterling) is presently introduced as a parameter in the system. (Recall that T_a stands for A's balance of trade expressed in dollars while T_a^* stands for A's balance of trade expressed in pounds sterling.) How does a dollar devaluation (i.e., an increase in R) affect Y_a, Y_b, and T_a^*?

In the rest of our analysis we assume that all prices and the rate of foreign exchange are initially equal to unity. This is a perfectly legitimate assumption, for at the current prices of A's and B's products and the rate of foreign exchange, we can always redefine the units of measurement of A's and B's products such that one new unit of each product costs 1 dollar, and then redefine the foreign currency as dollars. All prices and the rate of foreign exchange are now equal to unity.

In general, for any given value of R the system of eqs. (11.1) and (11.2) reduces to the system of eqs. (10.36) and (10.37) of chap. 10, and can be solved graphically by means of a pair of reaction curves as shown earlier. When R changes, both reaction curves shift. Once the precise shifts of these reaction curves (i.e., the changes in demand for each country's output at the initial equilibrium-income levels) are determined, the preceding chapter's multiplier theory can be easily applied to determine the effects of the exchange-rate adjustment on national incomes and the balance of trade.

The Direct Effects of a Change in R on D_a and D_b

What are the precise shifts of the two reaction curves following an increase in R by ΔR? Obviously, through partial differentiation of the aggregate demand functions, D_a and D_b, we have

$$\Delta D_a = \left(\frac{\partial D_a}{\partial R}\right) \Delta R = \left[\left(\frac{\partial Z_a}{\partial R}\right) + \left(\frac{\partial T_a}{\partial R}\right)\right] \Delta R \tag{11.3}$$

$$\Delta D_b = \left(\frac{\partial D_b}{\partial R}\right) \Delta R = \left[\left(\frac{\partial Z_b}{\partial R}\right) - \left(\frac{\partial T_a^*}{\partial R}\right)\right] \Delta R \tag{11.4}$$

It is interesting to note that the partial equilibrium (or elasticities) approach of chap. 4 has to do with the partial derivatives $(\partial T_a/\partial R)$ and $(\partial T_a^*/\partial R)$ only. Thus, if the stability conditions of chap. 5 are satisfied, both of these partial derivatives will be positive. In particular, starting from an initial situation in which $T_a^* = 0$ (and, therefore, $\partial T_a^*/\partial R = \partial T_a/\partial R$), we know that the Marshall-Lerner condition is necessary and sufficient for $(\partial T_a^*/\partial R) = (\partial T_a/\partial R) > 0$. (Recall that the supply elasticities for exports are presently infinite.)

With a little effort the preceding comment can be made rigorous. By definition $T_a^* \equiv S_£ - D_£$. Hence,

$$\frac{\partial T_a^*}{\partial R} = \left(\frac{1}{R}\right)(S_£ e_s^£ - D_£ e_d^£) = \left(\frac{1}{R}\right)[-S_£(1 + e_{mb}) - D_£ e_{ma}] \qquad (11.5)$$

The last equality follows from the fact that the supply elasticities for exports are infinite (see sec. 4.7). If the balance of trade is in equilibrium to begin with, i.e., if $S_£ = D_£$, eq. (11.5) reduces to

$$\frac{\partial T_a^*}{\partial R} = -\left(\frac{D_£}{R}\right)(1 + e_{ma} + e_{mb}) \qquad (11.6)$$

which is positive if, and only if, the Marshall-Lerner condition is satisfied.

The Laursen-Metzler Effect

Turn now to the partial derivatives $(\partial Z_a/\partial R)$, $(\partial Z_b/\partial R)$. Is there anything we can say about these derivatives *a priori?* Laursen and Metzler (1950, p. 286) claim from the statistical evidence that $(\partial Z_a/\partial R) > 0$, $(\partial Z_b/\partial R) < 0$. Their argument is very concise:

> With given prices at home, a decline in import prices increases the real income corresponding to any level of money income. Now the statistical evidence for the United States shows rather conclusively that the proportion of income saved tends to rise with a rise in real income and to fall with a fall in real income; . . . . We therefore believe that there is a strong presumption that, as import prices fall and the real income increases, the amount spent on goods and services out of a given money income will fall. The argument is applicable in reverse, of course, to a rise of import prices. In short, our basic premise is that, other things being the same, the expenditure schedule of any given country rises when import prices rise and falls when import prices fall.

Thus, as pounds sterling become more expensive A's imports (B's imports) become more expensive (cheaper). A's real income falls and B's rises. Accordingly, A's (B's) average propensity to spend out of a given money income increases (decreases). This argument is obviously based on the absence of *money illusion.*

Sohmen (1969, pp. 133–135) provides an elegant restatement of the Laursen-Metzler argument in simple mathematical language. Sohmen follows closely the Laursen-Metzler argument and considers the consumption function only. Nevertheless, we can generalize the argument by postulating that real spending (Z/P) is a function of real income (Y/P). Let the money expenditure Z on goods and services (domestic and foreign) be expressed as a function of money income Y and the price level P:

$$Z = Z(Y, P) \tag{11.7}$$

Absence of money illusion requires that the function $Z(Y, P)$ be homogeneous of the first degree in Y and P. Applying Euler's theorem on homogeneous functions, we obtain

$$Z = Z'Y + \left(\frac{\partial Z}{\partial P}\right)P \tag{11.8}$$

where $Z' \equiv (\partial Z/\partial Y)$ as before. Solving eq. (11.8) for $(\partial Z/\partial P)$ we finally obtain

$$\frac{\partial Z}{\partial P} = \left(\frac{Y}{P}\right)\left[\left(\frac{Z}{Y}\right) - Z'\right] > 0 \tag{11.9}$$

This derivative is positive since by assumption the proportion of income spent on goods and services (Z/Y) tends to fall with a rise in real income, which necessarily implies that $(Z/Y) > Z'$. Equation (11.9) holds for all countries.

In what follows it is necessary to evaluate the derivatives $(\partial Z_a/\partial R)$ and $(\partial Z_b/\partial R)$. Given eq. (11.9), this is easily accomplished. First, define as follows the price levels P_A and P_B of countries A and B, respectively:

$$P_A = (1 - \lambda_a)p_a + \lambda_a R p_b^* \tag{11.10}$$

$$P_B = (1 - \lambda_b)p_b^* + \lambda_b\left(\frac{p_a}{R}\right) \tag{11.11}$$

Hence, $(\partial P_A/\partial R) = \lambda_a$ and $(\partial P_B/\partial R) = -\lambda_b$, since by assumption $p_a = p_b^* = R = 1$. Let us further assume that the weight λ_i $(i = a, b)$ is given by the proportion of the ith country's expenditure spent on imports, i.e.,

$$\lambda_i = \frac{M_i}{Z_i} \quad (i = a, b) \tag{11.12}$$

Hence,

$$\frac{\partial Z_a}{\partial R} = \left(\frac{\partial Z_a}{\partial P_A}\right)\left(\frac{\partial P_A}{\partial R}\right) = \left(\frac{M_a}{Z_a}\right)\left(\frac{Y_a}{P_A}\right)\left[\left(\frac{Z_a}{Y_a}\right) - Z_a'\right] > 0 \tag{11.13}$$

$$\frac{\partial Z_b}{\partial R} = \left(\frac{\partial Z_b}{\partial P_B}\right)\left(\frac{\partial P_B}{\partial R}\right) = -\left(\frac{M_b}{Z_b}\right)\left(\frac{Y_b}{P_B}\right)\left[\left(\frac{Z_b}{Y_b}\right) - Z_b'\right] < 0 \tag{11.14}$$

The strength of the Laursen-Metzler (or terms-of-trade) effect presumably depends on the average propensity to import. The higher the average propensity to import, the stronger the terms-of-trade effect. In addition, the Laursen-Metzler effect depends crucially on the assumption that the basic relationship between real income and absorption is nonproportional. If a proportional relationship is postulated, then the average propensity to spend equals the marginal, and the right-hand sides of eqs. (11.13) and (11.14) become zero—the Laursen-Metzler effect disappears. Since we are presently concerned with short-run effects, however, we are justified in rejecting the proportionality hypothesis in favor of nonproportionality.

The Wealth Effect

An exchange-rate adjustment may affect aggregate spending through another channel: the *wealth effect*. Thus, as R increases, A's price level rises and B's falls. A's private sector suffers a reduction in the value of its cash balances and accumulated government bonds, while B's private sector enjoys an increase. (In addition, a redistribution of wealth may occur between the two countries to the extent that any international indebtedness exists.) It seems reasonable to assume that as a result of these wealth changes, A's expenditure will tend to fall while B's will tend to rise. Obviously the wealth effect works against the Laursen-Metzler effect. Nevertheless, in what follows the wealth effect is ignored for two reasons. First, the wealth effect must be of a transitory nature since its very existence generates forces for its elimination. Thus, the wealth effect can last only until the wealth in both countries is restored to its initial level. Second, the existence of the wealth effect depends on price expectations. Will prices remain at their current levels, will they return to their initial levels, or will they go higher? It all depends on circumstances. In the present context, of course, one may be justified in assuming inelastic expectations, but in part B, which deals with flexible-exchange rates, such an assumption may be unjustified. It is interesting to note that Sohmen (1969, p. 50) calls "the real balance effect of a rise in the domestic price level and the possibility of money illusion . . . as . . . mere curiosities."

11.2 THE EFFECT OF AN EXCHANGE-RATE ADJUSTMENT ON NATIONAL INCOME

What is the effect of an exchange-rate adjustment on the national incomes of countries A and B? Having determined the direct effects of the exchange-rate adjustment on the demand for each country's products (i.e., ΔD_a and ΔD_b), this question can be easily handled in terms of the national-income multiplier theory of the preceding chapter. Thus, in general, the national-income changes are given by the following equations:

$$\Delta Y_a = k_{aa}\,\Delta D_a + k_{ab}\,\Delta D_b \qquad (11.15a)$$

$$\Delta Y_b = k_{ba}\,\Delta D_a + k_{bb}\,\Delta D_b \qquad (11.16a)$$

or, dividing through by ΔR,

$$\frac{\Delta Y_a}{\Delta R} = k_{aa}\left(\frac{\partial D_a}{\partial R}\right) + k_{ab}\left(\frac{\partial D_b}{\partial R}\right) \qquad (11.15b)$$

$$\frac{\Delta Y_b}{\Delta R} = k_{ba}\left(\frac{\partial D_a}{\partial R}\right) + k_{bb}\left(\frac{\partial D_b}{\partial R}\right) \qquad (11.16b)$$

If the Laursen-Metzler effect is ignored, the balance of trade is initially balanced, the Marshall-Lerner condition is satisfied, and $R = 1$ by an appropriate choice of units of measurement, then $(\partial D_a/\partial R) = -(\partial D_b/\partial R) = (\partial T_a/\partial R) = (\partial T_a^*/\partial R) > 0$. In this case, eqs. (11.15b) and (11.16b) reduce to

$$\frac{\Delta Y_a}{\Delta R} = (k_{aa} - k_{ab})\left(\frac{\partial T_a}{\partial R}\right) > 0 \qquad (11.15c)$$

$$\frac{\Delta Y_b}{\Delta R} = (k_{ba} - k_{bb})\left(\frac{\partial T_a}{\partial R}\right) < 0 \qquad (11.16c)$$

The signs, of course, are deduced by applying theorem 10.4. Accordingly, a devaluation of A's currency leads, in this case, to an increase in A's national income and to a decrease in B's. We take it that this is the normal case.

The above result continues to hold if the Laursen-Metzler effect is included with the proviso that it is of the same strength in the two countries, that is, $(\partial Z_a/\partial R) = -(\partial Z_b/\partial R)$. In this case again, we continue to have $(\partial D_a/\partial R) = -(\partial D_b/\partial R) > 0$. Thus, eqs. (11.15$c$) and (11.16$c$) continue to hold with the minor difference that the partial derivative $(\partial T_a/\partial R)$ must now be replaced by $(\partial D_a/\partial R)$. Section 11.5 below shows that this result holds even when $(\partial Z_a/\partial R) \neq -(\partial Z_b/\partial R)$, provided only that the balance of trade is initially balanced.

Dropping the assumptions that the balance of trade is initially balanced and that the Laursen-Metzler effect is of the same strength in the two countries gives rise to many other outcomes which we need not study in detail. In general, if $-(\partial D_b/\partial R) > (\partial D_a/\partial R) > 0$, then B's income falls while A's income may either fall or rise. Similarly, if $(\partial D_a/\partial R) > -(\partial D_b/\partial R) > 0$, then A's income necessarily rises while B's income may either rise or fall.

11.3 THE EFFECT OF AN EXCHANGE-RATE ADJUSTMENT ON THE BALANCE OF TRADE

What is the *total effect* of a devaluation of A's currency on A's balance of trade? The preceding chapter's analysis can be effectively used to answer this question as well. The easiest approach is to apply eq. (10.64), keeping in mind that the difference $Z_b - Y_b$ gives T_a^*—not T_a. In addition, we normalize by dividing ΔT_a^* by ΔR. Accordingly,

$$\frac{\Delta T_a^*}{\Delta R} = \left(\frac{\partial Z_b}{\partial R}\right) - (1 - Z_b')\left(\frac{\Delta Y_b}{\Delta R}\right) \qquad (11.17)$$

From eq. (11.4) it follows that

$$\frac{\partial Z_b}{\partial R} = \left(\frac{\Delta D_b}{\Delta R}\right) + \left(\frac{\partial T_a^*}{\partial R}\right) \qquad (11.18)$$

Finally, substituting eqs. (11.18) and (11.16b) into eq. (11.17) and rearranging, we obtain

$$\frac{\Delta T_a^*}{\Delta R} = \left(\frac{\partial T_a^*}{\partial R}\right) - (1 - Z_b')k_{ba}\left(\frac{\partial D_a}{\partial R}\right)$$

$$+ [1 - (1 - Z_b')k_{bb}]\left(\frac{\partial D_b}{\partial R}\right)$$

$$= \left(\frac{\partial T_a^*}{\partial R}\right) - (1 - Z_b')k_{ba}\left(\frac{\partial D_a}{\partial R}\right) + (1 - Z_a')k_{ab}\left(\frac{\partial D_b}{\partial R}\right) \qquad (11.19)$$

Equation (11.19) is very significant and some interpretation of it is imperative. The right-hand side is the sum of three terms. The first term $(\partial T_a^*/\partial R)$ shows the direct effect of devaluation on A's balance of trade. This is the *price effect* of devaluation which is familiar to us from the partial equilibrium approach of part one of this book. If the Marshall-Lerner condition is satisfied, this first effect is favorable, that is, $(\partial T_a^*/\partial R) > 0$.

The second and third terms show the induced (or *income*) effects of devaluation on A's balance of trade. Both of these effects arise from the national-income changes generated by the devaluation. In particular, the second term, namely, $-(1 - Z_b')k_{ba}(\partial D_a/\partial R)$, shows the induced-income effect on T_a^* of the change $(\partial D_a/\partial R)$. This is in the spirit of eq. (10.64) once we realize that the product $k_{ba}(\partial D_a/\partial R)$ shows the change in B's national income following the change $(\partial D_a/\partial R)$. Similarly, the third term, namely, $(1 - Z_a')k_{ab}(\partial D_b/\partial R)$, shows the induced-income effect on T_a^* of the change $(\partial D_b/\partial R)$. Noting that the product $k_{ab}(\partial D_b/\partial R)$ shows the change in A's national income following the change $(\partial D_b/\partial R)$, this third term is in the spirit of eq. (10.63). On the reasonable assumption that both countries are stable in isolation, both income effects are unfavorable, i.e., the second and third terms are strictly negative.

Equation (11.19) reveals that the Marshall-Lerner condition is no longer sufficient for a successful devaluation. The trouble lies with the unfavorable income effects. If a devaluation is to be successful the favorable price effect must outweigh the unfavorable income effects. Thus, as Laursen and Metzler (1950) point out, a successful devaluation requires that the sum of the import-demand elasticities be much higher than unity.

11.4 THE HARBERGER CONDITION

We have just concluded that for a successful devaluation the sum of the import-demand elasticities must be higher than unity. But how much higher? Can we specify a critical value (higher than unity) for this sum of elasticities above which devaluation is successful? Harberger (1950), using the apparatus of formal demand theory, showed that such a critical value exists and in fact it is equal to unity plus the sum of the marginal propensities to import.

We can easily derive the Harberger condition with what we already know. First substitute eqs. (11.3), (11.4), (11.13), and (11.14) into eq. (11.19), noting that $P_A = P_B = 1$, to obtain

$$
\frac{\Delta T_a^*}{\Delta R} = \left(\frac{\partial T_a^*}{\partial R}\right) - (1 - Z_b')k_{ba}M_a\left(\frac{Y_a}{Z_a}\right)\left[\left(\frac{Z_a}{Y_a}\right) - Z_a'\right]
$$

$$
- (1 - Z_b')k_{ba}\left[T_a^* + \left(\frac{\partial T_a^*}{\partial R}\right)\right] - (1 - Z_a')k_{ab}M_b\left(\frac{Y_b}{Z_b}\right)
$$

$$
\times \left[\left(\frac{Z_b}{Y_b}\right) - Z_b'\right] - (1 - Z_a')k_{ab}\left(\frac{\partial T_a^*}{\partial R}\right)
$$

After regrouping and simplifying, we finally obtain

$$
\frac{\Delta T_a^*}{\Delta R} = m_a m_b (1 - Z_a')(1 - Z_b')\left(\frac{1}{\Delta}\right)
$$

$$
\times \left\{\left(\frac{\partial T_a^*}{\partial R}\right) - \left(\frac{M_a'}{1 - Z_a'}\right)T_a^* - M_a'\left(\frac{M_a}{1 - Z_a'}\right)\left(\frac{Y_a}{Z_a}\right)\right.
$$

$$
\times \left.\left[\left(\frac{Z_a}{Y_a}\right) - Z_a'\right] - M_b'\left(\frac{M_b}{1 - Z_b'}\right)\left(\frac{Y_b}{Z_b}\right)\left[\left(\frac{Z_b}{Y_b}\right) - Z_b'\right]\right\} \quad (11.20)
$$

where $\Delta \equiv 1 - m_a m_b M_a' M_b'$. A successful devaluation requires that the right-hand side of eq. (11.20) be positive.

To derive the Harberger condition, merely assume that the balance of trade is initially zero. That is, $T_a^* = 0$, which also implies that $Y_a = Z_a$, $Y_b = Z_b$, and $M_a = M_b$. Substituting these assumptions and eq. (11.6) into equation (11.20), we finally obtain

$$
\frac{\Delta T_a^*}{\Delta R} = m_a m_b (1 - Z_a')(1 - Z_b')\left(\frac{M_a}{\Delta}\right)(-1 - e_{ma} - e_{mb} - M_a' - M_b') \quad (11.21)
$$

For $(\Delta T_a^*/\Delta R) > 0$, it is required that the expression in the brackets be positive. That is,

$$
-1 - e_{ma} - e_{mb} - M_a' - M_b' > 0
$$

or
$$
-e_{ma} - e_{mb} > 1 + M_a' + M_b' \quad (11.22)
$$

Inequality (11.22) is the Harberger condition. It shows that with initially balanced trade devaluation improves the balance of trade if, and only if, the sum of the import-demand elasticities is greater than unity plus the sum of the marginal propensities to import. Thus once more we see that when the income effects are taken into consideration, the condition for a successful devaluation is more stringent than the simple Marshall-Lerner condition.

11.5 THE NATIONAL-INCOME CHANGES AGAIN

Assume that the balance of trade is initially balanced and the Harberger condition is satisfied. We can show that a devaluation of A's currency relative to B's currency causes unequivocally A's national income to increase and B's national income to fall.

Assume for simplicity that $R = 1$ initially, and recall that in the present case we have

$$\frac{\partial D_a}{\partial R} = \left(\frac{\partial Z_a}{\partial R}\right) + \left(\frac{\partial T_a}{\partial R}\right) = M[(1 - Z_a') + h + M_a' + M_b']$$

$$\frac{\partial D_b}{\partial R} = \left(\frac{\partial Z_b}{\partial R}\right) - \left(\frac{\partial T_a}{\partial R}\right) = -M[(1 - Z_b') + h + M_a' + M_b']$$

where $M \equiv M_a = M_b$ and $h \equiv (-1 - e_{ma} - e_{mb} - M_a' - M_b') > 0$. Substituting into eqs. (11.15b) and (11.16b) and using theorem 10.4, we obtain

$$\frac{\Delta Y_a}{\Delta R} = Mh(k_{aa} - k_{ab}) + M[k_{aa}(1 - Z_a')$$

$$+ M_a'(k_{aa} - k_{ab}) + M_b'(k_{aa} - k_{ab}) - k_{ab}(1 - Z_b')]$$

$$= Mh(k_{aa} - k_{ab}) + M[k_{aa}(1 - Z_a') + M_a'(k_{aa} - k_{ab})] > 0$$

$$\frac{\Delta Y_b}{\Delta R} = -Mh(k_{bb} - k_{ba}) - M[k_{bb}(1 - Z_b') + M_a'(k_{bb} - k_{ba})$$

$$+ M_b'(k_{bb} - k_{ba}) - k_{ba}(1 - Z_a')]$$

$$= -Mh(k_{bb} - k_{ba}) - M[k_{bb}(1 - Z_b') + M_b'(k_{bb} - k_{ba})] < 0$$

Note that

$$M_b'(k_{aa} - k_{ab}) - k_{ab}(1 - Z_b') = M_a'(k_{bb} - k_{ba}) - k_{ba}(1 - Z_a') = 0$$

PART B. THE FLEXIBLE-EXCHANGE RATES WITH BALANCED TRADE

11.6 INTRODUCTION

In the preceding chapter we learned that under fixed-exchange rates international trade is a powerful vehicle for the propagation of business cycles internationally. A boom (depression) in one country entails an expansion (contraction) in the rest of the world. But suppose that a flexible-exchange-rate system is adopted and the balance of trade remains always in balance. Would this act as a buffer and insulate, so to speak, each economy from disturbances which occur in the rest of the world? Would a country be able now to maintain an independent fiscal and monetary policy to stabilize domestic national income and employment, ignoring repercussions from foreign disturbances? Many economists have thought so. In their classic article Laursen and Metzler (1950) concluded that this is not the case. We shall presently discuss their thesis.

11.7 THE MODEL AND ITS STATIC SOLUTION

The mathematical model of the flexible-exchange-rate system with balanced trade is given by the following equations:

$$Y_a = Z_a(Y_a, R) \tag{11.23}$$

$$Y_b = Z_b(Y_b, R) \tag{11.24}$$

$$T_a^* = \left(\frac{1}{R}\right) M_b(Y_b, R) - M_a(Y_a, R) = 0 \tag{11.25}$$

We continue to assume that $p_a = p_b^* = 1$.

Observe that T_a (or T_a^*) does not appear in any of the national-income equilibrium eqs. (11.23) and (11.24) because it is by hypothesis zero. Thus, each country's circular flow of income might appear closed and raise the suspicion that the flexible-exchange-rate system cuts the link between the two economies and renders them independent of each other. In short, it might appear that business cycles originating in the rest of the world would have no effect on national income and employment at home, and vice versa. The suspicion is erroneous, of course, because of the terms-of-trade effect on absorption. Thus, the equilibrium value of R does depend on foreign trade as revealed by eq. (11.25), and in turn R is included in eqs. (11.23) and (11.24). Accordingly, the foreign-trade sector does affect income and employment, but only indirectly through its influence on the rate of foreign exchange (i.e., through the terms of trade).

Graphical Solution

The system of eqs. (11.23) to (11.25) consists of three equations in three unknowns: Y_a, Y_b, and R. Consequently, the system can be solved simultaneously for the equilibrium values of the three unknowns. Unfortunately, no single equation can be solved by itself to give the equilibrium value of one of the unknowns. This seems to create some difficulties when a graphical solution is pursued—three-dimensional surfaces cannot be easily manipulated in two dimensions. But this is illusory. The system can be solved graphically. In fact, technically speaking, it is simpler than the fixed-exchange-rate system of the preceding chapter.

Go back to eqs. (11.1) and (11.2) and consider the rate of exchange as a parameter. For each value of R this system can be solved for the equilibrium values of Y_a and Y_b. Given the equilibrium values of Y_a and Y_b, the balance of trade T_a^* can then be determined. But what does this have to do with the flexible-exchange-rate system? Merely this: the rate of exchange can be allowed to vary from zero to infinity and the resultant values of T_a^* can be shown graphically as in fig. 11.1. The value of the rate of exchange at which $T_a^* = 0$ is simply the equilibrium value of R *for the flexible-exchange-rate system* (eqs. (11.23) to (11.25)). Knowing the equilibrium value of R, eqs. (11.23) and (11.24) can then be solved graphically for the equilibrium values of Y_a and Y_b, respectively, as if each economy were closed.

Figure 11.1 portrays the case of multiple equilibria. Points E_1 and E_3 are stable while E_2 is unstable. Put differently, at E_1 and E_3 the Harberger condition is satisfied, and as R increases $T_a^* (\equiv \text{excess supply of pounds sterling})$ increases also. On the other hand, at E_2 the Harberger condition is not satisfied and as R

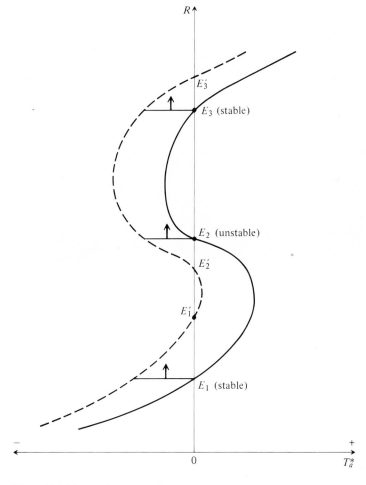

Figure 11.1 The excess supply of pounds sterling. The values of R at which $T_a^* = 0$ (that is, $0E_1$, $0E_2$ and $0E_3$) are equilibrium values for the flexible-exchange-rate system. The Harberger condition is satisfied at the stable points E_1 and E_3 only.

increases T_a^* falls. The corresponding equilibrium-income levels in countries A and B are different for each of these three equilibria. The higher the rate of exchange, the higher (lower) A's (B's) absorption and national income. Thus, A's national income is highest at E_3 and lowest at E_1 while B's national income is highest at E_1 and lowest at E_3.

11.8 COMPARATIVE STATICS

We proceed now to investigate how the present system reacts to disturbances. Does the flexible-exchange-rate system react to disturbances in the same way as the fixed-exchange-rate system? The answer turns out to be negative. In fact, the conclusions to be reached presently will appear quite perplexing and paradoxical at first.

To study the effects of any disturbance on the equilibrium levels of Y_a and Y_b—T_a^* is zero before and after the disturbance—we must first determine the influence on the equilibrium rate of exchange. How can we accomplish this? By determining how the excess-supply-of-pounds curve of fig. 11.1 shifts. In this connection, the balance-of-trade multiplier theory of the preceding chapter is of paramount importance.

Before proceeding with the study of concrete disturbances, it is important to emphasize that the rate of foreign exchange will tend to rise (fall) when A's balance of trade deteriorates (improves) at the initial equilibrium value of R irrespective of whether the initial equilibrium in the foreign exchange market is stable or unstable. For instance, suppose that a disturbance causes A's balance of trade to deteriorate. The excess-supply-of-pounds curve shifts to the left, as shown in fig. 11.1 by the broken curve. As explained in chap. 5 (see fig. 5.5), we should *not* conclude that if the system is initially at E_i it will move to E_i' ($i = 1, 2, 3$). This holds for the stable equilibria (E_1 and E_3) only. If the system is initially at the unstable equilibrium E_2, it will move to E_3'—not E_2'. Accordingly, R always increases in this case. A similar argument shows that when a disturbance causes A's balance of trade to improve, the rate of foreign exchange tends to fall irrespective of whether the system is initially at a stable or unstable equilibrium.

In the following analysis, we maintain the assumption that the marginal propensity to absorb of each country is less than unity, that is, $Z_a' < 1$, $Z_b' < 1$.

We are now ready to proceed with the comparative-statics effects of various disturbances. For comparison purposes, we propose to discuss the five disturbances we analyzed in sec. 10.13 in connection with the fixed-exchange-rate system.

Case (1) Consider an autonomous increase in A's demand for its own products produced solely by its own resources. That is, consider an increase in Z_{ad} by ΔZ_{ad}. Determine the effects on the rate of foreign exchange and national incomes.

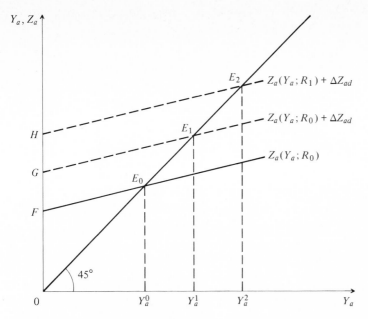

Figure 11.2 Comparative-statics effects on A's national income. The equilibrium of Y_a is determined at the point where the Z_a function (drawn for the equilibrium value of R) intersects the 45° line, as illustrated by point E_0. An autonomous increase in Z_{ad} by ΔZ_{ad} causes the Z_a schedule to shift upward, as indicated by the broken line GE_1. But this is not all, because R increases to, say, R_1. Because of the Laursen-Metzler effect, the Z_a function shifts upward for a second time to, say, HE_2. Hence, equilibrium shifts from E_0 to E_2.

SOLUTION In chap. 10 we learned that under a fixed-exchange-rate system an increase in Z_{ad} has the following effects: $\Delta Y_a > 0$, $\Delta Y_b > 0$, and $\Delta T_a^* < 0$. Accordingly, we may conclude that for *any* initial value of R an increase in Z_{ad} causes T_a^* to deteriorate. Hence the excess-of-supply-of-pounds curve of fig. 11.1 shifts to the left and the *rate of foreign exchange tends to rise*. What effects does a depreciation of the dollar and the autonomous increase in Z_{ad} have on the national incomes of countries A and B?

Figure 11.2 shows what happens to A's national income. Equilibrium occurs initially at E_0. The schedule FE_0 is drawn for the initial equilibrium value of the rate of exchange which is determined as explained earlier. Keep R fixed at its initial equilibrium value for the moment. When Z_{ad} increases, the schedule FE_0 shifts upward by ΔZ_{ad}, as shown by the broken schedule GE_1. If our economy were a closed one, or if the Laursen-Metzler (or terms-of-trade) effect were absent, equilibrium would shift to E_1 with A's income increasing to $0Y_a^1$. But A's economy is not closed and the Laursen-Metzler effect is not absent. As we saw, the dollar depreciates, A's terms of trade deteriorate, and A's absorption (Z_a) increases at every level of A's money income. In short, as R increases, the schedule GE_1 shifts upward, as shown by the broken schedule HE_2. Thus, eventually equilibrium shifts to E_2 and A's

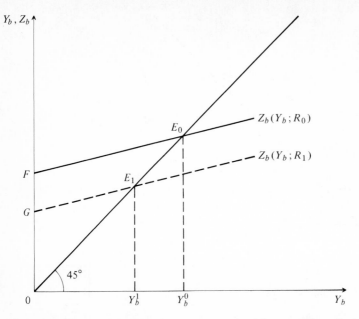

Figure 11.3 Comparative-statics effects on B's national income. When Z_{ad} increases, R increases also. As a result, the Z_b schedule shifts downward from FE_0 to GE_1, and equilibrium moves from E_0 to E_1. The paradox here is that, as Z_{ad} *increases*, B's income *falls*.

income increases to $0Y_a^2$. Note that *A's income increases faster in the present case than if country A were a closed economy.*

Figure 11.3 shows what happens to B's national income. Equilibrium occurs initially at E_0. As with country A, the schedule FE_0 is drawn for the initial equilibrium value of the rate of exchange. The autonomous increase in Z_{ad} has no direct influence on B's absorption. Nevertheless, the resultant depreciation of the dollar causes B's absorption to fall at every level of B's money income. Hence, the schedule FE_0 shifts downward, as shown by the broken curve GE_1. Accordingly, equilibrium shifts to E_1 and B's income *falls* to $0Y_b^1$. This result is paradoxical. *Under a fixed-exchange-rate system, B's income increases.* Now we find out that *under a flexible-exchange-rate system B's income decreases.*

Case (2) Consider an autonomous increase in B's demand for A's products. That is, consider an increase in Z_{bf} by ΔZ_{bf}. Determine the effects on the rate of foreign exchange and national incomes.

SOLUTION In the preceding chapter we learned that under a fixed-exchange-rate system an increase in Z_{bf} has the following effects: $\Delta Y_a > 0$, $\Delta Y_b > 0$, and $\Delta T_a^* > 0$. When the rate of foreign exchange is flexible, it follows that the initial improvement in A's balance of trade causes the rate of foreign exchange

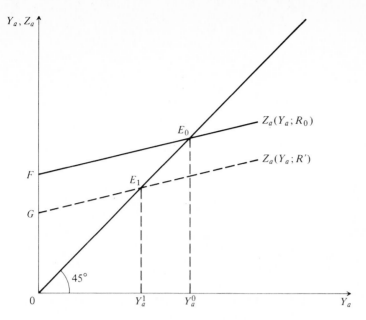

Figure 11.4 Comparative-statics effects on A's national income. An increase in Z_{bf} causes R to fall from R_0 to R'. As a result, the Z_a schedule shifts downward from FE_0 to GE_1, and equilibrium moves from E_0 to E_1. There is a paradox: as Z_{bf} *increases*, Y_a *falls*.

to fall—the excess supply curve for pounds sterling of fig. 11.1 shifts to the right.

The effect on A's national income is shown in fig. 11.4. Equilibrium occurs initially at E_0. As R falls, A's absorption function shifts downward, as shown by the broken curve GE_1. Hence A's income *falls*, which is paradoxical. B's increased spending on A's products results in a reduction of income and employment in A because A's currency appreciates relative to B's.

The effect on B's national income is shown in fig. 11.5. Equilibrium occurs initially at E_0. As B's total absorption increases autonomously and before A's currency appreciates, B's absorption function shirts upward, as shown by GE_1. If the terms-of-trade effect were zero, B's income would have increased to $0Y_b^1$. However, as R falls, B's absorption function shifts further upward to HE_2. B's national income increases finally to $0Y_b^2$.

Case (3) Consider an autonomous increase in B's demand for its own products. That is, assume that Z_{bd} increases by ΔZ_{bd}. Determine the effects on R, Y_a, and Y_b.

SOLUTION Under a fixed-exchange-rate system an increase in Z_{bd} has the following effects: $\Delta Y_a > 0$, $\Delta Y_b > 0$, and $\Delta T_a^* > 0$. When the rate of foreign exchange is flexible, this case is qualitatively similar to case (2). The only

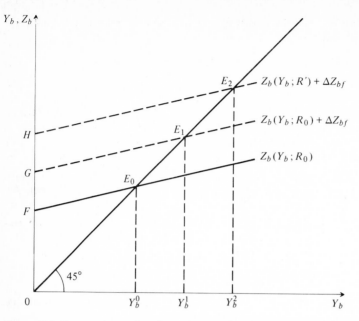

Figure 11.5 Comparative-statics effects on B's national income. As Z_{bf} increases by ΔZ_{bf}, the Z_b function shifts upward from FE_0 to GE_1 while R remains at its initial value R_0. Actually R falls from R_0 to R'. As a result, the Z_b schedule shifts upward for a second time, as illustrated by the broken curve HE_2. Thus, equilibrium moves from E_0 to E_2.

difference is that ΔT_a^* is larger for case (2) than for case (3) and, therefore, R falls deeper and the income changes are larger for case (2). Accordingly, figs. 11.4 and 11.5 can be used again to illustrate the effects on Y_a and Y_b.

Case (4) Consider an autonomous increase in A's demand for B's products. That is, assume that Z_{af} increases by ΔZ_{af}. Determine the effects on R, Y_a, and Y_b.

SOLUTION Under a fixed-exchange-rate system we have the following effects: $\Delta Y_a > 0$, $\Delta Y_b > 0$, and $\Delta T_a^* < 0$. (This case is similar to the second case except that the roles of the two countries are reversed.) For a flexible-exchange-rate system the solution is similar to the solution of case (1), and figs. 11.2 and 11.3 can be used to illustrate the present case as well.

The only difference between cases (1) and (4) is merely the fact that A's balance of trade deterioration under a fixed-exchange rate is smaller for case (1). Accordingly, under a flexible-exchange rate the rise in R and the income changes are smaller for case (1).

By looking at cases (1) to (4) we can easily conclude that, *under a flexible-exchange-rate system, an autonomous increase in a country's absorption of either domestic or foreign products results always in an expansion of domestic incomes and a contraction of foreign incomes.*

Case (5) Consider a diversion of B's demand away from its products to the products of country A. Determine the effects on R, Y_a, and Y_b.

SOLUTION Under a fixed-exchange rate we have the following effects: $\Delta Y_a > 0$, $\Delta Y_b < 0$, and $\Delta T_a^* > 0$. Nevertheless, when the rate of exchange is flexible the effects on Y_a and Y_b are reversed, that is, $\Delta Y_a < 0$ and $\Delta Y_b > 0$. Thus, since $\Delta T_a^* > 0$ under a fixed-exchange rate, the excess supply curve for pounds sterling of fig. 11.1 shifts to the right and A's currency appreciates relative to B's currency. Thus, as a result of the terms-of-trade effect, A's absorption function shifts downward, as shown in fig. 11.4, causing Y_a to fall. Similarly, B's absorption function shifts upward causing Y_b to rise. Accordingly, we reach the paradoxical conclusion that *when a country diverts part of its spending away from domestic products to foreign products, domestic incomes rise and foreign incomes fall.*

The results of the various disturbances under fixed- and flexible-exchange rates are summarized for convenience in table 11.1.

Table 11.1

Type of disturbance	Effects under fixed exchange rates			Effects under flexible exchange rates		
	ΔT_a	ΔY_a	ΔY_b	ΔR	ΔY_a	ΔY_b
1. Z_{ad} increases	−	+	+	+	+	−
2. Z_{bf} increases	+	+	+	−	−	+
3. Z_{bd} increases	+	+	+	−	−	+
4. Z_{af} increases	−	+	+	+	+	−
5. B diverts its spending from B's to A's products	+	+	−	−	−	+

SELECTED BIBLIOGRAPHY

Alexander, S. S. (1952). "Effects of a Devaluation on a Trade Balance." *International Monetary Fund Staff Papers*, vol. 2 (April), pp. 263–278.

Harberger, A. C. (1950). "Currency Depreciation, Income, and the Balance of Trade." *Journal of Political Economy*, vol. LVIII, no. 1 (February), pp. 47–60. Reprinted in AEA *Readings in International Economics*. Richard D. Irwin, Inc., Homewood, Ill., 1968.

Johnson, H. G. (1956). "The Transfer Problem and Exchange Stability." *Journal of Political Economy*, vol. LXIV, no. 3 (June), pp. 212–225. Reprinted in AEA *Readings in International Economics*. R. D. Irwin, Inc., Homewood, Ill., 1968.

Jones, R. W. (1960). "Depreciation and the Dampening Effects of Income Changes." *Review of Economics and Statistics*, vol. 42 (February), pp. 74–80.

Laursen, S., and L. A. Metzler (1950). "Flexible Exchange Rates and the Theory of Employment." *Review of Economics and Statistics*, vol. XXXII, no. 4 (November), pp. 281–299.

Machlup, F. (1955). "Relative Prices and Aggregate Spending in the Analysis of Devaluation." *American Economic Review*, vol. LXV (June), pp. 255–278. Reprinted in F. Machlup, *International Payments, Debts, and Gold*. Charles Scribner's Sons, New York, 1964.

—— (1956). "The Terms-of-Trade Effects of Devaluation Upon Real Income and the Balance of Trade," *Kyklos*, vol. IX, Fasc. 4, pp. 417–452. Reprinted in F. Machlup, *International Payments, Debts, and Gold*. Charles Scribner's Sons, New York, 1964.

Pearce, I. F. (1955). "A Note on Mr. Spraos' Paper." *Economica*, N.S., vol. XXII, no. 86 (May), pp. 147–151.

Sandler, T. M. (1974). "Devaluation, Capital Flows and the Balance of Payments: A Respecification." *Weltwirtschaft Archiv*, vol. 110, no. 2 (June), pp. 244–258.

Sohmen, E. (1969). *Flexible Exchange Rates*, revised ed. The University of Chicago Press, Chicago, Ill., chap. V.

—— (1974). "Exchange Rates, Terms of Trade and Employment: Pitfalls in Macroeconomic Models of Open Economies," *Kyklos*, vol. 27, no. 3, pp. 521–536.

Spraos, J. (1955). "Consumers' Behavior and the Conditions for Exchange Stability." *Economica*, N.S., vol. XXII, no. 86 (May), pp. 137–147.

—— (1957). "Stability in a Closed Economy and in the Foreign Exchange Market, and the Redistributive Effect of Price Changes." *Review of Economic Studies* vol. 24 (June), pp. 161–176.

Stern, R. M. (1973). *The Balance of Payments*. Aldine Publishing Company, Chicago, Ill., chap. 7.

Stolper, W. F. (1950). "The Multiplier, Flexible Exchanges, and International Equilibrium." *Quarterly Journal of Economics*, vol. 64 (November), pp. 559–582.

Vanek, J. (1962). *International Trade: Theory and Economic Policy*. R. D. Irwin, Inc., Homewood. Ill., chap. 8.

White, W. H. (1954). "The Employment-Insulating Advantages of Flexible Exchanges: A Comment on Professors Laursen and Metzler." *Review of Economics and Statistics*, vol. XXXVI, no. 2 (May), pp. 225–228.

TWELVE

THE TRANSFER PROBLEM

This chapter is divided into three parts. Part A deals with the nature of the transfer problem and its historical development. Part B considers the *classical transfer problem*, i.e., the transfer problem on the classical assumption of full employment and the added requirement that the economic system maintains automatically the equality between income and absorption (expenditure). Finally, part C considers the *Keynesian transfer problem*, i.e., the transfer problem in the context of the Keynesian, fixed-price model of chap. 10.

Valuable surveys of the transfer problem are those of Haberler (1936), Iversen (1936), Johnson (1961), Kindleberger (1968), Samuelson (1952, 1954), and Viner (1937). Johnson's paper was originally published in 1956.

PART A. THE NATURE OF THE TRANSFER PROBLEM

The transfer problem is mainly concerned with the difficulties associated with *unilateral payments* from one country to another. Such unilateral payments may occur as a result of *borrowing* (by economic units in a poor country from economic units in richer countries), *reparation payments* (made to the victors by defeated countries, such as France after the Franco-Prussian War of 1870–1871 and Germany after World War I), *grants-in-aid* (supplied by developed nations to industrially backward countries), and so forth. Such unilateral payments are usually called *transfers*.

The transfer is usually divided into two parts: the *money* or *financial* transfer (or the transfer of purchasing power), and the *real* transfer. The money transfer refers to the conversion of the currency of the transferor into the currency of the transferee through the foreign exchange market. The real transfer refers to the induced movement of goods between countries. The money transfer and the real transfer are closely interrelated. In general, the real transfer may precede, accompany, or follow the money transfer. Further and somewhat paradoxically, the money transfer is necessarily reversed when the real transfer is actually effected—in effect, the transferee returns the money to the transferor in exchange for real goods and services.

The real transfer is actually effected when the transferor country develops an export surplus, and the transferee country an import surplus, equal to the transfer. This is the only way in which real capital may be transferred between countries. The goods transferred need not be capital goods. Consumption goods and services may indeed be transferred by the transferor country to the transferee. These consumption goods and services enable the transferee country to free resources and channel them into the production of capital goods. Thus, the nature of the goods transferred is immaterial. In general, these goods reflect the comparative advantages and disadvantages of the transferor and transferee countries, respectively.

The transfer problem is not concerned with the long-run effects of the movement of real capital between countries, such as the effect on production, comparative advantage, marginal productivity of factors, income distribution, etc. Rather, the transfer problem is a standard exercise in the balance-of-payments adjustment mechanism and is mainly concerned with the difficulties and manner in which real capital is transferred between countries as a result of borrowing, reparations, aid, etc. This explains why unilateral payments which do not necessarily result in capital formation in the receiving country, such as reparations, are lumped together with payments which do give rise to capital formation, such as corporate borrowing and direct investment.

The transfer problem may be viewed as the inversion of the balance-of-payments problem, for any actual balance-of-payments disequilibrium involves a real transfer from the surplus to the deficit country. Thus, the correction of the balance-of-payments disequilibrium, brought about either automatically or by means of planned governmental policies, can be viewed as the problem of generating either a real transfer of equal amount in the opposite direction (i.e., from the deficit country to the surplus country), or a money transfer from the surplus to the deficit country. The latter case, in which the real transfer actually precedes the money transfer, is pursued further in chap. 19.

The transfer problem has been vigorously debated since the beginning of economic science. As noted in chap. 10, in the 1920s Professor Taussig (1927) and a group of his Harvard students—White (1933), Williams (1920), Viner (1924), and others—studied the transfer process and the balance-of-payments adjustment mechanism in connection with long-term capital movements to countries such as Argentina, Australia, and Canada. The object of these studies was to verify the classical theory of the price-specie-flow mechanism. Nevertheless, it was in relation with the problem of German reparations that economists fell into great dispute on the question of whether a unilateral transfer, aside from the primary burden of the payment itself, also causes a secondary burden as a result of an induced deterioration of the terms of trade of the transferor country.

It will be recalled (see Haberler, 1936, chap. VIII) that after World War I Germany was made at Versailles to pay war reparations to the Allies. Keynes (1929) upheld the so-called *orthodox position*, namely, the view that the transfer causes the terms of trade of the transferor to deteriorate, and claimed that Germany would have to experience a severe terms-of-trade deterioration in order to generate the necessary export surplus and effect the transfer. He even expressed fears that Germany would not be able to make the transfer at all because of the low elasticity of demand for her exports. He pointed out (see p. 167 in AEA *Readings*) that

> Historically, the volume of foreign investment has tended . . . to adjust itself . . . to the balance of trade, rather than the other way round, the former being the sensitive and the latter the insensitive factor. In the case of German Reparations, on the other hand, we are trying to fix the volume of foreign remittance and compel the balance of trade to adjust itself thereto. Those who see no difficulty in this . . . are applying the theory of liquids to what is, if not a solid, at least a sticky mass with strong internal resistances.

(Some of the implications of this remarkable passage are worked out below in chap. 19.)

Keynes was not alone in supporting the orthodox doctrine. Pigou (1932), Robertson (1931), Taussig (1917, 1927), Viner (1924), and many others upheld the orthodox view.

Ohlin (1929) and his followers adopted what they called the *modern view*, i.e. the proposition that a transfer need not necessarily worsen the terms of trade of the paying country. In particular, Ohlin pointed out that Keynes and his followers neglected the income effects and asserted that no clear-cut presumption existed regarding the direction in which the terms of trade would move. (It is indeed ironic that in this debate Keynes took the classical position while Ohlin emphasized the income-adjustment mechanism which was later linked with Keynes.) For a long time the discussion remained confused and inconclusive, both analytically and empirically.

Incidentally, Viner (1937) showed clearly that the modern view had its classical forerunners, e.g., Ricardo, Wheatley, Bastable, and others. On the other hand, the orthodox view was supported by Mill, Thornton, and others.

Perhaps the first rigorous formal treatment of the transfer problem was given by Pigou (1932). Pigou formulated the problem in terms of a model of pure exchange between two representative citizens in the two countries. He assumed independent utilities and in particular he made each commodity's utility a linear function of the quantity of that commodity alone. It is this assumption which obscured the meaning of his criterion for a change in the terms of trade and practically forced him to resort to considerations lying outside of his model (such as production and transportation costs) in order to justify his belief in the orthodox view.

In two rather exhaustive articles, Samuelson (1952, 1954) perfected Pigou's analysis and restated the criterion for a change in the terms of trade in terms of marginal propensities to consume. Samuelson concluded that in the absence of transport costs or impediments to trade there was no basis for the orthodox presumption. Only in the case of artificial tariff barriers did Samuelson find a presumption in favor of the orthodox thesis.

More recently, contributions to the transfer problem have been made by Chipman (1974), Johnson (1961, 1974), Jones (1970), Samuelson (1971), and others.

It is now realized that the transfer problem may be approached either on the classical assumption of full employment and price flexibility, as done by Pigou (1932) and Samuelson (1952, 1954), or on the Keynesian assumption of underemployment and constant prices, as done by Machlup (1943), Meade (1951), Metzler (1942, 1951), and others. The main issue in the classical transfer problem is whether the process by which the transfer is financed in the transferor country and disposed of in the transferee generates the trade surplus and deficit necessary to effect the transfer completely without any deterioration in the terms of trade of the transferor. Similarly, the main issue in the Keynesian transfer problem is how the transfer affects the national incomes and balance of trade of both the transferor country and the transferee, and in particular whether the process by which the transfer is financed and disposed of generates the necessary trade surplus and deficit and effects the transfer completely without requiring any further changes in the national incomes and/or the rate of exchange or even trade restrictions.

PART B. THE CLASSICAL TRANSFER PROBLEM†

12.1 THE MODEL

Consider two countries, A (transferor) and B (transferee), each producing under constant returns to scale two commodities, A-exportables and B-exportables. Country A exports A-exportables to country B in exchange for B-exportables. For the moment assume that no capital movements of any kind occur between the two countries. Also for convenience assume that tastes in each country are represented by a noninteracting social indifference map with regular convexity. Currently each country's value of exports equals the value of its imports and all markets are cleared. That is, long-run equilibrium prevails in both the labor and the commodity markets as well as the foreign exchange market. By assumption, absorption

---

† The present discussion of the classical transfer problem presupposes some knowledge of the pure theory of international trade. In this connection the reader may find it useful to refer to Chacholiades (1973) or any other book on the subject.

equals disposable income at all times. How does a series of annual transfer payments from country A to country B affect A's (i.e., the transferor's) terms of trade, $p \equiv (p_a/p_b)$?

Before proceeding any further there is a methodological point which must be cleared. As Samuelson (1952) points out, the transfer may be stipulated in terms of A-exportables, B-exportables, any combination of them, or even in some units of abstract purchasing power. *The qualitative effect of the transfer on the terms of trade is independent of the method by which the transfer is stipulated.* However, the *ex post* burden of the transfer depends very much on the commodity in which the transfer is expressed. Thus, the *ex post* burden of a transfer which is stipulated in terms of a commodity whose relative price increases because of the transfer is heavier than the *ex post* burden of an equivalent transfer (at the pre-transfer prices) which is stipulated in terms of a commodity whose price falls.

Nevertheless, as Samuelson (1952) and Johnson (1974) point out, the whole question of secondary burdens and benefits seems semantic or artificial. Certainly, what is important is the total effect of the transfer on the economic welfare of the transferor country and the transferee. One would then expect governments engaged in negotiating reparations payments to take into consideration the effects of the transfer on the terms of trade, although this argument need not apply to transfers effected by private economic units which behave as price takers.

To determine the effect of the transfer on the terms of trade of the transferor country, it is necessary to assume that equilibrium is unique and stable. The presence of multiple equilibria, some of which necessarily being unstable, creates difficulties and may give rise to strange results. For instance, Leontief (1936) presented a case in which the terms of trade changed so much in favor of the *transferor* country as to leave her actually better off after the unilateral transfer! The secondary improvement overcompensated the transferor country for the primary burden of the transfer. As Samuelson (1952, p. 284, fn. 1) points out, Leontief's paradoxical result is due to the existence of multiple and unstable equilibria. On this point, see also Mundell (1968) and Johnson (1974, pp. 80–81, fn. 1).

Given our assumption that international equilibrium is unique and stable both before and after (or, rather, during) the transfer, we can easily determine whether the transferor's terms of trade tend to deteriorate, improve, or remain unchanged by finding out whether the excess demand for either commodity increases or decreases with the transfer *at the pre-transfer equilibrium prices*. Note that we can concentrate on the excess demand of only one of the two commodities because of Walras' law (see Chacholiades, 1973, chaps. 3, 5, and 6.) Thus, for instance, when the excess demand for A-exportables increases, the excess demand for B-exportables necessarily decreases, and vice versa. Further, because of the assumed uniqueness and stability of equilibrium, when the excess demand for A-exportables increases (decreases), A's terms of trade improve (deteriorate).

Since we are basically interested in finding out what happens to the excess demand for either commodity at the pre-transfer equilibrium prices, it must be clear that any change in excess demand for either A-exportables or B-exportables can come about through a change in demand only—not supply. The production of A-exportables and B-exportables in both countries depends on relative prices; and since by assumption relative prices are kept constant at their pre-transfer levels, the production of A-exportables and B-exportables must necessarily also remain constant at the pre-transfer levels. How then does the demand for either A-exportables or B-exportables change as country A makes the transfer to B? And what is the effect of the transfer on the terms of trade of the transferor? The following discussion considers these questions under various circumstances where tariffs and transport costs may or may not be zero.

12.2 ZERO TARIFFS AND ZERO TRANSPORT COSTS

Assume now that there are no tariffs or other artificial trade impediments and that goods can move between countries in a costless fashion. In addition, international equilibrium prevails; for simplicity, assume that the equilibrium price ratio is unity. Under these circumstances country A undertakes an annual transfer to country B of U units of A-exportables. Clearly, A's disposable income (expressed in A-exportables) decreases by U while B's disposable income increases by U. Accordingly, A's demand for both commodities falls while B's demand for both commodities rises. By exactly what amounts do these demands change?

Recall that in a classical setting a country spends all of her income, and any marginal increases thereof, on A-exportables and B-exportables only. This means that the sum of the average propensities to spend on both commodities as well as the sum of the marginal propensities are equal to unity in both countries. Hence, letting the symbol M'_i indicate, as before, the ith country's marginal propensity to spend on imported goods, the demand changes in A and B may be summarized as follows:

Reduction in A's demand for A-exportables $= (1 - M'_a)U$

Reduction in A's demand for B-exportables $= M'_a U$

Increase in B's demand for A-exportables $= M'_b U$

Increase in B's demand for B-exportables $= (1 - M'_b)U$

Accordingly, the total change in the demand for A-exportables equals

$$\Delta Q_a = -(1 - M'_a)U + M'_b U = [(M'_a + M'_b) - 1]U$$

Similarly, the total change in the demand for B-exportables equals

$$\Delta Q_b = -M'_a U + (1 - M'_b)U = [-(M'_a + M'_b) + 1]U$$

Obviously, $\Delta Q_a + \Delta Q_b = 0$. Hence, in general ΔQ_a and ΔQ_b have opposite signs, and when one is zero the other is zero also. For this reason, we need to study the total change in the demand for only one of the two commodities. In what follows we choose to study the effect on the demand for A-exportables (ΔQ_a).

The change in the demand for A-exportables is given by $\Delta Q_a = [(M_a' + M_b') - 1]U$. Since U is by definition positive, it follows that the sign of ΔQ_a coincides with the sign of the bracketed expression $[(M_a' + M_b') - 1]$. Accordingly, if the sum of the two marginal propensities to import is *equal to unity* $(M_a' + M_b' = 1)$, the change in the demand for A-exportables is *zero* and no tendency exists for A's terms of trade to change. In this connection, note the following important statement by Keynes (1929, p. 163 in *AEA Readings*): "If £1 is taken from you and given to me and I choose to increase my consumption of precisely the same goods as those of which you are compelled to diminish yours, there is no Transfer Problem."

Similarly, if the sum of the two marginal propensities to import is *greater than unity* $(M_a' + M_b' > 1)$, the change in the demand for A-exportables is *positive* and a tendency exists for A's terms of trade to *improve*. Finally, if the sum of the two marginal propensities to import is *less than unity* $(M_a' + M_b' < 1)$, the change in the demand for A-exportables is *negative* and a tendency exists for A's terms of trade to *deteriorate* (orthodox view).

The preceding analysis shows that the effect on the transferor's terms of trade depends on the marginal propensities to import. In general, the transferor's terms of trade may improve, deteriorate, or remain the same. Nevertheless, as noted earlier, economists have been concerned with whether there is a presumption favoring the orthodox view. For this purpose, the assumption about tastes must be neutral. This is accomplished by adopting *Viner's hypothesis* of neutral tastes, namely, the assumption that tastes in each country are given by the same homothetic social-indifference map. This means that consumption patterns are identical between countries and income levels. Viner (1937, p. 343) justifies the *hypothesis of neutral tastes* as follows: "The assumption of 'similarity' of the utility functions is a reasonable one, not because 'similarity' is in fact probable, but because in the absence of specific information the 'dissimilarity' which is likely to exist is, *a priori*, as likely to be in the one direction as in the other." See also Samuelson (1952, pp. 295–298) and Chipman (1974, pp. 21–22).

In the present case of no tariffs and no transport costs and thus identical prices between countries, the hypothesis of neutral tastes implies $M_a' = 1 - M_b'$. Accordingly, no bias is revealed favoring the orthodox view. Only the agnostic position of the modern school is strengthened. This is the important conclusion reached by Samuelson (1952).

The above thesis has been challenged recently by Jones (1970). His argument is brief and elegant. Suppose tastes do differ between countries. Suppose, further, that factor (or commodity) endowments are independent of tastes. Then it is more likely that a country which has a taste bias toward a certain commodity will actually import that commodity. As Samuelson (1971, p. 328) puts it, "If I am a drunkard and you are a fop, I am more likely to export cloth and import rye than vice versa." In terms of our present model this means that A's tastes are biased toward B-exportables and B's tastes are biased toward A-exportables. That is,

$M'_a > 1 - M'_b$ or $M'_a + M'_b > 1$. Accordingly, a transfer from A to B *improves* A's terms of trade. On a probabilistic basis, therefore, Jones reaches an "anti-orthodox" (and, hence, partially anti-Ohlin) result.

Samuelson (1971) provides a model within which the orthodox conclusion is guaranteed. He considers the problem within the framework of the classical theory of international trade (see Chacholiades, 1973, chaps. 2 and 3, and especially app. 3A) but introduces leisure explicitly. In addition, Samuelson makes the crucial assumption that leisure's marginal utility is constant and then shows that a transfer worsens the terms of trade of the transferor country.

Samuelson's (1971) result can be established easily in terms of A's indirect supply of labor to B and B's demand for A's labor. (For this formulation, see Chacholiades, 1973, app. 3A.) Suppose country A makes a transfer to country B. At the pre-transfer terms of trade, A's citizens reduce their consumption of leisure and thus increase the indirect supply of A's labor to B by the amount of the transfer. Nevertheless, B's demand for A's labor remains the same because B's citizens use the proceeds of the transfer to merely increase their consumption of leisure. As a result, there emerges an excess supply of labor at the pre-transfer prices, causing A's factoral terms of trade to fall. But a deterioration of A's factoral terms of trade necessarily implies a deterioration in A's commodity terms of trade.

Samuelson's conclusion is in general correct. However, there is a special case in which the transferor's (A's) terms of trade actually remain the same even though the marginal utility of leisure is constant. This occurs when both countries produce one or more identical commodities at the pre-transfer equilibrium configuration and the transfer is relatively small. In this case, A's supply-of-labor-to-B schedule coincides with B's demand-for-A's-labor schedule over a horizontal stretch at the pre-transfer prices. Thus, provided the transfer is not too large, the pre-transfer prices will continue to be the equilibrium prices even after the transfer causes A's supply curve to shift to the right. However, when the transfer is "rather large," Samuelson's conclusion is unavoidable, unless both countries share the same labor coefficients.

12.3 POSITIVE TARIFFS AND ZERO TRANSPORT COSTS

In the presence of tariffs, prices are necessarily different between countries. Hence, there is a need to distinguish between the price ratio which exists in country A, say p, and that which exists in country B, say p^*.

Assume that t_a, t_b are the *ad valorem* tariff rates imposed by countries A and B, respectively. Let p_a and p_b be the prices of A-exportables and B-exportables in country A, and p_a^* and p_b^* the corresponding prices in country B. Then

$$p_a^* = (1 + t_b)p_a \tag{12.1}$$

$$p_b = (1 + t_a)p_b^* \tag{12.2}$$

$$p \equiv \frac{p_a}{p_b} = \left[\frac{1}{(1 + t_a)(1 + t_b)}\right]\left(\frac{p_a^*}{p_b^*}\right) \equiv \gamma p^* < p^* \tag{12.3}$$

where

$$\gamma \equiv \frac{1}{(1 + t_a)(1 + t_b)} < 1 \tag{12.4}$$

Accordingly, p is always a constant proportion (γ) of p^*. Moreover, the inequality $p < p^*$ simply means that a commodity is always cheaper in the country which exports it. In particular, A-exportables are relatively cheaper in country A and B-exportables are cheaper in country B.

Assume now that the system is in equilibrium at $\bar{p} < \bar{p}^*$, and let country A make a transfer to country B. What happens to A's terms of trade (p)?

Adopt again Viner's hypothesis of neutral tastes. Since the relative price of A-exportables is lower in country A $(\bar{p} < \bar{p}^*)$, it follows that A consumes, both on the average and on the margin, more units of A-exportables per unit of B-exportables relative to country B. As country A makes the transfer to country B, A reduces her consumption of A-exportables and B-exportables while B increases hers. However, at the pre-transfer prices country A is releasing more units of A-exportables per unit of B-exportables than country B is willing to absorb. Hence there emerges an excess supply of A-exportables and/or an excess demand for B-exportables, causing A's terms of trade to worsen. (Since $p = \gamma p^*$, both p and p^* must tend to fall.)

We therefore conclude that in the presence of tariffs there seems to be a presumption favoring the orthodox view. This is Samuelson's (1954) conclusion.

12.4 ZERO TARIFFS BUT POSITIVE TRANSPORT COSTS

How does the existence of transport costs affect the preceding conclusions regarding the effect of the transfer on the terms of trade of the transferor country? At first sight it appears that this question cannot be answered before a third industry (the transportation industry) is introduced explicitly into the model. However, Samuelson (1954) showed in an ingenious way how the introduction of the third industry can be avoided. In particular, Samuelson (1954, p. 268) assumed that:

> To carry each good across the ocean you must pay some of the good itself. Rather than set up elaborate models of a merchant marine, invisible items, etc., we can achieve our purpose by assuming that just as only a fraction of ice exported reaches its destination as unmelted ice, so will a_x and a_y be the fractions of exports X and Y that respectively reach the other country as imports. Of course, $a_x < 1$ and $a_y < 1$, except in the costless model, where they were each unity.

We find it easier to modify slightly Samuelson's convention and introduce transport costs as follows. Country B acquires 1 unit of A-exportables from country A when country A exports θ_a units $(\theta_a > 1)$. Similarly, country A acquires 1 unit of B-exportables from country B when country B exports θ_b units $(\theta_b > 1)$.

The differences $(\theta_a - 1)$ and $(\theta_b - 1)$ are the unit transport costs of A-exportables and B-exportables, respectively, expressed in terms of the same commodities. The present formulation is analytically identical to Samuelson's formulation. We prefer it, however, because the value of θ_a units of A-exportables (that is, $p_a\theta_a$) gives directly B's average cost of acquisition of A-exportables through trade. Similarly, the value of θ_b (that is, $p_b^*\theta_b$) gives directly A's average cost of acquisition of B-exportables through trade.

Given our convention of registering transport costs, we can formulate the following equations easily:

$$p_a^* = p_a\theta_a \tag{12.5}$$

$$p_b = p_b^*\theta_b \tag{12.6}$$

$$p \equiv \frac{p_a}{p_b} = \left(\frac{1}{\theta_a\theta_b}\right)\left(\frac{p_a^*}{p_b^*}\right) \equiv \lambda p^* < p^* \tag{12.7}$$

where

$$\lambda \equiv \frac{1}{\theta_a\theta_b} < 1 \tag{12.8}$$

As in the tariff case, $p < p^*$, that is, goods are relatively cheaper in their country of origin: A-exportables are cheaper in country A and B-exportables are cheaper in country B.

Assume now that the system is in equilibrium at $\bar{p} < \bar{p}^*$, and let country A make a transfer to country B. What happens to A's terms of trade (p)?

Adopt again Viner's hypothesis of neutral tastes. Since the relative price of A-exportables is lower in country A $(\bar{p} < \bar{p}^*)$, it follows that country A consumes again, both on the average and on the margin, more units of A-exportables per unit of B-exportables relative to country B. We may express this result mathematically as follows:

$$\xi_a > \xi_b \tag{12.9}$$

where ξ_i is the ratio of A-exportables to B-exportables consumed by the ith country. That is,

$$\xi_i \equiv \frac{\text{amount of A-exportables consumed by the } i\text{th country}}{\text{amount of B-exportables consumed by the } i\text{th country}}$$

$$(i = a, b) \tag{12.10}$$

As country A makes the transfer to country B, country A reduces, and B increases, her consumption of both commodities. In particular, country A reduces her consumption of A-exportables and B-exportables, at the pre-transfer prices, in the proportion $\xi_a : 1$. Similarly country B increases her consumption of A-exportables and B-exportables, at the pre-transfer prices, in the proportion $\xi_b : 1$. However, the amounts released by country A, say ΔQ_a and ΔQ_b, do not automatically become available to country B. In particular, when country A reduces her consumption of A-exportables by ΔQ_a, only $\Delta Q_a^* \equiv \Delta Q_a/\theta_a$ units are made available to country B. Similarly, when country A reduces her consumption of B-exportables by ΔQ_b, the bigger amount $\Delta Q_b^* = \theta_b \Delta Q_b$ is made available to country B. This is because initially country B had to export $\theta_b \Delta Q_b$ units of B-exportables to country A for the latter to receive ΔQ_b. Hence, as A's consumption of B-exportables falls by ΔQ_b, B's exports of B-exportables must fall by $\theta_b \Delta Q_b$, and therefore the availability of B-exportables in country B must increase by $\theta_b \Delta Q_b$.

We therefore conclude that the proportion in which A-exportables and B-exportables are made available to country B by country A is not ξ_a but

$$\xi_a^* \equiv \frac{\Delta Q_a^*}{\Delta Q_b^*} = \left(\frac{1}{\theta_a \theta_b}\right) \xi_a < \xi_a \qquad (12.11)$$

The effect of the transfer on A's terms of trade depends on the relationship between ξ_a^* and ξ_b and not between ξ_a and ξ_b. In particular, if $\xi_b < \xi_a^*$, there emerges, at the pre-transfer prices, an excess supply of A-exportables and/or an excess demand for B-exportables causing A's terms of trade to deteriorate. On the other hand, if $\xi_a^* < \xi_b$, there emerges, at the pre-transfer prices, an excess demand for A-exportables and/or an excess supply of B-exportables causing A's terms of trade to improve. Unfortunately, inequality (12.9) does not help eliminate either one of these two possibilities and we are therefore forced to conclude that in the presence of transport costs but no tariffs there is no presumption favoring the orthodox view. This again coincides with Samuelson's (1954) conclusion.

12.5 DOMESTIC GOODS

The introduction of transport costs into the model raises the possibility of a new class of commodities, namely, *domestic commodities*. These are defined as the commodities which are not tradable between countries because they have infinite transport costs, such as haircuts, houses, etc. The emergence of domestic commodities gives rise to several complications in the analysis of the transfer problem. Our purpose in this section is neither to review the literature on domestic commodities in relation to the transfer problem nor to extend our present model to incorporate such commodities. The present discussion serves merely as a warning to the reader about the limitations of the preceding analysis.

Viner (1937, pp. 348–349) provided a successful defense of the orthodox view by introducing domestic commodities into his discussion of the transfer problem. Samuelson (1952, p. 302) declared that Viner's model was to his knowledge "the only logically air-tight successful defense of the orthodox view. . . ." Viner's result depended on his special assumption that both countries specialized in the production of their domestic and export goods only.

Section 12.2 considered briefly Samuelson's (1971) model. It is now apparent that Samuelson's "leisure" is indeed a domestic (nontraded) commodity. For further insights into this aspect of Samuelson's model, see Samuelson (1971, pp. 344–350), and for further discussion concerning the consequences of domestic commodities in relation to the transfer problem, see Chipman (1974).

12.6 CONCLUDING REMARKS

There is no need to choose any one of the above competing models. They are all important because they bring to our attention the factors which ultimately influence the effect of the transfer on the terms of trade of the transferor country. The issue of whether the terms of trade of the transferor country deteriorate or improve with the transfer is clearly an empirical one. No amount of *a priori* reasoning can tell us what will actually happen in any particular situation. Each particular transfer must be studied on its own by means of patient econometric work.

PART C. THE KEYNESIAN TRANSFER PROBLEM

12.7 INTRODUCTION

With the advent of the Keynesian revolution the transfer problem was naturally recast into the newly developed macroeconomic model. Major contributions were made by Metzler (1942, 1951), Machlup (1943), Meade (1951, pp. 87–93 and 143–148), and Johnson (1961).

The model which forms the basis for the analysis of the Keynesian transfer problem is that of chap. 10. It will be recalled that the basic assumptions of the model are as follows. Unemployment prevails in all countries, production is carried out under constant returns to scale everywhere, all prices (i.e., commodity prices, money-wage rates, the rate of exchange, and the rate of interest) remain constant, all expenditures on exports are income generating, and all countries have sufficient stocks of foreign-exchange reserves.

As noted earlier in this chapter, the main issue in the Keynesian transfer problem is how the transfer affects the national incomes and the balance of trade of both the transferor country and the transferee. Does the process by which the transfer is financed and disposed of generate the necessary trade surplus and deficit to actually effect the transfer completely? Or are further changes in national incomes, the rate of exchange, and even trade restrictions necessary for this purpose? Alternatively, under what conditions is the transfer just effected, over-effected, or undereffected by the mere financing and disposal of the transfer? The answer to these questions necessarily depends on the particular fiscal policies pursued by both countries. For this reason, the Keynesian transfer problem is first studied in sec. 12.8 in very general terms, following the analysis of Johnson (1961). Then some important special cases are studied in sec. 12.9.

As Johnson (1961) observes, the Keynesian transfer problem differs from the classical in two respects. First, in the Keynesian transfer problem the financing and disposal of the transfer need not lead to changes in aggregate spending in the two countries equal to the amount of the transfer. The funds may merely come out of dissaving (in the transferor country) or go into saving (in the transferee country). Second, any changes in aggregate spending generated by the financing and disposal of the transfer (i.e., autonomous changes in spending from the viewpoint of the income-adjustment mechanism) necessarily have multiplier effects on the balance of trade. These multiplier effects must be taken into account before we can determine whether the financing and disposal of the transfer generates a surplus in the transferor's balance of trade which is smaller or larger than the transfer, or equal to it.

12.8 THE GENERAL CASE (JOHNSON)

Suppose that country A makes a unilateral transfer U to country B. How are A's national income Y_a and balance of payments B_a, and B's national income Y_b, affected by the transfer? To analyze this problem, we must first determine the autonomous change in demand for A's output (ΔD_a) and the autonomous change in demand for B's output as a result of the financing and disposal of the transfer, and then substitute these autonomous changes in the multiplier equations of chap. 10 to determine the resultant changes in A's national income (ΔY_a) and balance of payments (ΔB_a), and the change in B's national income (ΔY_b).

Let the symbols ζ_i and ζ_{if} represent the ith country's changes in demand for goods and services (domestic and foreign) and in imports, respectively, due to the financing or disposal of the transfer. The changes are expressed as proportions of the amount transferred. The change in demand for domestic goods alone as a proportion of the amount transferred is, of course, given by the difference $\zeta_i - \zeta_{if}$. Accordingly, the changes in demand for A's and B's products, respectively, are given by

$$\Delta D_a = (\zeta_{bf} + \zeta_{af} - \zeta_a)U \tag{12.12}$$

$$\Delta D_b = (\zeta_b - \zeta_{bf} - \zeta_{af})U \tag{12.13}$$

That is, the demand for A's products changes by the *increase* in B's demand for imports, $\zeta_{bf} U$, plus the *decrease* in A's demand for domestic goods, $-(\zeta_a - \zeta_{af})U$. Similarly, the demand for B's products changes by the *increase* in B's demand for domestic goods, $(\zeta_b - \zeta_{bf})U$, plus the *decrease* in A's demand for imports, $-\zeta_{af} U$.

The resultant changes in A's and B's national incomes and A's balance of payments are given by

$$\Delta Y_a = k_{aa} \, \Delta D_a + k_{ab} \, \Delta D_b \tag{12.14a}$$

$$\Delta Y_b = k_{ba} \, \Delta D_a + k_{bb} \, \Delta D_b \tag{12.15a}$$

$$\Delta B_a = \Delta T_a - U = (1 - Z_a') \, \Delta Y_a + \zeta_a U - U \tag{12.16a}$$

or $\qquad \Delta B_a = -\Delta T_b - U = -(1 - Z_b') \, \Delta Y_b + \zeta_b U - U \tag{12.17}$

The change in A's balance of payments equals the change in A's balance of trade minus the unilateral transfer. The multipliers k_{ij} $(i, j = a, b)$ are given in chap. 10 by eqs. (10.48), (10.49), (10.52), and (10.53).

Substituting eqs. (12.12), (12.13), (10.48), (10.49), (10.52), and (10.53) into eqs. (12.14a) and (12.15a), and then eq. (12.14a) into eq. (12.16a), we finally obtain

$$\Delta Y_a = [(\zeta_{bf} + \zeta_{af} - \zeta_a) + (\zeta_b - \zeta_{bf} - \zeta_{af})m_b M_b'] m_a \frac{U}{\Delta} \tag{12.14b}$$

$$\Delta Y_b = [(\zeta_{bf} + \zeta_{af} - \zeta_a)m_a M_a' + (\zeta_b - \zeta_{bf} - \zeta_{af})] m_b \frac{U}{\Delta} \tag{12.15b}$$

$$\Delta B_a = m_a m_b (1 - Z_a')(1 - Z_b') U \left(\frac{1}{\Delta}\right)$$

$$\times \left[\zeta_{bf} + \zeta_{af} - (1 - \zeta_a) \frac{M_a'}{1 - Z_a'} - (1 - \zeta_b) \frac{M_b'}{1 - Z_b'} - 1 \right] \tag{12.16b}$$

Actually, as Johnson (1961) observes, with some additional algebraic manipulation, eqs. (12.14b) and (12.15b) can be reduced to

$$\Delta Y_a = \frac{\Delta B_a + (1 - \zeta_a)U}{1 - Z_a'} \tag{12.14c}$$

$$\Delta Y_b = \frac{-[\Delta B_a + (1 - \zeta_b)U]}{1 - Z_b'} \tag{12.15c}$$

where ΔB_a is given, of course, by eq. (12.16a) or (12.16b). These equations may be easily verified by merely substituting into them eq. (12.16b) and then simplifying to obtain the initial eqs. (12.14b) and (12.15b).

Equation (12.16b) shows that, if both countries are stable in isolation (that is, $Z_a' < 1$, $Z_b' < 1$), the criterion for the transfer to be overeffected, just effected, or undereffected, is

$$\zeta_{af} + \zeta_{bf} \gtreqless 1 + (1 - \zeta_a) \frac{M_a'}{1 - Z_a'} + (1 - \zeta_b) \frac{M_b'}{1 - Z_b'} \tag{12.18}$$

The sign $>$ implies that $\Delta B_a > 0$ and therefore the transfer is overeffected. The sign $=$ implies that $\Delta B_a = 0$ and thus the transfer is just effected. Finally, the sign $<$ implies that $\Delta B_a < 0$ and thus the transfer is undereffected. Inequality (12.18) was first derived by Johnson (1961).

If either the transferor country or the transferee is unstable in isolation (i.e., either $Z_a' > 1$ or $Z_b' > 1$), then the inequality signs in (12.18) are reversed. That is, for $\Delta B_a > 0$ and $\Delta B_a < 0$ the signs $<$ and $>$, respectively, must hold in (12.18).

If the transferor country's (A's) marginal propensity to absorb is unity (that is, $Z_a' = 1$), the criterion for the transfer to be overeffected, just effected, or undereffected is $\zeta_a > 1$, $\zeta_a = 1$, $\zeta_a < 1$, respectively. This follows directly from eq. (12.16a). Similarly, when the transferee country's (B's) marginal propensity to absorb is unity ($Z'_b = 1$), the criterion for the transfer to be overeffected, just effected, or undereffected is $\zeta_b > 1$, $\zeta_b = 1$, $\zeta_b < 1$, respectively. This follows directly from eq. (12.17).

12.9 SOME SPECIAL CASES

We proceed now to apply the preceding general results to some special but nevertheless important cases.

The Metzler-Machlup Case

Metzler (1942) and Machlup (1943) showed that the transfer would necessarily be undereffected if both countries are stable in isolation (that is, $Z'_a < 1$, $Z'_b < 1$). Their analysis rests on the special assumption that the financing and disposal of the transfer changes the demand for domestic goods either by the amount of the transfer or not at all. In either case, the transfer is assumed not to affect the demand for imports directly. In other words, for the Metzler-Machlup case, we must set $\zeta_{af} = \zeta_{bf} = 0$, with ζ_a and ζ_b assuming either the value of unity or zero. Accordingly, we must consider four cases as follows.

Case (1): $\zeta_{af} = \zeta_{bf} = 0$ **and** $\zeta_a = \zeta_b = 1$
  Substituting the values $\zeta_{af} = \zeta_{bf} = 0$ and $\zeta_a = \zeta_b = 1$ into eqs. (12.14c), (12.15c), and (12.16b), we obtain

$$\Delta Y_a = \frac{\Delta B_a}{1 - Z'_a} \tag{12.19}$$

$$\Delta Y_b = \frac{-\Delta B_a}{1 - Z'_b} \tag{12.20}$$

$$\Delta B_a = -m_a m_b \left(\frac{1}{\Delta}\right)(1 - Z'_a)(1 - Z'_b)U \tag{12.21}$$

  Accordingly, if both countries are stable in isolation ($Z'_a < 1$, $Z'_b < 1$), then $\Delta B_a < 0$, $\Delta Y_a < 0$, and $\Delta Y_b > 0$. That is, the transfer is undereffected, the transferor country's income falls, and the transferee country's income rises.
  If the transferor country is unstable in isolation ($Z'_a > 1$), then $\Delta B_a > 0$ (i.e., the transfer is overeffected), $\Delta Y_a < 0$, and $\Delta Y_b < 0$.
  If the transferee country is unstable in isolation ($Z'_b > 1$), then $\Delta B_a > 0$ (i.e., the transfer is overeffected), $\Delta Y_a > 0$, and $\Delta Y_b > 0$.
  Finally, if either country's marginal propensity to absorb (Z'_i) is unity, the transfer is exactly effected, that is, $\Delta B_a = 0$. In addition, when $Z'_a = 1$, the transferor country's income falls ($\Delta Y_a < 0$) while the transferee country's income remains constant ($\Delta Y_b = 0$); and when $Z'_b = 1$, the transferor country's income remains constant ($\Delta Y_a = 0$) while the transferee country's income rises.

Case (2): $\zeta_{af} = \zeta_{bf} = \zeta_b = 0$ **and** $\zeta_a = 1$

Substituting again the values $\zeta_{af} = \zeta_{bf} = \zeta_b = 0$ and $\zeta_a = 1$ into eqs. (12.14b), (12.15b), and (12.16b), we obtain

$$\Delta Y_a = -m_a \frac{U}{\Delta} < 0 \tag{12.22}$$

$$\Delta Y_b = -m_a m_b M_a' \frac{U}{\Delta} < 0 \tag{12.23}$$

$$\Delta B_a = -m_a (1 - Z_a') \frac{U}{\Delta} \tag{12.24}$$

We therefore conclude that in this case both national incomes tend to fall. In addition, the transfer is undereffected, just effected, or overeffected according to whether the transferor country's (A's) marginal propensity to absorb is less than unity, equal to unity, or greater than unity (that is, $Z_a' < 1$, $Z_a' = 1$, or $Z_a' > 1$), respectively.

A very special case noted by Metzler (1942) is when $Z_a' < 1$ and $Z_b' > 1$, that is, when the transferee country is unstable in isolation. In this special case, not only is the transfer not completely effected but also the transferor country's balance of payments deteriorates by more than the transfer! That is, in this case the real transfer is perverse.

Case (3): $\zeta_{af} = \zeta_{bf} = \zeta_a = 0$ **and** $\zeta_b = 1$

Substituting again the values $\zeta_{af} = \zeta_{bf} = \zeta_a = 0$ and $\zeta_b = 1$ into eqs. (12.14b), (12.15b), and (12.16b), we obtain

$$\Delta Y_a = m_a m_b M_b' \frac{U}{\Delta} > 0 \tag{12.25}$$

$$\Delta Y_b = m_b \frac{U}{\Delta} > 0 \tag{12.26}$$

$$\Delta B_a = -m_b (1 - Z_b') \frac{U}{\Delta} \tag{12.27}$$

We therefore conclude that in this case both incomes always tend to rise and the transfer is undereffected when the transferee country is stable in isolation (that is, $Z_b' < 1$). On the other hand, when the transferee country is unstable in isolation ($Z_b' > 1$) the transfer is overeffected ($\Delta B_a > 0$), and when $Z_b' = 1$ the transfer is just effected ($\Delta B_a = 0$).

Metzler (1942) noted another case in which the real transfer is perverse, i.e., a case in which the transferor country's balance of payments deteriorates by more than the transfer. This occurs presently when the transferor country is unstable in isolation ($Z_a' > 1$).

Case (4): $\zeta_{af} = \zeta_{bf} = \zeta_a = \zeta_b = 0$

In this case, the reader may easily show that $\Delta Y_a = \Delta Y_b = \Delta B_a = 0$. In this connection, see Meade (1951, pp. 87–88 and 143–144).

The Meade Case

Meade (1951, pp. 87–93) showed that, if both countries are stable in isolation, the transfer would be overeffected, undereffected, or exactly effected according to whether the sum of the proportions of the transfer by which import demands are changed (that is, $\zeta_{af} + \zeta_{bf}$) is greater than, smaller than, or equal to unity, respectively. For this demonstration, he specifically assumed that the financing and disposal of the transfer changes each country's absorption by the amount of the transfer (that is, $\zeta_a = \zeta_b = 1$). Nevertheless, contrary to Metzler and Machlup, Meade allowed the transfer to affect imports directly (that is, $\zeta_{af} > 0$, $\zeta_{bf} > 0$).

Substituting Meade's assumptions ($\zeta_a = \zeta_b = 1$) into eqs. (12.14c), (12.15c), and (12.16b), we obtain

$$\Delta Y_a = \frac{\Delta B_a}{1 - Z'_a} \tag{12.28}$$

$$\Delta Y_b = \frac{-\Delta B_a}{1 - Z'_b} \tag{12.29}$$

$$\Delta B_a = m_a m_b (1 - Z'_a)(1 - Z'_b)\left(\frac{1}{\Delta}\right) U(\zeta_{af} + \zeta_{bf} - 1) \tag{12.30}$$

Equations (12.28) and (12.29) are identical to eqs. (12.19) and (12.20). Nevertheless, the resultant change in the transferor country's balance of payments (ΔB_a), as given by eq. (12.30), is different from that of the Metzler-Machlup case given by eq. (12.21). The difference, of course, is due to the fact that Meade permits the transfer to have an autonomous effect on imports whereas Metzler and Machlup do not. (Actually, Machlup does refer to the possibility of an autonomous effect on imports by the transfer but does not work out the consequences of this assumption.)

Equation (12.30) leads to the conclusion that, if both countries are stable in isolation ($Z'_a < 1$, $Z'_b < 1$), then $\Delta B_a \gtreqless 0$ according as $\zeta_{af} + \zeta_{bf} \gtreqless 1$. Further, the behavior of national incomes depends on whether the transfer is overeffected, undereffected, or exactly effected. Thus, if $\zeta_{af} + \zeta_{bf} > 1$ and therefore the transfer is overeffected (that is, $\Delta B_a > 0$), the national income of the transferor country increases ($\Delta Y_a > 0$) and that of the transferee decreases ($\Delta Y_b < 0$). On the other hand, if $\zeta_{af} + \zeta_{bf} < 1$ and therefore the transfer is undereffected, the national income of the transferor country falls and that of the transferee increases. Finally, if $\zeta_{af} + \zeta_{bf} = 1$ and therefore the transfer is exactly effected (that is, $\Delta B_a = 0$), the incomes of both countries remain unchanged ($\Delta Y_a = \Delta Y_b = 0$).

The consequences of the possibility that either country may be unstable in isolation are easy to study, and accordingly are left as an exercise for the reader.

The Classical Case

Johnson (1961, pp. 180–181) points out that "In general, there would seem to be less reason in a Keynesian model than in the classical model for identifying the direct effects of the transfer on demand with those of any other economic change."

Johnson proceeds, then, to show that if the usual assumption of the classical analysis is chosen, namely, that the transfer affects demands in the same way as any other income change (that is, $\zeta_a \equiv Z'_a, \zeta_b \equiv Z'_b, \zeta_{af} \equiv M'_a$, and $\zeta_{bf} \equiv M'_b$), then the transfer is necessarily undereffected when both countries are stable in isolation.

Substituting these assumptions (that is, $\zeta_a = Z'_a$, $\zeta_b = Z'_b$, $\zeta_{af} = M'_a$, and $\zeta_{bf} = M'_b$) into eq. (12.16b), we obtain

$$\Delta B_a = -m_a m_b (1 - Z'_a)(1 - Z'_b)\left(\frac{1}{\Delta}\right) U \qquad (12.31)$$

Obviously, if $Z'_a < 1$ and $Z'_b < 1$, the resultant change in the transferor country's balance of payments is negative ($\Delta B_a < 0$). Conversely, the transfer can be overeffected in the present case if, and only if, either country is unstable in isolation. This conclusion coincides with that reached by Metzler and Machlup.

The behavior of national incomes in the present case is indeterminate, as the reader may easily show.

SELECTED BIBLIOGRAPHY

Chacholiades, M. (1973). *The Pure Theory of International Trade.* Aldine Publishing Company, Chicago, Ill.

Chipman, J. S. (1974). "The Transfer Problem Once Again." In G. Horwich and P. A. Samuelson (Eds.), *Trade, Stability, and Macroeconomics: Essays in Honor of L. A. Metzler.* Academic Press, Inc., New York.

Haberler, G. (1936). *The Theory of International Trade.* The Macmillan Company, New York, chaps. VII and VIII.

Iversen, C. (1936). *Aspects of the Theory of International Capital Movements.* Levin and Munksgaard, Copenhagen.

Johnson, H. G. (1961). "The Transfer Problem and Exchange Stability." In *International Trade and Economic Growth: Studies in Pure Theory.* Harvard University Press, Cambridge, Mass., pp. 169–195. Reprinted in R. E. Caves and H. G. Johnson (Eds.), *Readings in International Economics.* Richard D. Irwin, Inc., Homewood, Ill., 1968.

———(1974). "The Welfare Economics of Reversed International Transfers." In G. Horwich and P. A. Samuelson (Eds.), *Trade, Stability, and Macroeconomics: Essays in Honor of L. A. Metzler.* Academic Press, Inc., New York.

Jones, R. W. (1970). "The Transfer Problem Revisited." *Economica,* N.S. (May), pp. 178–184.

Keynes, J. M. (1929). "The German Transfer Problem." *Economic Journal,* vol. XXXIX (March), pp. 1–7. Reprinted in H. S. Ellis and L. A. Metzler (Eds.), *AEA Readings in the Theory of International Trade.* Richard D. Irwin, Inc., Homewood, Ill., 1950.

Kindleberger, C. P. (1968). *International Economics,* 4th ed. Richard D. Irwin, Inc., Homewood, Ill., chap. 18.

Leontief, W. (1936). "Note on the Pure Theory of Capital Transfer." In *Explorations in Economics: Notes and Essays Contributed in Honor of F. W. Taussig.* McGraw-Hill Book Company, New York.

Machlup, F. (1943). *International Trade and the National Income Multiplier.* Reprints of Economic Classics, Augustus M. Kelly, Bookseller, New York, 1965.

Meade, J. E. (1951). *The Theory of International Economic Policy,* vol. I, *The Balance of Payments.* Oxford University Press, Inc., New York.

Metzler, L. A. (1942). "The Transfer Problem Reconsidered." *Journal of Political Economy*, vol. L (June), pp. 397–414. Reprinted in H. S. Ellis and L. A. Metzler (Eds.), AEA *Readings in the Theory of International Trade*. Richard D. Irwin, Inc., Homewood, Ill., 1950.

——— (1951). "A Multiple-Country Theory of Income Transfers." *Journal of Political Economy* (February), pp. 14–29.

Mundell, R. A. (1968). *International Economics*. The Macmillan Company, New York.

Ohlin, B. (1929). "The Reparation Problem: A Discussion I. Transfer Difficulties, Real and Imagined." *Economic Journal*, vol. XXXIX (June), pp. 172–178. Reprinted in H. S. Ellis and L. A. Metzler (Eds.), AEA *Readings in the Theory of International Trade*. Richard D. Irwin, Inc., Homewood, Ill., 1950.

Pigou, A. C. (1932). "The Effects of Reparations on the Ratio of International Exchange." *Economic Journal*, vol. XLII, pp. 532–542.

Robertson, D. H. (1931). "The Transfer Problem." In A. C. Pigou and D. H. Robertson (Eds.), *Economic Essays and Addresses*. King, London.

Samuelson, P. A. (1952). "The Transfer Problem and Transport Costs: The Terms of Trade When Impediments are Absent." *Economic Journal* (June), pp. 278–304. Reprinted in J. E. Stiglitz (Ed.), *The Collected Scientific Papers of Paul A. Samuelson*, vol. II. The MIT Press, Cambridge, Mass., 1966, pp. 985–1011.

——— (1954). "The Transfer Problem and Transport Costs, II: Analysis of Effects of Trade Impediments." *Economic Journal* (June), pp. 264–289. Reprinted in J. E. Stiglitz (Ed.), *The Collected Scientific Papers of Paul A. Samuelson*, vol. II. The MIT Press, Cambridge, Mass., 1966, pp. 1012–1037.

——— (1971). "On the Trail of Conventional Beliefs about the Transfer Problem." In J. N. Bhagwati, R. W. Jones, R. A. Mundell, and J. Vanek (Eds.), *Trade, Balance of Payments, and Growth: Papers in International Economics in Honor of Charles P. Kindleberger*. North-Holland Publishers, Amsterdam.

Taussig, F. W. (1917). "International Trade under Depreciated Paper: A Contribution to Theory." *Quarterly Journal of Economics* (May), pp. 380–403.

——— (1927). *International Trade*. The Macmillan Company, New York.

Viner, J. (1924). *Canada's Balance of International Indebtedness, 1900–1913*. Harvard University Press, Cambridge, Mass.

——— (1937). *Studies in the Theory of International Trade*. Harper and Brothers, New York, chap. VI.

White, H. D. (1933). *The French International Accounts, 1880–1913*. Harvard University Press, Cambridge, Mass.

Williams, J. H. (1920). *Argentine International Trade under Inconvertible Paper Money, 1880–1900*. Harvard University Press, Cambridge, Mass.

Wilson, R. (1931). *Capital Imports and the Terms of Trade*. University of Australia Press, Melbourne.

CHAPTER

THIRTEEN

CONFLICTS BETWEEN INTERNAL AND EXTERNAL BALANCE, AND MEADE'S RECONCILIATION

Our discussion so far has been concerned mostly with automatic processes and not with the determination of optimum policies. Even though the question of economic policy may seem more interesting, our approach was deliberate because optimum policies cannot be formulated unless the workings of the international economy are well understood. But the time has come to consider these interesting policy issues.

With the publication of his *General Theory*, Keynes (1936) dealt a definite blow to the classical notion of automatic full employment. However, the notion of automatic balance-of-payments equilibrium persisted longer. Today it is fair to say that both full employment (internal balance) and balance-of-payments equilibrium (external balance) are considered objectives of deliberate economic policy rather than targets which are attained automatically. Accordingly, in the last few decades economists have spent a great deal of time discussing the problem of how expenditure-adjusting policies can be combined with expenditure-switching policies to achieve simultaneously external and internal balance. The major contributors to this policy-oriented approach are Meade (1951) and Tinbergen (1952). Additional contributions have been made by Alexander (1952), Corden (1960), Johnson (1958), Nurkse (1956), Swan (1955), and others.

This chapter is divided into two parts. Part A deals with the conflicts between internal and external balance when expenditure-adjusting policies alone are pursued. Part B considers the conflicts between internal and external balance when expenditure-switching policies alone are pursued, and then shows how the conflicts are removed when both expenditure-adjusting and expenditure-switching policies are pursued simultaneously. The flexible-exchange-rate assignment is also discussed in the last section of part B as well as in the appendix to this chapter.

PART A.   EXPENDITURE-ADJUSTING POLICIES AND CONFLICTS BETWEEN INTERNAL AND EXTERNAL BALANCE

13.1 THE THEORY OF ECONOMIC POLICY (INTRODUCTORY)

The traditional approach to international equilibrium and adjustment which was expounded in earlier chapters deals primarily with the effects on such critical variables as income, employment, terms of trade, and the balance of payments of changes in any exogenously determined parameter. The Meade-Tinbergen policy model makes a sharp distinction between targets (objects of policy) and instruments (vehicles of policy), and inverts the traditional approach by taking the targets as given and then solving for the required values of the instruments. To achieve a given target there must be an *effective* instrument, and to achieve n *independent* targets there must be at least n independent and *effective* instruments. (This is the famous Tinbergen rule which we met earlier in part one of this book.) When there are n independent targets and m independent instruments with $m > n$, a large number of ways exist to achieve the n given targets. But when $m < n$, then in general only m targets can be achieved.

The targets must be mutually independent. For instance, suppose there exists a one-to-one correspondence between two variables, such as the level of employment and national output. It makes no sense to consider full employment and maximum output as independent targets. Another example of dependent targets is balance-of-payments equilibrium in countries A and B of our two-country model. When one balance of payments is in equilibrium, the other is also in equilibrium, ignoring any possible inconsistencies in the two countries' definitions.

The instruments must be effective and mutually independent. An instrument is effective when it affects the target variable (or variables) to an appropriate degree. A reduction in the interest rate, for instance, during a depression when investment is not interest-elastic is an ineffective means of increasing income and employment. In addition, the instruments must be mutually independent in the sense that their relative effectiveness on various target variables is different. For instance, full employment and balance-of-payments equilibrium cannot be achieved simultaneously by appropriate changes in taxes and government spending simply because the two instruments (taxes and government spending) are not independent—their relative influence on the two targets is the same. Thus, any changes in government spending and taxes which produce the same effect on employment also produce the same effect on the balance of payments. On the other hand, balance-of-payments equilibrium and full employment can be achieved simultaneously by appropriate changes in the exchange rate and government spending because the relative effectiveness of the latter instruments on the two targets is different. This is shown later in the present chapter.

The preceding principles are applied below to our two-country model. Two targets are specified for each country: full employment (internal balance) and balance-of-payments equilibrium (external balance). Since there is a one-to-one correspondence between A's and B's balances of payments, there are three independent targets in all: internal balance in A, internal balance in B, and external balance. According to Tinbergen's rule, three independent instruments are needed to achieve the three targets. The rest of the discussion in this part shows that the application of expenditure-adjusting policies by the two countries (two instruments) gives rise to conflicts between internal and external balance.

13.2 EXPENDITURE-ADJUSTING POLICIES AND FULL EMPLOYMENT (INTERNAL BALANCE)

Go back to the two-country, fixed-exchange-rate model of chap. 10 and rewrite the national-income equilibrium eqs. (10.36) and (10.37) as follows:

$$Y_a = F_a(Y_a; R) + T_a(Y_a, Y_b; R) + G_a \tag{13.1}$$

$$Y_b = F_b(Y_b; R) - T_a^*(Y_a, Y_b; R) + G_b \tag{13.2}$$

where

$$F_i(Y_i; R) \equiv C_i(Y_i; R) + I_i(Y_i; R) \qquad (i = a, b) \tag{13.3}$$

and $R = 1$ throughout the present section. Government spending G_i is separated from total absorption because for purely illustrative purposes it is treated in the present discussion as the main expenditure-adjusting policy parameter. Generally speaking, the same results can be achieved by any other expenditure-adjusting policy such as monetary policy, changes in taxes, or changes in transfer payments.

Suppose the full-employment incomes in A and B are given by Y_a^f and Y_b^f, respectively. What values should the policy parameters (instruments), G_a and G_b, assume so that both countries attain full employment? We are no longer interested in the effects of G_a or G_b on Y_a and Y_b. We invert the problem by taking Y_a and Y_b as given at their predetermined values Y_a^f and Y_b^f, respectively, and seek those values of G_a and G_b which give rise to the equilibrium solution, $Y_a = Y_a^f$ and $Y_b = Y_b^f$.

First consider those combinations of G_a and G_b which bring about full employment in A, that is, $Y_a = Y_a^f$, as shown in fig. 13.1 by A's internal-balance schedule NH. Since Y_a is fixed by assumption, eq. (13.2) gives Y_b as a function of G_b. From our foreign-trade multiplier theory we already know that

$$\left(\frac{\partial Y_b}{\partial G_b}\right)_{Y_a = Y_a^f} = \frac{1}{1 - Z_b' + M_b'} \equiv m_b \tag{13.4}$$

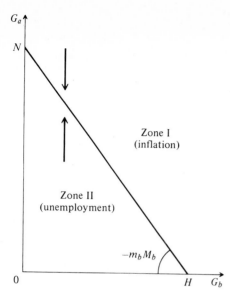

Figure 13.1 A's internal-balance schedule, shown by the curve NH. It gives all combinations of G_a and G_b which are consistent with full employment in country A.

Now for any value of Y_b and, therefore, G_b, eq. (13.1) gives Y_a as a function of G_a. Hence, it can be solved for that value of G_a for which $Y_a = Y_a^f$. As G_b increases by ΔG_b, Y_b increases by $\Delta Y_b = m_b \, \Delta G_b$ (ignoring foreign repercussion since $Y_a = Y_a^f$ by assumption). Hence B's imports ($\equiv$ A's exports) and, therefore, the aggregate demand for A's products at $Y_a = Y_a^f$ increases by $\Delta M_b = M_b' \, \Delta Y_b = M_b' m_b \, \Delta G_b$. To maintain equilibrium in A without inflation the aggregate demand for A's products must be reduced by ΔM_b. This is accomplished by setting

$$\Delta G_a = - M_b' m_b \, \Delta G_b \qquad (13.5a)$$

Accordingly,

$$\left(\frac{\Delta G_a}{\Delta G_b}\right)_{Y_a = Y_a^f} = - M_b' m_b \qquad (13.5b)$$

In summary, the curve NH in fig. 13.1 with slope equal to $- m_b M_b'$ gives all combinations of G_a and G_b which are consistent with full employment in country A. The curve NH, which we call A's internal-balance schedule, dramatizes the fact that one of the two instruments (G_a, G_b) is redundant in attaining the single goal of full employment in A. Thus, assuming that $G_b \le 0H$, country A can always determine a corresponding value for G_a at which $Y_a = Y_a^f$.

Reversing the roles of the two countries in the preceding discussion, we can easily determine B's internal-balance schedule, as shown in fig. 13.2 by the curve JK which is the locus of all combinations of G_a and G_b which are consistent with full employment in B. Again there is an infinite number of such combinations because the number of instruments (G_a, G_b) is larger than the number of targets (Y_b^f). The slope of B's internal-balance schedule is given by

$$\left(\frac{\Delta G_b}{\Delta G_a}\right)_{Y_b = Y_b^f} = - M_a' m_a \qquad (13.6)$$

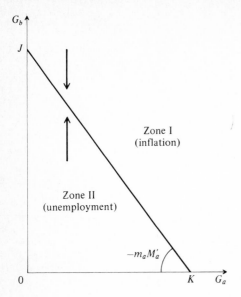

Figure 13.2 B's internal-balance schedule, shown by the curve JK. It is the locus of all combinations of G_a and G_b which are consistent with full employment in country B.

This follows directly from eq. (13.5b), where the subscripts a and b are reversed.

A's internal-balance schedule (NH) divides fig. 13.1 into two zones of economic unhappiness (Swan's phrase). At any point above and to the right of the line NH (zone I) the aggregate demand for A's products is higher than A's full-employment output, giving rise to inflation. On the other hand, at any point below and to the left of NH (zone II) the aggregate demand for A's products falls short of A's full-employment output, giving rise to unemployment. Similarly, B's internal-balance schedule (JK) also divides figure 13.2 into two zones. Again, in zone I country B experiences inflation, and in zone II, unemployment. (Note that the target level of income in each country could as easily correspond to some desired level of unemployment as to full employment, and that the argument does not require belief in the possibility of full employment without inflation.)

A's and B's internal-balance schedules are transferred to fig. 13.3. (The slope of A's internal-balance schedule with respect to the G_a axis is given by the reciprocal of $-m_b M'_b$, that is, $-1/m_b M'_b$, as shown in fig. 13.3.) A's internal-balance schedule is drawn steeper than B's. This is in accordance with the stability condition (see chap. 10)

$$\Delta \equiv 1 - m_a m_b M'_a M'_b > 0$$

which can also be written as

$$\text{Absolute slope of A's internal-balance schedule} \equiv \frac{1}{m_b M'_b} > m_a M'_a$$

$$\equiv \text{absolute slope of B's internal-balance schedule}$$

The two internal-balance schedules are drawn intersecting each other at F. (The possibility of multiple intersections or that the intersection may occur in any other

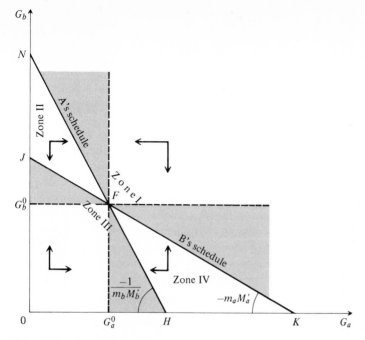

Figure 13.3 Expenditure-adjusting policies to achieve internal balance in A and B. A's and B's internal-balance schedules (NH and JK) divide the diagram into four zones of economic unhappiness as follows:

Zone I = general inflation
Zone II = unemployment in A and inflation in B
Zone III = general unemployment
Zone IV = inflation in A and unemployment in B

In the shaded areas, common sense directs one of the countries to change its spending in the wrong direction.

quadrant besides the first, giving rise to negative values, is presently ignored.) It is apparent, then, that both countries can reach full employment simultaneously if government spending in A and B is set at G_a^0 and G_b^0, respectively.

A's and B's internal-balance schedules divide fig. 13.3 into four zones of economic unhappiness. Any combination of G_a and G_b in any of these zones implies either unemployment or inflation in each country. Of course, if the full-employment point F is known and if the balance of payments is ignored, countries A and B could agree to set their respective government spending at G_a^0 and G_b^0 and move directly to full employment. But point F is not in general known to policy makers. All that is known to policy makers from the mere facts of employment is the zone in which their countries happen to be. Is this information sufficient to move the two countries closer to full employment? What rule should they follow?

Consider the two broken lines through F dividing the diagram into four quadrants. In each quadrant we can say unequivocally whether each country's

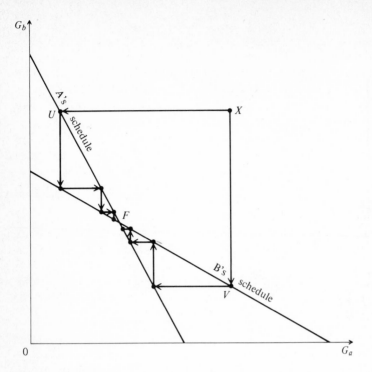

Figure 13.4 Application of the commonsense rule: unemployment → raise spending and inflation → reduce spending. Here internal balance in both countries is reached after the commonsense rule is applied several times.

government spending is higher or lower than the equilibrium levels indicated by point F. If the policy makers knew the quadrant they were in, they could move quickly and directly to F. Unfortunately, they only know the zone they are in—the data would only tell them that a country suffers from unemployment or inflation, but they would not give them the coordinates of point F. Now zone II falls entirely in the second and zone IV in the fourth quadrant. Hence, starting from a point in either zone II or IV, the policy makers would know the direction in which they should adjust their government spending. But each of zones I and III overlap with three quadrants. Thus, starting from a point in either zone I or III, the policy makers would have no idea how they should adjust their spending. The common-sense rule—that a country suffering from unemployment (inflation) should increase (decrease) its spending—while correct in zones II and IV may be misleading in zones I and III. In particular, in any of the four shaded cones of fig. 13.3 the commonsense rule directs one of the two countries to change its spending in the wrong direction. For instance, at any point in the triangle $G_a^0 HF$ country A suffers from unemployment and the commonsense rule calls for an increase in G_a. Nevertheless, increasing G_a is the wrong thing to do since G_a is already higher than G_a^0. Similar arguments can be provided by the reader for the rest of the shaded areas.

The commonsense rule that a country with unemployment (inflation) should increase (decrease) its spending can bring about full employment in both countries, but only after it is applied several times. This is shown in fig. 13.4. Starting from point X (zone I), let one country at a time adjust its spending until it attains full employment. Thus, assuming that A adjusts its spending first, the system would move from X to U and follow the arrows until it reaches F. On the other hand, if B adjusts its spending first, the system would move from X to V and follow the arrows until it reaches F again. In either case, the system seems to approach the full employment point F in a few steps.

The analysis of the present section illustrates Tinbergen's rule in the 2×2 case. Note that the two instruments (G_a, G_b) are indeed independent because the slopes of the two internal-balance curves are different. This independence of the two instruments guarantees the existence of the full-employment point F. If the two instruments were not independent, the two schedules would be parallel and in general full employment in both countries would not be feasible unless some other independent instrument was found.

13.3 EXPENDITURE-ADJUSTING POLICIES AND EXTERNAL BALANCE

In this section we wish to consider the use of expenditure-adjusting policies to achieve external balance. This prepares the ground for the discussion of the next section on the use of expenditure-adjusting policies to achieve internal and external balance simultaneously.

By external balance we mean a situation in which A's balance of trade is zero. (Capital movements are ignored.) Since $T_a \equiv M_b(Y_b^e) - M_a(Y_a^e)$ and Y_a^e and Y_b^e are functions of G_a and G_b, that is, $Y_a^e = Y_a^e(G_a, G_b)$ and $Y_b^e = Y_b^e(G_a, G_b)$, it follows that, other things remaining equal, T_a is in the final analysis a function of G_a and G_b, that is, $T_a = T_a(G_a, G_b)$. External balance prevails when

$$T_a(G_a, G_b) = 0 \qquad (13.7)$$

Equation (13.7) is illustrated graphically in fig. 13.5. The line MP, which we call the external-balance schedule, shows all combinations of G_a and G_b consistent with external balance. It slopes upward since an increase in G_a causes T_a to deteriorate while an increase in G_b causes T_a to improve. In particular, suppose we start from an initial combination of G_a and G_b satisfying eq. (13.7). If G_a changes by ΔG_a, then by applying eq. (10.64) we find that T_a changes by $-(1 - Z_b') \Delta Y_b = -(1 - Z_b')k_{ba} \Delta G_a < 0$. On the other hand, if G_b changes by ΔG_b, a similar application of eq. (10.63) reveals that T_a changes by $(1 - Z_a') \Delta Y_a = (1 - Z_a')k_{ab} \Delta G_b$.

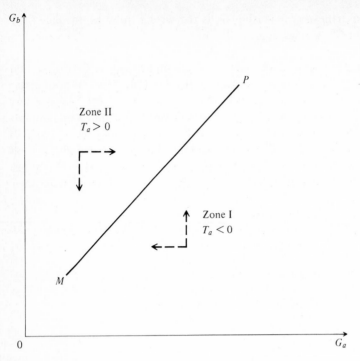

Figure 13.5 The external-balance schedule, shown by the line MP. It gives all combinations of G_a and G_b consistent with external balance, i.e., all those combinations of G_a and G_b which satisfy the equation: $T_a(G_a, G_b) = 0$.

External balance will continue to prevail if the sum of the two balance-of-trade changes is zero, i.e.,

$$(1 - Z'_a)k_{ab} \, \Delta G_b - (1 - Z'_b)k_{ba} \, \Delta G_a = 0 \tag{13.8}$$

Solving eq. (13.8) for $(\Delta G_b/\Delta G_a)$, we finally obtain

$$\frac{\Delta G_b}{\Delta G_a} = \left(\frac{1 - Z'_b}{1 - Z'_a}\right)\left(\frac{k_{ba}}{k_{ab}}\right) > 0 \tag{13.9}$$

on the reasonable assumption that both countries are stable in isolation, that is, $Z'_a < 1$, $Z'_b < 1$.

The external-balance curve (MP) divides fig. 13.5 into two zones. Above and to the left of MP (zone II) A's balance of trade is in surplus; below and to the right (zone I), it is in deficit. Only points on the line MP are consistent with external equilibrium. These points are infinite in number since two instruments (G_a, G_b) are used to attain a single goal $(T_a = 0)$. The attainment of external balance calls for either a decrease in G_a and/or an increase in G_b when the system is in zone I $(T_a < 0)$, and for either an increase in G_a and/or a decrease in G_b when the system is in zone II $(T_a > 0)$. This rule coincides with what common sense suggests.

13.4 EXPENDITURE-ADJUSTING POLICIES FOR INTERNAL AND EXTERNAL BALANCE

We have seen that expenditure-adjusting policies by both countries can achieve internal balance in both countries if external balance is ignored. We have also seen that such policies can achieve external balance if internal balance is ignored. But can the application of expenditure-adjusting policies alone achieve internal balance as well as external balance at the same time? Meade and Tinbergen showed that this is not possible. In particular, Meade showed that, when expenditure-adjusting policies alone are used, conflicts arise between internal and external balance. These conflicts arise because fewer instruments are used than the number of targets. As Meade showed, all conflicts are removed when another independent instrument (exchange-rate adjustment) is used.

The internal-balance schedules as well as the external-balance schedule are brought together in fig. 13.6. These three schedules divide fig. 13.6 into seven

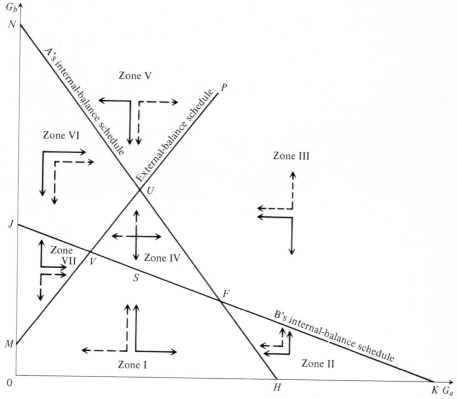

Figure 13.6 Conflicts between internal and external balance when expenditure-adjusting policies are pursued. Each arrow shows the direction in which each instrument must change in order to achieve one target at a time. There are conflicts in all zones except II and VI. The most difficult case is zone IV in which there are conflicts in both countries.

zones, but actually there are only four types of disequilibria, as Meade pointed out. Before discussing each one of these disequilibria in greater detail, this important truth must be brought out: simultaneous internal and external balance is possible if and only if the external-balance curve passes through the full-employment point F. Since in general there is no apparent reason why this should be so, our conclusion is that internal and external balance cannot be achieved simultaneously through the application of expenditure-adjusting policies alone.

Meade's four types of disequilibria are illustrated in zones I to IV. In each of these zones (as well as in zones V to VII) four arrows have been drawn to show how each instrument should change to achieve one target at a time. The suggested direction of change in G_i ($i = a, b$) to achieve internal balance in the ith country is indicated by the solid arrows. The direction of change in G_i to achieve external balance is indicated by the broken arrows. These arrows have been drawn on the basis of figs. 13.3 and 13.5. In all zones except II and VI there are conflicts in at least one country. The most difficult case is zone IV, in which there are conflicts in both countries. Let us consider each zone briefly.

Zone I Both countries suffer from unemployment and in addition A suffers from a balance-of-trade deficit (B has a surplus). To achieve internal balance both countries must increase their government spending, as shown by the solid arrows. But while increasing G_b tends to restore external balance as well, increasing G_a tends to aggravate A's deficit. Thus, country A faces a dilemma. If she increases G_a to increase employment, she aggravates the deficit. If she decreases G_a to eliminate the deficit, she aggravates the problem of unemployment. Clearly, there exists a conflict in country A between internal and external balance. Under such circumstances of general unemployment, it is the duty of the surplus country (in our case, B) to take the initiative and pursue an expansionary fiscal policy. But unfortunately even if the surplus country is agreeable to this course of action, full equilibrium (internal and external balance) cannot be reached. In general, three possibilities may be distinguished:

1. B's expansionary fiscal policy may bring about external balance first (see line segment MV). In this case, both countries could agree on a program to simultaneously increase their government spending until point V is reached, where external balance as well as internal balance in B are restored. A's unemployment will persist at a reduced rate.
2. B's expansionary fiscal policy may restore internal balance in B first (see line segment VF). Although A's deficit and unemployment are also reduced, they are not eliminated. Note the dilemma at a point such as S on the line VF. If G_a is decreased and G_b increased, we can move to point V. Alternatively, if G_a is increased while G_b is decreased, we could move to point F. In either case, an additional target is attained, but at the expense of moving further away from the third target.
3. Finally, B's expansionary fiscal policy may restore internal balance in A first (see line segment FH). Again A's deficit and B's unemployment are reduced but

not eliminated. Both countries could now agree on a program to increase G_b and decrease G_a and move to the full-employment point F, where A's deficit is also smaller.

Zone II In this zone, A suffers from inflation and a balance-of-trade deficit while B suffers from unemployment and a balance-of-trade surplus. This is the easiest case because no conflicts exist in either country. Thus, A must reduce spending for both internal and external balance. Similarly, B must increase spending for both internal and external balance. If the external-balance schedule lies above and to the left of the full-employment point F, as shown in fig. 13.6, and if these policies are coordinated properly, full employment in both countries and a smaller external imbalance can be attained (see point F). On the other hand, if the external-balance schedule lies below and to the right of point F, external balance will be reached first with smaller inflation in A and smaller unemployment in B. In either case, full equilibrium cannot be attained.

Zone III Here both countries suffer from inflation. In addition, A has a deficit and B a surplus. Country A can move closer to both internal and external balance by reducing spending. Thus, no conflict exists in A. Country B, on the other hand, must *increase* spending to achieve external balance and *reduce* spending to achieve internal balance. Thus, B has a conflict and faces a dilemma. As in zone I, the deficit country (A) which has no conflicts must reduce spending until either one or two targets are attained. Thus, with a little cooperation from the surplus country, a point may be reached somewhere on the line segment UF. Again full equilibrium is impossible.

Zone IV In this last case, A suffers from unemployment and a deficit while B suffers from inflation and a surplus. This is the most difficult case of all. Both countries face conflicts. Thus, A must increase spending for internal balance but reduce spending for external balance. Similarly, B must reduce spending for internal balance but increase spending for external balance. There is no such thing as a movement toward equilibrium in this zone. Moving closer to equilibrium in one area means moving further away from other equilibria. The conflicts in this zone assume greater significance when one realizes that any initial position in any other zone will sooner or later lead to the disequilibrium situation of zone IV (including the boundaries).

The types of disequilibria implied by zones V, VI, and VII correspond to the disequilibria of zones III, II, and I, respectively, with the minor difference that the roles of the two countries are reversed.

From the preceding discussion it follows that expenditure-adjusting policies conducted properly will lead the two countries eventually to the *triangle of conflict VUF*. Once in this triangle (or its boundaries), any movement in any direction implies that at least one disequilibrium is getting worse. Thus, while expenditure-adjusting policies take the world a long way toward achieving internal and external balance, they break down when the triangle of conflict is reached. Why is this so? What can be done? The answer has already been given by Meade and Tinbergen: an additional tool is needed. Since three independent targets are pursued, three—not two—instruments must be adopted. Meade (1951) chose the rate of exchange as the third instrument. Johnson (1958) generalized the procedure by showing that any expenditure-switching policy will do. This analysis is pursued below in part B.

PART B. INTRODUCTION OF EXPENDITURE-SWITCHING POLICIES

Expenditure-adjusting policies cannot possibly restore internal and external balance unless the triangle of conflict of fig. 13.6 is eliminated. This can be done through any effective expenditure-switching policy. We shall presently illustrate the argument by assuming that exchange-rate adjustments are used for this purpose.

13.5 THE EFFECTS OF EXCHANGE-RATE ADJUSTMENTS ON THE INTERNAL- AND EXTERNAL-BALANCE SCHEDULES

How does a change in the rate of exchange affect the internal- and external-balance schedules? The answer is implicit in the analysis of chaps. 10 and 11. As we have seen in chap. 11, an increase in R (depreciation of the dollar relative to the pound sterling) in general involves an increase in Y_a^e, a decrease in Y_b^e, and, assuming the Harberger condition is satisfied, an improvement in A's balance of trade. These results are sufficient for us to determine the shifts in the three schedules of fig. 13.6 following an increase in R. For instance, since an increase in R implies that Y_a^e increases for any given combination of G_a, G_b, it follows that internal balance in A may be restored through either a reduction in G_a or G_b. Accordingly, A's internal-balance schedule shifts downward and to the left. Similarly, since Y_b^e falls as R increases, internal balance in B is restored either through an increase in G_a or G_b. Thus, B's internal-balance schedule shifts upward and to the right. Finally, since T_a (and T_a^*) increases as R increases, external equilibrium can be restored if G_a increases and/or G_b decreases. Accordingly, the external-balance schedule shifts downward and to the right. (In all cases, the indicated changes in spending are not actual but merely intended. They show how spending ought to change to achieve a certain target, assuming that the target was met before the exchange-rate adjustment.) All of these shifts are illustrated in fig. 13.7 by the broken curves. The solid curves have been transferred from fig. 13.6 and indicate the initial situation before the exchange-rate adjustment.

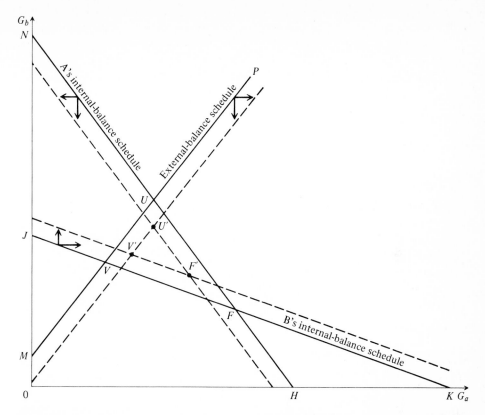

Figure 13.7 The effects of a devaluation of A's currency. The broken curves show how the three schedules shift when R increases (i.e., when the dollar depreciates relative to the pound sterling).

Figure 13.7 is important because it shows that with an appropriate exchange-rate adjustment the triangle of conflict shrinks. If the adjustment is pursued to the appropriate degree, the triangle of conflict can be made to disappear altogether. Accordingly, the introduction of exchange-rate adjustments as an additional policy instrument could force the external-balance schedule to pass through the full-employment point. Then expenditure-adjusting policies could be used to achieve both internal and external balance at the same time.

13.6 THE USE OF EXCHANGE-RATE ADJUSTMENTS TO ACHIEVE EITHER INTERNAL OR EXTERNAL BALANCE

Before considering the simultaneous application of both expenditure-adjusting and expenditure-switching policies for the achievement of internal and external balance, we wish to consider the required exchange-rate adjustments in each of the

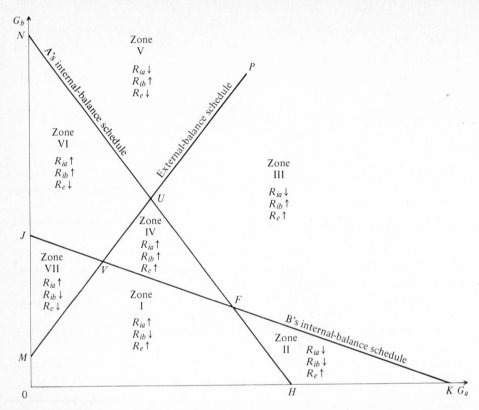

Figure 13.8 Conflicts between internal and external balance when expenditure-switching policies are pursued. The symbols R_{ia}, R_{ib} and R_e stand for the needed exchange-rate adjustment for achieving internal balance in A, internal balance in B, and external balance, respectively, with the arrows showing the direction of change. Conflicts exist in all zones except zone IV.

seven zones of economic unhappiness of fig. 13.6 for the achievement of the three targets: internal balance in A, internal balance in B, and external balance. This is done in fig. 13.8, which is similar to fig. 13.6. In each of the seven zones the symbols R_{ia}, R_{ib} and R_e stand for the needed exchange-rate adjustment for achieving internal balance in A, internal balance in B, and external balance, respectively, with the arrows showing the direction of change. When A suffers from unemployment (inflation) an increase (decrease) in R is called for. Similarly, when B suffers from unemployment (inflation) a decrease (increase) in R is needed. Finally, when A's balance of trade is in deficit (surplus) an increase (decrease) in R is called for.

Study fig. 13.8 carefully. Note that conflicts exist in all zones except zone IV, in which all arrows are pointing upward. Recall that zone IV was the most difficult case—the triangle of conflict—when expenditure-adjusting policies alone were pursued. As it turns out, this case can be handled by means of expenditure-switching policies. As noted in the preceding section, starting with the type of disequilibrium indicated by zone IV, the directive to increase R (i.e., devalue the dollar relative to the pound sterling) causes the triangle VUF to shrink. Thus, both countries move closer to internal and external balance.

13.7 COMBINING EXPENDITURE-ADJUSTING AND EXPENDITURE-SWITCHING POLICIES: (A) THE SINGLE-COUNTRY CASE

The time has come to consider the simultaneous application of expenditure-adjusting and expenditure-switching policies. For pedagogical reasons, our discussion is divided into two parts. In this section we wish to consider the simple case of a single country à la Swan. Then, in the following section, we shall open up the model to consider both countries simultaneously à la Meade.

To concentrate on the problems of a single country, assume that country B pursues expenditure-adjusting policies and maintains full employment at all times. Accordingly, $Y_b = Y_b^f$, and A's exports are a function of the rate of exchange only. In particular, for any given value of R, our system reduces to the simple foreign-trade multiplier model without foreign repercussion.

Consider now all combinations of R and G_a which are consistent with internal balance in A. This is shown by the internal-balance schedule KN in fig. 13.9. The schedule KN is sloping downward because, starting from an initial situation of full employment in A, an increase in G_a causes inflation which is removed by a decrease in R. Similarly, all combinations of R and G_a consistent with external balance are shown by the external-balance schedule VU. The latter is upward sloping because, starting from an initial situation of external balance, an increase in G_a gives rise to a deficit which is eliminated by an increase in R. The two schedules intersect each other at E. At this intersection, internal balance and external balance prevail simultaneously.

The internal- and external-balance schedules divide fig. 13.9 into four zones of economic unhappiness. But no matter which zone the system happens to be in initially, appropriate changes in spending and the rate of exchange can bring it to E, where internal and external balance prevail. Unfortunately, the direction of change for the two instruments is not always clear. Common sense and intuition may lead the system astray.

Consider the broken lines through E. They divide the diagram into four *regions*. Evidently, for the correct policy mix, knowledge of the region the system is in is necessary. However, the mere facts of employment and balance of payments tell us only which zone the system is in. Because the regions overlap with the zones mistakes are unavoidable.

Common sense would dictate that when unemployment (inflation) occurs the policy makers must increase (decrease) spending. Similarly, in the face of a balance-of-payments deficit (surplus) the policy makers must raise (lower) the rate of exchange. This commonsense rule, however, is the wrong thing to do in the four shaded cones. For instance, in the cone UEH where a deficit exists, common sense

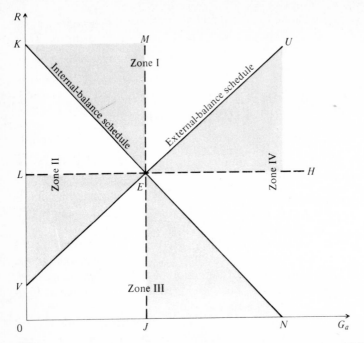

Figure 13.9 The use of expenditure-adjusting and expenditure-switching policies by a single country. The internal- and external-balance schedules (*KN* and *VU*) divide the diagram into four zones of economic unhappiness as follows:

   Zone I = inflation and balance-of-payments surplus
   Zone II = unemployment and balance-of-payments surplus
Zone III = unemployment and balance-of-payments deficit
Zone IV = inflation and balance-of-payments deficit

would dictate devaluation (i.e., an increase in *R*) whereas the correct policy is to *reduce R* and spending. In the cone *VEL* where a surplus exists, common sense would call for a reduction in *R* whereas the correct policy is to increase *R* (and spending). Similarly, the commonsense directive for changing spending is fallacious in the shaded cones *KEM* and *JEN*. In the former (*KEM*), common sense calls for a reduction in spending whereas the correct policy is to increase spending, and in the latter (*JEN*) the reverse is true. As Swan points out, these conflicts between the commonsense rule and the correct policy mix are the source of the problems and errors of economic policy; if one instrument is substantially out of line, the natural indications for the other may be quite misleading. This sounds a lot like Meade's theory of the second best.

    Finally, note that even though many conflicts exist in fig. 13.9, the commonsense directive for at least one of the two instruments is always in the right direction. The correct policy, then, is to use that instrument which helps both targets. Thus, in zone I a reduction in *R* is called for; in zone II, an increase in *G*; in zone III, an increase in *R*; and in zone IV, a reduction in *G*.

13.8 COMBINING EXPENDITURE-ADJUSTING AND EXPENDITURE-SWITCHING POLICIES: (B) THE GENERAL CASE

Turn now to the full model. What is the proper way to use expenditure-adjusting and expenditure-switching policies to achieve internal and external balance in both countries? Meade observed that in each zone of economic unhappiness there is always a certain policy mix for each country which can bring *that* country closer to internal and external balance. He therefore proposed that this policy mix, which is free from conflicts, is the correct strategy for each country. This is Meade's reconciliation of the conflicts between internal and external balance.

Figure 13.10 illustrates Meade's reconciliation. The internal- and external-balance schedules are similar to those of figs. 13.6 and 13.8. For the moment, ignore the broken lines through point E. The indicated changes of the three policy instruments G_a, G_b, and R have been determined by combining the policy changes

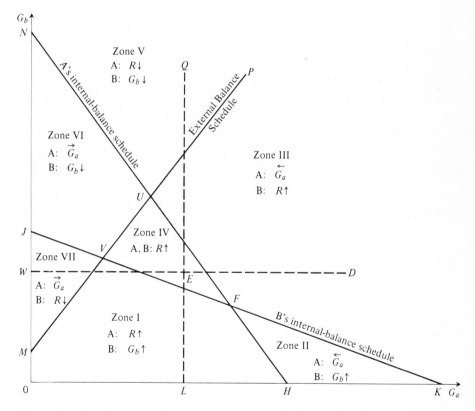

Figure 13.10 Meade's reconciliation. The correct strategy, according to Meade, is for each country to use that policy mix which can bring *that* country closer to internal and external balance. These are the policy mixes shown in all zones.

of figs. 13.6 and 13.8 and then rejecting those which presented conflicts for either country. Thus, in each zone of fig. 13.10 there is always a policy mix which brings each country closer to internal and external balance. All conflicts have been removed.

Suppose that Meade's recommendation is actually pursued by both countries. Does this mean that policy makers will always succeed in changing each instrument in the right direction? Unfortunately, this is not the case, as fig. 13.10 reveals. Consider the general-equilibrium point E which is determined by allowing the rate of exchange to vary until all schedules for internal and external balance pass through a common point such as E. (Point E must always lie in the triangle of conflict.) Through point E draw vertical and horizontal lines, as shown in fig. 13.10 by the broken lines LQ and WD. These lines through E divide fig. 13.10 into four regions. For the correct formulation of expenditure-adjusting policies we need to know the region we are in. Yet the mere facts of the employment situation tell us the zone we are in. Accordingly, as the reader can verify, spending is adjusted in the wrong direction in the two shaded areas. If point E were drawn closer to the line VU, either one or both shaded areas would shift to zone VI.

Consider now the rate of exchange. The correct change is that which causes the external-balance schedule MP to shift downward and pass through the general-equilibrium point E. As we have seen earlier, this can be accomplished in fig. 13.10 by *increasing R* (i.e., devaluing the dollar relative to the pound sterling). Nevertheless, Meade's reconciliation calls for a *reduction* in R in zones V and VII. This is obviously a move in the wrong direction.

13.9 THE ASSIGNMENT PROBLEM

Each country has two targets (external and internal balance) and two instruments (expenditure-adjusting and expenditure-switching policies). As Meade notes, there are two ways in which the authorities of each country may combine the use of expenditure-adjusting and expenditure-switching policies. One way is to assign the expenditure-adjusting policy to the preservation of internal balance and the expenditure-switching policy to the preservation of external balance. This is the case of the flexible-exchange-rate assignment and is pursued further in the following section and the appendix to this chapter. A second way is to assign the expenditure-adjusting policy to the preservation of external balance and the expenditure-switching policy to the preservation of internal balance. This is the case of the gold-standard assignment which is taken up in chaps. 15 and 16. It is interesting to note that the gold standard is a special case of Meade's general model.

The problem of pairing targets and instruments is called the *assignment problem*. The particular ways in which specific targets are paired with specific instruments are called *assignments*. In the general $n \times n$ case (n instruments and n targets) there are $n!$ different assignments. In our present 2×2 case there are only $2! = (1)(2) = 2$ assignments: the flexible-exchange-rate assignment and the gold-standard assignment.

13.10 THE FLEXIBLE-EXCHANGE-RATE ASSIGNMENT

Before concluding this chapter we wish to consider briefly the flexible-exchange-rate assignment. Under this assignment each country uses expenditure-adjusting policies for the preservation of internal balance while the exchange rate is left free to preserve external balance. In our model, we may say that the instruments G_a, G_b, and R are assigned to the targets: internal balance in A, internal balance in B, and external balance, respectively. Accordingly, G_a is increased (decreased) when there exists unemployment (inflation) in A; G_b is increased (decreased) when there is unemployment (inflation) in B; and R is increased (decreased) when A has a deficit (surplus).

Figure 13.11 summarizes in a convenient way the flexible-exchange-rate assignment. The arrows show the direction of change of the three instruments in each zone. Observe that not all indicated changes for G_a and G_b point toward the

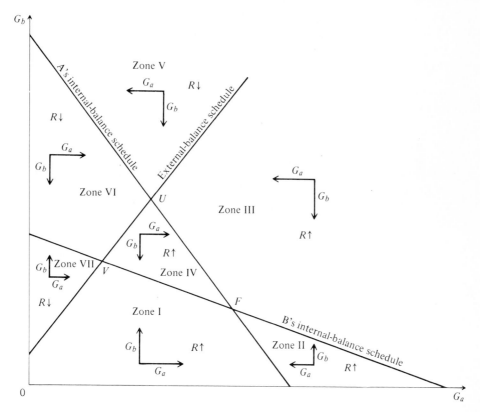

Figure 13.11 The flexible-exchange-rate system. Under the flexible-exchange-rate assignment, G_a is increased (decreased) when there exists unemployment (inflation) in A; G_b is increased (decreased) when there is unemployment (inflation) in B; and R is increased (decreased) when A has a deficit (surplus). See the arrows in all zones.

full-employment point F, and not all indicated changes in R cause the triangle of conflict VUF to shrink. The appendix to this chapter carries the analysis of the flexible-exchange-rate assignment a little further.

APPENDIX TO CHAPTER THIRTEEN. THE STABILITY OF THE FLEXIBLE-EXCHANGE-RATE ASSIGNMENT

This appendix discusses rigorously the flexible-exchange-rate assignment.

As explained in sec. 13.10, the flexible-exchange-rate assignment is the case where a flexible-exchange rate preserves external balance and each country preserves internal balance by pursuing expenditure-adjusting policies. Accordingly, we formulate the following dynamic system:

$$\dot{R} = k_1(-T_a^*) \tag{A13.1}$$

$$\dot{G}_a = k_2(Y_a^f - Y_a^e) \tag{A13.2}$$

$$\dot{G}_b = k_3(Y_b^f - Y_b^e) \tag{A13.3}$$

where $\dot{R}$, $\dot{G}_a$, and $\dot{G}_b$ are time derivatives, the parameters k_1, k_2, and k_3 are positive speeds of adjustment, and Y_a^e, Y_b^e are the roots of eqs. (11.1) and (11.2) for any given values of R, G_a, and G_b.

For small displacements around the equilibrium values $\bar{R}$, $\bar{G}_a$, and $\bar{G}_b$, the system of eqs. (A13.1) to (A13.3) is stable if the associated linear system is stable. Accordingly, expand the right-hand sides of these equations in the Taylor series about the equilibrium values $\bar{R}$, $\bar{G}_a$, and $\bar{G}_b$ and drop all popular terms to obtain

$$\dot{R} = -k_1\left(\frac{\partial T_a^*}{\partial R}\right)(R - \bar{R}) - k_1\left(\frac{\partial T_a^*}{\partial G_a}\right)(G_a - \bar{G}_a) - k_1\left(\frac{\partial T_a^*}{\partial G_b}\right)(G_b - \bar{G}_b) \tag{A13.4}$$

$$\dot{G}_a = -k_2\left(\frac{\partial Y_a^e}{\partial R}\right)(R - \bar{R}) - k_2\left(\frac{\partial Y_a^e}{\partial G_a}\right)(G_a - \bar{G}_a) - k_2\left(\frac{\partial Y_a^e}{\partial G_b}\right)(G_b - \bar{G}_b) \tag{A13.5}$$

$$\dot{G}_b = -k_3\left(\frac{\partial Y_b^e}{\partial R}\right)(R - \bar{R}) - k_3\left(\frac{\partial Y_b^e}{\partial G_a}\right)(G_a - \bar{G}_a) - k_3\left(\frac{\partial Y_b^e}{\partial G_b}\right)(G_b - \bar{G}_b) \tag{A13.6}$$

The solution of these differential equations has the following form:

$$R = \bar{R} + a_{11}e^{\lambda_1 t} + a_{12}e^{\lambda_2 t} + a_{13}e^{\lambda_3 t} \tag{A13.7}$$

$$G_a = \bar{G}_a + a_{21}e^{\lambda_1 t} + a_{22}e^{\lambda_2 t} + a_{23}e^{\lambda_3 t} \tag{A13.8}$$

$$G_b = \bar{G}_b + a_{31}e^{\lambda_1 t} + a_{32}e^{\lambda_2 t} + a_{33}e^{\lambda_3 t} \tag{A13.9}$$

where the constants a_{ij} depend on initial conditions at time $t = 0$, and λ_1, λ_2, and λ_3 are roots of the following determinantal equation:

$$
\begin{vmatrix}
-k_1\left(\dfrac{\partial T_a^*}{\partial R}\right) - \lambda & -k_1\left(\dfrac{\partial T_a^*}{\partial G_a}\right) & -k_1\left(\dfrac{\partial T_a^*}{\partial G_b}\right) \\[2ex]
-k_2\left(\dfrac{\partial Y_a^e}{\partial R}\right) & -k_2\left(\dfrac{\partial Y_a^e}{\partial G_a}\right) - \lambda & -k_2\left(\dfrac{\partial Y_a^e}{\partial G_b}\right) \\[2ex]
-k_3\left(\dfrac{\partial Y_b^e}{\partial R}\right) & -k_3\left(\dfrac{\partial Y_b^e}{\partial G_a}\right) & -k_3\left(\dfrac{\partial Y_b^e}{\partial G_b}\right) - \lambda
\end{vmatrix} = 0 \qquad \text{(A13.10)}
$$

Evidently the solutions given by eqs. (A13.7) to (A13.9) will converge to the equilibrium values $\bar{R}$, $\bar{G}_a$, and $\bar{G}_b$, respectively, if, and only if, the real parts of the roots λ_1, λ_2, and λ_3 are strictly negative. Expand the determinant (A13.10) and collect similar powers of λ to obtain

$$
\lambda^3 + A_1\lambda^2 + A_2\lambda + A_3 = 0 \qquad \text{(A13.11)}
$$

where

$$
A_1 = k_1\left(\frac{\partial T_a^*}{\partial R}\right) + k_2\left(\frac{\partial Y_a^e}{\partial G_a}\right) + k_3\left(\frac{\partial Y_b^e}{\partial G_b}\right) \qquad \text{(A13.12)}
$$

$$
\begin{aligned}
A_2 = {}& k_2 k_3\left[\left(\frac{\partial Y_a^e}{\partial G_a}\right)\left(\frac{\partial Y_b^e}{\partial G_b}\right) - \left(\frac{\partial Y_a^e}{\partial G_b}\right)\left(\frac{\partial Y_b^e}{\partial G_a}\right)\right] \\
&+ k_1\left(\frac{\partial T_a^*}{\partial R}\right)\left[k_2\left(\frac{\partial Y_a^e}{\partial G_a}\right) + k_3\left(\frac{\partial Y_b^e}{\partial G_b}\right)\right] \\
&- k_1 k_3\left(\frac{\partial T_a^*}{\partial G_b}\right)\left(\frac{\partial Y_b^e}{\partial R}\right) - k_1 k_2\left(\frac{\partial T_a^*}{\partial G_a}\right)\left(\frac{\partial Y_a^e}{\partial R}\right)
\end{aligned} \qquad \text{(A13.13)}
$$

$$
\begin{aligned}
A_3 = {}& k_1 k_2 k_3\Bigg\{\left(\frac{\partial T_a^*}{\partial R}\right)\left[\left(\frac{\partial Y_a^e}{\partial G_a}\right)\left(\frac{\partial Y_b^e}{\partial G_b}\right) - \left(\frac{\partial Y_a^e}{\partial G_b}\right)\left(\frac{\partial Y_b^e}{\partial G_a}\right)\right] \\
&+ \left(\frac{\partial T_a^*}{\partial G_a}\right)\left(\frac{\partial Y_a^e}{\partial G_b}\right)\left(\frac{\partial Y_b^e}{\partial R}\right) + \left(\frac{\partial T_a^*}{\partial G_b}\right)\left(\frac{\partial Y_b^e}{\partial G_a}\right)\left(\frac{\partial Y_a^e}{\partial R}\right) \\
&- \left(\frac{\partial T_a^*}{\partial G_b}\right)\left(\frac{\partial Y_a^e}{\partial G_a}\right)\left(\frac{\partial Y_b^e}{\partial R}\right) - \left(\frac{\partial T_a^*}{\partial G_a}\right)\left(\frac{\partial Y_b^e}{\partial R}\right)\left(\frac{\partial Y_a^e}{\partial G_b}\right)\Bigg\}
\end{aligned} \qquad \text{(A13.14)}
$$

It is known† that the necessary and sufficient conditions for the real parts of the roots of the third-degree eq. (A13.11) to be negative are

$$
A_1 > 0 \qquad A_1 A_2 - A_3 > 0 \qquad A_3 > 0 \qquad \text{(A13.15)}
$$

Assuming that the Harberger condition is satisfied (that is, $(\partial T_a^*/\partial R) > 0$) and recalling from chaps. 10 and 11 that $(\partial T_a^*/\partial G_a) < 0$, $(\partial T_a^*/\partial G_b) > 0$, $(\partial Y_a^e/\partial G_a) > (\partial Y_a^e/\partial G_b) > 0$, $(\partial Y_b^e/\partial G_b) > (\partial Y_b^e/\partial G_a) > 0$, $(\partial Y_a^e/\partial R) > 0$, and $(\partial Y_b^e/\partial R) < 0$, it

---

† See Samuelson (1947, app. B, esp. pp. 429–435). See also the Mathematical Appendix at the end of this book.

becomes clear from eqs. (A13.12) to (A13.14) that $A_1 > 0$, $A_2 > 0$, and $A_3 > 0$. However, substituting from eqs. (A13.12) to (A13.14) into the expression $A_1 A_2 - A_3$ and simplifying, we obtain

$$
\begin{aligned}
A_1 A_2 - A_3 = & -k_1 k_3 \left[k_1 \left(\frac{\partial T_a^*}{\partial R} \right) + k_3 \left(\frac{\partial Y_b^e}{\partial G_b} \right) \right] \\
& \times \left[\left(\frac{\partial T_a^*}{\partial G_b} \right) \left(\frac{\partial Y_b^e}{\partial R} \right) - \left(\frac{\partial T_a^*}{\partial R} \right) \left(\frac{\partial Y_b^e}{\partial G_b} \right) \right] \\
& - k_1 k_2 \left[k_1 \left(\frac{\partial T_a^*}{\partial R} \right) + k_2 \left(\frac{\partial Y_a^e}{\partial G_a} \right) \right] \left[\left(\frac{\partial T_a^*}{\partial G_a} \right) \left(\frac{\partial Y_a^e}{\partial R} \right) - \left(\frac{\partial T_a^*}{\partial R} \right) \left(\frac{\partial Y_a^e}{\partial G_a} \right) \right] \\
& + k_2 k_3 \left[k_2 \left(\frac{\partial Y_a^e}{\partial G_a} \right) + k_3 \left(\frac{\partial Y_b^e}{\partial G_b} \right) \right] \left[\left(\frac{\partial Y_a^e}{\partial G_a} \right) \left(\frac{\partial Y_b^e}{\partial G_b} \right) - \left(\frac{\partial Y_a^e}{\partial G_b} \right) \left(\frac{\partial Y_b^e}{\partial G_a} \right) \right] \\
& - k_1 k_2 k_3 \left[\left(\frac{\partial T_a^*}{\partial G_a} \right) \left(\frac{\partial Y_a^e}{\partial G_b} \right) \left(\frac{\partial Y_b^e}{\partial R} \right) - \left(\frac{\partial T_a^*}{\partial R} \right) \left(\frac{\partial Y_a^e}{\partial G_a} \right) \left(\frac{\partial Y_b^e}{\partial G_b} \right) \right] \\
& - k_1 k_2 k_3 \left[\left(\frac{\partial T_a^*}{\partial G_b} \right) \left(\frac{\partial Y_a^e}{\partial R} \right) \left(\frac{\partial Y_b^e}{\partial G_a} \right) - \left(\frac{\partial T_a^*}{\partial R} \right) \left(\frac{\partial Y_a^e}{\partial G_a} \right) \left(\frac{\partial Y_b^e}{\partial G_b} \right) \right]
\end{aligned}
$$

The first three terms of this last expression are positive. However, the last two terms can be either positive or negative. If they are negative, they could conceivably outweigh the rest of the positive terms and render the system unstable. Nevertheless, if the Laursen-Metzler effect is ignored (i.e., if $\partial Z_i / \partial R = 0$), then the last two terms become positive (as the reader should verify), and then the system is unequivocally stable. Actually, in the latter case $(\partial Z_i / \partial R = 0)$, the Marshall-Lerner condition becomes sufficient for stability.

SELECTED BIBLIOGRAPHY

Alexander, S. S. (1952). "Effects of a Devaluation on a Trade Balance." *IMF Staff Papers* (April), pp. 263–278. Reprinted in AEA *Readings in International Economics.* Richard D. Irwin, Inc., Homewood, Ill., 1968.

Corden, W. M. (1960). "The Geometric Representation of Policies to Attain Internal and External Balance." *Review of Economic Studies*, vol. 28, pp. 1–22. Reprinted in R. N. Cooper (Ed.), *International Finance: Selected Readings.* Penguin Books, Inc., Baltimore, Md., 1969.

Johnson, H. G. (1958). *International Trade and Economic Growth: Studies in Pure Theory.* George Allen and Unwin, Ltd., London, chap. VI. Reprinted in AEA *Readings in International Economics.* Richard D. Irwin, Inc., Homewood, Ill., 1968.

Keynes, J. M. (1936). *The General Theory of Employment, Interest and Money.* Macmillan and Company, Ltd., London.

Laursen, S., and L. A. Metzler (1950). "Flexible Exchange Rates and the Theory of Employment." *The Review of Economics and Statistics* (November), pp. 281–299.

Meade, J. E. (1951). *The Theory of International Economic Policy*, vol. I, *The Balance of Payments.* Oxford University Press, London, pts. III and IV.

Mundell, R. A. (1968). *International Economics.* The Macmillan Company, New York, chap. 14.

Nurkse, R. (1956). "The Relation Between Home Investment and External Balance in the Light of British Experience, 1945–55." *Review of Economics and Statistics* (May), pp. 121–154.

Samuelson, P. A. (1947). *Foundations of Economic Analysis.* Harvard University Press, Cambridge, Mass.

Swan, T. W. (1955). *Longer-Run Problems of the Balance of Payments.* Paper presented to Section G of the Congress of the Australian and New Zealand Association for the Advancement of Science, Melbourne. Reprinted in AEA *Readings in International Economics,* Richard D. Irwin, Inc., Homewood, Ill., 1968.

Tinbergen, J. (1952). *On the Theory of Economic Policy.* North-Holland Publishing Company, Amsterdam.

FOURTEEN

DIRECT CONTROLS

The preceding chapter showed how expenditure-adjusting policies may be combined with expenditure-switching policies to restore and preserve internal and external balance. Switching policies were illustrated by means of exchange-rate adjustments. Obviously the same analysis holds for price-level changes induced by inflation or deflation under fixed-exchange rates. Exchange-rate adjustments and price-level changes are *general* switching policies. That is, they are broad acts of policy which alter the general economic relationships between countries. These general switching policies influence the balance of payments indirectly—through their effect on national incomes and the price mechanism. The aim of these general policies is to switch expenditure both in the deficit and surplus country toward the domestic output of the deficit country.

The present chapter deals with *direct controls*. These are *selective* expenditure-switching policies whose aim is to control directly particular elements in the balance of payments. Usually direct controls are imposed on imports in an attempt to switch *domestic* expenditure away from foreign goods toward home goods. Less common is the use of controls to stimulate exports by switching *foreign* spending toward domestic output. Finally, controls may also be imposed on capital flows in an effort to either curb excessive capital outflows or induce capital inflows.

Following Meade (1951) we classify direct controls into three major categories as follows:

1. *Fiscal controls.* Taxes and subsidies on particular items in the balance of payments
2. *Commercial controls.* Quantitative restrictions (quotas) and state trading

3. *Monetary controls.* Exchange control, multiple-exchange rates, and advance-deposit requirements

Fiscal, commercial, and monetary controls are discussed in parts A, B, and C of this chapter, respectively. Part D considers the desirability of direct controls. Finally, part E considers briefly the question of whether direct controls should be imposed on a discriminatory or a nondiscriminatory basis.

Our entire discussion is based on three assumptions. First, the country imposing direct controls is assumed to suffer from a balance-of-payments deficit. This is justified by the fact that a balance-of-payments surplus is a less pressing problem. Nevertheless, the reader should have no difficulty in applying the present discussion to the case of a surplus country. Second, the rate of exchange is assumed fixed. Third, retaliation by foreign countries is disregarded. This last assumption is less justified since switching policies are, in general, beggar-thy-neighbor policies and are likely to provoke retaliation from foreign countries. However, the consideration of retaliation and counterretaliation would carry us too far afield. For our purposes, it is convenient to consider retaliation and counterretaliation as separate acts of policy and apply the present analysis to determine their effects.

PART A. FISCAL CONTROLS

Fiscal controls include all taxes and subsidies affecting particular items in the balance of payments. These items are usually the exports and imports of merchandise, mainly because such items lend themselves more readily to these fiscal devices. Invisible items, such as tourist expenditure, etc., are more difficult to cover by fiscal controls. In the case of capital movements these fiscal devices tend to break down completely unless they are reinforced by an effective system of exchange control.

14.1 INTRODUCTION

Taxes or subsidies may be imposed on exports or imports. Accordingly, there are four possible fiscal controls: import tax (tariff), export tax, import subsidy, and export subsidy. The most prominent fiscal devices are the import tax (tariff), whose aim is to switch domestic expenditure away from imports toward home goods, and the export subsidy, whose aim is to stimulate exports by switching foreign spending toward domestic output. The rest of our discussion is restricted to these two important fiscal devices (i.e., the tariff and the export subsidy).

In general, taxes and subsidies may be fixed legally in any of the following three ways:

1. *The ad valorem basis*, i.e., as a percentage on the *value* of the commodity imported or exported, inclusive or exclusive of transport cost

2. *The specific basis*, i.e., as an absolute amount of domestic currency per unit imported or exported
3. *The combined basis*, i.e., as a combination of an *ad valorem* tax (subsidy) *plus* a specific tax (subsidy)

Given the price of the commodity exported or imported, a specific tax or subsidy can always be converted into an equivalent *ad valorem* tax or subsidy. Nevertheless, the *ad valorem* incidence of a specific tax (subsidy) remains constant through time if, and only if, the price of the taxed (subsidized) commodity remains constant also. Now the price of a commodity may change for any number of reasons—some real (such as changes in tastes, technology, factor supplies, etc.) and some monetary (such as general inflation or deflation, exchange-rate adjustments, etc.). In particular, during an inflationary period when all prices tend to rise, the *ad valorem* incidence of a specific tax (subsidy) tends to fall. Similarly, during a deflationary period when all prices tend to fall, the *ad valorem* incidence of a specific tax (subsidy) tends to rise.

The *ad valorem* incidence of a specific tax (subsidy) is necessarily higher for cheaper qualities of a commodity than for the more expensive qualities. Conversely, for any given *ad valorem* tax (subsidy), the corresponding specific (per unit) tax (subsidy) is lower for cheaper qualities of a commodity than for the more expensive qualities.

Despite these differences between *ad valorem* and specific taxes and subsidies, the following discussion is based on the simplifying assumption that all taxes and subsidies are fixed on the *ad valorem* basis, for at any point in time there indeed exists a one-to-one correspondence between an *ad valorem* and a specific tax (subsidy). Any differences between them necessarily depend on future events, which our discussion does not cover.

Export and import taxes and subsidies are not normally levied indiscriminately on all imports or on all exports. An important feature of direct controls, as opposed to general switching policies, is their flexibility in operating differently on exports or imports of particular commodities, or on exports to and imports from particular foreign countries. This flexibility of direct controls enhances their effectiveness as an instrument of balance-of-payments adjustment. Nevertheless, because of the aggregative nature of the models we have been discussing so far, our further analysis will largely ignore this important aspect of direct controls.

14.2 THE SYMMETRY BETWEEN EXPORT AND IMPORT TAXES AND SUBSIDIES

Lerner (1936) showed that in a long-run, static equilibrium model (ignoring possible transitional difficulties such as unemployment and balance-of-payments disequilibria) a general export tax has the same effect as a general import tax of the same *ad valorem* percentage. This symmetry is also extended to subsidies. Thus, a general export subsidy has the same effect as a general import subsidy of the same *ad valorem* percentage.

Lerner's symmetry theorem is valid within the context of long-run equilibrium only. In the short run, which is relevant to our current analysis, an import tax tends to have similar effects on the balance of payments and national income as an export subsidy. Similarly, insofar as concerns their effects on the balance of payments and national income, an export tax is equivalent to an import subsidy. In other words, the import tax and the export subsidy operate in an expansionary, stimulating fashion and, in general, tend to improve the balance of payments as well, while the import subsidy and the export tax operate in an anti-inflationary, depressive manner and, in general, tend to worsen the balance of payments.

14.3 THE GENERAL EFFECTS OF TRADE TAXES AND SUBSIDIES

Trade taxes and subsidies have several effects. In addition to their effects on the balance of payments and national income (which are macroeconomic in nature and are studied below), trade taxes and subsidies have several other important microeconomic effects. In particular, trade taxes and subsidies influence the optimum allocation of resources between countries, the pattern of consumption, the distribution of income between countries through their effect on the terms of trade, the functional distribution of income within each country, etc. These microeconomic effects of trade taxes and subsidies belong traditionally to the pure theory of international trade and no attempt is made here to analyze them. In this respect, the reader may find the following works useful: Black (1959), Chacholiades (1973), Johnson (1971), Kindleberger (1968), Meade (1955), Mundell (1968), and Stern (1973).

Our present discussion is mainly concerned with the macroeconomic effects of trade taxes and subsidies, namely, their effects on national income and the balance of payments, and to a lesser extent, the terms of trade. In particular, the next section discusses the *direct* (or impact) effects of trade taxes and subsidies on the balance of payments and the terms of trade. The basic framework for this type of analysis is the partial equilibrium model of chap. 4. The effects of trade taxes and subsidies on national income and their *induced* effects on the balance of payments are discussed later on in sec. 14.5 within the context of the macroeconomic model of chaps. 10 and 11.

14.4 THE DIRECT EFFECTS OF TRADE TAXES AND SUBSIDIES ON THE BALANCE OF TRADE

Consider the partial equilibrium model of chap. 4. Assume that the rate of exchange is fixed and that country A is running a balance of payments deficit. What are the *direct* effects of an *ad valorem* import tax and an *ad valorem* export subsidy on A's balance of trade and the terms of trade?

The Direct Effects of an Import Tax (Tariff)

In general, the tariff reduces the volume of imports *and*, provided the foreign supply elasticity of exports is not infinite, the price paid to the foreign producers. Hence, both the balance of payments and the terms of trade of the country imposing the tariff tend to improve. This is illustrated in fig. 14.1, which shows the market for B-exportables. The solid curves show what happens before country A imposes the tariff. Equilibrium occurs at E_0. Country A imports $0Q_0$ units of B-exportables at a price (in pounds sterling) of $0P_0$. Thus, A's total expenditure on imports ($\equiv$ demand for pounds sterling) is given by the area of the rectangle $0Q_0 E_0 P_0$. When country A imposes the tariff, A's demand-for-imports schedule rotates counterclockwise through its horizontal-axis intercept (Q_3), as shown by the broken curve $P_3 Q_3$. This new demand-for-imports schedule gives the quantities of B-exportables demanded by country A at alternative prices (in pounds sterling) *net of the tariff*, i.e., prices which accrue to B's producers. Obviously, equilibrium moves to E_1. A's volume of imports falls to $0Q_1$, the price paid to B's producers falls to $0P_1$, and A's expenditure on imports falls to $0Q_1 E_1 P_1$. Hence, A's balance of payments improves by the amount shown by the shaded area. The actual tax per unit is given by the distance $E_1 E_2$ ($Q_1 E_2$ is the price paid by A's consumers while $Q_1 E_1$ is the price received by B's producers). The total tariff revenue accrued to A's authorities (revenue effect) is given by the area of the rectangle $E_1 E_2 P_2 P_1$.

To the extent that the price paid to B's producers falls, A's terms of trade improve. The reduction in the price paid to B's producers, and therefore the improvement in A's terms of trade, depends on two elasticities: A's elasticity of demand for imports and B's elasticity of supply of exports. In general, the *higher* A's elasticity of demand for imports and/or the *lower* B's elasticity of supply of exports, the larger the terms-of-trade improvement. In the limiting case where B's supply elasticity of exports is zero, or A's import-demand elasticity is infinite, the

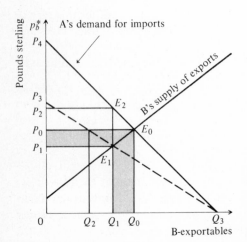

Figure 14.1 The direct effects of a tariff. When country A imposes a tariff, the demands-for-imports schedule rotates counterclockwise through its horizontal-axis intercept, as illustrated by the broken curve P_3Q_3. Equilibrium moves to E_1 and A's balance of payments improves by the amount shown by the shaded area.

terms-of-trade improvement is maximized—the total burden of the tariff is borne by the foreign producers. At the other extreme where B's supply elasticity of exports is infinite, or A's import-demand elasticity is zero, the terms-of-trade improvement is zero—the total burden of the tariff is borne by the domestic consumers.

The price paid by A's consumers and received by A's producers of B-exportables tends to increase after the tariff (except in the limiting case where B's supply elasticity of exports is zero). This encourages A's producers of B-exportables to expand their production (protection effect) and A's consumers to reduce their consumption (consumption effect).

Figure 14.1 is identical to fig. 4.3a. The latter shows the effects of a depreciation of the dollar (A's currency) relative to the pound sterling (B's currency). So far as concerns the volume of A's imports, the net price paid to B's producers of B-exportables, and A's expenditure on imports, an *ad valorem* tariff of, say, x percent is equivalent to an x percent depreciation of the dollar relative to the pound sterling. In this respect, it makes no difference whether A's importers pay a tariff or simply a higher price for B's currency. We therefore conclude that insofar as the market for B-exportables is concerned, a uniform *ad valorem* tariff levied on all imports is equivalent to a depreciation of the domestic currency (by the same percentage).

The Direct Effects of an Export Subsidy

In general, an export subsidy tends to increase the volume of exports and reduce the price paid by foreigners. Hence, while the terms-of-trade effect is in general unfavorable, the effect on the export revenue ($\equiv$ supply of foreign exchange) is indeterminate. In particular, it depends on the foreign elasticity of demand for imports. If the foreign demand for imports is elastic, the export revenue increases and the balance of payments improves. But if the foreign demand for imports is inelastic, the export revenue decreases and the balance of payments deteriorates. In the latter case, an export tax, not subsidy, is needed for a balance-of-payments improvement.

Figure 14.2 illustrates the case of an export subsidy. The solid curves show what happens before country A subsidizes exports. Equilibrium occurs at E_0. Country A exports $0Q_0$ units of A-exportables at a price (in pounds sterling) of $0P_0$. A's total export revenue is given by the area $0Q_0 E_0 P_0$. After the subsidy to exports, A's supply-of-exports schedule rotates clockwise (see broken curve) as if A's currency depreciated relative to B's. This new supply-of-exports schedule gives the quantities of A-exportables supplied by A's exporters at alternative prices (in pounds sterling) *exclusive of the subsidy*, i.e., prices paid by B's consumers. Equilibrium moves to E_1. A's volume of exports increases to $0Q_1$ but the price paid by B's consumers falls to $0P_1$. Whether A's balance of payments improves or deteriorates depends on whether the area of the rectangle $0Q_1 E_1 P_1$ is larger or smaller than the area $0Q_0 E_0 P_0$, and that depends on B's elasticity of demand for imports.

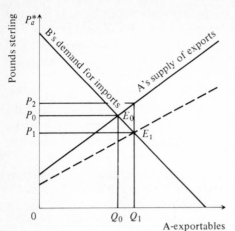

Figure 14.2 The direct effects of an export subsidy. A subsidy to exports causes the supply-of-exports schedule to rotate clockwise as if A's currency depreciated relative to B's. This is illustrated by the broken curve through E_1. Equilibrium moves to E_1. A's volume of exports increases to $0Q_1$ but the price paid by B's consumers falls to $0P_1$. Whether A's balance of payments improves or not depends on whether B's demand for imports is elastic or inelastic.

The price received by A's producers (inclusive of the subsidy) increases to $0P_2$. This encourages A's producers to increase their production, and at the same time causes A's consumers to decrease their consumption, of A-exportables.

Figure 14.2 is identical to fig. 4.3b. The latter shows the effects on the market for A-exportables of a depreciation of the dollar relative to the pound sterling. Obviously, insofar as concerns the volume of A's exports, the price paid by B's consumers for A-exportables, and A's export revenue, an x percent *ad valorem* export subsidy is equivalent to an x percent depreciation of the dollar relative to the pound sterling. Certainly it makes no difference to A's producers of A's exportables whether the higher price (in dollars) they receive for their exports to B's consumers is due to a subsidy to exports or a depreciation of the dollar relative to the pound sterling.

The Symmetry Between Import Taxes and Export Subsidies, and a Depreciation of the Domestic Currency

Given the preceding discussion, it becomes obvious that, insofar as concerns commodity trade, an x percent depreciation of a country's currency is equivalent to an x percent *ad valorem* tariff on all imports *plus* an x percent *ad valorem* subsidy to all exports.

14.5 THE EFFECTS OF TRADE TAXES AND SUBSIDIES ON NATIONAL INCOME AND THE BALANCE OF PAYMENTS

To study the effects of trade taxes and subsidies on national income and the balance of payments (including both the direct and the induced effects), we must turn to the model of chaps. 10 and 11. Recall that country A now specializes completely in the production of A-exportables, and B in B-exportables. Constant returns to scale prevail everywhere, and by an appropriate choice of units of measurement all prices are made equal to unity, that is, $p_a = p_b^* = R = 1$. Our approach is similar to the approach of chap. 11, part A, for an exchange-rate adjustment. That is, we first determine the direct effects on the aggregate demand for A's and B's products, and then use the foreign-trade multiplier theory of chap. 10 to determine the total effects on A's and B's national incomes and A's balance of trade.

The effects of a tariff depend crucially on how the government uses the tariff revenue. In general, the government may return the additional revenue to the consumers in the form of an income-tax reduction, or it may use it to increase its budget surplus (or reduce the budget deficit), or finally use it to finance government purchases of goods and services. These cases are treated separately below.

Similarly, the effects of an export subsidy depend crucially on the manner in which the subsidy is financed. In general, the government may impose an additional income tax to raise the necessary funds, or use already existing general revenues and thus reduce its budget surplus (or increase its budget deficit), or finally reduce its purchases of goods and services. Again these possibilities are considered separately below.

The Direct Effects of a Tariff

To determine the tariff's direct effects on the demand for A's products D_a, we must first determine its effect on A's balance of trade T_a and aggregate absorption Z_a. The direct effect of an *ad valorem* tariff t on A's expenditure on imports (ignoring the tariff revenue) is obviously given by

$$\left(\frac{\partial M_a}{\partial t}\right)_{t=0} = \left(\frac{\partial M_a}{\partial p_b}\right)\left(\frac{\partial p_b}{\partial t}\right) = M_a e_{ma} \tag{14.1}$$

(Note that $\partial p_b/\partial t = 1$, since by assumption B's supply of exports is infinitely elastic and thus $p_b = 1$ *before* the tariff is applied.)

When A's government redistributes the tariff revenue to its citizens in the form of an income-tax reduction, there is an additional increase in imports given by: tariff revenue $\times M_a'$. What is the tariff revenue equal to?

By definition, tariff revenue $\equiv T_r = tM_a$. Hence, $(\partial T_r/\partial t)_{t=0} = M_a + t(\partial M_a/\partial t) = M_a$. Accordingly, the effect on A's imports, following the redistribution of the tariff revenue, is given by $M_a M_a'$.

Finally, if the government actually spends the tariff revenue on goods and services, no direct effect on imports exists, since the usual assumption is that the goods and services so purchased by the government are produced solely by domestic resources.

What is the direct effect of the tariff on A's aggregate absorption? Here we have to distinguish again between three effects: (*a*) the terms-of-trade effect, (*b*) any autonomous change in government spending, and (*c*) any increase in private absorption, if the government redistributes the tariff revenue to its citizens.

Table 14.1 The direct effects of a tariff

(1) When the tariff revenue is saved by the government	(2) When the tariff revenue is redistributed	(3) When the government uses the tariff revenue to purchase goods and services
$\dfrac{\partial T_a}{\partial t} = -M_a e_{ma}$	$\dfrac{\partial T_a}{\partial t} = -M_a(e_{ma} + M'_a)$	$\dfrac{\partial T_a}{\partial t} = -M_a e_{ma}$
$\dfrac{\partial Z_a}{\partial t} = M_a(1 - Z'_a)$	$\dfrac{\partial Z_a}{\partial t} = M_a$	$\dfrac{\partial Z_a}{\partial t} = M_a(2 - Z'_a)$
$\dfrac{\partial D_a}{\partial t} = M_a(1 - Z'_a - e_{ma})$	$\dfrac{\partial D_a}{\partial t} = M_a(1 - M'_a - e_{ma})$	$\dfrac{\partial D_a}{\partial t} = M_a(2 - Z'_a - e_{ma})$
$\dfrac{\partial D_b}{\partial t} = M_a e_{ma}$	$\dfrac{\partial D_b}{\partial t} = M_a(e_{ma} + M'_a)$	$\dfrac{\partial D_b}{\partial t} = M_a e_{ma}$

Ignore for the moment the terms-of-trade effect. If the government spends the tariff revenue on goods and services, of course, A's absorption increases by the tariff revenue, that is, M_a. On the other hand, if A's authorities redistribute the tariff revenue, A's absorption increases by $M_a Z'_a$.

What is the terms-of-trade effect equal to? Noticing that A's price level is given by eq. (11.10) when $(1 + t)$ is substituted for R, we immediately conclude that the terms-of-trade effect is necessarily given by eq. (11.13), which is reproduced here for convenience:

$$\left(\frac{\partial Z_a}{\partial t}\right)_{t=0} = M_a\left(\frac{Y_a}{Z_a}\right)\left[\left(\frac{Z_a}{Y_a}\right) - Z'_a\right] > 0 \tag{14.2}$$

When the balance of trade is initially zero $(Y_a = Z_a)$, eq. (14.2) reduces to

$$\left(\frac{\partial Z_a}{\partial t}\right)_{t=0} = M_a(1 - Z'_a) > 0 \tag{14.3}$$

The preceding results are summarized in table 14.1 under the simplifying assumption that the balance of trade is initially zero. The total direct effect on the demand for A's products $(\partial D_a/\partial t)$ is given by the sum: $(\partial Z_a/\partial t) + (\partial T_a/\partial t)$. Similarly, $(\partial D_b/\partial t) = -(\partial T_a/\partial t)$ since $(\partial Z_b/\partial t) = 0$.

The Direct Effects of an Export Subsidy

The direct effects of an export subsidy s are summarized in table 14.2 under the simplifying assumption that A's balance of trade is zero initially. (Set $M_a = M_b = M$.) Consider the first column which shows the direct effects of the export subsidy when the government finances the subsidy by merely reducing its

Table 14.2 The direct effects of an export subsidy

(1) When the subsidy is financed by a reduction in the budget surplus	(2) When an income tax is imposed to finance the subsidy	(3) When the government finances the subsidy by reducing its purchases of goods and services
$\dfrac{\partial T_a}{\partial s} = -M_b(1 + e_{mb})$	$\dfrac{\partial T_a}{\partial s} = M_b M_a' - M_b(1 + e_{mb})$	$\dfrac{\partial T_a}{\partial s} = -M_b(1 + e_{mb})$
$\dfrac{\partial Z_a}{\partial s} = 0$	$\dfrac{\partial Z_a}{\partial s} = -M_b Z_a'$	$\dfrac{\partial Z_a}{\partial s} = -M_b$
$\dfrac{\partial Z_b}{\partial s} = -M_b(1 - Z_b')$	$\dfrac{\partial Z_b}{\partial s} = -M_b(1 - Z_b')$	$\dfrac{\partial Z_b}{\partial s} = -M_b(1 - Z_b')$
$\dfrac{\partial D_a}{\partial s} = -M_b(1 + e_{mb})$	$\dfrac{\partial D_a}{\partial s} = M_b(M_a' - Z_a' - 1 - e_{mb})$	$\dfrac{\partial D_a}{\partial s} = -M_b(2 + e_{mb})$
$\dfrac{\partial D_b}{\partial s} = M_b(e_{mb} + Z_b')$	$\dfrac{\partial D_b}{\partial s} = M_b(e_{mb} - M_a' + Z_b')$	$\dfrac{\partial D_b}{\partial s} = M_b(e_{mb} + Z_b')$

budget surplus. Obviously, the direct effect on A's balance of trade is due to the increase in B's expenditure on imports. Thus $(\partial T_a/\partial s) = [\partial(p_a^* M_b)/\partial p_a^*] \times (\partial p_a^*/\partial s) = -M_b(1 + e_{mb})$. There is no direct effect on A's absorption here since the prices paid by A's residents for A-exportables and B-exportables remain constant. Hence, $(\partial Z_a/\partial s) = 0$. Nevertheless, there is a terms-of-trade effect on B's absorption since the price B's consumers pay for A-exportables falls by the amount of the subsidy. The algebraic expression for this term is obtained directly from eq. (11.14). Finally, the total direct effect on the demand for A's products $(\partial D_a/\partial s)$ is given by the sum: $(\partial Z_a/\partial s) + (\partial T_a/\partial s)$. Similarly, $(\partial D_b/\partial s) = (\partial Z_b/\partial s) - (\partial T_a/\partial s)$.

Consider now the second column of table 14.2. The various effects here are obtained by adding the effects of an income tax in country A (equal to the total subsidy) to the corresponding effects of the first column. Since total subsidy $\equiv sM_b$, it follows that

$$\left[\frac{\partial(\text{total subsidy})}{\partial s}\right]_{s=0} = M_b + s\left(\frac{\partial M_b}{\partial s}\right) = M_b$$

Accordingly, the direct effects of A's income tax are (a) a reduction in A's absorption by $Z_a' M_b$ and (b) a reduction in A's imports by $M_a' M_b$.

Finally, when A's government reduces its spending on goods and services in order to finance the export subsidy (column 3), the various direct effects are again obtained from those of column (1) by merely adding the direct effects of a reduction in the purchases of goods and services by A's government. The only additional effect is, of course, a reduction in Z_a by M_b.

The Overall Effects of the Tariff and the Export Subsidy on National Incomes and the Balance of Trade

Given the direct effects of the tariff and the export subsidy, we can easily determine the overall effects on A's and B's national incomes and the balance of trade. Thus the effects of the tariff are computed as follows:

$$\frac{dY_a}{dt} = k_{aa}\left(\frac{\partial D_a}{\partial t}\right) + k_{ab}\left(\frac{\partial D_b}{\partial t}\right) \tag{14.4}$$

$$\frac{dY_b}{dt} = k_{ba}\left(\frac{\partial D_a}{\partial t}\right) + k_{bb}\left(\frac{\partial D_b}{\partial t}\right) \tag{14.5}$$

$$\frac{dT_a}{dt} = -\left(\frac{\partial Z_a}{\partial t}\right) + (1 - Z'_a)\left(\frac{dY_a}{dt}\right)$$

$$= \left(\frac{\partial Z_b}{\partial t}\right) - (1 - Z'_b)\left(\frac{dY_b}{dt}\right) \tag{14.6}$$

The same equations are used, of course, for the computation of the overall effects of the export subsidy, with the minor difference that all derivatives are now taken with respect to s—not t. The results are summarized in table 14.3.

From the results of table 14.3 we can formulate the following conclusions:

1. The imposition of a tariff always raises domestic income and employment (i.e., irrespective of the manner in which the tariff revenue is disposed of).
2. A tariff has a favorable effect on the balance of payments if, and only if, its effect on foreign incomes and employment is adverse (i.e., if, and only if, foreign incomes and employment fall).
3. The conditions under which the tariff has adverse effects on foreign incomes and employment $(dY_b/dt < 0)$ and therefore a favorable effect on the balance of payments $(dT_a/dt > 0)$ are:
   (a) When the tariff revenue is saved by the government:

$$-e_{ma} > M'_a$$

   (b) When the government redistributes the tariff revenue to its citizens:

$$-e_{ma} > M'_a + \left(\frac{M'_a}{1 - Z'_a}\right)$$

   (c) When the government spends the tariff revenue on goods and services:

$$-e_{ma} > M'_a + \left(\frac{M'_a}{1 - Z'_a}\right)$$

Accordingly, the condition for a favorable balance-of-payments effect is more stringent when the government does not save the tariff revenue than when it does.
4. Assume that the foreign demand for imports is elastic, that is, $e_{mb} < -1$. (A less-stringent condition is $e_{mb} < -Z'_b$.) Then the export subsidy has always an

Table 14.3 The overall effects of the tariff and the export subsidy

(1) Type of policy	(2) Overall effect on Y_a	(3) Overall effect on Y_b	(4) Overall effect on T_a
1. *Tariff*			
(*a*) When tariff revenue is saved by government	$\dfrac{dY_a}{dt} = \left(\dfrac{m_a m_b M_a}{\Delta}\right)\big[(1-Z_b)(1-Z_a) + M_b'(1-Z_a) - e_{ma}(1-Z_b)\big] > 0$	$\dfrac{dY_b}{dt} = \left[\dfrac{m_a m_b M_a(1-Z_a')}{\Delta}\right] \times (M_a' + e_{ma})$	$\dfrac{dT_a}{dt} = -(1-Z_b')\left(\dfrac{dY_b}{dt}\right)$
(*b*) When tariff revenue is redistributed	$\dfrac{dY_a}{dt} = \left(\dfrac{m_a m_b M_a}{\Delta}\right) \times \big[(1-Z_b')(1-M_a'-e_{ma}) + M_b'\big] > 0$	$\dfrac{dY_b}{dt} = \left(\dfrac{m_a m_b M_a}{\Delta}\right) \times \big[M_a' + (1-Z_b')(e_{ma}+M_a')\big]$	$\dfrac{dT_a}{dt} = -(1-Z_b')\left(\dfrac{dY_b}{dt}\right)$
(*c*) When the government spends the tariff revenue on goods and services	$\dfrac{dY_a}{dt} = \left(\dfrac{m_a m_b M_a}{\Delta}\right)\big[(2-Z_a')(1-Z_b') + M_b'(2-Z_a') - e_{ma}(1-Z_b')\big] > 0$	$\dfrac{dY_b}{dt} = \left(\dfrac{m_a m_b M_a}{\Delta}\right) \times \big[M_a'(2-Z_a') + (1-Z_a')e_{ma}\big]$	$\dfrac{dT_a}{dt} = -(1-Z_b')\left(\dfrac{dY_b}{dt}\right)$
2. *Export subsidy*			
(*a*) When budget surplus is reduced	$\dfrac{dY_a}{ds} = \left(\dfrac{m_a m_b M_b}{\Delta}\right) \times (1-Z_b')(-M_b'-1-e_{mb})$	$\dfrac{dY_b}{ds} = \left(\dfrac{m_a m_b M_b}{\Delta}\right)\big[(1-Z_a')(e_{mb}+Z_b') - M_a'(1-Z_b')\big] < 0$	$\dfrac{dT_a}{ds} = (1-Z_a)\left(\dfrac{dY_a}{ds}\right)$
(*b*) When income tax is imposed	$\dfrac{dY_a}{ds} = \left(\dfrac{m_a m_b M_b}{\Delta}\right)\big[(1-Z_b')(M_a' - Z_a'-1-e_{mb}) + M_b'(Z_b'-Z_a'-1)\big]$	$\dfrac{dY_b}{ds} = \left(\dfrac{m_a m_b M_b}{\Delta}\right)\big[-M_a'(1-Z_b') + (e_{mb}+Z_b')(1-Z_a') - M_a'\big] < 0$	$\dfrac{dT_a}{ds} = \left[\dfrac{m_a m_b M_b(1-Z_b')}{\Delta}\right] \times \big[(1-Z_a)(-1-e_{mb}-M_b') + M_a'\big]$
(*c*) When government purchases of goods and services are reduced	$\dfrac{dY_a}{ds} = \left(\dfrac{m_a m_b M_b}{\Delta}\right) \times \big[(1-Z_b')(-M_b'-2-e_{mb}) - M_b'\big]$	$\dfrac{dY_b}{ds} = \left(\dfrac{m_a m_b M_b}{\Delta}\right)\big[(1-Z_a')(e_{mb}+Z_b') - M_a'(2-Z_b')\big] < 0 \quad (e_{mb} < -1)$	$\dfrac{dT_a}{ds} = \left[\dfrac{m_a m_b M_b(1-Z_b')}{\Delta}\right] \times \big[(1-Z_a)(-1-M_b'-e_{mb}) + M_a'\big]$

adverse effect on foreign incomes and employment, that is, $(dY_b/ds) < 0$, irrespective of the method of financing the export subsidy.

5. When the export subsidy is financed through a reduction in the budget surplus, the effect on domestic income and employment as well as the balance of payment is favorable if and only if $-e_{mb} > 1 + M'_b$.

6. When the export subsidy is financed through a general income tax, the condition for a favorable balance-of-payments effect is $-e_{mb} > 1 + M'_b - [M'_a/(1 - Z'_a)]$ and the condition for a favorable effect on domestic income and employment $(dY_a/ds > 0)$ is $-e_{mb} > 1 + M'_b + (Z'_a - M'_a) + [M'_b Z'_a/(1 - Z'_b)]$. Obviously, the latter condition is more stringent than the former.

7. When the government reduces its purchases of goods and services in order to finance the export subsidy, the condition for a favorable balance-of-payments effect is $-e_{mb} > 1 + M'_b - [M'_a/(1 - Z'_a)]$, that is, it is the same as in the case where the government finances the export subsidy through a general income tax. The condition for a favorable effect on domestic income and employment is more stringent: $-e_{mb} > 1 + M'_b + [1/m_b(1 - Z'_b)]$.

8. As noted earlier, there is a symmetry between import taxes and subsidies, on the one hand, and a depreciation of the domestic currency, on the other. This symmetry may be verified here also. Thus, the reader can easily show that the combined effects of a tariff and an export subsidy are identical to the effects of a depreciation of the dollar. The only requirement is that the use of the tariff revenue should be symmetrical to the financing of the export subsidy. That is, if the tariff revenue is redistributed to the citizens, the subsidy must be financed through a general income tax, etc.

PART B. COMMERCIAL CONTROLS

Commercial controls include quantitative restrictions on the physical volume or value of imports (*import quota*) or exports (*export quota*), and state trading. The import quota is the most common commercial device, and the following discussion is restricted to it. The effects of state-trading monopolies are similar to those of quotas and fiscal controls. For this reason, state-trading monopolies are not explicitly discussed.

14.6 IMPORT QUOTAS

A quantitative restriction on the imports of a particular commodity may be administered either through an *open* or *global quota*, or through the issue of import licenses. A global quota allows a specified amount of imports of a particular commodity per year (or some other time period) but does not specify where the product may come from or who is entitled to import it. As soon as the specified amount is actually imported, further imports into the country are prohibited for the rest of the year.

The disadvantages of a global quota are obvious. Merchants (domestic importers and foreign exporters) will rush to get their shipments into the country before the limit is reached. Those who are lucky enough to get their goods into the country in time enjoy abnormal profits—domestic prices rise because of the increased scarcity. Those who are late suffer losses—storage costs and reshipment to the country of origin may even be involved. Goods originating in distant places are discriminated against in view of the longer transport time involved and the higher expected loss (because of higher transport costs) in case they arrive late. Also, large importing firms which are able to order large quantities on short notice (because of trade connections and good credit) have a distinct advantage over small importers. Finally, the rush to get commodities into the quota country as soon as possible may result in greater price fluctuation over the year, especially in the case of perishable goods.

To avoid the chaos of a global quota, governments usually issue import licenses which they either sell to the importers at a competitive price (or simply a license fee) or just give away on a first-come, first-served basis. The licenses may or may not specify the source from which the commodity is to be procured.

For every import quota there is an *equivalent tariff*. Consider again fig. 14.1. We saw earlier how A's government imposes a tariff which (a) reduces the volume of imports from $0Q_0$ to $0Q_1$, (b) raises the price paid by domestic consumers from $0P_0$ to $0P_2$, (c) lowers the price paid to the foreign producers from $0P_0$ to $0P_1$, and (d) generates a tariff revenue given by the area of the rectangle $P_1 E_1 E_2 P_2$. Exactly the same result could be accomplished by imposing an import quota of $0Q_1$ and auctioning off import licenses to domestic importers. The license fee per unit imported will be bid up to $E_1 E_2$, which is equal to the actual per unit tariff considered earlier. With the exception of the insignificant difference that the government's revenue (quota profit) is now collected in the form of a license fee instead of a tariff, the economic effects of the import quota are identical to those of the equivalent tariff. But this is not always the case as there are some important differences between an import quota and a tariff.

One considerable difference between an import quota and a tariff lies with the revenue effect. In the case of the tariff, the amount $P_1 E_1 E_2 P_2$ will unquestionably accrue to the government in the form of tariff revenue. In the case of an import quota, the outcome is not so certain. If the government actually auctions off import licenses to the highest bidder, Adam Smith's invisible hand will make sure that the amount $P_1 E_1 E_2 P_2$ accrues to the domestic government. Otherwise, depending on how the licensing system works, the amount $P_1 E_1 E_2 P_2$ may accrue to the domestic importers, consumers, or even government officials (who may have to be bribed in order to issue the necessary licenses), or the foreign exporters, or even the foreign governments. Thus, if the importers organize themselves into a monopoly while the foreign exporters remain unorganized, the importers are likely to get the profit. Of course, the domestic government, through an effective price control, may prevent the importers from raising the price of imports to consumers, and in that case all the profit accrues to the consumers. On the other hand, the foreign exporters may get organized while the domestic importers do not. In this case, the foreign exporters reap abnormal profits. Finally, it is not inconceivable for foreign governments to impose an equivalent export tax and collect all the revenue, assuming that neither the exporters nor the importers are organized and that the domestic government gives the import licenses away without any fee. On these points and others, see Heuser (1939) and Meade (1951, pp. 282–286).

Whether the quota profit accrues to the *domestic* importers, consumers, or government, on the one hand, or the *foreign* exporters or government, on the other, is important to the restricting country's balance of payments and terms of trade. Thus, if the quota profit accrues to the foreigners, the terms of trade of the restricting country necessarily worsen, and assuming that the demand for imports is inelastic and imports are restricted by volume, the expenditure on imports *increases*.

Kindleberger (1968, pp. 132–134; 1975, pp. 8–9) emphasizes another important difference between a quota and a tariff. Even though for every import quota there is always an equivalent tariff, the practical estimation of the equivalent-tariff rate is not easy because the supply and demand curves are not known in advance. In addition, the foreign supply of exports may be perfectly inelastic or very inelastic. If the object is to raise the domestic price of imports in order to protect the domestic producers, an import quota would be more effective. Kindleberger illustrates his point with a historical example. When the increase in the U.S. tariff diverted the bumper 1929–1930 Australian wheat crop to Europe, the French, who wanted higher wheat prices for French peasants, had to impose an import quota—no simple tariff could keep the Australian wheat out because of the inelastic supply of wheat from Australia to Europe once wheat was excluded from America.

A third and final difference between an import quota and a tariff is this: an import quota may convert a potential into an actual monopoly while a tariff does not. Consider fig. 14.3. A's domestic industry of B-exportables is a potential monopoly. The solid curves AC and MC are the monopolist's average and marginal cost curves, respectively. The world price of B-exportables is p_0, and this is also the equilibrium price in A before A's government interferes with tariffs and quotas (B's supply of exports is infinitely elastic at p_0). Thus, A's consumers consume $p_0 H$ units with $p_0 G$ produced by A's potential monopolist and GH units imported from country B. When country A imposes a tariff of $p_0 p_w$, the world price inclusive of an *ad valorem* tariff is p_w, which is also the current equilibrium price of B-exportables in A. A's consumers now consume $0Q_2$, with $0Q_1$ units produced by A's potential monopolist and $Q_1 Q_2$ units imported from country B.

Suppose now that the tariff is converted into an import quota allowing only $Q_1 Q_2$ units to be imported from B. Displace the AR curve to the left by $Q_1 Q_2$, as shown by the broken AR' curve. The relevant marginal revenue curve for A's monopolist is given by the broken curve $SEVUWFMR$. Hence he maximizes his profits at E (i.e., the point of intersection between the marginal cost and the

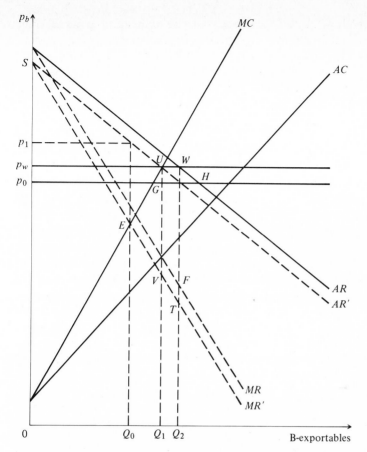

Figure 14.3 Potential monopoly converted to actual monopoly under import quota. B's supply of exports of B-exportables is infinitely elastic at p_0. When country A imposes the tariff $p_0 p_w$, the equilibrium price in A increases to p_w, and A's consumers consume $0Q_2$ of which $0Q_1$ is produced domestically by the potential monopolist and $Q_1 Q_2$ is imported from B. If A converts the tariff into a quota allowing only $Q_1 Q_2$ units to be imported from B, A's monopolist reduces his production to $0Q_0$ and raises his price to p_1, since his marginal revenue curve is now given by the broken line $SEVUWFMR$.

marginal revenue curves). A's monopolist reduces his production to $0Q_0$ and raises his price to p_1. For further details, see Bhagwati (1965), Heuser (1939, chap. XI), and Kindleberger (1968, app. E).

14.7 THE TARIFF QUOTA

Imports may also be restricted by means of a *tariff quota*. Under this scheme a certain amount of the commodity is imported free of any duty (or on the payment of a low import duty) while a heavier import duty is imposed on additional quantities. Thus, the ordinary tariff is the special case of the tariff quota in which the "quota" part is zero. Similarly, the ordinary import quota is also the special case of the tariff quota where the import duty of any additional quantities beyond the "quota" part is prohibitively high. The tariff quota does not raise any additional issues beyond those already discussed.

14.8 EXPORT QUOTAS

It is also possible that a country may desire to control directly the volume (or value) of exports. It may, therefore, decree that only a limited quantity or value of a particular commodity may be exported per unit of time. For this purpose the government may issue export licenses and either sell them to the country's exporters at a competitive price (or a license fee) or just give away on a first-come, first-served basis. In general, an export quota causes the price of the restricted commodity to rise in the foreign markets and fall in the domestic market. Thus, an export quota tends to create a margin between the price which the exporters in the restricting country are willing to sell the commodity and the price which the foreign consumers are willing to pay for it. This margin may accrue to the government of the restricting country in the form of export-license fees. If the government of the restricting country does not charge a fee for the issue of export licenses, the "margin" may accrue to domestic producers, middlemen, foreign consumers, or even as bribes to government officials issuing the licenses. The restricting country's export revenue (in foreign currency) tends to rise only if the foreign demand for imports is inelastic.

PART C. MONETARY CONTROLS

Monetary controls include exchange control, multiple-exchange rates, and advance-deposit requirements. This part discusses these monetary devices briefly.

14.9 EXCHANGE CONTROL

A deficit country may attempt to solve its balance-of-payments problem by means of exchange control; i.e., by arbitrarily *rationing* the limited supply of foreign exchange among all potential buyers at the prevailing rate of exchange. For this purpose, the deficit country may establish an *exchange-control authority*, and require by law all citizens who receive payment from abroad to sell their foreign currency to the exchange-control authority and all citizens who make payments abroad to buy the foreign currency they need from the exchange-control authority, at the official rate. Needless to say, the exchange-control authority will have to adopt an inventory policy with respect to foreign exchange and smooth out any seasonal variations in export revenue and/or expenditure on imports. The object is to keep the *flows* of sales and purchases in line *in the long run.*

An effective system of exchange control requires an elaborate bureaucratic machinery to oversee all foreign-exchange dealings. Both exporters and importers have an interest in evading the law—a fact which often leads to black markets in which the domestic currency is traded against foreign exchange at depreciated rates. An elaborate *postal control* is needed to prevent foreign-exchange transactions by mail. Tourists and other travellers should not be allowed to carry currency out of, or into, the country, except in limited amounts. All barter transactions should be banned. For this reason, an extensive bureaucratic inquiry at the ports is needed to determine the way all imports and exports are financed. Further, the exchange-control authority must make sure that licensed importers actually use their foreign-exchange allotment for the legal purpose for which it is approved. Importers should not be allowed to overstate the price of imported goods and use the surplus of foreign exchange for illegal purposes. Also, exporters should not be permitted to declare an artificially low price for the exported commodities. Finally, transfers between nonresident accounts (i.e., accounts with the domestic banking system held by foreigners and which are freely convertible) and resident accounts (i.e., accounts with the domestic banking system held by domestic residents which are not convertible) must also be controlled. Domestic importers should not be allowed to pay for their imports by means of a transfer to nonresident accounts, unless such a transfer is consistent with the exchange-control objectives. Similarly, exporters who are paid by means of a transfer from nonresident to resident accounts, and therefore have no foreign exchange to surrender to the exchange-control authority, must provide proof that they were actually paid by means of such a transfer.

The administration of an effective system of exchange control is not an easy matter. It is difficult, perhaps impossible, to plug all loopholes. For instance, how can the exchange-control authority prevent all leads and lags in international payments?

14.10 MULTIPLE-EXCHANGE RATES

The preceding discussion of exchange control assumes that all foreign-exchange transactions with the exchange-control authority are carried out at a single official rate of exchange. But there is no logical necessity for a uniform rate. The exchange-control authority may establish different rates for different transactions. For instance, the exchange-control authority may establish relatively high rates for imported luxury goods and relatively low rates for necessities. Similar arrangements may be established for different classes of exports. For our purposes, it is sufficient to note that a system of multiple-exchange rates is necessarily equivalent to a system of trade taxes and subsidies.

14.11 ADVANCE-DEPOSIT REQUIREMENTS

Imports may also be discouraged by requiring importers to deposit funds in a commercial bank in an amount equal to some specified percentage of the value of the imported goods for some specified period prior to the receipt of the goods. Such advance-deposit requirements impose an additional cost to the importer who must tie up his funds or borrow the necessary amount. Hence, they are similar to import taxes. One important reason for the adoption of this device is the comparative ease with which it can be administered, especially when international agreements hamper manipulation of other direct controls.

PART D. THE DESIRABILITY OF CONTROLS

How desirable is the use of direct controls by a deficit country instead of a general switching policy such as devaluation? Johnson (1958b) points out that two important issues are involved here. The first involves the effectiveness of controls, while the second involves their welfare effects, relative to devaluation.

As we have seen, devaluation is equivalent to an import tax plus an export subsidy. Further, an import tax necessarily reduces the need for foreign exchange, while an export subsidy increases the supply of foreign exchange only if the foreign demand for imports is elastic. Accordingly, an import restriction by itself tends to be more effective relative to devaluation if an export subsidy actually reduces the country's export revenue (i.e., if the foreign demand for imports is inelastic). In the latter case, i.e., when the foreign demand for imports is inelastic, exports should also be restricted—not encouraged as the export subsidy and devaluation do. On the other hand, an export subsidy by itself is always less effective relative to devaluation, since it fails to take into account the favorable effect of devaluation on imports. In general, controls are more effective than devaluation, mainly because of their flexibility. Thus, export and import commodities may be broken down into different classes according to their supply and demand elasticities. Then each class of commodities may be taxed or subsidized at different rates such as to maximize the balance-of-payments improvement.

Turn now to the second issue which concerns the effects on welfare. Alexander (1951) argues that the choice between controls and devaluation depends on the relation between the existing and the optimum degree of trade restriction.† If the current degree of controls falls short of the optimum degree (i.e., if the country possesses unexploited monopoly and monopsony power), then controls should be

---

† The optimum degree of trade restriction depends on real factors and ethical beliefs. Its study lies beyond the scope of this book, but the interested reader is referred to Chacholiades (1973), chap. 20, and the selected bibliography at the end of that chapter.

preferred until the optimum degree is reached. On the other hand, if the current degree of controls lies beyond the optimum degree, devaluation should be preferred. In fact, in the latter case trade restrictions should be relaxed until the optimum degree is reached, with further devaluation of the domestic currency being used to eliminate the resultant unfavorable effects on the balance of payments. This is the familiar optimum tariff argument.

Alexander's thesis is interesting but has several drawbacks. In the first place, the optimum degree of trade restriction is impossible to determine. But even if this were not the case and this optimum degree could be easily and uniquely determined, the case is still not proven that trade restriction ought to be preferred over devaluation, for once the optimum degree of trade restriction is reached, the country must turn, according to Alexander, to exchange-rate adjustments. Thus, even though Alexander's argument may be accepted in principle, the *continuous* use of trade restriction must be ruled out unless it were true that every balance-of-payments deficit necessarily created the required divergence between the existing and optimum degree of trade restriction which is, of course, absurd. Nevertheless, the balance-of-payments deficit may be offered as an excuse in intensifying trade restriction until the optimum degree is reached. Other countries may feel sympathetic toward the deficit country and may not retaliate.

PART E. DISCRIMINATION, THE BALANCE OF PAYMENTS, AND ECONOMIC WELFARE

Suppose that direct controls are employed by the countries of the world to keep their balances of payments in equilibrium. How should these controls be applied in order to minimize their economic inefficiencies? In particular, should the direct controls be imposed on a discriminatory or a nondiscriminatory basis? A theory which originated with Frisch (1947), Ekker (1950), and Flemming (1951) provides a convincing demonstration against the nondiscriminatory application of direct controls. An elegant statement of this theory is provided by Meade (1955, chap. XXXIV). A rigorous development of this theory is beyond the scope of this book. For the convenience of the reader, however, the main propositions as set out by Meade are summarized without proof below.

Consider a number of countries—A, B, C, D, etc. In each country, the money-wage rate, costs, and prices are all fixed in terms of the domestic currency. All rates of exchange are also fixed. Each country maintains internal balance by means of fiscal and monetary policy at all times. Currently, all balances of payments are kept in equilibrium by some arbitrary network of import restrictions imposed by the otherwise-deficit countries. What marginal adjustments should be made to the existing network of import restrictions so as to maintain external balance in all countries but raise economic welfare at the same time?

Subject to various assumptions and qualifications, Meade (1955, pp. 547–553) enumerates four principles which must be followed in the construction of an optimum network of import restrictions. These principles are:

1. The protective incidence† of the import restrictions of a country, say A, must be the same for all commodities imported from any other country, say B.
2. If two countries are restricting imports from each other, then they should simultaneously relax their import restrictions on each other's products until one of them has completely removed its restrictions on imports from the other.
3. If there are any three countries A, B, and C such that C is restricting imports from B, B from A, and A from C, then they should all relax their restrictions on imports from each other simultaneously until one of the countries has completely removed its restrictions on imports from the other two countries.
4. Consider any three countries A, B, and C such that C is restricting imports from both A and B, and B from A. Assume that principles (1) to (3) are fulfilled. Then C should discriminate in her import restrictions against A and in favor of B, until the excess of the protective incidence of C's restrictions on A's products over the protective incidence of C's restrictions on B's products is equal to the protective incidence of B's restrictions on imports from A.

SELECTED BIBLIOGRAPHY

Alexander, S. S. (1951). "Devaluation Versus Import Restriction as an Instrument for Improving Foreign Trade Balance." *IMF Staff Papers* vol. 1 (April), pp. 379–396.

Bernstein, E. M. (1950). "Some Economic Aspects of Multiple Exchange Rates." *IMF Staff Papers*, vol. 1, pp. 224–237.

Bhagwati, J. (1965). "On the Equivalence of Tariffs and Quotas." In R. E. Baldwin et al. (Eds.), *Trade, Growth and the Balance of Payments, Essays in Honor of Gottfried Haberler.* Rand-McNally and Company, Chicago, Ill.

Black, J. (1959). "Arguments for Tariffs." *Oxford Economic Papers*, N.S. 11, pp. 191–208.

Chacholiades, M. (1973). *The Pure Theory of International Trade.* Aldine Publishing Company, Chicago, Ill., pt. VII.

Ekker, M. H. (1950). "Equilibrium of International Trade and International Monetary Compensations." *Weltwirtschaftliches Archiv*, vol. 64, pp. 204–254.

Fieleke, N. S. (1971). *The Welfare Effects of Controls Over Capital Exports from the United States.* Essays in International Finance, no. 82, International Finance Section, Princeton University, Princeton, N.J.

Fleming, J. M. (1951). "On Making the Best of Balance of Payments Restrictions on Imports." *Economic Journal*, vol. 61 (March), pp. 48–71. Reprinted in AEA *Readings in International Economics.* Richard D. Irwin, Inc., Homewood, Ill., 1968.

Frisch, R. (1947). "On the Need for Forecasting a Multilateral Balance of Payments." *American Economic Review* vol. 37 (September), pp. 535–551.

---

† The protective incidence of the import restriction is defined to be the *ad valorem* rate of excess of the price in the importing country over the price in the exporting country.

Haight, F. A. (1935). *French Import Quotas.* P. S. King and Staples, London.

Hemming, M. F. W., and W. M. Corden (1958). "Import Restriction as an Instrument of Balance-of-Payments Policy." *Economic Journal,* vol. 48 (September), pp. 483–510.

Heuser, H. (1939). *Control of International Trade.* George Routledge and Sons, Ltd., London.

Johnson, H. G. (1958a). *International Trade and Economic Growth: Studies in Pure Theory.* George Allen and Unwin, Ltd., London, chap. VI. Reprinted in AEA *Readings in International Economics.* Richard D. Irwin, Inc., Homewood, Ill., 1968.

——— (1958b). "The Balance of Payments." *Pakistan Economic Journal,* vol. VIII, no. 2 (June), pp. 16–28. Reprinted in H. G. Johnson (Ed.), *Money, Trade, and Economic Growth.* George Allen and Unwin, Ltd., London, chap. I, 1962.

——— (1971). *Aspects of the Theory of Tariffs.* George Allen and Unwin, Ltd., London.

Kindleberger, C. P. (1968). *International Economics,* 4th ed. Richard D. Irwin, Inc., Homewood, Ill., chaps. 7 and 8.

——— (1975). "Quantity and Price, Especially in Financial Markets." *The Quarterly Review of Economics and Business* (Summer), pp. 7–19.

Lerner, A. P. (1936). "The Symmetry Between Import and Export Taxes." *Economica,* vol. III, no. 11 (August), pp. 306–313. Reprinted in AEA *Readings in International Economics.* Richard D. Irwin, Inc., Homewood, Ill., 1968.

Meade, J. E. (1951). *The Theory of International Economic Policy,* vol. I, *The Balance of Payments.* Oxford University Press, Inc., New York, pt. V.

——— (1955). *The Theory of International Economic Policy,* vol. II, *Trade and Welfare.* Oxford University Press, Inc., New York, chap. XXXIV.

Mikesell, R. F. (1954). *Foreign Exchange in the Postwar World.* Twentieth Century Fund, New York.

Modigliani, F. (1966). "International Capital Movements, Fixed Parities, and Monetary and Fiscal Policies" (mimeographed).

Mundell, R. A. (1968). *International Economics.* The Macmillan Company, New York, pt. I.

Schlesinger, E. R. (1952). *Multiple Exchange Rates and Economic Development.* Princeton University Press, Princeton, N.J.

Sohmen, E. (1969). *Flexible Exchange Rates,* revised ed. The University of Chicago Press, Chicago, Ill.

Stern, R. M. (1973). *The Balance of Payments.* Aldine Publishing Company, Chicago, Ill., chap. 9.

Yeager, L. B. (1966). *International Monetary Relations.* Harper and Row, Publishers, New York, chap. 7.

MONEY AND CAPITAL
MOVEMENTS

FIFTEEN

THE GOLD STANDARD:
I. THE CLASSICAL APPROACH†

Two centuries ago, the Scottish philosopher David Hume argued that there was an automatic self-correcting " price-specie-flow mechanism " at work which guaranteed balance-of-payments equilibrium.‡ Hume's explanation was that gold flows tended to produce price-level changes (according to the quantity theory) which in turn tended to restore equilibrium in the balance of payments and eventually check the flow of gold. The purpose of this chapter is to study Hume's mechanism rigorously.§

15.1 THE USE OF THE EQUATION OF EXCHANGE IN AN OPEN ECONOMY

The classical doctrine as expounded by many economists since its development by David Hume depends on the quantity theory of money. In particular, the equation

---

† Adapted from Chacholiades (1972).

‡ See Allen (1965, chap. 1), Blaug (1962, pp. 10–12), Bloomfield (1950, pp. 253–254), Clement, Pfister, and Rothwell (1967, pp. 216–219), Haberler (1959, pp. 26–29), Kindleberger (1958, chap. 4), Krueger (1969, p. 5), Lerner (1946, chap. 28), Samuelson (1961, p. 713), Scammell (1964, pp. 33–37), Scitovsky (1967, pp. 80–82), Vanek (1964, pp. 86–94), Viner (1937, pp. 292–293), Walter (1968, pp. 337–339), and Yeager (1966, pp. 63–64).

§ Several excellent surveys are available. See, for instance, Viner (1937) and Iversen (1935).

of exchange $(MV = PQ)$—which is used to determine the price level P in a closed economy given the full-employment rate of output Q, the money supply M, and the income velocity of circulation of money V—is often thought to apply to an open economy as well. Thus, an open economy's price level is taken to be proportional to its money supply.† Accordingly, the argument goes, under a regime of an international gold standard, gold flows tend to lower the price level of the gold-exporting country and raise the price level of the gold-importing country; these price-level changes tend to restore equilibrium in the balance of payments and eventually check the flow of gold.

Whatever the validity of the hypothesis that the price level is proportional to the money supply in a closed economy, such an hypothesis cannot be valid for an open economy. Prices are determined by supply and demand, and for a world economy it is *international* supply and demand relations that determine prices. The "mechanical application" of the quantity theory in each country separately ignores this important aspect of the problem.

To gain further insight into the classical approach, we must seek some valid interpretation of the equation of exchange. Three possibilities come easily to mind:

1. The product MV may be considered as an *aggregate demand for the open economy's output*.
2. The product MV may be considered as the open economy's *aggregate expenditure* (or absorption). This interpretation we call the *aggregate-expenditure approach*.
3. Finally, the ratio PQ/V may be considered as the demand for money. This interpretation we call the *demand-for-money approach*.

The first and second interpretations come to the same thing when the economy is closed. But when the economy is open they mean different things. Thus, in terms of the terminology and symbols adopted in chap. 10, the first interpretation sets $MV = D$, while the second interpretation sets $MV = Z$.

The first interpretation makes sense for a closed economy,‡ but not for an open economy. As we have seen, in an open economy exports are part of aggregate demand D, and no economist would argue that exports are *directly* determined by the domestic money supply. We therefore discard the first interpretation as invalid for an open economy.

The second and third interpretations are acceptable to the extent, of course, that the quantity theory of money is valid for a closed economy. Even then, however, the equation of exchange cannot be used directly to determine any price level. Instead, either of assumptions (2) or (3) above must be built into a dynamic model from which the equation of exchange emerges as a long-run equilibrium

† See, for instance, Haberler (1959, pp. 26–29), Vanek (1964, pp. 86–94), and Walter (1968, pp. 337–339).

‡ See Hansen (1953, p. 26).

property, which, like balance-of-payments equilibrium, is approached only gradually over time. The third interpretation is accepted, for instance, by Prof. Robert A. Mundell (1968, p. 114). Mundell carefully observes that:

> . . . it is not valid to assert in the context of an open economy, that the price level rises or falls according to whether there is excess or deficient liquidity. However valid this dynamic postulate may be in a closed economy, it is incorrect in an open economy. An excess supply of money implies an excess demand for goods in general and an excess of expenditure over income, but the *domestic* price level would only be pushed up insofar as the excess of expenditure reflected an excess demand for *domestic* goods. Insofar as an excess demand for goods can be expended on imports, the price level will have no tendency to rise (p. 116).

Therefore, the equation of exchange cannot be used directly to determine the domestic price level on the basis of the existing money supply. If this was done—as, of course, has been done mechanically by many economists—the money market would always be in equilibrium and, by Walras' law, Say's law would rule (i.e., income equals absorption) and thus no balance-of-payments disequilibrium would ever arise *no matter what the distribution of gold was.*

Similarly, the equation of exchange cannot be used to determine the price level when the second interpretation is adopted either. Such an approach would make national income ($= PQ$) equal to absorption ($= MV$), which again leads to continuous balance-of-payments equilibrium and total absence of gold flows. Therefore, in general, the determination of the price level by means of the equation of exchange is inconsistent with balance-of-payments disequilibrium and gold flows.

The rest of the present chapter shows how the equation of exchange, in either of its two valid interpretations for an open economy, can be rigorously incorporated into the classical adjustment mechanism.

15.2 LONG-RUN EQUILIBRIUM

Irrespective of which of the two valid interpretations of the equation of exchange one is willing to accept, the long-run equilibrium of the model must be common to both approaches. This much must be clear from the analysis of chap. 9. To prepare the ground for discussing the adjustment process under each of the two approaches, we review briefly in this section the long-run equilibrium of the model of chap. 9.

Recall that country A specializes completely in the production of A-exportables and B specializes in B-exportables. Constant returns to scale prevail in each country. Tastes in each country are represented by a nonintersecting social indifference map with regular convexity. Presently, we make the additional assumption that full employment is maintained through wage and price flexibility.

As in chap. 9, this model is best illustrated by means of the box-diagram technique, as shown in fig. 15.1. The distances 0_a0 and 0_b0 show, respectively, the full employment rates of output in A and B. The tangencies between the two social

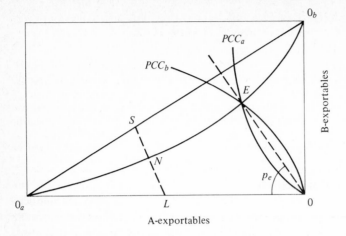

Figure 15.1 Long-run equilibrium. The distances $0_a 0$ and $0_b 0$ show, respectively, the full-employment rates of output in countries A and B. The tangencies between the two social indifference maps (not drawn) give rise to the contract curve $0_a E 0_b$. Long-run equilibrium occurs at E where the two price-consumption curves (PCC_a and PCC_b) intersect each other on the contract curve.

indifference maps (not drawn) give rise to the contract curve $0_a E 0_b$. As explained in chap. 9, long-run equilibrium occurs at E where the two price-consumption curves (PCC_a and PCC_b) intersect each other on the contract curve. (Multiple equilibria are excluded for simplicity.) The long-run equilibrium terms of trade of country A ($p \equiv p_a/p_b$) are given by the slope of the vector $0E$, that is, p_e. Further, at E "income = absorption" in every country. By Walras' law the money markets are also in equilibrium—in our present model only goods and money exist.

Presently, our primary interest lies not in the long-run equilibrium *per se* but in the adjustment process leading to it under an international gold standard. How does the system attain the long-run equilibrium at E? To consider this interesting problem some additional information is needed. This information is implicit in the interpretation of the equation of exchange one is willinng to accept. To be as general as possible, we consider each approach in turn. The trick is to determine a short-run equilibrium, i.e., a situation in which all markets are in equilibrium but with the balance of trade showing either a deficit or a surplus covered by a gold flow. As shown below, such short-run equilibria cannot persist. But note this: all short-run equilibria under either the aggregate-expenditure approach or the demand-for-money approach must by necessity occur on the contract curve of fig. 15.1. This follows from the principle of setting the marginal rate of substitution in each country equal to the common terms of trade.

15.3 THE AGGREGATE-EXPENDITURE APPROACH:
(a) THE INITIAL SHORT-RUN EQUILIBRIUM

Based on the assumption that the product MV gives aggregate expenditure on *all* commodities, we can formulate the following equations for countries A and B, respectively:

$$H_a V_a = Z_a \qquad (15.1)$$

$$H_b V_b = Z_b \qquad (15.2)$$

where H_i, V_i $(i = a, b)$ are, respectively, the money supply and the income velocity of circulation in the ith country.†

For simplicity it is also assumed that each country's money supply is identical to its gold supply. Thus, H_i stands both for the money supply and the stock of gold of the ith country. It is further assumed that the total world supply of gold is fixed, i.e.,

$$H_a + H_b = \bar{H} \qquad (15.3)$$

For any initial distribution of gold between A and B the aggregate world spending on A-exportables and B-exportables is given by

$$Z_a + Z_b = H_a V_a + H_b V_b = \bar{H} V_a + \delta H_b \qquad (15.4)$$

where

$$\delta \equiv V_b - V_a \qquad (15.5)$$

Further, the aggregate world spending must be equal to the value of A-exportables and B-exportables produced, i.e.,

$$Z_a + Z_b = p_a \bar{Q}_a + p_b \bar{Q}_b \qquad (15.6)$$

where $\bar{Q}_a$ and $\bar{Q}_b$ are the full-employment outputs of A-exportables and B-exportables, respectively.

Equation (15.6) places an important restriction on commodity prices p_a and p_b. Only combinations of p_a and p_b satisfying eq. (15.6) are allowed, i.e., combinations of prices which enable both countries together to buy the outputs $\bar{Q}_a$ and $\bar{Q}_b$—no more and no less. In terms of fig. 15.1, eq. (15.6) implies that the world budget line must pass through point 0_b, assuming that 0_a is the origin for world purchases of commodities.

Short-Run Equilibrium

Suppose now that the initial distribution of gold between A and B is given. How is a short-run equilibrium determined? At first glance, it appears that eqs. (15.1) and (15.2) cannot be used to draw the short-run budget lines of the two countries

---

† The change in notation from M to H is dictated by the fact that M is reserved for imports.

before p_a and p_b are known. However, as it turns out, the budget lines of the two countries always pass through a common point (say S) on the diagonal of the box diagram. This common point is independent of the absolute prices p_a and p_b as well as the terms of trade $p \equiv p_a/p_b$. Once point S is found, the short-run equilibrium is easily determined by rotating the budget line through point S until another point (say N) is found on the contract curve at which the budget line is tangent to the indifference curves of both countries. Point N is the short-run equilibrium point with the equilibrium terms of trade being given by the absolute slope of the vector SN. Thus, the first step in the determination of the short-run equilibrium solution is the determination of point S. How is point S determined?

Chacholiades (1972, p. 470) gives a rigorous solution to the problem of determining the common point S. For our purposes, it is sufficient to note that: (a) the ratio of aggregate expenditure of A and B, that is, Z_a/Z_b, is given when the initial distribution of gold is given; (b) given Z_a/Z_b and the world budget line through 0_b, A's budget line can be drawn such that any vector from the origin (0_a) to the world budget line will be bisected by A's budget line in the proportion Z_a/Z_b; (c) since point 0_b lies *always* on the world budget line, it follows that A's budget line must *always* bisect the diagonal 0_a0_b in the proportion Z_a/Z_b, that is, the location of point S is such that $(0_a S/S0_b) = Z_a/Z_b$; (d) finally, A's budget line through S becomes B's budget line when viewed from the origin 0_b.

Absolute Price Levels

How are the absolute price levels (p_a and p_b) determined at the short-run equilibrium point N? Very easily. The absolute slope of the vector SN gives the equilibrium terms of trade p_a/p_b. Knowing the equilibrium ratio p_a/p_b, both price levels are then determined from eq. (15.6).

15.4 THE AGGREGATE-EXPENDITURE APPROACH: (b) THE ADJUSTMENT PROCESS

The short-run equilibrium shown in fig. 15.1 at point N cannot by its nature last for long. As gold moves from one country to the other, the ratio Z_a/Z_b changes, causing point S to shift to a new position giving rise to a new short-run equilibrium. This process continues indefinitely until the system reaches a long-run equilibrium (i.e., point E of fig. 15.1).

We now proceed to analyze the adjustment process in detail. The straight line SL viewed from A's origin (i.e., point 0_a) is the budget line of country A. Therefore, A's expenditure in terms of Q_a is equal to $0_a L$. Since A's income in terms of Q_a is given by the distance 0_a0, which is greater than A's expenditure, country A must have a surplus in its balance of trade equal to the distance $L0$—expressed, of course, in terms of Q_a. Thus, country A must be gaining gold equal to $p_a^0(L0)$, where p_a^0 is the short-run equilibrium price of Q_a at N. As H_a increases, the ratio

Z_a/Z_b increases, too, and therefore point S moves in the northeast direction along the diagonal. The exact position depends upon the values of V_a and V_b.

There is a special case which can be easily handled, namely, when $V_a = V_b = 1$. In this case, the new position of point S can be determined as follows: simply draw a line parallel to SNL and passing through the southeast corner (i.e., point 0); the new position of S is the intersection between this auxiliary line and the diagonal. The truth of this proposition can be established as follows. First notice that when $V_a = V_b$ eq. (15.4) shows that the total world spending $(Z_a + Z_b)$ is independent of the distribution of gold, and therefore the values of p_a and p_b depend only on the equilibrium value of the terms of trade p. Further, since point S is unique and lies on the diagonal, we can determine it by drawing an auxiliary budget line for any value of p. In particular, we choose the value of p given by the slope of the straight line SNL. Thus, the auxiliary budget line must be parallel to SNL. Finally, notice that, for the chosen value of p, A's expenditure in terms of Q_a is equal to 0_a0, since, under the assumption that $V_a = V_b = 1$, A's expenditure in terms of Q_a must increase by $L0$.

The assumption $V_a = V_b = 1$ is necessary for the above procedure. Any thoughts that the less-stringent condition $V_a = V_b \neq 1$ might do as well can be quickly dispelled. Assume $V_a = V_b > 1$. As H_a increases, country A will be able to increase its expenditure in terms of Q_a at the original prices by more than $L0$ since the additional spending is now given by $(\Delta H_a)(V_a/p_a) = (L0)V_a > L0$. Normally, one would think that once $V_a = V_b$, the unit chosen to measure time could be selected without loss of generality so that $V_a = V_b = 1$. However, the unit of time has a special significance in the present model which makes such normalization impossible. Starting at a point in time, the two economies observe their current holdings of money H_i, set their respective rates of absorption equal to $H_i V_i$, and then continue that rate of absorption through time until a unit of time is completed, even though their holdings of money begin to change immediately. Thus, the larger the unit used to measure time, the more gold will be acquired (or given up) before its presence (or absence) is noticed and spending plans are changed. Because of this peculiarity, the model is recast later in the appendix to this chapter in continuous time.

Return now to the adjustment process. This is done in fig. 15.2 where, in addition to the assumption that $V_a = V_b = 1$, it is also assumed that both social indifference maps are homothetic to their respective origins (i.e., the income-consumption curves are straight lines through the origin) and that the contract curve lies below the diagonal. These assumptions do indeed guarantee the classical conclusion.

It is assumed that long-run equilibrium occurs at point E_L. The initial distribution of gold is assumed to put us at point S_0. Starting from point S_0, it is assumed that short-run equilibrium occurs at E_0. Gold in the amount $p_a^0(L_00)$ flows from B to A. Now draw the straight line $0S_1$ parallel to $S_0 E_0 L_0$. Point S_1 is the new common point on the budget lines of the two countries on the basis of which the equilibrium for period $t = t_1$ will be determined. Since in the region E_00_b of the contract curve all equilibrium values of p are higher than that implied

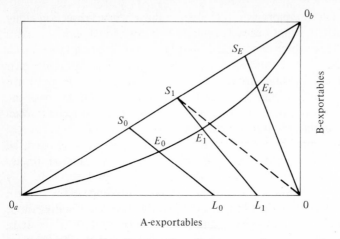

A-exportables

Figure 15.2 The adjustment process: the aggregate-expenditure approach. For any initial distribution of gold, a common budget line can be drawn through a point along the diagonal, such as S_0. (Point S_0 is such that $0_a S_0/S_0 0_b$ equals the ratio of aggregate spending by A and B, that is, Z_a/Z_b.) Allow the initial budget line to rotate through S_0 until it becomes tangent to both social-indifference curves along the contract curve, as illustrated by the short-run equilibrium point E_0. Assuming that $V_a = V_b = 1$, the short-run equilibrium for the following time period can be determined as follows: Draw a line through 0 and parallel to $S_0 E_0 L_0$, as illustrated by $S_1 0$. Now point S_1 (the intersection of $S_1 0$ with the diagonal) plays the same role as S_0. Hence, rotate the common budget line through S_1 until a second short-run equilibrium point (E_1) is determined, and so on.

by the slope of $S_0 E_0 L_0$, by assumption, the "equilibrium" budget line for the time period t_1 (say $S_1 L_1$) must be steeper than $S_0 E_0 L_0$. Thus point L_1 must lie to the left of point 0, gold will continue to flow from B to A, p will continue to increase, and point S will continue to march towards the equilibrium point S_E.

The preceding illustration conforms precisely to the conclusions of the price-specie-flow mechanism. Country A runs a surplus and B a deficit. Gold moves from B to A. Prices in A increase and prices in B decrease. The terms of trade turn against the gold-exporting country in favor of the gold-importing country. This process leads eventually to long-run equilibrium where the balance-of-trade disequilibrium is removed and the gold flow ceases completely. As becomes obvious from fig. 15.2, under the assumptions made country A cannot drain all the gold from country B. This is shown by the fact that all points $S_0, S_1, \ldots, S_n$ lie southwest (or to the left) of point S_E.

That the classical conclusions depend on particular assumptions which might or might not be true can be seen from the fact that if the contract curve lay above the diagonal, equilibrium would be approached cyclically, if at all—a result which seems to depend again on the peculiarity of the time unit noted above. Prices would tend to fall in the deficit country and rise in the surplus country, but the balance of trade of a country would fluctuate continuously from surplus to deficit and from deficit to surplus in an endless fashion until and when long-run equilibrium was attained. Those who mastered the technique of fig. 15.2 would have no difficulty in proving these statements.

Must the deficit country experience a terms-of-trade deterioration during the adjustment process? Certainly not. The point becomes obvious when it is realized that the present problem is an *inverted* transfer problem. That is, the transfer problem deals with the difficulties which arise *in creating a balance-of-trade deficit* equal to a predetermined transfer, while the present problem deals with the terms-of-trade effect of *the elimination of a current balance-of-trade deficit*. As with the transfer problem, the final outcome on the terms of trade depends on the characteristics of the two social indifference maps. Note that a contract curve below the diagonal implies that each country prefers its own goods, so that $M'_a + M'_b < 1$. On the other hand, a contract curve above the diagonal implies that each country prefers the other's goods, so that $M'_a + M'_b > 1$.

Although the preceding discussion is helpful in the sense that it gives us some insights into the adjustment mechanism, it must be admitted that the analysis is severely handicapped by the restrictive assumptions on which it is based. It is, therefore, necessary to extend the analysis beyond these specific assumptions. This is done in the appendix to this chapter. In the meantime, an alternative graphical solution is presented in the following section.

15.5 THE AGGREGATE-EXPENDITURE APPROACH: (c) AN ALTERNATIVE GRAPHICAL SOLUTION

While the box-diagram technique is convenient in illustrating the adjustment process under the aggregate-expenditure approach, the same technique becomes unworkable when the demand-for-money approach is pursued. For this reason and for gaining further insights into the adjustment process, it is considered useful to develop an alternative technique to handle both approaches.

A's Excess Demand for Money

Consider A's budget equation

$$p_a \bar{Q}_a + H_a = Z_a + L_a \qquad (15.7a)$$

where L_a is A's demand for money. Rewrite this budget equation as follows:

$$L_a - H_a = p_a \bar{Q}_a - Z_a \qquad (15.7b)$$

Equation (15.7b) shows that A's excess demand for money is given by the difference between A's national income $(p_a \bar{Q}_a)$ and expenditure (Z_a). For any initial distribution of gold, Z_a is given and A's excess demand for money is an increasing function of p_a, as shown in fig. 15.3. For $p_a > 0E$, country A has a positive excess demand for money; for $p_a < 0E$, A has a negative excess demand for money; and for $p_a = 0E$, A's excess demand for money is zero. In any short-run situation where the initial distribution of gold is given, A's gold exports or imports as well as the equilibrium value of p_a can be determined from fig. 15.3 if an excess supply schedule of gold were also derived as a function of p_a. How is this done?

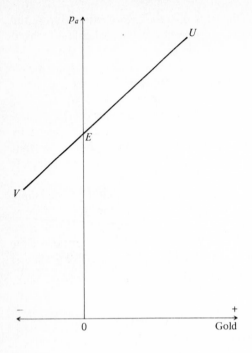

Figure 15.3 A's excess demand for gold is given by the difference between A's national income $(p_a \bar{Q}_a)$ and expenditure (Z_a). For any initial distribution of gold, Z_a is given and A's excess demand for gold is an increasing function of p_a, as shown by VEU.

The Price-Level Constraint

Consider eq. (15.6). For simplicity, assume that $V_a = V_b$ so that it may be combined with eq. (15.4) to give

$$\bar{H}V_a = p_a \bar{Q}_a + p_b \bar{Q}_b \qquad (15.8)$$

Equation (15.8) is illustrated graphically in fig. 15.4. The line UV is the constraint placed on the price levels p_a and p_b by the aggregate-expenditure approach. Given this constraint, it is obvious that there is a one-to-one correspondence between p and p_a.

A's Balance of Trade

Now consider the contract curve in fig. 15.2. As noted earlier, equilibrium, whether in the short or the long run, occurs on the contract curve. At every point on this curve draw the common tangent to the two tangential indifference curves, as illustrated by $S_0 E_0 L_0$. Then determine (a) the implied price ratio given by the absolute slope of the common tangent, and (b) A's balance of trade expressed in terms of A-exportables given by the distance $L_0 0$ as explained earlier. Repeat this experiment for all points on the contract curve and then plot the results as shown in fig. 15.5. A's balance of trade is a decreasing function of p in accordance with the homotheticity assumptions made earlier in relation to fig. 15.2.

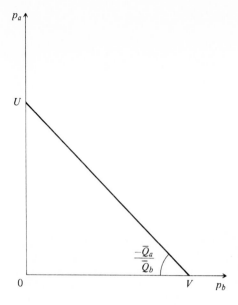

Figure 15.4 The price-level constraint of the aggregate-expenditure approach. The line UV is the constraint placed on the price levels p_a and p_b by the aggregate-expenditure approach (see eq. (15.8)).

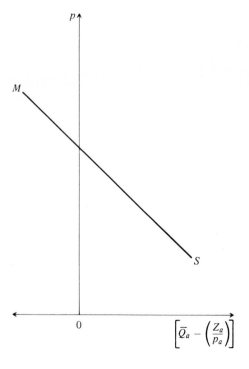

Figure 15.5 A's balance of trade. At every point on the contract curve of fig. 15.2 draw the common tangent to the two tangential indifference curves (such as $S_0 E_0 L_0$) and determine (a) the implied price ratio given by the absolute slope of the common tangent, and (b) A's balance of trade expressed in terms of A-exportables (such as $L_0 0$). Then plot the results on a new diagram, as shown by the curve MS.

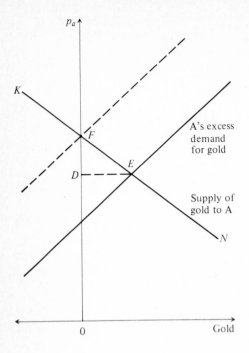

Figure 15.6 This adjustment process. Given the price-level constraint (fig. 15.4), A's balance-of-trade schedule (*MS*) given in fig. 15.5 is translated easily into a supply schedule of gold to A, as illustrated above by the line *KN*. Short-run equilibrium occurs at the intersection between A's excess demand-for-gold schedule and the supply-of-gold-to-A schedule, as illustrated above by point *E*. At *E*, A's gain of gold is given by the distance *DE*.

The Schedule of the Supply of Money to A and Short-Run Equilibrium

Given the constraint on price levels of fig. 15.4, the relationship of fig. 15.5 can be translated easily into a relationship between p_a and A's balance of trade expressed in terms of gold. This is shown in fig. 15.6 by the curve *KEN*. Let us refer to the latter curve as the *supply schedule of gold to A*. A's excess demand for gold given in fig. 15.3 is also reproduced in fig. 15.6. Evidently short-run equilibrium occurs at the intersection of the two schedules (i.e., point *E*). At *E* all equilibrium conditions are satisfied, as the reader should verify.

The Adjustment Process

The short-run equilibrium at *E* (fig. 15.6) cannot last for long. As country A imports gold (*DE*) from B, A's excess-demand schedule for gold shifts upward and to the left since, at every p_a, A's expenditure (Z_a) is now higher. Assuming that $V_a = V_b$, the supply schedule of gold to A should not shift since it depends only on the indifference maps, the full-employment levels of A-exportables and B-exportables, and the price-level constraint given by eq. (15.8). Accordingly, the short-run equilibrium of the system is expected to move gradually along the supply schedule of gold from *E* to *F* where long-run equilibrium is eventually attained. Note that the solution given in fig. 15.6 need no longer depend on discrete time--continuous time is perfectly satisfactory.

The preceding process is only slightly more complicated if the assumption $V_a = V_b$ is dropped. In this general case, which is left as an exercise for the reader, the international gold flow causes both the price-level constraint (fig. 15.4) and the supply schedule of gold to A to shift.

15.6 THE DEMAND-FOR-MONEY APPROACH

Turn now to the demand-for-money approach. In particular, it is now assumed that the demand for money in each country is proportional to money income or, assuming real output fixed at full employment, the price level.† Therefore, we have the following equations:

$$L_a = q_a p_a \tag{15.9}$$

$$L_b = q_b p_b \tag{15.10}$$

where
$$q_i \equiv \frac{Q_i}{V_i} \quad (i = a, b).$$

The gold market (or money market) will be in equilibrium if the following equation is satisfied:

$$L_a + L_b = \bar{H} \tag{15.11}$$

Substituting eqs. (15.9) and (15.10) into eq. (15.11), we get

$$q_a p_a + q_b p_b = \bar{H} \tag{15.12}$$

The interpretation of eq. (15.12) is rather simple. It gives all combinations of p_a and p_b which keep the world money market in equilibrium. Given the terms of trade p, eq. (15.12) can be used to determine the price levels of both countries. In effect, eq. (15.12) assumes now the role played by eq. (15.6) under the aggregate-expenditure approach. One minor difference between the two approaches is the fact that the absolute price levels are now independent of the distribution of gold between countries, whereas under the aggregate-expenditure approach the gold distribution is important. This difference can be verified by comparing eq. (15.6) with eq. (15.12).

Having established eq. (15.12), the supply schedule of gold to A can be derived step by step as with the aggregate-expenditure approach of the preceding section. The only difference, of course, is that now eq. (15.12) replaces eq. (15.6). Actually, this substitution makes the system simpler because it is no longer necessary to assume that $V_a = V_b$.

A's excess-demand schedule for gold is now given by $L_a - H_a = q_a p_a - H_a$. Thus, again for any given initial distribution of gold (i.e., given H_a), A's excess demand for gold is an increasing function of p_a; and as A gains (loses) gold, the

† For this type of argument see Mundell (1968, chap. 8) and Prais (1961).

excess-demand schedule shifts upward and to the left (downward and to the right). Accordingly, fig. 15.6 can be used to illustrate the adjustment process under the demand-for-money approach as well.

The demand-for-money approach is discussed further in the appendix to this chapter.

15.7 STOCK AND FLOW DEFICITS

Professor Harry G. Johnson (1968) has distinguished between "stock" deficits and "flow" deficits corresponding to the distinction drawn in monetary theory between "stock" decisions and "flow" decisions. A stock decision entails a once-and-for-all change in the composition of a community's assets by substituting other assets for domestic money. Accordingly, a stock deficit must necessarily be a temporary phenomenon. On the other hand, a flow deficit entails a decision to spend currently in excess of current national income. A flow deficit is not inherently of a limited duration.

All disequilibria we have discussed in this chapter so far are stock disequilibria—they are due to a bad distribution of the *stock* of gold between countries. As such they are only temporary phenomena since their very existence tends to produce gold flows, which in turn tend to bring about the desired distribution of gold between countries.

A stock disequilibrium may be converted into a flow disequilibrium if the third rule of the game is suspended. Thus, starting from a disequilibrium situation where gold is flowing from one country to the other, suppose that both countries decide to neutralize the effects of gold flows and keep their money supplies constant. The classical mechanism is then suspended and the stock disequilibrium is converted into a flow disequilibrium with no end in sight.

APPENDIX TO CHAPTER FIFTEEN. STABILITY CONDITIONS FOR THE CLASSICAL-ADJUSTMENT MECHANISM†

This appendix deals with the stability conditions of the classical adjustment mechanism studied in chap. 15. Thirty years ago, Lerner (1946) enunciated the theorem that the smooth functioning of the gold standard requires that the sum of the two elasticities of demand for imports (in absolute terms) be greater than unity. It is presently shown that the Marshall-Lerner condition is neither necessary nor sufficient for the stability of the system developed in chap. 15.

We are now assuming continuous time and cycles are impossible.

† Adapted from Chacholiades (1972).

A15.1 THE AGGREGATE-EXPENDITURE APPROACH

We proceed with the aggregate-expenditure approach first. Let us state the dynamic system explicitly. We have

$$H_a V_a + H_b V_b = \bar{H} V_a + \delta H_b = p_b(p\bar{Q}_a + \bar{Q}_b) \tag{A15.1}$$

$$\bar{Q}_a = Q_a^a(p; \lambda) + Q_a^b(p; 1/\lambda) \tag{A15.2}$$

$$\bar{Q}_b = Q_b^a(1/p; \lambda) + Q_b^b(1/p; 1/\lambda) \tag{A15.3}$$

$$T_a = p_b(pQ_a^b - Q_b^a) \tag{A15.4}$$

$$\dot{H}_a = T_a \tag{A15.5}$$

where $\lambda \equiv Z_a/Z_b$, $\dot{H}$ is a time derivative, and $Q_i^j \equiv j$th country's demand for $Q_i (i, j = a, b)$.

Equation (A15.1) is derived by substituting eq. (15.4) into eq. (15.6). Equations (A15.2) and (A15.3) equalize supply and demand for A-exportables and B-exportables, respectively. The quantities demanded (Q_i^j) are functions of two variables, namely, p and λ. The role of λ in eqs. (A15.2) and (A15.3) is that of a parameter. Given λ, therefore, we have two equations in only one unknown, p. However, one of these equations is redundant, as should be obvious from the discussion of chap. 15. Thus one of them can be eliminated. We choose to eliminate eq. (A15.3). Equation (A15.4) shows the balance of trade of country A (T_a) as the difference between the value of A's exports and imports. Finally, eq. (A15.5) states that the change in the gold stock of country A is equal to A's balance of trade.

How the System Works

We are now in a position to see how the system works. Given the distribution of gold at a point in time, we can determine λ and then use eq. (A15.2) to determine p. This equilibrium value of p can now be substituted into eq. (A15.1) which can be solved for the equilibrium value of p_b. Given p_b, p, and λ, we can then use eq. (A15.4) to determine A's balance of trade which, according to eq. (A15.5), is equivalent to the gold flow. As gold moves in or out of country A, the value of λ changes, and a second cycle through the system begins. This process comes to an end when $T_a = 0$. At that point the gold flow ceases and the value of λ is stabilized to produce the same equilibrium values of p_a, p_b, and p over time. Under what conditions is this long-run equilibrium position stable?

Stability

Let us rewrite eq. (A15.5) as follows:

$$\dot{H}_a = T_a(p_b, p; \lambda) \tag{A15.6a}$$

Now observe that p_b is a function of p (i.e., knowing p we use eq. (A15.1) to determine p_b); the variable p is a function of λ (i.e., knowing λ we use eq. (A15.2) to determine p); and λ is a function of H_a. Thus, in the final analysis T_a is a function of H_a.

Expanding eq. (A15.6a) in Taylor series around the long-run equilibrium point and dropping all nonlinear terms, we obtain

$$\dot{H}_a = \left\{ \left[\left(\frac{\partial T_a}{\partial p_b}\right)\left(\frac{\partial p_b}{\partial p}\right) + \left(\frac{\partial T_a}{\partial p}\right)\right]\left(\frac{\partial p}{\partial \lambda}\right) + \left(\frac{\partial T_a}{\partial \lambda}\right)\right\}\left(\frac{\partial \lambda}{\partial H_a}\right)(H_a - \bar{H}_a) \quad \text{(A15.6b)}$$

where $\bar{H}_a$ is the long-run equilibrium value of H_a and all derivatives are evaluated at the long-run equilibrium point.

For stability, it is required that

$$\left\{ \left[\left(\frac{\partial T_a}{\partial p_b}\right)\left(\frac{\partial p_b}{\partial p}\right) + \left(\frac{\partial T_a}{\partial p}\right)\right]\left(\frac{\partial p}{\partial \lambda}\right) + \left(\frac{\partial T_a}{\partial \lambda}\right)\right\}\left(\frac{\partial \lambda}{\partial H_a}\right) < 0 \quad \text{(A15.7)}$$

Inequality (A15.7) can be simplified in two ways. First note that $(\partial \lambda / \partial H_a) > 0$, and second that $(\partial T_a / \partial p_b) = pQ_a^b - Q_b^a = 0$ at the long-run equilibrium point. Introducing these simplifications into inequality (A15.7), we get

$$\left(\frac{\partial T_a}{\partial p}\right)\left(\frac{\partial p}{\partial \lambda}\right) + \left(\frac{\partial T_a}{\partial \lambda}\right) < 0 \quad \text{(A15.8)}$$

Before analyzing inequality (A15.8) any further, observe that the Marshall-Lerner condition deals only with the term $(\partial T_a / \partial p)$. Thus, if the Marshall-Lerner condition is satisfied, we must have $(\partial T_a / \partial p) < 0$. But this is neither necessary nor sufficient for condition (A15.8) to be satisfied because, as argued in chap. 15, the sign of the partial derivative $(\partial p / \partial \lambda)$ is indeterminate.

Partially differentiating T_a (as given by eq. (A15.4) with respect to λ, we get

$$\frac{\partial T_a}{\partial \lambda} = -p_b\left\{ \left(\frac{p}{\lambda^2}\right)\left[\frac{\partial Q_a^b}{\partial(1/\lambda)}\right] + \left(\frac{\partial Q_b^a}{\partial \lambda}\right)\right\} < 0 \quad \text{(A15.9)}$$

Hence, a *sufficient* condition for stability is

$$\left(\frac{\partial T_a}{\partial p}\right)\left(\frac{\partial p}{\partial \lambda}\right) < 0 \quad \text{(A15.10)}$$

When $(\partial p / \partial \lambda) < 0$, condition (A15.10) reduces to $(\partial T_a / \partial p) > 0$, which is the opposite of the Marshall-Lerner condition. Under these circumstances, the satisfaction of the Marshall-Lerner condition *might* give rise to *instability*—not stability. Finally, even in the classical case where $(\partial p / \partial \lambda) > 0$, the Marshall-Lerner condition, though sufficient, is not necessary for stability because $(\partial T_a / \partial \lambda) < 0$.

The Absolute-Price Levels

How do the absolute-price levels (p_a and p_b) behave through time? The usual interpretation of the classical theory simply states that the price level of the gold-importing country rises and the price level of the gold-exporting country falls in the same percentage as that by which the money supply of each country changes. Some economists, such as Haberler (1959, chap. 3), tried to relax this rigid version of the quantity theory by saying that the price level changes in the same direction but not necessarily by the same percentage as the money supply. Does this proposition hold in general even in its less rigid form where the percentage change in the money supply and price level are not equal, but only of the same sign?

Rewrite eq. (A15.1) as follows:

$$p_b = \frac{\bar{H}V_a + \delta H_b}{p\bar{Q}_a + \bar{Q}_b} \qquad (A15.11)$$

and differentiate p_b with respect to H_b to get

$$\frac{dp_b}{dH_b} = \left[\frac{1}{(p\bar{Q}_a + \bar{Q}_b)^2}\right]\left[\delta(p\bar{Q}_a + \bar{Q}_b) - (\bar{H}V_a + \delta H_b)\bar{Q}_a\left(\frac{\partial p}{\partial \lambda}\right)\left(\frac{\partial \lambda}{\partial H_b}\right)\right] \qquad (A15.12)$$

Now we can derive the following general conclusion: if $\delta \geq 0$ and $(dp/d\lambda) \geq 0$, then $(dp_b/dH_b) \geq 0$; if $\delta \leq 0$ and $(dp/d\lambda) \leq 0$, then $(dp_b/dH_b) \leq 0$.

What has been shown for country B can be extended by symmetry to country A as well. However, when we examine both countries simultaneously, we must bear in mind that the parameter δ for country A is the negative of that for country B, and the variable p is the reciprocal of p_a/p_b.

Graphical Illustration

The above conclusions can be very easily illustrated diagrammatically as shown in fig. A15.1. The straight line KL shows the locus of points which satisfy eq. (A15.1) for some initial distribution of gold.

Let us suppose that given the initial distribution of gold, the equilibrium value of p given by eq. (A15.2) is p_0. Thus, the coordinates of point R show the equilibrium price levels for the first period. Suppose now that this short-run equilibrium gives rise to a gold flow from country B to country A. If $V_a = V_b$, the line KL remains at the same position, and the effect on the price levels depends only on what happens to p. If p increases, p_a increases and p_b falls; if p decreases, p_a decreases and p_b increases.

If $V_a > V_b$, as gold moves from B to A, the line KL moves outward, say to $K'L'$. Now if p increases, the equilibrium point on the $K'L'$ line will lie in the region $K'R'$. Thus, p_a will definitely increase but nothing in general can be said about p_b. On the other hand, if p falls, the equilibrium point on the line $K'L'$ will lie in the region $R'L'$. Now, p_b definitely rises—quite contrary to the classical theory—but nothing can be said about p_a.

If $V_a > V_b$, as gold moves from B to A, the line KL moves inward, say to $K''L''$. In this case, it is quite conceivable that both p_a and p_b might fall. This will happen if the equilibrium point on the line $K''L''$ (as determined by the equilibrium value

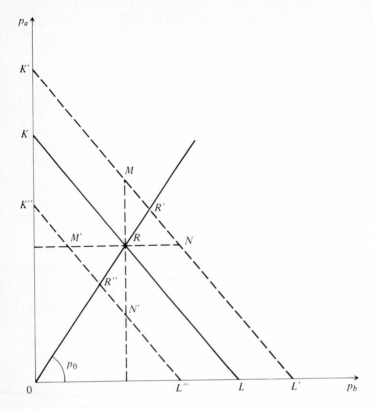

Figure A15.1 The absolute-price levels. KL is the constraint placed on absolute-price levels by eq. (A15.1). When gold moves from the country with the lower (higher) income velocity of money to the country with the higher (lower) income velocity of money, the price-level constraint shifts outward (inward). The equilibrium-price levels are determined at the intersection (say R) between the price-level constraint (say KL) and a vector through the origin (say OR) whose slope equals the equilibrium terms of trade.

of p) lies in the region $M'N'$. Further, p_a can increase only if p increases. However, if p increases it does not necessarily imply that p_a increases. A similar statement can be made about p_b. Finally, if p_a increases, then p_b necessarily falls, and vice versa.

A15.2 THE DEMAND-FOR-MONEY APPROACH

The solution under the demand-for-money approach proceeds along similar lines. The full dynamic system is summarized as follows:

$$p_b = \frac{1}{1 + p} \tag{A15.13}$$

$$f(p, \lambda) \equiv Q_a^a(p, \lambda) + Q_a^b(p, 1/\lambda) - \bar{Q}_a = 0 \tag{A15.14}$$

$$g(p, \lambda; H_a) \equiv h(p; H_a) - \lambda = 0 \tag{A15.15}$$

$$\dot{H}_a = \left(\frac{1}{1+p}\right)(pQ_a^b - Q_b^a) = T_a(p, \lambda) \tag{A15.16}$$

Equation (A15.13) is a simplification of eq. (15.12). It is assumed that the units of measurement of A-exportables and B-exportables are such that $\bar{Q}_i = V_i$ or $q_i = 1$, and $\bar{H} \equiv 1$. Equation (A15.14) is similar to eq. (A15.2), and eq. (A15.16) is similar to eq. (A15.5). The only real difference lies in eq. (A15.15) which states that the ratio of expenditures of A and B (λ) is no longer a function of H_a alone—it is also a function of the terms of trade p.

From eqs. (15.7a), (15.9), and the simplifying assumption that $q_i = 1$, we know that

$$Z_a = p_a \bar{Q}_a + H_a - p_a = p_a(\bar{Q}_a - 1) + H_a \tag{A15.17}$$

Similarly, for country B we have

$$Z_b = p_b \bar{Q}_b + H_b - p_b = p_b(\bar{Q}_b - 1) + H_b \tag{A15.18}$$

Accordingly,

$$\lambda \equiv \frac{Z_a}{Z_b} = \frac{p_a(\bar{Q}_a - 1) + H_a}{p_b(\bar{Q}_b - 1) + H_b} = \frac{p(\bar{Q}_a - 1) + (p + 1)H_a}{(\bar{Q}_b - 1) + (p + 1)H_b} \equiv h(p; H_a) \tag{A15.19}$$

Equation (A15.19) shows that λ is a function of p, H_a, and H_b. However, because $H_b = \bar{H} - H_a$, the expenditure ratio λ is only a function of p and H_a. On the reasonable assumption that $V_i = \bar{Q}_i > 1$, it is readily shown that

$$h_p > 0 \text{ and } h_{H_a} > 0 \tag{A15.20}$$

where the subscript indicates partial differentiation with respect to the said variable.

In the aggregate absorption version λ depended only on H_a and, therefore, once H_a was given, eq. (A15.2) could be solved for the equilibrium value of p. Under the present version, though, this cannot be done. Since λ depends on p as well, the equilibrium values of these variables must be determined simultaneously. But this is only a minor difference. The important thing is that eqs. (A15.2) and (A15.15) can be solved simultaneously for the equilibrium values of λ and p; then the absolute price levels can be recovered from eq. (A15.13). Thus, the short-run equilibrium system consists of eqs. (A15.2) or (A15.14), (A15.13), and (A15.15).

The Adjustment Process

Turn now to the adjustment process. Assume for the moment that eqs. (A15.14) and (A15.15) have been solved for $p(H_a)$ and $\lambda(H_a)$. Introducing these functions into the differential eq. (A15.16), we obtain

$$\dot{H}_a = T_a[p(H_a), \lambda(H_a)] \tag{A15.21}$$

Expanding the function T_a at the equilibrium point and dropping all nonlinear terms, we get

$$\dot{H}_a = \left[\left(\frac{\partial T_a}{\partial p} \right) \left(\frac{dp}{dH_a} \right) + \left(\frac{\partial T_a}{\partial \lambda} \right) \left(\frac{d\lambda}{dH_a} \right) \right] (H_a - \bar{H}_a) \tag{A15.22}$$

where $\bar{H}_a$ is the long-run equilibrium value of H_a. For stability it is required that

$$\left(\frac{\partial T_a}{\partial p} \right) \left(\frac{dp}{dH_a} \right) + \left(\frac{\partial T_a}{\partial \lambda} \right) \left(\frac{d\lambda}{dH_a} \right) < 0 \tag{A15.23}$$

From eq. (A15.9) we have $(\partial T_a / \partial \lambda) < 0$. Also, $(\partial T_a / \partial p) < 0$ when the Marshall-Lerner condition is satisfied. Therefore, the only thing that remains to be done is to determine the derivatives (dp/dH_a) and $(d\lambda/dH_a)$ from eqs. (A15.14) and (A15.15).

Differentiating eqs. (A15.14) and (A15.15) totally with respect to H_a, we get

$$\begin{bmatrix} f_p & f_\lambda \\ g_p & g_\lambda \end{bmatrix} \begin{bmatrix} \dfrac{dp}{dH_a} \\ \dfrac{d\lambda}{dH_a} \end{bmatrix} = \begin{bmatrix} 0 \\ -g_{H_a} \end{bmatrix} \tag{A15.24}$$

Solving the system by Cramer's rule, we get

$$\frac{dp}{dH_a} = \frac{g_{H_a} f_\lambda}{\Delta} \tag{A15.25}$$

$$\frac{d\lambda}{dH_a} = -\frac{f_p g_{H_a}}{\Delta} \tag{A15.26}$$

where

$$\Delta \equiv f_p g_\lambda - f_\lambda g_p \tag{A15.27}$$

Evaluating the various partial derivatives explicitly in terms of the original functions, we have

$$g_p = h_p > 0 \qquad g_\lambda = -1 < 0 \qquad g_{H_a} = h_{H_a} > 0$$

$$f_p = \left(\frac{\partial Q_a^a}{\partial p} \right) + \left(\frac{\partial Q_a^b}{\partial p} \right) < 0$$

$$f_\lambda = \left(\frac{\partial Q_a^a}{\partial \lambda} \right) - \left(\frac{1}{\lambda^2} \right) \left[\frac{\partial Q_a^b}{\partial (1/\lambda)} \right] \gtrless 0$$

Thus, the partial derivatives g_p and g_{H_a} are positive; the derivatives f_p and g_λ are negative; and the derivative f_λ can be either positive, negative, or zero. Therefore, the analysis can be broken down into the following three cases: (a) $f_\lambda < 0$; (b) $f_\lambda > 0$; and (c) $f_\lambda = 0$.

In case (a) where $f_\lambda < 0$, we have $\Delta > 0$, $(dp/dH_a) < 0$, and $(d\lambda/dH_a) > 0$. This case is illustrated in fig. A15.2. The curve marked f shows the locus of points which

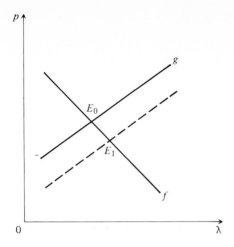

Figure A15.2 The effects of gold flows on p and λ when $f_\lambda < 0$. The f curve is downward sloping while the g curve is upward sloping. As gold flows from B to A the g curve shifts to the right (broken curve) and the system moves from E_0 to E_1.

satisfy eq. (A15.14) while the curve marked g shows the locus of points which satisfy eq. (A15.15). The f curve is unique in the sense that it does not depend on H_a. However, the g curve does depend on H_a. As H_a increases, the g curve shifts to the right because $h_{H_a} > 0$. Finally, the g curve must always be upward sloping because $-g_\lambda/g_p > 0$. The same statement cannot be made about the f curve which can be either rising or falling. In this case, the f curve must be downward sloping because $-f_\lambda/f_p < 0$.

Let us assume that the system is originally in short-run equilibrium at point E_0 and that gold flows from country B into A. The g curve shifts to the right and the new equilibrium values for λ and p are those shown by the coordinates of point E_1.

Finally, it should be pointed out that in this case (i.e., when $f_\lambda < 0$) the Marshall-Lerner condition works against the stability of the system. In fact it is readily seen from inequality (A15.23) that the nonsatisfaction of the Marshall-Lerner condition (that is, $(\partial T_a/\partial p) > 0$) is a sufficient though not a necessary condition for stability.

In case (*b*), we have $f_\lambda > 0$. The sign of both derivatives $(dp/dH_a, d\lambda/dH_a)$ depends only on the sign of Δ. Thus we may distinguish between two cases as follows:

1. $\Delta > 0$. This implies, of course, that $f_p g_\lambda > f_\lambda g_p$, or $-(g_\lambda/g_p) > -(f_\lambda/f_p) > 0$. Thus, in this case both the g curve and the f curve are upward sloping with the g curve being steeper. This is illustrated in fig. A15.3, whose interpretation is similar to that of fig. A15.2.

This case can be recognized as the classical case. The price level of the gold-exporting country is decreasing and that of the gold-importing country increasing. The expenditure ratio moves in favor of the gold-importing country. In this case, the Marshall-Lerner condition is sufficient (though not necessary) for stability.

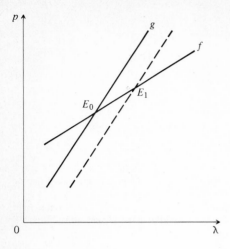

Figure A15.3 The effects of gold flows on p and λ when $f_\lambda > 0$ and $\Delta > 0$. Here both curves are upward sloping with the g curve being steeper.

2. $\Delta < 0$. This implies, of course, that $0 < -g_\lambda/g_p < -f_\lambda/f_p$. Here, the f curve is upward sloping and steeper than the g curve. This is illustrated in fig. A15.4.

   In this case, satisfaction of the Marshall-Lerner condition necessarily implies instability.

   Finally, case (c), where $f_\lambda = 0$, implies $\Delta > 0$, $(dp/dH_a) = 0$, and $(d\lambda/dH_a) > 0$. This is illustrated in fig. A15.5.

   The f curve is now horizontal. In this case all the points on the contract curve imply the same marginal rate of substitution. If tastes are homothetic, this case can be illustrated by a box diagram whose contract curve coincides with the diagonal. In this particular case, the Marshall-Lerner condition is simply *irrelevant*.

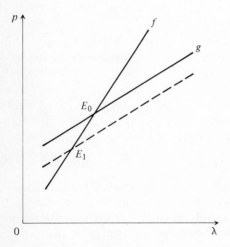

Figure A15.4 The effects of gold flows on p and λ when $f_\lambda > 0$ and $\Delta < 0$. Here both curves are upward sloping with the f curve being steeper.

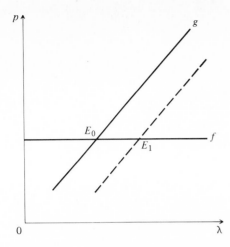

Figure A15.5 The effects of gold flows on p and λ when $f_\lambda = 0$. Here the g curve is upward sloping but the f curve is horizontal.

In summary, the Marshall-Lerner condition, believed to be necessary for the stability of the classical system, is neither necessary nor sufficient in general (although, in one classical case, it is sufficient).

SELECTED BIBLIOGRAPHY

Allen, W. R. (Ed.) (1965). *International Trade Theory: Hume to Ohlin.* Random House, New York.

Blaug, M. (1962). *Economic Theory in Retrospect.* Richard D. Irwin, Inc., Homewood, Ill.

Bloomfield, A. I. (1950). *Capital Imports and the American Balance of Payments 1934–39.* The University of Chicago Press, Chicago, Ill.

Chacholiades, M. (1972). "The Classical Theory of International Adjustment: A Restatement." *Econometrica* (May), pp. 463–485.

Clement, M. O., R. L. Pfister, and K. T. Rothwell (1967). *Theoretical Issues in International Economics.* Houghton Mifflin and Company, Boston.

Haberler, G. (1959). *The Theory of International Trade.* William Hodge and Company, Ltd., London.

Hansen, A. (1953). *A Guide to Keynes.* McGraw-Hill Book Company, New York.

Iversen, C. (1935). *Aspects of the Theory of International Capital Movements.* Ejnar Munksgaards Forlag, Copenhagen.

Johnson, H. G. (1958). *International Trade and Economic Growth: Studies in Pure Theory.* George Allen and Unwin, Ltd., London, chap. IV. Reprinted in AEA *Readings in International Economics.* Richard D. Irwin, Inc., Homewood, Ill., 1968.

Kindleberger, C. P. (1958). *International Economics,* 3d ed. Richard D. Irwin, Inc., Homewood, Ill.

Krueger, A. O. (1969). "Balance-of-Payments Theory." *Journal of Economic Literature,* vol. VII, pp. 1–26.

Lerner, A. P. (1946). *The Economics of Control.* The Macmillan Company, New York.

Mundell, R. A. (1968). *International Economics.* The Macmillan Company, New York.

Prais, S. J. (1961). "Some Mathematical Notes on the Quantity Theory of Money in an Open Economy." *IMF Staff Papers,* vol. 8, pp. 212–226.

Samuelson, P. A. (1961). *Economics,* 5th ed. McGraw-Hill Book Company, New York.

——— (1952). "The Transfer Problem and Transport Cost: The Terms of Trade When Impediments are Absent." *Economic Journal,* vol. 62, pp. 278–304.

———(1954). "The Transfer Problem and Transport Costs, II: Analysis of Effects of Trade Impediments." *Economic Journal,* vol. 64, pp. 264–289.

Scammell, W. M. (1964). *International Monetary Policy*, 2d ed. St. Martin's Press, New York.
Scitovsky, T. (1967). *Economic Theory and Western European Integration*. Stanford University Press, Stanford, Cal.
Vanek, J. (1964). *International Trade: Theory and Economic Policy*. Richard D. Irwin, Inc., Homewood, Ill.
Viner, J. (1937). *Studies in the Theory of International Trade*. Harper and Row, New York.
Walter, I. (1968). *International Economics*. The Ronald Press Company, New York.
Yeager, L. D. (1966). *International Monetary Relations*. Harper and Row, New York.

SIXTEEN

THE GOLD STANDARD:
II. THE KEYNESIAN APPROACH

This chapter continues the preceding chapter's discussion of the international adjustment process under a regime of an international gold standard. The interest is now focused on a Keynesian-type, fixed-price model. Price flexibility is discussed briefly in the appendix to this chapter.

The present discussion extends the income-adjustment model of chap. 10 by including explicitly the money and bond markets under various conditions of capital mobility. In particular, the discussion is divided into three parts. Part A deals with the adjustment process under a regime of perfect capital mobility, part B considers the implications of perfect capital immobility, and finally part C extends the analysis to the more general case of imperfect capital mobility.

PART A. PERFECT CAPITAL MOBILITY

16.1 THE BASIC ASSUMPTIONS

The discussion of this part is based on the assumption that there exists *perfect capital mobility* between countries. In other words, it is assumed that bonds issued by A's residents or government are perfectly substitutable for bonds issued by B's residents or government, and vice versa. The assumption of perfect capital mobility necessarily implies that the same rate of interest always prevails in both countries (law of one price).

It is assumed as before that there are two countries, A (home country) and B (foreign country), with national currencies the dollar and the pound sterling, respectively. Each country obeys the gold-standard rules of the game. In particular, each country is assumed to be on a gold-bullion standard. Each country's money supply is always a constant multiple of its gold reserve (fractional-reserve principle), as explained in chap. 7. The units of measurement are such that the rate of exchange (i.e., the mint parity) is unity. The distance between the gold points is assumed to be zero.

Countries A and B produce A-exportables and B-exportables, respectively, by means of a single factor of production, labor, and under constant returns to scale. Their respective money-wage rates are assumed rigidly fixed. The units of measurement of A-exportables and B-exportables are such that their respective prices are equal to unity.

The assumption of constant returns to scale is very convenient because it eliminates price changes which may occur as each country's level of output and employment vary. Nevertheless, the assumption of constant returns to scale does *not* preclude price changes altogether. Price changes may be introduced into the model through changes in the money-wage rates, as is done in the appendix to this chapter. Accordingly, the assumption of constant returns to scale frees the income-adjustment mechanism from any annoying price changes, but at the same time allows price changes into the adjustment process in the form of parametric shifts.

A country's aggregate spending Z_i and imports M_i depend on that country's income Y_i and the interest rate r. That is,

$$Z_i = Z_i(Y_i, r) \tag{16.1}$$

$$M_i = M_i(Y_i, r) \qquad (i = a, b) \tag{16.2}$$

with $0 < (\partial Z_i/\partial Y_i) < 1$, $0 < (\partial M_i/\partial Y_i) < 1$, $(\partial Z_i/\partial r) < 0$, and $(\partial M_i/\partial r) \leq 0$. The interest-rate effect on imports is strictly negative to the extent that the interest-rate-sensitive component of aggregate spending consists partly of imports. This happens especially when imports are partly used for investment purposes, and investment expenditure depends negatively on the interest rate. However, to simplify our analysis we shall assume from now on that imports are independent of the interest rate, that is, $(\partial M_i/\partial r) = 0$.

The demand for money L_i in each country depends on that country's national income and the interest rate. That is,

$$L_i = L_i(Y_i, r) \qquad (i = a, b) \tag{16.3}$$

This is in line with current macroeconomic thinking.

Finally, there exists a fixed amount of gold $\bar{g}$ in the world economy which is allocated between A and B on the basis of the economic transactions which have taken place between them in the past. That is,

$$\bar{g} = g_a + g_b \tag{16.4}$$

where g_i $(i = a, b)$ is the ith country's gold reserve. Given this historical allocation of gold between countries and each country's money multiplier k_i, the money supply H_i in each country is determined by

$$H_i = k_i g_i \qquad (i = a, b) \tag{16.5}$$

These are our basic assumptions. How is the long-run equilibrium determined? What are the long-run effects on Y_a, Y_b, r, g_a, and g_b of any parametric shifts such as changes in a country's spending on either its own or foreign products? Do business cycles continue to be transmitted internationally under the present circumstances in which the money and bond markets are incorporated into the model explicitly? What is the precise adjustment process which takes the system from a disequilibrium situation where a positive flow of gold between countries exists to the long-run equilibrium where the flow of gold ceases completely? These are important questions which we answer in the following sections.

16.2 THE LONG-RUN MARKET EQUILIBRIUM CONDITIONS

In our model we have several markets: the markets for A-exportables and B-exportables, the bond market, the money markets in A and B, and the foreign exchange market. In the long run all of these markets must be in equilibrium and the gold flow must be zero. How is this long-run equilibrium determined?

First we have the commodity-market equilibrium conditions as before:

$$Y_a = Z_a + T_a \equiv D_a(Y_a, Y_b, r) \tag{16.6}$$

$$Y_b = Z_b - T_a \equiv D_b(Y_a, Y_b, r) \tag{16.7}$$

Since in these two equations there are now three unknowns (Y_a, Y_b, and r), another independent equation must be added. This additional equation appears to be provided by the equilibrium condition in the bond market:

$$E_{ab} + E_{bb} \equiv E(Y_a, Y_b, r) = 0 \tag{16.8}$$

where E_{ib} $(i = a, b)$ stands for the ith country's excess demand for bonds.

What is the excess demand for bonds E_{ij} equal to? Consider the budget equations for countries A and B, respectively:

$$Y_a + H_a = Z_a + L_a + E_{ab} \tag{16.9}$$

$$Y_b + H_b = Z_b + L_b + E_{bb} \tag{16.10}$$

Solving these budget equations for E_{ab} and E_{bb}, respectively, we obtain

$$E_{ab} = (Y_a - Z_a) + (H_a - L_a) \tag{16.11}$$

$$E_{bb} = (Y_b - Z_b) + (H_b - L_b) \tag{16.12}$$

Finally, adding eqs. (16.11) and (16.12) and substituting their sum $(E_{ab} + E_{bb})$ into the equilibrium condition (16.8), and then using eqs. (16.6) and (16.7), we obtain

$$E(Y_a, Y_b, r) = (H_a - L_a) + (H_b - L_b) = 0 \qquad (16.13)$$

or
$$H_a + H_b = L_a + L_b \qquad (16.14)$$

That is, the bond market is in equilibrium when the total world supply of money (recall that R is unity) equals the total world demand for money.

Before completing the set of long-run equilibrium conditions there is a methodological point which must be cleared up. One might be tempted to consider a short-run equilibrium model consisting of the three equations: (16.6), (16.7), and (16.14). Given the initial distribution of gold between A and B, these three equations could be solved uniquely for the equilibrium values of the three variables Y_a, Y_b, and r. In general, when eqs. (16.6), (16.7), and (16.14) are satisfied simultaneously, all markets are in equilibrium except the foreign exchange market in which a gold flow may exist. In particular, the change in A's gold reserve (Δg_a) is given by

$$\Delta g_a = -H_a + L_a = -E_{ab} + (Y_a - Z_a) = -E_{ab} + T_a \qquad (16.15)$$

The change in B's gold reserve is necessarily the negative of A's, verified as follows:

$$\Delta g_b = -H_b + L_b = -E_{bb} - T_a = E_{ab} - T_a = (H_a - L_a) = -\Delta g_a \quad (16.16)$$

It could then be argued that if the money multipliers k_i were equal, i.e., if $k_a = k_b = k$, then the total world money supply would depend on the total supply of gold $\bar{g}$ only—not its distribution between countries. (Note that $H_a + H_b = k_a g_a + k_b g_b = k\bar{g}$.) In this case, the equilibrium values of Y_a, Y_b, and r would be *independent of the original distribution of gold between countries.* Accordingly, it could be argued, the only adjustment necessary to move the system from a short-run to a long-run equilibrium is purely monetary in nature. In fact, if the 100 percent money principle was adhered to by both countries (i.e., if $k_a = k_b = 1$), it would appear that the transition from short-run to long-run equilibrium would take place immediately with the first period's gold flow.

This view is too simplistic and in fact wrong. The international economy does not behave in this manner. When the system is out of long-run equilibrium, the adjustment process does not lead first to an artificially determined short-run equilibrium described by eqs. (16.6), (16.7), and (16.14) to be followed by a second type of adjustment process leading the system into the long-run equilibrium. Rather, a single type of adjustment process is set into motion, giving rise to a continuous gold flow until the system reaches the long-run equilibrium. The supposedly short-run system consisting of eqs. (16.6), (16.7), and (16.14) is an artificial construction and offers no help in understanding the adjustment process. All this becomes clear in sec. 16.5 below.

We continue now with the development of the long-run equilibrium conditions. In the long run, eqs. (16.4) to (16.7) and (16.14) must be satisfied. But we seem to have seven unknowns (Y_a, Y_b, r, g_a, g_b, H_a, and H_b) and only six equations. (In the long run the optimum distribution of gold between countries is an additional unknown. It is determined endogenously by the system.) Thus another equation is needed. This extra equation is provided by the condition that the flow of gold between countries is zero. Hence, we have the following system:

$$Y_a = D_a(Y_a, Y_b, r) \tag{16.6}$$

$$Y_b = D_b(Y_a, Y_b, r) \tag{16.7}$$

$$H_a + H_b = L_a(Y_a, r) + L_b(Y_b, r) \tag{16.14}$$

$$H_a = L_a(Y_a, r) \tag{16.17}$$

$$H_b = k_b \bar{g} - \left(\frac{k_b}{k_a}\right) H_a \tag{16.18}$$

where eq. (16.17) implies that the gold flow is zero and eq. (16.18) is a *money-supply constraint* obtained from the three equations (16.4) and (16.5) by eliminating g_a and g_b. Thus, $H_b = k_b g_b = k_b(\bar{g} - g_a) = k_b \bar{g} - k_b g_a = k_b \bar{g} - (k_b/k_a)H_a$.

The interpretation of eq. (16.18) is very simple. It gives all alternative combinations of H_a and H_b available to the two countries given the total stock of gold $\bar{g}$ and the money multipliers (k_a, k_b).

Actually, because of eq. (16.17), eq. (16.14) may be replaced by the simpler equation:

$$H_b = L_b(Y_b, r) \tag{16.19}$$

Accordingly, our long-run equilibrium system consists of the five equations (16.6), (16.7), and (16.17) to (16.19). The unknowns are five: Y_a, Y_b, r, H_a, and H_b. Knowing H_a and H_b, of course, we can recover g_a and g_b from eqs. (16.5). The solution of this system is given graphically in the following section.

16.3 LONG-RUN EQUILIBRIUM

Consider fig. 16.1. For any given rate of interest a pair of reaction curves are drawn in the first quadrant as shown by the two broken curves through E_1. These reaction curves are familiar to us from the income-adjustment mechanism of chap. 10. At their intersection, as illustrated by E_1, eqs. (16.6) and (16.7) are simultaneously satisfied for the given value of r. As r falls, A's reaction curve shifts upward and to the left while B's reaction curve shifts downward and to the right. Accordingly, the new intersection between the new pair of reaction curves lies northeast of E_1 on the curve labeled *commodity-market equilibrium locus*. The latter curve, as the name implies, is the locus of points at which both commodity markets are cleared at alternative values of r.

Turn now to the second quadrant. The curve through E_2 shows A's demand for money (L_a). Thus, from the construction of the commodity-market equilibrium locus it is apparent that there is a one-to-one correspondence between the interest rate and A's national income (and also B's national income). As r falls, Y_a increases. The quantity of money demanded by A (L_a) is a function of Y_a and r, as shown by eq. (16.3). In particular, L_a tends to increase when either Y_a increases or r falls. Hence, as we travel northeast on the commodity-market equilibrium locus, L_a tends to increase both because Y_a increases and at the same time r falls. This is shown by the curve labeled *A's demand for money*. The curve labeled *B's demand for money* in the fourth quadrant is similarly derived for country B.

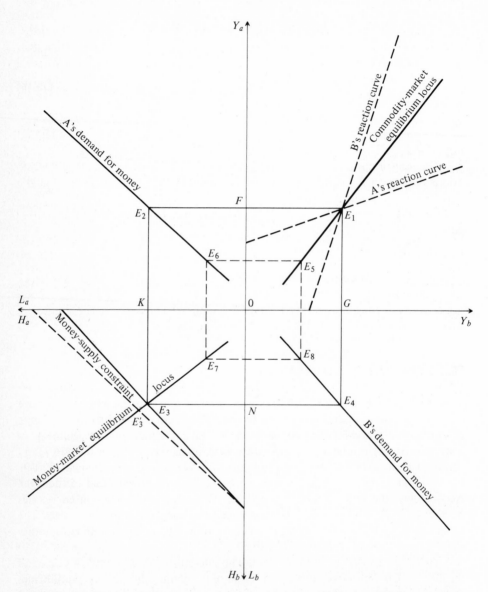

Figure 16.1 Long-run equilibrium with perfect capital mobility. Long-run equilibrium occurs in the third quadrant at the intersection between the money-supply constraint and the money-market equilibrium locus, i.e., point E_3.

Given the commodity-market equilibrium locus as well as A's and B's demand for money, we derive the *money-market equilibrium locus*, as shown in the third quadrant by merely completing the rectangles implied by the three given curves, as illustrated by $E_1 E_2 E_3 E_4$ and $E_5 E_6 E_7 E_8$. As we travel northeast on the commodity-market equilibrium locus, we necessarily travel southwest on the money-market equilibrium locus, since the rectangles tend to become bigger and bigger.

What does the money-market equilibrium locus show? It shows all alternative combinations of A's and B's money supply (H_a and H_b) which are consistent with equilibrium in all markets. Of course, not all of these equilibria are attainable because nothing has been said yet about the supply of money. The supply of money is the final link and is provided in the third quadrant in the form of a *money-supply constraint*, which is merely the graphical representation of eq. (16.18).

As noted above, the money-supply constraint in the third quadrant gives all alternative combinations of H_a and H_b available to the two countries given the total stock of gold $\bar{g}$ and the money multipliers (k_a, k_b).

The long-run equilibrium of the system is evidently shown in the third quadrant by the intersection E_3 between the money-supply constraint and the money-market equilibrium locus. Hence, the long-run equilibrium values of Y_a and Y_b are given by the coordinates of point E_1, that is, $0F$ and $0G$, respectively; and the equilibrium values of H_a and H_b, by the coordinates of point E_3, that is, $0K$ and $0N$, respectively. Knowing, of course, H_a and H_b we can easily determine from eq. (16.5) the long-run distribution of gold between A and B (that is, g_a and g_b). A minor disadvantage of our approach is that the long-run equilibrium interest rate is not shown explicitly although it is perfectly determined.

16.4 COMPARATIVE STATICS

Before turning to the adjustment process leading to the long-run equilibrium, it is important to consider the long-run effects of some parametric shifts in the system.

The Effects of an Increase in the Total Supply of Gold

Consider first an increase in the total supply of gold $\bar{g}$ in the system. In the long run it causes Y_a, Y_b, H_a, H_b, g_a, and g_b to expand and the interest rate to fall. This result is easily verified by observing that, as the total supply of gold increases, the money-supply constraint in the third quadrant of fig. 16.1 shifts downward and to the left (away from the origin). Hence the equilibrium rectangle expands. The rest is obvious.

The Effects of an Expansionary Monetary Policy in Country A

Similarly, an expansionary monetary policy in the ith country (by increasing the money multiplier k_i) causes both national incomes (Y_a and Y_b) to increase and the interest rate to fall, but the ith country loses gold to the other country even though *both* money supplies increase. This is easily verified in fig. 16.1 by observing that an increase in k_a causes the money-supply constraint to rotate, as shown by the broken curve in the third quadrant, so that equilibrium moves to E'_3.

The Effects of an Increase in A's Demand for Its Own Products

Consider now an autonomous increase in A's demand for its own products (A-exportables) either because of an expansionary fiscal policy or an investment boom. What are the long-run effects on Y_a, Y_b, H_a (and g_a), H_b (and g_b), and r? It will be recalled that in chap. 10 we concluded that, ignoring the money and bond markets, such a shift would cause both Y_a and Y_b to rise. Does this conclusion remain valid in our present model?

As we saw in chap. 10, for any given interest rate, an autonomous increase in Z_{ad} causes A's reaction curve to shift upward and to the left. Thus, the equilibrium point travels northeast on B's reaction curve because the latter does not shift. Accordingly, for any given r, both Y_a and Y_b tend to increase. This analysis holds for *any* value of r. In terms of fig. 16.1 it means definitely that the autonomous increase in Z_{ad} causes the commodity-market equilibrium locus to shift upward and to the left. But this is not all, for at every Y_a and Y_b a higher interest rate is now required since at any given interest rate both Y_a and Y_b are higher after the increase in Z_{ad}. Accordingly, each country's demand-for-money schedule (in the second and fourth quadrants) also shifts to the extent that a country's demand for money is sensitive to the interest rate. In general, both demand-for-money schedules will shift upward and to the right and a variety of results are possible. To clarify the problem, we consider first the following limiting case. Assume that the interest elasticity of demand for money is zero in both countries. This is the classical or monetarist position. Here neither country's demand-for-money schedule shifts, and the increase in Z_{ad} causes Y_a, H_a (and g_a) to increase and Y_b, H_b (and g_b) to decrease. *In this classical case, a boom in one country causes a depression in the other.*

The classical case is illustrated in fig. 16.2. The solid curves show the situation before Z_{ad} increases. Thus, equilibrium occurs initially at E_3. As Z_{ad} increases, the commodity-market equilibrium locus shifts upward and to the left, as shown by the broken curve NE'_1. The money-market equilibrium locus also shifts upward and to the left, as shown by the broken curve $E'_3 V$. (To see this, complete the rectangle $NE_2 VU$ and show that point V which lies on the new money-market equilibrium locus lies above and to the left of the initial locus.) Finally, the equilibrium rectangle shifts from $E_1 E_2 E_3 E_4$ to $E'_1 E'_2 E'_3 E'_4$, verifying our conclusion that Y_a, H_a, and g_a rise while Y_b, H_b, and g_b fall.

When the interest elasticity of demand for money is strictly negative, point E'_1 cannot be an equilibrium point because the interest rate is too high. At E'_1 there

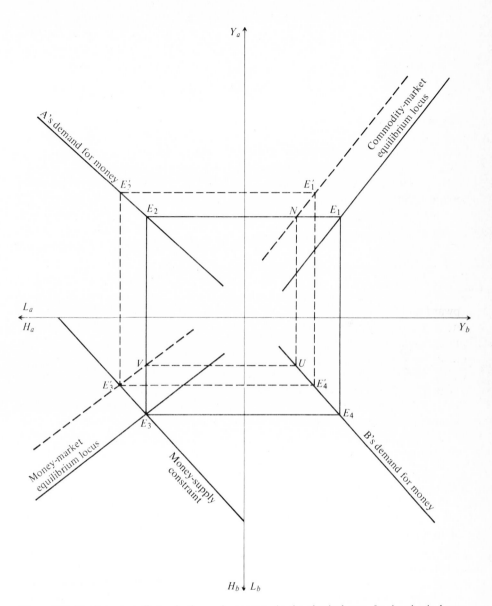

Figure 16.2 The long-run effects of a boom in country A: the classical case. In the classical case, the interest elasticity of demand for money is zero. Hence, a boom in A causes the commodity-market equilibrium locus (first quadrant) and the money-market equilibrium locus (third quadrant) to shift upward and to the left. Both A's and B's demand for money remain unaltered. Equilibrium shifts from E_3 to E'. Thus, Y_a, H_a, and g_a rise while Y_b, H_b, and g_b fall.

exists an excess supply of money in the international economy. To restore equilibrium, the interest rate must fall to a degree which depends on several parameters, such as the interest elasticity of demand for money in each country, the interest elasticity of aggregate spending in each country, and the various marginal propensities to spend. All we can say in general is that the final equilibrium point will lie on the new commodity-market equilibrium locus northeast of point E'_1. Thus, in general, both Y_a and Y_b will be higher than their respective values at point E'_1. Whether Y_b will increase beyond its initial level at E_1 depends on the various parameters. Nevertheless, it can no longer be asserted that a boom or depression in one country is necessarily transmitted to the rest of the world.

The Effects of Other Shifts

The preceding analysis holds step by step for an increase in B's demand for A's products. With a slight modification it can also be applied to a diversion of B's demand from B-exportables to A-exportables.

16.5 THE ADJUSTMENT PROCESS

We proceed now with the question of disequilibrium and adjustment. In this section we consider this question by means of an example. For the discussion of this section only, we make the simplifying assumption that $k_a = k_b = 1$ (i.e., the 100 percent money principle). A rigorous analysis is given later in the appendix to this chapter.

Assume that the system is initially in long-run equilibrium and suppose that this equilibrium is disturbed by a *net* reduction in B's demand for imports. (By "net reduction" is meant that B's total absorption and imports are reduced by the same amount.) What impact would this disturbance have on Y_a, Y_b, r, and the distribution of gold between A and B? How does the system move to a new long-run equilibrium?

Following the analysis of the preceding section, we can easily conclude that in the long run Y_a and r will tend to fall, while Y_b and g_a may either rise or fall. The most interesting question, however, concerns the precise adjustment process which the system follows to move to the new long-run equilibrium.

A net reduction in B's demand for imports does not affect B's reaction curve. But A's reaction curve shifts to the right. Thus, immediately after the shift in B's demand for imports the *observed point* (in the first quadrant of figs. 16.1 or 16.2) lies on B's, but not on A's, reaction curve. The money-supply constraint (in the fourth quadrant) continues to be satisfied, as explained below. Hence, it appears that there is a tendency for Y_a only to fall.

The shift in B's demand for imports necessarily implies another shift somewhere in the system because of B's budget constraint. Thus, when B decides to spend less on Y_a, it must simultaneously decide what to do with this "freed" amount of income. There are three possibilities as follows:

1. B can decide to increase its expenditures for its own output.
2. B can decide to increase its cash balances (i.e., its demand for money). In this case, the money market as well will be immediately out of equilibrium.
3. B can decide to increase its holdings of bonds, in which case the excess demand for bonds will be positive (immediately after the shift in B's demand for imports).

In what follows, it is assumed that the shift in B's demand for imports is followed by a shift in B's demand for bonds in the opposite direction. Does this mean that there is a tendency for the interest rate to fall at this stage? This depends on whether or not there is actually a positive excess demand for bonds at the interest rate prevailing at the initial equilibrium, say r_0, and before Y_a falls.

Suppose, then, that A's producers do not realize that the fall in foreign demand is of a permanent nature—they expect it to be a temporary phenomenon only. Such being the case, A continues to maintain its production and income at the initial level. Hence, A's *intended* expenditure for consumption and investment (i.e., intended absorption) remains at the original level. However, A's exports fall because of the autonomous reduction in B's demand for imports; therefore A's inventories start piling up. A's *actual* absorption rises above the initial equilibrium level—the rise in inventories being exactly equal to A's balance-of-trade deficit created by the fall of exports. How is this unintended inventory increase (or balance-of-trade deficit) financed? More specifically, does A export gold or bonds to B? Initially, and before A's producers realize that demand conditions have changed permanently, it seems natural to assume that A's producers allow their cash balances to fall *pari passu* with their inventory increase; and to this extent, indeed, gold flows from A to B. But this process cannot continue for long.

Financing unintended increases in inventories through continuous reductions of needed cash balances is hardly an ideal policy for A's producers. In addition, it is not the only means available to them! They do have two additional alternatives. First, they can issue new bonds; and, second, they can reduce the level of their production. Which of these two alternatives they actually pursue depends mainly on two things: (*a*) their expectations about the future and (*b*) the availability of credit capital. Assuming that they expect the reduction in foreign demand to be temporary, their first attempt is to borrow additional capital by selling bonds. Is there any part of the world economy which offers to buy these bonds at the current interest rate r_0? As we have seen earlier, B's residents happen to have an excess demand for bonds which is exactly equal to the new supply of bonds by A's producers. It seems, therefore, natural to conclude that, *during the initial stages of adjustment, the deterioration in A's balance of trade will be mainly financed through autonomous capital imports.*

To summarize: during this stage, B's residents want more bonds and less A-exportables. A's producers increase unintentionally their inventories, with the unintentional inventory increase being financed by the sale of bonds to B's residents. A's balance of trade deteriorates, but its balance of payments remains apparently in equilibrium, mainly because of autonomous capital imports. Note that under these circumstances, there is no tendency for the interest rate to fall.

What happens after A's producers realize that the drop of foreign demand for their products is actually a permanent phenomenon? They just have to reduce their production. By how much? By $\Delta Y_a = m_a \Delta M_b$, where ΔM_b represents the initial autonomous reduction in B's imports and m_a is A's foreign-trade multiplier defined in chap. 10. What are the immediate consequences of the reduction in Y_a? In the first place, since A's output and income fall, its demand for money as well as its demand for imports also fall. In the second place, A's producers produce only as much as they can sell. Therefore, their unintended inventory increase and the need for financing it disappears.

It is useful to determine the preceding changes more precisely. As we have seen, A's income falls by $\Delta Y_a = m_a \Delta M_b$. Further, A's imports fall by $M'_a \Delta Y_a = M'_a m_a \Delta M_b$ and A's demand for money falls by $\Delta L_a = (\partial L_a / \partial Y_a) \Delta Y_a$. Now A can afford to use an amount of gold equal to ΔL_a to finance initially its balance-of-trade deficit. Finally, A's balance-of-trade deficit during this second period of adjustment is given by $(1 - m_a M'_a) \Delta M_b$.

A's balance-of-trade deficit occurs because A's residents as a group actually spend more on commodities than they *actually* earn for producing A-exportables. Whether the spending is intended or unintended is immaterial. Initially, the deficit is financed by the excess supply of money (gold) which exists in A because Y_a falls. But as this excess supply of money disappears, A develops a need for financing the balance-of-trade deficit. Can this amount of needed financing be granted by B? To answer this question, we have to look at B's position.

Initially, B continues to produce the original level of output—B's exports have not as yet felt the adverse effects of the reduction of A's output. However, as Y_a falls and therefore A's imports ($\equiv$ B's exports) fall, B's inventories start piling up at the rate of $M'_a \Delta Y_a$ per unit of time. As a result, B's exporters start issuing new bonds at the rate of $M'_a \Delta Y_a$ to finance their unplanned inventories. What is the *net* supply of bonds of country B? It is negative and equal to A's balance-of-trade deficit because originally B had an excess demand for bonds equal to ΔM_b, which was satisfied by the issue of new bonds by A's producers to finance their unplanned inventories. But A's producers have no need for this financing any more. *Hence, B has an overall excess demand for bonds equal to* $\Delta M_b - M'_a \Delta Y_a = (1 - m_a M'_a) \Delta M_b$. Therefore, ignoring for the moment the amount of excess liquidity in A (ΔL_a) which is initially used to finance A's deficit, we conclude that B has an excess demand for bonds identically equal to A's supply of new bonds. Thus, the market for bonds is in equilibrium (ignoring, of course, the quantity ΔL_a) and A's balance-of-trade deficit is financed through autonomous capital imports. Gold flows from A to B temporarily and only to the extent that there exists excess liquidity in A.

To summarize: as in the preceding period, A's balance-of-trade deficit is being financed through autonomous capital imports from B. Further, at the end of this second period, there remain two signs of disequilibrium. In the first place, there exists an excess liquidity in B equal to the amount of gold which was transferred to B by A, that is, ΔL_a. Thus there exists a tendency for the interest rate to fall. (To the extent that A fails to finance its second-period balance-of-trade deficit with the export of unwanted gold, excess liquidity at the beginning of the third period could very well exist in A.) In the second place, there exists an excess supply of B-exportables and thus Y_b tends to fall. It will be useful to consider these tendencies in turn, as we enter the third period.

Assume that the interest rate falls first. In particular, assume that the interest rate falls to the level which is required to keep the money market in equilibrium. The exact amount by which it falls at this stage depends on two things: the existing excess liquidity and the interest elasticity of the demand for money in both A and B. Those residents of B who happen to have excess liquidity are out buying bonds, driving their prices higher. As the prices of bonds increase and the interest rate falls, both the resident of B *and* the residents of A substitute cash for bonds (i.e., they sell bonds) until, of course, they are satisfied with the composition of their portfolios. Accordingly, *as a result of the reduction in the interest rate there is a net supply of bonds from A to B, and, other things being equal, a corresponding flow of gold from B to A.* But whether gold actually flows from B to A depends upon whether other things do remain equal. As we shall see, other things do not actually remain equal. Now the reduction of the interest rate stimulates, of course, the demand for commodities in both countries. However, our analysis can be simplified by assuming that there exists a lag between the interest-rate reduction and the increase in the demand for commodities.

As mentioned earlier, another tendency in the world economy exists—a tendency for Y_b to fall. What happens as Y_b falls? In B, imports and the demand for money fall. In addition, the supply of new bonds to finance unwanted increases in inventories disappears, simply because the unintended accumulation of inventories disappears. On the other hand, there is an unplanned increase in inventories in A (equal to the reduction in B's imports) and a corresponding supply of new bonds to finance the increase in inventories. Hence, as Y_b falls, a new supply of bonds is generated in country A—a supply of bonds which is prompted by the unwanted increase in A's inventories. By a reasoning which is analogous to that given for the second period, it could be easily shown that this excess supply of new bonds by A matches exactly the excess demand for new bonds by B. Therefore, eventually A's balance-of-trade deficit is indeed financed by autonomous capital imports. In addition, because of the initial excess liquidity in B, there is an additional amount of capital imports into A which is accompanied by a flow of gold from B to A. Finally, note that, at the end of the third period, there exists in the system an excess amount of liquidity equal to the reduction of B's demand for money.

To summarize: during this third period of adjustment Y_b, M_b, and r fall, B's unwanted inventories disappear, and A's balance-of-trade deficit worsens. However, gold flows from B to A because of the increased capital flow from B to A. Finally, A's unplanned inventories increase and B finds itself with an excess amount of liquidity.

In the following period, the reduced interest rate will have a favorable effect on the expenditures of both countries. However, in country A, where there still exist unplanned inventories, the real possibility that the interest-rate reduction might not increase the demand for A's products sufficiently to eliminate the need for a reduction of Y_a cannot be ruled out. Nevertheless, Y_b will start improving, and this is the first sign for a recovery. Further, as a result of the existing excess liquidity, the interest rate will continue to fall, stimulating aggregate spending in both countries still further. This process will continue until a new long-period equilibrium is again established.

What important conclusions, if any, can be derived from the preceding analysis? Perhaps the following:

1. Disequilibrium in the world economy need not be reflected in gold movements. It may very well be reflected in unplanned inventory increases, excess liquidity, unemployment, etc.
2. Gold flows take place only to the extent that there exists excess liquidity in the gold-losing country.
3. When capital is perfectly mobile between countries, balance-of-payments equilibrium during the adjustment process is maintained mainly through autonomous capital movements.

PART B. PERFECT CAPITAL IMMOBILITY

We now turn from the world of perfect capital mobility to a world of perfect capital immobility. All other assumptions are retained. Since now the capital markets are totally disconnected—one country's bonds cannot be traded in the other—the interest rate will be different in the two countries and any gap in the balance of trade must be filled with gold flows. Long-run equilibrium requires now that each country's value of commodity exports be equal to the value of commodity imports. Our approach is to show first how long-run equilibrium is determined, and then study briefly the comparative statics of the system.

16.6 LONG-RUN EQUILIBRIUM

Our new long-run equilibrium system consists of the following equations:

$$Y_a = D_a(Y_a, Y_b, r_a) \tag{16.6}$$

$$Y_b = D_b(Y_a, Y_b, r_b) \tag{16.7}$$

$$H_a = k_a g_a = L_a(Y_a, r_a) \tag{16.17}$$

$$H_b = k_b \bar{g} - \left(\frac{k_b}{k_a}\right) H_a \tag{16.18}$$

$$H_b = k_b(\bar{g} - g_a) = L_b(Y_b, r_b) \tag{16.19}$$

$$T_a(Y_a, Y_b) = 0 \tag{16.20}$$

The only difference between the present model and the model of perfect capital mobility is that the equality $r_a = r_b = r$ has been dropped and replaced by eq. (16.20), which merely states that the balance of trade must be zero in the long-run equilibrium.

The solution of the present model is given graphically in fig. 16.3, which is very similar to figs. 16.1 and 16.2. In the first quadrant, the commodity-market

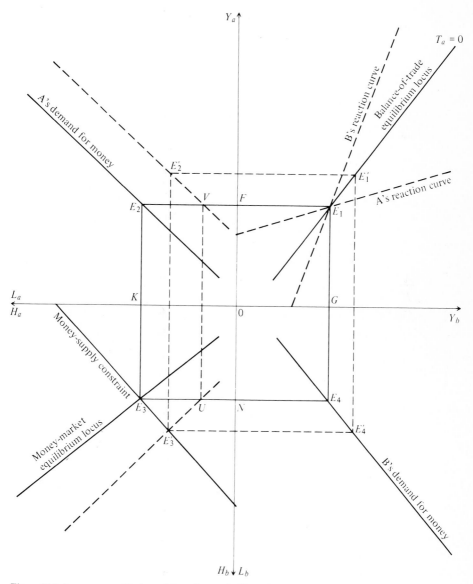

Figure 16.3 Long-run equilibrium with perfect capital immobility. The commodity-market equilibrium locus of figs. 16.1 and 16.2 is now replaced by the balance-of-trade equilibrium locus. The rest is the same. Thus, equilibrium occurs at E_3 (third quadrant).

equilibrium locus of figs. 16.1 and 16.2 is now replaced by the balance-of-trade equilibrium locus. The latter is simply the locus of all combinations of Y_a and Y_b which are consistent with balance-of-trade equilibrium. Now the interest rates r_a and r_b must be such that the two reaction curves intersect each other on the balance-of-trade equilibrium locus. When this happens, of course, eqs. (16.6),(16.7), and (16.20) are satisfied simultaneously. As we travel northeast along the balance-of-trade equilibrium locus both interest rates necessarily become smaller and smaller. Once the first quadrant is so constructed, the rest of the curves in the other three quadrants are derived as in figs. 16.1 and 16.2. Thus, equilibrium occurs at E_3 (in the third quadrant) and the long-run equilibrium values of Y_a, Y_b, H_a, and H_b are given, respectively, by the distances $0F$, $0G$, $0K$, and $0N$.

16.7 COMPARATIVE STATICS

The Effects of an Increase in the Total Supply of Gold

Consider now an increase in the total supply of gold $(\bar{g})$ in the system. As with perfect capital mobility, the money-supply constraint shifts downward and to the left (away from the origin), causing Y_a, Y_b, H_a (and g_a), and H_b (and g_b) to expand and both interest rates $(r_a$ and $r_b)$ to fall. An expansionary monetary policy in either country has the same effects as in the model of perfect capital mobility.

The Effects of an Increase in A's Demand for Its Own Products

Next consider an autonomous increase in A's demand for its own products, i.e., an increase in Z_{ad}, brought about either by an expansionary fiscal policy or an investment boom. Under the assumption of perfect capital mobility, the increase in Z_{ad} shifts the commodity-market equilibrium locus upward and to the left. However, under the assumption of perfect capital immobility the balance-of-trade equilibrium locus does not shift with the increase in Z_{ad}. This is a great simplification. The only thing that happens is that at each and every point on the balance-of-trade equilibrium locus a higher r_a is needed after the increase in Z_{ad} than before. In the classical/monetarist case where the demand for money is independent of the interest rate, A's demand-for-money schedule will remain at the initial position, and so will all the other schedules of fig. 16.3. Thus, in this classical/monetarist case, the autonomous increase in Z_{ad} has no long-run effect whatsoever on any of the variables Y_a, Y_b, H_a, H_b, g_a, g_b, and r_b. Only A's interest rate (r_a) rises sufficiently to choke off the additional demand for A-exportables.

On the other hand, suppose that A's demand for money is interest elastic. Then A's demand-for-money schedule shifts upward and to the right and causes the money-market equilibrium locus to shift downward and to the right, as shown in fig. 16.3. (The shift of the money-market equilibrium locus is verified by completing the rectangle $E_1 VUE_4$ and noting that point U must lie on the new locus.) Accordingly, equilibrium now shifts to E'_3, implying higher incomes in both countries, a higher gold reserve and money supply in B, a lower gold reserve and money supply in A, a lower interest rate in B, and a higher interest rate in A. (That r_a is higher at the new equilibrium follows from the fact that H_a is lower and Y_a higher than their initial equilibrium values.)

We therefore conclude that when capital is perfectly immobile between countries, booms and depressions are transmitted from one country to another, except in the classical/monetarist case where any effects on Y_a and Y_b of an upsurge in spending somewhere in the system are only ephemeral.

The Effects of an Increase in A's Demand for Imports

Consider finally a net increase in B's demand for imports of A-exportables (i.e., an increase in Z_b and M_b by the same amount). This is illustrated in fig. 16.4. The rectangle $E_1 E_2 E_3 E_4$ shows the initial equilibrium position as before. As B's imports increase, the balance-of-trade equilibrium locus shifts upward and to the left, as shown by the broken curve VM. Along this new locus a higher r_b is obviously implied at every Y_b as compared with the initial locus through E_1. Nevertheless, the *same* r_a is implied at the new as at the old locus at every Y_a. To see why, consider the initial equilibrium point E_1. As B's imports increase, A's reaction curve (at the initial interest rate at E_1) shifts upward and to the left, as shown by the broken curve through V. A's new reaction curve necessarily intersects the new balance-of-trade equilibrium locus at V. This must be clear from the analysis of chap. 11. Thus point V is reached as r_b is allowed to increase sufficiently to eliminate B's balance-of-trade deficit which exists at E_1 after the increase in B's imports. Since by assumption A's balance of trade remains unchanged, A's national income must remain unchanged also, since there was no shift in A's absorption Z_a. The same argument applies to all other points.

In the classical/monetarist case where the demand for money is independent of the interest rate and the demand-for-money schedules do not shift, the money-market equilibrium locus shifts upward and to the left, as shown by the broken curve $E'_3 N$. This is verified by completing the rectangle $VE_2 NU$. Equilibrium occurs at E'_3. Hence, Y_a, H_a, g_a, and r_b tend to increase while Y_b, H_b, g_b, and r_a tend to fall, as compared with their initial equilibrium values at E_1.

If the demand for money is interest elastic, B's demand-for-money schedule shifts upward and to the right (since now at every Y_b there corresponds a higher r_b) as shown by the broken curve in the fourth quadrant of fig. 16.4. A's demand-for-money schedule does not shift since at every Y_a there corresponds the same r_a. The shift in B's demand-for-money schedule pulls the money-market equilibrium locus $E'_3 N$ upward and to the left, as shown by the broken curve $E''_3 S$. This is easily verified by completing the rectangle $VE_2 SW$.

The new equilibrium point on the new balance-of-trade equilibrium locus in the first quadrant must lie somewhere between E'_1 and M, for at M there exists a *positive* excess demand for money since r_a is lower and Y_a and Y_b are higher than their respective values at the initial equilibrium point E_1. Similarly, at E'_1 there

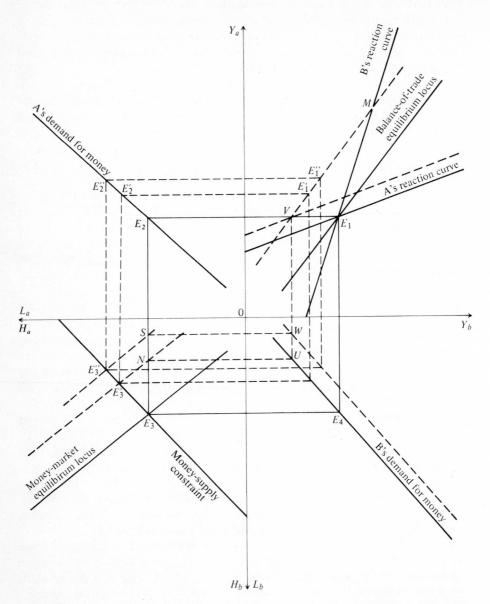

Figure 16.4 Long-run effects of an increase in B's demand for A-exportables under perfect capital immobility. An increase in B's demand for A-exportables causes the balance-of-trade equilibrium locus to shift upward and to the left, as shown by the broken curve VM. In the classical/monetarist case, the money-market equilibrium locus shifts to $E_3'N$ and equilibrium moves from E_3 to E_3''. When the demand for money is interest elastic, B's demand-for-money schedule also shifts upward and to the right (see the broken curve in the fourth quadrant), causing the money-market equilibrium locus to shift further upward and to the left, as illustrated by the broken curve $E_3''S$. Equilibrium now moves to E_3''.

exists a *negative* excess demand for money. (Recall that in the classical/monetarist case equilibrium occurs at E_1', but now there must exist at E_1' an excess supply of money in B since r_b is higher at E_1' than E_1 and B's demand for money is now interest elastic.) Equilibrium must, therefore, occur somewhere between E_1' and M, say E_1''. Accordingly, we can immediately conclude that r_a must fall and Y_a must rise compared with their equilibrium values at E_1' obtained in the classical/monetarist case. Further, A's demand for money is higher at E_1'' than at E_1'. Hence, H_a and g_a must also be higher. This means that A must import more gold from B compared with the classical/monetarist case. Finally, H_b, g_b, and Y_b fall while r_b rises, compared with their respective values at E_1. The decrease in Y_b, however, is smaller now than in the classical/monetarist case. (Both interest rates are, of course, lower at E_1'' than at E_1', that is, the point reached in the classical/monetarist case.)

Other disturbances can be analyzed by the reader in a similar fashion.

PART C. IMPERFECT CAPITAL MOBILITY

It remains to consider briefly the gold-standard system under a different, and perhaps more general, assumption concerning capital mobility between countries. In particular, we are presently concerned with the case of *imperfect capital mobility*, i.e., the case where each country's (positive) excess demand for foreign bonds is an increasing function of the interest-rate differential.

16.8 LONG-RUN EQUILIBRIUM

The long-run equilibrium system is now as follows:

$$Y_a = D_a(Y_a, Y_b, r_a) \qquad (16.6)$$

$$Y_b = D_b(Y_a, Y_b, r_b) \qquad (16.7)$$

$$H_a = k_a g_a = L_a(Y_a, r_a) \qquad (16.17)$$

$$H_b = k_b \bar{g} - \left(\frac{k_b}{k_a}\right) H_a \qquad (16.18)$$

$$H_b = k_b g_b = L_b(Y_b, r_b) \qquad (16.19)$$

$$T_a(Y_a, Y_b) + K(r_a - r_b) = 0 \qquad (16.21)$$

This system is similar to the model of perfect capital immobility studied in part B. The only difference is that eq. (16.20) of the earlier model is now replaced by eq. (16.21), where K shows the flow of bonds from one country to the other as a function of the interest-rate differential. In particular, when $K > 0$, bonds flow from A to B (B loans capital to A), and when $K < 0$, bonds flow from B to A (A loans capital to B). By assumption, $K' > 0$.

The graphical solution of the present system is only slightly more difficult than that of perfect capital immobility. The difficulty is to combine eqs. (16.6), (16.7), and (16.21) to generate an *external-balance locus* to replace the balance-of-trade equilibrium locus of figs. 16.3 and 16.4. Although it seems difficult to determine this external-balance locus graphically, we can study analytically its general properties and then use these properties to deduce the solution of the system.

Think of Y_b as a parameter and differentiate the system of eqs. (16.6), (16.7), and (16.21) totally with respect to Y_b in order to determine the derivatives (dY_a/dY_b), (dr_a/dY_b), and (dr_b/dY_b). Once this is done, all information needed for the completion of the solution of the system will be available.

The alert reader should note that under perfect capital immobility ($K \equiv 0$), we had $(dY_a/dY_b) > 0$, $(dr_a/dY_b) < 0$, and $(dr_b/dY_b) < 0$. Do these results still hold under imperfect capital mobility?

Performing the total differentiation indicated above and putting the results in matrix form, we obtain

$$\begin{bmatrix} \dfrac{1}{m_a} & -\left(\dfrac{\partial Z_a}{\partial r_a}\right) & 0 \\[2ex] -M_a' & 0 & -\left(\dfrac{\partial Z_b}{\partial r_b}\right) \\[2ex] -M_a' & K' & -K' \end{bmatrix} \begin{bmatrix} \dfrac{dY_a}{dY_b} \\[2ex] \dfrac{dr_a}{dY_b} \\[2ex] \dfrac{dr_b}{dY_b} \end{bmatrix} = \begin{bmatrix} M_b' \\[2ex] -\dfrac{1}{m_b} \\[2ex] -M_b' \end{bmatrix} \qquad (16.22)$$

where $(1/m_i) \equiv 1 - Z_i' + M_i'$ and $M_i'(i = a, b)$ is the ith country's marginal propensity to import as before.

Solving (16.22) by means of Cramer's rule, we finally obtain

$$\frac{dY_a}{dY_b} = \left(\frac{1}{\Delta}\right) \left[K'M_b'\left(\frac{\partial Z_b}{\partial r_b}\right) + K'\left(\frac{1}{m_b}\right)\left(\frac{\partial Z_a}{\partial r_a}\right) \right.$$

$$\left. - M_b'\left(\frac{\partial Z_a}{\partial r_a}\right)\left(\frac{\partial Z_b}{\partial r_b}\right) \right] > 0 \qquad (16.23)$$

$$\frac{dr_a}{dY_b} = \left(\frac{1}{\Delta}\right) \left[K'\left(\frac{1}{m_a m_b}\right)(1 - m_a m_b M_a' M_b') - M_b'\left(\frac{\partial Z_b}{\partial r_b}\right)(1 - Z_a') \right] < 0 \quad (16.24)$$

$$\frac{dr_b}{\partial Y_b} = \left(\frac{1}{\Delta}\right) \left[K'\left(\frac{1}{m_a m_b}\right)(1 - m_a m_b M_a' M_b') - M_a'(1 - Z_b')\left(\frac{\partial Z_a'}{\partial r_a}\right) \right] < 0 \quad (16.25)$$

and $\quad \Delta = M_a'\left(\dfrac{\partial Z_a}{\partial r_a}\right)\left[K' - \left(\dfrac{\partial Z_b}{\partial r_b}\right) \right] + K'\left(\dfrac{1}{m_a}\right)\left(\dfrac{\partial Z_b}{\partial r_b}\right) < 0 \qquad (16.26)$

Thus, the properties of the external-balance locus derived under the assumption of imperfect capital mobility are the same as those of the balance-of-trade equilibrium curve derived under the assumption of perfect capital immobility. Thus the external-balance locus is upward sloping as the balance-of-trade equilibrium locus of figs. 16.3 and 16.4. Further, as we travel along the external-balance locus in the northeast direction, both interest rates tend to fall. Accordingly, figs. 16.3 and 16.4 can again be used to demonstrate the long-run equilibrium of the present model as well.

16.9 COMPARATIVE STATICS

How does the present model respond to autonomous shifts? Obviously, an increase in the world supply of gold $\bar{g}$ will have similar results, as in the model of perfect capital immobility (and perfect capital mobility) if the balance-of-trade effect is ignored. The same is true for an expansionary monetary policy in either country. To determine how the system reacts to any autonomous changes in spending it is necessary to determine first how the external-balance locus shifts. To illustrate the problem we consider again an increase in A's spending for its own products, i.e., an increase in Z_{ad}.

The Effects of an Increase in A's Spending for A's Products

Consider fig. 16.5, which for simplicity shows the first quadrant only. Equilibrium occurs initially at E_0 where the interest rates of A and B are r_a^0, r_b^0, respectively. Freezing the interest rates at these levels for the moment, allow Z_{ad} to increase and cause A's reaction curve to shift upward and to the left, as shown by the broken line through E_1. At E_1, A's balance of trade is worse than it was initially at E_0, since $\Delta T_a = -(1 - Z_b') \Delta Y_b$ and $Z_b' < 1$ by assumption (see sec. 10.13, case 1). Since the interest-rate differential has been kept constant by assumption, it follows that A is running a balance-of-payments deficit at E_1. To determine a point on the new external-balance locus, allow r_a to rise gradually from its initial value r_a^0. As this happens, the commodity-market equilibrium point slides southwest on B's reaction curve from E_1 toward E_0. When is balance-of-payments equilibrium attained? Certainly r_a cannot be permitted to rise by as much as to shift the commodity-market equilibrium point down to E_0 because then a surplus would emerge in A's balance of payments—at E_0, A's capital inflow would be bigger now than it used to be initially since now r_a is higher. Accordingly, a point on the new external-balance locus must exist somewhere between E_0 and E_1, say E_2. Repeating the same experiment for all points on the initial external-balance locus leads to the conclusion that the external-balance locus shifts upward and to the left, as shown by the broken curve through E_2. In addition, at every Y_b a higher r_b is required now than initially; and, similarly, at every Y_a a higher r_a is required now also. This result is identical to that derived with the perfect capital mobility model of part A, and the long-run effects on Y_a, Y_b, H_a, H_b, g_a, and g_b are qualitatively the same for the two cases. Therefore, the reader may refer back to sec. 16.4.

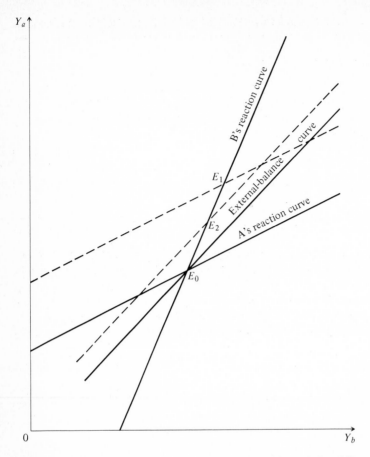

Figure 16.5 The effects of an increase in Z_{ad} under imperfect capital mobility. As Z_{ad} increases, the external-balance curve shifts upward and to the left, as shown by the broken curve through E_2.

APPENDIX TO CHAPTER SIXTEEN. THE STABILITY OF THE GOLD STANDARD

This appendix is divided into two parts. The first part deals with the stability of the fixed-price models studied in chap. 16. The second part considers briefly the problem of stability in the presence of price and wage flexibility. The analysis of both parts is carried out under various simplifying assumptions—an approach dictated by the mathematical complexity of the models involved.

PART A. STABILITY OF THE FIXED-PRICE MODELS

A16.1 PERFECT CAPITAL MOBILITY

Consider again the perfect capital mobility model of chap. 16. For simplicity, assume that the markets for A-exportables, B-exportables, and bonds adjust instantaneously. The dynamic movements of the model are then described by the following system of equations:

$$\dot{g}_a = c(L_a - k_a g_a) \tag{A16.1}$$

$$0 = D_a - Y_a \tag{A16.2}$$

$$0 = D_b - Y_b \tag{A16.3}$$

$$0 = k_a g_a + k_b(\bar{g} - g_a) - L_a - L_b \tag{A16.4}$$

Equations (A16.2) and (A16.3) are the market-equilibrium conditions for A-exportables and B-exportables. Equation (A16.4) is the market-equilibrium condition for bonds; it is actually eq. (16.13) of chap. 16. Finally, eq. (A16.1) says that the flow of gold into A is proportional to A's excess demand for money—the factor of proportionality c is actually a constant speed of adjustment. Equation (A16.1) is derived as follows. First, postulate that A's gold flow $(\dot{g}_a)$ is proportional to A's balance of payments surplus (or deficit). The latter is obviously given by $T_a - E_{ab} = Y_a - Z_a - E_{ab} = L_a - H_a = L_a - k_a g_a$. Equation (A16.1) now follows easily.

The solution of the associated linear system of eqs. (A16.1) to (A16.4) is of the form:

$$\begin{aligned} g_a &= g_a^e + a_1 e^{\lambda t} \\ Y_a &= Y_a^e + a_2 e^{\lambda t} \\ Y_b &= Y_b^e + a_3 e^{\lambda t} \\ r &= r^e + a_4 e^{\lambda t} \end{aligned} \tag{A16.5}$$

where the superscripts e indicate long-run equilibrium values, the constants $a_1, a_2, a_3,$ and a_4 depend on initial conditions at time $t = 0$, and λ is the root of the following equation:

$$\begin{vmatrix} -(ck_a + \lambda) & c\dfrac{\partial L_a}{\partial Y_a} & 0 & c\dfrac{\partial L_a}{\partial r} \\[2mm] 0 & -\dfrac{1}{m_a} & M_b' & \dfrac{\partial D_a}{\partial r} \\[2mm] 0 & M_a' & -\dfrac{1}{m_b} & \dfrac{\partial D_b}{\partial r} \\[2mm] k_a - k_b & -\dfrac{\partial L_a}{\partial Y_a} & -\dfrac{\partial L_b}{\partial Y_b} & -\dfrac{\partial L}{\partial r} \end{vmatrix} = 0 \tag{A16.6}$$

The multipliers m_a and m_b are given by $1/(1 - Z'_a + M'_a)$ and $1/(1 - Z'_b + M'_b)$, respectively, and $L \equiv L_a + L_b$. Obviously, the system is stable if, and only if, $\lambda < 0$.

Expanding the determinant (A16.6) in terms of the first column, we obtain

$$-\lambda\, \Delta_1 - ck_a\, \Delta_1 + k_b\, \Delta_2 - k_a\, \Delta_2 = 0 \qquad (A16.7)$$

where

$$\Delta_1 \equiv \begin{vmatrix} -\dfrac{1}{m_a} & M'_b & \dfrac{\partial D_a}{\partial r} \\[2ex] M'_a & -\dfrac{1}{m_b} & \dfrac{\partial D_b}{\partial r} \\[2ex] -\dfrac{\partial L_a}{\partial Y_a} & -\dfrac{\partial L_b}{\partial Y_b} & -\dfrac{\partial L}{\partial r} \end{vmatrix} > 0 \qquad (A16.8)$$

$$\Delta_2 \equiv \begin{vmatrix} c\dfrac{\partial L_a}{\partial Y_a} & 0 & c\dfrac{\partial L_a}{\partial r} \\[2ex] -\dfrac{1}{m_a} & M'_b & \dfrac{\partial D_a}{\partial r} \\[2ex] M'_a & -\dfrac{1}{m_b} & \dfrac{\partial D_b}{\partial r} \end{vmatrix} < 0 \qquad (A16.9)$$

recalling that $(1/m_a)(1/m_b) - M'_a M'_b > 0$.

Equation (A16.7) can be simplified by determining the sum $-ck_a\, \Delta_1 - k_a\, \Delta_2$. This can be accomplished easily by interchanging the first and second rows and then interchanging the second and third rows of Δ_2. This makes the first and second rows of the resultant matrix identical to the first and second rows of Δ_1, respectively. Hence,

$$-ck_a\, \Delta_1 - k_a\, \Delta_2 = -k_a \begin{vmatrix} -\dfrac{1}{m_a} & M'_b & \dfrac{\partial D_a}{\partial r} \\[2ex] M'_a & -\dfrac{1}{m_b} & \dfrac{\partial D_b}{\partial r} \\[2ex] 0 & -c\dfrac{\partial L_b}{\partial Y_b} & -c\dfrac{\partial L_b}{\partial r} \end{vmatrix} \equiv -k_a\, \Delta_3 < 0 \qquad (A16.10)$$

because $\Delta_3 > 0$.

Substituting these results into eq. (A16.7) and solving for λ, we finally obtain

$$\lambda = \frac{k_b\, \Delta_2 - k_a\, \Delta_3}{\Delta_1} < 0 \qquad (A16.11)$$

We therefore conclude that the system is stable.

A16.2 PERFECT CAPITAL IMMOBILITY

Turn now to the perfect capital immobility model. Assume again that the markets for A-exportables, B-exportables, and bonds adjust instantaneously. The dynamic system is now given by the equations:

$$\dot{g}_a = cT_a \tag{A16.12}$$

$$0 = T_a + k_a g_a - L_a \tag{A16.13}$$

$$0 = -T_a + k_b(\bar{g} - g_a) - L_b \tag{A16.14}$$

$$0 = D_a - Y_a \tag{A16.15}$$

$$0 = D_b - Y_b \tag{A16.16}$$

Since bonds are not traded between countries by assumption, A's balance-of-payments surplus coincides now with A's balance-of-trade surplus. Hence eq. (A16.12) now replaces eq. (A16.1). Equations (A16.15) and (A16.16) correspond to eqs. (A16.2) and (A16.3). The right-hand side of eq. (A16.13) gives A's excess demand for bonds. Similarly, the right-hand side of eq. (A16.14) gives B's excess demand for bonds. Since bonds are not traded between countries by assumption, eqs. (A16.13) and (A16.14) follow immediately.

We now have five equations in five unknowns: g_a, r_a, r_b, Y_a, and Y_b. The solution of the linear system associated with eqs. (A16.12) to (A16.16) is of the form

$$g_a = g_a^e + a_1 e^{\lambda t}$$
$$r_a = r_a^e + a_2 e^{\lambda t}$$
$$r_b = r_b^e + a_3 e^{\lambda t} \tag{A16.17}$$
$$Y_a = Y_a^e + a_4 e^{\lambda t}$$
$$Y_b = Y_b^e + a_5 e^{\lambda t}$$

where λ is the root of the following equation:

$$\begin{vmatrix} -\lambda & 0 & 0 & -cM_a' & cM_b' \\[2mm] k_a & -\dfrac{\partial L_a}{\partial r_a} & 0 & -\left(M_a' + \dfrac{\partial L_a}{\partial Y_a}\right) & M_b' \\[2mm] -k_b & 0 & -\dfrac{\partial L_b}{\partial r_b} & M_a' & -\left(M_b' + \dfrac{\partial L_b}{\partial Y_b}\right) \\[2mm] 0 & \dfrac{\partial D_a}{\partial r_a} & 0 & -\dfrac{1}{m_a} & M_b' \\[2mm] 0 & 0 & \dfrac{\partial D_b}{\partial r_b} & M_a' & -\dfrac{1}{m_b} \end{vmatrix} = 0 \quad \text{(A16.18)}$$

Expanding the determinant (A16.18) in terms of the first column, we obtain

$$\lambda \, \Delta_4 + k_a \, \Delta_5 + k_b \, \Delta_6 = 0 \qquad (A16.19)$$

where

$$
\Delta_4 \equiv
\begin{vmatrix}
-\dfrac{\partial L_a}{\partial r_a} & 0 & -\left(M_a' + \dfrac{\partial L_a}{\partial Y_a}\right) & M_b' \\[2ex]
0 & -\dfrac{\partial L_b}{\partial r_b} & M_a' & -\left(M_b' + \dfrac{\partial L_b}{\partial Y_b}\right) \\[2ex]
\dfrac{\partial D_a}{\partial r_a} & 0 & -\dfrac{1}{m_a} & M_b' \\[2ex]
0 & \dfrac{\partial D_b}{\partial r_b} & M_a' & -\dfrac{1}{m_b'}
\end{vmatrix}
> 0 \qquad (A16.20)
$$

$$
\Delta_5 \equiv
\begin{vmatrix}
0 & 0 & -cM_a' & cM_b' \\[2ex]
0 & -\dfrac{\partial L_b}{\partial r_b} & M_a' & -\left(M_b' + \dfrac{\partial L_b}{\partial Y_b}\right) \\[2ex]
\dfrac{\partial D_a}{\partial r_a} & 0 & -\dfrac{1}{m_a} & M_b' \\[2ex]
0 & \dfrac{\partial D_b}{\partial r_b} & M_a' & -\dfrac{1}{m_b}
\end{vmatrix}
> 0 \qquad (A16.21)
$$

and

$$
\Delta_6 \equiv
\begin{vmatrix}
0 & 0 & -cM_a' & cM_b' \\[2ex]
-\dfrac{\partial L_a}{\partial r_a} & 0 & -\left(M_a' + \dfrac{\partial L_a}{\partial Y_a}\right) & M_b' \\[2ex]
\dfrac{\partial D_a}{\partial r_a} & 0 & -\dfrac{1}{m_a} & M_b' \\[2ex]
0 & \dfrac{\partial D_b}{\partial r_b} & M_a' & -\dfrac{1}{m_b}
\end{vmatrix}
> 0 \qquad (A16.22)
$$

Finally, solving eq. (A16.19) for λ, we obtain

$$\lambda = -\frac{k_a \, \Delta_5 + k_b \, \Delta_6}{\Delta_4} < 0 \qquad (A16.23)$$

We therefore conclude that this system is stable also.

A16.3 IMPERFECT CAPITAL MOBILITY

We finally consider the model of imperfect capital mobility. To simplify our computations, we now assume that eqs. (A16.15) and (A16.16) are solved to give the equilibrium values of Y_a and Y_b as functions of r_a and r_b. Thus, we may write

$$Y_a^e = Y_a^e(r_a, r_b) \tag{A16.24}$$

$$Y_b^e = Y_b^e(r_a, r_b) \tag{A16.25}$$

where the superscript e indicates "equilibrium value." From the analysis of chapter 16 we also know that $(\partial Y_i^e/\partial r_j) < 0$ $(i, j = a, b)$.

Given the earlier assumption regarding instantaneous equilibrium in the bond markets as well, we write the dynamic system as follows:

$$\dot{g}_a = c(T_a + K) \tag{A16.26}$$

$$0 = T_a + k_a g_a - L_a + K \tag{A16.27}$$

$$0 = -T_a + k_b(\bar{g} - g_a) - L_b - K \tag{A16.28}$$

where K depends on the interest-rate differential $r_a - r_b$ and $K' > 0$, as explained in chap. 16. There are only three unknowns now, namely, g_a, r_a, and r_b. Note also that

$$\frac{dT_a}{dr_a} = \left(\frac{\partial T_a}{\partial Y_a^e}\right)\left(\frac{\partial Y_a^e}{\partial r_a}\right) + \left(\frac{\partial T_a}{\partial Y_b^e}\right)\left(\frac{\partial Y_b^e}{\partial r_a}\right) > 0$$

(A *reduction* in r_a has similar effects on T_a as an *increase* in Z_{ad}.)

$$\frac{dT_a}{dr_b} = \left(\frac{\partial T_a}{\partial Y_a^e}\right)\left(\frac{\partial Y_a^e}{\partial r_b}\right) + \left(\frac{\partial T_a}{\partial Y_b^e}\right)\left(\frac{\partial Y_b^e}{\partial r_b}\right) < 0$$

(A reduction in r_b has similar effects on T_a as an increase in Z_{bd}.)

$$\frac{dL_a}{dr_a} = \left(\frac{\partial L_a}{\partial Y_a^e}\right)\left(\frac{\partial Y_a^e}{\partial r_a}\right) + \left(\frac{\partial L_a}{\partial r_a}\right) < 0$$

$$\frac{dL_a}{dr_b} = \left(\frac{\partial L_a}{\partial Y_a^e}\right)\left(\frac{\partial Y_a^e}{\partial r_b}\right) < 0$$

$$\frac{dL_b}{dr_a} = \left(\frac{\partial L_b}{\partial Y_b^e}\right)\left(\frac{\partial Y_b^e}{\partial r_a}\right) < 0$$

and
$$\frac{dL_b}{dr_b} = \left(\frac{\partial L_b}{\partial Y_b^e}\right)\left(\frac{\partial Y_b^e}{\partial r_b}\right) + \left(\frac{\partial L_b}{\partial r_b}\right) < 0$$

The solution of the linear system associated with eqs. (A16.26) to (A16.28) is of the form:

$$g_a = g_a^e + a_1 e^{\lambda t}$$
$$r_a = r_a^e + a_2 e^{\lambda t} \tag{A16.29}$$
$$r_b = r_b^e + a_3 e^{\lambda t}$$

where λ is the root of the following equation:

$$
\begin{vmatrix}
-\lambda & c\left(\dfrac{dT_a}{dr_a}\right) + cK' & c\left(\dfrac{dT_a}{dr_b}\right) - cK' \\[2ex]
k_a & \left(\dfrac{dT_a}{dr_a}\right) - \left(\dfrac{dL_a}{dr_a}\right) + K' & \left(\dfrac{dT_a}{dr_b}\right) - \left(\dfrac{dL_a}{dr_b}\right) - K' \\[2ex]
-k_b & -\left(\dfrac{dT_a}{dr_a}\right) - \left(\dfrac{dL_b}{dr_a}\right) - K' & -\left(\dfrac{dT_a}{dr_b}\right) - \left(\dfrac{dL_b}{dr_b}\right) + K'
\end{vmatrix} = 0 \qquad \text{(A16.30)}
$$

Expanding the determinant (A16.30), we obtain

$$
A_0 \lambda + k_a A_1 + k_b A_2 = 0 \qquad \text{(A16.31)}
$$

where

$$
A_0 \equiv
\begin{vmatrix}
\left(\dfrac{dT_a}{dr_a}\right) - \left(\dfrac{dL_a}{dr_a}\right) + K' & \left(\dfrac{dT_a}{dr_b}\right) - \left(\dfrac{dL_a}{dr_b}\right) - K' \\[2ex]
-\left(\dfrac{dT_a}{dr_a}\right) - \left(\dfrac{dL_b}{dr_a}\right) - K' & -\left(\dfrac{dT_a}{dr_b}\right) - \left(\dfrac{dL_b}{dr_b}\right) + K'
\end{vmatrix}
$$

$$
A_1 \equiv
\begin{vmatrix}
c\left(\dfrac{dT_a}{dr_a}\right) + cK' & c\left(\dfrac{dT_a}{dr_b}\right) - cK' \\[2ex]
-\left(\dfrac{dT_a}{dr_a}\right) - \left(\dfrac{dL_b}{dr_a}\right) - K' & -\left(\dfrac{dT_a}{dr_b}\right) - \left(\dfrac{dL_b}{dr_b}\right) + K'
\end{vmatrix}
$$

and $\quad A_2 \equiv
\begin{vmatrix}
c\left(\dfrac{dT_a}{dr_a}\right) + cK' & c\left(\dfrac{dT_a}{dr_b}\right) - cK' \\[2ex]
\left(\dfrac{dT_a}{dr_a}\right) - \left(\dfrac{dL_a}{dr_a}\right) + K' & \left(\dfrac{dT_a}{dr_b}\right) - \left(\dfrac{dL_a}{dr_b}\right) - K'
\end{vmatrix}$

On the reasonable assumption that $(dL_a/dr_a) < (dL_a/dr_b)$ and $(dL_b/dr_b) < (dL_b/dr_a)$, the determinants A_0, A_1, and A_2 are all positive.

Finally, solving eq. (A16.31) for λ, we obtain

$$
\lambda = -\frac{k_a A_1 + k_b A_2}{A_0} < 0
$$

Accordingly, the system is again stable.

PART B. STABILITY IN THE PRESENCE OF WAGE AND PRICE FLEXIBILITY

We now proceed to study the stability of the gold standard under the assumption that money wages and prices are flexible in both directions. For simplicity we assume that perfect capital mobility prevails and that $k_a = k_b = k$. The dynamic system is now given by

$$\dot{g}_a = c_1(L_a - kg_a) \tag{A16.32}$$

$$\dot{p}_a = c_2(Y_a^e - Y_a^f) \tag{A16.33}$$

$$\dot{p}_b = c_3(Y_b^e - Y_b^f) \tag{A16.34}$$

$$0 = k\bar{g} - L \tag{A16.35}$$

where $L \equiv L_a + L_b$, Y_a^f and Y_b^f are the full-employment levels of A-exportables and B-exportables, respectively, and Y_a^e and Y_b^e are the solutions of the equations $Y_a = D_a$, $Y_b = D_b$ for any given values of $p \equiv p_a/p_b$ and r. The variables Y_a and Y_b are now expressed in *real* terms.

The solution of the linear system associated with eqs. (A16.32) to (A16.35) is of the form:

$$g_a = g_a^e + a_{11}e^{\lambda_1 t} + a_{12}e^{\lambda_2 t} + a_{13}e^{\lambda_3 t}$$

$$p_a = p_a^e + a_{21}e^{\lambda_1 t} + a_{22}e^{\lambda_2 t} + a_{23}e^{\lambda_3 t} \tag{A16.36}$$

$$p_b = p_b^e + a_{31}e^{\lambda_1 t} + a_{32}e^{\lambda_2 t} + a_{33}e^{\lambda_3 t}$$

where the superscripts e indicate long-run equilibrium values, and λ_1, λ_2, and λ_3 are roots of the following equation:

$$\begin{vmatrix} -(c_1 k + \lambda) & c_1\left(\dfrac{dL_a}{dp_a}\right) & c_1\left(\dfrac{dL_a}{dp_b}\right) & c_1\left(\dfrac{dL_a}{dr}\right) \\ 0 & c_2\left(\dfrac{\partial Y_a^e}{\partial p}\right)\left(\dfrac{1}{p_b}\right) - \lambda & -c_2\left(\dfrac{\partial Y_a^e}{\partial p}\right)\left(\dfrac{p}{p_b}\right) & c_2\left(\dfrac{\partial Y_a^e}{\partial r}\right) \\ 0 & c_3\left(\dfrac{\partial Y_b^e}{\partial p}\right)\left(\dfrac{1}{p_b}\right) & -c_3\left(\dfrac{\partial Y_b^e}{\partial p}\right)\left(\dfrac{p}{p_b}\right) - \lambda & c_3\left(\dfrac{\partial Y_b^e}{\partial r}\right) \\ 0 & -\dfrac{dL}{dp_a} & -\dfrac{dL}{dp_b} & -\dfrac{dL}{dr} \end{vmatrix} = 0$$

$$\tag{A16.37}$$

The following reasonable assumptions are made: $(\partial Y_a^e/\partial p) < 0$; $(\partial Y_b^e/\partial p) > 0$, $(dL/dp_a) > 0$, $(dL/dp_b) > 0$, $(\partial Y_a^e/\partial r) < 0$, and $(\partial Y_b^e/\partial r) < 0$.

Expanding the determinant (A16.37) in terms of the first column, we obtain

$$-(c_1 k + \lambda)\begin{vmatrix} c_2\left(\dfrac{\partial Y_a^e}{\partial p}\right)\left(\dfrac{1}{p_b}\right) - \lambda & -c_2\left(\dfrac{\partial Y_a^e}{\partial p}\right)\left(\dfrac{p}{p_b}\right) & c_2\left(\dfrac{\partial Y_a^e}{\partial r}\right) \\ c_3\left(\dfrac{\partial Y_b^e}{\partial p}\right)\left(\dfrac{1}{p_b}\right) & -c_3\left(\dfrac{\partial Y_b^e}{\partial p}\right)\left(\dfrac{p}{p_b}\right) - \lambda & c_3\left(\dfrac{\partial Y_b^e}{\partial r}\right) \\ -\dfrac{dL}{dp_a} & -\dfrac{dL}{dp_b} & -\dfrac{dL}{dr} \end{vmatrix} = 0$$

$$\tag{A16.38}$$

Expanding (A16.38) further, we obtain

$$A_0 \lambda^3 + A_1 \lambda^2 + A_2 \lambda + A_3 = 0 \qquad (A16.39)$$

where

$$A_0 = \frac{dL}{dr} < 0$$

$$A_1 = \left[c_1 k + c_3 \left(\frac{\partial Y_b^e}{\partial p} \right) \left(\frac{p}{p_b} \right) - c_2 \left(\frac{\partial Y_a^e}{\partial p} \right) \left(\frac{1}{p} \right) \right] \left(\frac{dL}{dr} \right)$$
$$+ c_3 \left(\frac{\partial Y_b^e}{\partial r} \right) \left(\frac{\partial L}{\partial p_b} \right) + c_2 \left(\frac{\partial Y_a^e}{\partial r} \right) \left(\frac{dL}{dp_a} \right) < 0$$

$$A_2 = -c_1 k \left[c_2 \left(\frac{\partial Y_a^e}{\partial p} \right) \left(\frac{1}{p_b} \right) \left(\frac{dL}{dr} \right) - c_2 \left(\frac{\partial Y_a^e}{\partial r} \right) \left(\frac{dL}{dp_a} \right) \right.$$
$$\left. - c_3 \left(\frac{\partial Y_b^e}{\partial p} \right) \left(\frac{p}{p_b} \right) \left(\frac{dL}{dr} \right) - c_3 \left(\frac{\partial Y_b^e}{\partial r} \right) \left(\frac{dL}{dp_b} \right) \right] - \Delta < 0$$

$$A_3 = -c_1 k \, \Delta < 0$$

and Δ is the determinant (A16.38) when $\lambda = 0$, that is,

$$\Delta \equiv -c_2 \left(\frac{\partial Y_a^e}{\partial r} \right) \left[c_3 \left(\frac{\partial Y_b^e}{\partial p} \right) \left(\frac{1}{p_b} \right) \left(\frac{dL}{dp_b} \right) + c_3 \left(\frac{\partial Y_b^e}{\partial p} \right) \left(\frac{p}{p_b} \right) \left(\frac{dL}{dp_a} \right) \right]$$
$$+ c_3 \left(\frac{\partial Y_b^e}{\partial r} \right) \left[c_2 \left(\frac{\partial Y_a^e}{\partial p} \right) \left(\frac{1}{p_b} \right) \left(\frac{\partial L}{\partial p_b} \right) + c_2 \left(\frac{\partial Y_a^e}{\partial p} \right) \left(\frac{p}{p_b} \right) \left(\frac{dL}{dp_a} \right) \right] > 0$$

For stability it is required that $A_1/A_0 > 0$, $A_2/A_0 > 0$, $A_3/A_0 > 0$, and $(A_1 A_2/A_0^2) - (A_3/A_0) > 0$. The first three conditions are obviously satisfied. To verify the last condition, rewrite it first as follows: $A_1 A_2 - A_0 A_3 > 0$, by multiplying by A_0^2. This condition is necessarily satisfied because the product $A_0 A_3 = -c_1 k(\partial L/\partial r) \Delta$ is one of the terms of the product $A_1 A_2$ and all other terms of the product $A_1 A_2$ are positive. Hence the system is stable. Internal and external balance are attained automatically.

SELECTED BIBLIOGRAPHY

(Please see the Selected Bibliography at the end of chaps. 7, 10, 15, and 17 and 18.)

CHAPTER

SEVENTEEN

MONETARY AND FISCAL POLICIES FOR INTERNAL AND EXTERNAL BALANCE: I. A SINGLE OPEN ECONOMY

As noted in chap. 8, the link between the balance of payments and the money supply was totally removed, especially after World War II when full employment was recognized as a primary objective of economic policy. The removal of this link gave rise to the international disequilibrium system. The primary objective of this and the following chapter is to reconsider the macroeconomic model of chap. 16 in the light of this new development, where each country's money supply is no longer endogenously determined but assumes the role of a policy instrument.

In chap. 13 monetary and fiscal policies were lumped together under the general heading of expenditure-adjusting policies. It was shown then, following Meade, that the use of expenditure-adjusting policies alone gives rise to conflicts between internal and external balance. Accordingly, we concluded then that for the attainment of external and internal balance expenditure-adjusting policies must be combined with expenditure-switching policies, such as exchange-rate adjustments and restrictions on trade and payments. Throughout our discussion, however, we have seen that the use of expenditure-switching policies is often avoided by policy makers for various reasons—some rational and others irrational. If expenditure-switching policies are actually excluded, how could internal and external balance be attained simultaneously? Mundell (1968, pp. 152–176 and 217–271) has shown that internal and external balance may be attained through an appropriate use of fiscal and monetary policies. As Mundell explained, this is possible in the presence of capital mobility because of the different impacts fiscal and monetary policies have upon the level of national income and the balance of payments.

Our analysis proceeds as follows. First, we show that the macroeconomic model of chap. 16 is converted into a disequilibrium model when the money supply is exogenous. Then we discuss the effects of devaluation and generalize the discussion to the flexible-exchange-rate system. Further, we discuss the effects of fiscal and monetary policies on national income and the balance of payments under fixed- and flexible-exchange rates. Finally, we consider the Mundellian thesis regarding the appropriate use of fiscal and monetary policy for the attainment of internal and external balance. Our analysis is carried out in two stages. In the present chapter we consider the problem from the point of view of a single open economy where all foreign repercussions are ignored. In the following chapter we extend the analysis to the full two-country model.

17.1 THE MODEL

For the purposes of this chapter assume an open economy producing with labor and under constant returns to scale a homogeneous product. The domestic money-wage rate is fixed and the units of measurement are such that the price of domestic output is unity. Foreign prices are assumed fixed and for simplicity equal to unity, exports are exogenous, and the domestic supply of money H (a policy parameter) is determined by the actions of the monetary authorities. The rate of foreign exchange is fixed. (The last assumption is removed later in this chapter to study the consequences of devaluation and flexible-exchange rates.) Finally, the net inflow of capital K is a function of the domestic interest rate r, since the foreign interest rate is taken as given. Capital inflow K is expressed in domestic currency. We may distinguish between perfect capital mobility, imperfect capital mobility, and perfect capital immobility according to whether $K' = \infty$, $0 < K' < \infty$, and $K' = 0$, respectively, where $K' \equiv (dK/dr)$.

The above model is summarized by the following market equilibrium conditions:

$$Y = F(Y, r; R) + T(Y; R) + G \tag{17.1}$$

$$H = L(Y, r; R) \tag{17.2}$$

where $F \equiv C + I$, and the rest of the symbols have the same meaning as before. Equation (17.1) is the familiar national-income equilibrium condition. Government spending G is separated from total absorption since it is later used as a policy parameter. Equation (17.2) is the money-market equilibrium condition. The bond market is eliminated by Walras' law. The two eqs. (17.1) and (17.2) can be solved for the equilibrium values of national income Y and the interest rate r.

The excess demand for foreign exchange at the current rate of exchange, i.e., the balance of payments surplus $(+)$ or deficit $(-)$, is given by the sum $T(Y; R) + K(r)$. In general, there is no reason why the balance of payments (or

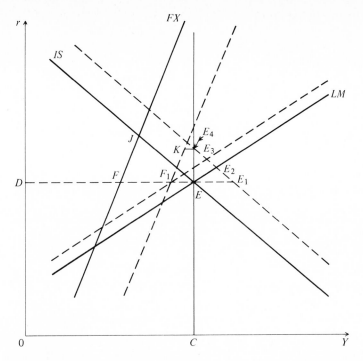

Figure 17.1 The effects of devaluation. National-income equilibrium occurs initially at E. The balance of payments is in deficit. Devaluation causes the FX and IS curves to shift to the right and the LM curve to the left, as shown by the broken curves.

the foreign exchange market) should be in equilibrium (that is, $T + K = 0$) when the commodity and money markets are in equilibrium, i.e., when eqs. (17.1) and (17.2) are satisfied.

The preceding model is illustrated graphically in fig. 17.1 by means of the widely known IS–LM apparatus. The IS curve traces out all combinations of interest rate and national income which keep the commodity market in equilibrium, i.e., those combinations which satisfy eq. (17.1). Similarly, the LM curve traces out all combinations of interest rate and national income which keep the money market in equilibrium, i.e., those combinations which satisfy eq. (17.2). Finally, the FX curve shows all combinations of interest rate and national income which produce balance-of-payments equilibrium, i.e., those combinations which satisfy the equation $T + K = 0$. When imperfect capital mobility prevails $(0 < K' < \infty)$, the FX curve is upward sloping, as illustrated in fig. 17.1. On the other hand, when perfect capital immobility $(K' = 0)$ or perfect capital mobility $(K' = \infty)$ prevail, the FX curve becomes vertical or horizontal, respectively. Perfect capital mobility presents some peculiarities and for this reason it is taken up separately in sec. 17.6 below.

The slope of the *IS* curve is obtained by differentiating eq. (17.1) totally. Similarly, the slope of the *LM* curve is obtained by differentiating eq. (17.2) totally. Finally, the slope of the *FX* curve is obtained by differentiating the equation $T + K = 0$ totally. Thus,

$$\text{Slope of } IS \text{ curve} = \frac{1/m}{\partial Z/\partial r} \leq 0 \tag{17.3}$$

$$\text{Slope of } LM \text{ curve} = -\frac{\partial L/\partial Y}{\partial L/\partial r} \geq 0 \tag{17.4}$$

$$\text{Slope of } FX \text{ curve} = -\frac{\partial T/\partial Y}{\partial K/\partial r} \geq 0 \tag{17.5}$$

National-income equilibrium occurs in fig. 17.1 at the intersection between the *IS* and *LM* curves (point *E*). Nevertheless, the foreign exchange market can be in equilibrium if, and only if, the *FX* curve passes through *E* also. Otherwise the country is either losing or gaining reserves.

The *FX* curve divides the whole quadrant into two regions. For points below and to the right of the *FX* curve, the country suffers from a balance-of-payments deficit—the national income is too high and/or the interest rate is too low. On the other hand, for the points above and to the left of the *FX* curve, the country runs a balance-of-payments surplus—the national income is too low and/or the interest rate too high. In the illustration of fig. 17.1 the national-income equilibrium point (*E*) lies below and to the right of the *FX* curve and the country is running a balance-of-payments deficit given by the product $FE \times M'$, where $M' \equiv$ marginal propensity to import.

Under the gold-standard rules of the game the equilibrium at *E* would be a temporary phenomenon only, for as the country loses reserves and its money supply falls, the *LM* curve shifts continuously to the left (at the same interest rate and a smaller supply of money, the money market can remain in equilibrium at a smaller national income) until it intersects the *IS* curve at *J*, where the balance of payments is in equilibrium and the money supply stabilized. *But the balance-of-payments deficit is removed at the expense of increased unemployment.* As a result countries no longer allow their money supply to fall automatically as they lose reserves. They undertake offsetting actions that *neutralize* or *sterilize* the negative effect of the loss of reserves on the money supply.

This neutralization or sterilization policy calls for the monetary authorities to buy securities at the same rate as the balance-of-payments deficit (or sell securities at the same rate as the balance-of-payments surplus). In essence, therefore, the neutralization or sterilization policy amounts to this: in the presence of a balance-of-payments deficit, the monetary authorities exchange foreign reserves for securities (bonds), and in the presence of a surplus, they exchange bonds for reserves. Because of this neutralization policy, the self-correcting *stock deficit* at *E* is converted into a persistent *flow deficit*, to use Harry G. Johnson's terminology.

To summarize: at the national-income equilibrium point E (fig. 17.1), the country is running a balance-of-payments deficit. The monetary authorities lose reserves to the rest of the world but gain bonds from the domestic consumers and producers. In effect, the private residents of the economy pay for their overspending (or overlending to the rest of the world, as the case may be) by giving up bonds not directly to the foreigners but to their monetary authorities. The latter seem to act as financial intermediaries (converting the bonds surrendered by domestic consumers and producers into an asset acceptable to the rest of the world, i.e., reserves) but their capacity is rather limited because they do not have access to unlimited foreign-exchange reserves. This idea is exploited further in the last chapter of the book.

17.2 THE EFFECTS OF DEVALUATION

Our earlier discussion of devaluation (chaps. 8 and 11) did not take into account the money and bond markets. In particular, the analysis of chap. 11 was based on the explicit assumption that the interest rate remained fixed. But it should be clear by now that the interest rate cannot remain fixed, for a devaluation of the domestic currency causes domestic output and the price level to increase. As a result, the interest rate tends to rise. What effect, if any, does the rise in the interest rate have on the final outcome of devaluation?

The interest-rate rise has a favorable effect on the balance of payments. For one thing, as the interest rate increases, aggregate spending tends to fall, and national income and, therefore, imports do not increase by as much. For another, the increase in the interest rate may give rise to an increased net capital inflow. For both of these reasons (reduced imports and increased net capital inflow), the final effect of devaluation is more favorable than our earlier analysis suggested.

The preceding analysis is illustrated in fig. 17.1. National-income equilibrium occurs initially at E and the balance-of-payments deficit is equal to FE times the marginal propensity to import. Devaluation causes all three curves to shift. In particular, the FX and IS curves shift to the right while the LM curve shifts to the left, as shown by the broken curves. The FX curve shifts to the right on the assumption that the Marshall-Lerner condition is satisfied. Thus, at any given interest rate, balance-of-payments equilibrium is attained at a higher income level since at the initial lower income level a surplus now prevails. Similarly, the IS curve shifts to the right since at every interest rate the aggregate demand for our economy's output tends to increase both because of the Laursen-Metzler effect and the balance-of-trade improvement (assuming the Marshall-Lerner condition is satisfied). The LM curve shifts to the left because of the increase in the economy's price level as imports become more expensive. Thus, at any interest rate, a lower income level is consistent with equilibrium in the money market.

If the interest rate remained constant as in the analysis of chap. 11, the balance-of-payments deficit would change from $FE \times M'$ to $F_1E_1 \times M'$. When the Harberger condition is satisfied, $FE \times M' > F_1E_1 \times M'$, or $FE > F_1E_1$, or $FF_1 > EE_1$. That is, when the Harberger condition is satisfied, the rightward shift of the IS curve (EE_1) is smaller than the rightward shift of the FX curve.

The analysis of chap. 11 shows the effect of devaluation on the balance of trade (and national income) on the assumption that the interest rate remains constant and the system moves from E to E_1. This would happen in the extreme Keynesian case of the liquidity trap (in which case the LM curve is horizontal) of if the monetary authorities expanded the money supply to make the LM curve pass through E_1.

In the extreme classical/monetarist case in which the demand for money is interest inelastic and the LM curve vertical, as shown in fig. 17.1 by the curve CEE_4, the interest rate would be bid up quickly with national-income equilibrium occurring at E_4 (assuming for the moment that the LM curve does not shift). In this classical/monetarist case the disturbing income effects of devaluation are eliminated and the Marshall-Lerner condition is sufficient for a balance-of-trade improvement. In fact, the balance-of-payments improvement is bigger when capital is mobile between countries because of the additional capital inflow prompted by the increase in the interest rate. Thus, $F_1E > KE_4$. In addition, to the extent that the LM curve shifts to the left, national income would tend to *fall* as the interest rate moves even higher. Here the unfavorable income effect is converted into a favorable one.

In general, then, we can say that in the classical/monetarist case the Harberger condition is too strong for a successful devaluation. Even the Marshall-Lerner condition appears to be too strong when a balance-of-payments improvement is sought—not a balance-of-trade improvement.

Both the liquidity-trap case and the classical/monetarist case are extremes. What happens when the interest elasticity of the demand for money is strictly negative and finite? Here the LM curve slopes upward, as shown in fig. 17.1. National-income equilibrium shifts from E to E_2, assuming the LM curve does not shift. To the extent that the LM curve shifts, the new national-income equilibrium point lies on the new IS curve northwest of E_2, as shown in fig. 17.1 by point E_3. Thus, in general, the interest-rate rise induces, on the one hand, a capital inflow and, on the other, mitigates the national-income increase of the devaluation, and to that extent partially reverses the negative income effect.

The preceding analysis rests on the assumption that aggregate spending in general and domestic investment in particular are interest elastic. If this is not so, i.e., if $(\partial Z / \partial r) = 0$, then the IS curve becomes vertical and the results of chap. 11 hold again. That is, national income would increase by the full multiplier effect and the balance of trade would improve if the Harberger condition is satisfied. The only difference from the results of chap. 11 is that the interest rate would now rise and cause a net capital inflow into the country. This case may be illustrated in fig. 17.1 by assuming that the vertical line CEE_4 is the initial IS curve. After devaluation the vertical IS curve passes through E_1, giving rise to the results mentioned above.

17.3 FLEXIBLE-EXCHANGE RATES WITH BALANCE-OF-PAYMENTS EQUILIBRIUM

Consider now a flexible-exchange-rate system. The rate of foreign exchange is free to vary until equilibrium is established in the foreign exchange market (or the balance of payments). The mathematical model for this system is given by the following equations:

$$Y = F(Y, r, R) + T(Y, R) + G \tag{17.6}$$

$$H = L(Y, r, R) \tag{17.7}$$

$$T(Y, R) + K(r) = 0 \tag{17.8}$$

Equations (17.6) and (17.7) correspond to our earlier eqs. (17.1) and (17.2), respectively. Equation (17.8) is the balance-of-payments equilibrium condition.

This system can be solved graphically in the same way as the flexible-exchange-rate system of chap. 11. Go back to eqs. (17.6) and (17.7) and consider the rate of exchange as a parameter. For each value of R this system can be solved for the equilibrium values of Y and r, as was done earlier in sec. 17.1. Given these equilibrium values of Y and r the change in reserves, $T + K$, can then be determined. Allow the rate of foreign exchange to vary from zero to infinity and plot the resultant values of $T + K$ against the corresponding values of R, as shown in fig. 17.2 by the curve SES'. This latter curve is actually an excess-supply

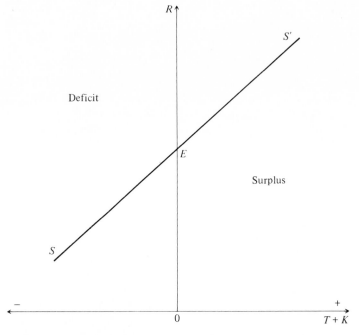

Figure 17.2 The flexible-exchange-rate system (excess supply of foreign exchange expressed in domestic currency). Equilibrium occurs at E where the excess supply of foreign exchange is zero.

schedule for foreign exchange, where the quantities ($\pm$) of foreign exchange supplied are given in terms of domestic currency. The analysis of the preceding section shows that, as R increases, the interest rate increases also (except in the extreme Keynesian case of the liquidity trap). Further, assuming that the Harberger condition is satisfied, both T and K tend to increase. Hence, the *SES'* curve must slope upward as shown. Along the *SES'* curve both the commodity market and the money market are in equilibrium. Obviously full equilibrium occurs at E where the balance of payments is also in equilibrium.

The appendix to this chapter studies the present system further.

17.4 FISCAL AND MONETARY POLICIES UNDER FIXED-EXCHANGE RATES

Consider again the fixed-exchange-rate system of sec. 17.1. How do fiscal and monetary policies (i.e., autonomous changes in G and H) affect national income and the interest rate as well as the balance of payments?

The Effects of Monetary Policy

Consider the effects of monetary policy first. An increase in the money supply H causes the *LM* curve to shift to the right. In general, therefore, the increase in the money supply causes the equilibrium level of national income to increase and the interest rate to fall. Accordingly, as H increases the balance-of-payments deficit worsens (or the surplus shrinks) because imports tend to rise (as income increases) and capital inflow tends to fall (as the interest rate falls). Reversing the argument, we can easily conclude that a decrease in the money supply causes Y to fall, r to increase, and the balance of payments to improve (since imports tend to fall and capital inflow tends to rise).

When either the interest elasticity of the demand for money is infinite (the liquidity-trap case) or the interest elasticity of aggregate spending is zero (vertical *IS* curve), the effect of money-supply changes on the equilibrium level of national income is nil. In the former case (liquidity trap), the effect of money-supply changes on the interest rate and the balance of payments is also nil since the *LM* curve is horizontal. In the latter case (vertical *IS* curve), the increase in the money supply causes the interest rate to fall (even though Y remains constant), and assuming capital is internationally mobile it also causes the balance of payments to deteriorate through a reduced capital inflow (or increased capital outflow). In the presence of perfect capital immobility, however, the only effect would be a fall in the interest rate, with the national income and the balance of payments remaining unaltered.

The Effects of Fiscal Policy

Turn now to fiscal policy. An increase in government spending G causes the IS curve to shift to the right. In general, with a downward-sloping IS curve and an upward-sloping LM curve, the increase in G causes both the national income and the interest rate to increase. The effect on the balance of payments is not clear, however, for as income increases imports also increase and cause the balance of payments to deteriorate. But as the interest rate rises, capital inflow is increased, causing the balance of payments to improve. The final outcome depends on which of these two effects is stronger. If capital is perfectly immobile between countries, the interest-rate effect is zero and the balance of payments deteriorates. The same is true in the liquidity-trap case in which the interest rate remains constant. On the other hand, in the classical/monetarist case where the LM curve is vertical, the effect of an increase in G on national income is zero while the interest rate rises. If capital is mobile, the balance of payments tends to improve because of the increased capital inflow. But if capital is perfectly immobile, the effect on the balance of payments is also zero.

17.5 FISCAL AND MONETARY POLICIES UNDER FLEXIBLE-EXCHANGE RATES

Consider now the flexible-exchange-rate system of sec. 17.3. How do fiscal and monetary policies affect the equilibrium values of R, Y, and r? As in chap. 11, for any autonomous change in the system we must first determine the effect on R by determining how the excess-supply schedule SES' of fig. 17.2 shifts. This presupposes knowledge of the results reached in the preceding section. Once the effect on R is determined, the effects on Y and r are determined as the sum of two effects: (a) the effect on Y and r at the initial value of R, as analyzed in the preceding section; plus (b) the effect on Y and r as R adjusts to its new equilibrium value, as explained in sec. 17.2.

The Effects of Monetary Policy

Consider monetary policy first. In general, for any given rate of exchange, an increase in the money supply causes Y to increase, r to fall, and the balance of payments to worsen. The balance-of-payments deterioration (at any given R) causes the excess-supply schedule for foreign exchange SES' of fig. 17.2 to shift to the left. Accordingly, *the rate of foreign exchange tends to rise.* Further, from the analysis of sec. 17.2 we know that, as the rate of exchange rises, both the national income and the interest rate tend to rise, and the balance of payments tends to improve. Under the flexible-exchange-rate system the rate of exchange rises sufficiently to restore equilibrium in the balance of payments. Obviously national income eventually increases since it increases twice. We can summarize this by saying that, in general, *monetary policy is more powerful (insofar as its effects on national income and employment are concerned) under a flexible- than under a fixed-exchange-rate system.*

What about the total interest-rate effect of the increase in the money supply? At first sight, it appears that nothing can be said *a priori* since the total interest effect is composed of two opposing influences, a negative and a positive, and the final result would depend on which of these opposing influences is stronger. Yet as it turns out the interest rate *falls.* A rigorous proof of this result is given in the appendix to this chapter. Here only a heuristic argument is provided.

As we saw, at the initial rate of exchange, the increase in the money supply causes Y to increase, r to fall, and the balance of payments to worsen. From this position allow the rate of exchange to increase *until the interest rate rises to its initial level,* and determine whether the balance of payments is still in deficit or not. If a deficit still exists, the rate of exchange must rise further and this will make the interest rate go higher than its initial equilibrium value. On the other hand, if the deficit is converted into a surplus, the increase in R and r must have gone too far. For balance-of-payments equilibrium the rate of exchange must be lowered. Therefore, the interest rate will be lower at the new equilibrium. What happens then to the balance of payments deficit as the rate of exchange rises until the interest rate reaches its initial value? We need to concentrate on the change in the balance of trade, since by assumption the capital flow depends on the interest rate and, therefore, must be the same.

Applying eq. (10.34), we obtain

$$\Delta T = -\Delta Z_{\text{aut}} + (1 - Z')\, \Delta Y = \left\{ -\left(\frac{\partial Z}{\partial R}\right) + m(1 - Z')\left[\left(\frac{\partial Z}{\partial R}\right) + \left(\frac{\partial T}{\partial R}\right)\right]\right\} \Delta R$$

$$= \left[(1 - Z')\left(\frac{\partial T}{\partial R}\right) - M'\left(\frac{\partial Z}{\partial R}\right)\right] m\, \Delta R$$

Accordingly, at the higher rate of exchange the balance of trade is improved ($\Delta T > 0$) if the last bracketed expression is positive. This condition is given as inequality (A17.15) or (A17.16b) in the appendix to this chapter. Suppose that this condition is indeed satisfied. In this case, when R is allowed to increase sufficiently to raise the interest rate to its initial value, the balance-of-payments deficit is converted into a surplus. The increase in R has gone too far. For balance-of-payments equilibrium R must remain at a lower level and so must the rate of interest as well. On the other hand, if inequality (A17.15) is not satisfied, the rate of interest must rise.

When the interest elasticity of the demand for money is infinite (the liquidity-trap case), the effect of a change in the money supply on R, Y, and r is nil. Essentially the same is true when the interest elasticity of aggregate spending is zero (vertical *IS* curve) and capital is perfectly immobile between countries. The only difference is that in this second case an increase (decrease) in the money supply causes the interest rate to fall (rise) while R and Y remain constant.

The Effects of Fiscal Policy

Turn now to fiscal policy. How does an increase in government spending G affect R, Y, and r? In general, for any given rate of exchange, an increase in government spending causes Y and r to increase while the balance-of-payments effect is indeterminate. Because of this indeterminacy of the balance-of-payments effect, the effect on the rate of exchange is also indeterminate. Does this mean that the *total* effects on Y and r are also indeterminate? At first sight it certainly looks like it. Nevertheless, the appendix to this chapter shows rigorously that both the interest rate and the equilibrium level of national income definitely increase. Here we provide a heuristic proof of this result.

Consider fig. 17.3, which is similar to fig. 17.1 except that the FX curve is now omitted for simplicity. Equilibrium occurs initially at E. An FX curve may be imagined passing through E also. As G increases (while R remains at its initial value), equilibrium moves to E_1. At E_1 there may be a deficit or a surplus in the balance of payments. If a deficit occurs at E_1, R will rise more and so will r and Y. Thus consider the case in which a surplus occurs at E_1. From the position reached at E_1 allow the rate of exchange to fall (appreciation of the domestic currency) until the interest rate is reduced to its initial value CE. Since as R falls the LM curve shifts downward and to the right, this auxilliary point must lie along the horizontal line EE_3 somewhere between E and E_3, say at E_2. At E_2 the interest

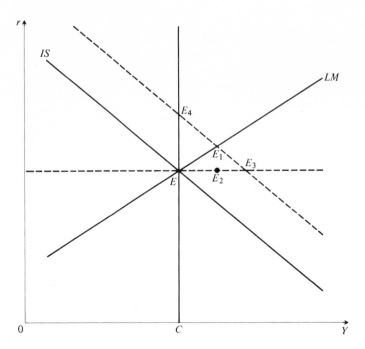

Figure 17.3 The effects of fiscal policy. Equilibrium occurs initially at E.

rate is at its initial level but national income is necessarily higher. What is the situation in the balance of payments? The capital inflow is obviously the same since r is the same at E_2 as at E. But the balance of trade has deteriorated both because national income is higher and R is lower (the domestic currency has appreciated). Accordingly, a *deficit* now exists in the balance of payments. To restore equilibrium in the balance of payments the rate of exchange must increase. This causes national income to increase further. The interest rate rises also from its level at E_2 (or E). We therefore conclude that an increase in government spending necessarily causes both the rate of interest and national income to increase.

If capital is perfectly immobile between countries, there will exist a balance-of-payments deficit at E_1 (fig. 17.3). Hence in this case the rate of exchange must increase and, therefore, the interest rate must rise *a fortiori*. In the liquidity-trap case, the rate of exchange increases also since at its initial value the national-income equilibrium moves from E to E_3 and the balance of payments necessarily deteriorates. The interest rate remains, of course, at its initial value CE. On the other hand, in the classical/monetarist case where the LM curve is vertical, the rate of exchange tends to decrease, since at its initial value the national-income equilibrium moves from E to E_4 and, in the presence of some capital mobility, the balance of payments improves. At the final equilibrium point, national income is higher than its initial value at E since as R falls the vertical LM curve shifts to the right. Similarly, the interest rate is also higher than its initial value at E— otherwise there would exist a deficit in the balance of payments. Should capital be perfectly immobile between countries, the only effect of the increase in G will be an increase in the interest rate. Thus, at the initial value of R, the system moves from E to E_4. At both points the balance of payments is in equilibrium and the rate of exchange has no tendency to change.

Is fiscal policy more powerful (or effective) insofar as its effects on national income and employment are concerned under a flexible- than under a fixed-exchange-rate system? It all depends on circumstances. In particular, if an expansionary fiscal policy causes a depreciation of the domestic currency (i.e., causes R to increase), then fiscal policy is more effective under a flexible-exchange-rate system. On the other hand, if an expansionary fiscal policy causes an appreciation of the domestic currency (i.e., causes R to decrease), then fiscal policy is more effective under a fixed-exchange-rate system.

17.6 PERFECT CAPITAL MOBILITY

Our discussion has ignored so far the case of perfect capital mobility. This was intentional. Perfect capital mobility appears to possess some unique peculiarities which are best handled separately.

The Effects of Monetary Policy

Consider fig. 17.4. Suppose that the initial equilibrium at E_0 is disturbed by an expansionary monetary policy. If the higher money supply could be sustained, the *LM* curve would shift to the right, as shown by the broken curve $E_2 E_1$; and if capital were only imperfectly mobile, equilibrium would move from E_0 to E_2. Thus, the interest rate would tend to fall and cause national income to increase. The balance of payments would tend to deteriorate. Is this possible under perfect capital mobility? Mundell (1968, chap. 18) shows that this is not the case. By assumption, domestic and foreign securities are perfect substitutes. When the monetary authorities attempt to increase the domestic money supply through purchases of securities in the open market, they only induce an inflow of foreign securities (capital outflow) at the same rate as their purchases of securities, leaving the interest rate unaffected. The monetary authorities' reserves start falling *pari passu* with the monetary authorities' purchases of securities. The money supply, on the one hand, tends to increase as the monetary authorities purchase securities and, on the other, tends to decrease as the monetary authorities sell foreign

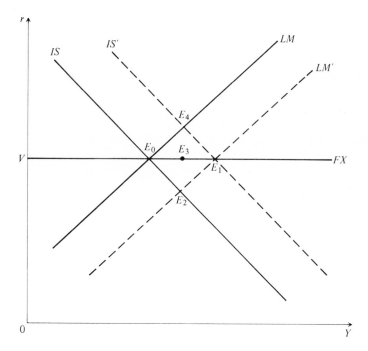

Figure 17.4 Perfect capital mobility. Ordinarily the monetary authorities can increase the money supply and raise national income. Not so under perfect capital mobility, since the interest rate is fixed in world markets. Thus, any attempt to increase the money supply (see broken *LM* curve $E_2 E_1$) will be frustrated and the system will become inconsistent. If R is flexible, equilibrium may move from E_0 to E_3. A similar inconsistency arises when the government increases spending, as illustrated by the broken *IS'* curve. Equilibrium cannot be sustained at E_4.

exchange. These two tendencies cancel out and the money supply remains constant. Thus, national income remains at E_0 since the interest rate remains at the initial level. As Mundell correctly points out, the system is now *inconsistent*.

Equilibrium can be restored in either one of the following two ways. (*a*) The monetary authorities may soon realize that it is not possible to increase the domestic money supply. Thus, they may stop buying securities in the open market. The system will then return to its initial equilibrium at E_0 where the annual loss of reserves is eliminated—although the *stock* of reserves is now lower because of the earlier losses. (*b*) Alternatively, the rate of exchange may be allowed to rise (i.e., the domestic currency may be allowed to depreciate). Under a flexible-exchange-rate system, the loss of reserves will force the domestic currency to depreciate automatically. In either case, as the rate of exchange increases, the *IS* curve shifts upward and to the right, the *LM'* curve shifts upward and to the left, until these two curves eventually intersect on the horizontal *FX* curve as illustrated by point E_3.

We therefore conclude that under a regime of perfect capital mobility and fixed-exchange rates an expansionary monetary policy will leave the interest rate and national income unaffected while causing a persistent balance-of-payments deficit and a persistent loss of reserves. Under a flexible-exchange-rate system the (potential or actual) loss of reserves causes the rate of exchange to increase, which in turn causes national income and employment to rise because of the balance-of-trade effect and the Laursen-Metzler effect.

The Effects of Fiscal Policy

Turn now to the effects of fiscal policy. Suppose that the initial equilibrium at E_0 (fig. 17.4) is now disturbed by an expansionary fiscal policy which shifts the *IS* curve to the right, as shown by the broken curve $E_4 E_1$. In the absence of perfect capital mobility and under a fixed-exchange-rate system, the national-income equilibrium would move from E_0 to E_4. Is this also possible when capital mobility is perfect? Not at all, for now the domestic interest rate cannot rise permanently above the world rate.

What actually happens is this. The government finances its additional spending by selling government bonds. Because the international demand for securities is infinitely elastic at the current interest rate, these bonds (or other domestic securities of equal value) find their way into foreign portfolios (capital inflow) inducing a balance-of-payments surplus. As the monetary authorities buy the excess supply of foreign exchange they create more money. In the absence of sterilization, the *LM* curve starts shifting to the right until equilibrium is reestablished at E_1. If, on the other hand, the monetary authorities attempt to sterilize the balance-of-payments surplus by selling securities of an equal amount, then the system becomes inconsistent. National income tends to increase to VE_1 but the money supply remains insufficient to sustain it at this level since the sterilization policy prevents it from expanding.

Again the inconsistency may be removed in any of the following two ways: (*a*) the monetary authorities may suspend the sterilization policy and allow the money supply to increase; or (*b*) the rate of exchange may be allowed to fall. Actually, under a flexible-exchange-rate system the rate of exchange will tend to fall automatically because of the excess supply of foreign exchange. When the sterilization policy is suspended, equilibrium shifts from E_0 to E_1. On the other hand, when the rate of exchange falls, the IS' curve shifts to the left and equilibrium returns to the initial point E_0 (or to the right of E_0 if the LM curve is affected by the appreciation of the domestic currency).

17.7 POLICIES FOR INTERNAL BALANCE IN THE FLEXIBLE-EXCHANGE-RATE SYSTEM

So far we have studied the effects of monetary and fiscal policies under fixed- and flexible-exchange rates. In this and the following section, we invert the problem and seek those policies which are consistent with internal and external balance. In particular, in this section we consider the use of either monetary or fiscal policy for internal balance while we leave the rate of exchange free to preserve external balance. (This problem is discussed more rigorously in the appendix to this chapter.) In the following section, we consider the Mundellian problem regarding the appropriate use of fiscal and monetary policy to preserve internal and external balance under fixed-exchange rates.

Consider the flexible-exchange-rate system, eqs. (17.6) to (17.8). For any given values of government spending G and money supply H this system can be solved for the equilibrium values of Y, r, and R. The balance of payments is necessarily in equilibrium. What should the money supply be, or, alternatively, what should government spending be, so that internal balance is also preserved?

Monetary Policy for Internal Balance

Consider monetary policy first. Assume that government spending G remains fixed at some level. For any value of R, eqs. (17.6) and (17.7) can be used to determine the appropriate value of H so that internal balance $(Y = Y_f)$ is preserved. As R changes to a new value, so also must H. In particular, as R increases, H must decrease, since both an increase in R and an increase in H cause national income to increase. Thus, starting from a particular combination of R and H for which $Y = Y_f$ and letting R increase, internal balance can be preserved if H decreases, and vice versa. This is shown in fig. 17.5 by the downward-sloping internal-balance schedule.

The combinations of R and H which are consistent with balance-of-payments equilibrium are shown in fig. 17.5 by the external-balance schedule. The latter is necessarily upward sloping since an increase in R causes the balance of payments to improve while an increase in H causes the balance of payments to deteriorate (as shown rigorously in the appendix, $(dR/dH) > 0$).

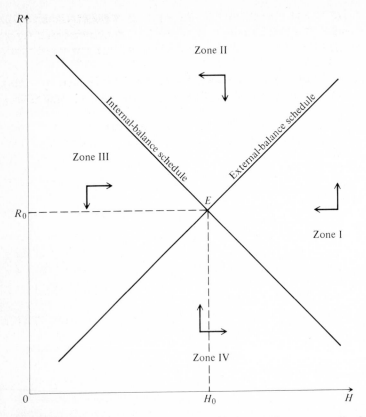

Figure 17.5 Exchange-rate policy for external balance and monetary policy for internal balance.

Zone I = inflation and deficit
Zone II = inflation and surplus
Zone III = unemployment and surplus
Zone IV = unemployment and deficit

    The point of intersection between the internal-balance schedule and the external-balance schedule gives the values of R and H (for some fixed value of G) which are consistent with internal and external balance. If point E is known, then internal and external balance can be attained quickly by choosing the values $H = H_0$ and $R = R_0$ (i.e., the coordinates of E). But point E is not generally known, and while the direction of change of one of the two instruments is always unambiguous, the direction of change of the other instrument is not. How then are internal and external balance attained?

    The internal and external balance schedules divide the diagram into four zones of economic unhappiness. In zones I and II (above and to the right of the internal-balance schedule) there exists inflation, while in zones III and IV (below and to the left of the internal-balance schedule) there exists unemployment. Similarly, in zones I and IV (below and to the right of the external-balance schedule) there exists a balance-of-payments deficit, while in zones II and III (above and to the left of the external-balance schedule) there exists a balance-of-payments surplus. Accordingly, in zones I and II there exists a tendency for H to fall and in zones III and IV there exists a tendency for H to rise (since monetary policy is by assumption used to preserve internal balance). Similarly, in zones I and IV there exists a tendency for R to rise and in zones II and III there exists a tendency for R to fall. All of these tendencies are shown by the arrows in each of the four zones. The appendix to this chapter shows that these tendencies will indeed direct the system to the full-equilibrium point E. The only requirement is that the demand elasticity for imports (in absolute terms) should be greater than unity plus the marginal propensity to import.

Fiscal Policy for Internal Balance

Internal and external balance may also be preserved if fiscal policy (instead of monetary policy) is combined with exchange-rate policy. This is shown in fig. 17.6, which assumes that the money supply remains fixed at some level. Again the internal-balance schedule shows all combinations of R and G consistent with full employment (internal balance). It slopes downward because both an increase in R and G cause Y to increase. The external-balance schedule shows all combinations of R and G which are consistent with balance-of-payments equilibrium (external balance). Because of the indeterminacy of the effect of G on the balance of payments (see sec. 17.4 above), the slope of the external-balance schedule is also indeterminate. Nevertheless, one important feature is certain: *if the external-balance schedule is actually negatively sloped, it must intersect the internal-balance schedule from below.* This feature is important since it preserves the stability of the system. (A rigorous proof for stability is provided in the appendix to this chapter.) How do we prove that this property must hold? (We ignore the case of an upward-sloping external-balance schedule because the analysis would be identical to that of monetary policy.)

Consider the full-equilibrium point E. Let G increase by ΔG. To preserve internal balance, R must fall by, say, ΔR^0. Thus we move to point V. What is the state of the balance of payments at V? It must be in *deficit*, for at V, as compared with E, we have the same Y but a lower interest rate and a lower rate of exchange. (The interest rate is lower because, as R falls, the LM curve shifts downward and to the right.) Accordingly, as G increases by ΔG, R must fall by a smaller amount than ΔR^0 in order to preserve external balance. (In fact, R may have to rise, depending on the degree of capital mobility, but we are only interested in a negatively sloped external-balance schedule.) Thus, to preserve external balance we must move to point U. Hence, the external-balance schedule is flatter than the internal-balance schedule.

As in fig. 17.5, the internal- and external-balance schedules divide the diagram into four zones and the arrows show the tendencies which actually exist in each zone. The appendix to this chapter shows rigorously that the present system is indeed stable, provided that the demand elasticity for imports (in absolute terms) is greater than unity plus the marginal propensity to import.

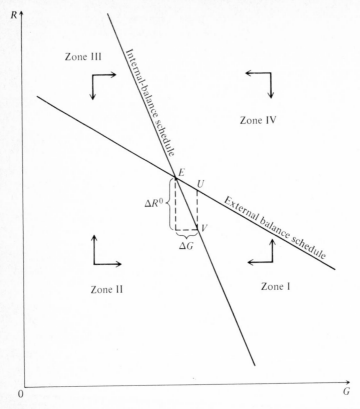

Figure 17.6 Exchange-rate policy for external balance and fiscal policy for internal balance. The internal- and external-balance schedules divide the diagram into four zones. The arrows show the tendencies which exist in each zone. Stability here seems obvious since zones I and III, once entered, can never be left except by moving to E, and the arrows in zones II and IV assure that either zone I or zone III must eventually be entered.

Redundancy of Instruments

The preceding analysis shows clearly that under a flexible-exchange-rate system there is a redundancy of instruments. External balance is preserved by exchange-rate policy while internal balance may be preserved by either monetary or fiscal policy. In fact, there is an infinite number of combinations of H and G which are actually consistent with internal and external balance. All these combinations can be obtained from eqs. (17.6) to (17.8) by putting $Y = Y_f$. Thus, this system of three equations in four unknowns (r, R, G, and H) can be condensed into one equation in two unknowns only: G and H. This relationship can be represented graphically by a downward-sloping curve as shown in fig. 17.7. The importance of fig. 17.7 is that the policy maker now has one degree of freedom. Accordingly, he may choose any point on the curve VU which, in addition to preserving internal and external balance, satisfies some other policy objective, such as the rate of growth.

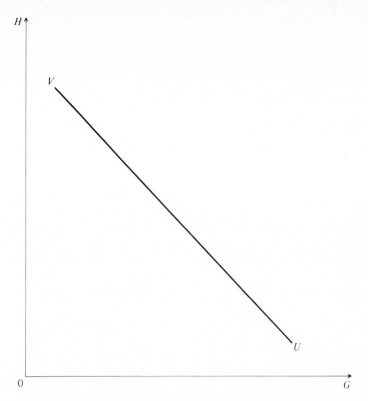

Figure 17.7 Combinations of fiscal and monetary policies consistent with internal balance under flexible-exchange rates. With flexible-exchange rates, there is an infinite number of combinations of monetary and fiscal policy which are consistent with internal and external balance, as shown by the curve VU. The policy maker now has one degree of freedom.

17.8 FISCAL AND MONETARY POLICIES FOR INTERNAL AND EXTERNAL BALANCE UNDER FIXED-EXCHANGE RATES

Turn now to the fixed-exchange-rate system. Can internal and external balance be achieved simultaneously by means of fiscal and monetary policies when the rate of exchange is fixed? As we saw in chap. 13 where international capital flows are ignored, expenditure-adjusting policies alone cannot be relied on to achieve internal and external balance. This view was predominant until the early 1960s when Mundell (1968, pp. 152–176 and 217–271) showed in a series of articles that fiscal and monetary policy may indeed lead to internal and external balance *under the proviso that capital flows are responsive to interest-rate differentials*. The rest of this section reviews the Mundellian thesis.

The Internal-Balance Schedule

Consider first the internal-balance schedule of fig. 17.8. It is derived formally from eqs.(17.1) and (17.2) by setting Y at the full-employment level Y_f and then using one of the equations to eliminate the rate of interest r. The result is one equation in two variables (or policy parameters): G and H. This is the equation which is represented graphically by the internal-balance schedule of fig. 17.8. The internal-balance schedule, which gives all combinations of G and H consistent with full employment, necessarily slopes downward. The reason is simple. An increase (decrease) in government spending G tends to increase (decrease) the level of

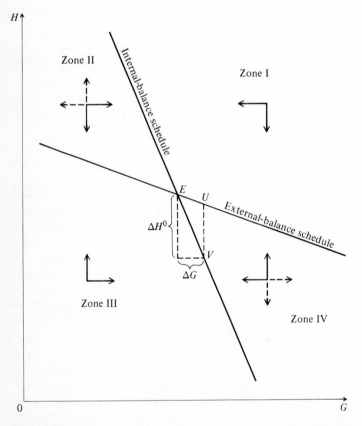

Figure 17.8 Fiscal and monetary policy for internal and external balance. The internal-balance schedule always slopes downward. The slope of the external-balance schedule is indeterminate, since the effect of G on the balance of payments is indeterminate. If the external-balance schedule actually slopes downward, it must be flatter than the internal-balance schedule as shown. When fiscal policy is assigned to internal balance and monetary policy to external balance (see solid arrows), the system is stable. But when fiscal policy is assigned to external balance and monetary policy to internal balance (see broken arrows), the system becomes unstable.

national income, whereas a decrease (increase) in the money supply H tends to decrease (increase) the level of national income. Thus, from any point on the internal-balance schedule an increase (decrease) in G would cause inflation (unemployment). To restore internal balance the money supply must be reduced (increased). Further, points above and to the right of the internal-balance schedule refer to inflation, while points below and to the left of the schedule represent unemployment.

The Importance of Capital Flows

Along the internal-balance schedule the *balance of trade* necessarily remains *constant*, for by assumption the balance of trade depends on the level of national income and the rate of exchange, and both of these variables remain constant along the schedule. Accordingly, if capital flows are ignored, as in chap. 13, the external-balance schedule (giving all combinations of G and H compatible with balance-of-payments equilibrium) would either coincide totally with the internal-balance schedule or never touch it at all. In this case (which is actually analyzed in chap. 13) internal and external balance can only be achieved fortuitously. In general, a conflict exists between the two goals, and an expenditure-switching policy must also be used if external and internal balance are to be attained simultaneously.

Suppose, however, that capital flows are responsive to interest-rate differentials. In particular, assume that $(\partial K/\partial r) > 0$. What difference does this new element make?

Even though the balance of trade remains constant along the internal-balance schedule, the interest rate and the capital inflow do not. Thus, as we travel northwest along the internal-balance schedule (i.e., in the direction of a higher money supply and lower government spending), both the interest rate and the net capital inflow tend to fall. (The interest rate tends to fall because as H increases the LM curve shifts downward and to the right, and as G decreases the IS curve shifts downward and to the left.) Hence, as we move in the northwest direction along the internal-balance schedule, the balance of *payments* tends to deteriorate. On the other hand, as we move in the southeast direction along the internal-balance schedule, the balance of payments tends to improve. In general, then, there should be a point on the internal-balance schedule which is consistent both with internal and external balance. To determine this point we need to derive explicitly the external-balance schedule shown in fig. 17.8.

The External-Balance Schedule

The slope of the external-balance schedule is in general indeterminate, since the effect of government spending on the balance of payments is indeterminate (see sec. 17.4 above). Thus, the external-balance schedule may slope upward or downward depending on the degree of capital mobility. Nevertheless, if it slopes downward, it must be flatter than the internal-balance schedule shown in fig. 17.8.

Thus, consider point E (i.e., the intersection between the internal- and external-balance schedules) and suppose that government spending increases by ΔG. To restore internal balance the money supply must be reduced, say, by ΔH^0. Thus, we move from E to V on the internal-balance schedule. But according to our earlier argument, at V there exists a balance of payments surplus, which could be eliminated by an *increase* in the money supply. Consequently, the external-balance schedule cannot be both negatively sloped and steeper than the internal-balance schedule.

The Four Zones of Economic Unhappiness

The internal- and external-balance schedules divide fig. 17.8 into four zones of economic unhappiness. Conclusions regarding the proper direction of change in the policy instruments can be drawn from fig. 17.8 as was done earlier for figs. 17.5 and 13.9. Note that while in zones II and IV the direction of change of both instruments is unambiguous, in zones I and III the direction of change of *neither* instrument is unambiguous. Further, when the external-balance schedule is upward sloping, then the direction of change of one of the two instruments is always unambiguous but the direction of change of the second instrument is ambiguous.

Internal and external balance occur simultaneously at E (fig. 17.8). If point E were known to policy makers, they could set the money supply and government spending at the appropriate levels (indicated by the coordinates of E) and move directly to full equilibrium. Nevertheless, neither the internal- and external-balance schedules nor their intersection are known to the policy makers. Accordingly, some guidance is needed in the search for full equilibrium. Should each instrument be assigned to a specific goal and, if so, which instrument (fiscal or monetary policy) should be assigned to internal balance and which to external balance?

The Principle of Effective Market Classification

Mundell (1968, pp. 152–176 and 233–239) offers a second-best criterion which he calls the *principle of effective market classification*. According to this principle, each policy instrument should be assigned to that target on which it has relatively the most influence. In our present problem this means that monetary policy should be assigned to external balance and fiscal policy to internal balance because monetary policy has a comparative advantage in working on external balance and fiscal policy on internal balance. This is seen from the fact that

$\quad$ – Slope of internal-balance schedule

$$> - \text{slope of external-balance schedule}$$

Thus, for a given increase in government spending, a smaller decrease in the money supply is needed to restore external than internal balance. Similarly, for a given increase in the money supply, a smaller decrease in government spending is needed to restore internal than external balance.

The appendix to this chapter shows rigorously that when Mundell's principle of effective market classification is followed and monetary policy is assigned to external balance and fiscal policy to internal balance, a stable dynamic system results (see the solid arrows in fig. 17.8). On the other hand, when fiscal policy is assigned to external balance and monetary policy to internal balance, the dynamic system is indeed unstable (see the broken arrows in fig. 17.8).

Mundell's approach has been criticized on several points. In the first place, fiscal and monetary policies may be subject to constraints and particularly political constraints. Thus, governments may not be willing to either reduce government spending to a low level or raise interest rates to high levels. Even in the absence of these political constraints, capital flows may fail to be sufficiently sensitive to interest-rate differentials, and, in addition, destabilizing speculation and lags may complicate the problem tremendously. Finally, some economists argue that Mundell's approach is not a true adjustment mechanism. The fiscal-monetary mix is merely viewed as a method of *financing* the balance-of-payments deficit. In the language of chap. 2, the short-term capital inflow prompted by monetary policy is an accommodating item—not autonomous. It simply fills a gap left by other transactions. Moreover, the short-term capital inflow may be ephemeral, as explained in part one of this book, although, when growth is allowed, this need not be the case.

Additional problems arise when more than one country is considered. These problems are discussed in the following chapter.

APPENDIX TO CHAPTER SEVENTEEN. STABILITY OF VARIOUS ASSIGNMENTS

This appendix deals mainly with the stability analysis of the various assignments considered in chap. 17. The appendix is divided into two parts. Part A deals with the flexible-exchange-rate system and part B with the fixed-exchange-rate system. For simplicity, the present discussion is restricted to the cases of perfect capital immobility and imperfect capital mobility. In addition, the special cases of the liquidity trap, the vertical *IS* curve, and the classical/monetarist case are also ignored.

PART A. THE FLEXIBLE-EXCHANGE-RATE SYSTEM AGAIN

This part of the appendix deals with the flexible-exchange-rate system of chap. 17. In particular, it deals with the problem of stability of the flexible-exchange-rate system and the comparative-statics effects of monetary and fiscal policies.

A17.1 STABILITY

The dynamic behavior of the flexible-exchange-rate system given by eqs. (17.6) to (17.8) is described by the following differential equations:

$$\dot{Y} = c_1[F(Y, r, R) + T(Y, R) + G - Y] \qquad (A17.1)$$

$$\dot{r} = c_2[L(Y, r, R) - H] \qquad (A17.2)$$

$$\dot{R} = -c_3[T(Y, R) + K(r)] \qquad (A17.3)$$

where c_1, c_2, and c_3 are positive speeds of adjustment and $\dot{Y}$, $\dot{r}$, and $\dot{R}$ are time derivatives.

As noted in similar problems earlier in the book, the system of differential eqs. (A17.1) to (A17.3) is stable for small displacement around the long-run equilibrium point defined by eqs. (17.6) to (17.8) if, and only if, the linear system associated with eqs. (A17.1) to (A17.3) is stable. Expanding the right-hand side of eqs. (A17.1) to (A17.3) around the equilibrium values Y^e, r^e, and R^e, and dropping all nonlinear terms, we obtain

$$\dot{Y} = c_1\left(-\frac{1}{m}\right)(Y - Y^e) + c_1\left(\frac{\partial Z}{\partial r}\right)(r - r^e)$$

$$+ c_1\left[\left(\frac{\partial Z}{\partial R}\right) + \left(\frac{\partial T}{\partial R}\right)\right](R - R^e) \qquad (A17.4)$$

$$\dot{r} = c_2\left(\frac{\partial L}{\partial Y}\right)(Y - Y^e) + c_2\left(\frac{\partial L}{\partial r}\right)(r - r^e) + c_2\left(\frac{\partial L}{\partial R}\right)(R - R^e) \qquad (A17.5)$$

$$\dot{R} = c_3 M'(Y - Y^e) - c_3\left(\frac{\partial K}{\partial r}\right)(r - r^e) - c_3\left(\frac{\partial T}{\partial R}\right)(R - R^e) \qquad (A17.6)$$

where $m \equiv \dfrac{1}{1 - Z' + M'}$

The solution of eqs. (A17.4) to (A17.6) is of the form:

$$Y = Y^e + a_{11}e^{\lambda_1 t} + a_{12}e^{\lambda_2 t} + a_{13}e^{\lambda_3 t} \qquad (A17.7)$$

$$r = r^e + a_{21}e^{\lambda_1 t} + a_{22}e^{\lambda_2 t} + a_{23}e^{\lambda_3 t} \qquad (A17.8)$$

$$R = R^e + a_{31}e^{\lambda_1 t} + a_{32}e^{\lambda_2 t} + a_{33}e^{\lambda_3 t} \qquad (A17.9)$$

where the constants a_{ij} ($i, j = 1, 2, 3$) depend on initial conditions at time $t = 0$, and λ_1, λ_2, and λ_3 are roots of the following characteristic equation:

$$\begin{vmatrix} -\left(\dfrac{c_1}{m}\right) - \lambda & c_1\left(\dfrac{\partial Z}{\partial r}\right) & c_1\left(\dfrac{\partial Z}{\partial R}\right) + c_1\left(\dfrac{\partial T}{\partial R}\right) \\[2mm] c_2\left(\dfrac{\partial L}{\partial Y}\right) & c_2\left(\dfrac{\partial L}{\partial r}\right) - \lambda & c_2\left(\dfrac{\partial L}{\partial R}\right) \\[2mm] c_3 M' & -c_3\left(\dfrac{\partial K}{\partial r}\right) & -c_3\left(\dfrac{\partial T}{\partial R}\right) - \lambda \end{vmatrix} = 0 \qquad (A17.10)$$

For stability it is required that the real parts of the roots λ_1, λ_2, and λ_3 are all negative. To determine the necessary and sufficient conditions for stability, expand the determinant (A17.10) and combine all like powers of λ to obtain

$$\lambda^3 + A_1\lambda^2 + A_2\lambda + A_3 = 0 \tag{A17.11}$$

where

$$A_1 = \left(\frac{c_1}{m}\right) - c_2\left(\frac{\partial L}{\partial r}\right) + c_3\left(\frac{\partial T}{\partial R}\right) \tag{A17.12}$$

$$A_2 = -c_2 c_3\left(\frac{\partial L}{\partial r}\right)\left(\frac{\partial T}{\partial R}\right) - c_2\left(\frac{c_1}{m}\right)\left(\frac{\partial L}{\partial r}\right) + c_2 c_3\left(\frac{\partial K}{\partial r}\right)\left(\frac{\partial L}{\partial R}\right)$$

$$- c_1 c_2\left(\frac{\partial L}{\partial Y}\right)\left(\frac{\partial Z}{\partial r}\right) + c_1 c_3\left[\left(\frac{1}{m}\right)\left(\frac{\partial T}{\partial R}\right) - M'\left(\frac{\partial Z}{\partial R}\right) - M'\left(\frac{\partial T}{\partial R}\right)\right] \tag{A17.13}$$

$$A_3 = + c_1 c_2 c_3\left\{-\left(\frac{\partial Z}{\partial r}\right)\left(\frac{\partial L}{\partial R}\right)M' + \left(\frac{\partial K}{\partial r}\right)\left(\frac{\partial L}{\partial Y}\right)\left[\left(\frac{\partial Z}{\partial R}\right) + \left(\frac{\partial T}{\partial R}\right)\right]\right.$$

$$+ \left(\frac{\partial K}{\partial r}\right)\left(\frac{\partial L}{\partial R}\right)\left(\frac{1}{m}\right) - \left(\frac{\partial T}{\partial R}\right)\left(\frac{\partial Z}{\partial r}\right)\left(\frac{\partial L}{\partial Y}\right)$$

$$\left. - \left(\frac{\partial L}{\partial r}\right)\left[\left(\frac{1}{m}\right)\left(\frac{\partial T}{\partial R}\right) - M'\left(\frac{\partial Z}{\partial R}\right) - M'\left(\frac{\partial T}{\partial R}\right)\right]\right\} \tag{A17.14}$$

Note that A_3 is simply equal to the *negative* of the determinant (A17.10) when $\lambda = 0$. For stability, the following conditions must be satisfied: $A_1 > 0$, $A_2 > 0$, $A_3 > 0$, and $A_1 A_2 - A_3 > 0$. (The second condition, $A_2 > 0$, may be eliminated because it is not independent.)

Assuming that the Marshall-Lerner condition is satisfied $(\partial T/\partial R > 0)$, it becomes obvious that $A_1 > 0$, but nothing can be said about A_2 and A_3 because of the indeterminancy of the last bracketed term in both cases. A sufficient condition for A_2 and A_3 to be positive is, therefore, that this last term be positive, i.e.,

$$\left(\frac{1}{m}\right)\left(\frac{\partial T}{\partial R}\right) - M'\left(\frac{\partial Z}{\partial R}\right) - M'\left(\frac{\partial T}{\partial R}\right) > 0$$

or

$$(1 - Z')\left(\frac{\partial T}{\partial R}\right) - M'\left(\frac{\partial Z}{\partial R}\right) > 0 \tag{A17.15}$$

But $T \equiv \bar{X} - RM(R)$, and $(\partial T/\partial R) = -M - R(\partial M/\partial R) = -M(1 + e_m)$, where $e_m \equiv$ demand elasticity for imports. Further, recall from chap. 11 that $(\partial Z/\partial R) = M(1 - Z')$. Substituting these results into (A17.15), we finally obtain

$$-(1 - Z')(1 + e_m)M - M'M(1 - Z') > 0$$

or

$$1 + e_m + M' < 0 \tag{A17.16a}$$

or

$$1 + M' < -e_m \tag{A17.16b}$$

Thus, a sufficient condition for $A_2 > 0$ and $A_3 > 0$ is that the demand elasticity for imports in absolute terms must be higher than unity plus the marginal propensity to import. (If the foreign demand elasticity for imports is not assumed zero, a weaker condition can be derived.) The present condition is stronger than the Marshall-Lerner condition. Accordingly, when inequality (A17.16a) is satisfied the Marshall-Lerner condition is satisfied *a fortiori*.

Consider, finally, the term $A_1 A_2 - A_3$. Thus, substituting the preceding results for A_1, A_2, and A_3 into the expression $A_1 A_2 - A_3$, we obtain

$$
\begin{aligned}
A_1 A_2 - A_3 = c_2 c_3 &\left[c_3 \left(\frac{\partial T}{\partial R}\right) - c_2 \left(\frac{\partial L}{\partial r}\right) \right] \left[\left(\frac{\partial L}{\partial R}\right)\left(\frac{\partial K}{\partial r}\right) - \left(\frac{\partial L}{\partial r}\right)\left(\frac{\partial T}{\partial R}\right) \right] \\
&- c_1 c_2 \left[c_3 \left(\frac{\partial T}{\partial R}\right) - c_2 \left(\frac{\partial L}{\partial r}\right) \right] \left(\frac{1}{m}\right)\left(\frac{\partial L}{\partial r}\right) - c_1^2 c_2 \left(\frac{1}{m}\right)^2 \left(\frac{\partial L}{\partial r}\right) \\
&- c_1 c_2 c_3 \left(\frac{1}{m}\right)\left(\frac{\partial L}{\partial r}\right)\left(\frac{\partial T}{\partial R}\right) + c_1 c_2 \left(\frac{\partial Z}{\partial r}\right)\left(\frac{\partial L}{\partial Y}\right)\left[c_2 \left(\frac{\partial L}{\partial r}\right) - \left(\frac{c_1}{m}\right) \right] \\
&+ c_1 c_3 \left[c_3 \left(\frac{\partial T}{\partial R}\right) + \left(\frac{c_1}{m}\right) \right] \left[\left(\frac{1}{m}\right)\left(\frac{\partial T}{\partial R}\right) - M' \left(\frac{\partial Z}{\partial R}\right) - M' \left(\frac{\partial T}{\partial R}\right) \right] \\
&+ c_1 c_2 c_3 \left\{ M' \left(\frac{\partial Z}{\partial r}\right)\left(\frac{\partial L}{\partial R}\right) + \left(\frac{\partial K}{\partial r}\right)\left(\frac{\partial L}{\partial Y}\right)\left[\left(\frac{\partial Z}{\partial R}\right) + \left(\frac{\partial T}{\partial R}\right) \right] \right\}
\end{aligned}
$$

Now even if inequality (A17.15) is satisfied, the term $A_1 A_2 - A_3$ need not be positive because the last bracketed expression in the above equation is negative. In what follows, it is assumed that $A_1 A_2 - A_3 > 0$.

A17.2 THE EFFECTS OF FISCAL AND MONETARY POLICIES

Consider now the system of eqs. (17.6) to (17.8), reproduced below for convenience:

$$ Y = F(Y, r, R) + T(Y, R) + G \tag{17.6} $$

$$ H = L(Y, r, R) \tag{17.7} $$

$$ T(Y, R) + K(r) = 0 \tag{17.8} $$

Assume that the stability condition (A17.16a) is satisfied. To determine the effects of fiscal policy, differentiate eqs. (17.6) to (17.8) totally with respect to G, assuming that H is a constant, to obtain

$$
\begin{bmatrix}
-\dfrac{1}{m} & \dfrac{\partial Z}{\partial r} & \left(\dfrac{\partial Z}{\partial R}\right) + \left(\dfrac{\partial T}{\partial R}\right) \\[2ex]
\dfrac{\partial L}{\partial Y} & \dfrac{\partial L}{\partial r} & \dfrac{\partial L}{\partial R} \\[2ex]
M' & -\dfrac{\partial K}{\partial r} & -\dfrac{\partial T}{\partial R}
\end{bmatrix}
\begin{bmatrix}
\dfrac{dY}{dG} \\[2ex]
\dfrac{dr}{dG} \\[2ex]
\dfrac{dR}{dG}
\end{bmatrix}
=
\begin{bmatrix}
-1 \\[2ex]
0 \\[2ex]
0
\end{bmatrix}
\tag{A17.17}
$$

Now solve system (A17.17) by means of Cramer's rule to obtain

$$\frac{dY}{dG} = \left(\frac{1}{\Delta}\right)\left[\left(\frac{\partial L}{\partial r}\right)\left(\frac{\partial T}{\partial R}\right) - \left(\frac{\partial K}{\partial r}\right)\left(\frac{\partial L}{\partial R}\right)\right] > 0$$

$$\frac{dr}{dG} = -\left(\frac{1}{\Delta}\right)\left[\left(\frac{\partial L}{\partial Y}\right)\left(\frac{\partial T}{\partial R}\right) + M'\left(\frac{\partial L}{\partial R}\right)\right] > 0$$

$$\frac{dR}{dG} = \left(\frac{1}{\Delta}\right)\left[\left(\frac{\partial L}{\partial Y}\right)\left(\frac{\partial K}{\partial r}\right) + M'\left(\frac{\partial L}{\partial r}\right)\right]$$

where Δ is the determinant of the system. We have already seen that Δ is given by $\Delta = -(1/c_1 c_2 c_3)A_3 < 0$. Thus, we conclude that an expansionary fiscal policy causes national income and the interest rate to increase, but the rate of exchange may go either way.

Finally, to determine the effects of monetary policy, differentiate eqs. (17.6) to (17.8) totally with respect to H, assuming that G is a constant, to obtain

$$\begin{bmatrix} -\dfrac{1}{m} & \dfrac{\partial Z}{\partial r} & \left(\dfrac{\partial Z}{\partial R}\right) + \left(\dfrac{\partial T}{\partial R}\right) \\[2ex] \dfrac{\partial L}{\partial Y} & \dfrac{\partial L}{\partial r} & \dfrac{\partial L}{\partial R} \\[2ex] M' & -\dfrac{\partial K}{\partial r} & -\dfrac{\partial T}{\partial R} \end{bmatrix} \begin{bmatrix} \dfrac{dY}{dH} \\[2ex] \dfrac{dr}{dH} \\[2ex] \dfrac{dR}{dH} \end{bmatrix} = \begin{bmatrix} 0 \\[2ex] 1 \\[2ex] 0 \end{bmatrix} \qquad \text{(A17.18)}$$

Now solve system (A17.18) by means of Cramer's rule to obtain

$$\frac{dY}{dH} = \left(\frac{1}{\Delta}\right)\left[\left(\frac{\partial Z}{\partial r}\right)\left(\frac{\partial T}{\partial R}\right) - \left(\frac{\partial K}{\partial r}\right)\left(\frac{\partial Z}{\partial R}\right) - \left(\frac{\partial K}{\partial r}\right)\left(\frac{\partial T}{\partial R}\right)\right] > 0$$

$$\frac{dr}{dH} = \left(\frac{1}{\Delta}\right)\left[\left(\frac{1}{m}\right)\left(\frac{\partial T}{\partial R}\right) - M'\left(\frac{\partial Z}{\partial R}\right) - M'\left(\frac{\partial T}{\partial R}\right)\right] < 0$$

$$\frac{dR}{dH} = -\left(\frac{1}{\Delta}\right)\left[\left(\frac{1}{m}\right)\left(\frac{\partial K}{\partial r}\right) - M'\left(\frac{\partial Z}{\partial r}\right)\right] > 0$$

where again $\Delta = -(1/c_1 c_2 c_3)A_3 < 0$. The effects of monetary policy are straightforward. An increase in the money supply causes Y and R to increase and, assuming that inequality (A17.15) is satisfied, r to fall.

A17.3 POLICIES FOR INTERNAL AND EXTERNAL BALANCE

Finally, consider the use of either monetary policy or fiscal policy for internal balance while external balance is preserved through the flexibility of the rate of exchange. Are these assignments stable?

Monetary Policy for Internal Balance

Consider first the use of monetary policy for internal balance. Write the dynamic system as follows:

$$0 = Z(Y, r, R) + T(Y, R) - Y$$
$$0 = L(Y, r, R) - H$$
$$\dot{R} = c_1[-T(Y, R) - K(r)] \qquad \text{(A17.19)}$$
$$\dot{H} = c_2(Y_f - Y)$$

where the parameters c_1 and c_2 are positive speeds of adjustment and Y_f is the full-employment level of national income. For simplicity, it is assumed that the commodity and money markets adjust instantaneously.

Expanding the right-hand side of eqs. (A17.19) around the equilibrium values Y_f, r^e, R^e, and H^e, and dropping all nonlinear terms, we obtain

$$0 = -\left(\frac{1}{m}\right)(Y - Y_f) + \left(\frac{\partial Z}{\partial r}\right)(r - r^e) + \left[\left(\frac{\partial Z}{\partial R}\right) + \left(\frac{\partial T}{\partial R}\right)\right](R - R^e)$$

$$0 = \left(\frac{\partial L}{\partial Y}\right)(Y - Y_f) + \left(\frac{\partial L}{\partial r}\right)(r - r^e) + \left(\frac{\partial L}{\partial R}\right)(R - R^e) - (H - H^e) \quad \text{(A17.20)}$$

$$\dot{R} = c_1 M'(Y - Y_f) - c_1\left(\frac{\partial K}{\partial r}\right)(r - r^e) - c_1\left(\frac{\partial T}{\partial R}\right)(R - R^e)$$

$$\dot{H} = c_2(Y_f - Y)$$

The solution of eqs. (A17.20) is of the form:

$$Y = Y_f + a_{11}e^{\lambda_1 t} + a_{12}e^{\lambda_2 t}$$
$$r = r^e + a_{21}e^{\lambda_1 t} + a_{22}e^{\lambda_2 t}$$
$$R = R^e + a_{31}e^{\lambda_1 t} + a_{32}e^{\lambda_2 t} \qquad \text{(A17.21)}$$
$$H = H^e + a_{41}e^{\lambda_1 t} + a_{42}e^{\lambda_2 t}$$

where the constants a_{ij} ($i = 1, 2, 3, 4; j = 1, 2$) depend on initial conditions at time $t = 0$, and λ_1 and λ_2 are roots of the following characteristic equation:

$$\begin{vmatrix} -\dfrac{1}{m} & \dfrac{\partial Z}{\partial r} & \left(\dfrac{\partial Z}{\partial R}\right) + \left(\dfrac{\partial T}{\partial R}\right) & 0 \\[2ex] \dfrac{\partial L}{\partial Y} & \dfrac{\partial L}{\partial r} & \dfrac{\partial L}{\partial R} & -1 \\[2ex] c_1 M' & -c_1\left(\dfrac{\partial K}{\partial r}\right) & -c_1\left(\dfrac{\partial T}{\partial R}\right) - \lambda & 0 \\[2ex] -c_2 & 0 & 0 & -\lambda \end{vmatrix} = 0 \qquad \text{(A17.22)}$$

For stability the real parts of λ_1 and λ_2 must be negative. To see what this means, expand the determinant (A17.22) and combine all like powers of λ to obtain

$$B_0 \lambda^2 + B_1 \lambda + B_2 = 0 \tag{A17.23}$$

where

$$B_0 = -\left[\left(\frac{1}{m}\right)\left(\frac{\partial L}{\partial r}\right) + \left(\frac{\partial L}{\partial Y}\right)\left(\frac{\partial Z}{\partial r}\right)\right] > 0 \tag{A17.24}$$

$$B_1 = -c_1 \Delta - c_2\left(\frac{\partial Z}{\partial r}\right) > 0 \tag{A17.25}$$

$$B_2 = c_1 c_2 \left\{\left(\frac{\partial K}{\partial r}\right)\left[\left(\frac{\partial Z}{\partial R}\right) + \left(\frac{\partial T}{\partial R}\right)\right] - \left(\frac{\partial Z}{\partial r}\right)\left(\frac{\partial T}{\partial R}\right)\right\} > 0 \tag{A17.26}$$

and Δ is the determinant of our earlier system (A17.17). We have seen that Δ is negative when inequality (A17.16a) is satisfied.

It is well known† that the real parts of the roots λ_1 and λ_2 are negative, and, therefore, the system is stable, when the coefficients B_0, B_1, and B_2 of the polynomial (A17.23) are all positive. We therefore conclude that when inequality (A17.16a) is satisfied the present system is stable.

Fiscal Policy for Internal Balance

Consider now the use of fiscal policy for internal balance and write the dynamic system as follows:

$$\begin{aligned}
0 &= F(Y, r, R) + T(Y, R) + G - Y \\
0 &= L(Y, r, R) - H \\
\dot{R} &= c_1[-T(Y, R) - K(r)] \\
\dot{G} &= c_2(Y_f - Y)
\end{aligned} \tag{A17.27}$$

This system can be tested for stability in the same way as system (A17.19). Without going through the various steps, we can easily conclude that stability requires that the real parts of the characteristic roots, λ_1 and λ_2, of the following equation are all negative:

$$\begin{vmatrix} -\dfrac{1}{m} & \dfrac{\partial Z}{\partial r} & \left(\dfrac{\partial Z}{\partial R}\right) + \left(\dfrac{\partial T}{\partial R}\right) & 1 \\[2ex] \dfrac{\partial L}{\partial Y} & \dfrac{\partial L}{\partial r} & \dfrac{\partial L}{\partial R} & 0 \\[2ex] c_1 M' & -c_1\left(\dfrac{\partial K}{\partial r}\right) & -c_1\left(\dfrac{\partial T}{\partial R}\right) - \lambda & 0 \\[2ex] -c_2 & 0 & 0 & -\lambda \end{vmatrix} = 0 \tag{A17.28}$$

† See Samuelson (1947, app. B. pp. 430–431) and also the Mathematical Appendix at the end of this book.

The determinant (A17.28) is very similar to the determinant (A17.22). The only difference is in the last column. Expanding the determinant (A17.28), we obtain

$$B_0' \lambda^2 + B_1' \lambda + B_2' = 0 \tag{A17.19}$$

where

$$B_0' = B_0 > 0$$

$$B_1' = -c_1 \, \Delta - c_2\left(\frac{\partial L}{\partial r}\right) > 0$$

$$B_2' = c_1 c_2 \left[\left(\frac{\partial L}{\partial R}\right)\left(\frac{\partial K}{\partial r}\right) - \left(\frac{\partial L}{\partial r}\right)\left(\frac{\partial T}{\partial R}\right) \right] > 0$$

and again Δ is the determinant of system (A17.17). Assuming that inequality (A17.16a) is satisfied, all coefficients (B_0', B_1', and B_2') are positive. Hence, this system is stable also.

We therefore conclude that, whether monetary or fiscal policy is used for internal balance while the rate of exchange preserves external balance, the system is stable provided inequality (A17.16a) is satisfied.

PART B. THE ASSIGNMENT PROBLEM UNDER THE FIXED-EXCHANGE-RATE SYSTEM

This part of the appendix deals with the stability of the two possible assignments of fiscal and monetary policies for internal and external balance. Section A17.4 deals with the problem of assigning monetary policy to external balance and fiscal policy to internal balance. Section A17.5 considers the problem of assigning monetary policy to internal balance and fiscal policy to external balance. In either case it is assumed that changes in the policy instruments proceed smoothly. Finally, sec. A17.6 considers some of the implications of income-sensitive capital movements.

A17.4 ASSIGNMENT RULE 1: ASSIGN MONETARY POLICY TO EXTERNAL BALANCE AND FISCAL POLICY TO INTERNAL BALANCE

The first assignment rule is to pair monetary policy with external balance and fiscal policy with internal balance. Assuming that the commodity and money markets adjust instantaneously, the dynamic system may be written as follows:

$$\dot{G} = c_1(Y_f - Y)$$

$$\dot{H} = c_2[T(Y) + K(r)]$$

$$0 = F(Y, r) + T(Y) + G - Y \tag{A17.30}$$

$$0 = L(Y, r) - H$$

The parameters c_1 and c_2 are constant speeds of adjustment and Y_f is the full-employment level of output. This is a system of four equations in four unknowns: G, H, Y, and r.

For the stability of the system of eqs. (A17.30) it is required that the real parts of the characteristic roots, λ_1 and λ_2, of the following characteristic equation are all negative:

$$\begin{vmatrix} -\lambda & 0 & -c_1 & 0 \\ 0 & -\lambda & -c_2 M' & c_2 K' \\ 1 & 0 & -\dfrac{1}{m} & \dfrac{\partial Z}{\partial r} \\ 0 & -1 & \dfrac{\partial L}{\partial Y} & \dfrac{\partial L}{\partial r} \end{vmatrix} = 0 \qquad (A17.31)$$

where $M' = (dM/dY)$, $K' = (dK/dr)$, and $(1/m) = 1 - Z' + M'$.

Expanding and collecting terms, we obtain

$$A_0 \lambda^2 + A_1 \lambda + A_2 = 0 \qquad (A17.32)$$

where

$$A_0 = -\left(\frac{1}{m}\right)\left(\frac{\partial L}{\partial r}\right) - \left(\frac{\partial Z}{\partial r}\right)\left(\frac{\partial L}{\partial Y}\right) > 0$$

$$A_1 = c_2 K'\left(\frac{1}{m}\right) - c_2 M'\left(\frac{\partial Z}{\partial r}\right) - c_1\left(\frac{\partial L}{\partial r}\right) > 0$$

$$A_2 = c_1 c_2 K' > 0$$

Since all coefficients (A_i) are positive the system is stable.

We therefore conclude that, if monetary policy is assigned to external balance and fiscal policy to internal balance, and changes in the policy instruments (G and H) proceed smoothly, then full equilibrium will always be attained.

A17.5 ASSIGNMENT RULE 2: ASSIGN MONETARY POLICY TO INTERNAL BALANCE AND FISCAL POLICY TO EXTERNAL BALANCE

The second assignment rule is to pair monetary policy with internal balance and fiscal policy with external balance. The dynamic system is now as follows:

$$\begin{aligned} \dot{H} &= c_1(Y_f - Y) \\ \dot{G} &= c_2[T(Y) + K(r)] \\ 0 &= F(Y, r) + T(Y) + G - Y \\ 0 &= L(Y, r) - H \end{aligned} \qquad (A17.33)$$

For stability it is required that the real parts of the characteristic roots, λ_1 and λ_2, of the following characteristic equation are all negative:

$$\begin{vmatrix} -\lambda & 0 & -c_1 & 0 \\ 0 & -\lambda & -c_2 M' & c_2 K' \\ 0 & 1 & -\dfrac{1}{m} & \dfrac{\partial Z}{\partial r} \\ -1 & 0 & \dfrac{\partial L}{\partial Y} & \dfrac{\partial L}{\partial r} \end{vmatrix} = 0 \qquad \text{(A17.34)}$$

Expanding and collecting terms, we obtain

$$B_0 \lambda^2 + B_1 \lambda + B_2 = 0 \qquad \text{(A17.35)}$$

where

$$B_0 = -\left(\frac{1}{m}\right)\left(\frac{\partial L}{\partial r}\right) - \left(\frac{\partial L}{\partial Y}\right)\left(\frac{\partial Z}{\partial r}\right) > 0$$

$$B_1 = -c_2 M'\left(\frac{\partial L}{\partial r}\right) - c_2 K'\left(\frac{\partial L}{\partial Y}\right) - c_1\left(\frac{\partial Z}{\partial r}\right)$$

$$B_2 = -c_1 c_2 K' < 0$$

Since $B_0 > 0$ and $B_2 < 0$ while the sign of B_1 is indeterminate, this system is necessarily *unstable*. Of course, if we make $c_2 < 0$ and if $K'(\partial L/\partial Y) > -M'(\partial L/\partial r)$, i.e., if the *FX* curve is actually flatter than the *LM* curve (or if we make c_2 sufficiently small in absolute terms), then the system becomes stable. But there is no guarantee that the *FX* curve is actually flatter than the *LM* curve. Therefore, it is not clear how fiscal policy should be assigned.

We therefore conclude that assigning monetary policy to internal balance and fiscal policy to external balance will *not*, in general, lead to full equilibrium (internal and external balance).

A17.6 INCOME-SENSITIVE CAPITAL MOVEMENTS

Professor Harry G. Johnson (1966) suggested that capital flows are responsive not only to changes in the interest rate but also to changes in the level of national income on the assumption that an increase in income leads to an increase in profitable-investment opportunities and a decrease in income to a decrease in such opportunities. Thus, as national income increases following an expansionary fiscal or monetary policy, in addition to the effects studied in chap. 17 there will be an additional capital inflow. If this income effect is strong enough, it may modify or reverse some of our policy recommendations.

The implications of income-sensitive capital movements for the two assignment rules are readily determined by writing $K = K(r, Y)$ with $(\partial K/\partial Y) > 0$. This change leads to the following minor modification in our earlier equations. The terms $-(1/m)$ and $(1/m)$ must now be replaced by the sums $-(1/m) + (\partial K/\partial Y)$ and $(1/m) - (\partial K/\partial Y)$, respectively. If $(1/m) - (\partial K/\partial Y) > 0$, then all of our earlier conclusions regarding stability hold, as the reader should verify. On the other hand, if $(1/m) - (\partial K/\partial Y) < 0$, then it is possible (but *not* certain) that the first assignment rule (monetary policy to external balance and fiscal policy to internal balance) may be rendered unstable, while the second assignment rule (monetary policy to internal balance and fiscal policy to external balance) may be rendered stable.

A sufficient condition for the inadequacy of income-sensitive capital movements to reverse any of our present conclusions is that *the marginal propensity to import goods* (M') *is higher than the marginal propensity to import capital,* that is, $(\partial K/\partial Y)$, for

$$(1/m) - (\partial K/\partial Y) = 1 - Z' + M' - (\partial K/\partial Y) = (1 - Z') + [M' - (\partial K/\partial Y)].$$

Since $1 - Z' > 0$, if $M' > (\partial K/\partial Y)$, then $(1/m) - (\partial K/\partial Y) > 0$.

SELECTED BIBLIOGRAPHY

Jones, R. W. (1968). "Monetary and Fiscal Policy for an Economy with Fixed Exchange Rates." *Journal of Political Economy,* vol. LXXVI, pt. II (July–August), pp. 921–943.

Johnson, H. G. (1958). "Towards a General Theory of the Balance of Payments." In *International Trade and Economic Growth.* George Allen and Unwin, Ltd., London. Reprinted in R. E. Caves and H. G. Johnson (Eds.), AEA *Readings in International Economics.* Richard D. Irwin, Inc., Homewood, Ill., 1968.

—— (1966). "Some Aspects of the Theory of Economic Policy in a World of Capital Mobility." In T. Bagiotti (Ed.), *Essays in Honor of Marco Fanno.* Cedam, Padua.

—— (1967). "Theoretical Problems of the International Monetary System." *Pakistan Development Review,* vol. VII (Spring), pp. 1–28. Reprinted in R. N. Cooper (Ed.), *International Finance: Selected Readings.* Penguin Books, Ltd., Middlesex, 1969.

Mundell, R. A. (1960). "The Monetary Dynamics of International Adjustment under Fixed and Flexible Exchange Rates." *The Quarterly Journal of Economics,* vol. 74 (May), pp. 227–257. Reprinted in R. A. Mundell, *International Economics.* The Macmillan Company, New York, 1968.

—— (1961*a*). "The International Disequilibrium System." *Kyklos,* vol. 14, pp. 154–172. Reprinted in R. A. Mundell, *International Economics.* The Macmillan Company, New York, 1968.

—— (1961*b*). "Flexible Exchange Rates and Employment Policy." *Canadian Journal of Economics and Political Science,* vol. 27 (November), pp. 509–517. Reprinted in R. A. Mundell, *International Economics.* The Macmillan Company, New York, 1968.

—— (1962). "The Appropriate Use of Monetary and Fiscal Policy under Fixed Exchange Rates." *IMF Staff Papers* (March), pp. 70–79. Reprinted in R. A. Mundell, *International Economics.* The Macmillan Company, New York, 1968.

—— (1963). "Capital Mobility and Stabilization Policy under Fixed and Flexible Exchange Rates." *Canadian Journal of Economics and Political Science,* vol. 29 (November), pp. 475–485. Reprinted in R. A. Mundell, *International Economics.* The Macmillan Company, New York, 1968.

—— (1968). *International Economics.* The Macmillan Company, New York.

Salop, J. (1974). "Devaluation and the Balance of Trade under Flexible Wages." In G. Horwich and P. A. Samuelson (Eds.), *Trade, Stability, and Macroeconomics.* Academic Press, New York.

Samuelson, P. A. (1947). *Foundations of Economic Analysis.* Harvard University Press, Cambridge, Mass.

Sohmen, E. (1967). "Fiscal and Monetary Policies under Alternative Exchange-Rate Systems." *Quarterly Journal of Economics*, vol. LXXXI (August), pp. 515–523.

———— (1969). *Flexible Exchange Rates*, 2d ed. University of Chicago Press, Chicago, Ill.

Sohmen, E., and H. Schneeweiss (1969). "Fiscal and Monetary Policies under Alternative Exchange Rate Systems: A Correction." *Quarterly Journal of Economics*, vol. LXXXII (May), pp. 336–340.

Stern, R. M. (1973). *The Balance of Payments*. Aldine Publishing Company, Chicago, Ill., chap. 10.

Takayama, A. (1969). "The Effects of Fiscal and Monetary Policies under Flexible and Fixed Exchange Rates." *Canadian Journal of Economics and Political Science*, vol. II-2 (May), pp. 190–209.

Tsiang, S. C. (1961). "The Role of Money in Trade-Balance Stability: Synthesis of the Elasticity and Absorption Approaches." *American Economic Review*, vol. LI (December), pp. 912–936. Reprinted in R. E. Caves and H. G. Johnson (Eds.), AEA *Readings in International Economics*. Richard D. Irwin, Inc., Homewood, Ill., 1968.

Whitman, M. V. N. (1970). *Policies for Internal and External Balance*. Special Papers in International Economics, no. 9, International Finance Section, Princeton University, Princeton, N.J.

MONETARY AND FISCAL POLICIES FOR INTERNAL AND EXTERNAL BALANCE: II. A TWO-COUNTRY MODEL

This chapter extends the analysis of chap. 17 to the two-country model. This step is indeed crucial to our discussion since it is only in the context of such a model that the consistency of policies pursued by various countries can be considered. The present chapter is divided into two parts. The first part deals with the fixed-exchange-rate system and the second part with the flexible-exchange-rate system.

PART A. THE FIXED-EXCHANGE-RATE SYSTEM

18.1 THE MODEL

The model of this part is very similar to the Keynesian-type, gold-standard model of chap. 16. The only difference is that now each country's money supply (a policy parameter) is exogenously determined by the monetary authorities. Thus, as in chap. 16, there are two countries, A and B, with national currencies, the dollar and the pound sterling, respectively. Countries A and B produce A-exportables and B-exportables, respectively, by means of a single factor of production (labor) and under constant returns to scale. Their respective money-wage rates are assumed rigidly fixed and the units of measurement are such that the dollar price of A-exportables and the pound sterling price of B-exportables are unity. The rate of exchange between the dollar and the pound sterling is also unity. (The rate of exchange is allowed to vary in part B.) Finally, the flow of capital from B to A ($K > 0$), or from A to B ($K < 0$), is a function of the interest-rate differential ($r_a - r_b$) as before. When perfect capital immobility prevails K is identically zero, but when capital is imperfectly mobile K may be either positive or negative with $K' > 0$. The case of perfect capital mobility is again treated briefly below in a separate section.

Following the discussion of chap. 16, the preceding model may be summarized by the following equations:

$$Y_a = D_a(Y_a, Y_b, r_a) \tag{18.1}$$

$$Y_b = D_b(Y_a, Y_b, r_b) \tag{18.2}$$

$$H_a = L_a(Y_a, r_a) \tag{18.3}$$

$$H_b = L_b(Y_b, r_b) \tag{18.4}$$

Equations (18.1) and (18.2) are the equilibrium conditions for the markets of A-exportables and B-exportables, respectively; and eqs. (18.3) and (18.4) are the equilibrium conditions for A's and B's money markets, respectively. This is a system of four equations in four unknowns (Y_a, Y_b, r_a, and r_b) since H_a and H_b are exogenous (policy parameters). In general, therefore, the system can be solved for the equilibrium values of the unknowns. This is done graphically in the following section.

Tsiang (1961) distinguishes between two alternative types of monetary policy: the *orthodox neutral monetary policy* and the *Keynesian neutral monetary policy*. Under the orthodox neutral monetary policy the monetary authority holds the nominal money supply constant. Under the Keynesian neutral monetary policy the monetary authority keeps the domestic interest rate constant by maintaining the supply of money and credit infinitely elastic at the existing rate of interest. Indeed, the analysis of part two of this book is based on the explicit assumption that both countries pursue a Keynesian neutral monetary policy. In fact, when r_a and r_b are kept constant, eqs. (18.1) and (18.2) reduce to eqs. (10.36) and (10.37), and nothing needs to be added to the analysis of part two. Accordingly, in what follows it is assumed that both countries pursue an orthodox neutral monetary policy.

As before, A's balance of payments is given by $T_a(Y_a, Y_b) + K(r_a - r_b)$. Nevertheless, as explained in the preceding chapter, the balance of payments need not be in equilibrium when eqs. (18.1) to (18.4) are satisfied. That is, the commodity, money, and bond markets may be in equilibrium and yet A's balance of payments may register either a deficit $(T_a + K < 0)$ or a surplus $(T_a + K > 0)$. Equilibrium in the foreign exchange market is maintained through purchases or sales of foreign exchange, as the case may be, by the monetary authorities.

18.2 GRAPHICAL SOLUTION

The solution of eqs. (18.1) to (18.4) is given in fig. 18.1 by means of the familiar *IS–LM* apparatus. In particular, A's *IS–LM* schedules are drawn in the second quadrant and those of country B in the fourth. For convenience, the subscripts *a* and *b* are used to distinguish between countries A and B, respectively. Equation (18.3) generates the unique LM_a curve in the second quadrant and eq. (18.4) the LM_b curve in the fourth quadrant. Equation (18.1) generates a family of IS_a curves in the second quadrant. Each IS_a curve is drawn for a specified value of Y_b as illustrated by the $IS_a(Y_b^0)$ curve in the second quadrant, which is drawn for the specific value $Y_b = Y_b^0$. Similarly, eq. (18.2) generates a family of IS_b curves in the fourth quadrant. Each IS_b curve is drawn for a specified value of Y_a as illustrated by the $IS_b(Y_a^0)$ curve in the fourth quadrant, which is drawn for the specific value $Y_a = Y_a^0$.

Consider now the second quadrant. For each value of Y_b and thus each IS_a curve, determine the equilibrium value of Y_a (and r_a) as given by the intersection between the LM_a curve and the relevant IS_a curve. Repeat this experiment for all values of Y_b and register the results in the first quadrant, as illustrated by A's reaction curve. Turn now to the fourth quadrant and repeat the same process for country B. Thus, for each value of Y_a choose the relevant IS_b curve and determine the equilibrium values of Y_b and r_b. Then use this information to derive B's reaction curve in the first quadrant. Because of the interest-rate effect, A's reaction curve must be flatter and B's steeper than the corresponding reaction curves of part two, where both countries pursued a Keynesian neutral monetary policy. Accordingly, the interest-rate effect is a strong stabilizing factor. Equilibrium occurs at the intersection between the two reaction curves, as illustrated in fig. 18.1.

There is nothing in the preceding solution to guarantee balance-of-payments equilibrium. Given the equilibrium values Y_a^0, Y_b^0, r_a^0, and r_b^0, A's balance-of-payments deficit $(-)$ or surplus $(+)$ can be determined by the expression $T(Y_a^0, Y_b^0) + K(r_a^0 - r_b^0)$. Since by assumption each country follows a sterilization or neutralization policy which in effect offsets the money-supply effect of the loss or gain of reserves, there does not exist any automatic mechanism to also bring about balance-of-payments equilibrium. Hence the current balance-of-payments disequilibrium, if any, may persist for a long time.

The preceding solution holds both for the case of imperfect capital mobility and perfect capital immobility. In the latter case, of course, the balance-of-payments deficit coincides with the balance-of-trade deficit, since by assumption $K = 0$. The case of perfect capital mobility is treated below in sec. 18.6.

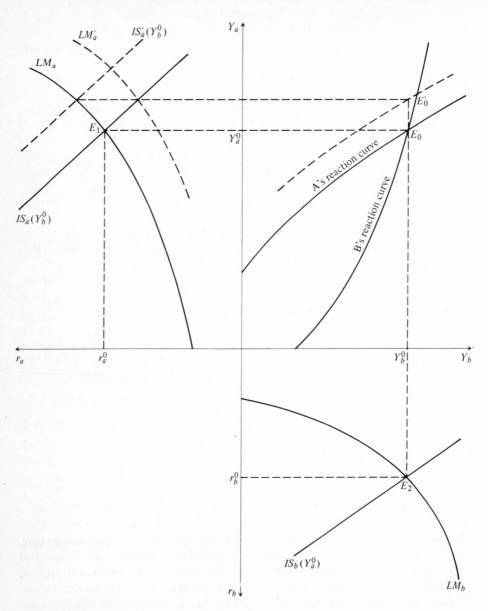

Figure 18.1 The effects of monetary and fiscal policy. Equilibrium occurs initially at E_0(i.e., the intersection between the two reaction curves). An increase in A's money supply causes the LM_a curve to shift to LM_a' (second quadrant); this causes A's reaction curve to shift upward and to the left, as shown by the broken curve through E_0' (first quadrant). Hence equilibrium moves to E_0'. If, alternatively, A increases G_a, then each IS_a curve shifts upward and to the left, as illustrated by the broken curve in the second quadrant. Again A's reaction curve shifts upward and to the left and equilibrium moves to E_0'.

18.3 THE EFFECTS OF MONETARY AND FISCAL POLICY

How does an expansionary monetary or fiscal policy in one country affect national incomes, interest rates, and the balance of payments? We must answer this question before we consider the Mundellian problem of the appropriate use of fiscal and monetary policy to preserve internal and external balance in the context of our two-country model.

The Effects of Monetary Policy

Consider monetary policy first. Assume that the system is in equilibrium at E_0 (fig. 18.1). How does an increase in A's money supply (H_a) affect Y_a, Y_b, r_a, r_b, and $T_a + K$? Briefly, A's *LM* curve (second quadrant) shifts to the right and, in general, causes A's reaction curve to shift upward and to the left, as shown by the broken curves. Thus, in general, Y_a, Y_b, and r_b tend to increase, r_a tends to fall, and A's balance of trade and balance of payments tend to deteriorate. Note that r_a must fall; otherwise aggregate demand and Y_a and Y_b could not have increased. A more rigorous proof of this result is given later in the appendix to this chapter.

If at the initial equilibrium country A's demand for money is infinitely elastic (liquidity trap), or if A's interest elasticity of investment is zero (fiscalist case), the increase in H_a leaves A's reaction curve (and, therefore, Y_a, Y_b, and r_b) unaltered. Further, r_a remains constant in the liquidity-trap case but falls in the fiscalist case. Accordingly, A's balance of payments remains the same in the liquidity-trap case but deteriorates in the fiscalist case (because of the induced capital outflow from A in the presence of some capital mobility).

Finally, assuming that A's reaction curve does shift, B's national income remains the same in the classical/monetarist case where B's interest elasticity of demand for money is zero (vertical *LM* curve). Also B's interest rate remains constant when B is at the liquidity trap.

The Effects of Fiscal Policy

Turn now to fiscal policy. Consider again the initial equilibrium at E_0 (fig. 18.1). Suppose that alternatively country A increases government spending. In this case, each IS_a curve shifts upward and to the left, as illustrated in fig. 18.1 by the pair $IS_a(Y_b^0)$, $IS_a'(Y_b^0)$. Again A's reaction curve shifts upward and to the left. Thus, in general, Y_a, Y_b, r_a, and r_b tend to increase and A's balance of trade tends to deteriorate. Nevertheless, A's balance of payments may either deteriorate or improve since the effect on the capital flow is indeterminate—both interest rates tend to rise.

If at the initial equilibrium point A's interest elasticity of demand for money is zero, then the increase in A's government spending leaves A's reaction curve unaltered. Accordingly, Y_a, Y_b, and r_b remain the same. However, r_a tends to rise and in the presence of capital mobility A's balance of payments tends to improve.

Finally, as with monetary policy, assuming that A's reaction curve does shift, B's national income remains the same in the classical/monetarist case where B's interest elasticity of demand for money is zero (vertical *LM* curve).

It is important to note that monetary policy still has a comparative advantage in working on external balance and fiscal policy on internal balance, because of their divergent effects on the domestic interest rate. Thus, in general, an increase in the domestic money supply still causes the domestic interest rate to fall, but an increase in government spending causes the domestic interest rate to rise.

18.4 THE ASSIGNMENT PROBLEM: GENERAL COMMENTS

As we have seen earlier, the assignment problem involves the pairing of a particular policy instrument with a particular policy target. The policy makers who control the policy instrument are instructed to achieve a specified value of the corresponding target variable. Essentially, the assignment problem arises from the fact that several policy makers work simultaneously but independently of each other to achieve their assigned policy targets. That is, the assignment problem is the product of decentralized decision making. Put differently, centralized decision making pursued by a unified policy authority to achieve simultaneously several interrelated targets involves no assignment problem.

Given a system of *n* targets and *n* independent instruments, a centralized policy authority with full information can simultaneously set all instruments at their appropriate values to achieve all targets. With decentralized decision making, however, an adjustment process takes place. The assignment problem is successfully solved only when this adjustment process leads eventually to the attainment of the targets. In other words, the assignment must be stable. Mundell's "principle of effective market classification" is specifically designed to solve the stability problem. Mundell's principle requires that each instrument be associated with that target on which it has relatively the greatest impact, i.e., on which it has a comparative advantage.

Even if stability of an unconstrained decentralized system can always be assured by proper assignment, several difficulties may arise, especially in the context of a multicountry world. First, a system of sovereign nations is characterized, almost by definition, by decentralized decision making, and in particular *each country's instruments are necessarily assigned to its own targets*. It is at least theoretically possible that stability for the system as a whole may require the assignment of one country's instrument(s) to another country's target(s). Under these circumstances some targets will not be attained.

Second, even if proper assignments do not cross national frontiers and national decision making ultimately leads to the attainment of all targets, the adjustment process takes time. During the transition when countries are off-target, a loss of welfare occurs. Cooper (1967, 1968, 1969) shows that the speed of adjustment depends on the sign and the size of the international repercussions of each country's actions, i.e., the side-effects of each instrument on target variables other than the one to which it is assigned. With strong side-effects decentralized decision making can be costly and the argument for coordinated decision making becomes more powerful. Centralized decision making could also provide for a more equitable distribution of the burden of adjustment among the countries concerned.

Third, the targets may not be compatible. For instance, if all countries aim at a trade surplus some of them are bound to be disappointed whatever policies are adopted. The same is true if each country aims at a zero balance of payments but the definitions adopted by the various countries are inconsistent, as explained in chap. 2.

Finally, there is what Mundell calls the "redundancy" problem. Consider an n country world in which all countries have compatible balance-of-payments targets. If each country has just enough instruments to reach its targets individually, then all of them together have one instrument to spare because of Cournot's law, namely, the proposition that the sum of all balances of payments is necessarily zero. Thus, only $n - 1$ countries in an n country world need achieve balance-of-payments equilibrium. Which country, if any, should be spared the balance-of-payments constraint? Which instrument should be considered redundant and how could it best be used?

18.5 FISCAL AND MONETARY POLICY FOR INTERNAL AND EXTERNAL BALANCE

Consider now the assignment problem within the context of our two-country model. Each country individually has two instruments (fiscal and monetary policy) and two targets (external and internal balance). Assuming that A's and B's balance-of-payments targets are consistent, as explained in sec. 18.4 above, the total number of independent targets is only three (full employment in A and B and balance-of-payments equilibrium) because of Cournot's law. Tinbergen's rule assures us that these three targets can be attained by the use of only three independent instruments. Since there are four instruments, there is one degree of freedom, i.e., one instrument is redundant. What alternative combinations of values should the instruments (H_a, H_b, G_a, and G_b) assume so that all three goals are simultaneously determined?

Consider fig. 18.2. The first quadrant gives the internal-balance schedule of the ith country ($i = a, b$). This schedule is similar to the one derived earlier in sec. 17.8 (see fig. 17.8), except that now we explicitly make the assumption that the other country's national income is at the full-employment level. The schedule VU in the second quadrant gives the resultant interest rate in the ith country as we move along the internal-balance schedule and H_i assumes different values. This schedule is sloping "upward" because a higher money supply necessarily implies a lower interest rate at the full-employment level of income. The schedule in the second quadrant is useful because, when the time comes to consider the balance-of-payments equilibrium, it is necessary to know explicitly the interest rate as well. The third quadrant gives a 45° line which helps to transfer the values of r_i from the

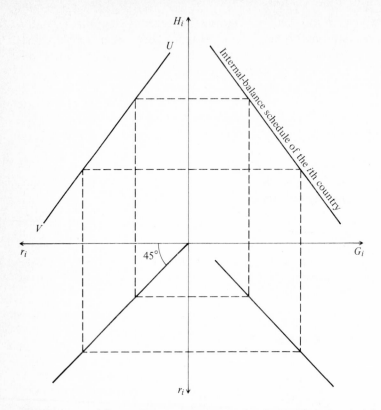

Figure 18.2 Internal balance in the *i*th country. The internal-balance schedule of the *i*th country (first quadrant) is drawn under the assumption that the other country is at full employment. The schedule VU (second quadrant) gives the resultant r_i as we move along the internal-balance schedule. By completing the rectangles as shown, a schedule is determined in the fourth quadrant which gives directly all combinations of r_i and G_i which are consistent with internal balance in the *i*th country. The term "internal-balance schedule" is reserved from now on for this schedule in the fourth quadrant.

horizontal to the vertical axis. Finally, by completing the rectangles as shown, a schedule is determined in the fourth quadrant which gives directly all alternative combinations of r_i and G_i which are consistent with internal balance in the *i*th country, with the understanding that the other country remains at full employment also. For the rest of the present discussion we shall use the term "internal-balance schedule" to refer to the schedule given in the *fourth* quadrant of fig. 18.2 since we are more concerned with the combinations of G_i and r_i rather than G_i and H_i.

Consider now fig. 18.3. The second and fourth quadrants give A's and B's internal-balance schedules, respectively. The first quadrant gives the external-balance schedule on the assumption that both countries are at full employment. Since the balance of trade is necessarily a constant (positive, negative, or even zero), external balance occurs when the interest-rate differential is such as to cause

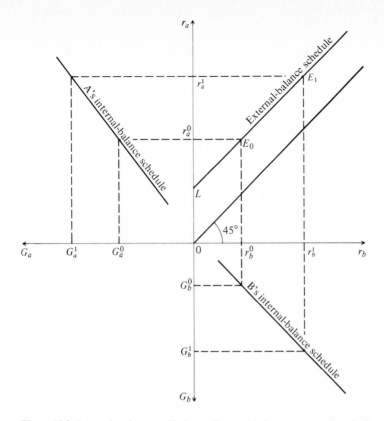

Figure 18.3 Internal and external balance. External balance occurs when the interest-rate differential is equal to $0L$. Now any point on the external-balance schedule (first quadrant), which is parallel to the 45° line, is consistent with both external and internal balance. Thus, there is one degree of freedom—one instrument is redundant.

the right amount of capital flow to satisfy the equation $T + K = 0$. In fig. 18.3 external balance occurs when the interest-rate differential $r_a - r_b$ is set equal to the distance $0L$. Presumably, country A is running a balance-of-trade deficit which is covered with autonomous capital imports from B. The external-balance schedule is always given by a straight line which is parallel to the 45° line.

Figure 18.3 illustrates the redundancy problem. Any point along the external-balance schedule is consistent with both external and internal balance. For instance, at E_0, country A must set $r_a = r_a^0$ and $G_a = G_a^0$ while country B must set $r_b = r_b^0$ and $G_b = G_b^0$. At E_1, the appropriate values of the instruments are: $r_a = r_a^1$, $G_a = G_a^1$, $r_b = r_b^1$, and $G_b = G_b^1$. Accordingly, there is one degree of freedom, and one of the instruments may be set arbitrarily at some level. In the following discussion and in the appendix to this chapter the extra degree of freedom is given to country B. Thus, country B may choose some arbitrary value for either r_b (or alternatively H_b) or G_b, and restrict the general equilibrium of the system to a single point on the external-balance schedule.

The appendix to this chapter considers rigorously the stability of various assignments. It shows that in the absence of income-sensitive capital movements stability prevails when country A adopts Mundell's assignment rule (i.e., fiscal policy for internal balance and monetary policy for external balance), while country B uses either monetary or fiscal policy to preserve internal balance.

18.6 PERFECT CAPITAL MOBILITY

The preceding analysis rests on the assumption of imperfect capital mobility. Now we consider briefly the limiting case of perfect capital mobility. This case assumes prominence in the last chapter.

In the presence of perfect capital mobility, the same interest rate prevails in both countries by definition. Accordingly, the number of unknowns in our system of eqs. (18.1) to (18.4) is reduced to three, with the possibility that the system may be rendered inconsistent as explained in the preceding chapter. In fact, following the analysis of the gold standard given in part A of chap. 16 (see especially fig. 16.1), we can immediately conclude that unless the money supplies of countries A and B coincide with the coordinates of some point of the money-market equilibrium locus (fig. 16.1) the system will be inconsistent. Thus, one country will continuously lose reserves to the other until the inconsistency is removed by proper coordination of monetary policies between the two countries. This result, which at first sight may seem paradoxical, dramatizes the fact that the various trading nations of the world are not entirely independent of each other in the exercise of their monetary policy. This interdependence is usually obscured since it may be more realistic to assume that capital is only imperfectly mobile between countries. And yet, as chap. 19 explains, it is only through recognition of this interdependence, the creation of an environment in which perfect capital mobility prevails, and the coordination of economic policies among sovereign nations that the balance-of-payments problem may be successfully solved.

Assume, then, that in the presence of perfect capital mobility countries do coordinate their monetary policies so that the system of eqs. (18.1) to (18.4) is indeed consistent at all times. Then the balance of payments must be in long-run equilibrium. This much follows from the analysis of the gold standard (chap. 16). How could internal balance in each country also be attained? Consider fig. 16.1 again and let the full-employment levels of Y_a and Y_b determine a point, say F (not shown), in the first quadrant. Internal and external balance may be achieved simultaneously in two steps: (a) for any given r, say $\bar{r}$, let each country adopt a fiscal policy such as to cause its reaction curve to pass through point F; and (b) let each country adjust its money supply and make it equal to the domestic demand for money, $L_i(Y_i^f, \bar{r})$, where $Y_i^f \equiv$ full-employment level of Y_i.

One instrument continues to be redundant because the interest rate in step (a) can be made to assume any value. (Note that the structure of the balance of payments remains the same as r is allowed to vary, since T is a function only of the parameters Y_a^f and Y_b^f and consequently remains constant.)

PART B. THE FLEXIBLE-EXCHANGE-RATE SYSTEM

This part considers briefly the flexible-exchange-rate system. That is, the rate of exchange is now allowed to vary until equilibrium is established in the foreign exchange market (or, alternatively, the balance of payments). We begin our discussion by considering the effects on the balance of trade and national incomes of a once-and-for-all change in the rate of exchange.

18.7 THE EFFECTS OF DEVALUATION

The effects of an exchange-rate adjustment on national incomes and the balance of trade have been discussed in chap. 11 under the simplifying assumption that each country pursued a Keynesian neutral monetary policy, i.e., that each country's interest rate remained constant. We concluded then that a devaluation causes, in general, the devaluing country's national income to increase and the rest of the world's national income to decrease. In addition, a devaluation improves the devaluing country's balance of trade when the sum of the import-demand elasticities in absolute terms is greater than unity plus the sum of the marginal propensities to import (Harberger condition). How are these conclusions amended when each country pursues an orthodox neutral monetary policy (i.e., when each country controls the nominal money supply) instead?

The conclusions of chap. 11 obviously continue to hold in the special cases of the liquidity trap and the fiscalist case where aggregate spending is perfectly interest inelastic. Further, in the classical/monetarist case of zero interest-demand elasticity for money, national incomes will either remain constant with devaluation or, to the extent that the *LM* curves are allowed to shift as explained in the preceding chapter, move in the opposite direction (i.e., the devaluing country's income will tend to fall and the rest of the world's income will tend to rise). In the latter case, of course, the national-income changes are *favorable* to a balance-of-trade improvement and the Marshall-Lerner condition becomes too strong for a successful devaluation.

In the general case where the interest-demand elasticities for money and aggregate spending are nonzero and finite the effects of devaluation are as follows. The national incomes of the devaluing country and the rest of the world will, in general, tend to increase and decrease, respectively. Nevertheless, because each country by assumption pursues an orthodox monetary policy, the interest rate will tend to rise in the devaluing country and fall in the rest of the world. These interest-rate changes have important implications, as emphasized by Tsiang (1961). Thus, the national-income changes are not as pronounced as when a Keynesian neutral monetary policy is pursued. Because of this, the unfavorable income effects on the devaluing country's balance of trade are somewhat restricted in such a way as to render the Harberger condition unnecessary for a balance-of-trade improvement. Accordingly, the monetary factors can play a vital stabilizing role in the foreign exchange market.

The preceding conclusions may be illustrated by the reader by means of a diagram similar to fig. 18.1. The appendix to this chapter provides rigorous proof.

18.8 FLEXIBLE-EXCHANGE RATES WITH BALANCE-OF-PAYMENTS EQUILIBRIUM

Consider now the following flexible-exchange-rate system:

$$Y_a = Z_a(Y_a, r_a, R) + RT_a^*(Y_a, Y_b, R) \quad (18.5)$$

$$Y_b = Z_b(Y_b, r_b, R) - T_a^*(Y_a, Y_b, R) \quad (18.6)$$

$$\bar{H}_a = L_a(Y_a, r_a, R) \quad (18.7)$$

$$\bar{H}_b = L_b(Y_b, r_b, R) \quad (18.8)$$

$$T_a^*(Y_a, Y_b, R) + K(r_a - r_b) = 0 \quad (18.9)$$

Equations (18.5) to (18.8) are similar to eqs. (18.1) to (18.4), except that in the present system the rate of foreign exchange R—which is now a variable—is introduced explicitly into the system. Equation (18.9) is the balance-of-payments

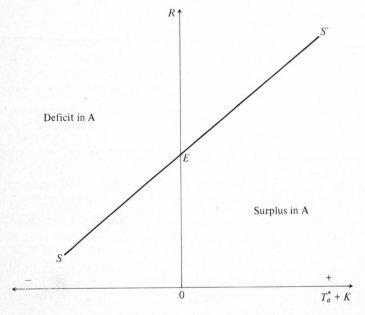

Figure 18.4 The flexible-exchange-rate system—excess supply of foreign exchange (that is, B's currency). The curve SES' shows the excess supply of B's currency in the foreign exchange market at alternative values of R. As we move along this curve, all other markets (except the labor markets) remain in equilibrium. Therefore, full equilibrium occurs at E.

equilibrium condition. The capital flow K is specified in terms of B's currency and, as before, is made an increasing function of the interest-rate differential.

This system can be solved graphically as the flexible-exchange-rate system of chap. 11, although the explicit introduction of the money markets does complicate the procedure slightly. Consider first eqs. (18.5) to (18.8) only, and treat R as a parameter. For each value of R determine the equilibrium values of Y_a, Y_b, r_a, and r_b as was done earlier in part A of this chapter. Given these equilibrium values, determine the change in A's reserves, $T_a^* + K$ (i.e., the excess supply of B's currency in the foreign exchange market). Allow R to vary from zero to infinity and plot the resultant values of $T_a^* + K$ against the corresponding values of R, as shown in fig. 18.4 by the curve SES'. This curve is drawn sloping upward since it is assumed that a devaluation of A's currency relative to B's tends to improve A's balance of trade. In addition, the capital flow from B to A tends to increase (or the capital flow from A to B tends to decrease) since in general the interest-rate differential $r_a - r_b$ tends to increase. Along the excess-supply curve SES' both the commodity and money markets are in equilibrium. Obviously full equilibrium occurs at E where the foreign exchange market is in equilibrium also.

18.9 THE EFFECTS OF FISCAL AND MONETARY POLICY

In considering the effects of fiscal and monetary policy in the context of the full flexible-exchange-rate system, we face several difficult questions. First, in what currency should the capital-flow function K be specified? There is no theoretical reason why one currency should be preferred over another. Yet, in general, the results are influenced by the choice of currency. Second, even if we assume that K is expressed in some currency, the effects of fiscal and monetary policy seem to depend on whether at the initial equilibrium the balance of trade is in deficit or surplus.

To solve these problems we make a simplifying assumption, namely, that at the initial equilibrium the balance of trade is zero. When this assumption is made, the effects of fiscal and monetary policy do not depend on the currency in which K is specified. This simplifying assumption of balanced trade at the initial equilibrium point is not unreasonable either. As explained in chap. 17 (and earlier in part one), the capital flow may be of a very short duration. Accordingly, the only lasting equilibrium is the one where the capital flow (and thus the balance of trade) is zero.

We proceed now with the effects of fiscal and monetary policy. Even with the simplifying assumption of balanced trade initially, the solution is rather complex and the diagrammatic approach cannot take us very far. For this reason, this problem is solved rigorously in the appendix to this chapter. The results are summarized in table 18.1. In this table, as well as in the appendix, only the general case is considered. Thus, the liquidity-trap, the fiscalist, and the classical/ monetarist cases are all ignored. In addition, capital is assumed imperfectly mobile between countries.

Each entry in table 18.1 shows the sign of the derivative of the variable indicated at the top of the column with respect to the parameter indicated at the left of the row. Thus, reading the first row from left to right, we find out that an increase in G_a causes Y_a, Y_b, r_a, and r_b to increase while the rate of exchange may go either way.

Table 18.1 The effects of fiscal and monetary policy when the balance of trade is initially zero

	Y_a	Y_b	r_a	r_b	R
G_a	+	+	+	+	?
G_b	+	+	+	+	?
H_a	+	−	−	−	+
H_b	−	+	−	−	−

Table 18.1 is useful in establishing the following general propositions, on the assumption, of course, that the balance of trade is initially zero:

1. An increase in government spending anywhere in the system is expansionary all around.
2. The effect of fiscal policy on the rate of exchange is indeterminate.
3. An expansionary monetary policy in any country causes the interest rate to fall in all countries.
4. An increase in the money supply of a country causes an *increase* in that country's income and employment but a *decrease* in the income and employment of the rest of the world.
5. An increase in the money supply of a country causes that country's currency to depreciate relative to the other currency.

18.10 POLICIES FOR INTERNAL BALANCE

Under our flexible-exchange-rate system, external balance is achieved automatically. What policy mix should countries A and B pursue to attain internal balance as well? There are three possibilities: (*a*) both countries may use fiscal policy; (*b*) both countries may use monetary policy; and (*c*) one country may use fiscal policy while the other uses monetary policy. Which of these three policy mixes must be pursued?

As shown rigorously in the appendix to this chapter, all of the preceding assignments are stable. Accordingly, any one of them may be used for internal balance.

APPENDIX TO CHAPTER EIGHTEEN. STABILITY OF ASSIGNMENTS AND COMPARATIVE STATICS IN THE TWO-COUNTRY MODEL

This appendix is divided into two parts. Part A deals with the comparative statics and stability of assignments in the fixed-exchange-rate system. Part B deals with the same problems in the flexible-exchange-rate system. The present discussion concentrates on the general case and ignores the limiting cases of the liquidity trap, the classical/monetarist, and the fiscalist.

PART A. THE FIXED-EXCHANGE-RATE SYSTEM

A18.1 KEYNESIAN NEUTRAL MONETARY POLICY

Consider the fixed-exchange-rate system of chap. 18 and assume that both countries pursue a Keynesian neutral monetary policy. We wish to study the stability of various assignments. Before doing so, however, we summarize for the convenience of the reader various results derived earlier in chap. 10:

$$\frac{\partial Y_a^e}{\partial G_a} = k_{aa} > 0$$

$$\frac{\partial Y_b^e}{\partial G_a} = k_{ba} > 0$$

$$\frac{\partial Y_a^e}{\partial G_b} = k_{ab} > 0$$

$$\frac{\partial Y_b^e}{\partial G_b} = k_{bb} > 0$$

$$k_{aa} > k_{ab} \qquad k_{bb} > k_{ba} \qquad \text{(Theorem 10.4)}$$

$$\frac{\partial T_a}{\partial G_a} = -(1 - Z_b')\left(\frac{\partial Y_b^e}{\partial G_a}\right) = -(1 - Z_b')k_{ba} < 0$$

$$\frac{\partial T_a}{\partial G_b} = (1 - Z_a')\left(\frac{\partial Y_a^e}{\partial G_b}\right) = (1 - Z_a')k_{ab} > 0$$

$$\frac{\partial Y_a^e}{\partial r_a} = \left(\frac{\partial Y_a}{\partial G_a}\right)\left(\frac{\partial Z_a}{\partial r_a}\right) = k_{aa}\left(\frac{\partial Z_a}{\partial r_a}\right) < 0$$

$$\frac{\partial Y_b^e}{\partial r_a} = \left(\frac{\partial Y_b^e}{\partial G_a}\right)\left(\frac{\partial Z_a}{\partial r_a}\right) = k_{ba}\left(\frac{\partial Z_a}{\partial r_a}\right) < 0$$

$$\frac{\partial T_a}{\partial r_a} = \left(\frac{\partial T_a}{\partial G_a}\right)\left(\frac{\partial Z_a}{\partial r_a}\right) = -(1 - Z_b')k_{ba}\left(\frac{\partial Z_a}{\partial r_a}\right) > 0$$

$$\frac{\partial Y_a^e}{\partial r_b} = \left(\frac{\partial Y_a}{\partial G_b}\right)\left(\frac{\partial Z_b}{\partial r_b}\right) = k_{ab}\left(\frac{\partial Z_b}{\partial r_b}\right) < 0$$

$$\frac{\partial Y_b^e}{\partial r_b} = \left(\frac{\partial Y_b}{\partial G_b}\right)\left(\frac{\partial Z_b}{\partial r_b}\right) = k_{bb}\left(\frac{\partial Z_b}{\partial r_b}\right) < 0$$

$$\frac{\partial T_a}{\partial r_b} = \left(\frac{\partial T_a}{\partial G_b}\right)\left(\frac{\partial Z_b}{\partial r_b}\right) = (1 - Z_a')k_{ab}\left(\frac{\partial Z_b}{\partial r_b}\right) < 0$$

We shall also use the symbol K' to indicate the derivative of K with respect to $(r_a - r_b)$. Thus,

$$K' = \frac{\partial K}{\partial r_a} = -\frac{\partial K}{\partial r_b} > 0$$

The superscript e means "equilibrium value." We proceed now with the stability of various assignments.

Assignment (1): *Country A uses monetary policy to attain external balance and fiscal policy to attain internal balance. Country B does nothing.* In particular, country B maintains both the interest rate and government spending at some fixed levels.

The dynamic system for this assignment may be written as follows:

$$\dot{G}_a = c_1(Y_a^f - Y_a^e) \tag{A18.1}$$

$$\dot{r}_a = -c_2(T_a + K) \tag{A18.2}$$

where c_1 and c_2 are positive speeds of adjustment, $\dot{G}_a$ and $\dot{r}_a$ are time derivatives, Y_a^f is A's full-employment national income, and Y_a^e is A's equilibrium level of income for given values of G_a, r_a, r_b, and G_b.

The system of eqs. (A18.1) and (A18.2) is stable when the following associated linear system is stable:

$$\begin{bmatrix} \dot{G}_a \\ \dot{r}_a \end{bmatrix} = \begin{bmatrix} -c_1\left(\dfrac{\partial Y_a^e}{\partial G_a}\right) & -c_1\left(\dfrac{\partial Y_a^e}{\partial r_a}\right) \\ -c_2\left(\dfrac{\partial T_a}{\partial G_a}\right) & -c_2\left(\dfrac{\partial T_a}{\partial r_a}\right) - c_2\left(\dfrac{\partial K}{\partial r_a}\right) \end{bmatrix} \begin{bmatrix} G_a - G_a^e \\ r_a - r_a^e \end{bmatrix} \tag{A18.3}$$

where G_a^e and r_a^e are the equilibrium values of G_a and r_a, respectively.

Substituting the results of chap. 10 into the matrix of (A18.3), we obtain

$$\begin{bmatrix} \dot{G}_a \\ \dot{r}_a \end{bmatrix} = \begin{bmatrix} -c_1 k_{aa} & -c_1 k_{aa}\left(\dfrac{\partial Z_a}{\partial r_a}\right) \\ c_2(1 - Z_b')k_{ba} & -c_2\left(\dfrac{\partial K}{\partial r_a}\right) + c_2(1 - Z_b')k_{ba}\left(\dfrac{\partial Z_a}{\partial r_a}\right) \end{bmatrix} \begin{bmatrix} G_a - G_a^e \\ r_a - r_a^e \end{bmatrix} \tag{A18.4}$$

For stability it is required that the real parts of the characteristic roots λ_1 and λ_2 of the following equation are negative:

$$\begin{vmatrix} -c_1 k_{aa} - \lambda & -c_1 k_{aa}\left(\dfrac{\partial Z_a}{\partial r_a}\right) \\[2ex] c_2(1 - Z_b')k_{ba} & -c_2\left(\dfrac{\partial K}{\partial r_a}\right) + c_2(1 - Z_b')k_{ba}\left(\dfrac{\partial Z_a}{\partial r_a}\right) - \lambda \end{vmatrix} = 0 \quad \text{(A18.5a)}$$

Expanding the determinant (A18.5a) and combining all like powers of λ, we obtain

$$\lambda^2 + A_1\lambda + A_2 = 0 \quad \text{(A18.5b)}$$

where

$$A_1 = c_1 k_{aa} + c_2\left[\left(\frac{\partial K}{\partial r_a}\right) - (1 - Z_b')k_{ba}\left(\frac{\partial Z_a}{\partial r_a}\right)\right] > 0$$

and A_2 is simply the determinant (A18.5a) when $\lambda = 0$. In particular, $A_2 = c_1 c_2 k_{aa}(\partial K/\partial r_a) > 0$. The real parts of λ_1 and λ_2 are negative when $A_1 > 0$ and $A_2 > 0$. These conditions are indeed satisfied.

If country A uses monetary policy to attain internal balance and fiscal policy for external balance, then the system becomes unstable. On this point see Mundell (1968) and Patrick (1968).

Assignment (2): *Country A uses monetary policy to attain external balance and fiscal policy to attain internal balance. Country B uses fiscal policy to attain internal balance.* Here the extra degree of freedom referred to in chap. 18 is given to country B. B's monetary policy is redundant.

The dynamic system for this assignment may be written as follows:

$$\dot{G}_a = c_1(Y_a^f - Y_a^e) \quad \text{(A18.6)}$$

$$\dot{r}_a = -c_2(T_a + K) \quad \text{(A18.7)}$$

$$\dot{G}_b = c_3(Y_b^f - Y_b^e) \quad \text{(A18.8)}$$

Equations (A18.6) and (A18.7) are identical to eqs. (A18.1) and (A18.2). Equation (A18.8) shows how fiscal policy is used by B to attain internal balance.

To study the stability of eqs. (A18.6) to (A18.8) determine the associated linear system as follows:

$$\begin{bmatrix} \dot{G}_a \\[2ex] \dot{r}_a \\[2ex] \dot{G}_b \end{bmatrix} = \begin{bmatrix} -c_1\left(\dfrac{\partial Y_a^e}{\partial G_a}\right) & -c_1\left(\dfrac{\partial Y_a^e}{\partial r_a}\right) & -c_1\left(\dfrac{\partial Y_a^e}{\partial G_b}\right) \\[2ex] -c_2\left(\dfrac{\partial T_a}{\partial G_a}\right) & -c_2\left[\left(\dfrac{\partial T_a}{\partial r_a}\right) + \left(\dfrac{\partial K}{\partial r_a}\right)\right] & -c_2\left(\dfrac{\partial T_a}{\partial G_b}\right) \\[2ex] -c_3\left(\dfrac{\partial Y_b^e}{\partial G_a}\right) & -c_3\left(\dfrac{\partial Y_b^e}{\partial r_a}\right) & -c_3\left(\dfrac{\partial Y_b^e}{\partial G_b}\right) \end{bmatrix} \begin{bmatrix} G_a - G_a^e \\[2ex] r_a - r_a^e \\[2ex] G_b - G_b^e \end{bmatrix}$$

$$\text{(A18.9)}$$

where G_a^e, r_a^e, and G_b^e are the equilibrium values of G_a, r_a, and G_b, respectively. This linear system is stable when its characteristic roots have negative real parts. Forming the characteristic equation and collecting all like powers of λ as we did in similar situations in the past, we obtain the polynomial

$$\lambda^3 + A_1 \lambda^2 + A_2 \lambda + A_3 = 0 \qquad (A18.10)$$

where

$$A_1 = c_1 \left(\frac{\partial Y_a^e}{\partial G_a}\right) + c_2 \left[\left(\frac{\partial T_a}{\partial r_a}\right) + \left(\frac{\partial K}{\partial r_a}\right)\right] + c_3 \left(\frac{\partial Y_b^e}{\partial G_b}\right) > 0$$

$$A_2 = c_3 \left(\frac{\partial Y_b^e}{\partial G_b}\right) \left[c_1 \left(\frac{\partial Y_a^e}{\partial G_a}\right) + c_2 \left(\frac{\partial T_a}{\partial r_a}\right) + c_2 \left(\frac{\partial K}{\partial r_a}\right)\right] + c_1 c_2 \left(\frac{\partial Y_a^e}{\partial G_a}\right) \left[\left(\frac{\partial T_a}{\partial r_a}\right) + \left(\frac{\partial K}{\partial r_a}\right)\right]$$

$$\quad - c_1 c_3 \left(\frac{\partial Y_a^e}{\partial G_b}\right)\left(\frac{\partial Y_b^e}{\partial G_a}\right) - c_2 c_3 \left(\frac{\partial Y_b^e}{\partial r_a}\right)\left(\frac{\partial T_a}{\partial G_b}\right) - c_1 c_2 \left(\frac{\partial T_a}{\partial G_a}\right)\left(\frac{\partial Y_a^e}{\partial r_a}\right)$$

$$\quad = c_2 c_3 \left(\frac{\partial Y_b^e}{\partial G_b}\right)\left[\left(\frac{\partial T_a}{\partial r_a}\right) + \left(\frac{\partial K}{\partial r_a}\right)\right] + c_1 c_2 \left(\frac{\partial Y_a^e}{\partial G_a}\right)\left(\frac{\partial K}{\partial r_a}\right) - c_2 c_3 \left(\frac{\partial Y_b^e}{\partial r_a}\right)\left(\frac{\partial T_a}{\partial G_b}\right)$$

$$\quad + c_1 c_2 \left[\left(\frac{\partial Y_a^e}{\partial G_a}\right)\left(\frac{\partial T_a}{\partial r_a}\right) - \left(\frac{\partial T_a}{\partial G_a}\right)\left(\frac{\partial Y_a^e}{\partial r_a}\right)\right]$$

$$\quad + c_1 c_3 \left[\left(\frac{\partial Y_b^e}{\partial G_b}\right)\left(\frac{\partial Y_a^e}{\partial G_a}\right) - \left(\frac{\partial Y_a^e}{\partial G_b}\right)\left(\frac{\partial Y_b^e}{\partial G_a}\right)\right]$$

and A_3 is the negative of the determinant of the system.

Substituting the results of chap. 10 into A_2 and A_3 and simplifying, we obtain

$$A_2 = c_1 c_3 (k_{aa} k_{bb} - k_{ab} k_{ba}) + c_2 (c_3 k_{bb} + c_1 k_{aa})\left(\frac{\partial K}{\partial r_a}\right)$$

$$\quad - c_2 c_3 k_{ba} \left(\frac{\partial Z_a}{\partial r_a}\right)[k_{bb}(1 - Z_b') + k_{ab}(1 - Z_a')] > 0$$

$$A_3 = c_1 c_2 c_3 \left(\frac{\partial K}{\partial r_a}\right)(k_{aa} k_{bb} - k_{ba} k_{ab}) > 0$$

For stability it is required that $A_1 > 0$, $A_3 > 0$, and $A_1 A_2 - A_3 > 0$. We have already shown that the first two conditions are indeed satisfied. To show that the third condition is satisfied also, substitute from the preceding results into the expression $A_1 A_2 - A_3$ and simplify to obtain

$$A_1 A_2 - A_3 = \left[c_1 k_{aa} + c_3 k_{bb} + c_2 \left(\frac{\partial K}{\partial r_a} \right) - c_2 (1 - Z'_b) k_{ba} \left(\frac{\partial Z_a}{\partial r_a} \right) \right]$$

$$\times \left\{ (c_2 c_3 k_{bb} + c_1 c_2 k_{aa}) \left(\frac{\partial K}{\partial r_a} \right) - c_2 c_3 k_{ba} \left(\frac{\partial Z_a}{\partial r_a} \right) \right.$$

$$\times \left[k_{bb} (1 - Z'_b) + k_{ab} (1 - Z'_a) \right] \Big\}$$

$$+ c_1 c_3 \left[c_1 k_{aa} + c_3 k_{bb} - c_2 (1 - Z'_b) k_{ba} \left(\frac{\partial Z_a}{\partial r_a} \right) \right]$$

$$\times (k_{aa} k_{bb} - k_{ab} k_{ba}) > 0$$

We therefore conclude that all stability conditions are indeed satisfied and thus the assignment is stable.

Again, if country A reverses its assignment and uses monetary policy for internal balance and fiscal policy for external balance, the system is rendered unstable. Also, the introduction of income-sensitive capital movements may destabilize the system.

Assignment (3): *Country A uses monetary policy to attain external balance and fiscal policy to attain internal balance. Country B uses monetary policy to attain internal balance. B's fiscal policy is now rendered redundant.*

The dynamic system for this assignment is as follows:

$$\dot{G}_a = c_1 (Y_a^f - Y_a^e) \tag{A18.11}$$

$$\dot{r}_a = -c_2 (T_a + K) \tag{A18.12}$$

$$\dot{r}_b = -c_3 (Y_b^f - Y_b^e) \tag{A18.13}$$

The matrix of the associated linear system now becomes

$$\begin{bmatrix} -c_1 \left(\dfrac{\partial Y_a^e}{\partial G_a} \right) & -c_1 \left(\dfrac{\partial Y_a^e}{\partial r_a} \right) & -c_1 \left(\dfrac{\partial Y_a^e}{\partial r_b} \right) \\[2ex] -c_2 \left(\dfrac{\partial T_a}{\partial G_a} \right) & -c_2 \left(\dfrac{\partial T_a}{\partial r_a} \right) - c_2 \left(\dfrac{\partial K}{\partial r_a} \right) & -c_2 \left(\dfrac{\partial T_a}{\partial r_b} \right) - c_2 \left(\dfrac{\partial K}{\partial r_b} \right) \\[2ex] c_3 \left(\dfrac{\partial Y_b^e}{\partial G_a} \right) & c_3 \left(\dfrac{\partial Y_b^e}{\partial r_a} \right) & c_3 \left(\dfrac{\partial Y_b^e}{\partial r_b} \right) \end{bmatrix} \tag{A18.14}$$

Again the characteristic equation takes the form given by (A18.10) where the parameters A_i $(i = 1, 2, 3)$ assume new values based on the elements of matrix (A18.14). For stability, it is again required that $A_1 > 0$, $A_3 > 0$, and $A_1 A_2 - A_3 > 0$. The first condition is obviously satisfied. The other two conditions are satisfied also.

After some elementary algebraic manipulations the expression for A_3 reduces to

$$A_3 = -c_1 c_2 c_3 \left(\frac{\partial K}{\partial r_a}\right)\left(\frac{\partial Z_b}{\partial r_b}\right)(k_{aa}k_{bb} - k_{ab}k_{ba}) > 0$$

Consider now the last condition: $A_1 A_2 - A_3 > 0$. Through direct algebraic manipulation and simplification, we obtain

$$
\begin{aligned}
A_1 A_2 - A_3 = c_2 c_3 &\left[c_1 k_{aa} - c_2(1 - Z_b')k_{ba}\left(\frac{\partial Z_a}{\partial r_a}\right) + c_2 K' - c_3 k_{bb}\left(\frac{\partial Z_b}{\partial r_b}\right) \right] \\
&\times \left\{ k_{bb}\left(\frac{\partial Z_b}{\partial r_b}\right)\left[(1 - Z_b')k_{ba}\left(\frac{\partial Z_a}{\partial r_a}\right) - K'\right] \right. \\
&\left. + (1 - Z_a')k_{ba}k_{ab}\left(\frac{\partial Z_a}{\partial r_a}\right)\left(\frac{\partial Z_b}{\partial r_b}\right) - k_{ba}K'\left(\frac{\partial Z_a}{\partial r_a}\right) \right\} \\
&- c_1 c_3 \left(\frac{\partial Z_b}{\partial r_b}\right)\left[c_1 k_{aa} - c_2(1 - Z_b')k_{ba}\left(\frac{\partial Z_a}{\partial r_a}\right) \right](k_{aa}k_{bb} - k_{ab}k_{ba}) \\
&+ c_1 c_2 k_{aa}K'\left[c_1 k_{aa} - c_2(1 - Z_b')k_{ba}\left(\frac{\partial Z_a}{\partial r_a}\right) + c_2 K' \right] \\
&- c_1 c_2 c_3 k_{aa}k_{bb}K'\left(\frac{\partial Z_b}{\partial r_b}\right) + c_1 c_3^2 k_{bb}\left(\frac{\partial Z_b}{\partial r_b}\right)^2 (k_{aa}k_{bb} - k_{ab}k_{ba}) > 0
\end{aligned}
$$

We therefore conclude that this assignment is stable also. Again, if country A reverses the assignment of its instruments and uses monetary policy for internal balance and fiscal policy for external balance, the system becomes unstable. Instability may also arise through the introduction of income-sensitive capital movements.

A18.2 ORTHODOX NEUTRAL MONETARY POLICY: COMPARATIVE STATICS

Turn now to the case where both countries pursue an orthodox neutral monetary policy. As explained in chap. 18, the equilibrium values of Y_a, Y_b, r_a, and r_b are functions of the policy instruments G_a, G_b, H_a, and H_b. We express this fact as follows:

$$Y_a^e = Y_a^e(G_a, G_b, H_a, H_b) \tag{A18.15}$$

$$Y_b^e = Y_b^e(G_a, G_b, H_a, H_b) \tag{A18.16}$$

$$r_a^e = r_a^e(G_a, G_b, H_a, H_b) \tag{A18.17}$$

$$r_b^e = r_b^e(G_a, G_b, H_a, H_b) \tag{A18.18}$$

where the superscript e indicates "equilibrium value." In this section we wish to study the comparative-statics effects of each of the instruments.

Return to eqs. (18.1) to (18.4) of chap. 18 and differentiate totally to obtain the following system:

$$
\begin{bmatrix}
1 - Z_a' + M_a' & -M_b' & -\dfrac{\partial Z_a}{\partial r_a} & 0 \\[2ex]
-M_a' & 1 - Z_b' + M_b' & 0 & -\dfrac{\partial Z_b}{\partial r_b} \\[2ex]
\dfrac{\partial L_a}{\partial Y_a} & 0 & \dfrac{\partial L_a}{\partial r_a} & 0 \\[2ex]
0 & \dfrac{\partial L_b}{\partial Y_b} & 0 & \dfrac{\partial L_b}{\partial r_b}
\end{bmatrix}
\begin{bmatrix}
dY_a^e \\[2ex]
dY_b^e \\[2ex]
dr_a^e \\[2ex]
dr_b^e
\end{bmatrix}
=
\begin{bmatrix}
dG_a \\[2ex]
dG_b \\[2ex]
dH_a \\[2ex]
dH_b
\end{bmatrix}
$$

$$(A18.19)$$

The determinant (Δ) of this system is positive, as the reader should verify. Obviously, it is different from the determinants of the systems we studied earlier in sec. A18.1.

The Effects of Fiscal Policy

To determine the effects of G_a, merely set $dG_b = dH_a = dH_b = 0$ and solve the system by Cramer's rule to obtain

$$
\frac{dY_a^e}{dG_a} = \left(\frac{1}{\Delta}\right)\left[(1 - Z_b' + M_b')\left(\frac{\partial L_a}{\partial r_a}\right)\left(\frac{\partial L_b}{\partial r_b}\right)\right.
$$

$$
\left. + \left(\frac{\partial L_b}{\partial Y_b}\right)\left(\frac{\partial L_a}{\partial r_a}\right)\left(\frac{\partial Z_b}{\partial r_b}\right)\right] > 0
$$

$$
\frac{dY_b^e}{dG_a} = \left(\frac{M_a'}{\Delta}\right)\left(\frac{\partial L_a}{\partial r_a}\right)\left(\frac{\partial L_b}{\partial r_b}\right) > 0
$$

$$
\frac{dr_a^e}{dG_a} = -\left(\frac{1}{\Delta}\right)\left[\left(\frac{\partial Z_b}{\partial r_b}\right)\left(\frac{\partial L_b}{\partial Y_b}\right)\left(\frac{\partial L_a}{\partial Y_a}\right)\right.
$$

$$
\left. + (1 - Z_b' + M_b')\left(\frac{\partial L_b}{\partial r_b}\right)\left(\frac{\partial L_a}{\partial Y_a}\right)\right] > 0
$$

$$
\frac{dr_b^e}{dG_a} = -\left(\frac{M_a'}{\Delta}\right)\left(\frac{\partial L_b}{\partial Y_b}\right)\left(\frac{\partial L_a}{\partial r_a}\right) > 0
$$

$$\left(\frac{dr_a^e}{dG_a}\right) - \left(\frac{dr_b^e}{dG_a}\right) = \left(\frac{1}{\Delta}\right)\left[M_a'\left(\frac{\partial L_b}{\partial Y_b}\right)\left(\frac{\partial L_a}{\partial r_a}\right)\right.$$

$$-\left(\frac{\partial Z_b}{\partial r_b}\right)\left(\frac{\partial L_b}{\partial Y_b}\right)\left(\frac{\partial L_a}{\partial Y_a}\right)$$

$$\left.- (1 - Z_b' + M_b')\left(\frac{\partial L_b}{\partial r_b}\right)\left(\frac{\partial L_a}{\partial Y_a}\right)\right]$$

$$\frac{dT_a}{dG_a} = -(1 - Z_b')\left(\frac{dY_b}{dG_a}\right) < 0 \qquad (Z_b' < 1)$$

Accordingly, an increase in G_a causes Y_a^e, Y_b^e, r_a^e, and r_b^e to increase and A's balance of trade to deteriorate. Since the effect on the interest-rate differential is indeterminate, the balance-of-payments effect is also indeterminate.

To determine the effects of G_b, set $dG_a = dH_a = dH_b = 0$ and solve system (A18.19) as before. Nevertheless, there is an easier way to get the answer: merely interchange the roles of the two countries in the preceding solution by interchanging the subscripts a and b.

The Effects of Monetary Policy

Turn now to the effects of monetary policy. To determine the effects of H_a, set $dG_a = dG_b = dH_b = 0$ and solve system (A18.19) by means of Cramer's rule to obtain

$$\frac{dY_a^e}{dH_a} = \left(\frac{1}{\Delta}\right)\left[\left(\frac{\partial Z_a}{\partial r_a}\right)\left(\frac{\partial Z_b}{\partial r_b}\right)\left(\frac{\partial L_b}{\partial Y_b}\right)\right.$$

$$\left.+ (1 - Z_b' + M_b')\left(\frac{\partial Z_a}{\partial r_a}\right)\left(\frac{\partial L_b}{\partial r_b}\right)\right] > 0$$

$$\frac{dY_b^e}{dH_a} = \left(\frac{M_a'}{\Delta}\right)\left(\frac{\partial Z_a}{\partial r_a}\right)\left(\frac{\partial L_b}{\partial r_b}\right) > 0$$

$$\frac{dr_a^e}{dH_a} = \left(\frac{1}{\Delta}\right)\left[(1 - Z_a' + M_a')(1 - Z_b' + M_b')\left(\frac{\partial L_b}{\partial r_b}\right)\right.$$

$$\left.+ (1 - Z_a' + M_a')\left(\frac{\partial L_b}{\partial Y_b}\right)\left(\frac{\partial Z_b}{\partial r_b}\right) - M_a'M_b'\left(\frac{\partial L_b}{\partial r_b}\right)\right] < 0$$

$$\frac{dr_b^e}{dH_a} = -\left(\frac{M_a'}{\Delta}\right)\left(\frac{\partial L_b}{\partial Y_b}\right)\left(\frac{\partial Z_a}{\partial r_a}\right) > 0$$

$$\left(\frac{dr_a^e}{dH_a}\right) - \left(\frac{dr_b^e}{dH_a}\right) < 0$$

$$\frac{dT_a}{dH_a} = -(1 - Z_b')\left(\frac{dY_b}{dH_a}\right) < 0$$

Accordingly, an increase in H_a causes Y_a^e, Y_b^e, and r_b^e to increase, r_a^e and $(r_a^e - r_b^e)$ to decrease, and A's balance of trade and balance of payments to deteriorate. To determine the effects of dH_b, merely reverse the subscripts a and b in the preceding solution.

A18.3 ORTHODOX NEUTRAL MONETARY POLICY: STABILITY OF POLICY ASSIGNMENTS

We proceed now with the stability of various assignments.

Assignment (1): *Country A uses monetary policy for external balance and fiscal policy for internal balance. Country B does nothing.* The dynamic system for this assignment may be written as follows:

$$\dot{G}_a = c_1(Y_a^f - Y_a^e) \tag{A18.20}$$

$$\dot{H}_a = c_2 B_a \tag{A18.21}$$

where

$$B_a \equiv T_a + K \tag{A18.22}$$

The matrix of the associated linear system is

$$\begin{bmatrix} -c_1\left(\dfrac{\partial Y_a^e}{\partial G_a}\right) & -c_1\left(\dfrac{\partial Y_a^e}{\partial H_a}\right) \\ c_2\left(\dfrac{\partial B_a}{\partial G_a}\right) & c_2\left(\dfrac{\partial B_a}{\partial H_a}\right) \end{bmatrix} \tag{A18.23}$$

The characteristic equation takes the form of (A18.5b). The parameters A_1 and A_2 now assume values based on the elements of (A18.23). For stability it is required that

$$(a) \quad \frac{\partial Y_a^e}{\partial G_a} > 0$$

$$(b) \quad \frac{\partial B_a}{\partial H_a} < 0$$

and

$$(c) \quad c_1 c_2\left[\left(\frac{\partial Y_a^e}{\partial H_a}\right)\left(\frac{\partial B_a}{\partial G_a}\right) - \left(\frac{\partial Y_a^e}{\partial G_a}\right)\left(\frac{\partial B_a}{\partial H_a}\right)\right] > 0$$

Condition (a) is obviously satisfied. Condition (b) is also satisfied, as shown in the preceding section.

To show that condition (c) is also satisfied, concentrate on the bracketed expression, since $c_1 c_2 > 0$. From the comparative-statics results of the preceding section, it follows easily that

$$\frac{\partial Y_a}{\partial G_a} = \alpha\left(\frac{\partial Y_a}{\partial H_a}\right) > 0 \tag{A18.24}$$

where
$$\alpha \equiv \frac{\partial L_a/\partial r_a}{\partial Z_a/\partial r_a} > 0 \qquad \text{(A18.25)}$$

Hence, condition (c) reduces to

$$\left(\frac{\partial B_a}{\partial G_a}\right) - \alpha \left(\frac{\partial B_a}{\partial H_a}\right) > 0 \qquad \text{(A18.26a)}$$

Through direct substitution from the results of the preceding section and further algebraic manipulation, inequality (A18.26a) is finally reduced to

$$\left(\frac{\partial r_a}{\partial G_a}\right) - \alpha \left(\frac{\partial r_a}{\partial H_a}\right) > 0 \qquad \text{(A18.26b)}$$

which is certainly satisfied since we already know that $(\partial r_a/\partial G_a) > 0$, $(\partial r_a/\partial H_a) < 0$, and $\alpha > 0$.

We therefore conclude that this assignment is stable. If country A reverses its assignment (i.e., if A uses monetary policy for internal balance and fiscal policy for external balance) the system becomes unstable. Similarly, if income-sensitive capital movements are introduced the system may become unstable and then stability can be restored by reversing the assignment.

Assignment (2): *Country A uses monetary policy to attain external balance and fiscal policy to attain internal balance. Country B uses fiscal policy to attain internal balance.* The dynamic system for this assignment may be written as follows:

$$\dot{G}_a = c_1(Y_a^f - Y_a^e) \qquad \text{(A18.20)}$$

$$\dot{H}_a = c_2 B_a \qquad \text{(A18.21)}$$

$$\dot{G}_b = c_3(Y_b^f - Y_b^e) \qquad \text{(A18.27)}$$

That is, eq. (A18.27) is added now to eqs. (A18.20) and (A18.21).

The matrix of the associated linear system is

$$\begin{bmatrix} -c_1\left(\frac{\partial Y_a^e}{\partial G_a}\right) & -c_1\left(\frac{\partial Y_a^e}{\partial H_a}\right) & -c_1\left(\frac{\partial Y_a^e}{\partial G_b}\right) \\ c_2\left(\frac{\partial B_a}{\partial G_a}\right) & c_2\left(\frac{\partial B_a}{\partial H_a}\right) & c_2\left(\frac{\partial B_a}{\partial G_b}\right) \\ -c_3\left(\frac{\partial Y_b^e}{\partial G_a}\right) & -c_3\left(\frac{\partial Y_b^e}{\partial H_a}\right) & -c_3\left(\frac{\partial Y_b^e}{\partial G_b}\right) \end{bmatrix} \qquad \text{(A18.28)}$$

Note that the partial derivatives in (A18.28) are nothing else but the comparative-statics solutions of (A18.19). The characteristic equation takes the form of (A18.10) where the parameters A_i ($i = 1, 2, 3$) assume values based on the elements of (A18.28). For stability it is again required that: (a) $A_1 > 0$; (b) $A_3 > 0$; and (c) $A_1 A_2 - A_3 > 0$.

The parameter A_1 is given by

$$A_1 = c_1\left(\frac{\partial Y_a^e}{\partial G_a}\right) - c_2\left(\frac{\partial B_a}{\partial H_a}\right) + c_3\left(\frac{\partial Y_b^e}{\partial G_b}\right) > 0 \qquad \text{(A18.29)}$$

Hence, condition (*a*) is satisfied.

Condition (*b*) is also satisfied since the parameter A_3 (after some algebraic manipulation) is given by

$$A_3 = c_1 c_2 c_3 K'\left(\frac{1}{\alpha}\right)\left[\left(\frac{\partial r_a}{\partial G_a}\right) - \alpha\left(\frac{\partial r_a}{\partial H_a}\right)\right]$$

$$\times \left[\left(\frac{\partial Y_a^e}{\partial G_a}\right)\left(\frac{\partial Y_b^e}{\partial G_b}\right) - \left(\frac{\partial Y_a^e}{\partial G_b}\right)\left(\frac{\partial Y_b^e}{\partial G_a}\right)\right] > 0 \qquad (A18.30)$$

where $K' \equiv \partial K / \partial(r_a - r_b)$, and α is defined by (A18.25).

The last condition is satisfied also. To see this, merely manipulate it algebraically into the following form:

$$A_1 A_2 - A_3 = c_1 c_3^2 \left(\frac{\partial Y_b^e}{\partial G_b}\right)\left[\left(\frac{\partial Y_a^e}{\partial G_a}\right)\left(\frac{\partial Y_b^e}{\partial G_b}\right) - \left(\frac{\partial Y_a^e}{\partial G_b}\right)\left(\frac{\partial Y_b^e}{\partial G_a}\right)\right]$$

$$+ c_1 c_2^2 \left(\frac{\partial B_a}{\partial H_a}\right)\left[\left(\frac{\partial Y_a^e}{\partial G_a}\right)\left(\frac{\partial B_a}{\partial H_a}\right) - \left(\frac{\partial Y_a^e}{\partial H_a}\right)\left(\frac{\partial B_a}{\partial G_a}\right)\right]$$

$$+ c_1^2 c_2 \left(\frac{\partial Y_a^e}{\partial G_a}\right)\left[\left(\frac{\partial Y_a^e}{\partial H_a}\right)\left(\frac{\partial B_a}{\partial G_a}\right) - \left(\frac{\partial Y_a^e}{\partial G_a}\right)\left(\frac{\partial B_a}{\partial H_a}\right)\right]$$

$$+ c_1^2 c_3 \left(\frac{\partial Y_a^e}{\partial G_a}\right)\left[\left(\frac{\partial Y_a^e}{\partial G_a}\right)\left(\frac{\partial Y_b^e}{\partial G_b}\right) - \left(\frac{\partial Y_a^e}{\partial G_b}\right)\left(\frac{\partial Y_b^e}{\partial G_a}\right)\right]$$

$$+ c_2 c_3 \left[c_2\left(\frac{\partial B_a}{\partial H_a}\right) - c_3\left(\frac{\partial Y_b^e}{\partial G_b}\right)\right]$$

$$\times \left[\left(\frac{\partial B_a}{\partial H_a}\right)\left(\frac{\partial Y_b^e}{\partial G_b}\right) - \left(\frac{\partial B_a}{\partial G_b}\right)\left(\frac{\partial Y_b^e}{\partial H_a}\right)\right]$$

$$- c_1 c_2 c_3 \left[\left(\frac{\partial Y_a^e}{\partial G_a}\right)\left(\frac{\partial Y_b^e}{\partial G_b}\right)\left(\frac{\partial B_a}{\partial H_a}\right) - \left(\frac{\partial Y_a^e}{\partial G_b}\right)\left(\frac{\partial Y_b^e}{\partial H_a}\right)\left(\frac{\partial B_a}{\partial G_a}\right)\right]$$

$$- c_1 c_2 c_3 \left(\frac{\partial Y_a^e}{\partial H_a}\right)\left(\frac{\partial Y_b^e}{\partial G_b}\right)\left[\alpha\left(\frac{\partial r_a}{\partial H_a}\right) - \left(\frac{\partial r_a}{\partial G_a}\right)\right]$$

$$- c_1 c_2 c_3 \left(\frac{\partial Y_a^e}{\partial H_a}\right)\left(\frac{\partial Y_b^e}{\partial G_b}\right)\left[\left(\frac{\partial B_a}{\partial G_a}\right) - \left(\frac{\partial B_a}{\partial G_b}\right)\right] > 0$$

To verify that the expression in the last brackets is negative (and therefore the last term is positive), rewrite it as follows:

$$\left(\frac{\partial B_a}{\partial G_a}\right) - \left(\frac{\partial B_a}{\partial G_b}\right) = M_b'\left[\left(\frac{\partial Y_b^e}{\partial G_a}\right) - \left(\frac{\partial Y_b^e}{\partial G_b}\right)\right] + M_a'\left[\left(\frac{\partial Y_a^e}{\partial G_b}\right) - \left(\frac{\partial Y_a^e}{\partial G_a}\right)\right]$$

$$+ K'\left[\left(\frac{\partial r_a}{\partial G_a}\right) - \left(\frac{\partial r_a}{\partial G_b}\right)\right] + K'\left[\left(\frac{\partial r_b}{\partial G_b}\right) - \left(\frac{\partial r_b}{\partial G_a}\right)\right] < 0$$

Also to verify that the bracketed expression of the sixth term is negative, rewrite it as follows:

$$\left(\frac{\partial Y_a^e}{\partial G_a}\right)\left(\frac{\partial Y_b^e}{\partial G_b}\right)\left(\frac{\partial B_a}{\partial H_a}\right) - \left(\frac{\partial Y_a^e}{\partial G_b}\right)\left(\frac{\partial Y_b^e}{\partial H_a}\right)\left(\frac{\partial B_a}{\partial G_a}\right)$$

$$= \left(\frac{\partial B_a}{\partial H_a}\right)\left[\left(\frac{\partial Y_a^e}{\partial G_a}\right)\left(\frac{\partial Y_b^e}{\partial G_b}\right) - \left(\frac{\partial Y_a^e}{\partial G_b}\right)\left(\frac{\partial Y_b^e}{\partial G_a}\right)\right]$$

$$- K'\left(\frac{\partial Y_a^e}{\partial G_b}\right)\left(\frac{\partial Y_b^e}{\partial G_a}\right)\left[\left(\frac{1}{\alpha}\right)\left(\frac{\partial r_a}{\partial G_a}\right) - \left(\frac{\partial r_a}{\partial H_a}\right)\right] < 0$$

All other terms are positive, as shown earlier in this appendix.

We therefore conclude that this assignment is stable. The same reservations expressed in earlier assignments in relation to the introduction of income-sensitive capital movements or the possibility of A reversing its assignment hold here as well.

Assignment (3): *Country A uses monetary policy to attain external balance and fiscal policy to attain internal balance. Country B uses monetary policy to attain internal balance.* The dynamic system for this assignment may be written as follows:

$$\dot{G}_a = c_1(Y_a^f - Y_a^e) \tag{A18.20}$$

$$\dot{H}_a = c_2 B_a \tag{A18.21}$$

$$\dot{H}_b = c_3(Y_b^f - Y_b^e) \tag{A18.31}$$

Now eq. (A18.31) is added to eqs. (A18.20) and (A18.21).

The matrix of the associated linear system is

$$\begin{bmatrix} -c_1\left(\dfrac{\partial Y_a^e}{\partial G_a}\right) & -c_1\left(\dfrac{\partial Y_a^e}{\partial H_a}\right) & -c_1\left(\dfrac{\partial Y_a^e}{\partial H_b}\right) \\[2mm] c_2\left(\dfrac{\partial B_a}{\partial G_a}\right) & c_2\left(\dfrac{\partial B_a}{\partial H_a}\right) & c_2\left(\dfrac{\partial B_a}{\partial H_b}\right) \\[2mm] -c_3\left(\dfrac{\partial Y_b^e}{\partial G_a}\right) & -c_3\left(\dfrac{\partial Y_b^e}{\partial H_a}\right) & -c_3\left(\dfrac{\partial Y_b^e}{\partial H_b}\right) \end{bmatrix} \tag{A18.32}$$

Again note that the partial derivatives in (A18.32) are nothing else but the comparative-statics solutions of (A18.19). The characteristic equation again takes the form of (A18.10) with the parameters A_i $(i = 1, 2, 3)$ assuming new values based on the elements of (A18.32). For stability it is again required that (a) $A_1 > 0$; (b) $A_3 > 0$; and (c) $A_1 A_2 - A_3 > 0$.

The first condition is obviously satisfied since

$$A_1 = c_1\left(\frac{\partial Y_a^e}{\partial G_a}\right) - c_2\left(\frac{\partial B_a}{\partial H_a}\right) + c_3\left(\frac{\partial Y_b^e}{\partial H_b}\right) > 0$$

The second condition reduces to

$$A_3 = c_1 c_2 c_3 \left[\left(\frac{\partial Y_b^e}{\partial H_b} \right) \left(\frac{\partial Y_a^e}{\partial H_a} \right) - \left(\frac{\partial Y_b^e}{\partial H_a} \right) \left(\frac{\partial Y_a^e}{\partial H_b} \right) \right]$$

$$\times \left[\left(\frac{\partial r_a}{dG_a} \right) - \alpha \left(\frac{dr_a}{dH_a} \right) \right] > 0$$

Note that both bracketed expressions are necessarily positive, as shown earlier in this appendix.

Finally, the last condition reduces to

$$A_1 A_2 - A_3 = c_1 c_3 \left[c_1 \left(\frac{\partial Y_a^e}{\partial G_a} \right) + c_3 \left(\frac{\partial Y_b^e}{\partial H_b} \right) \right] \left[\left(\frac{\partial Y_a^e}{\partial G_a} \right) \left(\frac{\partial Y_b^e}{\partial H_b} \right) - \left(\frac{\partial Y_b^e}{\partial G_a} \right) \left(\frac{\partial Y_a^e}{\partial H_b} \right) \right]$$

$$+ c_1 c_2 \left[c_1 \left(\frac{\partial Y_a^e}{\partial G_a} \right) - c_2 \left(\frac{\partial B_a}{\partial H_a} \right) \right] \left[\left(\frac{\partial Y_a^e}{\partial H_a} \right) \left(\frac{\partial B_a}{\partial G_a} \right) - \left(\frac{\partial Y_a^e}{\partial G_a} \right) \left(\frac{\partial B_a}{\partial H_a} \right) \right]$$

$$+ c_2 c_3 \left[c_3 \left(\frac{\partial Y_b^e}{\partial H_b} \right) - c_2 \left(\frac{\partial B_a}{\partial H_a} \right) \right] \left[\left(\frac{\partial Y_b^e}{\partial H_a} \right) \left(\frac{\partial B_a}{\partial H_b} \right) - \left(\frac{\partial Y_b^e}{\partial H_b} \right) \left(\frac{\partial B_a}{\partial H_a} \right) \right]$$

$$- c_1 c_2 c_3 \left(\frac{\partial Y_a^e}{\partial G_a} \right) \left(\frac{\partial Y_b^e}{\partial H_b} \right) \left(\frac{\partial B_a}{\partial H_a} \right) + c_1 c_2 c_3 \left(\frac{\partial Y_a^e}{\partial H_a} \right) \left(\frac{\partial B_a}{\partial H_b} \right) \left(\frac{\partial Y_b^e}{\partial G_a} \right)$$

$$- c_1 c_2 c_3 \left(\frac{1}{\alpha} \right) \left[\left(\frac{\partial Y_a^e}{\partial G_a} \right) \left(\frac{\partial Y_b^e}{\partial G_b} \right) \left(\frac{\partial B_a}{\partial H_a} \right) - \left(\frac{\partial Y_a^e}{\partial G_a} \right) \left(\frac{\partial Y_b^e}{\partial H_a} \right) \left(\frac{\partial B_a}{\partial G_a} \right) \right] > 0$$

Again all bracketed terms have been shown to be positive.

We therefore conclude that this assignment is stable. The earlier reservations regarding income-sensitive capital movements and a reversal in A's assignment hold here as well.

PART B. THE FLEXIBLE-EXCHANGE-RATE SYSTEM

A18.4 THE EFFECTS OF AN EXCHANGE-RATE ADJUSTMENT

Consider the following system:

$$Y_a = Z_a(Y_a, r_a; R) + T_a(Y_a, Y_b; R) \tag{A18.33}$$

$$Y_b = Z_b(Y_b, r_b; R) - \left(\frac{1}{R} \right) T_a(Y_a, Y_b; R) \tag{A18.34}$$

$$H_a = L_a(Y_a, r_a) \tag{A18.35}$$

$$H_b = L_b(Y_b, r_b) \tag{A18.36}$$

This system is similar to that given in chap. 18 by eqs. (18.1) to (18.4). Nevertheless, the rate of exchange is now shown explicitly simply because we presently wish to study the effects of exchange-rate changes. To facilitate our calculations, we make the simplifying assumption that the effect of exchange-rate changes on the demand for money is zero (that is, $(\partial L_a/\partial R) = (\partial L_b/\partial R) = 0$). For this reason the rate of exchange does not appear in the functions L_a and L_b.

To determine the effects of a once-and-for-all change in the rate of exchange on the equilibrium values of Y_a, Y_b, and T_a, we differentiate eqs. (A18.33) to (A18.36) totally with respect to R, assuming that initially $R = 1$ and $T_a = 0$. We obtain

$$
\begin{bmatrix}
(1 - Z_a' + M_a') & -M_b' & -\dfrac{\partial Z_a}{\partial r_a} & 0 \\[2ex]
-M_a' & (1 - Z_b' + M_b') & 0 & -\dfrac{\partial Z_b}{\partial r_b} \\[2ex]
\dfrac{\partial L_a}{\partial Y_a} & 0 & \dfrac{\partial L_a}{\partial r_a} & 0 \\[2ex]
0 & \dfrac{\partial L_b}{\partial Y_b} & 0 & \dfrac{\partial L_b}{\partial r_b}
\end{bmatrix}
\times
\begin{bmatrix}
\dfrac{dY_a}{dR} \\[2ex]
\dfrac{dY_b}{dR} \\[2ex]
\dfrac{dr_a}{dR} \\[2ex]
\dfrac{dr_b}{dR}
\end{bmatrix}
=
\begin{bmatrix}
\left(\dfrac{\partial Z_a}{\partial R}\right) + \left(\dfrac{\partial T_a}{\partial R}\right) \\[2ex]
\left(\dfrac{\partial Z_b}{\partial R}\right) - \left(\dfrac{\partial T_a}{\partial R}\right) \\[2ex]
0 \\[2ex]
0
\end{bmatrix}
\qquad \text{(A18.37)}
$$

The determinant of this system (Δ) is identical to the determinant of (A18.19) and, as we noted then, it is positive, that is, $\Delta > 0$.

Solving (A18.37) by means of Cramer's rule, we obtain (after simplification)

$$
\begin{aligned}
\frac{dY_a}{dR} = \left(\frac{1}{\Delta}\right)\left(\frac{\partial L_a}{\partial r_a}\right)\Bigg\{ &\left(1 - Z_b' + M_b'\right)\left(\frac{\partial L_b}{\partial r_b}\right)\left[\left(\frac{\partial Z_a}{\partial R}\right) + \left(\frac{\partial T_a}{\partial R}\right)\right] \\
&+ \left(\frac{\partial L_b}{\partial Y_b}\right)\left(\frac{\partial Z_b}{\partial r_b}\right)\left[\left(\frac{\partial Z_a}{\partial R}\right) + \left(\frac{\partial T_a}{\partial R}\right)\right] \\
&+ M_b'\left(\frac{\partial L_b}{\partial r_b}\right)\left[\left(\frac{\partial Z_b}{\partial R}\right) - \left(\frac{\partial T_a}{\partial R}\right)\right]\Bigg\}
\end{aligned}
\qquad \text{(A18.38)}
$$

$$\frac{dY_b}{dR} = \left(\frac{1}{\Delta}\right)\left(\frac{\partial L_b}{\partial r_b}\right)\Bigg\{\left(1 - Z'_a + M'_a\right)\left(\frac{\partial L_a}{\partial r_a}\right)\left[\left(\frac{\partial Z_b}{\partial R}\right) - \left(\frac{\partial T_a}{\partial R}\right)\right]$$

$$+ \left(\frac{\partial L_a}{\partial Y_a}\right)\left(\frac{\partial Z_a}{\partial r_a}\right)\left[\left(\frac{\partial Z_b}{\partial R}\right) - \left(\frac{\partial T_a}{\partial R}\right)\right]$$

$$+ M'_a\left(\frac{\partial L_a}{\partial r_a}\right)\left[\left(\frac{\partial Z_a}{\partial R}\right) + \left(\frac{\partial T_a}{\partial R}\right)\right]\Bigg\} \qquad (A18.39)$$

From eqs. (A18.35) and (A18.36) we obtain (by means of total differentiation with respect to R and rearrangement):

$$\frac{dr_a}{dR} = -\frac{(\partial L_a/\partial Y_a)(dY_a/dR)}{(\partial L_a/\partial r_a)} > 0$$

$$\frac{dr_b}{dR} = -\frac{(\partial L_b/\partial Y_b)(dY_b/dR)}{(\partial L_b/\partial r_b)} < 0$$

Because of the interest-rate effects, the Harberger condition now becomes too strong for a successful devaluation. To see this, we determine the balance-of-trade effect as follows:

$$\frac{dT_a}{dR} = \left(\frac{\partial T_a}{\partial R}\right) + M'_b\left(\frac{dY_b}{dR}\right) - M'_a\left(\frac{dY_a}{dR}\right)$$

$$= \left(\frac{1}{\Delta}\right)\left(\frac{\partial T_a}{\partial R}\right)\left[\left(\frac{\partial Z_b}{\partial r_b}\right)\left(\frac{\partial L_a}{\partial Y_a}\right)\left(\frac{\partial L_b}{\partial Y_b}\right)\left(\frac{\partial Z_a}{\partial r_a}\right)\right.$$

$$+ \left(1 - Z'_a\right)\left(\frac{\partial Z_b}{\partial r_b}\right)\left(\frac{\partial L_a}{\partial r_a}\right)\left(\frac{\partial L_b}{\partial Y_b}\right)$$

$$+ \left(1 - Z'_a\right)\left(1 - Z'_b\right)\left(\frac{\partial L_b}{\partial r_b}\right)\left(\frac{\partial L_a}{\partial r_a}\right)$$

$$+ \left(1 - Z'_b\right)\left(\frac{\partial L_b}{\partial r_b}\right)\left(\frac{\partial L_a}{\partial Y_a}\right)\left(\frac{\partial Z_a}{\partial r_a}\right)\right]$$

$$+ \left(\frac{1}{\Delta}\right)M'_b\left(\frac{\partial L_b}{\partial r_b}\right)\left[\left(1 - Z'_a + M'_a\right)\left(\frac{\partial Z_b}{\partial R}\right)\left(\frac{\partial L_a}{\partial r_a}\right)\right.$$

$$+ \left(\frac{\partial Z_b}{\partial R}\right)\left(\frac{\partial L_a}{\partial Y_a}\right)\left(\frac{\partial Z_a}{\partial r_a}\right) + M'_a\left(\frac{\partial Z_a}{\partial R}\right)\left(\frac{\partial L_a}{\partial r_a}\right)\right]$$

$$- \left(\frac{1}{\Delta}\right)M'_a\left(\frac{\partial L_a}{\partial r_a}\right)\left[\left(1 - Z'_b + M'_b\right)\left(\frac{\partial Z_a}{\partial R}\right)\left(\frac{\partial L_b}{\partial r_b}\right)\right.$$

$$+ \left(\frac{\partial Z_a}{\partial R}\right)\left(\frac{\partial L_b}{\partial Y_b}\right)\left(\frac{\partial Z_b}{\partial r_b}\right) + M'_b\left(\frac{\partial Z_b}{\partial R}\right)\left(\frac{\partial L_b}{\partial r_b}\right)\right]$$

Now recall from chap. 11 that under conditions of balanced trade $(\partial Z_a/\partial R) = M(1 - Z'_a)$ and $(\partial Z_b/\partial R) = -M(1 - Z'_b)$, where $M = M_a = M_b$. Substituting these results and rearranging, we finally obtain

$$\frac{dT_a}{dR} = \left(\frac{1}{\Delta}\right)\left(\frac{\partial T_a}{\partial R}\right)\left(\frac{\partial Z_b}{\partial r_b}\right)\left(\frac{\partial L_a}{\partial Y_a}\right)\left(\frac{\partial L_b}{\partial Y_b}\right)\left(\frac{\partial Z_a}{\partial r_a}\right)$$

$$+ \left(\frac{1}{\Delta}\right)(1 - Z'_a)\left(\frac{\partial Z_b}{\partial r_b}\right)\left(\frac{\partial L_a}{\partial r_a}\right)\left(\frac{\partial L_b}{\partial Y_b}\right)\left[\left(\frac{\partial T_a}{\partial R}\right) - MM'_a\right]$$

$$+ \left(\frac{1}{\Delta}\right)(1 - Z'_a)(1 - Z'_b)\left(\frac{\partial L_b}{\partial r_b}\right)\left(\frac{\partial L_a}{\partial r_a}\right)\left[\left(\frac{\partial T_a}{\partial R}\right) - M(M'_b + M'_a)\right]$$

$$+ \left(\frac{1}{\Delta}\right)(1 - Z'_b)\left(\frac{\partial L_b}{\partial r_b}\right)\left(\frac{\partial L_a}{\partial Y_a}\right)\left(\frac{\partial Z_a}{\partial r_a}\right)\left[\left(\frac{\partial T_a}{\partial R}\right) - MM'_b\right]$$

$$\text{(A18.40)}$$

The Harberger condition guarantees that the third term on the right-hand side of (A18.40) is positive. However, there are another three terms which are positive, even when the Harberger condition is not satisfied. Thus, the first term is positive when the Marshall-Lerner condition is satisfied $(\partial T_a/\partial R > 0)$. The second term is positive when $(\partial T_a/\partial R) > MM'_a$, or $M(-1 - e_{ma} - e_{mb}) > MM'_a$, or $(-e_{ma} - e_{mb}) > (1 + M'_a)$. Similarly, the last term is positive when $(-e_{ma} - e_{mb}) > (1 + M'_b)$. We therefore conclude that the Harberger condition, although sufficient, is no longer necessary for a successful devaluation. These results are strengthened when the exchange-rate effect on the demand for money is also included in the analysis.

A18.5 THE EFFECTS OF FISCAL AND MONETARY POLICY

Consider now the flexible-exchange-rate system given by the following equations:

$$Y_a = Z_a(Y_a, r_a) + T_a(Y_a, Y_b, R) \qquad \text{(A18.41)}$$

$$Y_b = Z_b(Y_b, r_b) - T_a^*(Y_a, Y_b, R) \qquad \text{(A18.42)}$$

$$H_a = L_a(Y_a, r_a) \qquad \text{(A18.43)}$$

$$H_b = L_b(Y_b, r_b) \qquad \text{(A18.44)}$$

$$T_a^*(Y_a, Y_b, R) + K(r_a - r_b) = 0 \qquad \text{(A18.45)}$$

This is a system of five equations in five unknowns: Y_a, Y_b, r_a, r_b, and R. (For simplicity, the Laursen-Metzler effect is ignored, that is, $(\partial Z_a/\partial R) = (\partial Z_b/\partial R) = 0$.) The capital-flow function K is specified in terms of pounds sterling (that is, B's currency). We wish to study the effects of fiscal and monetary policy on the equilibrium values of Y_a, Y_b, r_a, r_b, and R. As explained in chap. 18, we assume that the balance of trade is initially zero.

Differentiating eqs. (A18.41) to (A18.45) totally, assuming that $R = 1$ and $T_a = 0$ initially, we obtain

$$
\begin{bmatrix}
1 - Z'_a + M'_a & -M'_b & -\dfrac{\partial Z_a}{\partial r_a} & 0 & -\dfrac{\partial T_a}{\partial R} \\[2ex]
-M'_a & 1 - Z'_b + M'_b & 0 & -\dfrac{\partial Z_b}{\partial r_b} & \dfrac{\partial T_a}{\partial R} \\[2ex]
\dfrac{\partial L_a}{\partial Y_a} & 0 & \dfrac{\partial L_a}{\partial r_a} & 0 & 0 \\[2ex]
0 & \dfrac{\partial L_b}{\partial Y_b} & 0 & \dfrac{\partial L_b}{\partial r_b} & 0 \\[2ex]
-M'_a & M'_b & K' & -K' & \dfrac{\partial T_a}{\partial R}
\end{bmatrix}
\begin{bmatrix}
dY_a \\[2ex] dY_b \\[2ex] dr_a \\[2ex] dr_b \\[2ex] dR
\end{bmatrix}
=
\begin{bmatrix}
dG_a \\[2ex] dG_b \\[2ex] dH_a \\[2ex] dH_b \\[2ex] 0
\end{bmatrix}
$$

$$(A18.46)$$

where $K' \equiv \partial K / \partial (r_a - r_b)$. (Note that $(\partial T_a / \partial R) = (\partial T_a^* / \partial R)$ because initially $T_a = T_a^* = 0$ and $R = 1$.)

Expanding the determinant (Δ) of (A18.46), we obtain

$$
\Delta = \left(\frac{\partial L_a}{\partial Y_a}\right)\left(\frac{\partial L_b}{\partial Y_b}\right) \Delta_{11} + \left(\frac{\partial L_a}{\partial Y_a}\right)\left(\frac{\partial L_b}{\partial r_b}\right) \Delta_{12}
$$

$$
- \left(\frac{\partial L_a}{\partial r_a}\right)\left(\frac{\partial L_b}{\partial Y_b}\right) \Delta_{21} + \left(\frac{\partial L_a}{\partial r_a}\right)\left(\frac{\partial L_b}{\partial r_b}\right) \Delta_{22}
$$

where

$$
\Delta_{11} \equiv
\begin{vmatrix}
-\dfrac{\partial Z_a}{\partial r_a} & 0 & -\dfrac{\partial T_a}{\partial R} \\[2ex]
0 & -\dfrac{\partial Z_b}{\partial r_b} & \dfrac{\partial T_a}{\partial R} \\[2ex]
K' & -K' & \dfrac{\partial T_a}{\partial R}
\end{vmatrix}
$$

$$
= \left(\frac{\partial T_a}{\partial R}\right)\left[\left(\frac{\partial Z_a}{\partial r_a}\right)\left(\frac{\partial Z_b}{\partial r_b}\right) - K'\left(\frac{\partial Z_b}{\partial r_b}\right) - K'\left(\frac{\partial Z_a}{\partial r_a}\right)\right]
$$

$$\Delta_{12} = \begin{vmatrix} -M'_b & -\dfrac{\partial Z_a}{\partial r_a} & -\dfrac{\partial T_a}{\partial R} \\[2ex] 1 - Z'_b + M'_b & 0 & \dfrac{\partial T_a}{\partial R} \\[2ex] M'_b & K' & \dfrac{\partial T_a}{\partial R} \end{vmatrix}$$

$$= \left(\dfrac{\partial T_a}{\partial R}\right)(1 - Z'_b)\left[\left(\dfrac{\partial Z_a}{\partial r_a}\right) - K'\right]$$

$$\Delta_{21} = \begin{vmatrix} 1 - Z'_a + M'_a & 0 & -\dfrac{\partial T_a}{\partial R} \\[2ex] -M'_a & -\dfrac{\partial Z_b}{\partial r_b} & \dfrac{\partial T_a}{\partial R} \\[2ex] -M'_a & -K' & \dfrac{\partial T_a}{\partial R} \end{vmatrix}$$

$$= \left(\dfrac{\partial T_a}{\partial R}\right)(1 - Z'_a)\left[K' - \left(\dfrac{\partial Z_b}{\partial r_b}\right)\right]$$

and

$$\Delta_{22} = \begin{vmatrix} 1 - Z'_a + M'_a & -M'_b & -\dfrac{\partial T_a}{\partial R} \\[2ex] -M'_a & 1 - Z'_b + M'_b & \dfrac{\partial T_a}{\partial R} \\[2ex] -M'_a & M'_b & \dfrac{\partial T_a}{\partial R} \end{vmatrix}$$

$$= \left(\dfrac{\partial T_a}{\partial R}\right)(1 - Z'_a)(1 - Z'_b)$$

On the usual assumptions, namely, $(\partial T_a/\partial R) > 0$ (i.e., the Marshall-Lerner condition is satisfied), $(\partial L_a/\partial Y_a) > 0$, $(\partial L_b/\partial Y_b) > 0$, $(\partial L_a/\partial r_a) < 0$, $(\partial L_b/\partial r_b) < 0$, $(\partial Z_a/\partial r_a) < 0$, $(\partial Z_b/\partial r_b) < 0$, $Z'_a < 1$, $Z'_b < 1$, and $K' > 0$, it becomes apparent that $\Delta > 0$, since $\Delta_{11} > 0$, $\Delta_{12} < 0$, $\Delta_{21} > 0$, and $\Delta_{22} > 0$.

The Effects of Fiscal Policy

Consider now the effects of fiscal policy. To determine the effects of G_a, merely set $dG_b = dH_a = dH_b = 0$ and solve (A18.46) by means of Cramer's rule to obtain

$$\frac{dY_a}{dG_a} = \left(\frac{1}{\Delta}\right)\left(\frac{\partial L_a}{\partial r_a}\right)\left(\frac{\partial T_a}{\partial R}\right)\left[(1 - Z'_b)\left(\frac{\partial L_b}{\partial r_b}\right)\right.$$

$$\left. + \left(\frac{\partial L_b}{\partial Y_b}\right)\left(\frac{\partial Z_b}{\partial r_b}\right) - K'\left(\frac{\partial L_b}{\partial Y_b}\right)\right] > 0 \qquad \text{(A18.47)}$$

$$\frac{dY_b}{dG_a} = -\left(\frac{1}{\Delta}\right)K'\left(\frac{\partial L_b}{\partial r_b}\right)\left(\frac{\partial L_a}{\partial Y_a}\right)\left(\frac{\partial T_a}{\partial R}\right) > 0 \tag{A18.48}$$

$$\frac{dr_a}{dG_a} = -\left(\frac{1}{\Delta}\right)\left(\frac{\partial T_a}{\partial R}\right)\left(\frac{\partial L_a}{\partial Y_a}\right)$$

$$\times \left[(1 - Z_b')\left(\frac{\partial L_b}{\partial r_b}\right) - K'\left(\frac{\partial L_b}{\partial Y_b}\right) + \left(\frac{\partial L_b}{\partial Y_b}\right)\left(\frac{\partial Z_b}{\partial r_b}\right)\right] > 0 \tag{A18.49}$$

$$\frac{dr_b}{dG_a} = \left(\frac{1}{\Delta}\right)\left(\frac{\partial T_a}{\partial R}\right)K'\left(\frac{\partial L_a}{\partial Y_a}\right)\left(\frac{\partial L_b}{\partial Y_b}\right) > 0 \tag{A18.50}$$

$$\frac{dR}{dG_a} = \left(\frac{1}{\Delta}\right)\left\{K'\left(\frac{\partial L_a}{\partial Y_a}\right)\left[\left(\frac{\partial Z_b}{\partial r_b}\right)\left(\frac{\partial L_b}{\partial Y_b}\right) + (1 - Z_b' + M_b')\left(\frac{\partial L_b}{\partial r_b}\right)\right]\right.$$

$$\left. + M_a'\left(\frac{\partial L_a}{\partial r_a}\right)\left[(1 - Z_b')\left(\frac{\partial L_b}{\partial r_b}\right) + \left(\frac{\partial L_b}{\partial Y_b}\right)\left(\frac{\partial Z_b}{\partial r_b}\right) - K'\left(\frac{\partial L_b}{\partial Y_b}\right)\right]\right\} \tag{A18.51}$$

Similarly, to determine the effects of G_b, merely set $dG_a = dH_a = dH_b = 0$ and solve (A18.46) by means of Cramer's rule to obtain

$$\frac{dY_a}{dG_b} = -\left(\frac{1}{\Delta}\right)\left(\frac{\partial T_a}{\partial R}\right)\left(\frac{\partial L_a}{\partial r_a}\right)\left(\frac{\partial L_b}{\partial Y_b}\right)K' > 0 \tag{A18.52}$$

$$\frac{dY_b}{dG_b} = \left(\frac{1}{\Delta}\right)\left(\frac{\partial T_a}{\partial R}\right)\left(\frac{\partial L_b}{\partial r_b}\right)\left[(1 - Z_a')\left(\frac{\partial L_a}{\partial r_a}\right) - K'\left(\frac{\partial L_a}{\partial Y_a}\right) + \left(\frac{\partial L_a}{\partial Y_a}\right)\left(\frac{\partial Z_a}{\partial r_a}\right)\right] \tag{A18.53}$$

$$\frac{dr_a}{dG_b} = \left(\frac{1}{\Delta}\right)\left(\frac{\partial T_a}{\partial R}\right)K'\left(\frac{\partial L_a}{\partial Y_a}\right)\left(\frac{\partial L_b}{\partial Y_b}\right) > 0 \tag{A18.54}$$

$$\frac{dr_b}{dG_b} = -\left(\frac{1}{\Delta}\right)\left(\frac{\partial T_a}{\partial R}\right)\left(\frac{\partial L_b}{\partial Y_b}\right)$$

$$\times \left[(1 - Z_a')\left(\frac{\partial L_a}{\partial r_a}\right) - K'\left(\frac{\partial L_a}{\partial Y_a}\right) + \left(\frac{\partial L_a}{\partial Y_a}\right)\left(\frac{\partial Z_a}{\partial r_a}\right)\right] > 0 \tag{A18.55}$$

$$\frac{dR}{dG_b} = \left(\frac{1}{\Delta}\right)\left\{K'\left(\frac{\partial L_b}{\partial Y_b}\right)\left[\left(\frac{\partial Z_a}{\partial r_a}\right)\left(\frac{\partial L_a}{\partial Y_a}\right) + (1 - Z_a' + M_a')\left(\frac{\partial L_a}{\partial r_a}\right)\right]\right.$$

$$\left. + M_b'\left(\frac{\partial L_b}{\partial r_b}\right)\left[(1 - Z_a')\left(\frac{\partial L_a}{\partial r_a}\right) + \left(\frac{\partial L_a}{\partial Y_a}\right)\left(\frac{\partial Z_a}{\partial r_a}\right) - K'\left(\frac{\partial L_a}{\partial Y_a}\right)\right]\right\} \tag{A18.56}$$

Observe that eqs. (A18.52) to (A18.56) can be obtained directly from eqs. (A18.47) to (A18.51) by reversing the subscripts a and b, except in the derivative $(\partial T_a/\partial R)$.

The Effects of Monetary Policy

Turn now to the effects of monetary policy. To determine the effects of H_a, set $dG_a = dG_b = dH_b = 0$ and solve (A18.46) by means of Cramer's rule to obtain

$$\frac{dY_a}{dH_a} = \left(\frac{1}{\Delta}\right)\left(\frac{\partial T_a}{\partial R}\right)\left\{\left[(1 - Z'_b)\left(\frac{\partial L_b}{\partial r_b}\right) + \left(\frac{\partial L_b}{\partial Y_b}\right)\left(\frac{\partial Z_b}{\partial r_b}\right)\right]\right.$$

$$\left. \times \left[\left(\frac{\partial Z_a}{\partial r_a}\right) - K'\right] - K'\left(\frac{\partial Z_a}{\partial r_a}\right)\left(\frac{\partial L_b}{\partial Y_b}\right)\right\} > 0 \tag{A18.57}$$

$$\frac{dY_b}{dH_a} = \left(\frac{1}{\Delta}\right)\left(\frac{\partial T_a}{\partial R}\right)K'(1 - Z'_a)\left(\frac{\partial L_b}{\partial r_b}\right) < 0 \tag{A18.58}$$

$$\frac{dr_a}{dH_a} = \left(\frac{1}{\Delta}\right)\left(\frac{\partial T_a}{\partial R}\right)(1 - Z'_a)$$

$$\times \left[(1 - Z'_b)\left(\frac{\partial L_b}{\partial r_b}\right) - K'\left(\frac{\partial L_b}{\partial Y_b}\right) + \left(\frac{\partial L_b}{\partial Y_b}\right)\left(\frac{\partial Z_b}{\partial r_b}\right)\right] < 0 \tag{A18.59}$$

$$\frac{dr_b}{dH_a} = -\left(\frac{1}{\Delta}\right)\left(\frac{\partial T_a}{\partial R}\right)\left(\frac{\partial L_b}{\partial Y_b}\right)(1 - Z'_a)K' < 0 \tag{A18.60}$$

$$\frac{dR}{dH_a} = \left(\frac{1}{\Delta}\right)\left\{-K'(1 - Z'_a)\right.$$

$$\times \left[M'_b\left(\frac{\partial L_b}{\partial r_b}\right) + \left(\frac{\partial L_b}{\partial Y_b}\right)\left(\frac{\partial Z_b}{\partial r_b}\right) + (1 - Z'_b)\left(\frac{\partial L_b}{\partial r_b}\right)\right]$$

$$+ M'_a\left[\left(\frac{\partial Z_a}{\partial r_a}\right)\left(\frac{\partial Z_b}{\partial r_b}\right)\left(\frac{\partial L_b}{\partial Y_b}\right) - K'\left(\frac{\partial Z_a}{\partial r_a}\right)\left(\frac{\partial L_b}{\partial Y_b}\right) - K'\left(\frac{\partial Z_b}{\partial r_b}\right)\left(\frac{\partial L_b}{\partial Y_b}\right)\right.$$

$$\left.\left. - K'(1 - Z'_b)\left(\frac{\partial L_b}{\partial r_b}\right) + (1 - Z'_b)\left(\frac{\partial L_b}{\partial r_b}\right)\left(\frac{\partial Z_a}{\partial r_a}\right)\right]\right\} > 0 \tag{A18.61}$$

Finally, to determine the effects of H_b, set $dG_a = dG_b = dH_a = 0$ and solve (A18.46) to obtain

$$\frac{dY_a}{dH_b} = \left(\frac{1}{\Delta}\right)\left(\frac{\partial T_a}{\partial R}\right)K'(1 - Z'_b)\left(\frac{\partial L_a}{\partial r_a}\right) < 0 \tag{A18.62}$$

$$\frac{dY_b}{dH_b} = \left(\frac{1}{\Delta}\right)\left(\frac{\partial T_a}{\partial R}\right)\left\{\left[(1 - Z'_a)\left(\frac{\partial L_a}{\partial r_a}\right) + \left(\frac{\partial L_a}{\partial Y_a}\right)\left(\frac{\partial Z_a}{\partial r_a}\right)\right]\right.$$

$$\left. \times \left[\left(\frac{\partial Z_b}{\partial r_b}\right) - K'\right] - K'\left(\frac{\partial Z_b}{\partial r_b}\right)\left(\frac{\partial L_a}{\partial Y_a}\right)\right\} > 0 \tag{A18.63}$$

$$\frac{dr_a}{dH_b} = -\left(\frac{1}{\Delta}\right)\left(\frac{\partial T_a}{\partial R}\right)\left(\frac{\partial L_a}{\partial Y_a}\right)(1 - Z'_b)K' < 0 \tag{A18.64}$$

$$\frac{dr_b}{dH_b} = \left(\frac{1}{\Delta}\right)\left(\frac{\partial T_a}{\partial R}\right)(1 - Z'_b)$$

$$\times \left[(1 - Z'_a)\left(\frac{\partial L_a}{\partial r_a}\right) - K'\left(\frac{\partial L_a}{\partial Y_a}\right) + \left(\frac{\partial L_a}{\partial Y_a}\right)\left(\frac{\partial Z_a}{\partial r_a}\right)\right] < 0 \tag{A18.65}$$

$$\frac{dR}{dH_b} = \left(\frac{1}{\Delta}\right)\left\{-K'(1 - Z_b')\right.$$

$$\times \left[M_a'\left(\frac{\partial L_a}{\partial r_a}\right) + \left(\frac{\partial L_a}{\partial Y_a}\right)\left(\frac{\partial Z_a}{\partial r_a}\right) + (1 - Z_a')\left(\frac{\partial L_a}{\partial r_a}\right)\right]$$

$$+ M_b'\left[\left(\frac{\partial Z_b}{\partial r_b}\right)\left(\frac{\partial Z_a}{\partial r_a}\right)\left(\frac{\partial L_a}{\partial Y_a}\right) - K'\left(\frac{\partial Z_b}{\partial r_b}\right)\left(\frac{\partial L_a}{\partial Y_a}\right) - K'\left(\frac{\partial Z_a}{\partial r_a}\right)\left(\frac{\partial L_a}{\partial Y_a}\right)\right.$$

$$\left. - K'(1 - Z_a')\left(\frac{\partial L_a}{\partial r_a}\right) + (1 - Z_a')\left(\frac{\partial L_a}{\partial r_a}\right)\left(\frac{\partial Z_b}{\partial r_b}\right)\right]\right\} \tag{A18.66}$$

Again observe that eqs. (A18.62) to (A18.66) can be obtained directly from eqs. (A18.57) to (A18.61) by reversing the subscripts a and b, except in the derivative $(\partial T_a / \partial R)$.

A18.6 THE STABILITY OF POLICY ASSIGNMENTS FOR INTERNAL BALANCE

As explained in chap. 18, there are three possible ways in which fiscal and monetary policy can be used by countries A and B to attain internal balance: (1) both countries may use fiscal policy; (2) both countries may use monetary policy; and (3) one country (say A) may use fiscal policy while the other (say B) may use monetary policy. This section studies the stability of these assignments.

Assignment (1): *Both countries use fiscal policy for internal balance.* The dynamic system for this assignment is as follows:

$$\dot{G}_a = c_1(Y_a^f - Y_a^e) \tag{A18.67}$$

$$\dot{G}_b = c_2(Y_b^f - Y_b^e) \tag{A18.68}$$

The matrix of the associated linear system is given by

$$\begin{bmatrix} -c_1\left(\frac{\partial Y_a^e}{\partial G_a}\right) & -c_1\left(\frac{\partial Y_a^e}{\partial G_b}\right) \\ -c_2\left(\frac{\partial Y_b^e}{\partial G_a}\right) & -c_2\left(\frac{\partial Y_b^e}{\partial G_b}\right) \end{bmatrix} \tag{A18.69}$$

For stability it is required that

$$c_1\left(\frac{\partial Y_a^e}{\partial G_a}\right) + c_2\left(\frac{\partial Y_b^e}{\partial G_b}\right) > 0 \tag{A18.70}$$

and $\qquad c_1 c_2\left[\left(\frac{\partial Y_a}{\partial G_a}\right)\left(\frac{\partial Y_b^e}{\partial G_b}\right) - \left(\frac{\partial Y_a^e}{\partial G_b}\right)\left(\frac{\partial Y_b^e}{\partial G_a}\right)\right] > 0 \tag{A18.71}$

Recalling the earlier results given by eqs. (A18.47), (A18.48), (A18.52), and (A18.53), it becomes clear that both stability conditions are satisfied. Thus, inequality (A18.70) is obviously satisfied since all terms on the left-hand side are positive. Similarly, inequality (A18.71) becomes (after substitution of the earlier results and simplification)

$$
\left(\frac{\partial L_a}{\partial r_a}\right)\left(\frac{\partial L_b}{\partial r_b}\right)\left[(1 - Z_b')\left(\frac{\partial L_b}{\partial r_b}\right) + \left(\frac{\partial L_b}{\partial Y_b}\right)\left(\frac{\partial Z_b}{\partial r_b}\right) - K'\left(\frac{\partial L_b}{\partial Y_b}\right)\right]
$$

$$
\times \left[(1 - Z_a')\left(\frac{\partial L_a}{\partial r_a}\right) - K'\left(\frac{\partial L_a}{\partial Y_a}\right) + \left(\frac{\partial L_a}{\partial Y_a}\right)\left(\frac{\partial Z_a}{\partial r_a}\right)\right]
$$

$$
- \left(\frac{\partial L_a}{\partial r_a}\right)\left(\frac{\partial L_b}{\partial Y_b}\right)\left(\frac{\partial L_b}{\partial r_b}\right)\left(\frac{\partial L_a}{\partial Y_a}\right)(K')^2 > 0
$$

This last inequality is certainly satisfied, as the reader may verify.

We therefore conclude that if both countries use fiscal policy to attain internal balance the system will soon converge to long-run equilibrium where both internal and external balance prevails.

Assignment (2): *Both countries use monetary policy for internal balance.* The dynamic system for this assignment is as follows:

$$
\dot{H}_a = c_1(Y_a^f - Y_a^e) \tag{A18.72}
$$

$$
\dot{H}_b = c_2(Y_b^f - Y_b^e) \tag{A18.73}
$$

The matrix of the associated linear system is given by

$$
\begin{bmatrix}
-c_1\left(\dfrac{\partial Y_a^e}{\partial H_a}\right) & -c_1\left(\dfrac{\partial Y_a^e}{\partial H_b}\right) \\
-c_2\left(\dfrac{\partial Y_b^e}{\partial H_a}\right) & -c_2\left(\dfrac{\partial Y_b^e}{\partial H_b}\right)
\end{bmatrix} \tag{A18.74}
$$

For stability it is now required that

$$
c_1\left(\frac{\partial Y_a^e}{\partial H_a}\right) + c_2\left(\frac{\partial Y_b^e}{\partial H_b}\right) > 0 \tag{A18.75}
$$

and
$$
c_1 c_2\left[\left(\frac{\partial Y_a^e}{\partial H_a}\right)\left(\frac{\partial Y_b^e}{\partial H_b}\right) - \left(\frac{\partial Y_a^e}{\partial H_b}\right)\left(\frac{\partial Y_b^e}{\partial H_a}\right)\right] > 0 \tag{A18.76}
$$

To see whether these stability conditions are satisfied, we must substitute into inequalities (A18.75) and (A18.76) the earlier comparative-statics results given by eqs. (A18.57), (A18.58), (A18.62), and (A18.63). Obviously, inequality (A18.75) is satisfied since all terms on the left-hand side are positive. Similarly, inequality (A18.71) can be reduced to

$$\left\{\left[(1 - Z_b')\left(\frac{\partial L_b}{\partial r_b}\right) + \left(\frac{\partial L_b}{\partial Y_b}\right)\left(\frac{\partial Z_b}{\partial r_b}\right)\right]\left[\left(\frac{\partial Z_a}{\partial r_a}\right) - K'\right] - K'\left(\frac{\partial Z_a}{\partial r_a}\right)\left(\frac{\partial L_b}{\partial Y_b}\right)\right\}$$

$$\times \left\{\left[(1 - Z_a')\left(\frac{\partial L_a}{\partial r_a}\right) + \left(\frac{\partial L_a}{\partial Y_a}\right)\left(\frac{\partial Z_a}{\partial r_a}\right)\right]\left[\left(\frac{\partial Z_b}{\partial r_b}\right) - K'\right] - K'\left(\frac{\partial Z_b}{\partial r_b}\right)\left(\frac{\partial L_b}{\partial Y_b}\right)\right\}$$

$$- (K')^2(1 - Z_a')(1 - Z_b')\left(\frac{\partial L_a}{\partial r_a}\right)\left(\frac{\partial L_b}{\partial r_b}\right) > 0$$

through direct substitution of the earlier results and simplification. Now it becomes apparent that the second stability condition is also satisfied since the last inequality is obviously satisfied. Thus, this assignment is stable also.

Assignment (3): *Country A uses fiscal policy and country B uses monetary policy to attain internal balance.* The dynamic system for this assignment is as follows:

$$\dot{G}_a = c_1(Y_a^f - Y_a^e) \tag{A18.67}$$

$$\dot{H}_b = c_2(Y_b^f - Y_b^e) \tag{A18.73}$$

The matrix of the associated linear system is now given by

$$\begin{bmatrix} -c_1\left(\frac{\partial Y_a^e}{\partial G_a}\right) & -c_1\left(\frac{\partial Y_a^e}{\partial H_b}\right) \\ -c_2\left(\frac{\partial Y_b^e}{\partial G_a}\right) & -c_2\left(\frac{\partial Y_b^e}{\partial H_b}\right) \end{bmatrix} \tag{A18.77}$$

For stability it is now required that

$$c_1\left(\frac{\partial Y_a^e}{\partial G_a}\right) + c_2\left(\frac{\partial Y_b^e}{\partial H_b}\right) > 0 \tag{A18.78}$$

and

$$c_1 c_2\left[\left(\frac{\partial Y_a^e}{\partial G_a}\right)\left(\frac{\partial Y_b^e}{\partial H_b}\right) - \left(\frac{\partial Y_a^e}{\partial H_b}\right)\left(\frac{\partial Y_b^e}{\partial G_a}\right)\right] > 0 \tag{A18.79}$$

As the reader should verify, both conditions are satisfied. Thus this assignment is also stable.

We therefore conclude that internal balance can be achieved whether countries use fiscal or monetary policy for this purpose.

SELECTED BIBLIOGRAPHY

Cooper, R. N. (1967). *The Economics of Interdependence: Economic Policy in the Atlantic Community.* McGraw-Hill Book Company, New York.

——— (1968). "The Assignment Problem: A Characterization." In R. A. Mundell and A. Swoboda (Eds.), *Monetary Problems of the International Economy.* University of Chicago Press, Chicago, Ill.

——— (1969). "Macroeconomic Policy Adjustment in Interdependent Economies." *Quarterly Journal of Economics,* vol. LXXXIII (February), pp. 1–24.

Johnson, H. G. (1966). "The Objectives of Economic Policy and the Mix of Fiscal and Monetary Policy under Fixed Exchange Rates." In W. Fellner, F. Machlup, and R. Triffin (Eds.), *Maintaining and Restoring Balance in International Payments*. Princeton University Press, Princeton, N.J.

Kemp, M. C. (1966). "Monetary and Fiscal Policy under Alternative Assumptions about International Capital Mobility." *The Economic Record* (December), pp. 598–605.

Levin, J. H. (1972). "International Capital Mobility and the Assignment Problem." *Oxford Economic Papers*, vol. 24 (March), pp. 54–67.

Mundell, R. A. (1968). *International Economics*. The Macmillan Company, New York, chap. 18 and app. (pp. 250–271).

Mundell, R. A., and A. Swoboda (Eds.) (1968). *Monetary Problems of the International Economy*. University of Chicago Press, Chicago, Ill.

Niehans, J. (1968). "Monetary and Fiscal Policies in Open Economies under Fixed Exchange Rates: An Optimizing Approach." *Journal of Political Economy*, vol. LXXVI, pt. II (July–August), pp. 893–920.

Patrick, J. (1968). "The Optimum Policy Mix: Convergence and Consistency." In P. B. Kenen and R. Lawrence (Eds.), *The Open Economy: Essays on International Trade and Finance*. Columbia University Press, New York.

Swoboda, A. K., and R. Dornbusch (1973). "Adjustment, Policy, and Monetary Equilibrium in a Two-Country Model." In M. B. Connolly and A. K. Swoboda (Eds.), *International Trade and Money*. University of Toronto Press, Toronto.

Tsiang, S. C. (1961). "The Role of Money in Trade-Balance Stability: Synthesis of the Elasticity and Absorption Approaches." *American Economic Review*, vol. LI, no. 5 (December). Reprinted in R. E. Caves and H. G. Johnson (Eds.), *Readings in International Economics*, Richard D. Irwin, Inc., Homewood, Ill., 1968.

NINETEEN

THE NATURE OF BALANCE-OF-PAYMENTS DISEQUILIBRIUM

This last chapter takes a hard look at the nature of balance-of-payments disequilibrium. Unlike the analysis of the earlier chapters which follows the mainstream of economic thinking, the analysis of this chapter is rather unorthodox. A new view of balance-of-payments disequilibrium is put forward—a view which has been anticipated in the literature by Despres, Kindleberger, and Salant (1966), Ingram (1959, 1962), Kindleberger (1965), Salant (1966), and Scitovsky (1967). This new view of external disequilibrium leads naturally to a concrete proposal for reforming the international monetary system.

Before we set out to discuss the new approach, there is a methodological point which must be settled. One may object to the wisdom of appending at the end of a book ideas which in some sense may negate other ideas incorporated throughout the earlier discussion. This criticism is legitimate and our approach must be justified. First, there is the practical reason that most of the earlier discussion was already on paper before the new view occurred to the author. A second and more important reason is that the earlier discussion is indeed necessary for an understanding of the functioning of the international economy, even after the new view of external disequilibrium is accepted. This becomes clear from the rest of the discussion in this chapter.

This chapter is not addressed to the graduate students of international economics only. It is also addressed to the profession at large, both within and without the academic community.

19.1 THE NATURE OF EXTERNAL DISEQUILIBRIUM: FIRST APPROXIMATION

Consider again the two-country, fixed-exchange-rate system of the preceding chapter. To focus our attention primarily on the nature of external disequilibrium, assume that both countries are at full employment. In addition, assume that at the current equilibrium configuration country A is running a balance-of-payments deficit $(T_a + K < 0)$. In other words, assume that country A is losing reserves to country B at the rate of $-(T_a + K)$ per unit of time. What is the nature of this external disequilibrium and how can it be cured? The most important approaches to restoring external balance have been reviewed in earlier chapters. Here a new approach is sought.

Observe that all economic units in both countries, *except the monetary authorities*, are in equilibrium. The producers produce exactly what they want to produce and sell exactly what they want to sell. Similarly, the consumers buy the goods and services as well as the securities they want to buy. All factors are fully employed and all markets are cleared. Only the monetary authorities of both countries find themselves in disequilibrium. A's monetary authorities reluctantly lose reserves to B's monetary authorities. (For simplicity, we ignore the case where A's monetary authorities happen to possess excessive amounts of foreign exchange reserves and B's monetary authorities happen to have a corresponding deficiency in reserves.) Why are the monetary authorities in disequilibrium?

Fundamental Disequilibrium

As we saw earlier in this volume, an external disequilibrium reflects in the first instance a gap between "autonomous" purchases and sales of foreign exchange. This gap is closed by "accommodating" sales or purchases (as the case may be) of foreign exchange by the monetary authorities. But not every gap between autonomous international receipts and payments need present serious problems. In this connection the distinction between temporary and persistent balance-of-payments disequilibria is important. Thus, if in our illustration A's deficit is only temporary (i.e., expected to last for a short period of time and thereafter replaced either by external balance or by a surplus of approximately the same size as the current deficit) and if the stock of reserves of A's monetary authorities are sufficiently large, the external disequilibrium can and must be "financed." Any policy-induced adjustment to restore external balance would be totally unnecessary. If the stock of reserves is not sufficiently large, a strong case can be made for increasing international liquidity through, for instance, the creation of more SDR's. On the other hand, if A's deficit is persistent (i.e., expected to last indefinitely), no amount of reserves and external credit facilities, however large, can be adequate to finance it. It is in connection with such persistent deficits that the monetary authorities find themselves in a fundamental disequilibrium which needs to be taken care of immediately. According to current economic thinking, such disequilibria can only be corrected by means of a policy-induced adjustment which brings the autonomous international payments in line with the autonomous international receipts, as explained earlier in this volume.

Is A's deficit temporary or persistent? That depends very much on whether the current functional relationships (i.e., the consumption function, the investment-demand function, the demand for money, etc.) are expected to remain stable in the future. Now all economic units (besides the monetary authorities) are currently in equilibrium. Hence, they certainly have no incentive to change their behavior unless a change occurs in the fundamental data of the international economy. But such a change is necessarily exogenous and cannot always be counted on to occur when it is needed to restore external balance. We therefore conclude that on the basis of our model there exists no reason to expect a change in the flows of autonomous international receipts and payments. A's deficit is persistent. Johnson (1958) calls it a *flow deficit*.

The Gold Standard and the Flexible-Exchange-Rate System

It is, of course, possible for the monetary authorities to induce changes in the flows of autonomous international receipts and payments. Thus, the monetary authorities may permit their money supplies to decrease or increase as they lose or gain reserves, respectively. This is the case of the gold standard. As explained in great detail earlier in chaps. 15 and 16, these money-supply changes can indeed restore external balance. Nevertheless, following the Keynesian revolution and the greater understanding of the perhaps imperfect relationship between the money supply and aggregate demand, as well as the widespread adherence to the goal of full employment, countries refuse to follow blindly the gold-standard rules of the game which subordinate the domestic economic activity and price stability to the goal of external balance. Monetary authorities do indeed undertake offsetting actions which neutralize or sterilize the disturbing effects on the money supply of changes in international reserves. This thesis, of course, has been criticized by the new "monetary" approach to balance-of-payments theory which assumes—in some cases asserts—that the monetary flows associated with surpluses or deficits are not sterilized—or cannot be, within the relevant time period—but instead influence the domestic money supply. On this point, see Johnson (1972).

Alternatively, the monetary authorities may refuse to intervene in the foreign exchange market. The rate of exchange will then move to a new level at which external equilibrium is restored (disregarding, of course, the complications of destabilizing speculation).

In both instances the steps taken by the monetary authorities are sufficient to restore external balance. But this does not mean that the current external disequilibrium is not persistent (or fundamental). It only means that the monetary authorities, by means of deliberate policy measures, may restore external equilibrium *by inducing an appropriate adjustment in the behavior of all other economic units.* Now as we have seen all these other economic units were in equilibrium to begin with! Why, then, should their equilibrium be disturbed? In a sense, each and every economic unit is forced to shift to a new equilibrium only because their initial equilibrium creates problems for the monetary authorities. Is this adjustment necessary or can the problems of the monetary authorities be resolved in a different way—a way which does not interfere with the current equilibrium in the international economy (excluding the monetary authorities)?

The Constraint Imposed by the Monetary Authorities

It appears that the monetary authorities impose an additional constraint on the behavior of all other economic units. Not only should these units be in equilibrium; their equilibrium must be, in addition, such that the flow of autonomous international payments equals the flow of autonomous international receipts. Can we dispense with this additional constraint? The answer is "Yes." The clue is found in the interregional-adjustment mechanism which is the subject-matter of the following section.

19.2 THE INTERREGIONAL-ADJUSTMENT MECHANISM: A DIGRESSION

We digress briefly to consider the interregional-adjustment mechanism, or rather those aspects of the interregional-adjustment mechanism which are of crucial importance to the problem at hand.

There exists an extensive literature on the comparison between interregional and international balance-of-payments adjustment, but no attempt is made here to provide a review. What is striking in this literature is the general agreement that the interregional-adjustment mechanism is much smoother than the international-adjustment mechanism. Scitovsky (1967, p. 523) puts the matter thus: "There are two striking things about the balance-of-payments problem. One is the stubbornness with which it defies solution in the international realm; the other is the ease and smoothness with which the problem is resolved between regions of the same country." This is perhaps a rhetorical exaggeration but the point is well taken.

Meade's Thesis on the Differences Between Interregional and International Adjustment

In his authoritative monograph, Meade (1951) devotes a whole chapter to an almost exhaustive discussion of the differences between interregional and international adjustment. He lists several factors which may account for the smoother character of the interregional adjustment mechanism. In particular, Meade attributes the differences between interregional and international adjustment to the following factors: (a) the existence of a common monetary and banking system causing the interregional adjustment mechanism to work on the 100 percent money principle, thus making the adjustment more gradual and therefore easier than is the case with a percentage reserve system; (*b*) the fact that the movement of goods and services is likely to be more restricted, and thus the elasticity of demand for imports lower, in international than in interregional trade because of the protective policies adopted by national governments; (*c*) the likelihood that in different countries there are different financial policies or different institutional arrangements in other important economic respects than in different regions of the same country; and (*d*) the higher degree of factor (labor and capital) mobility in interregional than in international trade. Meade concludes that all these factors, *with the exception of capital mobility*, tend to make interregional adjustment smoother and easier.

The Thesis of Ingram and Scitovsky

On the other hand, Ingram (1959, 1962) and Scitovsky (1967, 1969) focus on the higher mobility of capital (securities) which exists between regions than countries and argue that this is *the* most crucial factor which accounts for the great difference between interregional and international adjustment. Scitovsky (1969, pp. 94–98) also emphasizes other factors such as the fact that the marginal propensity to import from another region is usually higher than the marginal propensity to import from another country, and also the role of a central government in the case of a single country as opposed to the world in relation to taxes, transfer payments, and government spending.

Our own analysis lends support to the Ingram-Scitovsky thesis but does not necessarily negate Meade's most general discussion. In general, the factors emphasized by Meade are indeed important and they do account for much, but not all, of the difference between interregional and international adjustment. That is, Meade's factors do create the presumption that interregional adjustment is much smoother than international adjustment but cannot really explain why a breakdown never occurs in the interregional balance-of-payments mechanism.

The Setting

Return now to our earlier model and suppose that A and B are merely two regions of the same country. Continue to assume that the economic units of the country, besides the banking system, are currently in equilibrium but that A's economic units make larger autonomous payments to B's economic units, than B's units to A's; in other words, region A is running a balance-of-payments deficit and region B is running a surplus. Thus, the banking system aside, the situation is the same whether A and B are two regions of the same country or two sovereign nations. Only by making such an assumption would we be able to isolate those factors, if any, which are responsible for the dramatic difference which exists between interregional and international balance-of-payments adjustment.

Does a balance-of-payments problem still exist? How is this problem handled now that A and B are two regions of the same country? Why do we not hear from time to time that a balance-of-payments problem exists among regions of a country as we hear about balance-of-payments problems among nations? What makes the interregional-adjustment mechanism so smooth and perfect?

A Unified Monetary System

We should not hasten to conclude that the interregional-adjustment mechanism is smooth because of the existence of a unified monetary system. Although this idea is basically sound, it does not really help us understand the nature of interregional adjustment. In fact such a response, if taken literally, may lead to the conclusion that the international balance-of-payments problem can be effectively attacked only through the creation of a unified international monetary system, i.e., a World Central Bank. Many would consider such a plan to be the best (or ideal) solution of the international balance-of-payments problem, but would not recommend it because of the political constraints. For instance, Robbins (1954, p. 82) notes that "balance of payments difficulties are essentially difficulties of money changing—difficulties of turning one money into another. And if there is only one money then, obviously, no such difficulties arise." And he continues (p. 84): "Just as the institution of an international army involves surrender of state sovereignty in the military sphere, so the institution of international money would involve the sur-render of state sovereignty in certain spheres of finance. To be concrete, it would mean the surrender of the money-creating power." He concludes (pp. 84–85): "It may well be that when the present wave of acute nationalism passes and as the universal element in the human soul once more asserts itself, there may come about supra-national integrations under which monetary arrangements of this sort will appear perfectly natural. But before this is likely to happen, there must be other changes too. There must be military integration."

The Irrelevance of Labor Mobility

Neither should we conclude prematurely that the international balance-of-payments problem is automatically solved through labor mobility. In the first place, the interregional mobility of labor, though higher than the international, is far from perfect. In addition, as Scitovsky (1967) points out, the mobility of labor by itself is at best a long-run equilibrating factor for two reasons: (a) adjustment still involves national-income changes which are presumably less painful because labor may migrate from the deficit region (in which income and employment tend to fall) to the surplus region (in which income and employment tend to rise); and (b) as people move from one region to the other they take with them liquid assets, and this aggravates the interregional-payments imbalance, at least in the short run. Finally, in our present case there does not appear any incentive for labor to migrate from one region to another. In fact, the assumption was made earlier that both (countries or regions) A and B are at full employment, and in addition at the current equilibrium configuration every economic unit (except the monetary authorities) is in equilibrium. This means that no producer has any incentive to either increase or decrease production, and no worker is unemployed. Why then should any worker move?

The Irrelevance of the 100 Percent Money Principle

Would money-supply changes (according to the 100 percent money principle) as envisioned by Meade bring about the desired smooth adjustment? It is highly unlikely. In effect money-supply changes need not take place at all. Surely the economic units of regions A and B (excluding the banking system) are by assumption content with their current money holdings. In other words, the collective decision of A's economic units to make larger payments to B's economic units than B's economic units make to A's does not coincide with a decision by A's units to reduce, and B's units to increase, their money holdings by A's deficit. If this were the case, of course, A's deficit would be corrected as Meade suggests, but at the same time such a deficit would no longer be a flow deficit—it would be a stock deficit. Our main problem is to determine how a flow deficit, not a stock deficit, is corrected.

Would the banking system itself initiate money-supply changes? Not necessarily. A well-integrated banking system will simply iron out the reserve positions of its member banks without necessarily affecting each region's money supply. What actually happens is this. Since A's economic units are currently content with their money holdings while, as a group, they make more payments to B's economic units than B's units make to A's, it follows that A's economic units must be financing these excess payments by selling securities to A's banks. (In general, A's banks extend credit to A's economic units.) At the same time, the opposite occurs in region B. That is, B's economic units use the excess receipts from A to buy securities from B's banks. (In general, B's economic units use the excess revenue from A to either make loans or repay old debts to B's banks.) Thus, in the final analysis, every economic unit in both regions does what it wants to do except that A's banks lose cash and gain securities, and B's banks gain cash but lose securities, at the rate of A's deficit.

Assuming that the banks' portfolios were in equilibrium to begin with, it now becomes apparent that A's banks would suffer from lack of liquidity while at the same time B's banks would enjoy excess liquidity. Therefore, A's banks would have an incentive to call in loans, or sell securities, while B's banks would have an incentive to extend new loans, or buy securities. In short, A's money supply would have a tendency to fall (by a multiple of A's deficit) and B's money supply would have a tendency to rise (by a multiple of B's surplus). Is this what will actually happen?

A well-integrated and efficient capital market will not permit the preceding tendencies to be realized. Actually, money-supply changes in the two regions are neither necessary nor desirable. *What needs to be done is essentially for A's banks to sell their excess securities to B's banks.* In the United States, for instance, there exists an active *federal funds market* which helps member banks trade off their excesses or deficiencies in reserves. When A's and B's banks iron out their reserve positions through, say, the federal funds market, then all economic units of both regions, including the banking system, will be in equilibrium. By means of such a simple transaction, the initial interregional balance-of-payments disequilibrium is well taken care of. In fact, it is no longer a disequilibrium at all! All economic units including the banking system are indeed in equilibrium and no one has any incentive to change his behavior. The current state of affairs can last indefinitely. The system is in a lasting equilibrium!

The Residual Capital Flow Effected by the Banking System

What happened? Why has the initial balance-of-payments problem disappeared? A's banks merely sold securities to B's banks at the rate of A's deficit. This simple, but extremely important, transaction corrected the disequilibrium of the banking system and simultaneously restored equilibrium in interregional payments. In other words, in the pursuit of its own interests the banking system transferred sufficient capital from the surplus region (B) to the deficit region (A) to *exactly* cover A's deficit. This *residual* capital flow effected by the banking system in the pursuit of its own interests and not in an effort to restore equilibrium in the interregional balance of payments is indeed *autonomous*. Accordingly, taking into consideration this additional capital flow effected by the banking system itself, it follows that A's autonomous payments to B equal B's autonomous payments to A. The interregional balance of payments is in equilibrium.

Conclusion

We therefore conclude that even though, in general, the factors listed by Meade may indeed account for much of the difference between interregional and international adjustment, the crucial factor remains the residual transfer of capital, by the banking system itself, from the otherwise surplus to the otherwise deficit region which is just sufficient to keep the interregional balance of payments in equilibrium. This residual transfer of capital eliminates the need for any balance-of-payments corrective measures. Finally, it should now be apparent that not only is the balance-of-payments problem a monetary phenomenon but in a deeper sense the balance-of-payments problem is indeed a problem of the monetary authorities only.

Given these important conclusions, we return now to the main theme of our investigation, i.e., the nature of the international balance-of-payments problem.

19.3 LACK OF INTERNATIONAL FINANCIAL INTERMEDIATION AS THE FUNDAMENTAL CAUSE OF INTERNATIONAL DISEQUILIBRIUM

Once the interregional-adjustment mechanism is well understood, the fundamental cause of international balance-of-payments disequilibrium is not hard to find.

Back to the International Economy

Return to the initial state of affairs in which A and B are two distinct sovereign nations with separate monetary systems. A's currency is the dollar and B's the pound sterling. Currently, country A is running a balance-of-payments (flow) deficit and is losing reserves to country B at the rate of $-(T_a + K)$ per unit of time. What is the fundamental cause of A's deficit?

As noted in sec. 19.1, the fundamental cause of A's deficit is not to be found in the neutralization (or sterilization) policies pursued by A's and B's monetary authorities. True, such policies do prevent money-supply changes which could restore external balance. But as we argued earlier, it is the absence itself of these sterilization policies which actually constitutes a policy—in fact, an unacceptable policy at that—to restore external disequilibrium. We should not fall into the trap of believing that (a) the adjustment process under an international gold standard is a natural process; (b) the sterilization policies pursued by A's and B's monetary authorities suspend this natural adjustment process, thus giving rise to a persistent balance-of-payments disequilibrium; and (c) therefore, the fundamental cause of persistent international disequilibrium is the existence of the sterilization policies. Our discussion of the interregional-adjustment mechanism provides convincing proof that there exists a more natural way of restoring external disequilibrium.

Aggregate Saving Equals Aggregate Investment

Recall the following national-income identities:

$$Y_a = C_a + I_a + T_a \tag{19.1}$$

$$Y_b = C_b + I_b - T_a \tag{19.2}$$

$$Y_a = C_a + S_a \tag{19.3}$$

$$Y_b = C_b + S_b \tag{19.4}$$

The government sector is omitted for simplicity.

By subtracting eq. (19.3) from eq. (19.1), and (19.4) from (19.2), and rearranging, we obtain

$$T_a = S_a - I_a = I_b - S_b \tag{19.5}$$

That is, A's balance of trade T_a is equal to (a) the difference between A's saving S_a and investment I_a, and (b) the difference between B's investment I_b and saving S_b.

To fix ideas, we assume in what follows that country A is running a balance-of-trade deficit, that is, $T_a < 0$, or $S_a < I_a$, or $I_b < S_b$.

Finally, by a mere rearrangement of eq. (19.5), we obtain the fundamental identity

$$S_a + S_b = I_a + I_b \qquad (19.6)$$

Equation (19.6) reveals the important result that aggregate saving equals aggregate investment in the world economy. This is nothing else but a straightforward generalization of the simple Keynesian identity $S = I$ for a closed economy. The world economy is indeed a closed economy.

The preceding *identities* hold irrespective of whether the national incomes of countries A and B are in equilibrium. For national-income equilibrium it is also required that the realized (or *ex post*) value of each variable equals the desired (or *ex ante*) value of the same variable. In what follows, we assume that national incomes are in equilibrium and that desired saving equals actual saving, and desired investment equals actual investment, in both countries.

The Identity "Saving-Investment" Does Not Hold for Each Country Separately

Obviously, as Keynes (1936) very appropriately pointed out, no single economic unit achieves perfect synchronization of saving and investment. If everyone did, there would be no Keynesian problem—or balance-of-payments problem for that matter. Similarly, no group of economic units can be expected, in general, to achieve perfect synchronization of its saving and investment activities either. Thus, while for the world as a whole saving equals investment, the same equality cannot be expected in general to hold for each country separately; and this is a necessary condition for the existence of international disequilibrium. While Keynesian unemployment occurs when there are not sufficient investment projects to absorb the full-employment saving, the balance-of-payments problem, as we shall see, arises from the difficulty of channeling one country's excess saving $(S - I > 0)$ to another country's excess investment $(I - S > 0)$. The solution, then, of the balance-of-payments problem requires the establishment of an effective mechanism of accomplishing this transfer of saving from the otherwise surplus to the otherwise deficit countries.

The Aggregate Demand and Supply of Securities

In general, a saver can use his savings in three ways: (a) he may add to his cash holdings; (b) he may—as an entrepreneur—purchase capital goods directly; or (c) he may buy securities. However, for our purposes, it is useful to view the various economic units in terms of their activities. Accordingly, alternative (b) may be eliminated. The purchase of capital goods directly by a saver may be decomposed into (a) a purchase of securities by the economic unit in its capacity as a saver from itself in its capacity as an entrepreneur, plus (*b*) a purchase of capital goods by the economic unit in its capacity as an entrepreneur.

The suppliers of the securities bought by the savers are, of course, the entrepreneurs (including savers who act in their capacity as entrepreneurs) who issue securities in order to finance their purchases of capital goods.

To simplify the analysis as much as possible, ignore for the moment the existence of a market for *old* securities. That is, assume that a person buying a security is " married " to it, and there exists no market for its resale. This restrictive assumption is indeed removed in the following section.

Given our earlier assumption that all economic units, excluding the monetary authorities, are in general in equilibrium and in particular content with their current money holdings, it follows that each country's saving and investment constitute a demand and supply of (new) securities, respectively. Equation (19.6) tells us, then, that the total world demand of securities by all economic units (excluding the monetary authorities) in their capacity as savers equals the total world supply of securities by all economic units (excluding the monetary authorities) in their capacity as entrepreneurs (investors).

The Importance of Perfect Capital Mobility

If the securities issued by A's entrepreneurs and the securities issued by B's entrepreneurs were perfect substitutes in the eyes of both A's and B's economic units (perfect capital mobility), there would be no international balance-of-payments problem. In this limiting case, illustrated in fig. 19.1, there exists a unified securities market and eq. (19.6) implies that A's economic units (excluding the monetary authorities) sell securities to B's economic units at the rate of $K \equiv (I_a - S_a)$ per unit of time. But $T_a + K = (S_a - I_a) + (I_a - S_a) = 0$ and, therefore, the balance of payments is in equilibrium.

Accordingly, a balance-of-payments *dis*equilibrium can exist if the securities issued by A's economic units are *not* perfect substitutes for the securities issued by B's economic units.

Perfect Capital Immobility

Consider now the other limiting case in which securities do not cross national frontiers at all, i.e., the case of perfect capital immobility. Here the securities markets of countries A and B are totally disconnected. Equilibrium, however, is maintained separately in each securities market because each country's monetary

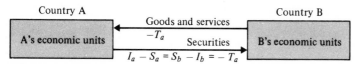

Figure 19.1 Flows of goods and services, and securities: perfect capital mobility.

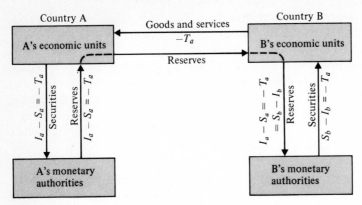

Figure 19.2 Flows of goods and services, securities, and reserves: perfect capital immobility.

authorities act as a residual buyer or seller as the case may be. In fact these residual purchases or sales of securities by A's and B's monetary authorities are what we earlier called sterilization operations. The purchases of securities by A's monetary authorities from A's economic units coincide with A's balance-of-payments deficit; and the sales of securities by B's monetary authorities to B's economic units coincide with B's balance-of-payments surplus. All these flows are shown schematically in fig. 19.2. Note that the money supply remains constant in both countries, all economic units (except the monetary authorities) in both countries are in equilibrium, and a new cycle is ready to begin.

Imperfect Capital Mobility

Finally, consider the intermediate and perhaps more realistic case of imperfect capital mobility. Here A's and B's securities are imperfect substitutes. B's economic units purchase some of the securities issued by A's entrepreneurs, say K, but these purchases fall short of A's excess supply of bonds $(I_a - S_a)$, that is, $K < (I_a - S_a)$. (K is assumed here to be positive, but theoretically it could also be negative.) Accordingly, A's monetary authorities purchase $(I_a - S_a - K)$ securities from A's economic units and pay for these securities with international reserves. In turn, A's economic units use the international reserves to pay for their excess purchases from B's economic units. Finally, B's economic units exchange the reserves for securities from B's monetary authorities. Figure 19.3 shows all these flows schematically. Again the money supply remains constant in both countries, all economic units (except the monetary authorities) in both countries are in equilibrium (i.e., they are content with what they are currently doing), and the whole process is ready to begin again. The only difficulty, of course, in the present case (and the preceding case of perfect capital immobility) is that A's monetary authorities will soon run out of reserves, and therefore something must be done to correct the current flow deficit.

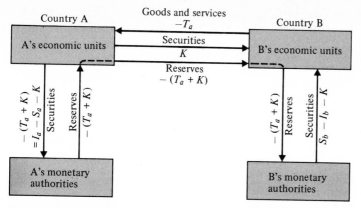

Figure 19.3 Flows of goods and services, securities, and reserves: imperfect capital mobility.

The Need for International Financial Intermediation

The preceding balance-of-payments disequilibrium does not arise because B's economic units are not willing to buy securities at the rate of A's excess supply of securities, that is, $I_a - S_a$. As we have seen, B's economic units have an excess demand for securities $(S_b - I_b)$ which matches precisely the excess supply of securities by A's economic units $(I_a - S_a)$. The problem arises because B's economic units, although in the market to buy securities, do not wish to buy the securities issued by A's economic units. Since the securities issued by A's economic units are not the kind of securities B's economic units wish to buy, some kind of international financial intermediation is called for to convert A's securities into some form acceptable to B's economic units. This international financial intermediation, or the lack of it, lies at the heart of the international balance-of-payments problem.

Sterilization Operations Viewed as International Financial Intermediation

To be sure, B's economic units do not wish to buy A's securities at the current price structure. Thus, if there was no intervention by the monetary authorities and the price mechanism were allowed to work freely in the securities markets, A's securities (which are in excess supply) would tend to become cheaper while B's securities (which are in excess demand) would tend to become dearer. Given some degree of substitutability between A's and B's securities, these changes in the market value of securities would tend to restore balance-of-payments equilibrium. The only trouble with this solution, of course, is that a reduction in the market value of A's securities amounts to an increase in A's interest rate; and an increase in the market value of B's securities amounts to a decrease in B's interest rate. These interest-rate changes would tend to reduce aggregate demand, income, and employment in A, and increase aggregate demand and money income, and create inflation in B. (Recall that A and B were assumed to be at full employment.) As explained repeatedly in this book, such a situation is totally unacceptable and the monetary authorities will interfere with such automatic tendencies which exist in the system. Such interference by the monetary authorities is what is known as sterilization or neutralization operations. Thus, A's deficit is settled through the transfer of reserves from A's monetary authorities to B's monetary authorities. If A's monetary authorities do not sterilize but, on the contrary, accept payment for the reserves they give up in terms of A's currency, A's money supply and the market value of A's securities would fall while A's interest rate would rise. Similarly, if B's monetary authorities do not sterilize but instead pay in B's currency for the reserves they acquire, B's money supply and the market value of B's securities would go up while B's interest rate would go down.

When A's monetary authorities actually sterilize the effects of the loss of reserves on the money supply, they merely act as a residual buyer of A's securities. Accordingly, A's monetary authorities absorb all excess supply of A's securities and prevent A's money supply from falling. The market value of A's securities and A's interest rate have no tendency to change. Similarly, when B's monetary authorities sterilize the effects of the inflow of reserves on the money supply, they merely act as a residual seller of B's securities. Accordingly, B's monetary authorities sell enough securities to satisfy the current excess demand for them at the current prices. B's money supply and interest rate remain constant. We therefore conclude that when A's and B's monetary authorities carry out their respective sterilization operations there is no tendency for the market value of securities or the interest rate to change in either country.

From the preceding discussion it becomes apparent that the sterilization operations by the monetary authorities amount to international financial intermediation. In particular, B's monetary authorities possess the kind of securities which B's economic units prefer. A's monetary authorities accept the excess supply of securities issued by A's economic units (and which are not acceptable to B's economic units) and they release in return an asset (international reserves) acceptable to B's authorities. Finally, B's authorities surrender to B's economic units the kind of securities which the latter find acceptable.

The Need to Improve the International Financial Intermediation Process

Unfortunately, the preceding international financial intermediation process cannot last for ever. Sooner or later A's monetary authorities will run out of reserves and the international financial intermediation process will break down. This badly needed intermediation process is founded on very shaky grounds and cannot normally continue for as long as is needed. There is no built-in mechanism to make it crisis-proof, as is the case with the interregional balance-of-payments adjustment process. As we know it, this mechanism of international financial intermediation is designed to handle minor problems only. When it comes to persistent balance-of-payments deficits the mechanism breaks down because it was never meant to cope with such problems. How can the current international financial intermediation process be improved and strengthened so that it becomes capable of coping with such persistent balance-of-payments disequilibria? This is basically the problem to which the rest of our discussion is addressed.

Incidentally, the often-quoted idea that A's balance-of-payments deficit is due to credit creation provides only a partial equilibrium view of the problem. The current balance-of-payments disequilibrium is not A's problem only; it is B's problem also. Furthermore, by necessity A's deficit is B's surplus. Whatever A's monetary authorities do, B's monetary authorities must do the opposite. A's credit creation, then, coincides with B's credit destruction. Therefore, for the world economy as a whole, credit is neither created nor destroyed.

19.4 A RESALE MARKET FOR SECURITIES

So far our analysis has been based on the assumption that only new securities are traded either nationally or internationally. What happens when this assumption is dropped and old securities are allowed to be traded side by side with the new securities?

To simplify our analysis as much as possible, assume that all securities issued by A's economic units are identical in the sense that they are considered to be perfect substitutes for each other. Similarly, all securities issued by B's economic units are also considered to be perfect substitutes for each other. Thus, there are only two types of securities in our model: A's securities and B's securities. But A's securities are not perfect substitutes for B's securities. Finally, at any moment in time, the accumulated stock of securities by A's economic units consists, in general, of both types of securities. The same is true of the accumulated stock of securities by B's economic units.

The assumption that old securities are not resold is, of course, equivalent to the assumption that the initial composition of the portfolios of A's economic units as a group, and also the initial composition of the portfolios of B's economic units as a group, is optimal at the current prices. Accordingly, new problems arise either when the initial composition of portfolios is not optimal to begin with, or when the initial optimal composition of portfolios is disturbed by a change in portfolio preferences or expectations.

What happens when a shift in demand occurs away from, say, A's securities to B's securities? In the absence of any intervention in the securities markets by the monetary authorities, the structure of market values of securities will change to accommodate the shift in portfolio preferences. There will be no *direct* effect on the balance of payments—exchanges of securities between A's and B's economic units leave no net capital flow. But there will be a direct effect on the international indebtedness position of the two countries as the market values of securities change, and an *indirect* effect on the balance of payments and the levels of economic activity in the two countries. In particular, in our illustration A's securities will tend to become cheaper and B's securities dearer, or, equivalently, A's interest rate will tend to rise and B's interest rate will tend to fall. Accordingly, aggregate spending will tend to fall in A and rise in B and, as shown earlier in this book, A's balance of trade will tend to improve. The effect on the flow of capital K is not clear because there are two opposing tendencies: (a) K tends to fall as a result of the shift in portfolio preferences and (b) K tends to increase as a result of the interest-rate changes.

On the other hand, if A's and B's monetary authorities pursue a Keynesian neutral monetary policy, country A will suffer from a *temporary* balance-of-payments deficit (stock deficit). Thus, A's monetary authorities will act as a residual buyer of A's securities and B's monetary authorities as a residual seller of B's securities. The shift in portfolio preferences will be fully accommodated by the monetary authorities. During this process, A's monetary authorities lose reserves to B's. The balance-of-payments disequilibrium disappears when the composition of portfolios becomes optimal.

19.5 AN OUTLINE OF A PLAN FOR REFORM OF THE INTERNATIONAL MONETARY SYSTEM

Economists have always emphasized *adjustment* for the restoration and preservation of international equilibrium. Without belittling the importance of adjustment (see sec. 19.6 below), we propose *international financial intermediation* as the means to restore international equilibrium in the short run. Actually, herein lies a modest reform of the international monetary system. In particular, it is proposed that the International Monetary Fund create a new department called the International Investments Department (or some other more appropriate title). The purpose of the International Investments Department (IID) is precisely to provide the mechanism for the needed international financial intermediation which cannot be provided on a continuing basis under the current arrangements.

The IID will be authorized to buy and sell securities (of any country) in the open market, perhaps with some limitations to be agreed upon by all countries. The IID will finance any new acquisitions of securities by issuing an interest-bearing asset, the international bond. The interest paid on these bonds should be commensurate with the interest and/or dividends received from the securities bought by the IID in the open market with due allowance made for running expenses. In short, the IID should work like an international mutual fund. The assets (international bonds) issued by the IID should enjoy general acceptability by both private economic units and monetary authorities.

How would the IID operations provide the necessary international financial intermediation and solve the balance-of-payments problem? The IID should simply buy the excess supply of securities of the deficit countries by issuing international bonds which in turn should find general acceptability in the surplus countries. Thus, the IID would merely convert the (unacceptable) securities of the deficit countries into (acceptable) international bonds. In effect, deficit countries would finance their deficits by giving up (within limits) ownership of real assets which the deficits themselves financed in the first place. In a deeper sense, then, the deficit countries may be viewed as intermediaries offering entrepreneurial services to the surplus countries by converting the excess savings of the latter into profitable investment projects. Such a scheme is feasible and should go a long way toward the restoration and preservation of economic order in the world economy. In addition, it could become a very powerful vehicle for channeling foreign aid to the industrially backward countries.

Triffin (1961) argued for the creation of an expanded International Monetary Fund (XIMF) which would make possible a programmed increase in international reserves by means of loans which "should fall into two broad categories, similar in many respects to those of national central banks' credit operations: 1. advances or rediscounts undertaken at the initiative of the borrowing country; 2. open market operations, or investments, undertaken at the initiative of the Fund itself (p. 115)." A major difference between Triffin's plan and the present proposal is, of course, the fact that Triffin proposes essentially the creation of a World Central Bank whereas the present proposal advocates for the creation of a new department of the existing IMF, with this new department operating on the same principles as a mutual fund. As mentioned earlier in this chapter, the creation of a World Central Bank is the ideal solution to the balance-of-payments problem. Nevertheless, it is not politically acceptable and for this reason we seek a second-best solution.

19.6 STRUCTURAL BALANCE VERSUS PORTFOLIO BALANCE

Under normal circumstances, international financial intermediation can potentially finance any balance-of-payments deficit. In addition, it brings the interest-rate structures of the economies of the world closer together, thus satisfying an important optimality condition. Yet such a solution need not be optimal because the current full-employment balance of trade (which signifies the real flow of capital between countries) is not determined by any optimization process but is instead arbitrarily determined by the current exchange rates, the current trade policies of the various countries, the relative strength of the labor unions in the various countries, and a host of other considerations which determine the current terms of trade.

Should international financial intermediation be used indiscriminately to finance any balance-of-payments deficit? It is useful to distinguish between two different balance-of-payments problems—a structural problem and a portfolio problem. The structural problem deals with the structure of the balance of trade while the portfolio problem deals with the composition of the portfolios of the asset holders. Portfolio balance prevails when the current composition of portfolios is considered optimal by the asset holders, and any increase (or decrease) in the size of portfolios is accommodated by the kind of assets preferred by the asset holders. On the other hand, structural balance prevails when the size of each country's balance-of-trade deficit or surplus is optimal. It must be perfectly clear that each of these problems must be handled separately. For an optimal allocation of resources in the world economy it is important to distribute real capital between countries until the rates of return are everywhere equal. All countries can benefit (potentially) when real capital flows from the capital-rich to the capital-poor countries. Thus, in principle, capital-rich countries should run balance-of-trade surpluses and capital-poor countries balance-of-trade deficits. Nevertheless, the precise numerical determination of the optimal sizes of these surpluses and deficits in any given situation may present difficulties and perhaps disagreement. But in principle there should be no difficulty—this problem is no different from any other optimization problem.

International financial intermediation is capable of restoring and preserving portfolio balance only. International financial intermediation *cannot* restore structural balance. It is made abundantly clear in this volume that structural balance can be restored only by the application of switching policies only. It would be a mistake to think that international financial intermediation is a panacea for all balance-of-payments problems. At the same time, it would also be a mistake to advocate for switching policies to correct a portfolio imbalance.

Most economists, frustrated and disillusioned with the fixed-exchange-rate system (mainly because of its basic inability to provide for a smooth adjustment process) and at the same time realizing that the creation of a World Central Bank must remain a dream for the future, turn to the flexible-exchange-rate system as the only known system capable of preserving international economic order in a world which is too hostile and too nationalistic. Our analysis shows that such a system may indeed create a high degree of instability and inefficiency in the world economy since it uses the same instrument—the rate of exchange—to attack both a structural and a portfolio imbalance. The main problem, of course, is that any portfolio imbalance would be allowed to exert a great influence on the economic structures of the economies of the world. But as Keynes (1929, p. 167) very aptly put it: "Those who see no difficulty in this . . . are applying the theory of liquids to what is, if not a solid, at least a sticky mass with strong internal resistances."

SELECTED BIBLIOGRAPHY

Despres, E., C. P. Kindleberger, and W. S. Salant (1966). "The Dollar and World Liquidity—A Minority View." *The Economist*, Feb. 5, pp. 526–529. Reprinted in B. J. Cohen (Ed.), *American Foreign Economic Policy*. Harper and Row, New York, 1968.
Ingram, J. C. (1959). "State and Regional Payments Mechanisms." *Quarterly Journal of Economics*, vol. 73, pp. 619–632.
——— (1962). "Some Implications of Puerto Rican Experience." *Regional Payments Mechanisms: The Case of Puerto Rico*. University of North Carolina Press. Chapel-Hill, N.C., pp. 113–133. Reprinted in R. N. Cooper (Ed.), *International Finance*. Penguin Books, Inc., Baltimore, Md., 1969.
Johnson, H. G. (1958). *International Trade and Economic Growth*. George Allen and Unwin Ltd., London, chap. VI. Reprinted in AEA *Readings in International Economics*. Richard D. Irwin, Inc., Homewood, Ill., 1968.
——— (1972). "The New Monetary Approach to Balance-of-Payments Theory." *Journal of Financial and Quantitative Analysis* (March), pp. 1555–1572. Reprinted in M. Connolly and A. Swoboda (Eds.), *International Trade and Money*. University of Toronto Press, Toronto, 1973.

Keynes, J. M. (1929). "The German Transfer Problem." *Economic Journal*, vol. XXXIX (March), pp. 1–7. Reprinted in AEA *Readings in the Theory of International Trade*. R. D. Irwin, Inc., Homewood, Ill., 1950, pp. 161–169.

——— (1936). *The General Theory of Employment, Interest and Money*. Macmillan and Company Ltd., London.

Kindleberger, C. P. (1965). "Balance-of-Payments Deficits and the International Market for Liquidity." Princeton Essays in International Finance, no. 46. International Finance Section, Princeton University, Princeton, N.J.

Machlup, F. (1966). "In Search of Guides for Policy." In W. Fellner, F. Machlup, and R. Triffin (Eds.), *Maintaining and Restoring Balance in International Payments*. Princeton University Press, Princeton, N.J.

Meade, J. E. (1951). *The Theory of International Economic Policy*, vol. I, *The Balance of Payments*. Oxford University Press, London, chap. XIX.

Mussa, M. (1974). "A Monetary Approach to Balance of Payments Analysis." *Journal of Money, Credit, Banking*, vol. 6, no. 3 (August), pp. 333–351.

Robbins, L. (1954). *The Economist in the Twentieth Century*. Macmillan and Company, Ltd., London.

Salant, W. S. (1966). "The Balance of Payments of a Financial Center." In W. Fellner, F. Machlup, and R. Triffin (Eds.), *Maintaining and Restoring Balance in International Payments*. Princeton University Press, Princeton, N.J.

Scitovsky, T. (1967). "The Theory of Balance-of-Payments Adjustment." *Journal of Political Economy* (Supplement), August.

——— (1969). *Money and the Balance of Payments*. Rand-McNally and Company, Chicago, Ill.

Triffin, R. (1961). *Gold and the Dollar Crisis*. Yale University Press, New Haven, Conn.

MATHEMATICAL APPENDIX

FIRST-ORDER LINEAR ORDINARY DIFFERENTIAL EQUATIONS WITH CONSTANT COEFFICIENTS

The simple dynamic systems considered in this book are examples of first-order linear ordinary differential equations with constant coefficients. This appendix shows briefly and without formal proof how such systems are solved.

MA.1 SINGLE DIFFERENTIAL EQUATION

Consider the following linear differential equation:

$$\dot{x} + ax = b \tag{A.1a}$$

or

$$Dx + ax = b \tag{A.1b}$$

where the real numbers a, b are constants, x is a function of t, and D is the differential operator (d/dt).

The general solution of eq. (A.1a) is the sum of two parts: (a) a *homogeneous solution* x_H, plus (b) a *particular solution* x_P. In other words, the general solution of eq. (A.1a) is given by

$$x = x_H + x_P \tag{A.2}$$

Our task is to determine x_H and x_P.

Homogeneous Solution

The homogeneous solution x_H is the solution of the following homogeneous equation, which is obtained from eq. (A.1b) by setting $b = 0$:

$$Dx + ax = 0 \qquad (A.3)$$

To determine x_H simply set

$$x_H = ce^{\lambda t} \qquad (A.4)$$

and substitute into eq. (A.3) in order to determine λ in terms of the given parameter a. Thus,

$$Dx_H + ax_H = \lambda ce^{\lambda t} + ace^{\lambda t} = 0$$

or, dividing through by $ce^{\lambda t}$,

$$\lambda + a = 0$$

or

$$\lambda = -a \qquad (A.5)$$

Accordingly, the homogeneous solution x_H becomes

$$x_H = ce^{-at} \qquad (A.6)$$

where c is a constant whose precise value depends on *initial conditions* as explained below.

Particular Solution

To determine the particular solution x_P set

$$x_P = p \qquad (A.7)$$

and substitute into eq. (A.1b) in order to determine the precise value of the constant p:

$$Dx_P + ax_P = 0 + ap = b$$

or

$$p = \frac{b}{a} \qquad (A.8)$$

We therefore conclude that the general solution of eq. (A.1a) is

$$x = x_H + x_P = ce^{-at} + \left(\frac{b}{a}\right) \qquad (A.9)$$

Initial Conditions

To determine the precise value of the constant c we must know the value of x at some value of t. For instance, assume that at time $t = 0$, x is x_0. Equation (A.9) must satisfy this initial condition. Setting $t = 0$ in eq. (A.9), and remembering that $x = x_0$ at $t = 0$, we obtain

$$x_0 = c + \left(\frac{b}{a}\right),$$

or
$$c = x_0 - \left(\frac{b}{a}\right) \tag{A.10}$$

Finally, substituting the value of c as given by eq. (A.10) into eq. (A.9), we obtain

$$x = \left[x_0 - \left(\frac{b}{a}\right)\right] e^{-at} + \left(\frac{b}{a}\right) \tag{A.11}$$

Equation (A.11) is the general solution of eq. (A.1a) and satisfies the initial condition, namely, that at $t = 0$, $x = x_0$.

Stability

The stability of eq. (A.1a) depends on the homogeneous solution only. Thus, if $a > 0$, $\lim_{t \to \infty} e^{-at} = 0$ and $\lim_{t \to \infty} x = b/a$. That is, if $a > 0$ (or $\lambda < 0$), as t tends to infinity, the term e^{-at} tends to zero and x tends to b/a. When this happens, we say that eq. (A.1a) is *stable* and its long-run equilibrium value is b/a. On the other hand, if $a < 0$ (or $\lambda > 0$), as t tends to infinity, the term e^{-at} and x tend to infinity also. When this happens we say that the solution is *explosive* and eq. (A.1a) is *unstable*.

Example A.1 Determine the general solution of the differential equation

$$10\dot{x} + 20x = 40 \tag{A.12}$$

assuming that at $t = 0$, $x = 100$.

SOLUTION To determine the homogeneous solution x_H ignore the constant term 40 and set $x_H = ce^{\lambda t}$. Upon substitution, we obtain

$$10\lambda ce^{\lambda t} + 20ce^{\lambda t} = 0$$

or
$$10\lambda + 20 = 0$$

or
$$\lambda = -2$$

For the particular solution, set $x_P = p$ and substitute into the given equation to obtain

$$0 + 20p = 40 \qquad \text{or} \qquad p = 2$$

Hence the general solution is of the form

$$x = ce^{-2t} + 2 \tag{A.13}$$

Finally, to determine c, substitute the initial condition into eq. (A.13) to obtain:

$$100 = c + 2 \qquad \text{or} \qquad c = 98$$

Thus, the final solution is

$$x = 98e^{-2t} + 2 \tag{A.14}$$

The solution is stable $(-2 < 0)$ and the reader may verify that eq. (A.14) can be obtained directly from eq. (A.11) by setting:

$$x_0 = 100 \qquad b = \frac{40}{10} = 4 \qquad a = \frac{20}{10} = 2 \qquad \frac{b}{a} = 2$$

MA.2 TWO FIRST-ORDER LINEAR DIFFERENTIAL EQUATIONS

With little effort, the preceding results can be extended to a system of two first-order linear differential equations. Consider the following system:

$$\begin{aligned} \dot{x}_1 + a_{11}x_1 + a_{12}x_2 &= b_1 \\ \dot{x}_2 + a_{21}x_1 + a_{22}x_2 &= b_2 \end{aligned} \tag{A.15}$$

or, in matrix form,

$$\begin{bmatrix} a_{11} + D & a_{12} \\ a_{21} & a_{22} + D \end{bmatrix} \begin{bmatrix} x_1 \\ x_2 \end{bmatrix} = \begin{bmatrix} b_1 \\ b_2 \end{bmatrix} \tag{A.16}$$

Where no ambiguity can result, system (A.16) can be written more concisely as

$$(a + DI)x = b \tag{A.17}$$

where x and b are the column vectors $[x_1, x_2]$ and $[b_1, b_2]$, respectively, and a and I are the matrix of coefficients and the unit matrix as follows:

$$a \equiv \begin{bmatrix} a_{11} & a_{12} \\ a_{21} & a_{22} \end{bmatrix} \qquad I \equiv \begin{bmatrix} 1 & 0 \\ 0 & 1 \end{bmatrix}$$

Equation (A.17) looks very much like eq. (A.1b).

The general solution of system (A.15) or (A.17) consists again of a homogeneous solution plus a particular solution.

Homogeneous Solution

To find the homogeneous solution consider the homogeneous system

$$\begin{aligned} \dot{x}_1 + a_{11}x_1 + a_{12}x_2 &= 0 \\ \dot{x}_2 + a_{21}x_1 + a_{22}x_2 &= 0 \end{aligned} \tag{A.18a}$$

or, in short,

$$(a + DI)x = 0 \tag{A.18b}$$

The homogeneous solution takes now the form

$$
\begin{aligned}
x_1 &= c_1 e^{\lambda t} \\
x_2 &= c_2 e^{\lambda t}
\end{aligned}
\tag{A.19a}
$$

or, in matrix form,

$$x_H = c e^{\lambda} \tag{A.19b}$$

where

$$x_H \equiv [x_1, x_2]$$

and

$$c \equiv [c_1, c_2]$$

Equation (A.19b) looks like eq. (A.4) except that now x_H and c are column vectors—not scalars.

To determine λ simply substitute from eqs. (A.19a) into eqs. (A.18a) as follows:

$$
\begin{aligned}
\lambda c_1 e^{\lambda t} + a_{11} c_1 e^{\lambda t} + a_{12} c_2 e^{\lambda t} &= 0 \\
\lambda c_2 e^{\lambda t} + a_{21} c_1 e^{\lambda t} + a_{22} c_2 e^{\lambda t} &= 0
\end{aligned}
\tag{A.20a}
$$

or, in matrix form,

$$e^{\lambda t}(a + \lambda I)c = 0 \tag{A.20b}$$

Dividing through by $e^{\lambda t}$ and rearranging, we obtain

$$
\begin{aligned}
(a_{11} + \lambda)c_1 + a_{12} c_2 &= 0 \\
a_{21} c_1 + (a_{22} + \lambda)c_2 &= 0
\end{aligned}
\tag{A.21a}
$$

or, in matrix form,

$$(a + \lambda I)c = 0 \tag{A.21b}$$

It is interesting to note that eq. (A.21b) can be easily obtained from eq. (A.18b) by substituting λ for D and the vector c for the vector x. This rule holds for the general case of n linear first-order differential equations.

It is well known that system (A.21a), or (A.21b), can have nontrivial solutions for c_1 and c_2 (or c) if, and only if, the determinant of the system vanishes, i.e.,

$$
\begin{vmatrix}
a_{11} + \lambda & a_{12} \\
a_{21} & a_{22} + \lambda
\end{vmatrix} = 0
\tag{A.22a}
$$

or, in more concise form,

$$|a + \lambda I| = 0 \tag{A.22b}$$

Equation (A.22a), or (A.22b), is called the *characteristic equation*, and the values of λ, say λ_1 and λ_2, which satisfy eq. (A.21a), the *characteristic roots* of the matrix a. Accordingly, for consistency, it is required that λ be a characteristic root of the matrix a.

Expand the characteristic determinant (A.22a) and collect all like powers of λ to finally obtain

$$\lambda^2 + A_1 \lambda + A_2 = 0 \tag{A.23}$$

where

$$A_1 \equiv a_{11} + a_{22} \tag{A.24}$$

$$A_2 \equiv |a| = a_{11}a_{22} - a_{12}a_{21} \tag{A.25}$$

Equation (A.23) can be solved for the two characteristic roots, λ_1 and λ_2, as follows:

$$\lambda_1 = \frac{-A_1 + \sqrt{A_1^2 - 4A_2}}{2} \tag{A.26}$$

$$\lambda_2 = \frac{-A_1 - \sqrt{A_1^2 - 4A_2}}{2} \tag{A.27}$$

For the moment assume that the two roots are distinct, i.e., $\lambda_1 \neq \lambda_2$. Accordingly, there are two homogeneous solutions, each corresponding to a characteristic root, as follows:

$$\begin{aligned} x_1 &= c_{11}e^{\lambda_1 t} \\ x_2 &= c_{21}e^{\lambda_1 t} \end{aligned} \tag{A.28}$$

and

$$\begin{aligned} x_1 &= c_{12}e^{\lambda_2 t} \\ x_2 &= c_{22}e^{\lambda_2 t} \end{aligned} \tag{A.29}$$

The second subscript of c_{ij} is inserted to indicate the corresponding root, λ_j.

Given two linearly independent solutions of the homogeneous system (A.18a), or (A.18b), such as eqs. (A.28) and (A.29), it is easily seen that any linear combination of the two individual solutions is also a solution. That is, the *general homogeneous solution* is of the form

$$\begin{aligned} x_1 &= c_{11}e^{\lambda_1 t} + c_{12}e^{\lambda_2 t} \\ x_2 &= c_{21}e^{\lambda_1 t} + c_{22}e^{\lambda_2 t} \end{aligned} \tag{A.30}$$

The precise values of the constants c_{ij} depend on initial conditions, on the one hand, and eqs. (A.21a), on the other. This is better explained by means of an example, as is done below.

Particular Solution

To obtain a particular solution we simply set

$$x_1 = p_1 \qquad x_2 = p_2 \tag{A.31}$$

and substitute into eqs. (A.15) to obtain

$$0 + a_{11}p_1 + a_{12}p_2 = b_1$$
$$0 + a_{21}p_1 + a_{22}p_2 = b_2$$

(A.32)

Solving eq. (A.32) for p_1 and p_2, we finally obtain

$$p_1 = \frac{1}{\Delta}\begin{vmatrix} b_1 & a_{12} \\ b_2 & a_{22} \end{vmatrix} = \frac{1}{\Delta}(b_1 a_{22} - b_2 a_{12})$$

$$p_2 = \frac{1}{\Delta}\begin{vmatrix} a_{11} & b_1 \\ a_{21} & b_2 \end{vmatrix} = \frac{1}{\Delta}(b_2 a_{11} - b_1 a_{21})$$

(A.33)

where

$$\Delta \equiv |a_{ij}| = a_{11}a_{22} - a_{12}a_{21}$$

(A.34)

General Solution

The general solution of eqs. (A.15) is merely the sum of the general homogeneous solution as given by eqs. (A.30) plus the particular solution given by eqs. (A.33). In other words,

$$x_1 = c_{11}e^{\lambda_1 t} + c_{12}e^{\lambda_2 t} + \frac{1}{\Delta}(b_1 a_{22} - b_2 a_{12})$$

(A.35)

$$x_2 = c_{21}e^{\lambda_1 t} + c_{22}e^{\lambda_2 t} + \frac{1}{\Delta}(b_2 a_{11} - b_1 a_{21})$$

Example A.2 Determine the general solution of the following system of linear differential equations:

$$\dot{x}_1 + 4x_1 - x_2 = 30$$
$$\dot{x}_2 + 2x_1 + x_2 = 90$$

(A.36)

with initial conditions at $t = 0$, $x_1 = 5$, and $x_2 = 40$.

SOLUTION To solve system (A.36), consider first the homogeneous system

$$\dot{x}_1 + 4x_1 - x_2 = 0$$
$$\dot{x}_2 + 2x_1 + x_2 = 0$$

(A.37)

To determine the general homogeneous solution set $x_1 = c_1 e^{\lambda t}$ and $x_2 = c_2 e^{\lambda t}$ and substitute into (A.37) to obtain (after simplification)

$$(4 + \lambda)c_1 - c_2 = 0$$
$$2c_1 + (1 + \lambda)c_2 = 0$$

(A.38)

Viewing c_1 and c_2 as the unknowns in eqs. (A.38), we immediately conclude that the condition of consistency requires the following characteristic equation to be satisfied:

$$\begin{vmatrix} (4 + \lambda) & -1 \\ 2 & (1 + \lambda) \end{vmatrix} = 0 \qquad\qquad (A.39a)$$

or
$$\lambda^2 + 5\lambda + 6 = 0 \qquad\qquad (A.39b)$$

Solving (A.39b) we obtain: $\lambda_1 = -3$ and $\lambda_2 = -2$. The general homogeneous solution takes the form:

$$\begin{aligned} x_1 &= c_{11} e^{-3t} + c_{12} e^{-2t} \\ x_2 &= c_{21} e^{-3t} + c_{22} e^{-2t} \end{aligned} \qquad\qquad (A.40)$$

Equations (A.38) impose some restrictions on the constants c_{ij}. Thus, for $\lambda_1 = -3$, eqs. (A.38) reduce to $c_1 = c_2$. Therefore, we must set $c_{11} = c_{21}$ in eqs. (A.40). (Recall that a second subscript is added to the constants c_1 and c_2 to indicate the corresponding characteristic root.) Similarly, for $\lambda_2 = -2$, eqs. (A.38) reduce to $2c_1 = c_2$. Hence, we must set $2c_{12} = c_{22}$ in eqs. (A.40). Making these substitutions into (A.40), we obtain

$$\begin{aligned} x_1 &= c_{11} e^{-3t} + c_{12} e^{-2t} \\ x_2 &= c_{11} e^{-3t} + 2c_{12} e^{-2t} \end{aligned} \qquad\qquad (A.41)$$

In eqs. (A.41) there are still two arbitrary constants, c_{11} and c_{12}, whose values depend on the initial conditions.

To get a particular solution set $x_1 = p_1$ and $x_2 = p_2$ in (A.36) and then solve for p_1 and p_2. Thus,

$$\begin{aligned} 4p_1 - p_2 &= 30 \\ 2p_1 + p_2 &= 90 \end{aligned} \qquad\qquad (A.42)$$

Solving by Cramer's rule or otherwise, we obtain $p_1 = 20$, $p_2 = 50$.

The general solution is

$$\begin{aligned} x_1 &= c_{11} e^{-3t} + c_{12} e^{-2t} + 20 \\ x_2 &= c_{11} e^{-3t} + 2c_{12} e^{-2t} + 50 \end{aligned} \qquad\qquad (A.43)$$

To determine the constants c_{11} and c_{12}, we require eqs. (A.43) to satisfy the initial conditions as follows:

$$\begin{aligned} 5 &= c_{11} + c_{12} + 20 \\ 40 &= c_{11} + 2c_{12} + 50 \end{aligned} \qquad\qquad (A.44)$$

Solving eqs. (A.44) for c_{11} and c_{12}, we obtain $c_{11} = -20$, $c_{12} = 5$. Accordingly, the solution to eqs. (A.36) which satisfies the given initial conditions is

$$x_1 = -20e^{-3t} + 5e^{-2t} + 20$$
$$x_2 = -20e^{-3t} + 10e^{-2t} + 50 \tag{A.45}$$

The Adjoint Matrix and the General Homogeneous Solution

The preceding procedure for determining the homogeneous solution may be formalized by the introduction of the adjoint matrix. This step facilitates the discussion of multiple roots also.

Consider a square matrix

$$a = [a_{ij}] = \begin{bmatrix} a_{11} & \cdots & a_{1n} \\ \vdots & & \vdots \\ a_{n1} & \cdots & a_{nn} \end{bmatrix} \tag{A.46}$$

Its *adjoint* is defined to be

$$A = [A_{ij}] = \begin{bmatrix} A_{11} & \cdots & A_{n1} \\ \vdots & & \vdots \\ A_{1n} & \cdots & A_{nn} \end{bmatrix} \tag{A.47}$$

where the element A_{ij} is the cofactor of the element a_{ij} in the matrix a. In other words, *the adjoint of matrix a is the transpose of the matrix of the cofactors of a.*

It is well known that the two matrices, a and A, satisfy the following important equation:

$$aA = Aa = |a| I_n \tag{A.48}$$

(The reader should test his understanding of eq. (A.48) by trying a few examples.) Now recall eq. (A.21b). Let A be the adjoint of the matrix $a + \lambda I$, that is,

$$A = \begin{bmatrix} (a_{22} + \lambda) & -a_{12} \\ -a_{21} & (a_{11} + \lambda) \end{bmatrix} \tag{A.49}$$

Theorem A.1 The solution x to eqs. (A.18a) is necessarily proportional to *any* column of the matrix $e^{\lambda t} A$, or

$$e^{\lambda t} A = \begin{bmatrix} (a_{22} + \lambda)e^{\lambda t} & -a_{12}e^{\lambda t} \\ -a_{21}e^{\lambda t} & (a_{11} + \lambda)e^{\lambda t} \end{bmatrix} \tag{A.50}$$

where λ is a root of eq. (A.22a), or (A.22b).

PROOF By direct substitution of $ke^{\lambda t} A$ for x into eq. (A.18b), where k is an arbitrary constant and depends on initial conditions only, we obtain

$$(a + DI)ke^{\lambda t} A = k(ae^{\lambda t} + \lambda e^{\lambda t} I)A$$
$$= ke^{\lambda t}(a + \lambda I)A = ke^{\lambda t}|a + \lambda I|I = 0 \tag{A.51}$$

The last equation follows from the fact that λ must be such that $|a + \lambda I| = 0$.

The preceding proof is general and holds for systems with n equations. For the benefit of the reader, we write out fully eq. (A.51) for the present 2×2 case.

$$(a + DI)ke^{\lambda t}A$$

$$= \begin{bmatrix} k(a_{11} + D)e^{\lambda t} & ka_{12}e^{\lambda t} \\ ka_{21}e^{\lambda t} & k(a_{22} + D)e^{\lambda t} \end{bmatrix} \begin{bmatrix} (a_{22} + \lambda) & -a_{12} \\ -a_{21} & (a_{11} + \lambda) \end{bmatrix}$$

$$= \begin{bmatrix} k(a_{11}e^{\lambda t} + \lambda e^{\lambda t}) & ka_{12}e^{\lambda t} \\ ka_{21}e^{\lambda t} & k(a_{22}e^{\lambda t} + \lambda e^{\lambda t}) \end{bmatrix} \begin{bmatrix} (a_{22} + \lambda) & -a_{12} \\ -a_{21} & (a_{11} + \lambda) \end{bmatrix}$$

$$= ke^{\lambda t} \begin{bmatrix} (a_{11} + \lambda) & a_{12} \\ a_{21} & (a_{22} + \lambda) \end{bmatrix} \begin{bmatrix} (a_{22} + \lambda) & -a_{12} \\ -a_{21} & (a_{11} + \lambda) \end{bmatrix}$$

$$= ke^{\lambda t} \begin{bmatrix} (a_{11} + \lambda)(a_{22} + \lambda) - a_{12}a_{21} & 0 \\ 0 & (a_{11} + \lambda)(a_{22} + \lambda) - a_{12}a_{21} \end{bmatrix}$$

$$= ke^{\lambda t} \begin{bmatrix} |a + \lambda I| & 0 \\ 0 & |a + \lambda I| \end{bmatrix} = 0 \qquad \text{(since } |a + \lambda I| = 0\text{)}$$

$$\text{(A.52)}$$

We therefore conclude that, for the present 2×2 case, the general homogeneous solution takes the form

$$x_1 = k_1(a_{22} + \lambda_1)e^{\lambda_1 t} + k_2(a_{22} + \lambda_2)e^{\lambda_2 t}$$
$$x_2 = -k_1 a_{21} e^{\lambda_1 t} - k_2 a_{21} e^{\lambda_2 t}$$

$$\text{(A.53)}$$

This solution is based on the first column of the matrix $e^{\lambda t}A$. For variety, the reader may consider the solution in terms of the second column of $e^{\lambda t}A$. The results are identical.

We can illustrate the above procedure by applying it to example A.2. Recall that $\lambda_1 = -3$, $\lambda_2 = -2$, $a_{21} = 2$, and $a_{22} = 1$. Hence, eqs. (A.53) become

$$x_1 = -2k_1 e^{-3t} - k_2 e^{-2t}$$
$$x_2 = -2k_1 e^{-3t} - 2k_2 e^{-2t}$$

$$\text{(A.54)}$$

The reader should verify that eqs.(A.54) are identical to eqs.(A.43), ignoring, of course, the constant terms, 20 and 50, of the latter equations. Since c_{11}, c_{12}, k_1, and k_2 are arbitrary constants, we can always set:

$$c_{11} = -2k_1 \qquad c_{12} = -k_2$$

Multiple Roots

Go back to eqs. (A.26) and (A.27) and assume that $A_1^2 = 4A_2$. In this special case, $\lambda_1 = \lambda_2$. Such roots are known as *multiple roots*, or in the present case, *double roots*. Multiple roots present some peculiarities and for this reason must be treated separately.

When $\lambda_1 = \lambda_2$, eqs. (A.53) collapse to

$$x_1 = k_1(a_{22} + \lambda_1)e^{\lambda_1 t}$$
$$x_2 = -k_1 a_{21} e^{\lambda_1 t}$$

(A.55)

Accordingly, one arbitrary constant (k_2) is lost and in general the solution to the differential eqs. (A.15) cannot be adapted to satisfy two initial conditions. For this reason an additional linearly independent solution to the homogeneous system (A.18a) is sought.

Differentiate the matrix $e^{\lambda t} A$ as given by eq. (A.50) with respect to λ. This is done by merely differentiating each element of $e^{\lambda t} A$ separately with respect to λ. We obtain

$$B \equiv \frac{d}{d\lambda}\left(e^{\lambda t} A\right) = te^{\lambda t} A + e^{\lambda t}\frac{d}{d\lambda}(A)$$

$$= te^{\lambda t}\begin{bmatrix}(a_{22} + \lambda) & -a_{12} \\ -a_{21} & (a_{11} + \lambda)\end{bmatrix} + e^{\lambda t}\begin{bmatrix}1 & 0 \\ 0 & 1\end{bmatrix}$$

$$= e^{\lambda t}\begin{bmatrix}(a_{22} + \lambda)t + 1 & -a_{12}t \\ -a_{21}t & (a_{11} + \lambda)t + 1\end{bmatrix}$$

$$= e^{\lambda t}(tA + I)$$

(A.56)

Theorem A.2 When $\lambda_1 = \lambda_2$, a second linearly independent solution to eqs. (A.18a) is provided by any column of the matrix B as given by eq. (A.56).

PROOF Set $x = kB$ and substitute into eq. (A.18b) to obtain

$$(a + DI)kB = k(a + DI)e^{\lambda t}\left[tA + \frac{d}{d\lambda}(A)\right]$$

$$= kae^{\lambda t}tA + kDIe^{\lambda t}tA + kae^{\lambda t}\frac{d}{d\lambda}(A) + kDIe^{\lambda t}\frac{d}{d\lambda}(A)$$

$$= ke^{\lambda t}taA + k(e^{\lambda t} + \lambda te^{\lambda t})IA + ke^{\lambda t}a\frac{d}{d\lambda}(A) + k\lambda e^{\lambda t}I\frac{d}{d\lambda}(A)$$

$$= ke^{\lambda t}t(a + \lambda I)A + ke^{\lambda t}\left[IA + a\frac{d}{d\lambda}(A) + \lambda I\frac{d}{d\lambda}(A)\right]$$

$$= ke^{\lambda t}t(a + \lambda I)A + ke^{\lambda t}\frac{d}{d\lambda}[(a + \lambda I)A]$$

$$= ke^{\lambda t}t|a + \lambda I|I + ke^{\lambda t}\frac{d}{d\lambda}(|a + \lambda I|)I$$

(A.57)

When $\lambda = \lambda_1$, the last expression necessarily vanishes. This follows from the fact that (a) $|a + \lambda_1 I| = 0$, and (b) $(d/d\lambda)(|a + \lambda I|)_{\lambda = \lambda_1} = 0$. That

$|a + \lambda_1 I| = 0$ is obvious since λ_1 is a characteristic root of a. But since λ_1 is a double root of $|a + \lambda I| = 0$, it follows that the derivative of the polynomial equation $|a + \lambda I| = 0$ with respect to λ, evaluated at $\lambda = \lambda_1$, must also vanish, for the term $(\lambda - \lambda_1)^2$ is necessarily a factor of the polynomial equation $|a + \lambda I| = 0$. This means that the term $(\lambda - \lambda_1)$ must be a factor of the derivative of $|a + \lambda I| = 0$ with respect to λ.

The preceding proof was intentionally cast in general terms since theorem A.2 holds for the general case of n differential equations. The reader is urged to test his understanding of the proof by directly using matrix B as given by eq. (A.56).

We therefore conclude that the general homogeneous solution in the case of double roots is given by:

$$x_1 = [(a_{22} + \lambda_1)(k_1 + tk_2) + k_2]e^{\lambda_1 t}$$
$$x_2 = -a_{21}(k_1 + tk_2)e^{\lambda_1 t} \tag{A.58}$$

This solution is merely a linear combination of the first columns of matrices $e^{\lambda t} A$ and B as given by eqs. (A.50) and (A.56), respectively.

Example A.3 Determine the general homogeneous solution of the system

$$\dot{x}_1 + 4x_1 - x_2 = 0$$
$$\dot{x}_2 + x_1 + 2x_2 = 0 \tag{A.59}$$

SOLUTION The characteristic equation is

$$\begin{vmatrix} 4 + \lambda & -1 \\ 1 & 2 + \lambda \end{vmatrix} = 0$$

or
$$\lambda^2 + 6\lambda + 9 = (\lambda + 3)^2 \tag{A.60}$$

Thus, $\lambda_1 = \lambda_2 = -3$. Substituting into eqs. (A.58), we finally obtain

$$x_1 = [-k_1 + (1 - t)k_2]e^{-3t}$$
$$x_2 = -(k_1 + tk_2)e^{-3t} \tag{A.61}$$

Complex Roots

If the expression under the radical sign in eqs. (A.26) and (A.27) is negative, then the characteristic roots, λ_1 and λ_2, will be complex numbers. It is in this case that the solution to differential equations gives rise to cyclical oscillations. Whether the cycles are damped or explosive depends entirely on the characteristic roots λ_1 and λ_2, and in particular their real part.

Suppose that $A_1^2 - 4A_2 < 0$ so that λ_1 and λ_2 are complex numbers. Write the two roots as

$$\lambda_1 = f + gi$$
$$\lambda_2 = f - gi$$

(A.62)

where $f = -A_1/2$, $g = (\tfrac{1}{2})\sqrt{4A_2 - A_1^2}$, and $i = \sqrt{-1}$. Substitute eqs. (A.62) into eqs. (A.53) to obtain

$$
\begin{aligned}
x_1 &= k_1(a_{22} + f + gi)e^{(f + gi)t} + k_2(a_{22} + f - gi)e^{(f - gi)t} \\
&= e^{ft}[k_1(a_{22} + f + gi)e^{tgi} + k_2(a_{22} + f - gi)e^{-tgi}] \\
x_2 &= -k_1 a_{21} e^{t(f + gi)} - k_2 a_{21} e^{t(f - gi)} \\
&= e^{ft}[-k_1 a_{21} e^{tgi} - k_2 a_{21} e^{-tgi}]
\end{aligned}
$$

(A.63)

Now recall Euler's formula

$$e^{iz} = \cos z + i \sin z$$

(A.64)

and from elementary trigonometry the simple formulas

$$\cos(-z) = \cos z$$

(A.65)

$$\sin(-z) = -\sin z$$

(A.66)

Substitute from eqs. (A.64) to (A.66) into eqs. (A.63) to obtain

$$
\begin{aligned}
x_1 &= e^{ft}[k_1(a_{22} + f + gi)(\cos gt + i \sin gt) \\
&\quad + k_2(a_{22} + f - gi)(\cos gt - i \sin gt)] \\
&= e^{ft}\{[k_1(a_{22} + f + gi) + k_2(a_{22} + f - gi)] \cos gt \\
&\quad + [k_1(a_{22} + f + gi) - k_2(a_{22} + f - gi)]i \sin gt\} \\
&= e^{ft}\{[(a_{22} + f)(k_1 + k_2) + g(k_1 - k_2)i] \cos gt \\
&\quad + [(a_{22} + f)(k_1 - k_2)i - g(k_1 + k_2)] \sin gt\} \\
x_2 &= e^{ft}[-k_1 a_{21}(\cos gt + i \sin gt) - k_2 a_{21}(\cos gt - i \sin gt)] \\
&= e^{ft}[-a_{21}(k_1 + k_2) \cos gt - a_{21}(k_1 - k_2)i \sin gt]
\end{aligned}
$$

(A.67)

Equations (A.67) give us the general homogeneous solution in terms of simple trigonometric functions. The reader should not be disturbed by the appearance of complex numbers in these solutions. In economic problems, of course, the actual values of x_1 and x_2 generated by eqs. (A.67) must be real instead of complex numbers. Nevertheless, this is usually assured by the initial conditions which help determine the values of the arbitrary constants k_1 and k_2. Thus when k_1 and k_2 are complex conjugates, the numbers $(k_1 + k_2)$ and $(k_1 - k_2)i$ are real, and all the coefficients in eqs. (A.67) become real. Accordingly, eqs. (A.67) can be reduced to

$$
\begin{aligned}
x_1 &= e^{ft}(C_1 \cos gt + C_2 \sin gt) \\
x_2 &= e^{ft}(C_3 \cos gt + C_4 \sin gt)
\end{aligned}
$$

(A.68)

where

$$C_3 = -a_{21}(k_1 + k_2) \tag{A.69}$$

$$C_4 = -a_{21}(k_1 - k_2)i \tag{A.70}$$

$$C_1 = -\left(\frac{a_{22}+f}{a_{21}}\right)C_3 - \left(\frac{g}{a_{21}}\right)C_4 \tag{A.71}$$

$$C_2 = -\left(\frac{a_{22}+f}{a_{21}}\right)C_4 + \left(\frac{g}{a_{21}}\right)C_3 \tag{A.72}$$

Stability The stability of eqs. (A.15) depends on the general homogeneous solution only. Stability requires that the various terms of the general homogeneous solution tend to zero as t tends to infinity. When does this happen? When the roots λ_1 and λ_2 have negative real parts. This is verified by inspecting eqs. (A.53), (A.58), and (A.68), which give the general homogeneous solution when the roots λ_1 and λ_2 are real and distinct, multiple, and complex conjugates, respectively. As we noted earlier for the single differential equation, the term $e^{\lambda t}$ tends to zero as $t \to \infty$ when $\lambda < 0$. Thus, when λ_1 and λ_2 are real, distinct, and negative, the right-hand sides of eqs. (A.53) necessarily tend to zero as $t \to \infty$. The same is true for eqs. (A.58) since the term $te^{\lambda t}$ also tends to zero as $t \to \infty$ when $\lambda < 0$. Finally, the right-hand sides of eqs. (A.68) tend to zero when $f < 0$, since the expressions $C_1 \cos gt + C_2 \sin gt$ and $C_3 \cos gt + C_4 \sin gt$ are cyclical and tend to repeat themselves every time gt increases by 2π.

Example A.4 Determine the general solution of the system

$$\begin{aligned} \dot{x}_1 + 4x_1 - 13x_2 &= 5 \\ \dot{x}_2 + x_1 - 2x_2 &= 15 \end{aligned} \tag{A.73}$$

assuming that, at $t = 0$, $x_1 = 50$ and $x_2 = 100$.

SOLUTION First determine the general homogeneous solution. The characteristic equation is

$$\begin{vmatrix} 4+\lambda & -13 \\ 1 & -2+\lambda \end{vmatrix} = 0$$

or $-(4 + \lambda)(2 - \lambda) + 13 = \lambda^2 + 2\lambda + 5 = (\lambda + 1 - 2i)(\lambda + 1 + 2i) = 0$

Thus, $\lambda_1 = -1 + 2i$, $\lambda_2 = -1 - 2i$. Hence, the general homogeneous solution takes the form (see eqs. (A.68):

$$\begin{aligned} x_1 &= e^{-t}(C_1 \cos 2t + C_2 \sin 2t) \\ x_2 &= e^{-t}(C_3 \cos 2t + C_4 \sin 2t) \end{aligned} \tag{A.74}$$

To obtain a particular solution, set $x_1 = p_1$, $x_2 = p_2$, and substitute into eqs. (A.73) to get

$$4p_1 - 13p_2 = 5$$
$$p_1 - 2p_2 = 15$$

Solving by means of Cramer's rule or otherwise, we obtain: $p_1 = 37$, $p_2 = 11$. Accordingly, the general solution takes the form:

$$x_1 = e^{-t}(C_1 \cos 2t + C_2 \sin 2t) + 37$$
$$x_2 = e^{-t}(C_3 \cos 2t + C_4 \sin 2t) + 11$$

(A.75)

Finally, to determine the constants C_1, C_2, C_3, and C_4 we use the initial conditions along with eqs. (A.71) and (A.72). Thus, substituting the initial conditions into eqs. (A.75), and remembering that $\cos(0) = 1$ and $\sin(0) = 0$, we obtain,

$$50 = C_1 + 37 \quad \text{or} \quad C_1 = 13$$
$$100 = C_3 + 11 \quad \text{or} \quad C_3 = 89$$

Substituting into eq. (A.71), we get

$$13 = -\left(\frac{-2-1}{1}\right)89 - \left(\frac{2}{1}\right)C_4$$

which yields $C_4 = (3 \times 89 - 13)/2 = 127$. Finally, substituting the values $C_3 = 89$, $C_4 = 127$ into eq. (A.72), we obtain

$$C_2 = -\left(\frac{-2-1}{1}\right)127 + \left(\frac{2}{1}\right)89 = 559$$

Substituting the preceding results into eqs. (A.75), we finally obtain

$$x_1 = e^{-t}(13 \cos 2t + 559 \sin 2t) + 37$$
$$x_2 = e^{-t}(89 \cos 2t + 127 \sin 2t) + 11$$

(A.76)

Equations (A.76) give us the general solution to eqs. (A.73), and they satisfy the initial conditions as well.

MA.3 SYSTEMS OF n DIFFERENTIAL EQUATIONS

The preceding results generalize easily to systems of n differential equations. Consider the system

$$\dot{x}_1 + a_{11}x_1 + a_{12}x_2 + \cdots + a_{1n}x_n = b_1$$
$$\dot{x}_2 + a_{21}x_1 + a_{22}x_2 + \cdots + a_{2n}x_n = b_2$$
$$\cdots\cdots\cdots\cdots\cdots\cdots\cdots\cdots\cdots\cdots\cdots\cdots\cdots$$
$$\dot{x}_n + a_{n1}x_1 + a_{n2}x_2 + \cdots + a_{nn}x_n = b_n$$

(A.77)

or, in matrix form,

$$(a + DI)x = b \tag{A.78}$$

where $a \equiv [a_{ij}]$ and the elements a_{ij} are real numbers, $x \equiv [x_1, x_2, \ldots, x_n]$, $b \equiv [b_1, b_2, \ldots, b_n]$, $D \equiv (d/dt)$, and I is the unit matrix of order n.

The general solution of system (A.77) is the sum of the general homogeneous solution plus a particular solution.

Homogeneous Solution

Consider the homogeneous system

$$(a + DI)x = 0 \tag{A.79}$$

Try again the solution

$$x_H = e^{\lambda t}c = e^{\lambda t}[c_1, c_2, \ldots, c_n] \tag{A.80}$$

where $c_1, c_2, \ldots, c_n$ are arbitrary constants. Substitute eq. (A.80) into eq. (A.79) to obtain

$$(a + DI)e^{\lambda t}c = (e^{\lambda t}a + De^{\lambda t}I)c = (e^{\lambda t}a + \lambda e^{\lambda t}I)c$$

$$= e^{\lambda t}(a + \lambda I)c = 0$$

or, dividing through by $e^{\lambda t}$,

$$(a + \lambda I)c = 0 \tag{A.81}$$

For consistency, it is again required that the determinant of system (A.81) vanishes, i.e.,

$$|a + \lambda I| = 0 \tag{A.82}$$

The last equation is nothing else but the characteristic equation which we met earlier (see eq. (A.22b)).

Expand the characteristic eq. (A.82) and collect all like powers of λ to finally obtain

$$\lambda^n + A_1 \lambda^{n-1} + A_2 \lambda^{n-2} + \cdots + A_{n-1}\lambda + A_n = 0 \tag{A.83}$$

The polynomial eq. (A.83) has n roots: $\lambda_1, \lambda_2, \ldots, \lambda_n$. These roots may be simple (distinct) or multiple (i.e., double, triple, quadruple, etc.). A root which is repeated m times is said to be a root of multiplicity m. When a root is a complex number, then its *conjugate is also a root.* If eq. (A.83) has a complex root $f + gi$ of multiplicity m, it has also the conjugate root $f - gi$ of the same multiplicity. If n is odd, eq. (A.83) must necessarily have a real root. The homogeneous solution corresponding to the simple root λ_s is necessarily proportional to any column of the matrix $e^{\lambda_s t}A$, where A is the adjoint of the matrix $a + \lambda I$. This result was proved earlier (see theorem A.1).

Consider now a root, λ_k, of multiplicity m. Form the following matrices:

$$B_1 = \frac{d}{d\lambda}(e^{\lambda t}A); \qquad B_2 = \frac{d}{d\lambda}B_1; \qquad \ldots; B_{m-1} = \frac{d}{d\lambda}B_{m-2}$$

Evaluate all derivatives at $\lambda = \lambda_k$. Then the columns of each of the matrices $e^{\lambda t}A$, $B_1, B_2, \ldots, B_{m-1}$ necessarily satisfy eq. (A.79). Choose one column from each of these m matrices. The homogeneous solution relating to the multiple root λ_k is a linear combination of these arbitrarily chosen columns. The proof of this proposition is very similar to that given earlier for theorem A.2, and for this reason is not pursued further.

Complex roots are treated in the same way, as shown earlier.

Particular Solution

To obtain a particular solution proceed as in the two-differential equations case and set

$$x = [p_1, p_2, \ldots, p_n] \equiv p \tag{A.84}$$

Substitute eq. (A.84) into eq. (A.77) or (A.78) to obtain

$$ap = b \tag{A.85}$$

and then solve system (A.85) by means of Cramer's rule for the values of p_1, $p_2, \ldots, p_n$.

General Solution

Again the general solution is the sum of the general homogeneous solution plus the particular solution. In this general solution there will be n arbitrary constants whose values must be determined from the initial conditions.

Stability

As in the simple 2×2 case, stability requires that the real parts of the characteristic roots of matrix a are negative.

MA.4 ROUTH'S THEOREM

There is a powerful theorem (due to Routh) which enables us to determine whether the (characteristic) roots of the polynomial equation (A.83) have negative real parts without actually solving the equation.

Consider the following nth-degree polynomial equation

$$a_0\lambda^n + a_1\lambda^{n-1} + a_2\lambda^{n-2} + \cdots + a_{n-1}\lambda + a_n = 0 \tag{A.86}$$

assuming $a_0 > 0$. Thus, compared with eq. (A.83), we have $a_0 = 1$, $a_1 = A_1$, $a_2 = A_2$, ..., $a_n = A_n$. Form the following sequence of determinants:

$$|a_1|; \quad \begin{vmatrix} a_1 & a_3 \\ a_0 & a_2 \end{vmatrix}; \quad \begin{vmatrix} a_1 & a_3 & a_5 \\ a_0 & a_2 & a_4 \\ 0 & a_1 & a_3 \end{vmatrix}; \quad \begin{vmatrix} a_1 & a_3 & a_5 & a_7 \\ a_0 & a_2 & a_4 & a_6 \\ 0 & a_1 & a_3 & a_5 \\ 0 & a_0 & a_2 & a_4 \end{vmatrix}; \quad ... \tag{A.87}$$

In this sequence of determinants all coefficients whose subscripts are greater than n are set equal to zero. Similarly, any negative subscript implies that the coefficient is zero.

Theorem A.3 (Routh) All the roots of the polynomial eq. (A.86) have negative real parts if, and only if, all determinants in the above sequence (A.87) are positive.

PROOF For a proof of this theorem the reader is referred to Routh (1955), Samuelson (1947), and Uspensky (1948).

Let us apply the preceding theorem to second- and third-degree polynomial equations. The polynomial eq. (A.23) has roots whose real parts are negative when the following conditions are satisfied:

(1) $|A_1| = A_1 > 0$

(2) $\begin{vmatrix} A_1 & 0 \\ 1 & A_2 \end{vmatrix} = A_1 A_2 > 0 \quad \text{or} \quad A_2 > 0$

since $A_1 > 0$.

For the third-degree polynomial equation

$$\lambda^3 + A_1 \lambda^2 + A_2 \lambda + A_3 = 0 \tag{A.88}$$

the conditions are:

(1) $|A_1| = A_1 > 0$

(2) $\begin{vmatrix} A_1 & A_3 \\ 1 & A_2 \end{vmatrix} = A_1 A_2 - A_3 > 0$

(3) $\begin{vmatrix} A_1 & A_3 & 0 \\ 1 & A_2 & 0 \\ 0 & A_1 & A_3 \end{vmatrix} = A_3(A_1 A_2 - A_3) > 0 \quad \text{or} \quad A_3 > 0$

since condition (2) requires $A_1 A_2 - A_3 > 0$.

SELECTED BIBLIOGRAPHY

Baumol, W. J. (1959). *Economic Dynamics*, 2d ed. The Macmillan Company, New York.
Frazer, R. A., W. J. Duncan, and A. R. Collar (1938). *Elementary Matrices and Some Applications to Dynamics and Differential Equations*. Cambridge University Press, Cambridge.
Routh, E. J. (1955). *Dynamics of a System of Rigid Bodies*. Dover Publications, New York, chap. VI.
Samuelson, P. A. (1947). *Foundations of Economic Analysis*. Harvard University Press, Cambridge, Mass, Mathematical Appendix B.
Uspensky, J. V. (1948). *Theory of Equations*. McGraw-Hill Book Company, New York.

NAME INDEX

Aghevli, B. B., 164
Alexander, S. S., 202, 235, 251, 272, 294, 314–316
Allen, C. L., 188
Allen, W. R., 188, 321n., 343
Auten, J. H., 36

Badger, D. G., 40, 76
Bagiotti, T., 407
Balassa, B., 184, 187
Baldwin, R. E., 188, 316
Bastable, C. F., 255
Baumol, W. J., 148, 149, 485
Beach, W. W., 164
Bernstein, E. M., 61, 64, 187, 316
Bhagwati, J. N., 150, 271, 311, 316
Bickerdike, C. F., xx, 77, 87, 113, 191, 194
Black, J., 233, 299, 316
Blaug, M., 321n., 343
Bloomfield, A. I., 165, 321n., 343
Boatler, R. W., xx
Branson, W. H., 36
Brown, W. A., Jr., 165

Canterbury, E. R., 149
Cassel, G., 184–187
Caves, R. E., 149, 270, 407, 446
Chacholiades, M., xvii, 33n., 36, 82n., 116, 124,
130, 149, 187, 188, 192n., 194, 202, 256n.,
257, 260, 270, 299, 314n., 316, 321n., 326,
334n., 343
Chalmers, E. B., 36
Chipman, J. S., 256, 259, 263, 270
Clement, M. O., 321n., 343
Cohen, B. J., 76, 464
Collar, A. R., 485
Connolly, M. B., 446, 464
Cooper, R. N., 52, 61, 62, 64, 69, 76, 113, 187,
294, 407, 414, 445, 464
Corden, W. M., 272, 294, 317

Deardorff, A. V., xx–xxi
Despres, E., 447, 464
Dornbusch, R., 113, 446
Duncan, W. J., 485

Edgeworth, F. Y., 187
Einzig, P. A., 36, 188
Ekker, M. H., 315, 316
Elliot, G. A., 187
Ellis, H. S., 76, 233, 234, 270, 271
Evans, T. G., 188

Fanno, M., 407
Fellner, W., 76, 446, 465
Fieleke, N. S., 61, 62, 76, 316
Fisher, I., 19, 21, 36
Flemming, J. M., 315, 316
Frazer, R. A., 485
Frenkel, J. A., 36
Friedman, M., 147–149
Frisch, R., 315, 316

Gailliot, H. J., 184, 188
Gardner, W. R., 76
Graham, F., 187

Haberler, G., 113, 184, 186–188, 204, 233, 253,
255, 270, 316, 321n., 322n., 337, 343
Haight, F. A., 317
Halm, G. N., 37, 150
Hansen, A. H., 184, 188, 322n., 343
Hansen, B., 188
Harberger, A. C., 113, 235, 241–243, 245, 251,
284, 293, 380, 382, 419, 437, 438
Harris, S. E., 188, 233
Harrod, R. F., 204, 233
Hawtrey, R. G., 165

SUBJECT INDEX